The Two Fundamental Problems of the Theory of Knowledge

In a letter of 1932, Karl Popper described *Die beiden Grundprobleme der Erkenntnistheorie – The Two Fundamental Problems of the Theory of Knowledge* – as "a child of crises, above all of . . . the crisis of physics. It asserts the permanence of crisis; if it is right, then crisis is the normal state of a highly developed rational science." Reporting in great detail on important research Popper carried out between 1930 and 1933, *Die beiden Grundprobleme der Erkenntnistheorie* was not published in German until 1979. Finally available in English, it is a major contribution to the theory of knowledge and a major contribution to twentieth-century philosophy.

The two fundamental problems of knowledge that lie at the centre of the book are the problem of induction, that although we are able to observe only a limited number of particular events, science nevertheless advances unrestricted universal statements; and the problem of demarcation, which asks for a separating line between empirical science and non-science. Popper seeks to solve these two basic problems with his acclaimed theory of falsifiability. He argues that science is separated from non-science not by the verifiability but by the falsifiability of its theories. He argues also that the inferences made in science are not inductive but deductive; science does not start out from observations and proceed to generalise them, as many presume, but starts with problems, which it attacks with bold conjectures.

The Two Fundamental Problems of the Theory of Knowledge contains the seed of many of the celebrated arguments that were later to find definitive expression in Popper's highly praised work, *The Logic of Scientific Discovery*. It is therefore essential reading for anyone interested in Karl Popper, in the history and philosophy of science, and in the methods and theories of science itself.

Translated by Andreas Pickel and edited by Troels Eggers Hansen.

Biography of Karl Popper

Karl Popper was one of the most provocative philosophers and thinkers of the twentieth century. His most celebrated books, *The Logic of Scientific Discovery* and *The Open Society and Its Enemies*, continue to have a profound effect on philosophers, scientists, politicians and others concerned for the future of freedom and democracy.

Born in Vienna in 1902, Popper grew up in a city witnessing great intellectual ferment and excitement. His first book, *The Logic of Scientific Discovery*, appeared in German in 1934. It marked Popper's break with the doctrines of the scientists and philosophers who formed the famous "Vienna Circle" and presented many of his most influential arguments, above all his theory of the growth of scientific knowledge. On its publication in English in 1959, the book was described in the *New Scientist* as "one of the most important documents of the twentieth century".

On the eve of World War Two, Popper's life took a dramatic turn. Forced to leave Austria by the threat of German invasion, he emigrated to New Zealand in 1937, where he took up a teaching post at Canterbury University College at Christchurch. It was there, reflecting on the tyranny that was sweeping through Europe, that he wrote *The Open Society and Its Enemies*, first published in 1945.

In 1946, Popper took up an invitation to teach philosophy at the London School of Economics, where he taught until retirement in 1969. This period saw the publication of *The Poverty of Historicism*, described in the *Sunday Times* in 1957 as "probably the only book published this year which will outlive this century".

Karl Popper was knighted in 1965 and appointed Companion of Honour in 1982. He continued to write and inspire colleagues, students and friends until his death in 1994.

Karl
Popper

The Two Fundamental Problems of the Theory of Knowledge

Edited by Troels Eggers Hansen

Translated by Andreas Pickel

Routledge
Taylor & Francis Group

LONDON AND NEW YORK

First published 2009 by Routledge
2 Park Square, Milton Park, Abingdon, Oxon OX14 4RN

Simultaneously published in the USA and Canada
by Routledge
270 Madison Avenue, New York, NY 10016

Routledge is an imprint of the Taylor & Francis Group, an informa business

First published in German as *Die beiden Grundprobleme der Erkenntnistheorie*,
Tübingen, 1979
© 2009 The Estate of Karl Popper

This English translation © 2009 Routledge

Editorial matter © 2009 Troels Eggers Hansen

Typeset in Joanna by RefineCatch Limited, Bungay, Suffolk
Printed and bound in Great Britain by MPG Books Ltd, Bodmin

British Library Cataloguing in Publication Data
A catalogue record for this book is available from the British Library

Library of Congress Cataloging in Publication Data
Popper, Karl Raimund, Sir, 1902–1994.
[Beiden Grundprobleme der Erkenntnistheorie. English]
The two fundamental problems of the theory of knowledge / Karl Popper;
edited by Troels Eggers Hansen; translated by Andreas Pickel.
    p. cm.
    Includes bibliographical references and index.
1. Knowledge, Theory of. 2. Induction (Logic) 3. Experience. I. Hansen, Troels
Eggers. II. Title.
BD163.P6413 2008
121—dc22
2008007767

ISBN10: 0–415–39431–7 (hbk)

ISBN13: 978–0–415–39431–4 (hbk)

I DEDICATE THIS BOOK TO MY WIFE

She has made great sacrifices for the book,
and also for *The Logic of Scientific Discovery*
and for my later books;
greater sacrifices than I should have
accepted, greater than better books
would have deserved.
November 1978

The answer to these questions has not, indeed, been such as a dogmatic and visionary insistence upon knowledge might lead us to expect – that can be catered for only through magical devices, in which I am no adept . . . it is the duty of philosophy to counteract their deceptive influence, no matter what prized and cherished dreams may have to be disowned. In this inquiry I have made completeness my chief aim . . .

Kant (1781)

Contents

BOOK II
THE PROBLEM OF DEMARCATION: EXPERIENCE AND METAPHYSICS

The Two Fundamental Problems of the Theory of Knowledge Volume II (Fragments)

PART ONE FRAGMENTS 1932

PART TWO FRAGMENTS 1933

Editor's foreword

TEXT

Words or groups of words in *square brackets* are additions that were not in the original manuscript copies (K_1, K_2, K_3 and K_4). A few of these additions were made by the editor; the remainder were made by the author when he revised the edited manuscript (MS) in 1975.

Sections 27 to 29 (inclusive) and 31 are set in smaller type: this indicates that the author wishes to dissociate himself clearly from these sections (see *Preface to the First German Edition 1978*).

NOTES

Notes with numbers: these are either from the original manuscript copies or by the editor. *Additions marked with an asterisk* (*) *before the number* are by the author (1975).

All the notes and all additions to the notes that have been supplied by the Editor are indicated by square brackets and normally also by "Ed.".

Notes supplied by the translator are indicated by a "plus" symbol (e.g. $^{+1}$) and the translator's additions to existing notes are also within square brackets and indicated by "Tr."

PUBLISHER'S ACKNOWLEDGEMENTS

The Publisher would like to thank Andreas Pickel for preparing the translation; Troels Eggers Hansen for his editorial work on the translation in its early and final stages; and John Kinory for his work in reading, revising and preparing the final version of the translation. The Publisher would also like to thank Gordon Wells for his assistance with the translation.

PREFACE TO THE FIRST GERMAN EDITION, 1978

The present book, *Die beiden Grundprobleme der Erkenntnistheorie*, can be seen as a collection of drafts and preliminary work from the years 1930 to 1933 for my first published book, *Logik der Forschung*, the first edition of which appeared in the autumn of 1934. The title is an allusion to Schopenhauer's *Die beiden Grundprobleme der Ethik* [1] (*The Two Fundamental Problems of Ethics*). Earlier preliminary work, as well as some of the work from the years 1930 to 1933, has been lost.

I had not planned on publishing this earlier work. As I have recounted in Section 16 of my autobiography, [2] it was Herbert Feigl who in 1929 or 1930 encouraged me to write a book for publication, and who later arranged for me to meet Rudolf Carnap. Carnap read the manuscript of *Die beiden Grundprobleme* in the summer of 1932, and subsequently several members of the Vienna Circle read it as well. Carnap reported on the manuscript in the journal *Erkenntnis*, [3] and Heinrich Gomperz wrote two

---

[1] Arthur Schopenhauer, *Die beiden Grundprobleme der Ethik, behandelt in zwei akademischen Preisschriften: I. Über die Freiheit des menschlichen Willens . . . , II. Über das Fundament der Moral . . .* (1841; 2nd ed, 1860).

[2] Karl Popper, "Intellectual Autobiography", *The Philosophy of Karl Popper I.* (edited by Paul Arthur Schilpp, 1974); *Unended Quest: An Intellectual Autobiography* (1976); *Ausgangspunkte: Meine intellektuelle Entwicklung* (German translation by Friedrich Griese and the author, 1979).

[3] Rudolf Carnap, "Über Protokollsätze", *Erkenntnis* 3 (1932), pp. 223 ff.

detailed letters on it, one to me and one to Oskar Siebeck of the publishing house J.C.B. Mohr, which now, forty-six years later, is publishing the book.

Aside from Herbert Feigl, my old friend Robert Lammer has done much for the book. He criticised the presentation of each new section, and as a result I learned much about how difficult it is to write a book in a clear fashion. My unattainable models were and still remain Schopenhauer and Russell.

The presentation in this book is much more detailed and broader than it is in *Logik der Forschung*, which was the result of drastic cuts. Of course, it is in part superseded by the somewhat later *Logik der Forschung*. But my friend Troels Eggers Hansen, who was kind enough to take on the editing of this book, drew my attention to the fact that many ideas that I rediscovered and published only years later were already anticipated in *Die beiden Grundprobleme*.

During his search for lost manuscripts, Hansen also found some old letters and suggested that a passage be quoted here, a passage taken from a letter of 30 June 1932 addressed to the Viennese poet and cultural historian Egon Friedell. In this letter I describe the book, *Die beiden Grundprobleme*, as "a child of crises, . . . above all of . . . the crisis of physics. It asserts the permanence of crisis; if it is right, then crisis is the normal state of a highly developed rational science."

I am deeply indebted to Troels Eggers Hansen for his years of work editing this book, and for the conscientiousness with which he carried out this task. Jeremy Shearmur, who, thanks to the Nuffield Foundation and the London School of Economics and Political Science, acts as my research assistant, has been of great help to both the editor and myself. Alfred Schramm read the editor's proofs and compiled the indexes. Axel Bühler and Erwin Tegtmeier read the galley proofs. Hans Albert has encouraged and supported the whole project. I am very grateful to all of them.

Penn, Buckinghamshire
November 1978

INTRODUCTION, 1978

1. *A brief historical comment on scientific knowledge as Socratic ignorance.* In Plato's *Apology of Socrates* – perhaps the most beautiful philosophical work I know – Socrates reports how surprised he was that the Delphic Oracle answered "No" to the question of whether anyone was wiser than Socrates. What does the god mean? Socrates asked himself, knowing full well that he was not wise. And he arrived at the following conclusion: "I am indeed a little wiser than the others because I know that I do not know. But the others do not even know that much; for they believe that they know something."

Socrates' insight into our ignorance, "I know that I know (almost) nothing", is of the greatest significance. Often this insight has not been taken very seriously; it has even been held to be paradoxical; and certainly, in the *Apology* the formulation is intended to sound rather surprising and paradoxical.[1]

---

[1] "I know that I know nothing" might be considered as a variant of the paradox of the liar ("What I say now is false"). Inserting the word "almost" formally avoids the appearance of the paradox. Therefore "scepticism" (at least in this sense) is certainly not "obviously nonsensical", as Wittgenstein says (*Tractatus Logico-Philosophicus*, 1918/1922, Proposition 6.51). Also the classic formulation of scepticism, "There is no universal criterion of truth", is far from being nonsensical: indeed, scepticism in this sense is a true theory. However, one certainly ought not to infer from this that there can be no progress in the sciences.

Socrates' pupil Plato abandoned the Socratic thesis of our ignorance, and with it the Socratic demand for intellectual modesty. Socrates and Plato both insisted that a statesman ought to be wise. But by this they mean fundamentally different things. According to Socrates, the statesman ought to be aware of his ignorance; whereas according to Plato, he ought to be a thoroughly instructed thinker, a learned philosopher.

The Socratic thesis concerning our ignorance has frequently been reasserted during the history of epistemology, for example during the middle period of the Academy (founded by Plato).

Essentially, there are three views in the theory of knowledge: (1) An optimistic view: We are capable of understanding the world. (2) A pessimistic view: Mankind is incapable of gaining any knowledge. This is the view that nowadays is referred to as scepticism. (3) The third view is that of scepticism (*skeptomai* = to examine, reflect, enquire) in the original sense of the "middle Academy". This is also the view of the pre-Socratic philosopher Xenophanes: We do not possess a criterion of truth, nor do we have any certain knowledge; but we can search and by searching we may eventually find something better.[2] According to this form of scepticism, it is possible for our knowledge to grow.

The two forms of scepticism had the stronger arguments on their side – until Newton. Newton's *Principia* (1687),[3] however, gave rise to an entirely new situation. It may be seen as the realisation of the research programme of the pre-Socratics and Plato; a realisation going far beyond the most daring dreams of the ancients. The predictions of Newton's theories were confirmed with incredible precision; and what at first appeared as a deviation from his predictions led to the discovery of the planet Neptune. This, without any doubt, was knowledge; certain knowledge, *episteme*, in Plato's and Aristotle's sense. Certain knowledge of the cosmos; knowledge of a kind that the pre-Socratics and Plato could hardly have dreamt of.

Socrates' thesis concerning our ignorance is not the oldest form of scepticism. A far older form may be found in Xenophanes; see Hermann Diels and Walther Kranz, *Die Fragmente der Vorsokratiker* (below cited as D-K), B 34. Xenophanes' scepticism is particularly interesting, since it explicitly admits progress in our knowledge (D-K B 18). See Book I: Section 11, text to notes 28a and 28b, and my *Logik der Forschung* (3rd ed., 1969; and subsequent editions), Preface to the 3rd ed., esp. p. XXVI.

[2] See D-K B 18; cf. also Book I: Section 11, text to note 28a.

[3] Isaac Newton, *Philosophiae Naturalis Principia Mathematica* (1687).

The sceptics were defeated, so it appeared, although they did not immediately realise it. Fifty-two years after Newton, Hume, one of the greatest sceptics, wrote his *Treatise*[4] in the hope of creating a theory for the social sciences to be compared with Newton's theory of gravitation.

It was Kant, converted to scepticism by Hume, who most clearly recognised the almost absurd character of the new knowledge. Astonished by the success of Newton's theory and under the influence of Hume, a hundred years after Newton's *Principia*, Kant posed the following question,[5]

"How is a pure science of nature possible?"

By the phrase *pure science of nature* (or "pure natural science"), he understood primarily the laws of Newtonian mechanics, and also the dynamic-atomistic theory of matter that Kant himself (and Boscovic) had developed.[6]

Kant's question can be understood only in the sense that, starting from Hume's scepticism, he felt that the existence of Newtonian physics was paradoxical. His question led him to another one, which he regarded as even more fundamental:[7]

"How is pure mathematics possible?"

And he wrote:[8]

---

[4] David Hume, *A Treatise of Human Nature* (1739/40).

[5] Immanuel Kant, *Kritik der reinen Vernunft* (2nd ed., 1787), Introduction, p. 20. [English translation by N. Kemp Smith (1929), 1965: *Critique of Pure Reason*, p. 56. Tr.]

[6] See Immanuel Kant, *Metaphysische Anfangsgründe der Naturwissenschaft* (1786). [English translation by James W. Ellington, 1970: *Metaphysical Foundations of Natural Science*. Tr.]

[7] Immanuel Kant, *Kritik der reinen Vernunft* (2nd ed., 1787), Introduction, p. 20. [English translation by N. Kemp Smith (1929), 1965: *Critique of Pure Reason*, p. 56. Tr.] Kant posed the question concerning the possibility of pure mathematics (probably for systematic reasons) prior to the question concerning the possibility of pure natural science. However, I suspect that, historically, he first hit upon the second question as a result of Newton's theory and only later came to the question concerning the possibility of mathematics.

[8] Immanuel Kant, *loc. cit.* In a footnote (pp. 20 ff. [English translation, *loc.cit.*]) relating to the cited passage, Kant writes: "Many may still have doubts as regards pure natural science [that is, its reality]. We have only, however, to consider the various propositions that are to be found at the beginning of (empirical [thus not 'pure']) physics properly so called, those, for instance, relating ... to inertia [Newton's first law], to the equality of action and reaction [Newton's third law], etc., in order to be convinced that they constitute a *physica pura*, or *rationalis* ..." [Comments inserted in *square brackets* are comments by the present author, not by Kant. Tr.]

"Since these sciences [pure mathematics and pure natural science] actually exist, it is quite proper to ask *how* are they possible; for that they are possible is proved by the fact that they exist."

It has often been felt that Kant formulated the question in a curiously indirect fashion. But if one recalls that he started from Hume's scepticism, it is only natural and quite straightforward: the existence of Newton's mechanics is paradoxical for a sceptic; and it directly leads to the question: How is this possible? How is it possible that such a science exists?

Kant's answer was:[9] *"The understanding does not derive its laws* [namely, the laws of pure natural science] . . . *from, but prescribes them to, nature."*

In other words, Newton's theory was not empirically gleaned from the phenomena, with the aid of our senses. Rather, it is non-empirical, a "pure" creation, created by our understanding; it is something that our understanding prescribes to nature.

I believe this to be both correct and very important; but in contrast to Kant, I would say: a theory is something our understanding *attempts* to prescribe to nature; it is, however, a prescription that nature does not always tolerate; it is a *hypothesis* created by our understanding, but — and here is the difference from Kant — it is *not necessarily successful*. A hypothesis that we try to force on nature may be defeated by nature.

My formulations allude to an event that did not occur until many years after Kant: the Einsteinian revolution.

Einstein's theory of gravitation, which showed the Newtonian one to be hypothetical or conjectural, has a long prehistory, and so have Einstein's theoretical ideas on the status of scientific knowledge. Some of the most important names in this prehistory are Bernhard Riemann, Hermann Helmholtz, Ernst Mach, August Föppl and Henri Poincaré.

It is no coincidence that these names belong to the prehistory both of Einstein's theory of gravitation and of Einstein's epistemology.

In the 1920s I realised for the first time the significance of the Einsteinian revolution for epistemology. If Newton's theory, which had been subjected to the most severe tests and had been corroborated better than any scientist could ever have dreamt of, was shown to be an uncertain and

---

[9] Immanuel Kant, *Prolegomena* (1783), § 36, p. 113. [English translation by Paul Carus, extensively revised by James W. Ellington (1977), p. 62. Tr.]

temporary hypothesis, it was hopeless ever to expect any physical theory to attain more than hypothetical status.

This realisation was by no means generally accepted at the time. Admittedly, there were many theorists of knowledge who emphasised the hypothetical character of our scientific knowledge, but almost all of them assumed that through corroboration, a hypothesis would become more and more probable until it reached a degree of certainty indistinguishable from a probability of 1. Once a hypothesis has reached this degree of certainty, it no longer needs to be called a hypothesis but can receive the honorary name of *theory*. Only if it is *certain*, and if its certainty can be justified, is it admitted into the body of scientific knowledge. For *science is knowledge*, and knowledge implies both *certainty* and *justification*: the capacity for being either empirically or rationally established (or grounded).

No significant changes in this view of scientific knowledge occurred between Kant's *Critique of Pure Reason* and Carnap's *Der logische Aufbau der Welt*.[10] And even the two great adversaries in the assessment of the inductive sciences, John Stuart Mill and William Whewell, concurred on this point.

I had now come to the realisation that if any theory could attain the highest conceivable degree of corroboration, it would have to be Newton's theory. On the other hand, all successful scientific predictions that were derived with the help of Newton's theory could also be derived with the help of Einstein's. All the so-called empirical grounds in favour of Newton thus also spoke in favour of Einstein. There were, moreover, predictions derivable by means of Newton's theory which contradicted some of Einstein's. The two theories were thus logically *incompatible*; and *crucial experiments* (*experimenta cruces*) between them were possible.

Most of the crucial experiments that Einstein suggested were not carried out at the time (with the exception of the bending of light rays in the gravitational field of the sun and, possibly, the perihelion movement of Mercury; however, both phenomena might have been explained in ways other than by Einstein's theory). Today, however, all the experiments suggested by Einstein, as well as a number of others, have been performed. The results seem to be in favour of Einstein and against Newton. However, in all cases, measurements are difficult and the results not very reliable. I

---

[10] Rudolf Carnap, *Der logische Aufbau der Welt* (1928); see, for example, p. V, where Carnap raises the "demand for justification and compelling proof of every thesis". (The passage quoted is in the 2nd ed., 1961, and in the 3rd ed., 1966, on p. XIX.)

therefore do not wish to claim that Newtonian theory is refuted (falsified). Nevertheless, the logico-epistemological situation revealed by Einstein's theory is revolutionary. It shows that even for the empirically most successful theory T1 (that is, for an allegedly certain and inductively justified or established – or confirmed – theory), there may well be a competing theory T2 such that, on the one hand, T2 is logically *inconsistent* with T1 (so that at least one of the two must be false) and, on the other hand, T2 has been corroborated by all the previous experiments corroborating T1. In other words, though mutually inconsistent, T1 and T2 may nonetheless lead to empirically indistinguishable predictions within arbitrarily large regions and within any such region, both may be highly corroborated.

Since the two theories T1 and T2 are mutually inconsistent, evidently they cannot both be "certain". Thus, even the most thoroughly corroborated theory can never be certain: *our theories are fallible and will remain fallible, even when exceedingly well corroborated.*[11]

---

[11] At the time of writing *The Two Fundamental Problems*, and for many years after that, I did not move significantly beyond the following intuitive insights: (1) Newton's theory is exceedingly well corroborated. (2) Einstein's theory is at least equally well corroborated. (3) Newton's and Einstein's theories largely agree with each other; nevertheless, they are logically inconsistent with each other because, as for instance in the case of strongly eccentric planetary orbits, they lead to conflicting predictions. (4) Therefore, corroboration cannot be a probability (in the sense of the calculus of probabilities).

Unfortunately, until recently I have neglected to think through the intuitively very plausible point (4) in detail and to prove it through points (1), (2) and (3). But the proof is simple. If corroboration were a probability, then the corroboration of "Either Newton or Einstein" would be equal to the sum of the two corroborations, for the two logically exclude each other. But as both are exceedingly well corroborated, they would both have to have a greater probability than ½ (½ would mean: no corroboration). Thus, their sum would be greater than 1, which is impossible. It follows that corroboration cannot be a probability.

These thoughts may be generalised: they lead to a proof that the probability of even the best corroborated universal laws is equal to zero. Peter Havas ("Four-Dimensional Formulations of Newtonian Mechanics and their Relation to the Special and the General Theory of Relativity", *Reviews of Modern Physics* 36 (1964), pp. 938 ff.) has shown that Newton's theory may be rendered in a form that is very similar to Einstein's theory, with a constant k that in Einstein's case becomes $k = c$ (c is the velocity of light) and in Newton's case $k = ¥$. But then there will be more mutually exclusive theories with $c \leq k \leq \infty$ that are denumerable, all of them being at least as well corroborated as Newton's theory. (We avoid randomly distributed *a priori* probabilities.)

At that time I read through Einstein's writings, hoping to find this consequence of his revolution in his work. What I did find was his paper *Geometrie und Erfahrung*, in which he wrote:[12]

"In so far as the statements of mathematics speak about reality, they are not certain, and in so far as they are certain, they do not speak about reality."

At first, I generalised from mathematics to science in general:[13]

"In so far as scientific statements speak about reality, they are not certain, and in so far as they are certain, they do not speak about reality."

(By those certain statements which do not speak about reality, evidently Einstein alluded to Poincaré and to conventionalism, or to the idea that the law of inertia is an implicit definition of motion without force, and thus of the concept of force.)

This idea of uncertainty or of the fallibility of all human theories, even of the best-corroborated ones, I later called "fallibilism". (To the best of my knowledge, Charles Sanders Peirce was the first who used this term.)

But fallibilism, of course, hardly differs from Socratic ignorance. In brief, we have the following:

(1) Socrates: I know that I know nothing. (And nobody knows more than that.)

In any case, from this set of theories one can select denumerable sets; for example, theories with $k = c$; $k = 2c$; . . .; $k = nc$; . . .; $k = ¥$. Since any two different theories in this infinite sequence are logically inconsistent with each other, the sum of their probabilities cannot be greater than 1. From this it follows that Newton's exceedingly well-corroborated theory with $k = ¥$ has a vanishing probability. (Therefore, the degree of corroboration cannot be a probability in the sense of the calculus of probabilities.) It would be interesting to hear what the theoreticians of induction – such as the Bayesians, for instance, who identify the degree of corroboration (or the "degree of rational belief") with a degree of probability – would have to say about this simple refutation of their theory.

[12] Albert Einstein, *Geometrie und Erfahrung* (1921), pp. 3 f.

[13] Karl Popper, "Ein Kriterium des empirischen Charakters theoretischer Systeme (Vorläufige Mitteilung)", *Erkenntnis* 3 (1933), p. 427: "*In so far as a scientific statement speaks about reality, it must be falsifiable, and in so far as it is not falsifiable, it does not speak about reality.*"

This "preliminary communication" was published again in *Logik der Forschung* (2nd ed., 1966; and subsequent editions) [*The Logic of Scientific Discovery* (1959; 2nd ed., 1968; and subsequent editions). Tr.], New Appendix *I (see text to note 4). Cf. also below, Appendix: Section V, text to note 4.

(2) Kant: Newton's theory is justifiable science, and therefore certain knowledge. (Hence Socrates is refuted by the fact of the existence of science.) Thus he arrives at the question: How is science possible?

(3) Einstein: Scientific knowledge about reality is uncertain. (Therefore, scientific knowledge is not knowledge in the traditional sense of the word; neither in the sense of ordinary language, nor in the sense of philosophical usage, at least up to and including Carnap's *Aufbau* [14]). Thus, in spite of Newton's great achievement, ultimately Socrates' fallibilism is right.

Here I would like to express my hope that the modest Socratic insight into our ignorance will finally become a common intellectual good once again. This insight was probably shared by all the great natural scientists: by Galilei, who in his *Dialogue* (Fourth Day) speaks of "those wise and modest words 'I do not know' ",[15] from Kepler and Newton[16] to Einstein and beyond. All the great natural scientists were opponents of dogmatic belief in the authority of science: they were all opponents of what today is called *scientism*.

But today's opponents of scientism have not yet understood that. They have also failed to understand that fallibilism destroys scientism. They are not so much opponents of dogmatic belief in the authority of science as they are uncritical opponents of science; they are dogmatic proponents of an anti-scientific ideology.

2. *Some critical comments on the text of this book, particularly on the theory of truth.* (1) At the time when I was writing The Two Fundamental Problems and also The

---

[14] Rudolf Carnap, loc. cit. (See above, note 10.)

[15] Galileo Galilei, *Dialogo . . . Doue ne congressi di quattro giornate si discorre sopra due massimi sistemi del mondo Tolemaico, e Copernicano* (1632), Giornata quarta, p. 439; *Dialog über die beiden hauptsächlichsten Weltsysteme: Das Ptolemäische und das Kopernikanische* (German translation by Emil Strauss, 1891), Vierter Tag, p. 465. [English translation by Stillman Drake (1953), 2nd ed., 1967: *Dialogue Concerning the Two Chief World Systems*, p. 445. Tr.]

[16] In Volume II, Chapter 27 of Sir David Brewster's *Memoirs of the Life, Writings, and Discoveries of Sir Isaac Newton* (1855), p. 407, the following famous quotation of Newton can be found: "I do not know what I may appear to the world, but to myself I seem to have been only like a boy playing on the seashore, and diverting myself in now and then finding a smoother pebble or prettier shell than ordinary, whilst the great ocean of truth lay all undiscovered before me."

Logic of Scientific Discovery, Alfred Tarski's great work on the concept of truth[1] had not yet been published. Like many others, I myself was not clear on the idea of truth.

The idea of truth is of fundamental importance for the theory of knowledge, and particularly of scientific knowledge. *Science is searching for truth*: not the possession of truth, but the quest for truth.

This formulation, which can also be found in the penultimate paragraph of *The Logic of Scientific Discovery*, presupposes the crucial distinctions between truth and certitude (certainty), or between truth and justifiability, and between objective truth and subjective belief. In *The Two Fundamental Problems*, sometimes I did not keep these things sufficiently separate.

It is no excuse that this confusion is suggested by common linguistic usage; that it can be traced back to Xenophanes and even to Homer; that the idea of truth being *manifest* is widespread;[2] and that even today, this confusion can still be found in many philosophical books.

(2) In my view, there is only *one* theory of truth that is to be seriously entertained: the *correspondence theory*. It states that a statement is true if it agrees with, or corresponds to, the facts, or to reality. This theory immediately gives rise to a problem: it looks as though it would be very difficult to explain what is meant by "agreement" or "correspondence" between a statement and a fact. Alfred Tarski has completely solved this problem, and he has done so in a surprisingly simple and intuitively satisfactory fashion.

Normally we use our language to speak about facts; for example, about the fact that A cat is sleeping here. If we want to explain the correspondence between statements and facts, we need a language in which we can speak both about statements — that is, about certain linguistic entities — and about facts. Since Tarski, a language in which we can speak about

[1] Alfred Tarski, "Der Wahrheitsbegriff in den Sprachen der deduktiven Disziplinen [Summary]", *Anzeiger der Akademie der Wissenschaften in Wien: Mathematisch-naturwissenschaftliche Klasse* 69 (1932), pp. 23 ff.; "Pojęcie prawdy w językach nauk dedukcyjnych", *Travaux de la société des sciences et des lettres de Varsovie, Classe III: Sciences mathématiques et physiques* 34 (1933); "Der Wahrheitsbegriff in den formalisierten Sprachen", *Studia Philosophica* 1 (1935), pp. 261 ff.; "The Concept of Truth in Formalized Languages" (English translation by Joseph Henry Woodger), in: A. Tarski, *Logic, Semantics, Metamathematics* (1956), pp. 152 ff.

[2] For Xenophanes (D-K B 34), see my translation ("certain truth") in Book I: Section 11, text to note 28b; also in *Logik der Forschung* (3rd ed., 1969; and subsequent editions), Preface to the Third Edition. In Homer the truth is often the opposite of a lie; it is thus what is believed to be the truth. For the historically important theory that the truth is manifest, see my *Conjectures and Refutations* (1963), Introduction.

linguistic entities has been called a "metalanguage". The language about which, and about the entities of which, we speak in the metalanguage is called an "object language". A metalanguage in which we can speak not only about an object language but in addition (as in an ordinary language) about facts, is what Tarski calls a "semantical metalanguage". In order to explain the correspondence between statements and facts, we obviously need a semantical metalanguage.

If we use the English language as a semantical metalanguage, we can speak, for example, about a statement in the German language (object language), such as "Eine Katze schläft hier". We can then say in our semantical metalanguage:

The statement in German (object language), "Eine Katze schläft hier", corresponds to the facts if, and only if, A cat is sleeping here.

Thus, if one has a metalanguage in which one can not only speak *about statements* but also describe *facts* such as a cat sleeping here, then it becomes almost trivial that — and how — one can speak about the correspondence between statements and facts.

That one needs such a metalanguage — or that one must use one's language as a metalanguage — in order to speak about the correspondence between a statement and a fact, is surely not trivial; but it is easy enough to understand.

With this explanation of the correspondence between an (object language) statement and a fact described in the semantical metalanguage, the basic objection to the correspondence theory of truth is invalidated, and we can say in very general terms that a statement is true if it corresponds to, or agrees with, the facts.

(3) I shall briefly mention two further points here.

(a) When we say,

"The statement in the object language, 'Eine Katze schläft hier', corresponds to the facts",

then this English statement about the German statement belongs to the (English) metalanguage. Tarski has demonstrated that in order to avoid paradoxes, the metalanguage must be strictly distinguished from the object language. The predicates "corresponds to the facts" and "is true" belong to the metalanguage, and relate to statements of a certain object language. Moreover, if we speak about these metalanguage predicates, then we speak in a meta-metalanguage. As a result, there is a hierarchy of metalanguages. As long as we keep this in mind — as long as we are aware of the fact that the predicates of the metalanguage are one step higher in this hierarchy than the expressions of the object language (for instance, the statements) to which they relate – then it does not matter if we use the same natural language (more precisely, different parts of the same natural language), such as English, as metalanguage and as object language.

(b) The word "true" does not belong to the metalanguage in all of its uses: the predicate

". . . is true"

always belongs to the metalanguage, where ". . ." may be replaced by a name (or a designator) of a statement in the object language. However, the expression

"It is true that . . ."

is not an expression of the metalanguage, but a phrase of the same object language to which the phrase to be substiuted for ". . ." belongs. For example, the statement

"It is true that a cat is sleeping here"

belongs to the same language as

"A cat is sleeping here",

and neither of these two statements has a metalinguistic character: both speak about a cat, neither speaks about any linguistic expressions. And from a logical point of view, both statements have the same truth value: either they are both true (if a cat is sleeping here) or they are both false (if no cat is sleeping here). From a logical point of view, the two statements are equivalent statements of one and the same language.

In contrast, the statement

"The statement 'A cat is sleeping here' is true"

or, more briefly,

" 'A cat is sleeping here' is true"

belongs to the metalanguage of that object language to which the statement "A cat is sleeping here" belongs.

In the example we have just considered, the predicate ". . . is true" at first seems to have no significant function – hardly more so than the phrase "It is true that . . .". But we can lay down important metalinguistic rules, such as:

"From a class (or a system) of statements that are all true, no false statement can be logically derived."

Here it is evident that the metalinguistic term "true" can play an important role. This will become even clearer if we translate this rule in accordance with the correspondence theory:

"From theories (systems of statements) that correspond to the facts, no statements are logically derivable that do not correspond to the facts."

This rule explains, in part, why in science we search for truth; that is, for theories that are true.

(4) The correspondence theory of truth may be extended in the following fashion:

If a statement in the English language is a true statement, then evidently its equivalents in German, French, Greek, etc. translation will also be true: a statement is true or false together with its class of equivalent translations. Therefore, truth or falsity should be regarded not so much as a property of an individual statement, but as a property of its meaning; and the meaning of a statement can be regarded as the class of its equivalent translations, or as what all equivalent translations have in common. Thus, a statement is true if its meaning is true; that is, if a statement and all its equivalents correspond to the facts.

Similarly, a conviction or an idea may be called true if a statement that formulates this conviction or this idea is true.

Evidently, all these extensions of Tarski's correspondence theory do not change anything of significance. They all have in common the idea that truth or falsity is fundamentally a property of linguistically formulated, descriptive statements.

The widespread idea – which is also held by Bertrand Russell[3] – that the correspondence consists in the similarity between our mental images or conceptions and the facts – in the similarity, as it were, between a mental photograph and its object – seems to me fundamentally misconceived. However, this idea is correct to the extent that it contains the correspondence theory as such. But what is overlooked is that even somebody who is blind and deaf-mute can comprehend the idea of truth if, as did Helen Keller, the individual learns to master a language. However, a human being who has not learned to use language cannot comprehend it.

(5) If we accept the correspondence theory – the thesis that the truth of a statement consists in its correspondence with the facts – then it becomes evident that we must clearly distinguish truth from certitude or certainty, or from justifiability, decidability or demonstrability.

---

[3] Bertrand Russell, *Human Knowledge: Its Scope and Limits* (1948), p. 170.

We may be more or less certain or sure that a statement is true, or that a statement is false. This clearly shows the difference between certitude or certainty on the one hand, and truth on the other.

The demonstrability or justifiability of a statement entails its truth; but not *vice versa*: a statement may correspond to the facts (it may be true) without being demonstrable or in any other way justifiable.

(6) It is particularly important for a critical assessment of certain poor formulations in *The Two Fundamental Problems*, that we must sharply distinguish between the question of whether a statement is *decidable* – the question of whether we can prove it to be true or false – and the question of its truth. At that time I was not always sufficiently clear in my own mind about this distinction. Now and again I spoke of "type of validity", meaning decidability (verifiability, falsifiability); that is, the possibility of *proving* a statement to be true or perhaps false. It is clear that I did not always distinguish between *decidable* truth or falsity on the one hand, and truth value (that is, true and false)[4] on the other: sometimes I used "true" in the sense of "decidably true".

(7) Universal theories are fundamentally hypothetical or conjectural, because they are not decidably true. This does not, however, mean that they may not be true. It is only that we cannot be certain of their truth. But if "true" is not sufficiently clearly distinguished from "decidably true" or "certainly true", one may easily get to the point of calling hypotheses "fictions" (in Vaihinger's sense). This is another mistake I occasionally make in *The Two Fundamental Problems*; a serious one.[5]

In spite of these mistakes, which are also found in other authors (and even many years later), other passages in the book are without these same flaws; and to the best of my knowledge, such mistakes no longer occur in *The Logic of Scientific Discovery*.

(8) I shall now discuss my so-called *criterion of demarcation*, the criterion for the empirical-scientific character of theories (systems of statements).

As is well known, I have proposed empirical refutability ("falsifiability") as a criterion of demarcation. A theory may be refuted empirically or falsified, if there exist observation statements ("basic statements", "test statements") whose truth would refute the theory; that

---

[4] See especially Book I: Section 6, text to note *1 and the phrase "finally decidable" occurring there, as well as the term "truth value" in the subsequent paragraph.

[5] See Book I: Section 34, notes *4 and *5 as well as the text to these notes.

is, prove it to be false. Or, instead of requiring the existence of such statements for falsifiability, we may equally well require the existence of possible observable events; that is, events whose occurrence is excluded, "prohibited", by the theory in question. Sometimes I call such possible events "potential falsifiers".

To give an extreme example: a reversal in the direction of the (apparent) motion of the sun for (say) six hours would be a potential falsifier of almost all astronomical theories, from Anaximander and Ptolemy to Newton and Einstein. Therefore, all these theories are falsifiable: they are empirical-scientific theories (they have "empirical content").

(9) My criterion of demarcation has frequently been misunderstood in fanciful ways. The term "falsifiability", for example, has been explained as "liability to be counterfeited or corrupted" instead of "refutability" – obviously by someone who conscientiously looked it up in *Duden*[6] or in some other dictionary.

Or else, the aim of demarcation has been completely misunderstood by assuming that I wanted to characterise the *currently accepted* theories in the empirical sciences; whereas it was my intention to demarcate all propositions which can genuinely be regarded as empirical-scientific theories, including outdated or refuted ones – that is, all true *and false* empirical theories – from pseudo-scientific theories, and also from logic, pure mathematics, metaphysics, epistemology and philosophy in general. Another assumption has been that I have proposed that all statements excluded by the demarcation criterion should be regarded as "meaning-less", or "non-rational", or "inadmissible".

Almost every interested student (and more than one professor) initially responded to my criterion of demarcation with the question: "But is this criterion of demarcation itself empirically refutable?" It is, of course, not empirically refutable, for it is after all not an empirical-scientific hypothesis but a philosophical thesis: a thesis of metascience. And besides, it is not a dogma but a proposal: a proposal which, in serious discussions, has been well corroborated.

Thus, the criterion of demarcation is non-empirical. It was not obtained by observing what scientists do or don't do, whether by

---

[6] Cf. Duden: *Das große Wörterbuch der deutschen Sprache* II. (ed. Günther Drosdowski, 1976), p. 794. [See also *A Dictionary of the English Language*, Vol. I (ed. Samuel Johnson, 1755/1967): "FALSIFIABLE: liable to be counterfeited or corrupted." Tr.]

studying living scientists or by studying the history of science. But it is of help to us in the history of science; for it tells us what to include and what not to include in the history of empirical science.

If a potential falsifier actually occurs, and thus an observation statement, a "basic statement" inconsistent with a given theory, is true; or – which amounts to the same thing – if an event prohibited by the theory does occur, then the theory is falsified; it is false, refuted. Such a false, falsified theory is evidently falsifiable, and therefore it has an empirical-scientific character, even though, on account of its refutation, it is excluded as false (but not as unscientific) from the hypotheses of accepted science.

Thus, should the sun (apparently) come to a standstill or the earth suddenly cease to rotate without a catastrophe, then Newtonian and Einsteinian astronomy and physics will be refuted. They will also be refuted if the event occurs after the human race has become extinct, hence cannot be observed by anyone: an "observable event" is an event which can, in principle, be observed if a suitable observer in a suitable place is available.[7]

Theories such as the Einsteinian and Newtonian theories of gravitation have an infinite number of potential falsifiers. Many possible motions of the planets and the moons are absolutely prohibited by these theories.

Some motions would, at first glance, seem to be excluded ("prohibited"), but they are prohibited only *under certain conditions*; for example, only on the assumption that we know all the planets and have taken them into account.

As we know, a deviation in the calculated orbit of the planet Uranus led to the discovery of Neptune. An event which at first looked like a falsification of Newton's theory became a convincing victory for the theory.

I have frequently pointed this out. But some of my former students have misunderstood this example. They believe that any putative falsification of Newtonian theory may be turned into a victory by assuming the existence of an unknown (and perhaps invisible) mass.

However, this is simply a physical (or mathematical) error. First, there are many motions that in principle are observable but that cannot be explained by any such auxiliary hypothesis (for instance, a sudden reversal

---

[7] See Karl Popper, *Logik der Forschung* (1934; 2nd ed., 1966; and subsequent editions) [*The Logic of Scientific Discovery*, 1959 (2nd ed., 1968; and subsequent editions). Tr.], Section 28, penultimate paragraph.

of motions). Second, with our space probes we can find out whether the inferred invisible planet, or an invisible heavy mass, does exist in the calculated position.

Thus, as already mentioned, there are an infinite number of possible planetary motions that are excluded by Newton's theory. But there is no possible human behaviour that is excluded by psychoanalytic theories (Freud, Adler, Jung).[8]

Here we have a crucial contrast which, as was to be expected, many have denied.

(10) So far I have spoken about falsifying actual events (i.e. actual events that falsify) or of true falsifying statements.

It is an entirely different question whether we can be *sure* that such a falsifying event did in fact occur, and that a corresponding falsifying statement is true.

This question has nothing to do with the criterion of demarcation as such. The criterion of demarcation only concerns events and basic statements that are possible in principle. And quite clearly, here there exists an asymmetry between verifiability and falsifiability. Certain universal theories may, in principle, be falsified, refuted, by an observable event (or by a corresponding descriptive basic statement); but they can never be justified or verified by such an event or by such a statement.

This asymmetry is a fundamental logical fact that is not affected by any of the problems of attaining empirical certainty by means of our observations.

(11) These problems do exist, and I have stressed this fact in *The Logic of Scientific Discovery*.[8] But they have nothing to do with falsifiability as a criterion of demarcation.

They only have to do with the question of whether we have, in fact, falsified a theory by observations. The question of whether the falsification really did occur may be an important and difficult question; but it is to be strictly separated from the question of potential falsifiability in principle (that is, the question of the criterion of demarcation).

The term "falsificationism", which some of my critics bandy about too freely, tends to confound these two questions. But perhaps my presentation has not always been sufficiently clear.

---

[8] See Karl Popper, *op. cit.*, Sections 29 and 30. Cf. also Book I: Section 11 near the end; and Appendix: Sections VIII (C, D) and IX.

(12) In *The Two Fundamental Problems* I spoke in particular of such things as "final falsifiability".[9] Now final falsifiability, as already suggested, does exist. Nevertheless, as I have strongly emphasised in *The Logic of Scientific Discovery*,[10] there is almost certainly no such thing as indubitable (or final) falsification by observation. This is precisely where Socratic ignorance, fallibilism, the uncertainty of all scientific knowledge comes in. It is always possible – or at least *almost* always in all non-trivial cases – that we might have been wrong.

That there are cases – trivial cases – where we can hardly be wrong, may of course be admitted.[11] Certainly, there are any number of such examples, but they are of little interest. Scientific theories can generally be *immunised* against falsification. (The term "immunisation" was first used by Hans Albert,[12] in *The Logic of Scientific Discovery* I speak instead, in a somewhat awkward fashion, about a "conventionalist stratagem".[13]) But the very important immunisability of all, or at least of most, scientific theories does not affect what I call their falsifiability; that is, their falsifiability in the sense of the demarcation criterion: the existence of "potential falsifiers".

(13) In connection with the term "falsificationism" (which now I tend to avoid), I would like to note that I have never said that falsification is important, or that it is more important than verification. Falsifiability is important (and more important than verifiability, precisely because the latter is not applicable to scientific theories); but what is especially important is the *critical attitude*: the *critical method*.

The critical attitude is characterised by the fact that we try not to verify our theories but rather to falsify them. Verifications are cheap: they are easy to come by if one is looking for them. The only verifications of significance are serious attempts at falsification that have not achieved their objective, thus resulting in a verification rather than a falsification.

---

[9] See e.g. Book I: Section 37, text to note *2.

[10] See note 8.

[11] Russell's example is: There is now "no [fully-grown] rhinoceros in the room." Cf. Ronald W. Clark, *The Life of Bertrand Russell* (1975), pp. 170, 680; Bertrand Russell, "Ludwig Wittgenstein", *Mind*, N.S., 60 (1951), p. 297.

[12] See Hans Albert, *Traktat über kritische Vernunft* (1968; 4th ed., 1980) [English translation by Mary Varney Rorty, 1985: *Treaties on Critical Reason*. Tr.].

[13] See Karl Popper, *Logik der Forschung* (1934; 2nd ed., 1966; and subsequent editions), Section 20. [*The Logic of Scientific Discovery* (1959; 2nd ed., 1968; and subsequent editions), Section 20. Tr.]

But even in such cases it is, of course, always possible that the next test of the same theory will result in a falsification.

The critical attitude is – evidently – the attitude of searching for an error. This applies not only to the testing of empirical theories but also, more generally, to the criticism of philosophical theories. Naturally, one should not dwell on errors that are easily repaired but, if possible, correct them before embarking on serious criticism.

The importance of the critical attitude, of the search for falsifications as opposed to the almost always successful search for verifications, was already seen by the inductivist Francis Bacon; what he did not see was that verifications are of no significance – unless they are unsuccessful falsifications.

(14) In *The Two Fundamental Problems* I frequently speak about a *principle of induction*, that is, a principle which, if it were true, would make inductive inferences valid. What I cite as an example for a principle of induction[14] (albeit probably not important to my argument) is inadequate as a principle of induction. I doubt whether it is possible to formulate a principle of induction that would, at least initially, appear satisfactory. A possible principle of induction might be the following:

"The structure of the world is such that a possible (hypothetical) rule that is supported by at least 1,000 verifying singular cases ('instances' in Bacon's sense) is a universally valid rule."

Such a principle could be used as a major premise for an inductive inference from 1,000 premises describing individual cases to a conclusion that is a universal law.

But of course *any* such principle is false. Regardless of how much we enlarge the number of cases, it will always be false. The pendulum of a clock may be found on the left side any number of times; but it is not always on the left. This leads us to Bacon's exhortation to search for negative cases in order to guard against premature generalisations.

But even that is insufficient. A series of any length of positive cases in conjunction with an absence of negative cases, does not suffice to establish a law-like regularity. There are innumerable examples of this – examples of inductive laws that for a long time appeared to be valid

---

[14] See Book I: Section 5, note *3 and text to this note.

(I shall formulate them in the form "there-is-not statements"[15]), supported by a series of positive cases of arbitrary length and by the objective absence of negative cases, but ultimately refuted by an entirely new negative case. Examples: "Clouds over 1,000 metres in length and less than 30 metres in width do not exist." – "Birds or flying machines weighing over 2 tonnes do not exist." We immediately see that with every new invention and its consequences, a host of possible inductions are refuted that up to that time, for many thousands of years or even longer, appeared to be valid. To be seriously entertained, a theory of induction would have to exclude such inductions. I do not know of any such theory; not even of one aspiring to do anything like this.

Not only does the demand for a valid inductive inference lead to the formulation of a principle of induction and thereby to infinite regression; apparently, it is not even possible to formulate a principle of induction that is moderately plausible.

(15) Wherein lies the fundamental weakness of inductivism? It does not lie in its objective: inductivism and deductivism agree on the fact that it is the aim of knowledge to discover law-like regularities, with the help of which we can explain and understand natural events. The final weakness of inductivism lies in its extremely popular but fundamentally erroneous theory of the human mind, in the *tabula rasa* theory, which I have called the "bucket theory of the mind". According to this theory, the human mind is essentially passive. The senses provide the "data" ("sense data"), and our knowledge is, in essence, a passive expression of these "givens".

By contrast, my theory is that nothing is "given" to us; that our sense organs are already active adaptations, the result of mutations, i.e. they are the precursors of hypotheses; and that all hypotheses are active attempts at adaptation.

We are active, creative, inventive, even if our inventions are controlled by natural selection. Thus, the stimulus-response scheme is replaced by a mutation-selection scheme (mutation = new action). The life of higher

---

[15] On laws in the form of "there-is-not statements", see Karl Popper, *Logik der Forschung* (1934; 2nd ed., 1966; and subsequent editions), Section 15 [*The Logic of Scientific Discovery* (1959; 2nd ed., 1968; and subsequent editions), Section 15. Tr.]; and Karl Popper, "The Poverty of Historicism II.", *Economica*, N.S., 11 (1944), pp. 121 f. (*The Poverty of Historicism*, 1st ed., 1957; and subsequent editions, pp. 61 f.).

animals, and especially of humans, is not routine. And in particular, the acquisition of knowledge, and science, are not routine.

This unusual conception of the acquisition of knowledge will not easily gain acceptance. For everyday experience seems to teach us that we only need to close our eyes to reduce our knowledge of the external world calamitously; and that we only need to open them, immediately to be once again passively instructed by the external world. But this description is misleading. Our perception is active, it is the active formation of hypotheses, even if we are not conscious of this.

Until this new conception of the acquisition of knowledge (and, indeed, of human life) gains acceptance, most philosophers will probably continue to believe in induction.

(16) As the final point in this introduction, I wish to note that I have come to an agreement with the editor to set certain sections[16] in small type because I wish to dissociate myself particularly from those sections. First, they are not important, because they are, at least in part, of a terminological nature; and second, because the terminology (partly based on Carnap's highly original *Abriß der Logistik*[17]) is outdated. Among the terms that nowadays are rarely used (or rarely used in the sense in which Carnap then used them) is the term "logistic". One now speaks of "symbolic" or "mathematical logic". Carnap also uses the phrase "general implication" (occasionally he uses it to refer to a natural law). Also outdated is the analysis of the central logical idea of deduction. We have to distinguish not only between an implication (material as well as formal) and logical derivability or deducibility, but also between logical deduction and logical proof. However, this really became clear – at least to me – only after Carnap's *Abriß der Logistik*.

Penn, Buckinghamshire
November 1978

---

[16] Book I: Sections 27 to 29 (inclusive) and 31.
[17] Rudolf Carnap, *Abriß der Logistik* (1929).

Exposition [1933][See Editor's Postscript, Section 6: D). Ed.]

[1.] *Comments on the content.* This book constitutes a theory of knowledge. It is a "theory of experience", that is, of *scientific* experience. It shows that all scientific "experiences" *presuppose hypotheses*, and that *scientific experience* may be characterised as a *method* of formulating and testing theories.

The book attempts to identify the two fundamental problems that are at the root of both the classical and the modern problems of epistemology (the relationship between these two problems is partly misunderstood while their significance is – partly – not appreciated). It attempts ultimately to reduce these problems to *one* problem. It systematically presents the most important epistemological solutions that have been proposed since Hume and Kant, subjects each to an *immanent critique,* and shows how the internal contradictions of each position necessarily lead to the next attempt at a solution. Above all, however, the book proposes a new *solution* by *eliminating* the previously unrecognised and unexamined *presuppositions* that have led many to conclude that these problems are insoluble.

[2.] *Comments on the relationship of the book to the current theory of knowledge.* On account of its formulation of the problem and its method, which is oriented towards natural science, the book is close to modern

---

¹ [See Editor's Postscript, Section 6: D). Ed.]

("logistically" oriented) "*positivism*" (Bertrand Russell, Moritz Schlick, Philipp Frank, Rudolf Carnap, Hans Reichenbach, Ludwig Wittgenstein). Yet for this very reason, it devotes its most detailed *criticisms* to this movement, and it attempts to expose the "fundamental contradiction of positivism" through which this philosophy fails. (The book contains the first extensive discussion of Wittgenstein's *Tractatus Logico-Philosophicus*,[1] which can almost be called the bible of the most modern form of positivism.) Among other modern philosophies, conventionalism (Henri Poincaré, Hugo Dingler) receives special critical attention.

---

[1] [Ludwig Wittgenstein, *Tractatus Logico-Philosophicus* (1918/1922). Ed.]

Book I

The Problem of Induction

Experience and Hypothesis

The Two Fundamental Problems
of the Theory of Knowledge
Volume I

Chapter I

FORMULATION OF
THE PROBLEM

1. *The problem of induction and the problem of demarcation.* This analysis focuses on two questions: the problem of induction and the problem of demarcation.

The *problem of induction*:

We are only able to observe particular events, and always only a limited number of them. Nonetheless, the empirical sciences advance *universal propositions*, such as the natural laws; that is, propositions which should hold true for an unlimited number of events. What is the justification for advancing such propositions? What is actually meant by these propositions? These questions indicate in outline the problem of induction. The "problem of induction" will denote the question concerning the validity or justification of universal propositions of the empirical sciences. Or, put another way, can empirical propositions that are based on experience be universally valid? (Or more simply, can we know more than we know?)

The *problem of demarcation*:

Most of the empirical sciences, as their history shows, have sprung from the womb of metaphysics. Their last pre-scientific form was speculative-philosophical. Even physics, the most highly developed among them, has perhaps to this day not completely freed itself from the last remnants of its metaphysical past. Especially in recent times, it has been subjected to a revolutionary cleansing process. Metaphysical reasoning (for example, Newton's absolute space and absolute time, Lorentz's ether at rest) has been ruthlessly eliminated. The less highly developed sciences (for example, biology, psychology, sociology) have always been much more strongly laced with metaphysical elements than has physics, and the same is still true today. Indeed, even the view that metaphysics must be eliminated as "unscientific" is explicitly rejected by some proponents of these sciences.

Is metaphysics rightly rejected or not? What is actually meant by the terms "metaphysics" and "empirical science"? Is it possible at all to establish strict distinctions, to determine certain limits? These questions, which indicate in outline the problem of demarcation, are of general and decisive importance. Any form of empiricism must, above all, demand from the theory of knowledge that it secures empirical science against the claims of metaphysics. The theory of knowledge must establish a strict and universally applicable criterion that allows us to distinguish between the statements of the empirical sciences and metaphysical assertions ("criterion of demarcation"). The question concerning the criterion of demarcation is what I call the "problem of demarcation". Or put another way: in case of doubt, how can one decide whether one is dealing with a scientific statement or "merely" with a metaphysical assertion? (Or more simply, when is science not science?)

This investigation will have to demonstrate that these two questions, the (Humean) *problem of induction* and the *problem of demarcation* (Kant's question concerning the limits of scientific knowledge), can rightly be called *the two fundamental problems of the theory of knowledge*. The problem of demarcation deserves our primary interest. It is by no means of only theoretical-philosophical significance. Rather, it is of the greatest relevance for the separate sciences, particularly for the research practices of the less highly developed ones. But even from a philosophical-epistemological point of view, it proves to be the central problem to which probably all other questions of the theory of knowledge, including the¯problem of induction, can be reduced.

These *epistemological* questions are of an entirely different nature from the *psychological* question of how our knowledge actually comes into being. The question is not about the way in which scientific statements are discovered, or how they develop, but about their *justification*, and about their *validity*. The *epistemological* questions, as questions of *justification* or *validity* (Kant: "*quid juris?*"), must be strictly distinguished from *psychological* (and historical-genetic) *questions of fact* ("*quid facti?*"), that is, from questions concerning the *discovery* of knowledge.

(In the present work, factual psychological and historical-genetic questions of cognition will be discussed only to the extent necessary in order to separate these questions from the epistemological problem formulation and to eliminate them from the analysis.)

The view that the theory of knowledge should deal exclusively with questions of validity but not with questions of fact, makes it, so to speak, into a general methodology for empirical science. For method in science is not the way in which something is *discovered*,*[1] but a procedure by means of which something is *justified*.

---

*[1] Thus, methodology is distinguished here from heuristics. This does not mean, however, that heuristics has nothing to learn from methodology.

Chapter II

DEDUCTIVISM AND INDUCTIVISM

2. *Comments on how the solutions are reached and preliminary presentation of the solutions.* Are we justified in calling the problem of induction, but even more so the problem of demarcation, the fundamental problems of the theory of knowledge?

Are we justified in regarding the theory of knowledge as the methodology of the empirical sciences?

Evidently, these questions can only be answered through an analysis that *takes into account* the *historical* circumstances. However, such analysis need *not*, as a consequence, have a *historical interest*. It will only have to show that the typical problems that have, time and again, been dealt with by the theory of knowledge, are reducible to the problem of induction and then to the problem of demarcation; and it will also have to show that these problems may be viewed as methodological problems, and that such a view is a *productive* one.

For these reasons if not for others, much attention will be devoted to the presentation and *criticism* of the most important epistemological approaches; at all times, however, an attempt will be made to make this criticism productive; that is, to penetrate to the *positive* questions, to the methodological questions underlying the positions criticised.

According to the view advocated here, the "epistemological problems" can be divided into two groups. The first group contains *methodological* questions; the second contains *speculative-philosophical* questions, which in most cases may be described as *misinterpretations* of methodological problems. For the most part, typical *epistemological prejudices* (for instance, the psychologistic, the inductivist, the logicistic or the language-critical prejudice) can be held responsible for these misinterpretations. If this view is justified, then the productivity of the epistemological method and of a successful formulation of the epistemological problem will prove itself by allowing *replacement of the questions from the second group by those of the first*; in other words, not simply by dismissing the epistemological misinterpretations as pseudo-problems, but by identifying and solving the genuine and concrete methodological problems that underlie them.

For the following critical and positive analyses to be understood and assessed from a unified viewpoint, the most important points of the epistemological position advocated in this work will now be briefly high-lighted. They will not be further explained at this point; this will be the task of the analysis itself (cf. Section 47).

a) On the method of the theory of knowledge:

The term "*transcendentalism*" will denote the view that epistemological assertions and concepts can and must be critically examined – exclusively – in terms of the actual justification procedure of the empirical sciences. This "methodological method" may (for reasons suggested in Section 9) be called the "transcendental method". The theory of knowledge is a science of science. It relates to the individual empirical sciences in the same way as the latter relate to empirical reality; the transcendental method is an analogue of the empirical method. The theory of knowledge would, accordingly, be a theoretical science. It also contains free stipula-tions (such as definitions); yet it consists *not only of arbitrary conventions* but also of statements that are refutable by comparison with the actual and *successful* methods of the individual empirical sciences. All other epistemo-logical methods (psychological, language-critical, etc.) *are altogether rejected by transcendentalism* – of course with the exception of logical criticism, the exposing of internal contradictions in the opponent's position.

b) Fundamental ideas of the epistemological solution:

The view advanced here may be called radical "*deductivism*". It holds that all scientific methods of justification are, without exception, based on strictly logical deduction, and that there is no *induction* of any sort qua scientific method.

Theories of knowledge may have either a *deductivist* or an *inductivist* orientation, depending on how they assess the significance of deduction (logical derivation) and of induction (generalisation). Thus, classical rationalism (Descartes, Spinoza), for example, has a strictly *deductivist* orientation (its model is geometrical deduction [Euclid]), whereas classical empiricism is *inductivist*. Radical inductivist positions (such as Mill's) deny that deduction has any significance at all; for, it is argued, what can be deduced is only that which induction has originally placed in the major premises. But even intermediate positions (such as that of Jevons), which seek to characterise the empirical-scientific method as a synthesis of induction and deduction, will be rejected here as "inductivist". The deductivist view advocated here denies that induction has any significance.

The only admissible inferences in an *inductive direction* – that is, proceeding from a theory's minor premises to its major premises – are the *deductive* inferences of the *modus tollens*, the falsification of major premises by way of falsifying the conclusions deduced from them.

(The idea of a strictly *deductivist* theory of knowledge, if consistently applied, leads to simple solutions of epistemological problems. *All the following considerations* are based on this idea.)

A further consequence of deductivism and the rejection of induction may be denoted by the term "hypotheticalism"; that is, the view that empirical-scientific theories (*universal* empirical statements) can never be more than *tentative assumptions*, or unfounded anticipations,*[1] because an *empirical verification* of theories – a reduction of *universal* empirical statements to *singular* empirical statements (induction) – is logically inadmissible.

The position advanced here is *empiricist* by virtue of its fundamental principle (the *fundamental thesis of empiricism*) that only *experience* can decide the truth or falsity of an empirical statement.

---

*[1] Or conjectures.

According to the *deductivist-empiricist view* advocated here, there is only *one* relationship between natural laws, theories and *universal* empirical statements, on the one hand, and *singular empirical statements* (the "empirical basis": cf. Section 11) on the other, namely that of logical deduction. With the help of theories, *predictions* are deduced and tested by experience.

Natural laws thus constitute the *bases of deduction* for the deduction of predictions, that is, for the deduction of *singular* empirical statements, the truth or falsity of which can be decided by experience. *Universal* empirical statements, natural laws and theories possess those logical properties – and *only* those – that "deductive bases" must have if they cannot be *tested directly, but only indirectly through their consequences*: they are (as will be further explained in Section 31) *empirically falsifiable, but not verifiable*. While they cannot be justified in an inductive fashion, they can always (by means of the *modus tollens*) be conclusively *refuted by experience*.

(If the fundamental deductivist idea is consistently applied, the concept of "experience" can be defined as a *methodological* concept.)

The idea of the one-sided *falsifiability* of universal empirical statements (theories), in addition to that of deductivism, may be characterised as the *second fundamental idea* of this analysis. Most of the earlier epistemological attempts (perhaps the only exception being the probability positions: cf. Sections 12 ff.) have in common the unfounded presupposition that all genuine empirical statements must be fully decidable (either verifiable or falsifiable); more precisely: that *both* empirical verification and empirical falsification must be *logically possible* for all genuine empirical statements. (In view of the fact that what is discussed here is *logical* possibility – rather than *empirical reality* – it would be better to speak of "verifiable *and* falsifiable statements" instead of "verifiable *or* falsifiable statements".) This unfounded presupposition that all genuine empirical statements must be *fully decidable*, leads to serious epistemological problems. If this presupposition is abandoned, thus also admitting *partially decidable* empirical statements, then the epistemological problems can easily be solved. (Partially decidable statements are those that *for logical reasons* are not verifiable *and* falsifiable, but either exclusively verifiable – e.g. "there is a sea-serpent" – or *exclusively falsifiable*, and according to what has been said above, the latter include all natural laws).

c) On the problem of induction:

The question of the validity of universal empirical statements may be tentatively answered by suggesting that universal empirical statements are not verifiable, but *only falsifiable*. In other words, on the basis of scientifically admissible methods of justification, universal empirical statements can never be assigned a positive degree of validity, but may well be assigned a negative one. The method of testing them consists of attempts at falsification, that is, by deducing fully decidable predictions.

d) On the problem of demarcation:

The *criterion of falsifiability* may serve as the criterion of demarcation. Only statements that can be refuted by empirical reality tell us something about such reality; that is, statements for which we can specify the conditions under which they are to be considered *empirically refuted*.

According to the criterion of falsifiability, fully decidable and exclusively falsifiable statements are declared to be *empirical-scientific*, while other statements (including one-sidedly verifiable there-is statements) – in so far as they are not logical tautologies (analytic judgements such as mathematical statements) – are demarcated from empirical-scientific statements as *metaphysical statements*.

Much like Einstein's demarcation between applied mathematics and pure mathematics, the criterion of falsifiability demarcates applied theory from pure theory, and empirical systems from metaphysical (and tautological) systems. Einstein's[1] statement that "In so far as the statements of mathematics speak about reality, they are not certain, and in so far as they are certain, they do not speak about reality" may be generalised (if we replace "not certain" by "falsifiable" or "refutable") into the following definition of empirical science: in so far as scientific statements speak about reality, they must be falsifiable, and in so far as they are not falsifiable, they do not speak about reality.

The simple fundamental ideas of the proposed solution ("deductivism" – "empiricism" – "one-sided falsifiability") will have to prove themselves critically and positively. *Critically*, by demonstrating that every attempted

---

[1] Albert Einstein, *Geometrie und Erfahrung* (1921), pp. 3 f.

epistemological solution encounters (internal, immanent) problems precisely at those points where there is a deviation from the solution proposed here. (In the theory of knowledge, not only the statement *simplicitas sigillum veri* applies, but even *difficultas indicium falsi*.) Positively, by showing that a consistent application of the fundamental ideas (especially of the criterion of falsifiability) permits the deduction of a theory of scientific method that is in agreement with the methods successfully employed by the individual sciences.

3. *Rationalism and empiricism — deductivism and inductivism*. The deductivist-empiricist theory of knowledge advocated here may be represented as a synthesis of two classical theories of knowledge: as a synthesis of elements of *rationalism* and those of *empiricism*.

Classical rationalism maintains that the truth or falsity of propositions that make statements about reality may (under certain conditions) be decided "on grounds of reason", that is, "*a priori*", which means: without referring to experience. From this basic assumption, classical rationalism (for example, Spinoza) draws *deductivist* conclusions. It is, above all, the universal fundamental laws of natural science that are known rationally; other statements are derived deductively from them.

Classical empiricism represents the opposite standpoint. Its fundamental thesis is that the truth or falsity of an empirical statement can be decided solely "*a posteriori*", that is, by experience. From this fundamental thesis, classical empiricism draws *inductivist* conclusions. It believes that it can infer from this thesis that natural laws must be *derived*, that is, *induced*, from experience.

The view advanced here combines the fundamental *empiricist* thesis with the *deductivist* method of classical rationalism, and in this way emphatically rejects both the *rationalist* fundamental assumption, in its strict sense, and (empirical) *inductivism*.

Using Kant's classical terminology and formulation of the problem, the contrast between rationalism and empiricism, on the one hand, and the proposed synthesis, on the other, will now be described in more precise terms.

The dispute between rationalism and empiricism concerns the question of the grounds of validity of statements about reality.

Empirical statements are to be contrasted here with *purely logical statements*.

The falsity of an internally inconsistent statement (a contradiction) may be asserted on logical grounds. The contradiction may be demonstrated as false in an a priori fashion (without referring to experience). Rationalism and empiricism concur in this, as they also do on the a priori truth of a tautology. A tautology is a statement whose negation is inconsistent, i.e. a contradiction. (Thus, for example, every statement asserting the falsity of a contradiction is tautological.)

Thus, the dispute between rationalism and empiricism concerns not the validity of tautological or analytic judgements (acknowledged by both), but solely the validity of non-logical empirical statements, which are synthetic judgements.

The question at issue between rationalism and empiricism may be represented with the help of Table 1 (which, as I have learned, was also used by Leonard Nelson[1]).

(The table is explained in the following.)

Let us begin by discussing the distinction between analytic and synthetic judgements.

The (Kantian) criterion for this distinction is a purely logical one:

Analytic judgements are tautological (as already noted by Kant and emphasised by Schopenhauer): they "depend on the principle of contradiction",[2] that is, their denial or their negation is a contradiction. They may be rationally proved by logical transformation.

In contrast, a synthetic judgement is, by definition, one whose truth or falsity cannot be decided by logic alone: it is contradictable, that is, it can be contradicted without arriving at an internally inconsistent statement or a contradiction. Logically, its negation is free from contradiction, it is logically possible.

Accordingly, a statement such as "Today Methuselah is celebrating his 300th birthday in the best of health" is a (false) synthetic judgement, while

---

[1] [Cf. Leonard Nelson, Fortschritte und Rückschritte der Philosophie von Hume und Kant bis Hegel und Fries: Vorlesungen (1919–1926) gehalten an der Universität Göttingen (posthumous works edited by Julius Kraft, 1962), p. 195. Ed.]

[2] [Cf. Immanuel Kant, Prolegomena (1783), § 2, pp. 25, 30 [English translation by Paul Carus, extensively revised by James W. Ellington (1977), pp. 12, 14. Tr.]; I. Kant, Kritik der reinen Vernunft (2nd ed., 1787), p. 16. [English translation by N. Kemp Smith (1929), 1965: Critique of Pure Reason, p. 54. Tr.] See also Arthur Schopenhauer, Die Welt als Wille und Vorstellung II. (2nd. ed., 1844), pp. 36 ff. [English translation by E.F.J. Payne, The World as Will and Representation, 2 vols (1958), p. 32. Tr.] Ed.]

Table 1

		(Logical distinction)	
		analytic judgements	synthetic judgements
(Distinction by	a priori	+	?
grounds of validity)	a posteriori	−	+

the statement "If today Methuselah is celebrating his 300th birthday, then there are men who reach the age of 300" is an *analytic* judgement, for it is demonstrable by a logical transformation of the definitions of the concepts involved. The statement "All analytic judgements are *a priori* valid" is also an analytic judgement, for it follows from the definition of an analytic judgement.

Here is an example (the *problem of causality*) that will be *of considerable importance for the subsequent analysis*. The following statement is also an analytic judgement (or a definition): "To give a *causal explanation* of an event means to reduce it to natural laws; *to deduce it from natural laws; to derive it deductively from natural laws.*"*¹ In the same way, the statement "In principle, all natural events can be causally explained" is analytic, for it is always possible to introduce, in an *ad hoc* fashion, a hypothesis that allows one to deduce a particular natural event (even a "miracle"; one only needs to generalise the singular statement in question, which is always logically possible). However, in the following form, a *causal statement* is a *synthetic* judgement: "In principle, all natural events must be predictable through being deducible from natural laws"; for since it is a common experience that scientific predictions fail, the assumption that there are natural events that present insuperable obstacles to deductive predictions is surely not *logically inconsistent*. Indeed, even the much more modest assertion that *there actually are natural laws* − that is, universal rules that are applicable without exception and can serve as a basis for predictions − is no doubt a *synthetic*

---

*¹ As emphasised in *Logik der Forschung* (1934; 2nd ed., 1966; and subsequent editions) [*The Logic of Scientific Discovery* (1959; 2nd ed., 1968; and subsequent editions). Tr.], Section 12, the more precise formulation should be: "to *deduce* it from natural laws and initial conditions".

judgement;*² for it is not logically inconsistent to assume that there are, in this sense, no natural laws at all, that is, that every regularity for which there seem to be no exceptions, nevertheless is somehow incomplete (cf. Sections 5 and 11).

These examples should provide an adequate illustration of the distinction between analytic and synthetic judgements. They also show that all statements about reality (about the world of experience, or nature) are synthetic judgements. (The question whether, conversely, all synthetic judgements are empirical statements, as well as a *closer analysis of the concept of an empirical statement*, of empirical reality, etc., will be broached later – in the context of the analysis of the problem of demarcation;³ initial references can also be found in Section 11, in the discussion of the empirical basis. For the time being, "synthetic judgements" and "empirical statements" may be used synonymously.)

While the distinction between analytic and synthetic judgements is a purely logical one, the second distinction in Table 1 – the distinction between *a priori* and *a posteriori* statements – is a specifically epistemological one. The concepts of *a priori* and *a posteriori* refer to the *validity* of a judgement, to the method of its justification and to its "ground of validity".+¹

The validity of a judgement is *a posteriori* (or *empirical*) if *experience* is its ground of validity. I may *suspect*, for example, that it will rain tomorrow. However, only experience can decide (afterwards, *a posteriori*) whether my suspicion proves correct.

But one may assert *a priori* (from the start, without turning to experience) that it either will or will not rain tomorrow. And this assertion can be justified. Its ground of validity is logic (the law of the excluded middle*³).

The terms "*a priori*" and "*a posteriori*" are not fully on a par. While the term "*a posteriori*" indicates a certain ground of validity, namely empirical testing or verification by experience, "*a priori*" only means that the validity of the statement in question does not depend on experience. How its validity is to be justified is not indicated by the term "*a priori*" as such. One

---

*²   See Ludwig Wittgenstein, *Tractatus Logico-Philosophicus* (1918/1922), Propositions 6.31 and 6.36.

³   [Cf. Section 11, text to note 55; see also Editor's Postscript. Ed.]

+¹   [The slightly awkward phrase "ground of validity" has been adopted here and in the following for the German term "*Geltungsgrund*", which the author uses as distinct from "*Begründung*" ("justification"). Tr.]

*³   Here the text, wrongly, said: "of contradiction".

a priori ground of validity is, in any case, logic (the laws of logic). The contrasting of a priori and a posteriori does not determine whether, in addition to logic, there are other ways of justifying judgements in an a priori fashion. This remains a problem.

All analytic judgements are, in any case, a priori valid (shown in Table 1 as "+"). They are valid on logical grounds: indeed, they might even be defined as logical statements. They are not decidable through experience; they are compatible with any experience.

It follows from this that all statements that are valid a posteriori must be synthetic statements (shown in Table 1 as "−" and "+" on the a posteriori line). This does not mean, however, that there cannot be any synthetic statements that are a priori valid.

Are there synthetic a priori judgements? This is the controversial issue between [classical] rationalism*⁴ and [classical] empiricism.

One may also ask: Is there any ground of validity for non-logical statements other than experience? For if synthetic judgements were valid a priori, then − in addition to the method of empirical testing and the logical method, which is ruled out for synthetic judgements − there would have to be another method ensuring the truth of a statement. For logic is ruled out as the ground of validity of synthetic judgements, since a synthetic judgement is, after all, defined by the fact that its negation is also logically possible.

Rationalism answers in the affirmative the question whether there are synthetic a priori judgements.

Rationalism thus assumes that, without resorting to (or consulting) experience, we can ascertain (a priori) the truth of statements whose negation is by no means contradictory. Therefore, since it cannot appeal to logic as a ground of validity, either it must do without any ground of validity, or it must state some other such ground a priori. Indeed, it believes it can find such grounds in the "evidence": the proposition "is immediately evident to the understanding", is "true on rational grounds", is "intuitively grasped". (All such assumptions will be subsumed under the heading of "the doctrine of self-evidence".)

Empiricism, on the other hand, contends that even highly plausible synthetic judgements may turn out to be false (i.e. that this is always

---

*⁴ Only many years later did I sometimes refer to my own position as that of "critical rationalism".

logically possible) and that in fact there have been such surprises. There-fore – in addition to logic as a ground of validity for analytic judgements – it admits no ground of validity other than "empirical verification", or testing by experience. It rejects the assumption that synthetic judgements can be *a priori* valid.

As also emphasised by Kant, Euclidean geometry is the model of classi-cal rationalism (Kant speaks about "dogmatism"). In the past, the major premises of geometry (the "axioms" or "postulates") used to be charac-terised as "immediately plausible". At any rate, they stand at the top of the system, without either proof or inductive justification, and all other statements are *deduced* from them in a purely logical fashion (axiomatic-deductive method).

Rationalism, which postulates the most fundamental principles of its system *a priori* (in the manner of geometrical axioms), also obtains the entire scientific structure in an axiomatic-deductive fashion, purely by way of logical deduction. For classical rationalism, the axiomatic-deductive method is the most important method for justifying a scientific statement.

In contrast, classical empiricism must demand that the most general statements (the axioms) themselves first be justified before serving as a basis for the justification of other statements. It demands that they be grounded in experience. The "derivation" of universal statements from empirical statements – from statements that can be tested directly by experience, that is, from singular statements – is, however, nothing but "induction".

I believe that the fundamental *rationalist* idea – "there are *a priori* synthetic judgements" – can be separated from the idea of *deductivism* with which it is connected, and that these two ideas are by no means logically tied to each other; in the same way, inductivism [may be separated] from the fundamental idea (the fundamental thesis) of empiricism.

The combinations that such separation makes possible can best be illustrated, once again, by means of a simple table (Table 2).

Four combinations are possible:

1. Classical rationalism, which is deductivist and rationalist.
2. Classical empiricism: inductivist and empiricist.
3. An inductivist rationalism. This combination, too, has been realised by some philosophical systems. One example would be Wittgenstein's

Table 2

	Inductivism	Deductivism
Rationalism	3	1
Empiricism	2	4

conception, which in the present analysis will be the subject of detailed criticism. It is strictly inductivist (cf. Section 44) and, even if unintentionally, rationalist (cf. Sections 45 and 46).

4. Finally, the view advanced here combines a strictly deductivist standpoint with a strictly empiricist one. Like rationalism, this view assumes that the most general statements (axioms) of natural science are (tentatively) adopted without logical or empirical justification. However, unlike rationalism, they are not *a priori* assumed to be *true* (in view of their self-evidence), but are adopted only as *problematic*, as unjustified anticipations or tentative assumptions [conjectures]. They are corroborated or refuted, in strictly empiricist fashion, only by experience: by deducing statements (predictions) that can be empirically tested in a direct manner.

One could show that this deductivist-empiricist theory of knowledge is informed by the modern conception of geometry, in much the same way as classical rationalism was informed by the older conception.

Before the discovery of non-Euclidean geometry, Euclid's axioms could well be regarded as the only possible ones, as "immediately plausible" and "*a priori* true". Modern developments have shown, however, that Euclid's geometry represents only one possibility among many and that other, *a priori* equally warranted systems can be developed in the same non-contradictory and compelling fashion as Euclid's system. The different systems are to be understood as *freely postulated* (freely chosen within the confines of logic), and none of them should be given *a priori* preference.

The question of which system best corresponds to real space can only be decided by experience: by *deducing consequences* that can be empirically tested ("predictions"). For practical purposes and terrestrial dimensions, the Euclidean system proves to be by far the most appropriate. However, for the purposes of treating certain problems of theoretical physics and cosmic dimensions this system proves to be unsuitable (cf. Section 30).

If we apply this conception of geometry to the problem of theory formation in natural science in general, then natural laws (the axioms of natural scientific theory) can also be regarded as freely postulated statements (or similar). One will, at any rate, see them as assumptions that are not derived from experience but tentatively adopted as logical constructs, to be corroborated or refuted by experience through their consequences.

In the case of the systems of natural science too, there are always several systems that are logically admissible. In deciding between the rival axiomatic-deductive theories under discussion at any particular time, experience does so by means of the *empirical verification* or *falsification* of the deduced predictions.

This is roughly the way in which the deductivist-empiricist view might be represented as a further development of the rationalist orientation towards the axiomatic-deductive systems of geometry, linked with the empirical principle that the axiomatic-deductive systems too – in so far as they are applied to reality – can only be decided (*a posteriori*) by experience. It is thus a synthesis of elements of rationalism and empiricism.

Kant's theory of knowledge (leaving aside the preliminary work of his friend J.H. Lambert) is the first attempt at a critical synthesis of the classical opposition between rationalism and empiricism. Kant set himself the task of determining, through this synthesis, the "formal" and the "material" side of knowledge: the formal side by taking over elements of rationalism, the material side by taking over empiricist elements. (Perhaps this tendency is expressed in its purest form in the first two "Postulates of Empirical Thought in General",[4] here quoted in Section 11, as well as in his famous formulation: "Thoughts without content are empty, intuitions without concepts are blind."[5])

In this way Kant's critique of pure reason attempts to solve essentially the same problems that I called here (Section 1) the fundamental problems of the theory of knowledge.

[4] Immanuel Kant, *Kritik der reinen Vernunft* (2nd ed., 1787), pp. 265 f. [English translation by N. Kemp Smith (1929): *Critique of Pure Reason*, p. 196, A. Pickel (2nd version c.1993), pp. 239 f. Tr.].

[5] Immanuel Kant, *op. cit.*; p. 75 [English translation, *op. cit.*, p. 93. Tr.].

The "transcendental analytic" is dedicated to the treatment of the problem of induction (in the form of Hume's problem), while the "transcendental dialectic" is devoted to the problem of demarcation. Kant himself seems to regard the latter as the more important problem (even though the former is probably the more difficult one). The restriction of scientific knowledge to the realm of *experience* through a critique of the claims of rationalism – "knowledge from pure reason" (doctrine of self-evidence) – is after all what gives the entire work its title.

In my view, Kant's "transcendental analytic", that is, his solution of the problem of induction, is *not* satisfactory. The synthesis between rationalism and empiricism attempted by Kant restricts the epistemological claims of classical empiricism by making concessions to rationalism. These concessions, however, seem to me excessive. In order to take account of the formal element of knowledge (all knowledge is rationally formed, it takes the form of understandable or meaningful statements), Kant concedes to rationalism the *possibility of a priori synthetic judgements*: but on the other hand, he restricts admissible *a priori* judgements to purely *formal* judgements (example: the principle of causality) while rejecting the material *a priori* synthetic judgements of rationalism. He further demands an (*a priori*) *justification* for all formal *a priori* synthetic judgements that are to be accepted as valid, and rejects the mere appeal to "evidence" and such like. By demanding such a justification of *a priori* synthetic judgements (he finds a method for their justification in the "transcendental deduction", cf. Section 9) and by restricting *a priori* synthetic judgements to *formal* judgements (material judgements must be empirically justified), Kant believes he has distanced himself sufficiently from "dogmatic" rationalism.

(Even in this formal apriorism, the deductivist-empiricist view still detects [the influence of classical] rationalism. Indeed, it advances the empiricist thesis that there are no synthetic judgements which are *a priori* valid; cf. the "Critique of Apriorism", Sections 10 and 11.)

In direct contrast to the "analytic", the "transcendental dialectic" that contains Kant's solution to the problem of demarcation restricts the epistemological claims of rationalism by making concessions to empiricism. But these concessions are very radical. Kant develops a synthesis between rationalism and empiricism that is largely identical with the one advocated here (in my opinion, of a strictly empiricist nature). He restricts the scientific "Employment of the Ideas of Pure Reason" to the realm of experience, explaining these "ideas" as *problematic* while referring to the realm of experience as the *"touchstone of the truth of its rules"*.[6]

Kant's solutions are not entirely satisfactory. Therefore, Kant's position will certainly not be defended in its entirety. Rather, it will be criticised precisely on that point that is frequently taken to be the decisive one of his doctrine. However, regarding the modern disdain for Kant, I should emphasise here that the present work will advocate Kant's *formulation of the problem* and his *method*, and also very significant parts of his *solutions*.

First and foremost, I shall have to defend the deductivist standpoint against the modern positivists (the successors to classical empiricism); in particular, against "logical positivism" (Russell, Schlick, Wittgenstein, Carnap and others). I consider "logical positivism" – a name coined in a programmatic article [by Blumberg and Feigl[7]] – one of the most interesting attempts to solve Kant's problems since Kant himself. It also attempts a synthesis between rationalism and empiricism. It ascribes eminent importance to the "formative components of knowledge".[8] These are logical forms, in particular the forms of the logistical relational calculus, in which the empirical material of knowledge appears; on the other hand, "all substantive (i.e. not purely formal) knowledge originates in experience".[9] In the following discussion, the criticism of logical positivism, especially the criticism of Schlick and Wittgenstein, will take up the greatest space. It will be shown (cf. Sections 44–46) that logical positivism, too, is defeated by its typically *inductivist prejudice*, which in perhaps no other theory of knowledge has found such consistent elaboration as in Wittgenstein's.

4. *The possibility of a deductivist psychology of knowledge.* The dominant psychology of knowledge is *inductivist*; and like any other inductivist psychology, it is also more or less explicitly *sensualist*.

It assumes that starting from singular experiences – especially perceptual experiences – we attain our knowledge and experience through

---

[6] Immanuel Kant, *op. cit.*, p. 675 [English translation, *op. cit.* p. 535. Tr.]; cf. the more extensive quotation in Section 47 [text to note 6. Ed.].

[7] [Albert E. Blumberg and Herbert Feigl, "Logical Positivism: A New Movement in European Philosophy", *The Journal of Philosophy* 28 (1931), pp. 281 ff. Ed.]

[8] Rudolf Carnap, *Der logische Aufbau der Welt* (1928), p. 260.

[9] Rudolf Carnap, *loc. cit.*

generalisation. For example, it assumes that we order our experiences according to their similarities (by an "association in terms of similarity"), thus arriving at "circles of similarity" and "classes of abstraction" [Carnap].[1] In this way we ascend progressively, always in an inductive direction, from the singular to the universal until finally we reach the concepts and knowledge of science.

Now, clearly it is not one of the tasks of the present analysis to deny that what *psychological inductivism* asserts may, in fact, be the case. No claims or assumptions will be made here as to whether psychological inductivism is right or wrong.

A *neutral* standpoint will be adopted with respect to such questions. Only *one* thing will be required: strict separation between questions of fact in the discovery of knowledge and questions of validity in the theory of knowledge.

Yet precisely in order to strengthen this neutral position, and in order to safeguard the autonomy of the theory of knowledge vis-à-vis the psychology of knowledge, it is imperative to demonstrate that the inductivist psychology of knowledge is not the only conceivable or possible one. It must be shown *that a deductivist psychology of knowledge is also possible.*

Thus, the arguments in this section are directed not against the inductivist psychology of knowledge as such, but against the inductivist prejudice that holds induction to be the only possible form of acquiring knowledge. Such a concept would pose a most serious threat to the independence of the theory of knowledge from the psychology of knowledge. The strict distinction advocated here between psychological questions of fact and epistemological questions of validity would become inapplicable, since facts can decide only in cases where more than one possibility exists. (Synthetic judgements must be contradictable without becoming logical contradictions.)

If one then assumes, with respect to the manner in which we gain knowledge, that things are *necessarily* the way psychological inductivism claims them to be, the only consistent assumption would be that not merely the facts but also *logical* or *epistemological* considerations will decide this question.

---

[1] Cf., for instance, Rudolf Carnap, *Der logische Aufbau der Welt* (1928).

An inductivist prejudice concerning the question of how knowledge is gained will also necessarily lead to an *inductivist prejudice in the field of epistemology*.

Only the *latter* prejudice shall be opposed here. For this purpose, however, it will be necessary to return to the psychological root of this prejudice and to show that psychological deductivism would not have to contend with any serious intellectual difficulties.

Therefore, this digression into the field of psychology should not be interpreted as a concession to psychologism. Psychological arguments are not being introduced into the discussion; on the contrary: the autonomy of the epistemological standpoint is being safeguarded.

In addition to this main task, the present section has a further (if less important) purpose: it seeks to draw attention to the fact that the conflict between deductivism and inductivism remains important in all areas related to our *knowledge*: in the historical-genetic as much as in the psychological field (in the narrower sense), and in logic as much as in the theory of knowledge.

Before the analysis proceeds to the acquisition of knowledge – to the historical-genetic and, subsequently, to the psychological field – some brief comments on the *logic of knowledge* will therefore be added.

Without a doubt, the proper domain of logic is the *theory of deduction*. Thus, classical logic is purely deductivist; inductivist reasoning has played a very minor part (in spite of various attempts going back to Aristotle and perhaps to the Socratic method).

Notwithstanding Mill, who further developed Bacon's and Herschel's approaches, attempts to develop a *logic of induction* have not succeeded in dislodging the theory of deduction from its dominant position in logic.

Inductivist lines of thought can also be discerned in modern developments of mathematical or symbolic logic, in "*logistic*" [Carnap] and in related endeavours. Thus, in addition to deductivist reasoning, Whitehead and Russell's *Principia Mathematica* also contains inductivist reasoning (e.g. the theory of abstraction). This emerges with particular force in the introduction to the second edition that, under Wittgenstein's influence, grounds logic in the doctrine of the truth functions of elementary statements – "atomic propositions".[2] (Cf. also my comments towards the end

---

[2] [Alfred North Whitehead and Bertrand Russell, *Principia Mathematica* I. (2nd ed., 1925), "Introduction to the Second Edition", pp. XV f. Ed.]

of Section 44. It seems to me that the assumption – however fictitious – that an inventory of all true elementary statements can be compiled, completely misconceives the task of logic. The individual sciences are far from being logical products of elementary statements; the latter are of relevance only for verification. However, these questions cannot be pursued here.) In contrast, the analyses of modern *axiomatics* (starting primarily with David Hilbert) are purely deductivist. From the standpoint of a deductivist theory of knowledge, they deserve the greatest attention.

In principle, deductivist reasoning in the field of *the acquisition of knowledge* may be compatible with both an inductivist and a deductivist theory of knowledge; and vice versa. (In principle, any conceivable combinations may be put forward here.)

It must be admitted that combining the deductivist theory of knowledge advocated here with deductivism in the field of the acquisition of knowledge will yield a far more unified overall picture, and is, in any case, easier than combining it with psychological inductivism. The present theory of knowledge definitely aims to show (if possible) that a historical-genetic and psychological deductivism not only is conceivable, but is supported by significant facts.

An inductivist theory of knowledge will obviously have an analogous interest, even if it is sufficiently unbiased to claim the independence of the theory of knowledge from its psychology. It will, at any rate, give preference to the inductivist theory of the acquisition of knowledge, unless there are compelling facts arguing against this.

The fact that an inductivist theorist of knowledge, in the light of the historical-genetic facts, accepts that deductivism is justified in the field of the acquisition of knowledge, is a powerful argument in favour of my assertion that a deductivist psychology of knowledge is possible.

Such a position is put forward, for example, by Herbert Feigl (in his work *Theorie und Erfahrung in der Physik* [Theory and Experience in Physics]).

As a *theorist of knowledge*, he emphasises that:[3] "If we proceed from *all* the facts explained by a theory – in the case of a well-confirmed theory, this is not simply a possible or imagined, but actually observed states of affairs – the theory can actually be constructed by inductive generalisation." (Similar statements can be found in many other places.)

---

[3] Herbert Feigl, *Theorie und Erfahrung in der Physik* (1929), e.g. p. 116.

However, Feigl distinguishes strictly between theory of knowledge and psychology of knowledge:[4] "If contemporary philosophy has any merit at all, it consists in the fact that it has learned to distinguish clearly between the historical and the systematic, the psychological and the logical, genesis and validity."

This strict distinction makes it possible for Feigl to accept a deductivist position in the acquisition of knowledge:[5] "Some thinkers (particularly the conventionalists) have sought to demonstrate that physical theories are never simple inductive generalisations, but rather conceptual constructs which have to fulfil the . . . purpose of integrating experimental laws into a *deductive context*. In this, they base themselves on the historical state of research and come up with impressive examples."

Earlier he has already stated in the same vein:[6] "Theories almost always precede experience, and it is the soundness of these theories that is tested by observation. Even in the case of investigations designed to follow up on an accidental discovery, they are of course always based on a programme, on a guiding idea in one form or another.

"All these conceptual operations, which have their place *prior to* obser-vation, are no doubt of the utmost importance for the emergence and development of scientific knowledge. They are extremely interesting from the standpoint of the *historian* of science and of the *psychologist* of knowledge. Thus in the writings of Mach and Duhem, who chiefly adopt such a perspective, we also find valuable insights concerning these intellectual activities that are so relevant to the genesis of science."

With respect to these deductivist thought processes, Feigl is content to emphasise that his own *epistemological* position is not affected by such arguments:[7] "What the aforementioned examples prove is relevant solely to the genesis of physical theories. Indeed, the idea of universal gravity is an absolute novelty vis-à-vis Kepler's laws, as is the idea of molecular motion vis-à-vis the laws of gases. Therefore, these theories are not simply inductively *acquired* from experience. Nevertheless, the *validity* of these theories can be justified only inductively."

[4] Herbert Feigl, *op. cit.*, p. 115.
[5] Herbert Feigl, *op. cit.*, p. 114. Emphasis not in the original.
[6] Herbert Feigl, *op. cit.*, pp. 30 f.
[7] Herbert Feigl, *op. cit.*, p. 115.

Without internal contradiction, he can thus summarise his own position in the following words:[8] "Even if research does not discover them by induction, the theories still have to be evaluated as inductions with regard to their validity."

I have discussed Feigl's view in such detail, because it seems to me particularly impressive as a clear recognition – from the opponent's, namely the inductivist, camp – of *genetic deductivism*.

(For the sake of completeness, however, I should like to note that this deductivist line of thought that Feigl alludes to – in particular Pierre Duhem's *The Aim and Structure of Physical Theory*[9] – is, in my opinion, not only genetically but also epistemologically important. The most significant elaboration of Duhem's deductivist standpoint I consider to be Viktor Kraft's[10] *Die Grundformen der wissenschaftlichen Methoden*. Cf. also the comments at the end of Section 24.)

In the *psychology of knowledge* (or "cognitive psychology") proper, the deductivist line of thought is found primarily among *biologically* oriented psychologists.

In my presentation I shall start from a comment by Mach who, in his *Prinzipien der Wärmelehre*,[11] discusses the question of the genesis of thought and of concepts in a biological-psychological sense. (Very similar ideas can already be found earlier: in the writings of Ernst Mach and in those of Heinrich Gomperz.[12])

Mach shows that in (objectively) *different situations*, the *same reactions* (sniffing, licking, crunching) may occur. The *similar aspects* that can perhaps be identified in those situations are frequently "recognised" only through the mediation of such *reactions*; for they, in turn, result in new typical sense perceptions (smell, taste) which in their turn will be decisive for further

---

[8] Herbert Feigl, *op. cit.*, p. 116.

[9] Pierre Duhem, *Ziel und Struktur der physikalischen Theorien* (German translation by Friedrich Adler, 1908). [*The Aim and Structure of Physical Theory*, English translation by Philip P. Wiener, (Princeton, 1954). Tr.]

[10] Viktor Kraft, *Die Grundformen der wissenschaftlichen Methoden* (1925).

[11] Cf. Ernst Mach, *Die Prinzipien der Wärmelehre* (2nd ed., 1900), pp. 415, 422.

[12] Ernst Mach, *Die Analyse der Empfindungen und das Verhältnis des Physischen zum Psychischen*, Ch. XIV, Sections 8 ff. [6th ed., 1911, pp. 262 ff. Ed. English translation by C.M. Williams and S. Waterlow: *The Analysis of Sensations* (Chicago, 1914). Tr.]; Heinrich Gomperz, *Zur Psychologie der logischen Grundtatsachen* (1897), p. 26; cf. also H. Gomperz, *Weltanschauungslehre* II. (1908), pp. 117 f., 251.

reactions (devouring, discarding). In this mutual relationship between reaction and reception, Mach sees the "psychological foundation of a concept":

"Whatever calls forth the *same* reaction is subsumed under *one* concept. There are as many concepts as there are reactions."[13]

This approach of Mach's*[1] contains the view – incidentally, also supported by cerebral physiology – that a *reactive side* must be distinguished from a *receptive side* in our mental apparatus, and that for the processes of cognition or thinking, the *reactive* side is of decisive importance. Cognition is related to the *assigning of reactions to receptions*, that is, it is itself a particular *kind of reaction* to certain situations and to certain (objective) stimuli.

As will be shown in the following, this idea may be used as a basis upon which to construct a deductivist psychology of knowledge. That it contradicts (inductivist) *sensualism* is, of course, self-evident. Our cognition and our thinking should not be understood as the combining or the associative grouping of perceptual experiences, of *receptions*. Rather, our thoughts should be characterised as *intellectual reactions*.

It is true of *physiological reactions* in general (and not only of intellectual reactions) that they may be *triggered* by a stimulus (a reception), yet the specific form of the reactive process largely depends on the subjective *conditions of the reacting apparatus itself*. The objective triggering stimulus may be regarded as the *material* condition of the reaction, for it is the condition of its actual occurrence; the reacting apparatus contains the *formal* conditions for the reactive process. Reactions may therefore be called "*subjectively preformed*".

But how can such subjectively preformed reactions match the (objective) stimuli? In other words, how can we explain why it is that reactions, which are subjectively preformed, that is, not "acquired from experience", prove to be successful in the objective situations of the environment, and thus prove to be biologically valuable?

An answer to this question might, for example, be Jennings' *theory of trial movements*.[14] Jennings shows that a lower organism, especially a unicellular

---

[13] [Ernst Mach, *Die Prinzipien der Wärmelehre* (2nd ed., 1900), p. 416. Ed.]

*[1] It will be seen that Mach's approach, which I describe here, sharply contrasts with his sensualist approach in *The Analysis of Sensations*.

[14] Herbert Spencer Jennings, *Das Verhalten der niederen Organismen* (German translation by Ernst Mangold, 1910). [H.S. Jennings, *The Behaviour of Lower Organisms* (1906). Tr.]

one, will try out *all* the reactions at its disposal*[2] in response to certain (particularly harmful) stimuli, until one of them "fits the situation" and is biologically successful (that is, releasing it from the harmful stimulus). If the stimulus recurs, the whole procedure will start over again. Once more all the trial movements are sequentially modified. Even multiple repetitions will not change this, or rather only the *speed* of the process will change. The "matching" reaction occurs more and more swiftly, but only because the sequence of trial movements is completed increasingly rapidly. Repetition and practice effect a *"speeding up of the process"*.

Thus, through "trial behaviour" (Selz[15]), failure and finally success, subjectively preformed reactions could *adapt* to the objective situation.

These ideas, only briefly sketched out here, could perhaps also be interpreted in the sense of an inductivist psychology of knowledge. But they could certainly serve as building blocks for a conception that may be called deductivist.

If our subjective ideas and our subjective knowledge – our belief in "causality", that is, in law-like regularities ("rule-consciousness", Bühler[16]) etc. – can be conceived as *intellectual reactions*, then what has just been outlined for reactions in general might apply to intellectual reactions, too.

Intellectual reactions would be *subjectively preformed*; they would be triggered by objective stimuli or receptions, which would be their material conditions – but they would in no way be derived from the receptions.

If the *assigning* of intellectual reactions to the objective situation always results from trial behaviour, then the assigning always occurs *prior to* its success. The assigning is, therefore, *anticipatory* relative to its success (as long as the reaction remains unsuccessful, it may be called an "unjustified prejudice"). Often, success will not occur. The anticipatory assignment of reaction to stimulus is a *tentative* one.

---

*[2] Later, I introduced the phrase "repertoire of behaviour" for this. [See Karl Popper, "The Rationality of Scientific Revolutions", in *Problems of Scientific Revolution: Progress and Obstacles to Progress in the Sciences* (The Herbert Spencer Lectures 1973, ed. Rom Harré, 1975), pp. 74 ff. Ed.]

[15] [Otto Selz, *Über die Gesetze des geordneten Denkverlaufs* II. (1922), pp. 645 ff.; cf. also O. Selz, *Die Gesetze der produktiven und reproduktiven Geistestätigkeit* (1924), pp. 16 ff. Ed.]

[16] [Karl Bühler, "Tatsachen und Probleme zu einer Psychologie der Denkvorgänge I.", *Archiv für die gesamte Psychologie* 9 (1907), pp. 334 ff. Ed.]

That is why I call subjectively preformed intellectual reactions simply "*anticipations*".*[3].

According to the deductivist view, we do not attain our empirical knowledge by abstraction or generalisation from sense-perceptions, but by trying out anticipations tentatively assigned to the "material" of the receptions. Whether this tentative assignment will be abandoned or not is decided by its biological value. The method of deciding is a *selective* one. If the anticipations prove useless, they will be eliminated; either they are replaced by other reactions, or their "carrier" – the reacting organism – will perish with them.

Success in the environment determines the fate of preformed anticipations.

(It is the "method of Trial and Error", as Bernard Shaw[17] calls it in his "metabiological Pentateuch".)

In order to illustrate the application of the schema, we may ask how, for example, the process of *re-cognition* should be interpreted?

Inductivism will simply assume that the later reception is linked with the earlier one by an association ("memory of similarity", Carnap[18]), reproducing the earlier one. (The serious problems concealed in this apparently very elementary conception will not be further discussed here.*[3a])

According to the deductivist view, a reaction has adapted to the first stimulus. Through new trials, the same reaction is also successful with respect to the later stimulus. In so far as in both cases the same reaction has been successful, the two cases must have something in common, regardless of how different they may be in other respects. This explains the fact that becoming conscious of, that is, cognising, what is *common* in objectively *different* situations (all situations are objectively more or less

---

*[3] The term "anticipation" is used by Bacon in a deprecating sense (as a synonym for "prejudice"); I use it in a positive sense, as a synonym for "expectation" (or assumption). Cf. *Logik der Forschung* (1934; 2nd ed., 1966; and subsequent editions) [*The Logic of Scientific Discovery* (1959; 2nd ed., 1986; and subsequent editions). Tr.], Section 85.

[17] [Bernard Shaw, *Back to Methuselah: A Metabiological Pentateuch* (1921), pp. LV and 82. Ed.]

[18] [Rudolf Carnap, *Der logische Aufbau der Welt* (1928). Ed.]

*[3a] For a discussion, see *Logik der Forschung* (1934; 2nd ed., 1966; and subsequent editions) [*The Logic of Scientific Discovery* (1959; 2nd ed., 1968; and subsequent editions). Tr.]. New Appendix *X; cf. also *Conjectures and Refutations* (1963), pp. 44 f.).

different) always depends on subjective factors as well ("method of exhaustion"). As Mach[19] says (cf. above): "Whatever calls forth the *same* reaction is subsumed under *one* concept . . ."

According to this view, receptions are not assigned directly to each other. Rather, reactions are first assigned to them, and the (indirect) links between receptions come about only via this reference system.

The great *rapidity* of even indirect assignment may be explained by a radical speeding up of the process. (By the "miracle of condensed repetition", says Shaw.[20])

There is one thing the deductivist theory cannot explain: how new reactions emerge, how new anticipations are generated and how new knowledge is conceived.

But whereas inductivism purports to provide an explanation, deductivism does not even attempt fully to explain the generation of the new. It only seeks to explain the method by which the *decision* about the assignment of the reaction to the reception is made. *Cognition* lies precisely in this *decision*.

This method is a law-like, rational one, and it is therefore subject to explanation, that is, to being reduced to a law-like regularity. It is the "method of Trial and Error",[21] the method of *selection*.

Deductivism, however, would give only *one* answer (and that scarcely worthy of the name) to the question of how the conceiving of new knowledge comes about: in the same way that anything new emerges biologically, or in the same way that any mutations are produced.

According to deductivism, there is *no law-like dependence* between new receptions, or between new objective conditions and the emergence of new reactions. (Or rather, there is only *one* dependence, namely, the *selective* one, which renders unadapted reactions worthless, sometimes confronting the organism with the alternative of producing something new or perishing; however, this fails to account for the unexplained element.)

Whereas inductivism not only seeks to show how new knowledge emerges from new receptions (namely, by comparison of perceptions, etc.), but also "explains" why the newly created knowledge is adequate to the receptions (because it has emerged from them); for deductivism it

---

[19] [See note 13 and text to this note. Ed.]
[20] [Bernard Shaw, *op. cit.*, pp. XXIV ff. Ed.]
[21] [See note 17. Ed.]

is not necessary to assume such *correspondence* between newly conceived knowledge and receptions. On the contrary: it assumes (of course, only schematically) that new reactions – once they have emerged – are in no way dependent on the receptions. The majority of them, after all, are discarded: the "method of Trial and Error" employed by nature presupposes *overproduction*.

According to the deductivist view, no law-like or rational way leads from new receptions to new reactions or to new "ideas"; their emergence may be called, if you will, *accidental*. At any rate, it seems to contain an *irrational*, creative element (cf. the comments on "intuitionism" in Section 47).

The question regarding the emergence of *new* conceptions leads us, once again, to a comparison of the inductivist and the deductivist views, a comparison that reveals their fundamental opposition in sharp focus.

Inductivism reduces the cognition of *law-likeness* – the emergence of a belief in a regularity or a natural law – to *habituation* as a result of regular *repetition* (Hume's *habituation theory of induction*).

Deductivism does not see anything in repetition that might produce something new; on the contrary, repetition can only make something *disappear* (*speeding up the process*); habit and practice only *eliminate* the detours of the reaction process by streamlining it. Thus, nothing comes into being through repetition. The increasing rapidity of a reaction should not be mistaken for its gradual re-creation (natura facit saltus).

The deductivist approach can see nothing in the search for rules [and] in general "rule-consciousness" but a preformed anticipation – with the help of which we "*make* our experiences" (rather than being *made* by them); although it is probably the most general *fundamental form of all intellectual reaction*, the very precondition for successful adaptation.

("... the *understanding* ... we may ... characterise as the *faculty of rules*", says Kant in the first edition of the *Critique of Pure Reason*;[22] and further: "The latter is always occupied with the investigation of appearances, in order to detect some rule in them.")

Whether this schematic outline of a deductivist psychology of knowledge comes even close to corresponding with the facts, or whether it is

---

[22] Immanuel Kant, *Kritik der reinen Vernunft* (1st ed., 1781), p. 126. [English translation by N. Kemp Smith (1929), 1965: *Critique of Pure Reason*, pp. 146 f. Tr.]

perhaps completely misdirected empirically, will not be discussed here. (I happen to suspect that the facts probably support it; however, further details regarding this subject will be reserved for a work as yet unpublished, "Theory of the Intellect".[23])

It is perhaps not self-evident why the psychological view described is called "deductivist". It might be granted that there is here a certain analogy to the deductivist-empiricist theory of knowledge (outlined in the two preceding sections); that "unjustified anticipations" correspond approximately to "tentative assumptions", and the "method of corroboration" to that of the "empirical verification of predictions". But what actually constitutes the *deductivist* aspect may not yet be quite evident at this point.

I could respond to such an objection by explaining in greater detail that the relationship between this undoubtedly deductivist theory of knowledge (which for this purpose would first have to be discussed in more precise terms) and the deductivist psychology of knowledge just delineated, is in fact one of perfect analogy. For it was constructed by direct transference*[4] of the theory of knowledge to psychological questions.

For present purposes it is, however, entirely irrelevant whether the term "deductivist" is or is not accepted. What matters here is this: that the psychology of knowledge outlined above *contradicts* the dominant *inductivist* view.

---

[23] [This work cannot be located and must be presumed lost. "Theorie des Intellekts" was the theoretical part of *"Gewohnheit"* und *"Gesetzerlebnis"* in der Erziehung: Eine pädagogisch-strukturpsychologische Monographie [*"Habit" and "Experience of Lawfullness," in Education: A pedagogical-structural-psychological monograph.* Tr.]. A part of this monograph, namely "Vorbemerkung", "Einleitung", 1. Teil: "Psychologie des Gesetzerlebnisses", 1. Abschnitt: "Phänomenologie", und "Literaturverzeichnis" ["Preliminary Note", "Introduction", Part I: *"Experience of Lawfullness"*, Section 1: "Phenomenology", and "Bibliography". Tr.], was submitted as "Thesis" in 1927 to the Pädagogisches Institut der Stadt Wien; only this "Thesis" has been preserved. Cf. Karl Popper, Zur Methodenfrage der Denkpsychologie (Dissertation, Vienna 1928), p. V; Karl Popper, Conjectures and Refutations (1963), p. 50; Karl Popper, "Intellectual Autobiography", The Philosophy of Karl Popper I. (ed. Paul Arthur Schilpp, 1974), pp. 34 ff., 59 ff., 161: note 55 (= Karl Popper, Unended Quest: An Intellectual Autobiography, 1976, pp. 44 ff., 75 ff., 205: note 55). Ed.]

*[4] I described this "principle of transference" from logic or epistemology to psychology somewhat more precisely, many years later, in my book Objective Knowledge (1972).

Whether *inductivism in the psychology of knowledge* is right or wrong, it is surely not the only possibility: it is not the *only conceivable option*.

But this is all that was to be demonstrated.

The deductivist psychology of knowledge has important similarities with Kant's psychology of knowledge, which nowadays is held in such low esteem.

The contrast between *receptions* and intellectual *reactions*, the conception of the triggering stimulus – or of the reception – as the material condition for the reaction – the formal conditions of which lie in the reacting apparatus itself (which is why they have been called "subjectively pre-formed") – all this is largely in accordance with Kantian views. Kant[24] analogously distinguishes between the "*receptivity of sensibility*" and the acts of "*spontaneity of knowledge*". The term "spontaneous" does not at all mean "self-generating" or "freely arising" or anything of this sort, but should only emphasise – in my terminology – the subjectively preformed element of the reactive. Kant rightly regards receptions as also being subjectively preformed, even if not to the same degree as the intellectual reactions of the "understanding".

(Therefore, following Helmholtz,[25] Johannes Müller's Law of the Specific Energies of the Senses can to some extent be justifiably regarded as an empirical corroboration of Kant's doctrine; but this would of course only be a corroboration of Kant's *psychology*. A number of works on cognitive psychology by Oswald Külpe's Würzburg School might, in this sense, be understood as experimental corroborations of Kant's ideas, such as Karl Bühler's *Tatsachen und Probleme zu einer Theorie der Denkvorgänge*,[26] in which Kant's ideas on this matter are addressed, and Otto Selz's *Über die Gesetze des geordneten Denkverlaufs*.[27])

---

[24] [Cf. Immanuel Kant, *Kritik der reinen Vernunft* (1st ed., 1781), p. 126. Ed.; English translation by N. Kemp Smith (1929): *Critique of Pure Reason*, p. 147. Tr.]

[25] [Cf. Hermann von Helmholtz, *Über das Sehen des Menschen* (1855), pp. 19, 41 f. (*Vorträge und Reden* I., 3rd ed., 1884, pp. 379, 396; 4th ed., 1896, pp. 99, 116); H. von Helmholtz, *Handbuch der physiologischen Optik* (1867), § 17, p. 208 (2nd ed., 1896, p. 249) [English translation by J.P.C. Southall, *Handbook of Physiological Optics* (1924–1925). Tr.]; H. von Helmholtz, *Die Tatsachen in der Wahrnehmung* (1879), pp. 8, 42 (*Vorträge und Reden* II., 3rd ed., 1884, pp. 222 f., 248; 4th ed., 1896, pp. 218 f., 244). Ed.]

[26] Karl Bühler, *Archiv für die gesamte Psychologie* 9 (1907), pp. 297 ff.; 12 (1908), pp. 1 ff., 123.

[27] Otto Selz, *Über die Gesetze des geordneten Denkverlaufs* I. (1913); II. (1922).

Kant's own distinction between theory of knowledge and psychology of knowledge was often not sufficiently strict. ·

His term "*a priori*", for example, is no doubt primarily of *epistemological* significance; it might be translated as "*valid independently of all experience*", thus referring not to genesis but to validity. (In the present analysis it will always be used in this sense.)

But it is, of course, also possible to give the term "*a priori*" a psychological meaning, perhaps one such as "not *generated* on the basis of experience". Though Kant explicitly rejects a nativist interpretation of the *a priori* ("innate concepts", etc.), psychological-genetic elements still play quite a significant part in his usage of the word.

In this psychological usage, however, the term "*a priori*" is almost equivalent to what has here been called "anticipatory".

If, for the sake of argument, we accept this usage of the term "*a priori*", then "*anticipations*" should be defined as "*a priori synthetic judgements*". The anticipatory aspect of the reaction of "rule-consciousness" (the method of tentatively searching for law-like regularities) would roughly correspond to an *a priori* "principle of causality".

But these "*a priori* synthetic judgements" would only be *tentative anticipations*, they would only exist *a priori*, that is, prior to being empirically corroborated; *a posteriori* they could still be rejected, refuted by experience. Thus it might, for example, prove futile to search for rules in certain empirical fields, such as in games of chance.

Whether the epistemological-psychological equivocation of the term "*a priori*" is of greater significance for Kant's doctrine will not be examined here (but cf. Section 11). Anyway, Kant himself always claimed universal validity and necessity for all *a priori* synthetic judgements.

But it is interesting that Kant[28] takes into consideration an *interpretation of his "result"* that fully conforms with the view presented here. This is very clearly shown by the two arguments he advances *against* such a subjective "*preformation system* of pure reason".

He holds, first, that such a preformation system would have to assume that our intellect, our subjective "dispositions of thought implanted in us", are in harmony with the "laws of nature", that they are in accordance with them (that they are adapted to them, as we would say today). If one

---

[28] Immanuel Kant, *Kritik der reinen Vernunft* (2nd ed., 1787), § 27 [English translation by N. Kemp Smith (1929), 1965: *Critique of Pure Reason*, p. 174 f. Tr.].

does not want to assume that this correspondence is an accidental one, then one is compelled to adopt the hypothesis that this correspondence was ordered by our Creator (as a kind of pre-established harmony). Kant rightly holds "that on such a hypothesis we can set no limit [to the assumption of pre-determined dispositions to future judgements]". This objection is directly related to the view advanced here (and also to the problem of adaptation in general). We have dealt with this question above ("method of Trial and Error",[29] theory of selection).

Kant's second objection is that this kind of subjectively preformed *a priori* synthetic judgement would lack the (objective) "*necessity of the categories, which is part of their very conception*". Again, this is in agreement with the view advanced here that anticipations are not necessarily *true*, and indeed that they can prove useless, and may be *a posteriori* false.

Using the term "*a priori*" in its (genetic) meaning of "anticipatory", one might characterise the psychological (and also the epistemological) "theory of preformation" advocated here, the deductivist-empiricist view, by means of the formulation:

There are, indeed, synthetic a priori judgements, but a posteriori they are often false.

---

[29] [See note 17. Ed.]

Chapter III

THE PROBLEM OF INDUCTION

5. *The infinite regression (Hume's argument).* Hume[1] was the first who presented, with exemplary clarity, the difficulties surrounding the problem of universal empirical statements, or the problem of induction ("Can we know more than we know?"). He demonstrated that every attempt at *inductive generalisation* will be defeated by a *circular inference*.

This argument will be presented here in detail: it is the crucial idea of the whole problem area. The presentation will deviate from Hume on some points of only minor relevance to the subject. (In particular, Hume's circular inference will be replaced by a so-called *regressus in infinitum*.[*1]) This does not, however, alter Hume's fundamental idea that in analysing any inductive generalisation, one will necessarily encounter impermissible logical operations.

Let us briefly mention that the concept of circular inference would be confronted here with certain logical objections (in particular from

---

[1] [David Hume, *A Treatise on Human Nature* (1739/1740), Book I, Part III, Section VI. Ed.]

[*1] The infinite regression already appears quite explicitly in Hume. See *Logik der Forschung* (2nd ed., 1966; and subsequent editions) [*The Logic of Scientific Discovery* (1959; 2nd ed., 1968; and subsequent editions). Tr.], New Appendix *VII, notes 4, 5 and 6 with references to Hume, and the text to these notes.

Russell's "theory of types"; compare this with Wittgenstein's self-contradictory formulation:[2] "No proposition can say anything about itself"). The concept of "infinite regression" is not open to these objections, but otherwise it accomplishes the same task, namely that of demonstrating the existence of an impermissible operation.

A further deviation from Hume consists in the fact that what will be primarily considered here is not so much the principle of causation, as a more general formulation of the "principle of induction"; such a "generalisation of the Humean problem" has, however, long been common practice thanks to Kant.

Apart from these changes, which are of no significance for the fundamental ideas, the presentation will merely attempt to restate Hume's argument against the admissibility of induction in its purest form.

The argument is this:

We make a sequence of observations, and may notice that a certain discovered regularity holds for all our observations without exception.

Based on these experiences, we are then quite justified in regarding as valid a statement – an empirical statement – that says something like "In all these observations, this particular regularity has always occurred."

This statement is not a strictly universal statement. It does not formulate a natural law. It is merely a *summary report* of particular events.

However, if we want to formulate the observed regularity as a natural law (because it was, indeed, identifiable in all observations without exception), that is, if we want to propose a strictly universal rule – a *strictly universal empirical statement* – we have to *induce*, or to generalise.

The generalised statement (the *inductum*) might then read as follows: "Under specified conditions, this particular regularity will always occur."

Can this generalisation be justified?

The observation material that furnished us with a basis for the summary report is, by itself, certainly not capable of providing a sufficient basis for this strictly universal proposition. For in the latter, we are asserting *more* than we are able to justify by those experiences.

From a logical point of view, whenever we make an induction, we

---

[2] [Ludwig Wittgenstein, *Tractatus Logico-Philosophicus* (1918/1922), Proposition 3.332. Ed.] *Wittgenstein's proposition is self-contradictory, because it says something about *all* propositions and therefore "about itself" – in contrast to what he himself claims.

(tacitly or explicitly) make certain *assumptions* that are not justified by the observation material on which the generalisation is directly based.

But perhaps these assumptions can be justified by different, previous and more general experiences?

In order to establish this, we must above all know exactly what assumptions we are making if we want to perform an induction.

In the most general (and, for the time being, very imprecise) terms, the assumptions of induction to be examined would have to contain something along the following lines: "Generalisation is admissible." This statement, however, should not be understood to imply that every generalisation will necessarily be correct. We know from experience that often we generalise quite incorrectly (that is, when subsequently experience proves us wrong). We might, therefore, prefer to say, "Generalisation is *possible*,"*² to express the idea that our assumption consists only in the fact that (with due caution and good luck) it is *possible* to arrive at correct generalisations. This tentative formulation, "Generalisation is possible", would thus have to express the notion that generalisation may allow us to arrive at a statement that is *true*.

In order to improve the assumption's formulation, a terminological consideration must be inserted here.

What an empirical statement reproduces, what it describes, what it *represents*, we call a "state of affairs". Every empirical statement can thus be regarded as the representation of a state of affairs. If the state of affairs represented by a statement actually *exists* (if, in fact, *there is* such a state of affairs), then the statement is *true*; if the state of affairs represented does not exist, then the statement is *false*.

With the help of this terminology, we can attempt to formulate more adequately the assumptions we make with every induction. The assumption should state that universal empirical statements may be *true*. Universal empirical statements can, however, be true only if such *states of affairs*, as represented by universal empirical statements or by natural laws, do in fact exist. If we call such a state of affairs "a universal state of affairs" or a "*law-like regularity*", we can say in brief: what we presuppose whenever we induce is that there are universal states of affairs, law-like regularities.

---

*² For example: "There is a procedure for justifying strictly universal statements." See also the following note (*3).

This presupposition would indeed suffice to justify the method of induction.*³ For if there are law-like regularities, it should in principle be possible to derive them from singular observations. For if knowledge of a true natural law permits us to deduce particular events, then, conversely, it should be possible (with luck and due caution) to find a description of a singular event such that it can be generalised into a natural law. (It must be possible to infer the law hidden behind the events, as it were, from the circumstantial evidence.) But this does mean that "induction is possible".

The assumptions we make with every inductive process (and without which this method would serve no purpose) might accordingly be formulated as follows:

"There are law-like regularities (states of affairs), i.e. states of affairs of the kind that are represented by strictly universal empirical statements – by natural laws."*⁴

This proposition I call the (first) *principle of induction*.

This principle of induction is formulated in such general terms that it probably contains only a minimum of assumptions. At any rate, there are other statements that might also be adopted as "*principles of induction*" (since they contain assumptions sufficient for an induction), but that contain more assumptions than is absolutely necessary. Such a "principle of induction", for example, would be the "principle of causality" that (according to the common view) not only asserts that there are law-like

---

*³ Below, in Section 10 (towards the end) I write: "*Obtaining knowledge means searching for laws; or, more precisely, proposing laws and systematically testing them* (irrespective of the question whether or not strictly universal laws actually exist)." In contrast to what my text says (here as well as in Section 10), this (it seems to me now) applies to both an inductivist and a deductivist concept of knowledge (see my *Introduction* 1978). That there are law-like regularities does not seem to me to be *sufficient* to justify the *procedure of induction* (in contrast to what my text seems to be saying here). What would be necessary is a metatheoretical principle such as: *There is a procedure for demonstrating the truth of strictly universal synthetic statements*.

*⁴ Cf. Ludwig Wittgenstein, *Tractatus Logico-Philosophicus* (1918/1922), propositions 6.31 and 6.36 (the reference in proposition 6.361 is to Heinrich Hertz's *Prinzipien der Mechanik*, 1894 [English translation by D.E. Jones and J.T. Walley (1899): *The Principles of Mechanics*. Tr.]). On this important point I was obviously influenced by Wittgenstein. As a principle of induction, however, the proposition is inadequate.

regularities but that, in addition, may be roughly formulated as follows: "It must be possible to predict every change in nature with any arbitrary degree of completeness (including the details of time and place) through deduction from natural laws." (In direct opposition to Schlick's[3] view, the principle of causality may thus be understood as representing a "sufficient condition of the inductive method", but not a "necessary condition".)

Whichever statement*[5] one wishes to adopt as a principle of induction, it must in any case be an empirical one (a synthetic judgement), and it must state something about the law-like character or uniformity of "nature" or the "world of experience" – about the justification for making universal statements about reality such as those proposed by natural laws.

Now how can we establish which principle of induction is the correct one and whether a valid principle of induction exists at all? Everything depends on the validity of the principle of induction, for every induction of a natural law presupposes a principle of induction. It is, therefore, logically untenable if the principle of induction is invalid.

One might simply declare one of the principles (for example, the one I have formulated, or the "principle of causality") to be an indispensable intellectual precondition, to be immediately plausible, self-evident, etc.; in a word, to be valid for the reason that its soundness cannot be doubted. The principle of induction would, then, have to be accepted as a synthetic *a priori* judgement: a concession to rationalism that would certainly be quite problematic.*[6] While this step might be considered as a last resort (it will be discussed in Sections 9–11), it will not be taken into account for the moment.

Here we shall take the position of not accepting synthetic *a priori* judgements and of allowing experience alone to make the final decision about synthetic judgements. Accordingly, we must demand that the principle of induction also be justified by experience (*a posteriori*).

---

[3] Moritz Schlick, *Allgemeine Erkenntnislehre* (2nd ed., 1925), p. 362.

*[5] From here on, the argument of this section seems to me essentially unobjectionable, provided the "second-order principle of induction" is corrected according to the correction of the first-order principle.

*[6] Kant made this concession, later unconsciously followed by Bertrand Russell, in spite of Wittgenstein's remark in the *Tractatus Logico-Philosophicus* (1918/1922), proposition 6.31. Cf. Bertrand Russell, "The Limits of Empiricism", *Proceedings of the Aristotelian Society* 36 (1936), pp. 131 ff.

At first glance, this does not seem to be very difficult.

After all, it was established above only that *those* sequences of observations that lead directly to the formulation of a particular natural law are not sufficient for its induction. The principle of induction is nothing but a formulation of the assumptions that, in addition to these observations, are necessary for the induction.

The principle of induction itself might, therefore, be justified by *other* observations.

We would, then, have to assume (roughly as Mill did) that the principle of induction is justified by an immense number of experiences, or more precisely, by an incomparably greater number than any particular natural law.

The lesson of these experiences is that in countless cases of practical life, induction has met with complete, and indeed often surprising, success. We may infer from this that generalisation really is possible, that is, that the principle of induction is valid. Moreover, not only do we have the argument concerning the large number of observations; we might also assert that each advance in our knowledge of nature opens up profound and increasingly startling insights into the fact that the world is ruled by "eternal laws".

And yet, all these arguments together still do not suffice to guarantee the validity of the principle of induction.

The inference from our observations as to the validity of the principle of induction in turn represents a generalisation, an inductive inference. And in this generalisation *again* we (tacitly or explicitly) make an *assumption* analogous to the earlier assumption formulated in the principle of induction. The only difference is that this time it consists not in the induction of a natural law, but in the induction of a principle of induction.

A natural law may be understood as a statement about singular empirical statements; a principle of induction – as a statement about natural laws.

Accordingly, the new assumption will have to be slightly modified in roughly the following terms:*[7]

---

*[7] The following statement should be corrected according to the correction of the earlier (first-order) principle of induction, as follows: "There is a procedure for demonstrating the truth of the (first-order) principle of induction."

"There are law-like regularities, there are universal states of affairs of the kind represented by statements about natural laws, that is, by propositions of the type of a principle of induction."

This statement I call the "second-order principle of induction". (The preceding "principles of induction" may now be called "first-order principles of induction".)

The second-order principle of induction is analogous to the first-order principles of induction. While the latter may be regarded as statements about statements of the type of natural laws, the former may be regarded as a statement about statements of the type of principles of induction.

Assuming such a second-order principle of induction as given, a first-order principle of induction can be induced. Which of the possible first-order principles of induction is to be adopted would then be decided by the experiences discussed above, in the same way as the decision about the content of a particular natural law is made on the basis of experience. That is why corrections may still become necessary. (Even if a principle of induction is given, the *inductum* should not be regarded as given but as a "task that is set" for cognition, as the neo-Kantians put it.)

In fact, until recently*[1] most natural scientists held the view that experience favours a principle of induction as formulated in the "principle of causality". Today, on the basis of more recent observations about atomic processes (cf. also Section 19), the preference seems to be for a more general formulation (such as I have introduced as the first principle of induction).

Now everything depends on the validity of the second-order principle of induction.

It requires no further explanation that considerations analogous to those concerning the validity of a first-order principle may be brought to bear on the validity of the second-order principle of induction. If its validity is to be based on an induction, a third-order principle of induction would have to be presupposed, which would then be a statement about statements of the type of the second-order principle of induction.

In this way, a hierarchy of types emerges:

---

*[1] This was written in about 1930. The allusion is to Heisenberg's indeterminacy relations (1927).

Natural laws (these may be understood as statements about singular empirical statements, and as of a higher type than the latter*[9]). The induction of a natural law requires a

First-order principle of induction, which as a statement about natural laws is of a higher type than the latter; the induction of a first-order principle of induction, in turn, requires a

Second-order principle of induction, which as a statement about first-order principles of induction is, in turn, of a higher type than the latter; *and so on.*

Every universal empirical statement requires a principle of induction of a higher type than the *inductum*, if it is to possess any *a posteriori* validity value at all (either true or false) as an inductum.*[10]

Therein consists the infinite regression.

This line of argument is the foundation of the critique of inductivism.

The infinite regression ("regress of induction") formulates, in more precise terms, Hume's argument against the admissibility of induction. It states that a pure inductive inference cannot be logically justified, that universal statements can never be derived from singular observations; in brief, it states something that (at least for every empiricist) is self-evident: that we cannot know more*[11] than we know.

6. *Inductivist positions.* What are the conclusions to be drawn from Hume's argument? Is there no gap in Hume's reasoning? How are natural laws, universal empirical statements, now to be understood?

It is clear that Hume's argument has *posed* the problem of induction exhaustively. What solutions are there?

The different possible answers to these questions will be discussed systematically. An attempt will be made to show that none of the inductivist theories of knowledge deals successfully with the problem. Following this somewhat lengthy examination (and in part during this examination), the deductivist-empiricist standpoint will be discussed in

---

*[9] Today I would not regard natural laws as of a higher "type" (in the sense of a theory of types) than singular empirical statements (basic statements). The view outlined here in the text, however, does not seem to affect what follows.

*[10] Should read: ". . . if it is to be accepted as true as an *inductum*" or perhaps "to be assigned the validity value true . . ."

*[11] Formulated more clearly: that we do not know more than we know.

order to show that it is capable of furnishing a satisfactory answer to the problem of induction (and to questions related to it).

The large number of inductivist attempts to cope with the problem of induction makes it necessary to proceed in a *systematic* fashion if the criticism is to aim at completeness and, as far as possible, to take all approaches into account.

The tentative inductivist solutions will be treated [here], in turn, in the following groups.

1. *Normal-statement positions*: these solutions assume that all empirical statements have a "normal" type of validity, that is, that they are in principle *finally decidable*, that they are [demonstrably*[1]] either true or false. If there are any *universal* empirical statements, then this must also apply to them. However, *whether* there are universal empirical statements is precisely what is at issue between these competing solutions to the problem.

2. *Probability positions*: these tentative solutions assume that the price that empirical statements are obliged to pay for universal validity is an abnormal type of validity; that is, universal empirical statements possess no normal truth value, but only an (objective) *probability value.*[2]

3. *Pseudo-statement positions*: these assume − like the normal-statement positions − that all empirical statements have a normal type of validity. In addition, however, they advance the view that the so-called "universal empirical statements" can, in principle, be assigned *no* normal validity value since they can never be finally proved to be true. They conclude that these universal empirical statements are *not genuine statements* at all. They are frequently taken to be statements simply because one is easily deceived by their grammatical form (the *statement* form). But the "statements" of our language are not always "statements" in the logical sense. According to this view, *universal* empirical statements should, from the logical stand-point, be regarded as *pseudo-statements*. Therefore, they themselves are not knowledge, but they do have an important function in the cognitive process; not a theoretical function, admittedly, but a *practical* one: they are "*instructions*" for the formation of genuine (i.e. *individual*) empirical statements.

---

*[1] See my *Introduction* 1978.
*[2] This was Hans Reichenbach's position (in 1930).

A further comment on this classification:

It takes into account only the attitude towards the *epistemological* problem of induction. It does not take into account psychological aspects, such as the *belief* in truth or in probability. These elements will only be incorporated into the closer analysis of the different positions if they are important for an understanding of these positions.

Chapter IV

THE NORMAL-STATEMENT POSITIONS

7. *The normal-statement positions: naive inductivism, strict positivism and apriorism.*
The normal-statement positions on inductivism assume that all empirical
statements are "normal" statements, that is, that they are *decidably true or
false.**¹ It "is essential for a genuine statement", says Schlick,¹ "that it be in
principle finally verifiable or falsifiable". If "strict universal empirical
statements" exist at all, then the same will also apply to them.

But are there universal empirical statements (in the sense of strict
universality)?

Naive inductivism – prior to Hume – readily affirms the existence of universal empirical statements. Bacon believes in *inductio vera*, a scientific
method that in principle is capable of establishing, through systematic
generalisation, true and universally valid laws. (Errors may, of course,
always occur – but the same is true for deduction.) This is the position
against which Hume's arguments are actually directed. It seems to me that

---

*¹ What is meant is: "normal" statements have a logical form such that, if they are
true, their truth is *decidable*, and if they are false, their falsity is *decidable*; that is, decidable
by *experience*.

¹ Moritz Schlick, "Die Kausalität in der gegenwärtigen Physik", *Die Naturwissenschaften*
19 (1931), p. 156.

this position has been finally overcome by Hume (in spite of Mill) and will not, therefore, be treated any further in this analysis.

As a result of Hume's argument, only two views remain logically admissible among the normal-statement positions, since all the others lapse into infinite regression. With great acumen, Kant described these two still-admissible views in the following terms:

". . . experience never confers on its judgements true or strict but only putative and comparative *universality*, through induction. We can properly say, therefore, only that *so far as we have hitherto observed*, there is no exception to this or that rule." (The latter emphasis is not in the original.) "If, then, a judgement is thought with strict universality . . . it is not derived from experience, but is completely valid *a priori*."[2]

Kant's two statements formulate with clarity the only two positions still admissible among the "normal-statement positions":

Either, one takes a consistently empiricist standpoint, refusing to make any concession to rationalism – then there are no [demonstrably true] universal statements but only *summary reports* of observations (*"so far as we have hitherto observed . . ."*). The linguistic form of universality in these statements is only a *façon de parler*, a convenient form of reporting. The position that interprets "universal" empirical statements as summary reports is what I call "*strict positivism*".

Or, one is intent on saving the strictly universal empirical statements, and then one is forced to concede to rationalism the existence of *synthetic a priori judgements*; at least, the *a priori* validity of a principle of induction (for instance, in the form of a principle of causality). This is the position of "*apriorism*".

In his clear formulation of this (apparently so self-evident) alternative, Kant shows himself to be far ahead of a number of his modern critics (in particular, the proponents of the probability positions): not only as a better logician but, as we shall see, also as a better student of Hume.

Does one of these two positions succeed in satisfactorily solving the problem of induction? The following sections (8–11) will show that neither solution is satisfactory, and thus that the normal-statement position as such should be abandoned.

---

[2] [Immanuel Kant, *Kritik der reinen Vernunft* (2nd ed., 1787), pp. 3 f. Ed.; English translation by N. Kemp Smith (1929), 1965: *Critique of Pure Reason*, pp. 43 f. Tr.]

8. *Critique of strict positivism — twofold transcendence of natural laws.* Can empirical statements be universally valid [demonstrably universally valid] solely on the basis of experience?

Strict positivism and apriorism concur that this question must be answered in the negative: since Hume, no other response is possible.

But the two approaches draw very different conclusions from Hume's argument.

Strict positivism (not to be confused with the approach that in this work is referred to as logical positivism) abandons the strict universality of natural laws. In this way, it is able to preserve the fundamental empiricist thesis. It concludes: If empirical statements cannot be [are not demonstrably] strictly universally valid through being based on experience alone, then natural laws simply are not strictly universal statements (but are only summary reports of what we have hitherto observed). For (as empirical statements) they can be valid only on the basis of experience.

Apriorism draws the opposite conclusion: If empirical statements cannot be universally valid on the basis of experience alone, then natural laws are not valid *solely* on the basis of experience (but they contain an apriorist element). For they are strictly universal empirical statements.

Both positions do accept Hume's argument. They diverge, however, in their *assessment* of the two assumptions – the *fundamental empiricist thesis* on the one hand, the *strict universality* of natural laws on the other – one of which has to be abandoned since it seems that they cannot both together be compatible with Hume's argument. Strict positivism regards the *fundamental empiricist thesis* as more valuable, sacrificing strict universality. Apriorism believes that natural laws must not be conceived as summary reports. While saving the *strict universality* of natural laws, it must in return abandon the fundamental empiricist thesis and concede to [classical] rationalism the *a priori* validity of a principle of induction.

(A schematic representation of these relationships may be found in the Appendix, Table II.)

Of the two, strict positivism seems to be the position closer to the empirical sciences, for it is *radically empiricist*. It also seems to be the more cautious of the two, and to make fewer assumptions.

Strict positivism may be called radically empiricist, because not only does it fully and programmatically accept the fundamental empiricist thesis: it goes even further. Not merely does it hold that experience alone *decides* the truth or falsity of a statement, but it asserts (the characteristic assertion of *every* form of positivism) that all scientifically admissible (all "legitimate") statements, all empirical-scientific knowledge, must be *completely reducible to experience* (perceptual experiences).

This assertion that "it must be possible in principle to transform all scientific statements into statements about the 'given', or about experiences", might be called the "fundamental positivist thesis". Its bias is clear. Positive facts from our immediate experience (especially from our perceptual experience) are the only thing that in the empirical realm can be called "strict" or "completely certain". For this reason, an exact factual science must not assert more than what we know for certain, and [it] should not attempt to offer more than is actually "given" to us.

Positivist arguments will be thoroughly discussed in subsequent sections (cf. especially the criticism of logical positivism in Sections 44–46). At this point, general positivist arguments will be briefly considered as far as is necessary for an understanding of the normal-statement positions – of strict positivism and of apriorism.

The positivist theory of knowledge has been called, quite correctly, a "doctrine of immanence", because it is not content with a decision by experience, but (if at all possible) wants to remain in the realm of the immediately given, of what can be immediately experienced. In its fundamental approach, positivism is directed against any "*transcendence*", that is, against any attempt to go beyond this realm of the "given", even where it only happens tentatively, as when a hypothesis is adopted conjecturally and pending further trials.

Schlick[1] characterises this "immanence philosophy" quite correctly when he speaks of the "positivist desire to stop at the purely factual, anxiously avoiding additions from thought, and restricting itself to the mere description of what exists through propositions, without adding hypotheses".

Of course, any attempt to apply the idea of immanence in its *perfect* purity would be defeated by the fact that it would render all knowledge com-

---

[1]   Moritz Schlick, *Allgemeine Erkenntnislehre* (2nd ed., 1925), p. 182.

pletely impossible. Every proposition, *every representation*, but especially every scientific proposition *transcends* the immediately given, and is more than a pedantically precise description of pure experience.

This applies not only to universal statements but to *all* empirical statements, that is, also to singular empirical statements. For example, if a chemist notes – apparently in a purely descriptive fashion – that this (particular) fluid produced foam when this (particular) piece of metal was thrown into it, this description incorporates a large number of assumptions that are not "given", i.e., they are transcendent: among other things, for instance, the assumption that quite different experiences (such as those relating to "non-effervescent fluid" and "effervescent fluid") somehow refer to the *same* ("genidentical"*[1]) *object*; further, that not *all* experiences (e.g. a simultaneous "feeling of thirst") are to be included in the description, not even all simultaneous perceptual experiences (a car sounding its horn), indeed, not even all directly related visual perceptions (the glint of the test tube), etc.

Any representation, even the simplest, thus contains more (and less) than what is immediately "given". (Incidentally, from the point of view of non-sensualist cognitive psychology – the *psychology of intellectual reactions* – this should come as no surprise.)

I call the form of transcendence just outlined, which is inevitable in *all* empirical knowledge, including singular empirical statements, the "*transcendence of representation in general*". This transcendence will prove to be relevant to the arguments of the next section and especially those of Section 11.

Hence, the radical demand to restrict oneself to *pure immanence* must be rejected. It is in no way capable of elucidating empirical knowledge, and is far from solving the epistemological problems in a satisfactory fashion. Schlick views the situation in much the same way. He writes (immediately following the above quotation):[2]

"Alas, however, it is self-evident that the pedantically strict application of this programme would amount to a renunciation of knowledge in

---

*[1] The term "genidentical" (from genetically identical) was coined by Kurt Lewin. [See K. Lewin, *Der Begriff der Genese in der Physik, Biologie und Entwicklungsgeschichte: Eine Untersuchung zur vergleichenden Wissenschaftslehre* (1922). Ed.]

[2] Moritz Schlick, *op. cit.*, pp. 182 f.

general. For knowledge presupposes thought, and this requires concepts, and they can only be acquired by working on the factual material, which immediately creates the possibility of errors and contradictions. Scientific description, which is explanation, consists after all in the fact that, with the help of acts of re-cognition, facts are related to each other and interpreted in terms of each other.

"Thus, if strictly applied, this extreme standpoint is self-defeating; though one can still hope that its advantages may continue to be enjoyed if a minimum of added thought is permitted."

The epistemological position that is here called strict positivism, holds the view that this "minimum of added thought" certainly does not include the acceptance of strictly universal empirical statements (or even that of a synthetic-apriori principle of induction).

For in contrast to singular empirical statements, strictly universal statements – if one were to accept them as "legitimate" – would be transcendent in two ways. Not only do they transcend immediate experience; as Hume's argument demonstrates, they even transcend the realm of what is empirically verifiable in general. Their transcendence is not only the unavoidable but hardly disquieting transcendence of representation in general, but they are also burdened with a second form of transcendence, the transcendence of generalisation.

This second form of transcendence is undoubtedly a much more serious problem than the first.

A pure doctrine of immanence that seeks to avoid even the transcendence of representation in general, preferring to do without any knowledge of reality rather than accepting transcendence – such a view simply cannot be recognised as an epistemological position. Its argumentation has a strong psychologistic tinge, and it is of no practical significance at all for the problems of scientific justification. There are no systematic experiences that would cause science to approach simple ("elementary") empirical statements (in so far as they "report observations" without theoretically interpreting them) in a particularly sceptical fashion. Such scepticism would be merely a matter of speculation. (On the question of "elementary empirical statements", the "empirical basis", cf. final part of Section 11).

In contrast, the view here referred to as strict positivism may be called a strictly epistemological position. That an unequivocal empirical verification of an elementary empirical statement is possible, may be [provisionally*²] accepted as unproblematic. But the fact that we have no way of guaranteeing the truth of a strictly universal empirical statement does indeed have *practical consequences* for scientific methods (and for our life in general). In numerous instances, later observations have demonstrated a presumed law to be false, or a presumed law-like regularity to be non-existent (for example, Koch's tuberculin treatment³).

Thus, the rejection of the transcendence of generalisation ought indeed to be taken seriously; it is not possible to defend the transcendence by appealing simply to the transcendence of representation in general, perhaps by arguing that it is arbitrary to permit one form of transcendence while excluding the other. Strict positivism is protected against such superficial objections by Hume's argument against the admissibility of induction.

Thus, strict positivism attempts to do without any generalisation, and without induction.

It views natural laws as summary reports, that is, it simply stops short of taking the impermissible step of generalising. That natural laws are linguistically formulated as strictly universal statements is no argument in support of taking the (impermissible) inductive step, but [it] occurs only for reasons of economy in linguistic expressions: drawing any conclusions from this as to the logical character of natural laws would be entirely misconceived.

Theoretical physics, too, seeks to represent its statements in the axiomatic-deductive form of mathematics. But all physicists know that mathematical and physical statements must nevertheless be distinguished from each other: with respect to *physical* statements they are, in principle, always prepared to be corrected by experience and to revise these statements; yet no experience will persuade them to revise a purely mathematical statement.

Thus the physicist – so the "strict positivist" concludes – tacitly makes the following proviso with respect to all "universal" statements (in

---

*² In Volume II this will become a problem. See *Introduction 1978*.

³ [Robert Koch, *Verhandlungen des 10. internationalen medizinischen Kongresses Berlin 1890* (1891), pp. 45 ff.; *Deutsche medizinische Wochenschrift* 16 (1890), pp. 757, 1029 ff.; 17 (1891), pp. 101 f., 1189 ff.; 23 (1897), pp. 209 ff. See also Bernhard Möllers, *Robert Koch: Persönlichkeit und Lebenswerk 1843–1910* (1950), pp. 556 ff. Ed.]

Kant's[4] formulation; cf. preceding section): "so far as we have hitherto observed". Yet natural laws become summary reports precisely on account of this *reservatio mentalis*.

According to strict positivism, the problem of induction arises only as a result of misjudging these simple facts.

Undoubtedly, the epistemology of strict positivism cannot be refuted by purely logical means. (Incidentally, the same applies to apriorism.) It is entirely consistent and free of internal contradictions. Nevertheless, it is not satisfactory as an epistemological solution. It is defeated by the *fundamental positivist contradiction*.

This contradiction is not an internal or *logical* one, but a *specifically epistemological* contradiction: the *positivist interpretation* of scientific knowledge is inconsistent with the *actual method* of the empirical sciences, and in particular with the methods of scientific testing.

If the pure doctrine of immanence completely fails to do justice to the fact of scientific knowledge and therefore must be rejected from a specifically epistemological standpoint, the situation is analogous in the case of strict positivism; the latter, too, is unable to do justice to scientific knowledge.

The view that natural laws are summary reports contradicts the method used by natural science for testing natural laws.

Schlick's work "Die Kausalität in der gegenwärtigen Physik"[5] contains a section in which the objections against strict positivism suggested here are convincingly formulated. One reason for my quoting this section is that Schlick himself (as a logical positivist) advances arguments that, as will be shown below (especially in Section 41), are closely connected with strict positivism. Schlick writes:[6]

"After we have successfully discovered a function linking a series of observation results with each other in a satisfactory fashion, we tend not to be fully satisfied, even if this function has a very simple structure; rather, we are only now approaching the main question that our previous considerations have not yet touched upon: we examine whether the formula

---

[4] [Immanuel Kant, *Kritik der reinen Vernunft* (2nd ed., 1787), pp. 3 f. Ed.; English translation by N. Kemp Smith (1929), 1965: *Critique of Pure Reason*, p. 43 f. Tr.]

[5] Moritz Schlick, *Die Naturwissenschaften* 19 (1931), pp. 145 ff.

[6] Moritz Schlick, *op. cit.*, pp. 149 f.

obtained, also correctly represents those observations that we have not yet used in arriving at the formula. For the physicist as an explorer of reality, the absolutely decisive and essential thing, the only thing of real importance, is that equations derived from a set of data are now also corroborated by new data. Only if this is the case, will he consider his formula to be a natural law. In other words, the true criterion of law-likeness, and the essential characteristic of causality, is *successful prediction*.

"A successful prediction, then, can only be understood as the corroboration of a formula by data not used in constructing the formula. Whether these data have already been observed earlier or are only subsequently ascertained, is completely irrelevant. This is a principle of the greatest importance. In this respect, past and future data have exactly the same status, i.e. the future does not have a special status; the criterion . . . is not corroboration in the future, but corroboration in general."

Schlick summarises his view to the effect "that empirical knowledge coincides with the possibility of making predictions".[7]

Strict positivism, however, is incompatible with the methodological facts described by Schlick.

First, conclusions about unknown events or about "new data" can never be derived from a summary report. This is precisely the significance of Hume's argument that nothing justifies our drawing conclusions from the known and the observed about the unknown and the hitherto unobserved.

The success of predictions can only be a criterion of law-likeness if the predictions stand in a logical relationship with the established law, that is, if they are *logically entailed* by the established law. However, in order for us logically to infer a hitherto unobserved event, the natural law cannot be a summary report, but must be a *universal* statement.

"A direct application of what was valid in a number of individual cases to a similar new case can . . . represent only a psychological event, not a *logical* connection," writes Victor Kraft,[8] and he continues: "*One is justified* . . . in inferring a new case only through the medium of the *universal*. Only if there is universality over and above the individual cases is one . . . justified in applying to a new case a state of affairs holding for known individual cases."

---

[7] Moritz Schlick, *op. cit.*, p. 150
[8] Viktor Kraft, *Die Grundformen der wissenschaftlichen Methoden* (1925), p. 220.

It seems to me that even more important than this argument – that one may infer unobserved cases only through the "medium of the universal" – is the fact that the method presented by Schlick is a method of (empirically) *testing* natural laws. This alone is enough to refute strict positivism.

Strict positivism is interested in natural laws being empirically decided. It regards them as summary reports because it is only the latter that confine themselves to what we know and can be conclusively verified in a strictly empirical fashion. However, the decision in fact *never* depends exclusively on the observations that, according to strict positivism, ought to determine the acceptance or rejection of natural law. Other observations are decisive, namely, those that were not used in formulating the law. Thus, natural laws are more than (or at any rate something different from) mere reports about what we already know.

In addition to this decisive argument, there is another of lesser significance that nevertheless seems to me quite noteworthy. It is the argument that the transcendence of all generalisations, especially in the case of the most important natural laws, assumes a particularly pronounced form that seems hardly compatible with strict positivism.

The argument for strict positivism is based on the assumption that the [Kantian] proviso, "so far as we have hitherto observed", is sufficient to transform any natural law into a summary report about sequences of observations (or, more precisely, to make it evident that it is nothing but a summary report). This idea, however, is applicable only if the natural law (conceived as a universal statement) is, in terms of its content, nothing but a simple generalisation, a mere *extrapolation of a sequence of observations*.

However (as Duhem[9] in particular has shown), it is precisely the most significant and typical natural laws that are the furthest removed from simple extrapolations. They always contain a new idea, which is indeed *new* vis-à-vis the "sequences of observations" – an idea extending far beyond the realm of the sequence of observations. This is demonstrated by the fact that its consequences may be observed in entirely different fields of scientific experience.

---

[9] [Cf. Pierre Duhem, *Ziel und Struktur der physikalischen Theorien* (German translation by Friedrich Adler, 1908). Ed. English translation by Philip P. Wiener (1954): *The Aim and Structure of Physical Theory*. Tr.]

Thus, this special (and if you like, "higher") form of the transcendence of generalisations consists in that typical natural laws (theories) make assertions not merely about hitherto unobserved cases of a sequence of scientific observations (an observed regularity), but even about very distant and often still unexplored areas of experience.

For example, even if one were to view Kepler's laws as mere generalisations or as simple extrapolations, such a view would appear to be definitely inapplicable to Newton's theory of gravitation. True, the law of gravity is itself a generalisation of Kepler's laws (and Newton himself even held the erroneous view that he was able logically [inductively] to reduce his theory to these laws). But the law of gravity is something completely different; [it] is at any rate *much more* than a mere extrapolation from Kepler's laws or from the corresponding sequences of observations exhaustively covered by Kepler's laws. For according to Kepler's second law (and according to one of Newton's theorems), planetary motion is a "central motion" caused by the planets being subjected to a force directed towards the sun. The force operating in this central motion would affect *only* the planet, i.e. it would be *one-sided*. The *mutual* attraction between the masses of the sun and the planet asserted by the law of gravity can therefore never be derived by mere extrapolation from this approach. Another reason why the theory of gravitation cannot be a simple generalisation of Kepler's laws is that it directly contradicts them. According to Kepler, the sun is not in motion, whereas according to Newton, it revolves around the common centre of gravity of sun and planet. A *generalisation* of Kepler's laws would at least have to assume that they hold in all cases (even if perhaps only as approximations). According to the theory of gravitation, even as approximations they hold only if the mass of the planet is very small compared with that of the sun. The idea of general gravitation thus contains something new vis-à-vis Kepler's laws; this is also borne out by the fact that it is applicable to other fields of observation, and not only to celestial mechanics.

It would probably be even more difficult to view modern theories of physics, such as the theory of relativity, as mere extrapolation from a number of observations.

What is characteristic of these theories connecting distant fields of knowledge is that, while under specific conditions they may produce results similar to those of the older theory, they nevertheless flatly contradict a simple generalisation of it. The older theory is, after all, not *strictly* a special case of the new one, but a (more or less crude) *approximation*.

The applicability of theories to *different* fields of empirical research*[3] is of great interest. Some fields of research*[4] were opened up only in this way, and new and fruitful problems are always being posed. For the method of empirically testing theories, this form of the transcendence of generalisation also proves significant. Corroboration from a very remote field carries particular weight in science, and is regarded (cf. on this the considerations in Sections 15 and 16) as a particularly convincing form of justification.

Strict positivism – at first glance appealing owing to its radical empiricism – proves on closer inspection to be unsatisfactory, especially from the perspective of empirical science.

Theorising in natural science strives for the highest degree of generalisation, for the greatest unification and the utmost level of abstraction – in short, for ever higher transcendence; and (as will be seen) it does so without violating the fundamental empiricist thesis. It is impossible to pursue the idea of immanence, even in a moderate form, while simultaneously keeping one's sights on [the practice of] science. The interests of science are different from those of positivism; and this is the *fundamental positivist contradiction*.

Just as the pure doctrine of immanence implies a renunciation of all knowledge, so the epistemology of strict positivism implies a renunciation of theorising, or of the methods of theoretical natural science.

Yet there is no reason to fear that positivist philosophy will threaten the existence of theoretical natural science; rather, the opposite is the case: the very fact of the existence of theoretical knowledge in natural science makes strict positivism a logically unobjectionable but epistemologically insignificant philosophical ideology.

---

*[3] What is meant is that (for example) Newton's theory brings together Kepler's theory of planetary motion and Galileo's theory of free fall near the earth's surface (while at the same time correcting them).

*[4] For instance, the observations of fixed stars situated almost in line with the sun were inspired by Einstein's theory.

9. *The transcendental method – presentation of apriorism.* At the end of Section 2, the *method* of the present investigation was characterised – only *tentatively* – as that of a *critique of proposed epistemological solutions.*

The first of these critiques being completed, an attempt can now be made to spell out this critical method at somewhat greater length; I shall, however, return to the question of method later on (in Section 47) and provide an answer in more precise terms.

All scientific criticism consists in identifying *contradictions.*

A contradiction may (in the simplest case) be a *purely logical* one, an "internal contradiction" of an assertion. In this case, the method of criticism, or the method of demonstrating this contradiction, can be called a *logical method.* An example of the logical method in epistemological criticism is provided by Hume's argument: the logical demonstration that naive inductivism is an internally inconsistent position.

The *empirical method of criticism* is of the greatest importance for the criticism of *empirical statements,* e.g. of physical propositions; this is in addition to the purely logical method, for such a statement might also be internally inconsistent. The empirical method of criticism consists in demonstrating a contradiction with the facts, that is, with experience. For every empirical statement *asserts* something empirical (the existence of a state of affairs) and can in this way become inconsistent with experience.

The logical *and* the empirical methods of criticism may be called methods of *immanent criticism* (for they do not go beyond the realm of what is asserted by the thesis criticised), and may be contrasted with the entirely different kind of criticism known as *transcendent criticism.* (Whether the logical and empirical methods are the *only* methods of immanent criticism need not concern us for the moment.)

Transcendent criticism, which as a method of criticism and argumentation should never*[1] be allowed to play a part in the epistemological debate, consists in confronting one thesis, one position, with another; more precisely, in using a contradiction between one position assumed to be true and another that is being criticised, as evidence against the latter. Such criticism, combating one position by means of presuppositions extraneous to it (which is why such criticism is said to be transcendent),

---

*[1] I now hold a completely different view on this matter: even a transcendent criticism may be exceedingly illuminating, although it will never be sufficient for a clear refutation.

and setting out to assess one theoretical construct in terms of an entirely different one, can in principle always be directed with equal justification against either position; hence, it is completely *irrelevant* for our discussion (however persuasive it may sound). One must therefore insist that all epistemological criticism be *immanent criticism*.

Yet time and time again one encounters this untenable method of transcendent criticism in the epistemological debate; probably because it is not sufficiently distinguished from the following (critical) procedure; a procedure that is based on the method of *immanent criticism*, and is the only one that makes this method into one of positive *corroboration*.

This procedure, also used in the present work, may perhaps be best described by some remarks on its structure.

If the proposed solution is correct — which will always be only tentatively presupposed — then all other solutions will be *false where* they contradict the proposed solution. Admittedly, in itself a ("transcendent") contradiction between two solutions is insignificant. If, however, we can successfully demonstrate in a *different* way, by way of a *strictly immanent* criticism, that all other solutions are untenable precisely in those respects in which they also contradict the proposed solution, then this will no longer be completely insignificant. Admittedly, such a procedure cannot be regarded as a method of *proving* the proposed solution to be the correct one, but if this solution *proves* to be a key, or a guide, to the *immanent* weaknesses of all other positions, then this may well be regarded as a serious argument in its favour.

It is, however, as we can see, absolutely crucial for this method that finding the weakness of an opponent's position (through a transcendent comparison with one's own position) should not be regarded as an *argument*, and that the presumed weakness should be *demonstrated* only through a *strictly immanent* criticism.

Thus, only immanent criticism is of objective significance and only such criticism will be presented in the following analysis (cf. also Section 37). Only *after* completing the (immanent) critical discussion of the problem of induction will I return (in Section 47) to the procedure of corroborating the proposed solution.

At this point, however — as a preliminary step in the immanent criticism of the positions to be discussed — the following question needs to be answered:

How can an *epistemological solution* be immanently criticised? Which *methods of immanent criticism* can be applied to it?

So far we have discussed two methods of immanent criticism, the *logical* and the *empirical* method. Now our question is:

Can both methods be used for epistemological criticism? With respect to the logical method at least, the answer should be affirmative; but what about the empirical method? And if it cannot be used, will the logical method suffice? If not: *are there other admissible methods*, methods of immanent criticism?

This can be seen in schematic representation in Table 3.

Aside from the *purely logical* method – the admissibility and applicability of which requires no further justification – the *empirical* method of the *psychology of knowledge* (especially since Locke) has been recommended time and again as the method of the theory of knowledge. This method is rejected here. The question about the *validity* of natural laws cannot be answered by appealing to psychological facts – for example, by appealing to our beliefs (cf. Sections 1, 2 and 4, later also Section 11).

Shall we, therefore, have to be content with the purely logical method? If there were no admissible method apart from logic, then a logically consistent theory of knowledge could never be immanently criticised.

Is there, in addition to the logical method (and the psychological-empirical method, which has been rejected), a method of epistemological criticism that could be a substitute for the inapplicable empirical method? *Is there a specifically epistemological method?*

Table 3

	Immanent criticism			*Transcendent criticism*
	Purely logical method	*Empirical method*	*Other methods?*	(confronting different positions with each other)
(Methods *admissible* in general)	(+)	(+)	(?)	(–)
Applicable to *epistemological* criticism	+	?	?	–

This question gives no indication whatever as to how, in more concrete terms, such a method might proceed. The phrase "specifically epistemological" does not contain an answer, but only a *problem*.

Kant was the first who saw this problem. What is alluded to here by the phrase "*specifically epistemological*", in Kant's terminology would have to be rendered by the term "*transcendental*". And a method such as the one under consideration here – a method proceeding neither *purely logically* nor *empirically*, and specifically relating to *epistemological* assertions, that is, to the question whether or not these assertions are *justified* – would accordingly, in Kant's terminology, be a "*transcendental method*".

Taking this linguistic usage into account, the schematic representation of our question takes the form shown in Table 4.

In Kantian terminology, to be subsequently also employed here, our question would now have to be formulated as follows:

Is there a transcendental, that is, a specifically epistemological, procedure of immanent criticism?

And what might such a transcendental procedure be?

It has often been doubted that there is another procedure of immanent criticism in addition to the logical and the empirical testing procedures; for while Kant's definition of the *task* of his "transcendental method" is quite unequivocal, his *solution* of this task, and the more concrete description of the transcendental *procedure itself*, are often rather abstruse and contradictory. It is, therefore, quite understandable that even

Table 4

	Immanent criticism			Transcendent criticism
	Purely logical method	Psychological-empirical method	Transcendental method	
Methods of *epistemological* criticism	+	–	?	–

[1] [Jakob Friedrich Fries, *Neue Kritik der Vernunft* I. (1st ed., 1807), pp. XXVII, XXXV ff.; 2nd ed. (*Neue oder anthropologische Kritik der Vernunft* I.), 1828, pp. 21, 28 ff. Ed.]

Fries[1] (who otherwise is probably one of the most faithful keepers of the Kantian tradition) speaks of Kant's "prejudice in favour of the transcendental", declaring empirical psychology to be the only admissible method of the theory of knowledge ("anthropological method of the critique of reason"; cf. Section 11).

Yet despite such reservations, the question of the admissibility of a transcendental method must undoubtedly be answered in the affirmative.

There is a specifically epistemological method, that is, a *transcendental method* (in the sense of the task that Kant formulated for such a method); a method that, if handled properly, is not only completely *unobjectionable* but virtually *unavoidable*; a method that probably *every* theorist of knowledge (since Kant) has utilised more or less consciously.

In the present work too, such a transcendental method – without mentioning this term – has repeatedly been used.

In particular, the *critique of strict positivism* was purely transcendental. There it was explicitly emphasised that this position is *logically* unassailable, and that the contradiction it confronts is not an internal, that is, a *purely logical* one, but a contradiction between the epistemological position and the *actual method of the empirical sciences.*

"The very fact of the existence of theoretical knowledge in natural science makes strict positivism a logically unobjectionable but epistemologically insignificant philosophical ideology." That was the conclusion of the preceding section.

According to the view advocated here, this criticism employs the specifically epistemological, the transcendental, method; it appeals to the *fact that empirical science exists,* and above all to the *methods* of testing and justifying results that are actually used in the empirical sciences.

It should be evident that such a method is justified and that such a criticism is an immanent one.

Epistemological assertions are not, after all, arbitrary (if logically unobjectionable) definitions. For example, no theorist of knowledge would, without any regard to natural science, consider solving epistemological problems by creating an arbitrary definition of the term "natural law" in such a way that those problems will no longer arise. Rather, every such theorist attempts to take into account the actual method of natural science. *That is his task,* just as it is the task of the scientist to have due regard to the facts of the empirical world. It is almost self-evident that examining whether this task has been successfully discharged is the method of an immanent critique.

Thus, the "transcendental method" is analogous to the empirical method; and the theory of knowledge is related to science in much the same way as science is related to the empirical world.

In the following discussion, the phrase "transcendental method" will be employed in the sense described here; the practical demonstration of this method in the preceding section and the discussion in this one should have provided a sufficiently clear definition of this phrase.

However, in order to dispel any doubts concerning the view advanced here, I will formulate it – in analogy with the fundamental thesis of empiricism – as the following fundamental transcendental thesis:

Epistemological assertions and definitions must be critically examined in the light of the actual procedure of justification employed by the empirical sciences; and only this – transcendental – examination can determine the fate of such assertions.

The conception of the "transcendental method" as presented here is by no means new. For example, Külpe (who refers, among others, to Natorp, Cohen, Riehl, Schuppe, Wundt and Rehmke[2]) has described the transcendental method in various places, explaining that rather than examining our subjective cognition through psychological analysis, the method involves examining knowledge as it actually occurs in the objectively existing sciences. Thus in his lectures on logic,[3] when criticising Husserl's phenomenological method, he states:

"Now there is, however . . . another method first recommended by Kant, the *transcendental method*. The analysis . . . of scientific knowledge as an objective fact constitutes the essence of this method."

It is beyond the scope of this study to list all those theorists of knowledge who have employed the transcendental method without referring to it as such. As already mentioned, almost every one of them has made use of it to a greater or lesser degree.

Nevertheless, this method has rarely been applied with sufficient consistency. It appears almost always in conjunction with psychological

---

[2] Cf. Oswald Külpe, *Einleitung in die Philosophie* (11th revised edition, ed. August Messer, 1923), § 5.
[3] Oswald Külpe, *Vorlesungen über Logik* (ed. Otto Selz, 1923), p. 151.

considerations (such as those concerning the human "faculty of know-ledge", especially in Kant); or "instead of investigations into the human 'faculty of knowledge' . . . one reflects upon the essence of all expressions, of all representations, that is, of every possible 'language' in the most general sense of the word" (thus, for example, in Wittgenstein[4]). How-ever interesting such investigations may be, they cannot replace the transcendental method.

If "investigations" and "reflections" of this kind yield results that fail to do justice to the actual method of the sciences, then – just like strict positivism – they are epistemologically irrelevant; they must be rejected.

More particularly (usually with a disdainful glance at "traditional philosophy", i.e. Kant), the various currents of modern *positivism* tend to espouse the transcendental method but without employing this Kantian expression. But since, aside from their transcendental programme, they chiefly pursue entirely different (namely *positivist*) ideas, they fail to apply consistently either the logical or the transcendental method. (As will be shown below, even Schlick, whose excellent transcendental reflections in the preceding section were directed against strict positivism, maintains a position that does not stand up to a transcendental critique.) The critique of logical positivism, one of the main criticisms presented in this work, will demonstrate the incompatibility of positivist and transcendental tendencies: the *fundamental positivist contradiction*.

This fundamental contradiction was already recognised by Kant; and it is this insight that leads him beyond Hume's positivism ("scepticism"). Kant's objection to Hume is exactly the same as the objection to strict positivism proposed here (which *roughly* corresponds to the implications that Hume himself derives from his argument). It is the transcendental objection that such a standpoint does not take into account [the fact of] the *theoretical* knowledge of nature.

Kant realised – as briefly pointed out in Section 7 – that the implications of Hume's argument leave only two possibilities: the position that has been referred to here as *strict positivism* (roughly Hume's position) and that of apriorism.

Confronted with the choice of abandoning either the fundamental empiricist thesis or strict universality – and with it the theoretical sciences

[4] Quoted in Moritz Schlick, "Die Wende der Philosophie", *Erkenntnis* 1 (1930), p. 7.

in general*² – the choice for him is clear; it is mapped out by the transcendental task of the theory of knowledge.

That the theoretical natural sciences exist is a fact. It is the task of the theory of knowledge not to *doubt* this fact, but rather to *explain* it. [In Kant's words]:⁵

"Since these sciences actually exist, it is quite proper to ask *how* they are possible; for *that* they must be possible is proved by the fact that they exist."

In this way Hume's argument turns into "*Hume's problem*", the fundamental problem of the "transcendental analytic":

Hume's argument – the claim that there is no way of grounding a proposition such as the principle of causality, that a principle of induction cannot be justified – this argument *must* be defective; this is demonstrated by the fact that there *is* theoretical knowledge of nature. The only question is, where is the flaw in this argument?

This question, or, in other words, the task of furnishing a proof for the *justification* of a principle of induction (such as the principle of causality) and thus also for theoretical-scientific propositions, is precisely what [for Kant] constitutes "*Hume's problem*".

But Hume's argument *is* compelling proof (and *here* it cannot be defective) that for strictly universal statements, a purely empirical, *a posteriori* validity is inadmissible; if at all, such statements can only be valid *a priori*.

Therefore, Kant is forced to formulate "Hume's problem" in terms of the more general question:

"*How are synthetic a priori judgements possible?*" In other words: how can a proof of the justification of such statements be furnished?

It is already evident at this point, that Kant's "*critical*" apriorism differs in several respects from any "*dogmatic*" rationalism that does not put limits on arbitrary speculation.

First, because of his transcendental starting point: only the actual presuppositions of the empirical sciences are to be sought out and their validity substantiated.

---

*² Especially Newton's theory of gravitation: when Kant speaks of "pure natural science", he is almost always thinking of this theory.

⁵ Immanuel Kant, *Kritik der reinen Vernunft* (2nd ed., 1787), p. 20. [English translation by N. Kemp Smith (1929), 1965: *Critique of Pure Reason*, p. 56. Tr.]

Second, however, because of Kant's demand for objective *justification*, Kant forcefully rejects the rationalist *doctrine of self-evidence* (cf. Section 3). In order for synthetic judgements to be accepted as *a priori* valid, he demands an objectively testable justification with (at least) the same degree of reliability and objectivity as is guaranteed by experience and observation for singular empirical statements. (When in this context Kant speaks about "*deduction*", he does not have in mind the *logical-deductive form* of justification in particular, but justification in general.) Thus for example, in his *Critique of Pure Reason* (just before the "General Note on the System of the Principles" of the second edition[6]), with reference to the doctrine of self-evidence that sets out "to pass off a proposition as being immediately certain, without justification or proof", he writes:

". . . for if, in dealing with synthetic propositions, we are to recognise them as possessing unconditioned validity independently of any deduction . . . then, no matter how evident they may be, all critique of understanding is given up."

In regard to the "audacious pretensions", which in a "confident tone . . . demand to be accepted as actual axioms", Kant[7] requires (in the same place) that for synthetic *a priori* statements "it is indispensable that, if not a proof, at least a deduction of the legitimacy of such an assertion should be supplied".

But how is such a deduction (the "*transcendental deduction*") possible?

One might consider supplying the desired demonstration of legitimacy with the help of the transcendental method, expressed in the following form:

If the theoretical sciences exist, then there must also be a principle of induction; and that this must be "possible" is – according to Kant – proved by the "reality" of those sciences.

Such a view misunderstands the Kantian question (Kant's emphasis on the distinction between "*that* they are possible" and "*how* they are possible"); the "demonstration of legitimacy" outlined above would represent a misuse of the transcendental method: this method may be used for the purpose of *criticism*. "This fact *disproves*" Hume's standpoint

---

[6] Immanuel Kant, *op. cit.*, p. 285. [English translation by N. Kemp Smith, *op. cit.*, p. 251. Tr.]

[7] Immanuel Kant, *op. cit.*, pp. 286 f. Ed. [English translation by N. Kemp Smith, *op. cit.*, pp. 251. Tr.]

(cf. [the] "Transition to the transcendental deduction of the categories"[8]) by showing that it is incompatible with scientific knowledge (namely that of theoretical natural science); the transcendental appeal to this fact may *raise problems.* However, if this fact (the existence of theoretical sciences) constitutes the *problem* of the theory of knowledge, then it cannot simultaneously contain its *solution.* The question about the *legitimacy* of the theoretical sciences cannot be answered by appealing to their existence; the question of justification (quid juris?) must be strictly distinguished from the question of fact (quid facti?).

The problem of a "transcendental deduction" is thus posed in its most acute form; yet at the same time all hope of solving the problem seems to have vanished: it appears that Kant has blocked all his own escape routes.

One way of justifying a synthetic statement immediately springs to mind; namely, to let experience decide. This *empirical route* is blocked by Hume's argument. An analogous "*transcendental*" *route* might also be conceivable, in the sense of deriving validity from fact; according to Kant himself this route is not permissible, and the same is true of what is apparently the only remaining way out, namely, the *doctrine that truth is manifest.* No fourth route seems to exist, however.

Kant nonetheless finds a way for the "transcendental deduction" to succeed; a way of claiming *a priori* validity for propositions like the principle of induction and a way of justifying this claim.

I will begin by outlining the *plan* for this particular justification procedure, the *plan of the* "*transcendental deduction*"; it is based on the following considerations.

Hume's argument is directed against the admissibility of strictly *universal* empirical statements. It consists in the logical proof that they cannot be grounded in experience.

Thus here (as well as elsewhere) Hume presupposes, as a matter of course, that "*experience*" *may be a ground of validity*; that experience may very well be capable of securing the validity of knowledge – of course only the validity of *singular* empirical statements.

I do not propose to question this presupposition that we have, in general, the right to test some (if not all) statements about reality and to justify them by experience – or that experience is acceptable as a ground

---

[8] [Immanuel Kant, *op. cit.,* pp. 127 f. Ed.; English translation by N. Kemp Smith, *op. cit.,* p. 128. Tr.]

of validity in general; at any rate, all the science of experience, indeed all empirical knowledge, is dependent on it. This presupposition – Kant described it as the "possibility of experience"[9] – may without hesitation be accepted as a final datum. Hume (surely rightly) no longer regarded it with scepticism; at any rate, he did not consider it capable of further analysis – in so far as he ever attained clarity about this presupposition at all. For Hume, "*experience*" was merely a *programme*, never a *problem*.

Thus, without wishing to call into question the principle of the "possibility of experience", it may nevertheless be important to have a clear understanding of its importance.

If – in analogy with Hume's analysis of *universal* empirical statements and their presuppositions – we also subject *singular* empirical statements to analysis, we shall find that every *singular* empirical statement accepted as valid on the basis of experience can only be valid on the basis of this universal formal presupposition – only on the basis of the principle of the "possibility of experience"; and just as it cannot be permissible to ground a principle of induction on experience alone, since this would presuppose another principle of induction, likewise it is logically impossible to ground the principle of the "possibility of experience" in turn on experience; for every empirical statement already presupposes it.

Therefore the formal principle of the "possibility of experience" cannot be an empirical statement, it cannot be *a posteriori* valid; it is inconceivable that among our individual material experiences, a particular one could be identified that corresponds to this principle, or on the basis of which the latter could be asserted.

(Whether this non-empirical principle is perhaps a logical proposition, a tautology, will not be examined at this point; cf., however, Sections 10 and 11.)

While these considerations might not suffice to undermine Hume's argument, they may yet point the way to the "transcendental deduction".

What Hume's argument unassailably proves may also be expressed in the following way: it is futile to search for a (formal) principle of induction among our material empirical statements. This is, no doubt, correct. But the arguments presented above strongly suggest that empirical statements are not at all the place where we ought to search for such formal

---

[9] [Immanuel Kant, *op. cit.*, pp. 5, 126. Ed.; English translation by N. Kemp Smith, *op. cit.*, pp. 45, 126. Tr.]

principles, and that the latter could possibly be found by inquiring into the formal presuppositions of our individual material experiences, rather than by searching amongst these experiences. (This may, then, be the gap in Hume's argument that we are looking for.)

"How is experience possible?" should be the central question in such an investigation.

The [Kantian] plan of the "transcendental deduction" thus consists in proving that among the general formal presuppositions of *all* material experiences, there are statements of the type of a principle of induction. Such a proof would also satisfy the requirements formulated above: if successful, it would have at least the same degree of reliability and objectivity as any empirical proof. For in both cases, the proof rests on the presupposition that experience is an admissible ground of validity. Of course, the two cases make use of this presupposition in very different ways: the one by assuming that experience can decide *material* statements; the other by presupposing, along with the admissibility (the "possibility") of any such decision, the validity of certain *formal* principles.

If the "transcendental deduction" can be carried out according to the plan just outlined, and if it can be shown that *all* empirical knowledge is based on the same kind of presuppositions as induction, then this would undermine all sceptical conclusions drawn from Hume's argument. With his own empiricist presuppositions, Hume would unconsciously have presupposed those very principles he doubts; indeed, he would virtually have made them into the foundations of all validity, since they would ultimately form the basis for the validity of all experience – and experience for Hume represents the highest authority in questions of validity. Hume's scepticism would have proved contradictory, and Hume's problem would be solved.

The *success of the "transcendental deduction"* depends on the proof that *all* experience, even singular empirical statements, and thus *all* knowledge of reality, are made possible only by specific presuppositions, and that these presuppositions are of the same type as principles of induction; this means, however, that these presuppositions are statements about *law-like regularities*.

This may be put more simply: it must be shown that all knowledge of nature, even every singular empirical statement, presupposes the existence of *law-like regularities*.

Thus, the most general presuppositions of *any experience* would be identical with the most general *a priori* laws that we call principles of induction (or at least be of the same type as the latter, which of course would be sufficient to escape the infinite regression). On the one hand, these most general *a priori* principles would make experience in general possible. On the other, based on these most general laws *as well as* on experience, various natural laws could be discovered and be validated. Indeed, this is also Kant's view[10] of the function of these most general and "original" *a priori* laws: "Empirical *laws* can exist and be discovered only through experience, and indeed in consequence of those original laws through which experience itself first becomes possible."

After what has been said, the idea should no longer appear strange that *all* knowledge of reality, including every *singular* (scientific) empirical statement, is possible only on the basis of certain presuppositions (which in turn cannot be *a posteriori* valid) – and hence that any experience is *impossible* without certain *a priori* presuppositions. As has already been shown in the presentation of strict positivism, that is, in the discussion of the pure doctrine of immanence, *all* knowledge goes beyond and transcends the immediately "given".

This general transcendence of any representation was examined in only a rather superficial fashion. Now the task of the transcendental deduction may be explicitly formulated as follows: it should analyse the transcendence of representation in general, in a way similar to Hume's analysis of the transcendence of generalisation.

If this analysis succeeds, it will probably uncover certain *formal* presuppositions underlying every observation. For all knowledge is formed; it has the logical-grammatical form of a statement, or a judgement. Every judgement, in turn, is a structured (articulated) connection of signs (concepts). The "transcendental deduction" will, therefore, primarily attempt to determine the formal aspect of knowledge more specifically.

In *carrying out the "transcendental deduction"*, Kant employs both *psychological* and – in our sense – *transcendental* arguments (that is, specifically methodological, epistemological arguments) in order to establish the formal components of all knowledge.

---

[10] Immanuel Kant, *op. cit.*, following the discussion of the "Third Analogy", p. 263 [English translation by N. Kemp Smith, *op. cit.*, p. 237. Emphasis added. Tr.]

The *psychological arguments* demonstrate that in the "apperception" (per-ception) in which all empirical knowledge originates, formative elements, which in turn are not reducible to apperceptions, play a major role.

The most general and fundamental of these formal and psychologically *a priori* presuppositions of every apperception is the fact called *unity of consciousness*. Without the "synthetic unity of apperception", there would be no "consciousness" at all; unconnected sensations would become "either impossible, or at least would be nothing to me",[11] and they could constitute no consciousness, or ego.

However, this "supreme principle of all use of the understanding" is not the only formative component. Our consciousness is not a mere bundle of sensations that, *simply* because they are connected (as Hume and Mach believe), form a conjunction, an ego; rather, it is characterised by very specific forms of order. Above all, it may be compared to a *stream* (a stream of consciousness) that flows along in "time". But even this stream of consciousness is not *merely temporally* ordered while otherwise remaining a chaotic sequence of a "multiplicity of sensations". It is not a mere "rhapsody of perceptions", but is *structured*. While our experiences are interconnected and can never be sharply separated from each other, the fact that they are structured – their combination into (complex and inter-related) *units* – is just as much a fact as is the stream of experience itself. The structure of these units (say, of these individual "apperceptions") is in part dependent on "ourselves", that is, on our attentiveness, our inter-ests, etc. The *same* groups of sensations may be combined into *different* units, a process in which we feel like *active* participants. The order-creating elements should thus be characterised (at least in part) as *"acts"* ("acts of spontaneity of our understanding"). This applies in particular to the (psychological) process of *cognition*. Every "cognition" is to be understood as a "recognition", and every apperception that is to provide the basis of (objective) knowledge must contain such a recognition; but this pre-supposes the possibility of *reproducing* past experiences and of *comparing* them with others, and thus of relating them. These represent additional formative elements of experience.

In addition to these more psychologically oriented arguments concern-ing the formal elements of the unity of consciousness and apperception

---

[11] [Immanuel Kant, *op. cit.*, p. 132. Ed.; English translation by N. Kemp Smith, *op. cit.*, p. 153. Tr.]

(in part, also determined by logical and transcendental considerations), there are, as already mentioned, methodological-transcendental arguments in Kant, that from the viewpoint of the present work are of even greater significance. (Hume's arguments are directed not only against the validity of the *principle* of causality but, above all, against the admissibility of the *concept* of causality. This is why Kant first provides the more psychologically coloured deduction of the "pure forms of thought" – or "concepts of the understanding", "categories" – and only then the deductions or proofs of the synthetic *a priori* "*principles*" that contain the most important transcendental observations.)

Transcendental considerations have already made their appearance in the "exposition" preceding the "transcendental deduction", in the "search" for the *a priori* forms of knowledge (to be subsequently deduced). Since all scientific knowledge takes the form of statements (judgements), Kant based his inventory of the forms of knowledge on a table of the forms of judgement. All knowledge must appear in one of these forms; and the synthetic *a priori principles* that are to be deduced must correspond to them.

It is primarily the *deductions of the principles*, or their proofs "from the possibility of experience", that are *transcendental* in our sense. These transcendental arguments are undoubtedly the most important ones in the "Transcendental Analytic", that is, in the [Kantian] treatment of "Hume's problem".

Here, Kant actually proves that *any* scientific experience, and thus *any* knowledge with a claim to "*objectivity*", is possible only if there are *law-like regularities*. In other words, he demonstrates that all scientific objectivity *presupposes* the existence of *law-like regularities*, regardless of whether the knowledge in question is the representation of a *singular* observation or the formulation of a natural law, i.e. the formulation of a strictly universal empirical statement.

The argument underlying Kant's proof is simple, although the same cannot be said of his presentation (and the examples he chose in order to elucidate the concept of the objectivity of experience, especially in the *Prolegomena*,[12] are rather unfortunate). This is why I shall develop Kant's

[12] [Immanuel Kant, *Prolegomena* (1783), § 19, pp. 80 f.; § 20, pp. 82 f. Ed.; English translation by Paul Carus, extensively revised by James W. Ellington (1977), § 19, pp. 42 f.; § 20, pp. 43 ff. Tr.]

argument with reference to a concrete example; this example is intended to show what is to be understood by "objectivity" in the sense of the methods employed by the empirical sciences (and to show that scientific objectivity presupposes the existence of law-like regularities, since without such regularities scientific objectivity is not "possible" at all).

A natural scientist observes a specific, individual and well-researched process, such as the process of a chemical reaction in a test tube. He sees a familiar light-green bubbling fluid.

Suddenly he observes a change in the colour of the fluid. Contrary to all previous observations and expectations, he sees a colour that he recognises as purple. But immediately after this (just as the scientist is becoming fully aware of his surprise) the fluid has taken on its usual colour again. Retrospectively, the observer estimates that the change in colour lasted for about one-quarter of a second.

Let this be the observational basis. Now, will the scientist immediately publish his observation as a discovery (or, perhaps, only as a chemical observation that might be important)? Certainly not. If the event in question, as postulated, has been well researched but involves no current scientific problem, then the chemist will probably attach no significance at all to the observed change in colour, but simply assume that he was mistaken.

Nevertheless, if he attaches any importance to the observation, he will above all check whether he can reproduce that remarkable observation. He might first consider whether a reflection of light (perhaps caused by a glossy object in the laboratory, etc.) could explain the observation. In order to test this conjecture, he will try to position the test tube in front of himself in the same way as before; or he may conjecture that a special admixture or impurity can explain the observation, and he will repeat the experiment, successively testing for each of the various potential impurities.

Should he succeed in reproducing the observation in this way, then and only then will he attribute any *objective significance* to it; but if there is *no way* of successfully reproducing the observation, he will simply assume that he was mistaken. Yet he does not have to let the matter rest at this point. If he is interested in *objectively* useful results, he may attempt to investigate this sensory illusion more closely from a *psychological* viewpoint, in which case he will in principle have to follow the same procedure as before. He must attempt to create the same, or a similar, sensory illusion.

Objectivity in the sense of empirical science is, in principle, only conferred on *testable* (that is, intersubjectively testable) observations. Indeed, the possibility of testing an observation should be regarded as the very *definition* of scientific objectivity (*objectivity* = intersubjective testability).

However, any such *testing* is based on *repetitions* (more precisely, repeatability) and thus on regularities, on *law-like dependences*; the *object* of natural science − "*nature*" − can be determined objectively only through these regularities and law-like dependences. Or, as Kant[13] puts it:

"By nature, in the empirical sense, we understand the connection of appearances . . . according to laws."

Specific questions of natural philosophy will not be further discussed here, either in descriptive or in critical terms. The subject under discussion is solely the problem of induction, or the problem of law-like regularities. It may, therefore, merely be briefly noted that Kant distinguishes three groups of law-like connections, which (depending on their respective relationship to time) are subsumed under the "concept of substance", the "concept of causality" and the "concept of reciprocity". ("Substance" − following e.g. Schlick[14] − might be conceived as the connection of the law-like alternation of "accidents" or of "qualities"; "causality" as the law-like connection within processes that enables one to make predictions in the precise sense of predictions *in time*; without "reciprocity", e.g. reciprocal light signals or reciprocal gravitation, the simultaneous coexistence of different processes could never be established empirically.)

What is of crucial importance for our problem is Kant's discovery that *all knowledge of reality*, the "possibility of experience" and the *objectivity of cognition are based on the existence of law-like regularities.* In this form, this discovery may appear *trivial* (like many great discoveries), but as will be shown by our further discussion (especially by the critique of logical positivism), its implications are by no means yet fully appreciated.

Kant's solution of Hume's problem (which as a result of the extensive scope of the "Transcendental Analytic" has frequently failed to be recognised as constituting the latter's fundamental problem) may be summarised as follows:

---

[13] Immanuel Kant, *op. cit.*, following the discussion of the "Third Analogy", p. 263. [English translation by N. Kemp Smith, *op. cit.*, p. 237. Tr.].

[14] Moritz Schlick, *Allgemeine Erkenntnislehre* (2nd ed., 1925), p. 346.

Just like singular empirical statements, universal empirical statements can be true or false, as the latter presuppose as much, or as little, as the former.

Or, using the terminology introduced here in the discussion of strict positivism:

The transcendence of generalisation is reducible to the transcendence of (scientific) representation in general.

This would dispose of the problem of induction.

10. *Critique of apriorism.* This section will provide a critique, as well as an appreciation, of the proof structure of the "transcendental deduction". (Immanent) criticism is fundamental: it is directed not only at the "transcendental deduction" in the Kantian form, but also at the conclusiveness of any proof attempting to found the *validity of synthetic a priori judgements* – especially of a *principle of induction* – on the principle of the "possibility of experience".

The task required of the "transcendental deduction", and the purpose of carrying it out, is to justify the *synthetic a priori proposition that "law-like regularities"* exist.

In order to make the *a posteriori* statement that in our world – so far as we have hitherto observed – "law-like regularities" *seem* to exist; that in our world everything is *as if* there were "law-like regularities"; in order to make this statement we do not need a "transcendental deduction": we know this from experience.

The crucial point about the "transcendental deduction", therefore, concerns only the *a priori character* of the statement that "law-like regularities" exist; the point is to prove that this statement has the character of *necessity*, or, phrased differently, that "law-like regularities" must exist *unconditionally*.

Can the "transcendental deduction" furnish such proof?

The following view will be advanced here:

If we are not willing to accept a synthetic *a priori* judgement without proof – if, like Kant,[1] we maintain that a justification (quid juris?) is "indispensable" for any synthetic *a priori* assertion, and that without this, its claim to validity must be rejected – then we must consistently *reject all*

---

[1] [Immanuel Kant, *Kritik der reinen Vernunft* (2nd ed., 1787), p. 286. See Section 9, text to note 7. Ed.; English translation by N. Kemp Smith (1929), 1965: *Critique of Pure Reason*, p. 251. Tr.].

synthetic a priori judgements as unprovable and deny them any scientific validity. This view is based on the fact that, for logical reasons, a synthetic a priori judgement can be proved only by presupposing that another synthetic a priori judgement is valid. But since this, in turn, would also have to be proved, any attempt to prove a synthetic a priori judgement must ultimately lead to an infinite regression or circle.

The view articulated here, which states that it is logically impossible to prove synthetic a priori judgements (already asserted in a similar way by Fries and his school; cf. the next section), will be presented in greater detail in the following discussion; it will be based on the line of argument used in the "transcendental deduction".

The argument of the "transcendental deduction" centres on the proof that there can be knowledge of reality in the sense of natural science (or that experience is possible) only if "law-like regularities" exist.

As the previous section has shown, this proof is based on the objectivity or testability of scientific knowledge. The proof thus consists of a logical analysis of the concept of knowledge of reality, or of the concept of experience in the sense of empirical science. The result of this conceptual analysis is the analytic judgement that without "law-like regularities" there can be no scientific knowledge. Phrased in more informal terms:

In so far as there is experience at all, there are also "law-like regularities".

This analytic judgement has the form of a hypothetical judgement (or an "implication"; cf. Section 31). By itself it is not sufficient for the deduction that "law-like regularities" really do exist; this would require the further presupposition that experience exists (or that experience is possible).

The whole deduction now runs like this:

(1) There is experience (or: experience is possible);

(2) if there is experience (if experience is possible), then there must also be "law-like regularities" (analytic-hypothetical statement);

(3) hence "law-like regularities" exist.

The final proposition of this deduction may be considered as proved only if the presupposition "There is experience" (or: "Experience is possible") is valid. If this presupposition becomes untenable, then the chain of reasoning breaks down.

It follows that, based on this argument, "unconditional" validity for this final proposition may be claimed only if the presupposition is also "unconditionally" (that is, a priori) valid.

In order to prove the *a priori* validity of the statement "There are law-like regularities", one would first have to prove the *a priori* validity of the statement "There is experience" ("Experience is possible").

In systematic representation:

The analysis of the concept of experience leads to the proposition:

(1) Only if "law-like regularities" exist is experience possible.

This is an *analytic judgement*.

With its help, the following proposition can be deduced:

(2) "Law-like regularities" exist, since experience is in fact possible.

But this proposition can be asserted only as a *synthetic a posteriori* judgement; for in order to prove the synthetic *a priori* judgement:

(3a) "Law-like regularities" must exist under any circumstances – one would have to be able to presuppose:

(3b) Experience must be possible under any circumstances.

Kant believed that the presupposition that experience is possible would be sufficient for the "transcendental deduction"; since there actually is experience, such a presupposition did not appear to be particularly problematic.

It becomes evident, however, that for the deduction of a synthetic *a priori* judgement much more would have to be presupposed – namely, that experience must be unconditionally possible.

This synthetic *a priori* turn of the "transcendental deduction" is, however, obviously inadmissible. For as a synthetic *a priori* judgement, the presupposition that experience must be unconditionally possible would itself first have to be proved. To presuppose it without justification is impermissible according to Kant's own principles, for it would be "*dogmatic*".

But how can we prove that experience must necessarily, unconditionally, be possible?

If – according to the view just presented – Kant's *synthetic a priori turn of the "transcendental deduction"* is rejected, then we arrive at the conclusion that the statement "There are law-like regularities" may only be asserted *a posteriori*.

But this means that we are not entitled to claim the existence of "law-like regularities" in the sense of strictly universal natural laws, since we are only justified in stating that (so far as we have hitherto observed) everything happens *as if* strictly universal laws exist.

Now in Section 5, the term "law-like regularity" was defined as referring exclusively to a strictly universal state of affairs – in the sense of a strictly universal empirical statement. According to this linguistic usage, there simply cannot be such an *a posteriori* statement as "There are law-like regularities". This statement could be asserted only *a priori*, if at all.

Thus, when in the present section we have spoken about the *a posteriori* statement that "There are law-like regularities", we have used this phrase in a different sense from that established in Section 5. (In order to indicate this, the term ["law-like regularity"] has always been put in quotation marks.)

Two concepts must therefore be distinguished:

1. "Law-like regularity" in the sense of strictly universal natural laws (*"a priori"* or *"strictly universal law"*);

2. "Law-like regularity" in the sense of the Kantian "so far as we have hitherto observed, there is no exception to this . . . rule".[2] This second (that is, the *"a posteriori"*) "law-like regularity" might be called an *"as-if law"*: everything (so far) has been as if there are strictly universal laws.

Only in the sense of this "as-if law" can the statement "There are laws" be an *a posteriori judgement* at all.

This, however, necessarily implies the following:

If one rejects the synthetic *a priori* usage of "transcendental deduction", then the phrase "law-like regularity" may be conceived only in the sense of an "as-if law" *in the entire chain of reasoning.*

One would therefore have to show that even the analytic judgement from which our criticism starts (the hypothetical-analytic statement: "If experience is possible, then there must be 'law-like regularities' ") is only to be understood in the sense of an "as-if law".

Indeed, this is the case. Upon re-examining the conceptual analysis of objectivity or testability of scientific knowledge with respect to this question, we must conclude that this analytic judgement can be asserted only in the sense of an "as-if law". In order for the objectivity of experience to be possible, it suffices that everything should happen as though strict universal laws exist. As long as this is always the case, experiences can be tested – say, by repeated observations.

---

[2] [Immanuel Kant, *Kritik der reinen Vernunft* (2nd ed., 1787), pp. 3 f. Ed.; English translation N. Kemp Smith: *Critique of Pure Reason* (1965), p. 44. Tr.]

This realisation, however, undermines any attempt at a synthetic *a priori* version of the "transcendental deduction".

Various *objections* can be raised to this critique of the "transcendental deduction", which in spite of their differences (as will be shown in the following) can all be basically reduced to a common denominator.

The most basic of these objections would be an attempt to secure the *a priori* character of the statement "There are law-like regularities" with the help of a *definition of "nature"* (or of the "world" or of "reality"). Thus, for example, following Kant,[3] one can *define* "nature" as the "connection of appearances . . . according to (strictly universal) laws"; or one might define "world" in the same way. Or one might suggest the definition: "real" (or "existent") is whatever is governed by (strictly universal) laws. Now it is assumed that with the help of such definitions, the *a priori* existence of laws can be proved; perhaps because there must be laws if there is any reality at all, etc.

One of Kant's greatest achievements was to have demonstrated that no progress whatever can be made in this way. It can never be proved that something does or does not exist by means of ("dogmatic") concepts. (All these attempts — as well as those still to be discussed — to save the "transcendental deduction" are similar in form to the ontological proof of the existence of God: they assert an existence *by definition*.) The objections discussed can be refuted by pointing out that in this way one can arrive only at an analytic and tautological, but never at a synthetic, judgement that "There are law-like regularities".

Attempts aimed at proving the *a priori character of the possibility of experience* would be somewhat more sophisticated.

If it could be proved that the statement "Experience is possible" (or "There is experience") is *a priori* valid, then the proposed criticism would be untenable.

Let us now briefly mention arguments of the kind: That experience exists cannot itself be an experience (from which it is to be inferred that the statement "There is experience" must be *a priori* valid). While these arguments may lead to certain formal-logical problems (theory of

---

[3]   [Cf. Immanuel Kant, *op. cit.*, p. 263. Ed.; English translation by N. Kemp Smith, *op. cit.*, p. 237. Tr.]

types), which should be taken seriously, they are completely unrelated to the particular problem to be treated here. (They are of the same kind as statements such as: That there is knowledge cannot be knowledge, or: That there are true statements cannot itself be a true statement.)

The other objections to the criticism of the "transcendental deduction", objections that I think ought to receive more attention than these attempts, are those related to the old *idealism vs. realism* controversy.

Idealism ("the world, the objects, exist only in my imagination") is, as Lichtenberg[4] has already emphasised, "simply impossible to refute". The antithesis between idealism and realism ("the world, the objects, do not exist in my imagination alone; they exist independently of my imagination; they only stimulate my imagination") is, however, equally irrefutable.

The idealism–realism antithesis may be regarded as an example of undecidable *antinomy*.

An important conclusion should be drawn from the fact that (undecidable) antinomies exist. Nothing permits us to infer the *truth* of a doctrine from its *irrefutability* (as Lichtenberg,[5] for example, does), for the *antithesis* of the particular doctrine, that is, its very opposite, might be equally irrefutable. Kant was the first who described this relationship in his *doctrine of antinomies*, specifically with respect to the conflicting theses of "rational cosmology" (which are formally analogous to the theses mentioned above): he puts up a number of irrefutable theses against a number of equally irrefutable antitheses. Kant arrives at the conclusion (and rightly so – as will be shown in the analysis of the problem of demarcation[6]) that in those cases where there is an undecidable antinomy, both assertions are to be rejected as unjustifiable and therefore as *unscientific* (dogmatic-metaphysical).

The antinomy between idealism and realism cannot be discussed further until we proceed to the analysis of the problem of demarcation;[7]

---

[4] [*Georg Christoph Lichtenbergs vermischte Schriften* II. (ed. Ludwig Christian Lichtenberg and Friedrich Kries, 1801), *Bemerkungen vermischten Inhalts: 1. Philosophische Bemerkungen*, p. 62; 1844 ed. I., p. 82. Ed.]

[5] [Georg Christoph Lichtenberg, *op. cit.*, pp. 61 ff; 1844 ed. I., pp. 81 ff. Ed.]

[6] [Cf. Vol. II (Fragments): [VI.] Philosophy, Section 1, text to note 1; Immanuel Kant, *op. cit.*, pp. 448 ff. (English translation by N. Kemp Smith, *op. cit.*, pp. 393 ff. Tr.) See also *Editor's Postscript*. Ed.]

[7] [See Editor's Postscript. Ed.]

here I only wish to show that from the position of certain idealist conceptions, my criticism of the "transcendental deduction" *cannot* appear compelling; in particular, from the position of Kantian "*transcendental idealism*".

The demonstration that the criticism of the "transcendental deduction" is untenable from the standpoint of so-called transcendental idealism does not – this is important to note – in any way undermine the *immanent character* and conclusiveness of that criticism. For Kant's *proof of transcendental idealism* itself presupposes the conclusiveness of the "transcendental deduction"; it is therefore impossible in principle to reject an attack on the conclusiveness of the "transcendental deduction" from the position of transcendental idealism. Moreover, this "proof of transcendental idealism" itself – that is, the argument leading from the results of the "transcendental deduction" to the "lesson" of transcendental idealism – does not stand up to criticism: it would be inadequate even if its foundation, the "transcendental deduction", were unassailable (more on this point in the next section).

Any objections to this criticism that might be raised from the position of transcendental idealism can thus be rejected before they have even been formulated. They cannot strengthen the disputed conclusiveness of the proof of the "transcendental deduction", since they themselves make unprovable assumptions.

Nevertheless, I propose briefly to present these objections.

Kant's *transcendental idealism* tells us that natural objects (the "objects of experience") are given to us only as representations (in this it does not differ significantly from ordinary idealism). But in contrast to ordinary (or *material*) idealism, "transcendental" (or *formal*) idealism emphasises that these representations can be given to us only under those formal conditions impressed upon them by our cognitive apparatus.

Any representation, or any intuition, can appear only in our "forms of intuition" of space and time; and by processing the representations, our "understanding" impresses on them *its laws:* "The understanding does not derive its laws . . . from, but prescribes them to, nature";[8] the most

---

[8] Immanuel Kant, *Prolegomena* (1783), § 36, p. 113. [English translation by Paul Carus, extensively revised by James W. Ellington (1977), § 36, p. 62. Tr.]

general laws of nature are "quite the same"[9] as the most general formal condition of experience, the mere universal conformity to law.

It is for Kant, quite rightly, a foregone conclusion that we cannot experience objects and processes of the external world (physical objects) as they are "in themselves", that is, that we never get to know them (as Schlick[10] puts it) the way they are "in themselves". But transcendental idealism claims more than that: not only can we never experience ("be acquainted with") these "things in themselves", but we can never know them – for we cannot know the formal conditions, the laws, that may govern them.

Our scientific knowledge is absolutely restricted to the world of experience: to the representations governed by the laws of the understanding. And only what belongs to this world of experience can (in the sense of empirical science) be called "real" or "existent".

These are roughly the fundamental ideas of transcendental idealism.

It hardly requires any further explanation as to why, from this standpoint, any criticism of the "transcendental deduction" will be futile; and this also applies to the criticism put forward here.

"The objects of experience . . . are . . . given . . . only in experience, and have no existence outside it", we read in the Critique of Pure Reason,[11] and further: "That there may be inhabitants in the moon, although no one has ever perceived them . . . only means that in the possible progress of experience we may encounter them."

For such a concept of experience and reality, the a priori character of the statement "Experience is possible" cannot be called into question.

It cannot be doubted that experience must be possible "unconditionally", "always" and "everywhere", for "conditions" of any kind, as well as specific times and locations, can exist only in the world of experience. There is (in the sense of the Kantian concept of reality) no world outside the world of experience. The concepts of "existence", "world" and "experience" are related to each other in such a way that the assumption

---

[9] Immanuel Kant, op. cit., § 36, p. 112. [English translation by Paul Carus, op. cit., § 36, p. 61. Tr.]

[10] [Moritz Schlick, Allgemeine Erkenntnislehre (2nd ed., 1925), p. 213. Ed.]

[11] Immanuel Kant, Kritik der reinen Vernunft (2nd ed., 1787), "Der Antinomie der reinen Vernunft", Section 6, p. 521. [Emphasis added. Ed.; English translation by N. Kemp Smith (1929), 1965: Critique of Pure Reason, p. 440. Tr.]

of the existence of a world that would not be a world of experience (not an "object of possible experience") would be contradictory (or at least unscientific, *metaphysical*).

Arguments of the kind just outlined, designed to prove the *a priori* character of the possibility of experience, are without exception closely related to *positivist ideas*. They identify the world of experience with reality, and reject the assumption of a reality transcending experience as metaphysical (or "meaningless"; cf. Sections 43 ff.).

It is evident that these questions touch on the *problem of demarcation*; a more specific definition of the – by no means simple – concepts of "experience" and "reality" and their mutual relations will become possible only in the course of our analysis of this problem[12] (except for the preliminary though important notes in the next section on the *empirical basis*). (In the meantime, these concepts will be used in a general and cautiously indeterminate manner, so that all the results will remain tenable under subsequent examination.)

The "transcendental deduction", the attempt *to prove* the existence of law-like regularities in the sense of strictly universal and valid laws, is not conclusive. The thesis that experience is unconditionally possible or, phrased differently, that the world can be unconditionally known, is unprovable.

However, it is not only unprovable but also absolutely *irrefutable*. For the thesis that experience is possible can indeed never be *empirically falsified*, that is, we could never know that we cannot obtain knowledge about the world. As long as there is experience, and as long as there is knowledge about reality, it must be possible to obtain knowledge about the world.

But this equally unprovable and irrefutable thesis – that *we can gain knowledge of the world* – also gives rise to an *undecidable antinomy*.

The *thesis* that the world can be unconditionally known must not be considered true on account of its irrefutability, for it is opposed by an antithesis that is as irrefutable, but also as unprovable, as the thesis itself.

The *antithesis* asserts that the statement that knowledge of the world must be possible is *false*, that knowledge of the world is not necessarily possible unconditionally, that is, that there may be conditions under which the

---

[12] [See Editor's Postscript; cf. also Section 11, text to note 55. Ed.]

world cannot be known, under which as-if laws no longer exist; thus, it asserts (and this assertion too can only be made *a priori*) *that there are no strictly universal laws*, in short – that our cosmos will (at some time) dissolve into chaos.

It is clear that this assertion, too, is unprovable and irrefutable.*¹

It is only by having an insight into this "antinomy of the knowability of the world" that the critique of apriorism can succeed in penetrating to the roots of the problem.

Kant's apriorism, as we have seen, entails the assertion of the *thesis* of this antinomy, for it is synonymous with the synthetic *a priori* principle of induction that we are discussing.

At this point in the analysis, which is devoted to the critique of apriorism, the *antithesis* cannot be presented in more detail. The investigations in Section 46 will show that the antithesis has its proponents, too. It is entailed by the epistemological considerations underlying the pseudo-statement position of the logical positivist Wittgenstein.

Only an analysis of the problem of demarcation¹³ will establish whether (and how) both the thesis and the antithesis of the antinomy of the knowability of the world can be eliminated from the theory of knowledge as unscientific, as *metaphysical*.¹⁴

At this point I shall not employ such arguments. Here it is sufficient to show that the antinomy is undecidable. The "transcendental deduction", as a *proof of the thesis*, is inconclusive; no proof of the same kind as the "transcendental deduction" can stand up to an immanent critique.

The claim to validity of a synthetic *a priori principle of induction cannot be justified*.

Is the "transcendental deduction" therefore a complete failure? It seems so. We must content ourselves with the *a posteriori* realisation that there are "as-if laws"; and no such realisation (as we have learned in Section 5) can take the problem of induction any further.

---

*¹ The thesis that our cosmos will dissolve into chaos is most interestingly discussed and defended in John Archibald Wheeler's "From Relativity to Mutability", in *The Physicist's Conception of Nature* (ed. Jagdish Mehra, 1973), pp. 202 ff.

¹³ [See Editor's Postscript. Ed.]

¹⁴ [Cf. Section 46; see also Karl Popper, *Logik der Forschung* (1934; 2nd ed., 1966; and subsequent editions) (*The Logic of Scientific Discovery*, (1959, 2nd ed., 1968) Tr.), Section 78. Ed.]

Even though undoubtedly this is correct, nevertheless I believe that Kant's "transcendental deduction", properly understood, signifies a very *decisive step in the development of the problem of induction.*

I take the *synthetic turn* that Kant gave to the "transcendental deduction" to be a misunderstanding of his own discovery (for some comments on the ultimate reasons for this misunderstanding, see the next section).

In my view, the true achievement of the "transcendental deduction", Kant's real discovery, lies in the *analytic statement* (based on the *concept of objectivity*) that experience, or knowledge in the sense of empirical science, is impossible without "laws"; more precisely, that such knowledge is impossible unless everything behaves as if strictly universal laws exist.

Observations that cannot be related to some kind of law have no scientific significance, because they are not *objective*, i.e. not *intersubjectively testable: every objective test thus consists in the verification or falsification of a prediction* proposed on the basis of a supposed law (repeatability). (Cf. also the next section.)

This result of the "transcendental deduction", i.e. this analytic statement, is actually only a *definition* of the concept of "knowledge" as understood by natural science. Formulated in radical terms, the definition would be something like this:

Obtaining knowledge means searching for laws; or, more precisely, proposing laws and systematically testing them (irrespective of the question whether or not strictly universal laws actually exist).

Other philosophers have repeatedly stressed that such a definition (it might be called a *transcendental definition of knowledge*) is the true achievement of the "transcendental deduction". But, to my knowledge, the full import of this result has still not been understood. (Its ultimate implications, as will be shown later,[15] lead directly to *deductivism*.)

For example, Feigl,[16] in his critique of apriorism, states quite correctly that the real end-result of "Kantianism" is "merely a definition of the concept of knowledge". However, he regards this definition not as an epistemologically important discovery, but as trivial: "What was and is understood everywhere by obtaining knowledge is bringing to light some kind of order, discovering laws."[17] But this charge of triviality is very

---

[15] [See Editor's Postscript; cf. also Section 5, note *3. Ed.]
[16] Herbert Feigl, *Theorie und Erfahrung in der Physik* (1929), p. 104.
[17] Herbert Feigl, *loc. cit.*

unfair. The most eminent proponents of logical positivism such as Carnap, Schlick and Wittgenstein (Feigl himself belongs to this school) base their epistemological investigations on a concept of knowledge completely different from Kant's. (Cf. Sections 19 ff., especially Section 44; there it will also be shown that one of the reasons why logical positivism fails is that it ignores Kant's concept of knowledge.)

Hume, too, would certainly have posed and assessed the problem of induction in a different way, had he realised that all knowledge consists of "bringing to light some kind of order", or "discovering a law".[18]

We must search for natural laws, for law-like regularities, if we want to obtain any knowledge at all. But this does not in any way require us to assume the existence of strictly universal laws; it is enough for us to know that knowledge consists in *searching for strictly universal laws* – as if they existed.

However, the assumption that they do not exist would also be unfounded. The question whether they really do or do not exist – whether there can be knowledge of the world or not – is *undecidable;*[*2] for this reason (and because it lies outside the question of method) it does not enter into the discussion.

Strict positivism is untenable: if we want to gain any knowledge, we have to search for laws, we have to propose and test natural laws, strictly universal empirical statements.

But *apriorism* must also be rejected; the theses formulated at the end of the preceding section are not tenable. Universal empirical statements cannot "simply be true or false in the same way as singular empirical statements"; for although singular empirical statements also presuppose that laws exist (in order for their claims to validity to be testable), they do so only in the *a posteriori* sense of as-if laws. Yet in order to be able to assert that it must be possible to discover strictly universal empirical statements (or natural laws) that are *true*, one would have to be able to prove a principle of induction. The synthetic *a priori* judgement that there are strictly universal laws would have to be provable.

[18] Herbert Feigl, *loc. cit.*; see above.

[*2] Today I would write: "This question is *scientifically* undecidable"; and I would stress that (even if not decidable) it is an interesting metaphysical question, and that metaphysical realism gives an affirmative answer. Cf. also *Logik der Forschung* (1934; 2nd ed., 1966; and subsequent editions) [*The Logic of Scientific Discovery* (1959; 2nd ed., 1968; and subsequent editions). Tr.], Section 79.

We are, then, faced with the strange situation that, while the natural sciences must *propose and test natural laws*, the truth of *these laws can in principle never be scientifically proved*. These very important universal empirical statements can, in principle, never lose the character of unproven assertions or of *hypotheses*. We must never assign them the value *true* [neither *a priori* nor *a posteriori*].

The normal-statement position has been defeated.

Thus, the problem of induction has entered a new stage. The question now is:

How should we understand these curious universal empirical statements whose truth can never be demonstrated? Is there no difference at all, with respect to their validity, between a universally accepted *natural law* and a tentative *hypothesis* not yet thoroughly tested? A theory of knowledge that aims to do justice to the actual procedure of science cannot simply ignore the fact that science regards some natural laws as well corroborated, whereas it has little or no confidence in others.

Yet, it is perhaps this varying degree of certainty of hypotheses that points the way forward. It strongly suggests that universal empirical statements are statements that *can have values of validity lying between true and false*; that *hypotheses* should *never* be called "true", but rather *more or less* "*probable*".

Chapter V

KANT AND FRIES

11. *Supplement to the critique of apriorism. (Psychologism and transcendentalism in Kant and Fries. – On the question of the empirical basis.)* The present rather lengthy section ought, strictly speaking, to be characterised as a *digression*. While in this part of the book there is otherwise no digression from the analysis of the problem of induction, this section will present a number of related problems in some detail. It will not, however, change the position we have already reached in discussing the problem of induction. *The next section will therefore resume the argument from the end of the preceding section.*

Thus, the analysis in this section is intended not to move the discussion forward but rather to deepen it, particularly with respect to the question of the *epistemological method*. Although, in a certain sense, this section represents merely a collection of critical reflections, nevertheless it serves the important purpose of showing that *a systematic comparison of the transcendental and the psychological methods* is an illuminating and promising way of getting closer to the solution of epistemological problems.

As I have already suggested, the confusion of aspects of the *psychology* of knowledge with those of the *theory* of knowledge is quite significant in Kant. This inadequate distinction between psychological and epistemological aspects is connected with the problem-situation of classical empiricism. The latter poses the problem in terms of the "legitimate" (that is, sensualist-empiricist) *sources of concepts* – such as the concept of causality – rather than in terms of the *validity of statements* – such as the *principle of causality*. In principle, Kant overcomes this formulation (which may be characterised as *misconceived**¹) by distinguishing between *analytic* and *synthetic statements* that are *a priori* or *a posteriori* valid. (He thus became the founder of a specifically epistemological set of problems.) Nevertheless, he himself reverted time and again to a genetic-psychological formulation of the problem. Both the (epistemological) *a priori–a posteriori* distinction (in the sense of "originating in experience") and the (logical) distinction between *analytic* and *synthetic* judgements (in psychological terms: judgements that only elucidate or analyse what "we already know", and judgements that expand and increase our knowledge) can be interpreted genetically. The genetic-psychological conception is also prominent in Kant's terminology, and leads to certain *ambiguities*. Thus, Kant asks whether a specific item of knowledge "*springs from experience*" instead of asking whether and how it may be *proved* by experience (perceptual judgements). Accordingly, Kant refers to "experience", "understanding", etc. as "*sources of knowledge*" (a vague metaphor with obvious genetic overtones) instead of putting forward experiences, logical demonstrations, etc. as *grounds* for knowledge. This also accounts for the fact that the problematic character of the attempt to justify *statements* by "experience" (such as sense perception) was not recognised until Fries (cf. the "trilemma" in the final part of this section).

One of the problems that can be resolved as soon as one avoids confusing psychological and transcendental questions is Kant's argument (which is peculiar to him) that transcendental idealism derives from "transcendental deduction" (Kant's proof of transcendental idealism). This argument was already mentioned in the previous section and at the end of Section 4 (in the context of Kant's psychological-genetic use of the term "*a priori*").

I will link the presentation of this Kantian "proof of transcendental

*¹ Here for the first time, a theme is raised that is very important for my later views. (Cf. for example, my *Logic of Scientific Discovery*, 1959, 2nd ed., 1968, and subsequent editions, note *1 to Section 4 and text.) As is evident, I attribute this distinction to Kant, although it should be noted that Kant did not always consistently follow it.

idealism" to his formulation (already quoted in Section 9) of the results of the "transcendental deduction":[1]

"There are many laws of nature that we can only know by means of experience, but *conformity to law* in the connection of appearances . . . in general, we cannot discover by any experience, because experience itself requires laws which are *a priori* at the basis of its possibility.

"The possibility of experience in general is therefore at the same time the universal law of nature, and the principles of experience are the very laws of nature."

However, Kant is by no means satisfied with this result. It seems to him to be in need of interpretation or *explanation*.

The conditions of the "possibility of experience in general" are, after all, the most general formal and ordering conditions of *our cognitive process* (or, to put it in more psychological terms, of our cognitive apparatus, our "understanding"). *How can these subjective conditions at the same time be the most general laws of nature?* How can "such a necessary agreement of the principles of possible experience with the laws . . . of nature"[2] be *explained*?

While not explicitly formulating this problem, Kant nevertheless does discuss it (in the *Prolegomena*[3]). It is this discussion that contains the "*proof of transcendental idealism*". It justifies Kant's view that his "main proposition . . . that universal laws of nature can be known *a priori* . . . leads naturally to the proposition that the highest legislation about nature must lie in ourselves, in our understanding".[4]

In order to answer the question of how an "agreement of the principles of possible experience with the laws . . . of nature" is to be explained, Kant argues as follows:

---

[1] Immanuel Kant, *Prolegomena* (1783), § 36, p. 111 [English translation by Paul Carus, extensively revised by James W. Ellington (1977), § 36, p. 61. Tr.]. Emphasis added.

[2] Immanuel Kant, *op. cit.*, § 36, p. 112 [English translation by Paul Carus, *op. cit.*, p. 61. Tr.].

[3] Immanuel Kant, *loc. cit.*; regarding the following, see, however, also the Preface and especially § 27 of the *Kritik der reinen Vernunft* (2nd ed., 1787) [English translation by N. Kemp Smith (1929), 1965: *Critique of Pure Reason*, pp. 173 f. Tr.] as well as the corresponding "Summary Representation" of the 1st ed. (1781), pp. 128 ff. [English translation, *op. cit.*, pp. 149 ff. Tr.].

[4] Immanuel Kant, *Prolegomena* (1783), § 36, pp. 111 f. [English translation by Paul Carus, *op. cit.*, § 36, p. 61. Tr.].

Only three possibilities are conceivable in order to explain the agreement of any knowledge with its object.

First possibility: our knowledge is determined by its object.

Second possibility: the object is determined by our knowledge.

A middle course: we have knowledge as an (inborn) disposition that is *preformed* such that it agrees with its object.

Kant rejects the first possibility for *a priori* principles. It can only apply to *a posteriori* knowledge; the assumption that *a priori laws* "are drawn from nature by means of experience . . . is self-contradictory, for the universal laws of nature can and must be known *a priori* (that is, independently of all experience) and be the foundation of all empirical use of the understanding".[5]

Kant rejects the middle course because it does not offer any *explanation*; it leads, according to Kant, to the pseudo-explanation "that a Spirit, who can neither err nor deceive, originally implanted these laws in us".[6] The "middle course", therefore, does not lead to any (or only to a fantastic metaphysical) explanation. Moreover, "there is this decisive objection against the suggested middle course" that in such a case of "strange agreement . . ." the "*necessity* would then have to be sacrificed".[7]

Thus, we are left with the second possibility, that is, with the seemingly paradoxical assumption that the objects are determined by our knowledge (Kant's "Copernican revolution" in the problem of knowledge):

"*The understanding does not derive its laws (a priori) from, but prescribes them to, nature.*"[8]

---

[5] [Immanuel Kant, *op. cit.*, § 36, p. 112. Ed.; English translation by Paul Carus, *op. cit.*, § 36, pp. 61 f. Tr.]

[6] [Immanuel Kant, *loc. cit.* Ed.] In the *Prolegomena* [*loc. cit.*] Kant strangely enough invokes "only" Christian August Crusius regarding this "middle course"; in the *Metaphysische Anfangsgründe der Naturwissenschaft* (1786), Preface, footnote 2 near the end [XIX], Kant speaks of the "unaccountable agreement of the phenomena with the laws of the understanding" and rejects the explanation of this "agreement" in terms of a "*pre-established harmony*" [*i.e. rejects Leibniz's explanation]; the relation of the "compromise" to the doctrine of the "*veracitas dei*" [*i.e. to Descartes' explanation] seems to have escaped him. [See English translation by E.B. Bax in *Kant's Prolegomena and Metaphysical Foundations of Natural Science* (1983), p. 146. Tr.]

[7] Immanuel Kant, *Kritik der reinen Vernunft* (2nd ed., 1787), § 27, pp. 167 f. [English translation by N. Kemp Smith (1929), 1965: *Critique of Pure Reason*, p. 175. Tr.]

[8] [Immanuel Kant, *Prolegomena* (1783), § 36, p. 113. Ed.; English translation by Paul Carus, extensively revised by James W. Ellington (1977), § 36, p. 62. Tr.]

However, this Copernican revolution already contains the thesis of *transcendental idealism*.

Not only is nature given to us solely in our perceptions and our ideas, but all objects and processes of nature are (necessarily) *given to us only in those forms which our understanding has prescribed to them.*

According to this view, the process of cognition (the process of apperception) is comparable to the process of taking in food (assimilation); the product of assimilation is partly determined and formed by the subjective formal conditions of the organism, and much the same applies to the process of cognition.[9] The formal conditions, the most general regularities of the cognitive product (cognised nature), agree with the most general principles of the empirical use of the understanding, because the former are prescribed and generated by the latter.

This, then, is the argument underlying Kant's "proof of transcendental idealism".

Before critically analysing this argument, I will comment on its role in the system of Kant's apriorism.

In the preceding section it was claimed that transcendental idealism is wholly based on the results of the "transcendental deduction". This claim is of considerable importance, since it protects the critique of apriorism advocated here – the critique of the "transcendental deduction" – from any objections that already assume transcendental idealism. It must, therefore, itself be protected against the view that transcendental idealism can be proved even without the "transcendental deduction", say through Kant's doctrine of the subjectivity of the categories of intuition of space and time (that is, through his transcendental aesthetics), or by resolving the cosmological antinomies (that is, through his transcendental dialectic). These objections can be dealt with in the following way. The only aspect of transcendental idealism relevant to the problem of induction is the doctrine of the *subjectivity of natural laws*, or the doctrine of the *understanding as nature's lawgiver.* This is the core of transcendental idealism. It is only on account of the subjectivity of natural laws that the "things in themselves" are *unknowable* (and not simply *unknown;* cf. the preceding section), since all possibly existing objective laws that might govern them

---

[9] On this subject, see e.g. Jakob Friedrich Fries, *Neue Kritik der Vernunft* II (1st ed., 1807), § 95, pp. 65 f. [2nd ed. (*Neue oder anthropologische Kritik der Vernunft* II.), 1831, § 95, pp. 76 f. Ed.].

are replaced by the categories of the understanding that can apply only to the representational material (the "appearances"). However, this doctrine *cannot* be proved by the doctrine of the subjectivity of the categories of intuition, or by the doctrine of the antinomies.

The following criticism of the "proof of transcendental idealism" is designed to show that the argument presented above is a typical example of the confusion of epistemological with genetic-psychological aspects.

The criticism has to take as its point of departure the problem area that leads from the results of the "transcendental deduction" to transcendental idealism. Kant's formulation of the problem is something like this:

How can the agreement of the (subjective) conditions of possible experience with (objective) laws of nature be explained?

It will be shown that such a question – in whatever way one may try to *reformulate* it – can never be understood as an *epistemological question*, but only as a *genetic-psychological one*. In order to show this, the question will be reformulated in such a way that it becomes as unobjectionable as *possible* from a purely *epistemological* point of view. Thus, the question is:

According to the transcendental definition of empirical knowledge, "knowing" consists in formulating and testing natural laws. For knowledge to exist, the precondition to be fulfilled is that we be able to formulate and test natural laws. As it turns out, this precondition in fact is fulfilled since empirical knowledge exists objectively. How can this be explained?

It is evident that the formulation of the problem that leads Kant into transcendental idealism is basically a demand for an explanation of *the fact that there is knowledge*.

However, epistemology cannot pose (let alone answer) this question.

Epistemology can, however, examine the question: "How is knowledge *possible?*" That is, it can analyse the concept of knowledge and examine the preconditions that have to be fulfilled for empirical knowledge to exist ("transcendental definition" of the concept of knowledge). Moreover, it can ascertain that there really is experience, i.e., that in fact these preconditions are fulfilled.

But it can never demand an *explanation* for this fact; it can never ask: "In what sense is knowledge *real?* Why is there *real* knowledge?"

Similarly, a physicist cannot ask why, for instance, the conditions formulated in Maxwell's equations are, in fact, fulfilled in nature. He can only *formulate* these conditions, and he can try to deduce them logically from more general laws and thus explain them (since "to explain" means: to derive from a general law).*² And just as a physicist cannot ask why one law or other does hold, an epistemologist cannot ask why in fact the conditions for knowing are fulfilled, that is, why regularities do exist.

It is clear that this question is inadmissible and unscientific, since any explanation could in turn be given only in terms of a general law.

That there is knowledge, that regularities do exist, means only that the task of natural science to formulate and test natural laws can be *carried out*, and that testing generally – or at least frequently – has positive results. The positive result of a test, that is, a successful *prediction* deduced from a particular natural law, cannot be further explained than by this particular (or any other) natural law. The fact that the natural law is corroborated, that is to say, that the prediction is fulfilled, cannot be explained any further. A successful prediction is to be considered a final datum that cannot be further reduced.

In itself it is neither deducible nor predictable. There are *not two* hierarchically ordered predictions: a scientific one predicting a specific event and an epistemological one predicting that this event will, in fact, occur. There is only *one* prediction, the scientific one.

The task of knowing (predicting) *reality* is accomplished *only* by *natural science*, using any means at its disposal. (Epistemology simply is not an empirical science.)

Any attempt to *explain* the fact that we can *successfully* test certain natural laws – or, what amounts to the same thing, any attempt to explain that we can really have knowledge – *lies beyond the scope of science* (it is "meta-physical"). It does not matter if, like Kant, one looks for the basis of explanation *in ourselves* – in the properties of our understanding, which prescribes laws to nature – or perhaps in the general *properties of the world* (such as simplicity, etc.).

---

*² This concept of explanation (nowadays usually referred to as the "deductive-nomological model") is further discussed in *Logik der Forschung* (1934; 2nd ed., 1966; and subsequent editions) [*The Logic of Scientific Discovery* (1959; 2nd ed., 1968; and subsequent editions). Tr.], Section 12.

We know the properties of the world (to which our understanding also belongs) through natural laws, for which we search with the methods of natural science – regardless of whether these laws have a "precise character" ("causal character") or a "statistical character". Other "properties" that make such laws "possible" cannot be known by scientific methods, neither by those of natural science nor by those of philosophy – nor even by the methods of any epistemology.

While Kant's formulation of the problem is completely unacceptable as an epistemological question, it can nevertheless be successfully interpreted as a *psychological* and a *genetic-biological* one. Kant's formulations, such as the "strange agreement of appearances with the laws of the understanding"[10] (and many others), point to such a (psychological) interpretation.

In this sense (that is, excluding any epistemological considerations), the question might be formulated in the following way:

How can the agreement of the (subjective) conditions of our cognitive apparatus – of the laws governing the functioning of our mind – with the (objective) conditions of our environment be explained?

It can be shown that this question may be reduced to the general *biological* question of how the *adaptation* of living organisms to objective environmental conditions can be explained. This is a theoretical question in natural science – it is a factual question.

Once again, one should not ask why there is such a thing as adaptation at all, or why there are law-like environmental conditions to which organisms are able to adapt. One may well enquire into the objective and subjective conditions of adaptation, but one cannot ask why they are fulfilled.

No doubt, in addition to objective conditions such as the constancy (law-like regularity) of the environment, certain subjective conditions (conditions of the adapting subject) must be fulfilled so that there can be adaptation and so that one can speak of any adaptation at all (such as the existence of organic life, reactivity, etc.). Obviously, the fact that these basic subjective conditions exist cannot itself be explained *in terms of adaptation.* (If one wanted to attempt such an explanation, one would have

---

[10] [Immanuel Kant, *Metaphysische Anfangsgründe der Naturwissenschaft* (1786), Vorrede, footnote 2 near the end, p. XIX. Ed.; English translation by E.B. Bax in *Kant's Prolegomena and Metaphysical Foundations of Natural Science* (1983), p. 146. Tr.]

to take a different route.) This might be put in the following terms: The genesis of the preconditions of all adaptation is "*a priori*" vis-à-vis *adaptation* in a sense *analogous* to Kant's ideas.

These conditions are the prerequisite for the "possibility" of adaptation.

Proceeding now from these general considerations to the specific case of our *cognitive apparatus*, that is, our *intellectual functions*, the characteristic fact that we search everywhere for regularities (according to Kant, the "*understanding* [is] . . . the faculty of rules";[11] on this subject and on what follows, cf. Section 4) may be seen as such a fundamental condition of our intellectual adaptation.

Since the *process of intellectual adaptation*, that is, cognition, consists in the search for rules, the fact that we possess an intellect and search every-where for rules cannot itself be regarded as a process of *intellectual adaptation*. The peculiarity of searching for rules is *a priori* vis-à-vis the process of intellectual adaptation, and in this case *entirely* *[*3] in the Kantian sense.

Only the existence of this basic intellectual function, namely, the search-ing for regularities, makes *possible* the process of intellectual adaptation (cognition).

Thus, although the existence and genesis of the basic intellectual func-tion cannot be explained in terms of a process of *intellectual* adaptation, it can nevertheless be *explained* – as a (non-intellectual) *process of adaptation*.

In other words, the fact that we possess intellectual functions can be explained (given the present state of our biological knowledge) by the hypothesis that they have gradually developed through adaptation (of course, non-intellectual).

In this way the question is only pushed further back. Like all the fun-damental problems of biology, the problem of adaptation remains largely unresolved.

This at least, however, has been achieved: the Kantian question concern-ing the "strange agreement" between our intellect and the properties of the environment has been reduced to the more general biological question of adaptation. As such, *it does not have any special epistemological status over and above other questions of biological adaptation.*

---

[11] [Immanuel Kant, *Kritik der reinen Vernunft* (1st ed., 1781), p. 126. Ed.; English translation by N. Kemp Smith (1929), 1965: *Critique of Pure Reason*, p. 147. Tr.]

*[*3] Today I would say "*almost entirely*".

The *apriorism* of the basic intellectual functions turns out to be a *genetic* apriorism: these basic functions are *inborn*; they exist as conditions of, and prior to, any knowledge of reality. The question as to why, *in spite of this*, they suit our environment is fundamentally on the same level as the question of how a bird could have come by its wings even before it had a chance to use them in the air.

After analysing the Kantian *formulation of the problem*, we now have to examine Kant's *three possible answers*.

The view just presented implies a decision in favour of the "*middle course*".

The basic intellectual functions are *preformed*, and are "subjective dispositions of thought, implanted in us from the first moment of our existence".[12] But in order to explain this "system of preformation", we need not resort either to any pre-established harmony or to the *veracitas* of our creator: the question has the same status as other questions of "preformation", that is, of inborn adaptation.

Kant's objection that no *necessary* agreement with the environment can be ascribed to such a system of preformation, once again clearly shows his confusion of genetic and epistemological arguments; only this time it is the epistemological intruding on the genetic side.

The genetic-*apriori* system of preformation is certainly not "necessarily in agreement" with its environment, that is, at any time our cognitive apparatus might fail (and we go down in chaos). Kant, however, remembers that his (*epistemological*) concept of the *a priori* has the character of "necessity", that is, validity *under any circumstances*, and he employs this argument in discussing a problem that, as already shown, cannot really be treated as epistemological.

Once all such epistemological aspects have been eliminated, the gulf between the "middle course" and the two other possibilities is no longer unbridgeable.

The *first possibility* in the now established view would correspond to the environment determining the process of adaptation; and the environment, no doubt, partly determines (e.g. through *selection*) any process of adaptation; this is implicit in the concept of "adaptation".

[12] Immanuel Kant, *Kritik der reinen Vernunft* (2nd ed., 1787), § 27, p. 167. [English translation by N. Kemp Smith (1929), 1965: *Critique of Pure Reason*, p. 174. Tr.]

The *second possibility* would correspond to the subject of adaptation, the adapting organism, determining its environment and *prescribing* its subjective-formal conditions to its environment. And this undoubtedly is also the case. An ant population or a termite state live in a different "world" from that of their (local) neighbours among the birds and mammals (a fence that obstructs our way may be a road for an army of ants). Seen in this light, the subjective structuring of the "environment" (which Kant put at the centre of his doctrine) is a well-founded biological *hypothesis*.

"Environment", in this sense, is the totality of all biologically relevant, external conditions; however, what is *biologically relevant* and in what way it is relevant depends largely on internal conditions (according to this hypothesis).

Applied to human knowledge, we have to conclude that:

Our knowledge is *anthropomorphic*.

The idea of *anthropomorphism* is of fundamental importance for Kantian epistemology. The doctrine of transcendental idealism and the concept of the thing in itself – translated into a more biological terminology – imply that we cannot go beyond our subjectively coloured and subjectively structured "environment": that it is impossible for us to transcend our anthropomorphic limitations.

But can one really derive epistemological conclusions from this biological hypothesis? Or are these ideas, perhaps, also based on an anthropomorphism understood in epistemological terms?

Because of the typically circular reasoning to which its analysis leads, the so-called "problem of anthropomorphism", or the problem of the subjectivity of our knowledge, appears banal rather than subtle.

This applies more particularly to the two *antinomous views* that appeal (with the same apparent justification) to the idea of anthropomorphism: epistemological pessimism and epistemological optimism (as I wish to characterise these views).

There is no knowledge at all, says the *epistemological pessimist*, the *sceptic*; or, at any rate, there is no knowledge in the strict sense: there are no absolutely true statements. ("I know that I know nothing – and this I barely know.") The reason: our knowledge, by necessity, is always *subjectively coloured*. The (less significant) *individual-subjective* colouring – the one so conspicuous, for example, in any legal dispute – may be overcome to a certain degree by the intersubjective methods of science, which transcend the individual; however, the far more significant *species*-subjective colouring (which is precisely what anthropomorphism means) is insurmountable for us human beings. We can, therefore, never attain objectivity of knowledge or absolute truth. (If, following Husserl,[13] for example, one wished to raise the objection that "What is true is absolutely, 'intrinsically' true: truth is one and the same, whether humans or non-humans, angels or gods apprehend and judge it", then the pessimist could respond to such an ontological proof of truth by saying: "Precisely because the concept of truth entails absolute truth, we cannot grasp it, for none of our judgements can deny its anthropomorphic character.")

It is evident that this sceptical-pessimistic view is *contradictory*. First, because it is, after all, founded on *knowledge*. (Individual-subjective colouring is an *empirical claim*, and so is the idea of general anthropomorphism, which presupposes biological considerations.) Thus, by eliminating the truth of its presuppositions, the sceptical view simultaneously eliminates itself.

In order to demonstrate the internal inconsistency of such a general scepticism, it will suffice to recall the "Cretan syllogism".*⁴ It may be formulated here as follows: If there is no true knowledge, then (since the knowledge claim just stated is thus not true) there would have to be true knowledge after all, . . . etc.

(This internal inconsistency remains unaffected even if the *sceptical thesis itself* is not claimed to be true, but is merely proposed as an uncertain conjecture as it has been proposed by all consistent sceptics since Pyrrho and Arcesilaos, and probably even since Socrates.)

This formalistic refutation of scepticism may not be very appealing, and it is certainly not entirely satisfactory (for which internal reasons will also emerge below). In order to provide a more transparent formulation of this criticism, one may attempt to apply the sceptic's doubt, which is expressed in very general terms, to specific cases. You doubt – one might try to argue in an *ad hominem* fashion with the sceptic – you doubt that you hear the song of a blackbird? But we happen to *call* the sound you hear the

---

[13] [Edmund Husserl, *Logische Untersuchungen* I. (1900), § 36, p. 117. Ed.; English translation from the 2nd German ed. by J.N. Findlay, *Logical Investigations* I. (1970), p. 140. Tr.]

*⁴ This remark is from a time before I became acquainted with Tarski's theory of truth.

singing of a bird (regardless of what it may be "in itself"), and this dark something that you see over there we happen to *call* a blackbird. If you doubt whether we really *call* it *that*, you can easily convince yourself by asking us, or by consulting a book, etc. If, however, you doubt whether it really *is* a blackbird, we can only respond: Our statement "This *is* a blackbird" is not intended to be, and must not be, understood in any other way than "We *call* that a blackbird." It is true that we can never penetrate to the "essence of things", etc. with this *merely stipulative* ("semantic"*[5]) *method of knowledge*; but because we do not intend to do anything of the kind, and because more particularly our statements certainly do *not claim* to represent the essence of things but are only designed unambiguously to *label* them, this fact does not contradict but supports the possibility of knowledge.

However, such considerations may not satisfy the sceptic. (Incidentally, they are not entirely unexceptionable in other respects either: not because of the *semantic view of knowledge* that is advocated, but because of the psychologistic form of argumentation.) Anthropomorphism, or subjectivism, the sceptic might respond, is clearly evident in your own arguments. You simply call it the "semantic method of knowledge". I gladly admit [he might continue] that our knowledge is merely "semantic"; but the inevitable anthropomorphism consists *precisely in this*, since it reveals the dependence of knowledge on *our* assignments of symbols. In short, your thesis that our knowledge is merely semantic represents to me just another way of expressing the sceptical thesis that we cannot actually know anything at all (that we cannot possess any *genuine* knowledge – scepticism here borders on mysticism).

But then, the sceptic would also have admitted that we have knowledge (of course, "only" semantic knowledge); and what he now attacks is *our* (*semantic*) *concept of knowledge*, and our concept of *truth*, which is closely connected with it.

This, however, brings us back to our point of departure; we have gone round in a circle. The sceptic, who at first doubted the absolute truth of our knowledge, is in turn compelled to explain this (absolute) concept of truth as anthropomorphic. But what he still doubts can now no longer be expressed; for it is evident that even the concept of *doubt* presupposes the concept of truth.

---

*[5] Of course I did not use the term "semantic" in Tarski's sense. At the time I did not know anything about Tarski or about metalanguages.

Moreover, the sceptic cannot escape these implications by explaining logic itself – and with it, all consistency – as anthropomorphic; for the concept of truth stands or falls with our logic (which may, incidentally, be understood as an implicit definition of the concepts of "true" and "false").

Wittgenstein's characterisation of the situation in which general scepticism, or epistemological pessimism, finds itself, can therefore hardly be improved upon:[14]

"Scepticism is *not* irrefutable, but obviously non-sensical, when it tries to raise doubts where no questions can be asked."

The result of this dispute might be interpreted to mean that anthropomorphism has proved to be *absolutely inescapable*. It permeates our logic, our concept of truth, indeed, even our scepticism.

This interpretation, however, leads to epistemological *optimism*; it leads to a view of the question of anthropomorphism as represented, for example, by Kant's *apriorism*.

According to this view, we have no choice: we are forced to accept the anthropomorphic framework – the forms of our understanding – as something ultimate. We can know these *forms themselves*, though not in order to transcend them but, on the contrary, in order to establish them as the ultimate limits that cannot be transgressed and simultaneously as the ultimate, and now irrefutable, principles of our knowledge.

Thus, *transcendental idealism* may also be seen as the radical consequence of the idea that all our knowledge is *subjectively coloured*, that is, *anthropomorphic*.

This Kantian view has specific implications for the use of the concepts "*objective*" and "*subjective*" (which account for certain terminological inconsistencies in Kant's work), for radical subjectivism also renders the concept of "*object*" subjective.

The objects of science are given to us only in our experience and in our knowledge; in order for something to become an object at all, it must already be formed subjectively.

The *objectivity* of knowledge cannot therefore be sought in any knowledge that grasps its object "in itself"; rather, it consists in scientifically determining the object according to *universally valid* (*intersubjective*) methodological principles (for the use of our understanding). (In Kant's terminology, this objectivity might be called "*empirical objectivity*".)

---

[14] Ludwig Wittgenstein, *Tractatus Logico-Philosophicus* (1918/1922), Proposition 6.51.

Corresponding to this concept of (empirical) *objectivity*, in the sense of being universally valid and of conforming to scientific-empirical standards,[+1] (of *intersubjective testability*; cf. end of Section 9 and this section below), there would be a concept of (empirical) *subjectivity*, in the sense of a conviction (a "belief"), justification of which could not be tested according to scientific, or universally valid, methods.

However, in contrast to this linguistic usage, which most closely corresponds to transcendental idealism, there is another, less important and evidently older usage that has nothing to do with the concept of objectivity used in the present study. It may be characterised as equating *"objective"* with *"absolute"*: knowledge would be *objective* if it comprehended its *object as it is* − "in itself" − detached from all relations to the knowing subject; it would be *subjective* if its determination of the object were only *relative*, related to other components of knowledge, as well as to the basic formal precondition of a knowing subject or scientific knowledge.

If one avoids this second (transcendent) usage that hardly corresponds to transcendental idealism − which can easily be done, since we have the conceptual pair of "absolute" and "relative" at our disposal − and only employs the concepts "objective" and "subjective" in the sense referred to above as "empirical", then the result of the Kantian critique of knowledge can be summarised in the following formula:

The *"absolute"* can be grasped only *subjectively* (that is, "believed");

all *objective* (that is, universally valid, intersubjectively testable *scientific*) *knowledge* is *"relative"*.

"It seems to me that this pair of opposites, *subjective-absolute* and *objective-relative*, contains one of the most fundamental epistemological insights that can be gleaned from science," writes Weyl,[15] admittedly without reference to Kant's doctrine; and he continues: "Whoever desires the absolute must take the subjectivity and egocentricity as part of the

---

[+1] [The German phrase rendered as "conforming to scientific-empirical standards" is "*wissenschaftlich-empirische Dignität*". A.P. (Tr.)]

[15] Hermann Weyl, *Philosophie der Mathematik und Naturwissenschaft* (1927), p. 83. [English translation by Olaf Helmer: *Philosophy of Mathematics and Natural Science*, rev. and augm. English ed. (1949), p. 116. Emphasis as in the German original. Tr.]

bargain; whoever feels drawn toward the objective faces the problem of relativity."[16]

It can hardly be doubted that this insight is implicitly contained in Kantian epistemology (even if the terminological confusion mentioned above [slightly] detracts from it) – indeed, it contains one of the most important ideas in all of Kantian philosophy (cf., for example, Section 3 of the "Transcendental Doctrine of Method"[17] but also Kant's *practical philosophy*); it marks that aspect of Kantian philosophy that is empiricist without being positivist. Kant's extremely important *concept of objectivity* and its "relativist" implications will be discussed later in this section. (Obviously, this "relativism" has nothing to do either with platitudes such as "Everything is relative" or with a relativisation of the concept of truth.[18])

At this point, *apriorism* needs to be further criticised. Even Kant's *optimistic* view that we are compensated for the necessary anthropomorphic limitations of our knowledge (i.e., for its relativisation) by having *a priori* valid, objective-synthetic insights is not tenable; transcendental idealism cannot be founded on the idea of an anthropomorphism that can in no way be transcended; the optimistic apriorist is caught in contradictions analogous to those of the pessimistic sceptic.

Kant seeks to explain and secure the epistemologically *a priori* status of a principle of induction, or the "necessity" of the existence of universal natural laws, using the assumption that our understanding prescribes its laws to nature and imposes its forms upon it. However, this assumption in no way delivers what Kant demands from it. It *explains nothing*, it is *circular*, and ultimately it even proves *incompatible* with Kant's fundamental

---

[16] As Weyl himself emphasises, this idea is also found in Max Born, *Die Relativitätstheorie Einsteins und ihre physikalischen Grundlagen* (1920), Introduction; and even earlier, Reininger offered a very similar statement; cf. Robert Reininger, *Das Psycho-Physische Problem* (1916), pp. 290 f.

[17] [Immanuel Kant, *Kritik der reinen Vernunft* (2nd ed., 1787), Transzendentale Methodenlehre, 2. Hauptstück, 3. Abschnitt, pp. 848 ff. Ed.; English translation by N. Kemp Smith (1929), 1965: *Critique of Pure Reason*, Transcendental Doctrine of Method, Chapter II, Section 3, pp. 645 ff. Tr.]

[18] On the concept of "relativity" see also Jakob Friedrich Fries, *Neue Kritik der Vernunft II.* (1st ed., 1807), § 111: 3, p. 121. [2nd ed. (*Neue oder anthropologische Kritik der Vernunft II.*), 1831, § 110: 3, p. 129. Ed.]

presuppositions and with his definition of the notions of analytic and synthetic judgements.

To begin with, even if one could successfully reduce the *problem of law-like regularities in nature* to that of the *laws of the understanding* – what would be gained by this? Even the assertion that the laws of our understanding have universal and strict validity would have to *presuppose a principle of induction*.

Thus Kant assumes, for example, a universal uniformity among the intellects of all mentally healthy human beings. However, this assumption is empirical and therefore requires a principle of induction.

In order to escape this circle, one would have to start from "methodological solipsism" [Carnap]. My understanding prescribes laws to nature (as it appears to me), hence there are laws of my own nature; based on this [or another*⁶] *principle of induction*, I am now able to assert the uniformity of human minds (which are part of "nature" as it appears to me), etc. But even this step does not eliminate the circular inference. What would justify my asserting something like a uniformity, or law-likeness, of my intellect – *without* presupposing, that is, *a priori* presupposing, a principle of induction?

(Transcendental idealism could explain the *a priori* status of natural laws only in *psychological* respects, but never in *epistemological* ones. Once again, it becomes evident that at crucial points Kant confuses these two concepts of the *a priori*.)

Such uniformity of my intellect can by no means be taken for granted. It is an empirical fact that the human understanding (in its ontogenetic and phylogenetic aspects) changes and develops. And these changes are primarily of a *formal* nature. They consist not so much in changes of material knowledge, but primarily affect the intellectual *functions*, methods and unexamined presuppositions of our thinking.

It is, therefore, not intuitively evident (unless one confuses the psychological and the epistemological *a priori*) why the laws of my understanding should be more certain or more stable or more easily comprehensible (or even more evident?) than natural laws. (Thus in geology, for example, it is a well-tested assumption that the most general geophysical conditions – that is, conditions determined by natural laws – have not changed in different geological periods; yet no one doubts the fact that great

---

*⁶ Cf. my new comments on Section 5, above.

phylogenetic changes have occurred in human intellectual functions within much shorter periods of time.)

Hence, reducing natural laws to the laws of our understanding explains nothing. Such a reduction, moreover, contains a circularity that cannot be eliminated; and it must contain such a circularity: we ourselves are natural (and not supernatural) beings, we ourselves belong – with our understanding, our reason, our knowledge, our science (even after Kant) – to that "nature" which is said to be formed, to become "nature", only through us.

One objection that is closely related to the one just presented (even though it contains no suggestion of the circular inference) is raised by Russell,[19] specifically to Kant's philosophy of arithmetic and of logic: "The thing to be accounted for is our certainty that the facts must always conform to logic and arithmetic. To say that logic and arithmetic are contributed by us does not account for this. Our nature is as much a fact of the existing world as anything, and there can be no certainty that it will remain constant. It might happen, if Kant is right, that tomorrow our nature would so change as to make two and two become five. This possibility seems never to have occurred to him, yet it is one which utterly destroys the certainty and universality which he is anxious to vindicate for arithmetical propositions."

It seems to me that an even more serious objection to optimistic apriorism than that of circularity, is that this position is *incompatible* with Kant's very significant distinction between *analytic* and *synthetic* judgements.

Kant believed that there had to be synthetic judgements *a priori*, but (in contrast to "dogmatic" rationalism, which presupposed *material* synthetic judgements *a priori*) only those that are *valid for formal reasons*. He believed that they must be valid for everything (thus being *a priori*) because they are nothing but the *most general rational forms* that we imprint upon every substance, and in which therefore *any* substance must appear if it is to be rationally determined, that is, *known*.

This *synthetic formalism* of Kant – his view that synthetic judgements can have validity for *formal reasons* – is, as can easily be shown, incompatible with Kant's definition of a synthetic judgement, according to which every synthetic judgement can be *negated* without contradiction.

---

[19] Bertrand Russell, *The Problems of Philosophy* (1912), VIII [p. 135].

Kant's idea of synthetic formalism is roughly that every substance, every sense impression, is subsumed by our understanding (by means of certain schemata) under certain formal concepts; the pure concepts of the understanding, or *categories*, are applied to the substance (according to four different aspects); every thing is rationally processed, categorically formed.

However, "*negation*" too is a *category*, and one that – *in purely formal terms* – can be applied to any statement whatsoever, regardless of its form.

In a certain class of statements it becomes evident that by applying the category of negation, by negating (which can always formally be done), a statement is obtained that *cannot be valid* for formal reasons because it is internally *inconsistent*. These are the *analytic* statements, whose negations are *contradictions*.

In contrast, according to Kant[20] a *synthetic judgement* can never "be established by the law of contradiction". This means, however, that its negation is never contradictory, and that applying the category of negation to a synthetic judgement will never result in a statement that is invalid for *formal reasons*.

If, therefore, a particular thing can appear in a certain form as a (synthetic) judgement, then – for formal reasons – another form can *always* be applied to the same thing, namely, the *negation* of the first judgement.

Thus, the *choice* between these two mutually contradictory (mutually exclusive) forms cannot be based on a decision according to *formal* criteria. Only the *material* side of knowledge (empirical testing) can decide which of these (in formal terms equally "possible") synthetic judgements is to be regarded as *true*, and which as *false*.

Kant himself clearly saw this: the first two (previously quoted[21]) "postulates of empirical thought in general" state:[22]

"1. That which agrees with the formal conditions of experience . . . is *possible*.

---

[20] [Immanuel Kant, *Prolegomena* (1783), § 2, p. 28; I. Kant, *Kritik der reinen Vernunft* (2nd ed., 1787), p. 14. Ed. Immanuel Kant, *Prolegomena*, English translation by Paul Carus, extensively revised by James W. Ellington (1977), § 2, p. 13; I. Kant, *Critique of Pure Reason*, English translation by N. Kemp Smith (1929), 1965: p. 52. Tr.]

[21] [See Section 3, text to note 4. Ed.]

[22] [Immanuel Kant, *Kritik der reinen Vernunft* (2nd ed., 1787), pp. 265 f. Ed. English translation by N. Kemp Smith, *Critique of Pure Reason* (1929), 1965: p. 239. Tr.]

"2. That which is connected with the material conditions of sensual experience . . . is *actual*."

This sums it up concisely:

A priori, one cannot know of any form whether it, or its equally possible (formally equally applicable) negation, will be applicable to a particular case in empirical reality (to a particular thing). This will be decided – *a posteriori* – by the material conditions of experience.

All statements that for formal reasons are *a priori* true are *analytic*. If a statement containing a particular assertion about a *thing* is (*a priori*) valid *on account of its form alone*, it must, in addition to this assertion, also admit the possibility of its negation (and thus become an analytic statement; for example, "The sun will rise tomorrow – or it won't").

Synthetic statements, therefore, are never valid for formal reasons; they can only be valid *a posteriori*.

Kant considered formal synthetic statements possible, partly because of his conception of mathematics but above all because he was misled by an *equivocation*; he confused his *logical* concepts "synthetic" and "analytic" with other, more particularly, with *psychological* concepts. Any "form", any order, *combines* "elements"; it is – if you like – a "*synthesis* of the manifold" and *to that extent* it may be called "synthetic". But *this* concept of synthesis has nothing to do with "synthetic judgements" (in the sense of non-analytic, non-tautological assertions).

Those statements that Kant held to be formal synthetic *a priori* judgements are partly *material* (and *synthetic*) and *not a priori* – these include, for example, his statements of "pure natural science" (some of which have, accordingly, proved to be false*[7]) – and partly genuinely *formal* and *a priori*, but *analytic*. These include all of Kant's epistemologically more important statements. Examples from this group are the aforementioned "postulates of empirical thought in general", which Kant[23] states are nothing but explanations of the concepts of "possibility" and "actuality", and thus[24]

---

*[7] An allusion to Einstein's theory of gravitation and Heisenberg's uncertainty relations.

[23] [Immanuel Kant, *op. cit.*, p. 266. Ed. English translation by N. Kemp Smith, *op. cit.*, p. 239. Tr.]

[24] [Immanuel Kant, *op. cit.*, p. 286. Ed. English translation by N. Kemp Smith, *op. cit.*, p. 251. Tr.]

"not objectively synthetic" (hence "objectively analytic"?) but only "subjectively synthetic" (that is, "synthetic" in some psychological sense).

Transcendental forms – forms to which our scientific knowledge is tied – are therefore only the forms of *analytic* statements, or logical or mathematical tautologies. (Echoing Wittgenstein,[25] though in a different sense, one might say: "*Only logic is transcendental*.")

This is all I propose to say by way of a critique of Kantian apriorism, in particular of Kant's optimistic position on the question of anthropomorphism.

The rather high hopes that Kant derived from the correct insight that a general scepticism is self-contradictory have proved to be unjustified. But how is the question of anthropomorphism to be resolved? From the position we have reached in the discussion of the problem of induction, can we perhaps find a third and more satisfactory view besides pessimism and optimism?

The sterile and banal character of the whole debate between epistemological pessimism and optimism has its roots in its excessively general and unspecific formulation of the question. The general epistemological question concerning the validity of "our knowledge in general" will have to be replaced by more concrete problems arising from empirical-scientific methodology. In fact, with his distinction between analytic and synthetic judgements, Kant took the first decisive step in this direction.

Seen from the perspective of empirical science, *analytic* judgements do *not pose a methodological problem*. To the empirical scientist, the sceptical view of analytic judgements (which of course also means of logic) appears futile; our analysis has, moreover, demonstrated that such scepticism is untenable.

Synthetic judgements are, however, a different matter.

On the one hand, the reason why a summary rejection of *scepticism* is unsatisfactory is clearly that, in the light of the methodological development of empirical science, a certain scepticism regarding some synthetic judgements appears to be *not entirely unjustified*. Since there are no synthetic judgements *a priori* – and thus no principle of induction – a *logically unobjectionable, final justification of universal synthetic judgements is impossible*.

[25] Cf. Ludwig Wittgenstein, *Tractatus Logico-Philosophicus* (1918/1922), Propositions 6.13 and 6.421.

We must, on the other hand, also agree with Kant's view that anthropomorphism imposes on human knowledge limits that cannot be transcended; but in contrast to Kant's view, this limitation of our knowledge (according to the view advocated here) does not consist in the fact that it is tied to synthetic *a priori* dogmas; rather, its force is, above all, the *impossibility of ever obtaining a final verification of universal empirical statements*.

In view of the previous discussion of the problem of induction, the idea of *anthropomorphism* should be linked to a *sceptical view* of the problem of knowledge (a view that originally had quite different motives); to be sure, it should be linked to a *limited* scepticism relating primarily to the validity of *natural laws* (universal empirical statements), thus avoiding the contradictions of a general form of scepticism.

But this is not enough. A sceptical view of natural laws remains a rather empty idea, and is methodologically almost meaningless unless it is supplemented by a statement of the *approximate character* of our empirical knowledge, thus pointing it again in a more optimistic direction.

So long as we have only a general *suspicion* that some particular item of knowledge has an anthropomorphic character (or that it has not been finally proved [and may therefore be incorrect]) without being able to justify this suspicion, we move within the domain of rather futile speculation. It is an entirely different matter if we point out that often we *transcend particular scientific theories, that we replace them with better ones*. In such cases we can usually establish in a very concrete fashion which (unproved) *prejudices* the older theory was based on. We can examine these prejudices; in many cases the trait described as "anthropomorphic" can be identified. Thus, only the (epistemological) *fact of approximation, of a theory being transcended by a better one*, gives a tangible content to the idea of anthropomorphism (and of scepticism).

A position such as the one just outlined is, however, not too far removed from epistemological optimism. This can be clearly seen in the affinity of this position with certain of Kant's ideas that have been pursued by the *neo-Kantians* in particular. The doctrine that the "object" of our knowledge is never "given" but is always merely "postulated" as the unknown *x*, emphatically underscores the approximate character and the incompletability of our knowledge (even if this is understood in a sense somewhat different from the one advocated here). There is, however, an almost unbridgeable conflict between the view advocated here and the radical optimism of Wittgenstein, who – wholly in the spirit of positivism and in opposition to any form of scepticism – states:[26]

"The riddle does not exist.

If a question can be framed at all, it is also possible to answer it."

The methodological importance of the approximate character of our knowledge is evident. It is, perhaps, not quite so obvious that the impossibility of any final verification of universal empirical statements has practical methodological consequences. (This will be sufficiently emphasised in the further course of this study.) If the idea of anthropomorphism (which, of course, was originally a biological idea) is at all applicable to the field of methodology and epistemology, then it can be applied only with the aid of the concept of approximation and that of the incompletability of our empirical knowledge. The former only derives its full import from the discovery of the latter, as well as positively complementing the discovery itself.

The view presented here of the problem of anthropomorphism is not exactly new. It can hardly be considered a coincidence that Xenophanes (c.500 BCE), the first to highlight the significance of anthropomorphism, also expressed the two other ideas – the approximate character of our knowledge of nature and the impossibility of its definitive verification.

I will here render the passages in question from Xenophanes' preserved fragments (in my own translation[27]). I shall first quote his classical formulation of the critical idea of anthropomorphism:

> The Ethiops say that their gods are flat-nosed and black
> While the Thracians say that theirs have blue eyes and red hair.
> Yet if cattle or horses or lions had hands and could draw
> And could sculpture like men, then the horses would draw their gods
> Like horses, and cattle like cattle, and each would then shape
> Bodies of gods in the likeness, each kind, of its own.[28]

---

[26] Ludwig Wittgenstein, op. cit., Proposition 6.5; cf. also Sections 19 and 43 f.

[27] [In the 1994 German edition of Die beiden Grundprobleme, Popper provided his own German translation of Xenophanes. For this English translation we have used Popper's English translation of the verse. In the German edition, footnotes 27, 28, 28a, 28b and 28c consist of comments by Popper on his German translation. The standard German translation of Xenophanes is found in Hermann Diels and Walther Kranz, Die Fragmente der Vorsokratiker. Tr.]

[28] [B16 and 15. Tr.]

This, perhaps, led Xenophanes to the insight that we acquire our knowledge (at best) through step-by-step improvements – through approximations to the truth.

[Xenophanes' verse continues:]

> The gods did not reveal, from the beginning,
> All things to us; but in the course of time,
> Through seeking we may learn, and know things better . . .[28a]

According to Xenophanes, these approximations are uncertain and even if they could be completed, this could *never be finally verified* (Xenophanes' "scepticism" – when modernised, that is, extended to *natural laws* – agrees with the one advocated here).

[Xenophanes' verse continues]:

> But as for certain truth, no man has known it,
> Nor will he know it; neither of the gods
> Nor yet of all the things of which I speak.
> And even if by chance he were to utter
> The perfect truth, he would himself not know it;
> For all is but a woven web of guesses.[28b]

These wonderful verses of Xenophanes showed me that 2,500 years ago, he had anticipated my epistemological insights – those insights that I formulated for myself in the winter of 1919–1920 and that were, for the first time, developed in this book. I am referring, above all, to the fallibilism that we cannot overcome; and to absolute and objective truth, which we seek and sometimes even find, though without ever being able to know with certainty that we have, in fact, found it. All this Xenophanes knew.

There are plenty of examples showing that the fallibility of our knowledge often springs from our anthropomorphism, but that our errors can, nonetheless, be rectified. An example of this kind is the development that begins with Zeus hurling bolts of lightning and leads to electromagnetic field theory. A similar development leads from the birth of our material

---

[28a] [B18. Tr.]
[28b] [B34. Tr.]

world out of the marriage of heaven and earth (Uranus and Gaia) all the way to unified field theory. A characteristic trait of all these series of developments is the move from the *concrete* to the *abstract*. This tendency towards the abstract (not towards a *lack of imagination* but towards *abstraction*, towards *rational design*) is already very evident in Xenophanes. He himself emphasises abstraction in the following six hexameters, in which he opposes to primitive anthropomorphic polytheism a monotheistic idea of *God = Spirit*:

> *One* God, alone among gods and alone among men, is the greatest,
> Neither in mind nor in body does he resemble the mortals.
> Always in one place, he remains, without ever moving.
> Nor is it fitting for him to wander now hereto now thereto.
> Effortless he swings the All, by mere thought and intention.
> All of him is sight; all is knowledge; and all is hearing.[28c]

Among many examples of such a development towards the abstract, the *development of the problem of causality* is, more than anything, relevant to the present analysis; this question will therefore be discussed here in somewhat greater detail.

In Section 3 of this study, the following definition was proposed for the concept of causal explanation: "To give a *causal explanation* of an event means . . . to *derive it deductively* from natural laws." This definition, which reduces the *concept of causality* to that of *natural law*, will be explained by contrasting it with other, more anthropomorphic, views.

Historically, the *concept of causality* is closely related to the concept of *genesis*, of creating, generating, coming into being, *by someone* and *out of something*. The German word *Ur-Sache*,[+2] the Ionian speculation about an original substance, and also religious theories of the genesis of the world and the cosmological proofs of the existence of God, clearly point to this method of *explanation*.

It is equally certain that an *animistic* element has been preserved in our *instinctive* attitude towards natural events (take notions such as the maxim

---

[28c] [B23, 26, 25 and 24. Tr.]

[+2] [The German word *Ursache* means "cause". Literally, the two parts comprising the word, i.e. the prefix *Ur* and the noun *Sache*, mean "original matter" or "original thing". Tr.]

"If something can go wrong, it will"). The primitive concept of causality obviously contains the notion of a *sympathetic understanding* of the cause ("*endopathy*" in H. Gomperz's sense[29]); the cause is regarded as active, as an acting person "bringing forth the effect".

This view of causality is so deeply rooted in our instincts that it is likely to persist for a long time to come. It is present not only when a cause is understood to produce its effect (*causa causans*), but also when "natural necessity", or a "necessary connection" between cause and effect, is assumed. Any assumption of a "real relationship" between two particular events of the kind in which one is said *necessarily* to follow the other "*according to a rule*" – or merely always *does* follow the other (*causa vera*) – still has animistic and thus also anthropomorphic overtones.

The *criticism* of this animistic conception of causality is very old. Starting around 200 CE with the sceptical physician Sextus Empiricus (whose predecessors had, however, paved the way for him), continuing with the Arab Al-Gazzâlî (eleventh century CE), Nicolaus of Autrecourt (fourteenth century), Malebranche and Joseph Glanvill (seventeenth century) through to Hume, the critics of the concept of causality stress that the assertion of causal necessity in the sequence of individual events cannot be justified either logically or empirically (and the same applies to the assertion of a universal law-governed natural order – [or*[8]] of a principle of induction).

We can never observe that one event causes another, but only that one event of this type has (so far) *regularly followed* one of another type, or more precisely, that certain events occur *as if they conformed to a universal rule, a natural law*.

If we eliminate the problem of induction from the discussion of the problem of causality (which contains the former), that is, from the question whether there are exception-less and always valid regularities, or whether strict natural laws exist, then we are left with the following crucial point:

When we speak of causality, we always speak about the regularity and the law-like behaviour of sequences of events, and not about the unique, unrepeatable coincidence of certain individual events.

---

[29] Cf. Heinrich Gomperz, *Weltanschauungslehre* I. (1905), p. 166.
*[8] See Section 5, note *3.

We can never claim with respect to an individual, isolated occurrence (a pair of events) that it is causally determined (that its members stand in a causal relationship), for observation can only tell us about the actual sequence of events, and an isolated observation gives us no reason to assume that this sequence is *typical*, that it constitutes a *causal relationship*, and is thus distinguishable from an accidental concurrence. We would never call the movement of this table an "effect" and my pressure against it its "cause", if we did not assume that this movement *regularly* follows upon the pressure. We have postulated a *universal law* (a *hypothesis*) from which this particular occurrence can be derived (predicted) by *deductive logic*.

"*The natural law thus takes the place of causation,*" writes Weyl.[30] In the same context he also stresses that "[t]he abandonment of the metaphysical quest for the *cause* in favour of the scientific quest for the *law* is preached by all great scientists", citing evidence from Galilei, Newton, D'Alembert and Lagrange; it almost goes without saying that Hertz, Kirchhoff and Mach too are important in this connection.

Causal statements such as "Everything that *happens* (begins to be), presupposes something that it follows *according to a rule*",[31] or "All alterations take place in conformity with the law of the connection of cause and effect",[32] or "Same cause, same effect", etc., should be replaced with the less anthropomorphic formulation (already presented in Section 3 above): "All natural events must, in principle, be predictable by deduction from natural laws [and initial conditions]." (Such a formulation also helps fully to clarify the often misinterpreted analogy between "reason and (logical) consequence", on the one hand, and "cause and effect", on the other.)

While the former statements of the principle of causality have to be rejected as outmoded because of their *anthropomorphism* and their animistic character, the discussion of the *problem of induction*, in particular of *apriorism*, has shown that even a principle of causality of the latter form cannot be justified.

---

[30] Hermann Weyl, *Philosophie der Mathematik und Naturwissenschaft* (1927), p. 145. [English translation by Olaf Helmer: *Philosophy of Mathematics and Natural Science*, rev. and augm. English ed. (1949), p. 189. Emphasis as in the German original. Tr.]

[31] Immanuel Kant, *Kritik der reinen Vernunft* (1st ed., 1781), p. 189. [The first emphasis is not in the original. Ed.; English translation by N. Kemp Smith, *Critique of Pure Reason* (1929), 1965: p. 218. Tr.]

[32] Immanuel Kant, *Kritik der reinen Vernunft* (2nd ed., 1787), p. 232. [English translation by N. Kemp Smith (1929), 1965: *Critique of Pure Reason*, p. 218. Tr.]

Indeed, it cannot be justified even as a working hypothesis. It is, no doubt, true that our *practical behaviour*, for example *scientific research*, presupposes universal natural laws; it is probably true that neither in practical life nor in research will we ever cease *our search for laws*.*[9] But this fact does not require us to adduce the principle of causality (even in the form of a working hypothesis).

Our *practical behaviour* (as well as our *inclination to engage in research*) is sufficiently explained by the biological importance that *knowledge* has for us as a form of adaptation. And, as far as *systematic scientific research* is concerned, it can, and indeed it must, be satisfied with the *transcendental definition* of its task (to gain knowledge), from which the hypothetical statement (analytically) follows: "If you want to gain knowledge, you must search for laws." However, we can only hope (but not predict) that our search for knowledge will be successful – *it must make itself manifest*.

(Wittgenstein[33] writes: "If there were a law of causality, it might be put in the following way: 'There are laws of nature'. But of course that cannot be said; it makes itself manifest." But one may well say: If there is knowledge at all, then only through natural laws; and what "makes itself manifest" is *only that there is knowledge*.)

Clearly, the (subjective) *belief* in causality is *genetically a priori*. "This by no means compels us, however, to create a new mysticism out of what is instinctive in science, and to regard this factor as infallible," states Mach.[34] The criticism shows that this instinctive and anthropomorphically coloured principle of (epistemological) apriorism cannot be refuted – but neither can it be *in any way justified*.

The result of the critical appraisal of the *psychologistic traits in Kant's theory of knowledge* can be summarised in the following fashion:

Kant holds that while temporally (genetically) "all our knowledge begins with experience",[35] synthetic principles of knowledge exist that are epistemologically *a priori*.

---

*[9] Including the search for statistical laws.

[33] Ludwig Wittgenstein, *Tractatus Logico-Philosophicus* (1918/1922), Proposition 6.36.

[34] Ernst Mach, *Die Mechanik in ihrer Entwicklung* (8th ed., ed. Joseph Petzoldt, 1921), p. 27. [English translation by Thomas J. McCormack: *The Science of Mechanics* (6th ed., 1960), p. 35. Tr.]

[35] [Immanuel Kant, *Kritik der reinen Vernunft* (2nd ed., 1787), Introduction, p. 1. Ed.; English translation by N. Kemp Smith (1929, 1965: *Critique of Pure Reason*, p. 41. Tr.]

The critique presented here leads to a view that virtually reverses this relationship: temporally, psycho-genetically (it was conjectured in Section 4), all "knowledge" could precede its confirmation by experience (genetic *a priori*); epistemologically, however, the *validity* of all our knowledge always begins "with experience": there are no synthetic principles that are *a priori* valid.

At this point we should discuss the interesting view of J.F. Fries and the Friesian school (whose most eminent representatives were E.F. Apelt and the recently deceased Leonard Nelson). Even though Fries and Apelt were apriorists, they were respected by positivists: in giving them due recognition, Mach[36] states that they "have strongly promoted . . . many aspects of scientific methodology". However, as will be demonstrated in the following, Mach is also correct in further suggesting that they had "never succeeded in freeing themselves fully from preconceived philosophical views".

Fries takes over Kant's most important *results* (with modifications that are not relevant to the discussion of the problem of induction), but he firmly opposes Kant's *method*. In particular, he recognises the impossibility of Kant's "transcendental deduction", the impossibility of *demonstrating* the validity of synthetic *a priori* principles; his argument that any such attempted proof must lead to circularity (or to an infinite regression) was also employed in the previous section.

Drawing on old philosophical arguments (Carneades), Fries[37] attacks the *prejudice of proof*. The demand that *everything* must be proved before it can be accepted as scientifically justified is *contradictory*, for every proof of a synthetic statement requires *premises*.

Thus, the prejudice of seeking to prove everything must lead to a form of general *scepticism* (which itself is contradictory). If, on the other hand, one gives up this prejudice and if one accepts the necessity of assuming unprovable presuppositions as true, then this could open the floodgates to the arbitrariness of *dogmatism*.

---

[36] Ernst Mach, Erkenntnis und Irrtum (2nd ed., 1906), p. VI.

[37] [Cf. Jakob Friedrich Fries, *Neue Kritik der Vernunft* I. (1st ed., 1807), Introduction. (2nd ed., *Neue oder anthropologische Kritik der Vernunft* I., 1828, Introduction.) Ed.]

Between *dogmatism* and *scepticism*, that is, between the prejudice of self-evident knowledge intuited by reason and the prejudice of proof, Fries attempts to find a critical *middle way*.

This "critical stance" must accept the necessity of unprovable premises, but it must demand for them a *justification*, which *must not*, however, *be a logical proof*.

That it is possible to justify a statement without providing a logical proof can be seen in *perceptual judgements*. If I am to justify the assertion "The moon is shining now", then I can only ask the sceptic to convince himself through the evidence of his *own eyes*; I cannot logically prove my statement.

If there are synthetic statements that are *a priori* valid, then their validity cannot be proved; their justification must take a different route, one that will in some ways be analogous to that of justifying a perceptual judgement. Instead of attempting to *prove the objective validity of a priori principles*, one must try to *point out the subjective, psychological facts* that justify us in taking them to be true.

(How this is to be done will be shown below.)

Fries' ideas, which I have just outlined, are directed against Kant's "transcendental" theory of knowledge and have been generalised by Nelson into a *critique of epistemology in general* (also with reference to Carneades and other Pyrrhoneans, specifically to their arguments against the Stoic doctrine of the "criterion of truth").

Nelson's "proof of the impossibility of a theory of knowledge"[38] proceeds in roughly the following way.

The "*theory of knowledge*" [as it is called] sets itself the task of analysing and assessing the objective *validity* of our knowledge – such as ascertaining its "conditions" or justifying it by providing it with a "final justification". But any such task is *contradictory*. If our knowledge were in need of such an analysis, of such a "final justification", what would entitle us to make an exception for the *knowledge of the theory of knowledge*? If we make no exception and also require an analysis of the theory of knowledge (by an epistemology of a higher order), we will obviously end up in an infinite regression. If, on the other hand, the theory of knowledge is granted a special status, then this step (which is, in any case, open to objection) will

---

[38] [Cf. Leonard Nelson, "Über das sogenannte Erkenntnisproblem", § 3, Abhandlungen der Friesschen Schule neue Folge, 2 (1908), p. 444. Ed.]

itself require an epistemological justification – as a result of which we again end in an infinite regression.

Therefore, the task of the "theory of knowledge" is contradictory; hence, *a "theory of knowledge" is impossible.*

Nelson derives the same conclusion from this argument as does Fries.

The contradictory *epistemological* ("transcendental") formulation of the problem must be replaced by a *psychological* formulation. The *justification,* which is necessary in order to protect *a priori* principles from dogmatic arbitrariness, does not take the form of a proof of the objective *validity* of these principles. Rather, it is merely the empirical-psychological "self-analysis of knowing reason" that uncovers our subjective, internal foundations of belief in truth.

Whether such a procedure is capable of dispelling our doubts and of completely satisfying our *need for justification* can be demonstrated only by the application of this psychological method.

For this purpose, let us begin by examining a relatively simple case: the justification of our *perceptual judgements.* Perceptual judgements, like all synthetic statements, cannot be *proved*; rather, their justification takes the form of an appeal to a *perception* (or "intuition", as Kant and Fries usually call it).

Such a perception is an *experience,* that is, a *psychological fact.* The presentation of such a fact is all that we can adduce for the justification of a perceptual judgement. The question of justification (*quid juris?*) is reduced to a question of fact (*quid facti?*); the (epistemological) *proof* is replaced by a (psychological) *fact.*

However, the demonstration of such a fact, and the experience of the perception, are *sufficient for us* to consider a perceptual judgement as justified; it satisfies all our needs for justification. This is also a fact, a *psychological one.* We might formulate this fact as the "principle of the self-assurance of perception".[+3]

Only this empirical-psychological analysis is capable of demonstrating the basis on which the justification of our perceptual judgements rests: by returning to the ultimate psychological facts which as such are simply "given". An *epistemological* formulation of the problem not satisfied with these facts – perhaps demanding a justification of the "principle of the certainty of perception" – will necessarily lead nowhere (to a regression).

[+3] [The German term *"Selbstgewißheit"*, which has been rendered as "self-assurance", literally means that someone or something is certain of itself. A.P. (Tr.)]

Thus, synthetic judgements (and according to Fries, even analytic judgements) can be justified only by presenting psychological facts. Fries[39] calls this type of ultimate psychological fact, such as perception, "*immediate knowledge*". (This terminology is rather unfortunate. It would be advisable to refer exclusively to *statements* as "knowledge", and perhaps to say that even though a perceptual judgement is subjectively *based on a perception*, a perception itself is not therefore knowledge. Schlick's[40] argument, which opposes the doctrine of "immediate knowledge", is no doubt correct; but this questionable term of Fries, which has caused real confusion, could be eliminated from his doctrine without affecting its crucial point; Schlick's criticism is thus justified, but not decisive.)

In order to be able to justify a *synthetic a priori judgement*, there would have to be corresponding psychological facts that are *not* perceptions (for "perceptual judgements" are *a posteriori*). In Friesian terminology: "immediate knowledge" would have to exist not only in our "intuition", but also in our "*reason*"; such knowledge would have to be *demonstrated*.

These psychological facts cannot be apprehended by intuition ("evident") in the way that our perception is. It is (according to Fries, but also according to Kant) a psychological fact that we do *not* possess *any* "*intellectual intuition*". The psychological facts that form the basis of synthetic *a priori* judgements (I am referring here only to discursive synthetic judgements, and not to the Kantian–Friesian philosophy of mathematics) are not intuitive, not "evident", but rather "primevally obscure"; however, they can be made comprehensible through reflection.

This indicates the chief task of the [Friesian] "anthropological critique of reason", or of the empirical "self-analysis of cognitive reason".

It has, first, to show the empirical existence of those psychological facts (of "immediate knowledge") that underlie the synthetic *a priori* principles, and it has to make them understandable; second, it has to establish the psychological fact that such an empirical demonstration satisfies all our needs for justification, i.e. that for psychological reasons we cannot doubt our "immediate knowledge intuited by reason" ("principle of the self-confidence of our reason").

---

[39] [Cf. Jakob Friedrich Fries, *Neue Kritik der Vernunft* I. (1st ed., 1807), pp. XXXVIII and 288 ff. (2nd ed., *Neue oder anthropologische Kritik der Vernunft* I., 1828, pp. 31, 347 ff.) Ed.]

[40] Moritz Schlick, *Allgemeine Erkenntnislehre* (2nd ed., 1925), p. 80.

This methodological programme is carried out through an empirical-theoretical psychology of knowledge, through a *"theory of reason"* (which formulates universal psychological natural laws). The existence of those psychological facts ("immediate knowledge") is *deduced* from this theory. This Friesian *"deduction of immediate knowledge"* should not be confused with the Kantian *"transcendental deduction"*. Both "deductions" are designed to justify *a priori* principles; in the case of Kant this is by proving their objective validity, whereas in that of Fries (reducing the question *quid juris?* to *quid facti?*) it is by demonstrating the existence of corresponding psychological facts.

So much for the Friesian *methodological* argument.

Criticisms of Fries have suggested that his "anthropological method" attempts to ground *a priori* knowledge in *a posteriori*, empirical knowledge. This criticism, however, is unjustified. Just as the analysis of our perceptual knowledge outlined above is not designed to justify the validity of particular perceptual judgements, so the "self-analysis of cognitive reason" is (according to Fries) not designed to ground (prove) the *validity of a priori* principles – such as the principle of induction. Rather, the *validity* (whether of a perceptual judgement or of an *a priori* principle) is, according to Fries, grounded in the corresponding "immediate knowledge", that is, in a particular psychological fact, and not in the theoretical-empirical analysis and description of this fact.

Thus, the Friesian view is far from transforming *a priori* into *a posteriori* principles. According to Fries, only the *method of the justification of a priori* principles is empirical – the principles themselves are valid *a priori*.

The criticism of the Friesian view may be divided into two parts: the criticism of Nelson's "proof of the impossibility of a theory of knowledge", and the criticism of the "anthropological method of the critique of reason".

Of course, every theory of knowledge seems to have a strong interest in refuting Nelson's proof. Thus, Schlick[41] (in a very interesting account) feels compelled to refute this proof by showing that Nelson is confusing the concepts of "cognition" [*Erkennen*] (in the sense of "identifying") and "knowing" [*Kennen*] (in the sense of "experiencing"). Nelson's chain of reasoning cannot, however, be broken in this way (as the Friesian

---

[41] Moritz Schlick, *op. cit.*, p. 83.

philosopher Kraft[42] has rightly argued against Schlick); in my view, Nelson's proof is unassailable. The assumption that there exists a science – namely the "theory of knowledge" – of which the task is to pronounce a final verdict on the objective validity of all knowledge, is no doubt contradictory.

Fortunately, however, the present analysis (and many other "epistemological" studies, including Schlick's) does not set itself such a task. What Nelson calls a "theory of knowledge" has almost nothing to do with what is here designated a "theory of knowledge".

Admittedly, the "theory of knowledge" – in the sense of the phrase advocated here – also deals with *questions of validity*, and – just like the "theory of knowledge" in Nelson's sense – is sharply opposed to any *psychological* perspective concerned with empirical *questions of fact*. But it certainly does not set itself the task of deciding the objective validity of empirical knowledge in individual scientific disciplines; and even less that of supplying a "final justification" of *all* knowledge.

By contrast, here the task of the theory of knowledge has been defined as that of analysing the procedure of justification – that is, the *methods* of individual sciences – and that of removing the contradictions that arise from the misinterpretations of the methods (and results) of individual disciplines.

This theory of knowledge does not aim to discover any knowledge – except its *own* (methodological) knowledge; it takes the position that *every science* – regardless of whether it is an individual discipline or a theory of knowledge – *should take care of itself*; every science is responsible for its claims and must itself yield the "justification" of its knowledge (regardless of whether it is a "final" or an "initial" justification); for *only* by systematically *justifying* its claims – by its critical arguments – does it become a *science*.

Such a view has, therefore, nothing in common with the contradictory assumption that individual sciences present knowledge that is in need of, and is amenable to, a "final justification" by means of the theory of knowledge. Hence too, in no way is it threatened by the contradictory implications of this assumption – the infinite regression of a hierarchy of sciences.

---

[42] Julius Kraft, *Von Husserl zu Heidegger* (1st ed., 1932), p. 31. [2nd ed., 1957, p. 31. Ed.]

Moreover, the theory of knowledge does not justify the *methods* of individual sciences, though they may well be subject to epistemological criticism. Thus, the failure of some sciences might be explained by a *methodological critique* – for example, that these sciences attempt to imitate the successful methods of physics without, however, being able correctly to interpret the relationships between [physical] theory and experience (experiment).

That such a general methodology and methodological critique may rightly call itself a "theory of knowledge" has been sufficiently "justified" here. The traditional *epistemological problems* are reduced to the general methodological problems of the natural sciences. On the other hand, Nelson's own methodological investigations of the "problem of knowledge" (for instance, his "proof of the impossibility of a theory of knowledge"[43]) demonstrate that the task of such a descriptive as well as critical methodology is not contradictory. They deal, for the most part, with general considerations of methodological criticism rather than with the psychology of knowledge.

If the theory of knowledge is defined as a general methodology of empirical science, then a hierarchy of possible sciences, and thus the *appearance* of an infinite regression, may well arise. After all, the theory of knowledge also uses particular methods; these may be described (and perhaps even criticised) by a "second-order theory of knowledge", which in turn uses its own methods, etc.

However, this infinite hierarchy is not an impermissible infinite regression in the logical sense. For none of these sciences is *dependent* on a higher science or requires the validity of higher knowledge for the justification of its statements. A "regression" is therefore not logically necessary. It can be interrupted at any time when there is no longer a need for, or an interest in, the (increasingly more *specialised*) higher "theory of knowledge". That *such* a hierarchy is not contradictory may be illustrated by the following example. We can practise an *empirical psychology* of, say, processes in the formation of physical theories. We can then try to do theoretical work on this special psychology of knowledge itself, by psychologically examining the accompanying psychological processes of theory formation (now in the theory formation of the psychology of knowledge), and we can form

---

[43] [See note 38. Ed.]

further theories, etc. *ad infinitum*. We *can* go on with this hierarchy of psychologies of knowledge as long as we wish; but the regression *can* also be stopped as soon as there is neither a need for nor an interest in an increasingly specialised analysis.

Nelson's "proof of the impossibility of a theory of knowledge" does not affect the theory of knowledge in the sense of the view advocated here. It does, however, affect Nelson's own position. *Any justification of apriorism,* including Fries' (and Nelson's) "anthropological method", must fall victim to the circularity indicated by Nelson (or to an infinite regression).

All apriorism must subscribe to the position that the universal synthetic statements of the natural sciences can be justified only by a *synthetic a priori principle of induction*; the natural sciences cannot, therefore, stand on their own; their knowledge is in need of, and is amenable to, a final justification through *a priori* principles (of natural philosophy). The *justification of these* principles, in turn, can only proceed in an *a priori* philosophical fashion (which is Kant's project: [the] "transcendental" or "epistemological" method in the terminology of Fries and of Nelson). The result is an infinite regression. Alternatively, the justification of *a priori* principles may (according to Fries' method) follow an empirical-scientific approach (whether psychological or physical). The result is circularity.

This *circularity*, which the critique of the Friesian "*anthropological method*" has to expose, is the same as the circularity identified above in the critique of Kant's *optimistic position* on the question of anthropomorphism.

The same objection can be raised against Friesian transcendental idealism and subjectivism.

Nothing is achieved by reducing the problem of the *laws of nature* (or of "natural necessity", as Fries says) to that of the *laws of the understanding* (or of rational necessity), and thus to a factual question in empirical psychology. To be able to assert the strict and universal validity of psychological statements, the *validity of a principle of induction must also be presupposed*.

The Friesian method must, therefore, also be circular. This circle will now be demonstrated in strictly *immanent* fashion.

Fries is fully aware of the fact that individual psychological observations (*singular* empirical statements of psychology) are not sufficient to demonstrate the existence of "immediate knowledge" of *a priori* principles.

"Necessary knowledge and its origin in reason are the whole riddle in philosophy,"[44] we read in his *Neue Kritik der Vernunft*, and shortly thereafter[45] he maintains that "momentary self-observation" never corresponds to "necessity" (apodictic *a priori* knowledge), but only to "reality" (assertoric knowledge).

The existence of *a priori*, that is, universally valid and necessary, "immediate knowledge" can thus be demonstrated only through *universal* psychological statements, or through *psychological laws*; Fries therefore speaks of an (empirical-psychological) "*theory of reason*", from which the existence of "immediate knowledge" of *a priori* statements is said to be deducible.

This "theory of reason", however, can only be obtained by *induction*. The Friesian critical-empirical method is distinguished from the dogmatic methods of a "one-sided rationalism" and of a "one-sided empiricism" precisely by the fact that "in the struggle against these two . . . it has been forced . . . to derive the highest principles of our *theory* of transcendental apperception by *inductions* from our internal experience".[46]

The theory of reason thus presupposes the admissibility of induction, and presupposes that universal empirical statements can be formulated and verified in an inductive fashion.

According to Fries' apriorist premises,[47] the inductive procedure is admissible only if an *a priori principle of induction* is valid. We find this very clearly and simply formulated in Fries' supreme "principle of natural philosophy" as the *fundamental law of natural necessity*:[48] "*The world of appearances is under the universal rule of natural laws.*"

Like all empirical theories, the "theory of reason" presupposes the truth of this fundamental law. According to Fries, however, this simply means that it *presupposes the existence of a corresponding* "*immediate knowledge*" (i.e., the immediate knowledge of this "principle").

---

[44] Jakob Friedrich Fries, *Neue Kritik der Vernunft* II. (1st ed., 1807), § 88, p. 25. [2nd ed. (*Neue oder anthropologische Kritik der Vernunft* II.), 1831, § 88, p. 18. Ed.]

[45] Jakob Friedrich Fries, *op. cit.* (1st ed., 1807), § 88, p. 26. [2nd ed., 1831, § 88, p. 19. Ed.]

[46] Jakob Friedrich Fries, *op. cit.* (1st ed., 1807), § 95. p. 63. [2nd ed., 1831, § 95, p. 74. Ed.] Emphasis added.

[47] On this subject, cf. especially Ernst Friedrich Apelt, *Theorie der Induktion* (1854).

[48] Jakob Friedrich Fries, *op. cit.* (1st ed., 1807), § 114, p. 133. [Cf. 2nd ed., 1831, § 116, p. 150. Ed.]

The task of the "theory of reason" is, however, to demonstrate the existence of this "immediate knowledge". Since it presupposes what it should demonstrate, the task is incorrectly set: (the) Friesian "anthropological method" (itself therefore once again) contains Nelson's circle.

Only a discussion of this critique, and the objections that may be raised against it from the Friesian standpoint, will allow us fully to reveal the peculiar character of the "anthropological method".

The following objections in particular might be raised.

An existential proof cannot be circular. For example, if a physical theory were to presuppose that the energy principle is not valid and that a perpetuum mobile exists, the existential proof (the practical technical construction of a perpetuum mobile) would obviously not be facilitated by such a physical-theoretical presupposition. The same applies to the "theory of reason". While it assumes the existence of the "immediate knowledge" in question, this by no means guarantees a positive result for the empirical existential proof (for the "deduction"). There still remains the possibility that the corresponding psychological facts cannot be found.

This objection is partly justified, but it fails to save the "anthropological method".

Evidently, an existential proof of psychological facts cannot be pre-judged by the universal formal presupposition that there is a theoretical psychology of knowledge (a "theory of reason").

(Incidentally, this statement can be interpreted in different ways: it could perhaps be used against the doctrine of "immediate knowledge" just as easily as in support of the admissibility of the Friesian method; but this argument will not be utilised here.)

On the other hand, a favourable outcome of an existential proof – should this be actually achieved – can never, without the use of a circular argument, be interpreted as a proof of the "immediate knowledge" of a principle of induction [or of the "principle of natural philosophy"].

For we are dealing with an interpretation: even in the most favourable cases, the observed psychological facts can never be more than a basis for an induction or confirmation for the (general) existential claim of "immediate knowledge". In order to infer the justification of the general existential claim ["there is a theory of reason"] from the observations, this existential claim would already have to have been justified.

Thus, the objection raised is incapable of justifying the admissibility of the Friesian method. While a positive outcome of the existential proof of the "immediate knowledge" in question depends *not solely* on the theoretical presuppositions but also on empirical findings, even the "most favourable" empirical finding can be interpreted as an existential proof of the "immediate knowledge" in question *only on the basis of the theoretical presuppositions*.

An objection to Fries' critique that is more radical than the one just discussed would be the following.

Even if we grant the existence of circular inference, and that this circular inference is necessarily inherent in the Friesian method – this method might nevertheless succeed in providing the required justification. For in the case at hand, the circular inference is harmless, that is, it is not a prohibited *vicious circle*.

According to Fries, there cannot be any empirical science *without presuppositions*. Every empirical science presupposes the "principles of natural philosophy". That the (empirical-psychological) "theory of reason" also presupposes these principles – and along with their truth, also the existence of a corresponding "immediate knowledge" – is, therefore, simply a matter of course.

Whoever concludes from this fact that the Friesian method is inadmissible obviously misunderstands Fries' intentions. Fries neither doubts the validity of empirical-scientific knowledge nor does he want to prove it. Rather, he only wants to propose a systematic scientific procedure for critically examining the *a priori* presuppositions of all individual sciences, instead of simply asserting them (naively or dogmatically) without critical examination.

Now, the empirical method is admittedly a scientific method, though it is not without presuppositions (like *all* science, by the way). While in the special case of the "theory of reason", the existence of those presuppositions actually does lead to a kind of circle, it is *harmless* since this circle is only produced by the indispensable presuppositions of *all* empirical science. This can be more precisely shown by the following argument.

It is evident that a circle is only inevitable, i.e., that it necessarily inheres in the method, if a *genuine principle* is to be deduced, that is, a principle that of necessity *must* be presupposed by *any* theoretical-empirical science (thus also by the "theory of reason"). Circularity, then, is unavoidable only in the case of *indispensable* and therefore *justified presuppositions of all empirical science*; in the case of all others, e.g. in the case of "*a priori* principles" mistakenly held to be justified, circularity can obviously be avoided.

The *result* of a carefully conducted deduction will therefore *not be influenced* by circularity. The outcome of the deduction will be *positive* in the case of indispensable and therefore justified principles – for here circularity could only lead in the *same* direction, that is, to a *positive* result. Its outcome will be *negative* if the principles are dispensable and thus turn out to be unjustified; for in this case, circularity – which could change a negative result into a positive one – can be avoided.

Circularity thus proves to be harmless, because it *does not falsify the result of the deduction*; and the results of the empirical "theory of reason" are as solid as any other scientific results.

Only this last objection to the criticism presented here seems to me fully to exhaust the possibilities of the Friesian argument. But even this objection is untenable; for the circularity defended by Fries is *by no means harmless*, regardless of whether or not it is accepted as a genuine *vicious circle*. This can best be shown in the following way.

If one assumes that there is *no* valid principle of induction, and thus that we can *not* assert the existence of strictly universal laws – then empirical-scientific hypotheses can never be finally verified, and the truth of a universal empirical statement can never be scientifically justified. The "theory of reason" will, then, also remain an [unverified and] unverifiable hypothesis, [and] the "existence" of universal-anthropological (that is, law-like) "immediate knowledge" can never be considered as proved. If *no principle of induction* is presupposed, the result of the deduction can *only be a negative one*, even if an empirical-anthropological method is applied.

Conversely, if a principle of induction is presupposed (and if favourable observations are available), the result *may*, as already shown, be a *positive* one.

Therefore this procedure does, indeed, produce exactly what has been put into it by way of presuppositions; thus, the circularity defended by Fries must not be considered harmless.

In this way it has been demonstrated that the Friesian method of "deduction", or the "anthropological method of the critique of reason", is inadmissible.

The Friesian method might perhaps be capable of bringing about a decision between justified and unjustified "*a priori* principles" – *provided that a priori valid principles exist at all*. However, as the preceding arguments have shown, it is utterly *incapable of deciding between a non-apriorist position and apriorism as such*. This points to the crucial weakness in its chain of reasoning. The circle is rooted not in the presupposition of a *particular* principle of induction, but rather in the dogmatic claim that an *a priori* valid principle of induction *does in fact* exist, that is, in the (general and unspecific) claim of *apriorism*. This *petitio principii* is concealed by the assumption that the "deduction" of *particular a priori* principles implicitly provides a proof that something like this principle does in fact exist.

The Friesian conception thus founders on the same point as the Kantian one. While teaching apriorism, it is incapable of resolving the "*antinomy of the knowability of the world*". According to Fries, moreover, laws must exist by apodictic necessity – because knowledge in general would otherwise be impossible. (The fact of "synthetic reflective knowledge" proves [according to Fries] the existence of "immediate knowledge" corresponding to the principles of natural philosophy.) But this derivation (just like the Kantian one) presupposes that knowledge of the world must be possible by apodictic necessity; thus it replaces, in a completely uncritical fashion, the simple (assertoric) *fact* that knowledge exists with the claim that knowledge must exist by apodictic necessity (under all circumstances). Thus, Friesian apriorism also advocates the *position that the "world" must necessarily be knowable*. But this means: it is based on the *thesis* of the "antinomy of the knowability of the world".

It may be regarded as certain that the Friesian method is incapable of resolving this antinomy. What (empirical) psychological *facts* could possibly guarantee that, under all circumstances, "our reason" can have knowledge of "the world"?

Fries' apriorism has, therefore, not moved beyond that of Kant. Instead, turning away from the "transcendental" method, it could even be said to represent a step back compared with Kant. It amplifies Kant's most serious mistakes, that is, his tendency to slip back into psychologism (subjectivism) and, in this way, surrenders one of his most crucial discoveries: the analysis of the concept of scientific knowledge (Kant's "transcendental definition" of empirical knowledge).

At the centre of this analysis of Kant (as already mentioned in Section 9) is the concept of science or of *scientific objectivity*. "Objectivity" means *intersubjective testability*, that is, testability by anyone (who makes the effort and meets the technical prerequisites).

The way in which Friesian psychologism surrenders this concept of science will be illustrated with reference to the examples of Fries' evaluation of "*intuitionism*" ("intellectual intuition") and his view of "*perception*".

Intuitionism, the doctrine of "intellectual intuition", may best be defined as the view that we can have a pictorial and intuitive "grasp" not only of *particular individual cases*, but also of *universal "essences"* (universal concepts, law-like regularities, etc.).

Fries rejects this doctrine. Following a similar psychologistic thesis of Kant, he maintains that we do not possess any intellectual intuition. His rejection is thus supported by a psychologistic assertion. But this assertion, the "non-existence of intellectual intuition", is denied by intuitionists of all shades. They claim that they are able to establish intellectual-intuitive experiences; and Husserl[49] declares the Kantian proposition of the non-existence of intellectual intuition to be the most serious error of the critical approach.

From the viewpoint of scientific methodology, that is, of the "transcendental" method (as advocated in the present work), the question about the actual existence or non-existence of psychological processes for which the phrase "intellectual intuition", or something of this sort, might be appropriate, appears to be of no relevance for the theory of knowledge. Consistent transcendentalists can easily admit that intellectual intuitions actually exist; they will only note that these experiences, which may be very important in the genesis of scientific knowledge, have no epistemological significance (i.e., from the perspective of a method of justification). For science requires that all knowledge – even if it has been intuitively discovered – must be justified *objectively*, that is, systematically, in an intersubjectively testable fashion. (To give some rather hetero-

---

[49] [Cf. Edmund Husserl, *Logische Untersuchungen* II.: 2. Teil (3rd ed., 1922), p. 230 (English translation from the second German edition by J.N. Findlay: *Logical Investigations* II, 1970, pp. 833 f. Tr.); see also Julius Kraft, *Von Husserl zu Heidegger* (1st ed., 1932), p. 23 (2nd ed., 1957, p. 24). Ed.]

geneous examples, this principle applies to psychology or sociology just as much as it does to mathematics; in all cases, even the most profound intuition can never be a substitute for an objective justification.) That "*intuition" is not an objective method of justification* – that is, the correct core of the Kantian rejection of intuition (provided one disregards its psychologistic guise and reconstructs Kant's [intended] transcendental meaning). The reasons why "intuitive knowledge" has to be denied objectivity and thus scientific status will be further discussed in this section (in the analysis of the theory of perception).

Fries and his students even sought to prove the psychological "fact" of the "non-existence of intellectual intuition". Take, for example, Julius Kraft.[50] The argument that is to serve as proof is that intuitionism entails *mysticism*. But this attempted proof only reveals the mistakes of the psychological method, and it also shows that this method always unconsciously presupposes transcendental considerations. Indeed, the undeniable fact that something like mysticism exists is powerful evidence for intellectual intuition qua psychological fact. And only the – evidently transcendental – presupposition that empirical science and mysticism are completely heterogeneous can account for the Fries–Kraft view that intuitionism is reduced *ad absurdum* by its mystical consequences.

Thus in Fries' thinking, the transcendental insight into the methodological inadequacy of intuitionism is replaced by a denial of the psychological fact that intuitions exist. And since he fails to appreciate the fundamental importance of intuition for the discovery of knowledge – and his ill-founded assertion of the *psychological* "impossibility of intuitionism" provokes *legitimate* opposition – he indirectly only strengthens the *epistemological*-intuitionist position, opposition to which was supposed to be one of the most important missions of the critical approach.

In the Friesian *theory of perception*, the situation is analogous to that of his theory of intuition (though exactly the other way round).

In the rendering provided above (which is a slight modification of Fries' original one), the situation is that perception (in Fries: "intuition") is a final psychological fact to which we appeal in justifying particular knowledge claims (perceptual judgements), and which does not, in turn,

---

[50] Julius Kraft, *op. cit.* (1st ed., 1932), pp. 120 f. [2nd ed., 1957, pp. 108 f. Ed.]

require any further justification ("principle of the self-assurance of perception"[+4]). Fries[51] calls "immediate knowledge" this final fact by which we justify our knowledge. Accordingly, the formulation of the theory of perception is: "All intuition is immediate knowledge, which does not demand, and is in no need of, any further reduction in order to establish itself as true."[52] While it may to a certain degree reflect the *psychological* state of affairs rather well, this conception is *epistemologically*, at any rate, quite untenable. (Here is an insight that contains within itself one of the strongest arguments in favour of the transcendental concept of objectivity.)

Once again, the strict separation between the *psychology* and the *theory* of knowledge provides the basis for both our critical and our positive considerations.

The view, advocated by Fries, that perception (or "intuition") constitutes a final, an absolute basis for our empirical knowledge, and that this is where we have to look for our *empirical basis*, is (according to the view advocated here) *psychologistic*. Fries is not alone, however, in his psychologistic conception of the basis. On the contrary, almost all hitherto existing theories of knowledge (conventionalism might be mentioned as the only exception, and even that only with many reservations) confuse transcendental with psychological aspects when faced with questions concerning the "basis" of our empirical knowledge.

The reason for this is simple enough; and Fries himself has underlined it more strongly than anyone (cf. also the presentation above): if statements are not to be introduced *dogmatically*, they have to be *justified*. Should one insist on avoiding all psychologistic, i.e., all subjective answers, however, the question of the justification of statements will lead nowhere. For if one does not want to appeal to one's conviction, perception, evidence, "immediate knowledge" or the like (all this is subjective, psychologistic), then *statements can only be justified by other statements* that, if they are not to be introduced dogmatically, will again evidently stand in need of justification. Faced with this trilemma (*dogmatism − infinite regression of justification − psychologistic basis*), Fries − with almost all other theorists of knowledge with an empiricist orientation − opts for *psychologism*, which means that he opts

---

[+4] [See note +3. Tr.]
[51] [See note 39. Ed.]
[52] Julius Kraft, *op. cit.* (1st ed., 1932), p. 120. [2nd ed., 1957, p. 108. Ed.]

for the subjective experience of perception or intuition as the absolute foundation and justification of the final, most fundamental statements (*basic statements*) of the system, or of perceptual judgements.

But this widespread view (which for reasons that will become clearer below seems to accord so closely with common sense) *does not withstand the test of transcendental, or methodological, critique.*

This critique shows that perceptions and observations (more precisely, perception and observation reports) *are never taken seriously in science* unless they are *objective*, that is, intersubjectively testable – not even if they are backed up by a subjectively intense experience of conviction. Reports that are not intersubjectively testable do not even enter *natural science* as preliminary material (*history* may sometimes evaluate them as such), but are, *at best*, suggestions and formulations of problems.

This assertion can be supported by a large amount of transcendental evidence.

A rather entertaining contribution is the example of the so-called "*Tatzel worm issue*": reports repeatedly*[10] emerge from the Alpine regions of sightings of a "*Tatzel worm*" or "*Bergstutz*", a supposedly dangerous animal half a metre in length, thick as a human arm, in the shape of a worm and with the eyes of a basilisk. Reading the reports,[53] it is hardly possible to doubt the subjective experience of conviction or the credibility of the informants. What they had seen and heard is, nevertheless, not enough to ensure the *scientific objectivity* of the *Tatzel* worm. (At best, they *provoke debate* about whether such a creature really exists.) If there were an intersubjective method of testing the reports – the best course would be to put a *Tatzel* worm on show in a museum – scientific objectivity would be assured. It should be noted that scientific objectivity could be assured in ways other than through a museum exhibit. Other *corpora delicti* could be sufficient – such as individual parts, marks, traces or perhaps even an appropriately certified photograph, etc. – to render the existence of the *Tatzel* worm an objective, that is, an intersubjectively testable scientific *hypothesis*. This would be the case if we could infer the existence

---

*[10] When this was written (1932), the "*Tatzel* worm issue" was still fairly topical in Austria. A similar problem is that of the existence of a so-called "Yeti" in the Himalayas.

[53] Cf. Hans Flucher, "Noch einmal die Tatzelwurmfrage: Ein Überblick über das Ergebnis unserer Rundfrage", *Kosmos: Handweiser für Naturfreunde* 29 (1932), pp. 66 ff., 100 ff.

of the *Tatzel* worm from the existing testable evidence with the aid of well-corroborated universal laws. Even weak but intersubjectively testable evidence is of disproportionately greater significance in science than are the most detailed observation reports if these are incapable of being tested, even if they come from trained observers of proven reliability and match each other down to the last detail.

(There is a wealth of examples of the "*Tatzel* worm question" type. Take, for instance, the often very plausible reports of sea serpents, also certain reports from spiritualist circles.)

With respect to all these examples, one must emphasise that it is not the truth, but the scientific character or objectivity of a statement ("A *Tatzel* worm exists") that is dependent on its intersubjective testability. Perhaps there really is a *Tatzel* worm, a fact that may in the future be objectively demonstrated; in such an event, the statement (untestable today) would already have been true today. Accordingly, science does *not negate* this statement or call it false, but, so to speak, *ignores* it. Science does not take any position on it.

In science, *subjective convictions* – even if they are very intensely and directly experienced – can *never be of methodological, but only of historical-genetic significance.* This insight is opposed not only to the Friesian doctrine of "immediate knowledge", but also to the view that perceptual statements, observation reports and the like can constitute the "*empirical basis*" of science. The "*basic statements*" of empirical science – like all scientific statements – must possess the character of *objectivity.*

This, of course, also applies to scientific psychology (regardless of whether a behaviourist-physicalist or an introspective approach is adopted). From a psychological-scientific standpoint, every psychological statement must be intersubjectively testable. That I now have a particular perceptual experience may be subjectively *certain for me*; but for scientific psychology, the statement "*A* has a particular perceptual experience" has merely the character of a *hypothesis* that can be tested by means of different (objective) procedures. (This can be achieved experimentally, for example, by examining different *stimuli* – e.g. questions – and my responses to them – e.g. my answers – to see whether they are consistent with that hypothesis, based on well-corroborated psychological laws.)

Thus, the principle of the *objectivity of basic statements* is generally valid for all sciences; it must therefore also apply to the *psychology of knowledge.* Experiences of perception and conviction can never form the basis of objective science, for the simple reason that in objective science they can occur only as an object of psychological hypotheses, so that their existence [more precisely, the hypothesis of their existence] must be objectively tested according to the same methodological principles as any other hypothesis, that is, *by the logical deduction of singular statements, of singular, objectively testable predictions.*

The *psychology of knowledge,* whose (universal) statements, therefore, have only a hypothetical character, can in its psychological analysis of the process of knowledge be expected to arrive at conclusions largely analogous to those of an epistemological analysis (cf. Section 4). It will be able to establish that for an experience of conviction to come about, perceptions, or the "testimony of the senses", are exceedingly important. (This is probably the reason why the psychologistic theory of knowledge, based on "self-reflection", together with common sense, holds fast to the perceptual basis.) But even from the *psychological* perspective, perceptions by no means prove to be the final, absolute and indubitable foundations of our convictions; quite the reverse.

As already stated in the context of the analysis of the concept of objectivity (towards the end of Section 9), we will always have doubts, concerning those perceptions we cannot test at will (repeatedly), as to whether we may not have been mistaken after all. Greater certainty of a subjective experience of conviction can, however, be achieved through the agreement of *different perceptions* with one another (which do not, individually, have absolute persuasive power); this means, however, that they are in agreement with some (well-corroborated) theories. Thus, for example, a visual perception can be supported by a tactile one (based on the theory that it must be possible to touch visible bodies – "*inter-sensational testing*"), or by other visual perceptions, or by a comparison with other people's *statements* that we have heard or read. It is a *trivial* point that *for every* subject the experience of conviction must occur as a result of his or her *own* experiences, because he or she must *hear* – or see – and *understand* the reports of others. (It is *misleading* to characterise this *psychological* triviality as "*methodological solipsism*"[54] or the like, for this masks the opposition between the theory of knowledge – that is, methodology – and the psychology of knowledge.)

---

[54] [See Hans Driesch, *Ordnungslehre: Ein System des nichtmetaphysischen Teiles der Philosophie* (2nd ed., 1923), p. 23; Rudolf Carnap, *Der logische Aufbau der Welt* (1928), pp. 86 f. Cf. also Karl Popper, *Conjectures and Refutations* (1963), pp. 265 ff. Ed.]

The emphasis on the objective character of all scientific propositions, including the "basic statements" (the elementary empirical statements, as they are also referred to here), and the *elimination of subjectivist psychologism from the theory of knowledge*, which is connected with it, is the important positive result of the (at least partly immanent, because partly psychological) critique of the Friesian theory of perception. But this does not yet seem to have resolved the "*trilemma*" described above.

The resolution of this trilemma will not be presented in detail at this point. The question about the basic statements of science is equivalent to the question about a suitable concept of "*experience*"; only the analysis of the *problem of demarcation* [55] can fully clarify this issue. (It should be noted in passing that the positive discussion of this question should by no means be considered as an immanent criticism of Kant or of Fries.)

As repeatedly mentioned, the "empirical basis" of science is formed by *singular empirical statements*, that is, by singular *predictions* deduced with the aid of a theoretical system.

Now, it is of great significance that in most cases of scientific *practice* the verification or falsification of such singular predictions does not lead to any methodological difficulties, and does not contain any practical-methodological problems.*[11] We are thus confronted with one of those epistemological questions (cf. Section 2) that become a problem not because of the requirements of scientific practice but only when epistemological misinterpretations occur. With such questions, the danger of falling victim to epistemological prejudices is especially great (hence the widespread attempts at a psychologistic solution); the application of the transcendental method, and the orientation towards actual scientific practice, thus become all the more important – but also more difficult. It is therefore advisable to start from an analysis of those (rare) cases of scientific practice, in which the verification or falsification of singular predictions raises difficulties as well as doubts as to whether the statements in question should be regarded as verified or falsified.

How does science actually proceed in such cases? Are such cases submitted to a vote? Or are they, perhaps, assigned some value lying between "true" and "false" (such as the value "probable")?

---

[55] [See Editor's Postscript; cf. also Section 10, text to note 12. Ed.]

*[11] The problem of the experimenter is solved if his experiment can be reproduced; however, sometimes the problem is very difficult to solve.

In order properly to evaluate the actual procedure of science in deciding singular statements, it is necessary to recall the significance of singular statements for natural science.

According to the *deductivist view*, *singular statements* are utilised for the testing of *laws* and of *theoretical systems*, that is, of *universal* statements. The testing of universal statements is carried out by *deducing singular predictions* that can be verified and falsified.

If, therefore, a decision about the verification or falsification of any particular singular prediction creates difficulties, scientific practice usually adopts the expedient of dispensing with a decision and, in order to test these laws, deduces *other* predictions that do not give rise to such difficulties.

This is the reason why (in the natural sciences) it is relatively rare for a decision to be taken about a particular singular statement where such difficulties have arisen.

But even an analysis of those cases in which singular statements are further examined, tested and supported does not – *prima facie* – lead to an illuminating result.

For such problematic singular statements are always supported by *other singular statements* – that do not, in turn, pose any difficulties or do not give rise to a practical-methodological problem. These other singular statements are *deduced* from the singular statement to be tested with the aid of theories; thus the singular statement in question plays, in turn, the role of a hypothesis, of a *natural law of the lowest level of universality*, and is tested through the deduction of predictions, that is to say: supported or refuted by other singular statements.

Take the following example. If doubts arise as to whether the singular statement "This powder is a red precipitate" is to be considered falsified or verified, *predictions* arising from the statement in question and the chemical laws are tested; for example, the powder is heated, the escaping gas subjected to an oxygen test with the aid of a glowing taper, etc. This process leads to other singular statements (for example, "This taper ignites as soon as it is inserted into the tube" or "There is a mercury deposit in this test tube"), and if these statements in turn give any reason for doubt, they are submitted to analogous tests. This procedure is continued until a result is considered to have sufficient support and any further doubts are considered superfluous or mere hair-splitting.

If possible, especially if the testing was important and difficult, the procedure stops at those statements for which the subjective testing by *all* subjects present during the test (or whatever else it may be) is particularly easy (for example, "This taper has now been inserted into the test tube four times, and each time it ignited"). They are thus intersubjectively testable, *objective* statements about which all subjects present can easily form subjective convictions.

(It is important that these *subjective convictions themselves should not enter the scientific procedure of justification and testing*: for science never appeals to subjective convictions. While encouraging everyone to form an opinion, it is left to the individual to convince himself.)

An analysis of all the cases in which singular scientific statements are tested leads to analogous results.

If difficulties arise, then the measuring instruments, clocks, for example, may be tested — which can obviously [be done] only by deducing other predictions (e.g. "After about 20 days, this clock will deviate from that one by less than 15 seconds"), and [by] verifying or falsifying these predictions. It may happen that the individuals performing the measurements are tested rather than the measuring instruments, e.g. for colour-blindness or for their "personal equation", as it is called (their response times). These tests too, will always have the same (objective) character. From the hypothesis that Mr *A* is colour-blind, predictions about certain responses are derived; these singular, objective predictions that any subject can easily test are verified or falsified.

As mentioned above, the outcome of the methodological analysis does not seem to lead to an illuminating result.

In order to support problematic singular statements, less problematic (or unproblematic) singular statements are derived from them. But clearly, this only shifts the problem elsewhere:

What is it that supports unproblematic singular statements (that any subject can easily test)? What does it mean to say that such a statement is verified or falsified?

With this problem, we still seem to find ourselves in the midst of the *trilemma*. Are such statements (1) simply dogmatically postulated as true, or are they (2) justified *ad infinitum* by other statements (a process that seems to be interrupted only for practical reasons), or are they (3) after all supported by the subjective convictions (perceptions) of the various subjects?

As will be seen in a moment, all three positions of the trilemma prove to be justified, though of course only in a *very limited fashion* – that is, if one takes the position proposed here as a solution.

According to this view, the *endpoints of the deduction*, that is, the *basic statements* of science (the "elementary empirical statements"), are adopted *by decision*, by a *convention* that in one sense is arbitrary but in another is regulated. To the extent (but *only* to the extent) that these statements are adopted (qua basic statements) by decision *without any further justification of* what they assert, the first position of the trilemma can be described as justified, that is, the decision can be called "dogmatic".

But this "dogma" is far from dangerous, for the decision follows certain methodological principles: above all, the principle that the only statements to be adopted are those that do not give rise to any methodologically admissible doubt; should such doubts arise, then the deduction is carried further. *Such a continuation is, in principle, always possible.* For, since it can be tested, every *objective* scientific statement has, in a certain sense, the character of a universal law and all testing is based on law-likeness (or on repeatability) – such as the law-like regularities on the basis of which the event in question can be photographed or filmed (or observed). (*Objective singular* statements can therefore be called "natural laws of the lowest level of universality".) This universal character of every objective statement is precisely what accounts for the fact that, in principle, *more predictions* can be *deduced* from any such statement than can be tested; and that such a statement always implies more than can be ascertained by "observation", etc. (transcendence of representation in general; cf. Sections 8 and 9). Hence, if continued testing is always in principle possible, this means that in a certain limited sense, the second position of the trilemma is correct: as long as one does not *decide* to accept a statement without further justification, i.e., to adopt it by decision as "true" or as "false", hypothetical-deductive testing must be carried further – which would in principle be possible *ad infinitum*. The deduction never comes to a natural end; no statement is marked out by its form or content as the endpoint of the deduction, or predestined to be a basic statement.

But the third position of the trilemma is also valid (of course, in an even more limited fashion). Admittedly, a scientific statement can never be justified by an appeal to subjective convictions (such as a *consensus omnium*); but a *methodological rule for its adoption* will always take account of whether or not various subjective convictions are in mutual agreement.

This final remark may be regarded as a concession to psychologism, and thus as a backdoor through which psychologism can, at the last moment, slip back into the system. For this reason – and in order to show that this criticism does not affect the position advocated here – the *distinction between the justification of a statement* (or an assertion) and the *methodological rule of decision making* must be further explained; it has, moreover, to be shown that although the methodological rule of decision making *takes account of subjective convictions*, it does not depend on the latter but represents a thoroughly "*objective*" *procedure*.

In order to show that the *methodological rule of decision making* is a completely different matter from the *justification of a statement*, the example of the (older, "classical") jury may be cited.

As is well known, the verdict of the jury is on *questions of fact (quid facti?)*. Thus, through the jury's decision, an assertion about a *concrete event* is made: a *singular empirical statement*. The significance of the decision, its practical and theoretical function, is that in conjunction with the universal statements of the legal system (penal code), certain conclusions can be *deduced* from it. In other words, the decision forms the basis for the *application* of the general system of the penal code; the verdict is *used* like a true statement, and it plays the role of a true statement in the logical deductions.

It is clearly not the case that the statement is necessarily true simply because it was decided by the jury. (This is also acknowledged in legal procedure, for under certain conditions such a "verdict" may, as we know, be quashed or revised.)

The decision is reached through a precisely regulated *procedure*. This procedure is built on certain principles that are by no means designed exclusively to safeguard the discovery of some objective truth. Rather, they leave room not only for subjective convictions but even for subjective bias. However, even if one disregards the special conditions governing (classical) juries and imagines a procedure based *exclusively* on the principle of finding the truth in as objective a fashion as possible, one can at least state the following.

The methodological rule of the decision-making procedure *in no way justifies the jury's verdict, or the truth of the empirical statements it has issued*. One obvious reason for this is that the regulation of decision making is *general*, and remains the same for all cases, while the statements decided upon propose rather diverse and always very specific assertions.

Moreover, the subjective convictions of the jurors can in no way be regarded as justifying the validity of the statements adopted (even though they are, of course, causally related to the decision making, that is, they are *motives* for decision making; cf. Section 12). This is brought out by the fact that the decision-making procedure can be regulated in very different ways (certain questions can, for instance, be decided only unanimously or by a qualified majority, while others require only a simple majority), so that depending on the rule, the relationship between subjective convictions and decisions may assume very different forms.

In contrast to the jury's *verdict*, the *judgement* of a judge must be *justified* because it must be logically derived from other statements. A *decision*, on the other hand, can be tested only with respect to whether it has been reached *in accordance with a procedure governed by rules*, that is, with respect only to form, not to content. (The correct expression for justifications of decisions in terms of content is actually "reasoned judgement" rather than "justification".)

In deciding the basic statements of science, the situation is analogous to the example above.

The methodological rule governing such decisions contains what may be called "*empirical verification and falsification*", or "*empirical method*".

This is not the place to discuss these methodological rules in detail (this will be done in the demarcation analysis,[56] where these methodological rules are derived from the principle of *methodological realism*). Just two points will be emphasised here, as they shed particular light on the Kant–Fries problem of perception.

The *fundamental principle* of this rule for deciding basic statements is that *only singular empirical propositions may be adopted by decision as* "*true*" *or* "*false*". Which basic statements in particular are hypothetically postulated depends on the theoretical system (much as the questions presented to the jury depend on legal regulations). But the decisions concerning basic statements settle the fate of the theoretical systems – not vice versa. ("Empiricism" – in contrast to "conventionalism" – means "*singularism*" *of the adopted basic statements*.)

The empiricist rule for the adoption of basic statements is distinguished from any kind of dogmatism – especially from *perceptual absolutism* (Fries, the *positivists*) – by the proposition that in any case of *methodologically*

---

[56] [See Editor's Postscript; cf. also Appendix: Section IX, text to note 1. Ed.]

admissible doubt, the hypothetico-deductive process of testing through the deduction of predictions must continue; or that no basic statement may, in such a case, be accepted.

In order to be able to accept any basic statement at all, however, it is necessary to restrict the concept of methodologically admissible doubt in some definite way; we know that we are dealing with a methodologically admissible doubt if it is easy to test (to verify with the aid of permissible stipulations) the *objective, sociological statement* that the *subjective convictions* of different testers of a singular statement *diverge*, and that an *intersubjective agreement* (*consensus omnium*) does not exist. In this case, further testing must occur (or some stipulation must be given up). As mentioned above, this testing can also be extended to the participating observers – say, by determining their personal equations – as a way of eliminating inconsistencies, that is, of removing methodologically justified doubts. Thus, the aim is not to achieve the consistency of any subjective experiences of conviction (it is not even clear what this would be); rather, the *consistency of objective basic statements* is a fundamental methodological requirement that should not be violated by any stipulation. (The principle of eliminating such inconsistencies through continued testing – by deduction of objective predictions – is also characteristic of *methodological realism*.)

But why do we adopt such statements? Why do we decide to introduce basic statements, or endpoints of deductive testing, into science as "*true*" or "*false*" propositions?

The jury example is enlightening with respect to this question, too. The decision of the jury forms the basis for the *application* of the law.

In much the same way we can say: the decision by which we introduce certain basic statements is nothing but the decision to *apply* science or to apply a theoretical system. Just as it is only the verdict of the jury that makes it possible logically to deduce concrete statements – thus allowing for the application of the law – so, too, deciding whether specific basic statements are "true" or "false" consists precisely in the decision to introduce these statements into the system in order to make the concrete *application* of the system possible (deduction of singular predictions). The *decision as to whether a basic statement is* "true" *or* "false" *is equivalent to applying the system*. (If the propositions of logic can, in a manner of speaking, be called implicit definitions of the concepts "true" and "false", then it can also be said that by specific *applications* of the logical rules of transformation and inference certain statements can be implicitly defined as "true" or "false".) Therefore, usually basic statements are not expressly decided upon but, instead, science itself gets applied – which amounts to the same thing. (And this is why, in a certain sense, singular basic statements belong not to the scientific system as such – not even within so-called "applied sciences" – but to the *actual, practical application* of the system, to technical-practical action; this does not, however, deprive them of their propositional character – cf. Section 41.)

As was promised, we shall now move on to discuss the extent to which the methodological rule of decision making, while admittedly *taking account of subjective convictions*, nevertheless represents an *objective procedure*.

Subjective convictions are taken into account through the rule that no decision may be made in the face of the objective (and itself easily testable) sociological proposition that the decision commands no *consensus omnium*.

It is important to bear in mind the *negative form of this rule*. For if a *positive consensus omnium* were necessary for *every* decision, then a *decision could never be reached* – or the procedure would have to surrender its objective character. For if the *consensus omnium* were to influence the procedure only in the form of an *objective, sociological, singular statement* (of an easily testable sociological, or socio-psychological, hypothesis of the lowest level of universality), then – if there were simultaneously a *positive* rule that every decision requires a *consensus omnium* – this consensus would first have to be tested, which in turn would be possible only with the aid of basic statements, that is, of new decisions, and so on. We would then again find ourselves in the second position of the trilemma, with the unimportant difference that instead of a *sequence of justifications ad infinitum*, we would be dealing with a *sequence of decisions ad infinitum*.

In order to redress this situation, the concession to the first position of the trilemma must come into play; this occurs by way of a *negative* formulation of the decision-making rule, or by utilising the (objective and in part sociologically determined) concept of "methodologically admissible *doubt*". Singular statements, which the various subjects can easily test, may *always be adopted by decision, unless* such doubts arise.

(With respect to the question of how to regulate decision making, the deductivist-empiricist theory of knowledge also takes a position that is, by and large, analogous to its conception of the formation and of the testing of hypotheses: the basic statements to be decided are first adopted tentatively and provisionally. They are held to be decided – for each specific case to be *finally* decided – if *no objections* are raised.)

Knowledge is, then, "possible" only by virtue of the fact that "*unproblematic*" *basic statements* exist (an analogue to the immediately certain perceptual statements), that is, basic statements that do not need to be further tested, and for which no intersubjective agreement need be sought. It should be recorded, as a fundamental methodological fact, that such statements *do* exist, that we are successful with our decisions and with our elementary empirical statements and that we do not thereby encounter any contradictions. We can, of course, never know whether this fact will hold at all times and in all cases. (*Why* such statements exist – why objections are not raised against every decision or why some decisions do not lead to contradictions – this question, like all questions concerning the grounds of the possibility of knowledge, is scientifically inadmissible and leads *to metaphysics* – not to methodological but *to metaphysical realism*; cf. above.)

Why, in spite of a certain dogmatic method of deciding basic statements (the dogmatism is inherent in the very concept of an "unproblematic" basic statement), does the *scientific method* have a far less dogmatic character than, say, the *method of juries*? The major reason is that in all cases that are not unproblematic, it *makes no decision at all*; either it completely refrains from making a decision (the statement is declared scientifically undecidable and not "objective"), or the statement is further tested. There is, moreover, always the possibility that any basic statement might no longer be considered unproblematic and will be *further tested* (*relativity of basic statements*). Finally – and this point is perhaps the crucial one – scientific method (as repeatedly mentioned above) is primarily interested not in particular and individual *singular basic statements*, but rather in *universal laws*; that is, in statements that it never directly decides, statements that can and must be tested, over and over again in a deductive fashion (by many and very different singular statements).

One further *objection* should be discussed. It is directed against the *sociological character of science*, and against the *sociological concept of objectivity* (which – according to the view advocated here – is to be strictly separated from the non-sociological *concept of truth*). It is the "*Robinson objection*".

Let us imagine that a *Robinson* [*Crusoe*], who is completely isolated from other human beings but has command of a language, develops a physical theory (say, for the purpose of controlling nature more effectively). One may assume – although this assumption is *psychologically* anything but plausible – that this "physics" is (as it were, literally) *identical* with our modern physics; further, that Robinson, who has built himself a physical laboratory, subjects his physics to experimental tests. Such an occurrence, unlikely though it may be, is at least conceivable. Hence, concludes the "Robinson objection", the sociological character of science is not of fundamental importance. Admittedly, owing to our limited life span, the fact of a cooperation among many subjects may be *psychologically* necessary, but it is epistemologically inessential.

Confronted with this argument, it must initially be conceded that *continued testing by one individual is somewhat similar to intersubjective testing*. (Therefore, the sociological character is – at least in some cases – not of decisive importance for such testing.) Moreover, even the concept of intersubjectivity or of a plurality of subjects is, in certain respects, somewhat imprecise. Yet the Robinson objection is *not valid*. The physics Robinson has constructed for himself is simply *not science*. And this is not because we arbitrarily *define* "science" in a way that only allows intersubjectively testable theories to be called science; rather, it is because the Robinson objection starts from the false assumption that science is characterised by its *results*, and not by its *methods*.

Thus, for example, a theory identical with our physics, which has perhaps been *discovered* through intellectual intuition but which has not been systematically *tested*, would by no means represent science. For *objectivity* is inherent in scientific testing, i.e., in the scientific method, and this, for a Robinson, is in principle not fully attainable.

That Robinson's physics is identical with ours, and that he carries out the same experiments as our physicists, appears from the methodological point of view as a mysterious accident, if not as a miracle. For *the methods at his disposal do not guarantee* *[12] *the elimination of certain errors that could be eliminated by our methods*. However, the methodological mechanism of scientific *development* and of scientific *progress* consists in the *method of selection*. The methodologist will therefore have to issue a very *unfavourable prognosis* even for the brilliant "physicist" Robinson. His prognosis will state that

---

*[12] Today I would write "do not permit" instead of "do not guarantee".

Robinsonian science will before long be significantly different from ours – because the apparent equivalence was after all nothing but an accident.

If Robinson arrives at correct results, then he will have been lucky. Correct results are, admittedly, always *partly* a matter of luck, but our methods at least enable us to identify and eliminate many of those theories with which we have had no luck. But if Robinson happens to have bad luck, then he may just not notice it, and he will thus not give up a theory that *we* could falsify, so that his physics subsequently develops in a completely different direction from our intersubjective [physics]. It can easily happen that the distinction between the world of things, which for us is intersubjective and can be localised and perceived, and his (subjective) experience will start to blur (and that he takes *his feeling of fear*, for example, to be a thing similar, say, to the sun or to the night).

Certainly, it is conceivable that there may be subjective analogues to our objective science. The example shows, however, that it is a mistake to view science only *statically* (that is, as a system of results at a given point in time) and that, from a methodological point of view, the *development* of science is of the greatest interest; for it is only in the *changing* of the system and in the methodological conditions of scientific *progress* that the character of a science that is corrigible by reality and by experience is clearly revealed.

How can we justify the doctrine of the singularism of basic statements (decided by convention) that we have propounded here?

The only "justification" possible is a methodological analysis showing that the view developed here is in agreement with the method of the natural sciences.

But why does science follow such a method? Because its *methodological experiences* (which are generated in the same way as other experiences, that is, by trial and error) have taught us that this method is *successful*.

Therefore, only *success* decides between scientific methods.

Thus, for example, if we assert here that *intuition* does not constitute an objective scientific method,*[13] then this is to say that methodological experience has shown that this method does not lead to any *success*. It does not lead to intersubjective agreement, and in the case of contradictory

---

*[13] Of course, only the appeal to intuition as a *justification* is attacked here, and not intuition as an important intellectual "faculty", albeit one that frequently leads to untenable results. (See the discussion of intuitionism earlier in this section.)

results, it does not allow for further testing and for the elimination of contradictions.[57]

So far, science has been lucky with *singular empirical statements*, the unproblematic, objective, singular basic statements that any subject can easily test by observation. The method has, in this way, simply developed by trial and error; it is empiricist, and it takes account of subjective experience to the extent that is consistent with the principle of scientific objectivity (and evidently it produces only that minimum of "dogmatism" without which we could not find our way in the chaos of reality). The rule in accordance with which the "verification" and the "falsification" of singular basic statements are decided is related to (hypothetical) *observations* and *perceptions* in the way already described. The common view that refers to basic statements as "*observation statements*" or "*perceptual statements*" is, therefore, not unjustified, and this terminology is not inadequate – once the view of the absolute validity of the subjective perceptual basis has been abandoned and the objectivity requirement fulfilled. Hence, only this last point matters; only this point, i.e., the question of objectivity, is of positive methodological significance; and it was only in order to combat subjectivist-psychologistic and absolutist misconceptions and to show that an empiricist method can be developed without a subjective basis, that it was necessary to criticise the "doctrine of perception" at such length. In the further course of the analysis, the ordinary and naive terminology ("observation", "observation basis", etc.) will therefore be retained wherever no danger of misunderstanding can arise. For the problem of induction, only *singularism* is of importance: the doctrine that the basis or the endpoints of the deduction are *singular empirical statements* that are "fully decidable", i.e., are finally *verifiable and falsifiable* (by decision).

The objection raised against the doctrine of Kant and Fries of the *non-existence of intellectual intuition* was that from a psychological point of view it is incorrect, while from an epistemological point of view it is irrelevant. The objection raised against the Kant–Friesian doctrine of the *absolute perceptual basis of empirical knowledge* was that, from an epistemological point of view, it is incorrect, while, from a psychological point of view, it represents an exaggeration.

---

[57] Cf, for example, Viktor Kraft, "Intuitives Verstehen in der Geschichtswissenschaft", *Mitteilungen des österreichischen Instituts für Geschichtsforschung*, Ergänzungsband 11 (1929), pp. 1 ff.

If, however, these two doctrines are purged of their psychologistic residue and *translated into a transcendental mode of thinking*, then the position of Kant and Fries can be equated with the *singularism of the basis* as advocated here. The *non-existence of intellectual intuition* becomes a rule against adopting by decision universal statements (theories) as "true" or "false" (thus, it is also opposed to modern conventionalism, among other things). The doctrine of the foundational character of *perception* or *of empirical intuition* becomes the thesis that only singular statements may be adopted as basic statements. As a result of the methodological rule of these decisions, more particularly of the possibility of deductively moving the basis if necessary to an ever deeper level, science is made into an empirical science, into a science of reality.

Therefore, the empirical basis of objective science has *nothing absolute* about it. Science does not rest on solid bedrock. The whole towering structure, the often fantastic and audacious construction of scientific theories, is built over a swamp. Its foundations are pillars driven from above into the swamp – not down to any natural, "given", ground, but driven just as deeply as is necessary to support the structure. The reason why we stop driving the pillars deeper into the ground is not that we have reached solid rock. No, our decision is based on the hope that the pillars will support the structure. (If the structure becomes too heavy and starts to shift, then driving the pillars more deeply into the ground is unlikely to help. A new structure may be necessary, but the foundation of its construction must rest on the ruins, on the sunken pillars of the collapsed structure.)

So what has been said above[58] bears repeating here (following Kant, Reininger, Born and especially Weyl): *The objectivity of science can be gained only at the price of relativity* (and whoever seeks the absolute, must search for it in the subjective).

These last considerations throw into sharp relief the peculiar character of the transcendental method and its opposition to psychologism; and this is true also of the importance of the transcendental concept of objectivity and of the Kantian transcendental definition of empirical knowledge. In this way we return to the concluding thoughts of the preceding section, at a point where the discussion can now be resumed.

---

[58] [See notes 15, 16 and 17 and the text to these notes. Ed.]

Chapter VI

THE PROBABILITY POSITIONS

12. *The probability positions — subjective belief in probability.* The normal-statement positions cannot be satisfactory:

Naive inductivism is *logically* untenable; it is directly refuted by Hume's argument.

Strict positivism is logically consistent, but *epistemologically* (trans-cendentally) unsatisfactory. It does not provide an explanation for the existence of natural laws, and cannot give an adequate interpretation of theoretical natural science. It offers *too little.*

Apriorism, on the other hand, offers *too much.* It "proves" the absolute *a priori* validity of certain empirical statements; but empirical science will find it hard to accept the view that there are empirical statements that are necessarily valid and in principle irrefutable by experience.

This is where the *probability positions* enter, which seem to overcome all of these difficulties. They agree with positivism (and empirical science) that universal empirical statements can never be ultimately verified; like apriorism (and again like empirical science) they acknowledge that natural laws are strictly universal empirical statements.

The probability statement positions manage to overcome these apparently irreconcilable antagonisms by abandoning an assumption that all normal-statement positions have in common, one that — according to the probability positions — causes all the difficulties of the problem of induction. It is the (unproved) assumption that statements can only have the values "*true*" and "*false*".

According to the probability positions, it is only if this assumption is abandoned that the problem of induction can be solved.

(A schematic representation of these relationships can be found in the Appendix, Table III.)

The *probability positions* assume "that inductively obtained statements do not possess the property of certainty".[1] They can never "shed their hypothetical character";[3] nevertheless, they have some *degree of validity*: they are *probable*. This view is so widely held that Schlick[3] says: "Recent philosophy and science have long become accustomed to claiming only probability for empirical knowledge."

A closer analysis of this position does reveal problems. Schlick, who still advocates this position in his *Erkenntnislehre* (he has since abandoned it), is already forced to admit[4] "that the concept of probability in its application to the empirical world still contains profound puzzles".

However, such "puzzles" in the theory of knowledge are frequently an indication of the existence of fundamental misconceptions. And this is why I wish here to present one result of my analysis of this position: I will flatly reject the view that an empirical statement can have an objective degree of validity other than "*true*" or "*false*".

In my view, it is indefensible to speak of the "probability" of a statement in terms of an objective degree of validity between "true" and "false". (I fully agree on this with Waismann's "Logical Analysis of the Concept of Probability".[5]) Of course, I am far from disputing the fundamental concept of objective probability (in the sense of the probability of an event).

Regrettably, as a result of a large number of misconceptions, the problem of probability seems to be so confused that a detailed account will be necessary. I shall, therefore, make every effort to keep to a minimum any discussion of side-issues that do not immediately touch on the problem of induction.

---

[1]   Moritz Schlick, *Allgemeine Erkenntnislehre* (2nd ed., 1925), p. 357.

[3]   [Hans Reichenbach, *op. cit.*, p. 171. Ed.]

[3]   Moritz Schlick, *loc. cit.*

[4]   Moritz Schlick, *op. cit.*, p. 360.

[5]   Friedrich Waismann, "Logische Analyse des Wahrscheinlichkeitsbegriffs", *Erkenntnis* 1 (1930), pp. 228 ff.

Once again, it was Hume who pointed out the significance of the *belief in probability*. The most important prerequisite for any study of the problem of probability is to distinguish clearly the *subjective* belief in probability from whatever can be said about *objective* validity and grounds of validity, more particularly, about "objective probability statements".

When a friend tells me about an event, or when I study the weather forecast before setting out on a mountain walk, many things may have a bearing on how my opinion or belief is formed. Liking for and trust in my friend, courage or cowardice, are just as likely to play a part as a sober assessment of different options. I call all these influences *motives of belief* in order to distinguish them from objective *grounds of validity*.

Motives and grounds of validity can easily be confused, because grounds of validity may very well figure as motives. Indeed, if I want to reveal the motives for my belief to myself or to others, I will surely try to support it primarily with objective considerations. I may believe in something because it is justified – very often belief rests on a very different motivation; but this relationship can never be reversed. My belief can never provide an objective ground of validity.

It is the fundamental error of [classical] rationalism to regard subjective belief (for example, the notorious category of self-evidence) as a ground of validity.

The fact that we believe in the hypotheses of science, or that we are completely convinced of the truth of some hypothesis, has nothing directly to do with the problem of validity. The importance of this belief for practical life has been emphasised often enough. It may be an object of interest for the theory of knowledge, or it may be in need of clarification; reference to it may perhaps enable us to identify as psychological problems (problems of fact) certain problems that we took to be problems of validity.

But since belief alone can never constitute a ground of validity, it alone can never raise any problem of validity.

Subjective probability, therefore, concerns our topic only indirectly.*[1] But as stated in Schlick's *Erkenntnislehre*,[6] "without doubt probability statements claim objective significance beyond their subjective meaning".

---

*[1] With this remark, the subjective theory of knowledge as a whole and the doctrine of knowledge as a variant of belief are rejected. See also my book *Objective Knowledge* (1972).

[6] Moritz Schlick, *op. cit.*, p. 358.

What might this significance, i.e., "objective probability", consist in?

13. *Statements about the objective probability of events.* With respect to *objective probability*, Waismann[1] states: "The term probability has two different meanings. On the one hand, one may speak about the probability of an event. The term is used in this sense in probability calculus. Or, on the other hand, one may speak about the probability of a hypothesis or of a natural law ... These two meanings have nothing whatsoever in common." Now, my topic has to do with the "*probability of hypotheses*". But in order to be able to show how little this concept has to do with the *probability of events*, I shall first have to discuss in brief, in this section, the question of the probability of events.

A trivial example of a statement about the probability of an event would be the following: "The probability of throwing '2' with the next throw in a game of dice equals 1/6."

This statement is about the next throw, about the future. We are, thus, evidently dealing with a scientific *prediction* (whose central importance in science has already been mentioned).

But what an odd prediction it is! It really says nothing at all. Indeed, it is an obvious admission of the fact that one can simply make *no* prediction about this throw. For with the next throw I can throw any number – and I will then definitely not know whether the prediction was true or false.

Therefore, this probability statement is in urgent need of clarification. Such clarification, I believe, is not too difficult to provide.

First, a few words on the making of predictions.

A prediction is usually obtained by deduction from a number of hypotheses (universal empirical statements) by supplementing them with specific assumptions and conditions. There can be various intermediate levels between the universal hypotheses (natural laws) forming the basis for the deduction and the singular predictions; that is, statements, or hypotheses that are *derived* from the basis of the deduction with the aid of certain *additional assumptions*, but which nevertheless are *universal statements*. An example would be the (approximately) parabolic shape of all trajectories, derived from the law of gravity. Such derived hypotheses are, admittedly, on a lower level of universality than the hypotheses from which they are

---

[1] Friedrich Waismann, "Logische Analyse des Wahrscheinlichkeitsbegriffs", *Erkenntnis* 1 (1930), p. 228.

deduced, and they are valid only for the more limited range demarcated by the assumptions; but within this range, they can still be strictly universal.

We now turn to probability statements.

In my view, all probability statements belong to these *derived* universal hypotheses (derived from natural laws and other assumptions); or to predictions deduced from derived hypotheses – for there are also singular probability statements.

Thus, the feature distinguishing probability statements from other derived hypotheses has not yet been touched on.

I characterise probability statements as derived hypotheses (or predictions) about *sequences of events*.*[1] (They do not establish any laws or predictions about the properties of individual events, but rather laws or predictions about the properties of sequences of events.) This constitutes their distinguishing feature.

In order to underscore the fact that the special character of probability statements must also be deducible from the character of the assumptions, I have stressed that these statements are derived hypotheses. We can only appreciate that which is important about probability statements when we understand what typifies their assumptions.

The typical features of these assumptions are characterised: (1) by the fact that the assumptions known to us (natural laws and special conditions ["initial conditions"]) are *not sufficient* for the deduction of a prediction about an individual element in the sequence of events; (2) by the fact that we cannot formulate a law for the *missing conditions*; from this we infer the proposition that these randomly changing conditions *partly compensate* each other (if, as it were, a plurality of events gives them the opportunity of doing so); so that the sequence of events rather than its individual elements can be assumed to be *partly independent* "of the conditions about which we have no detailed knowledge". (This is similar to what is claimed by Wittgenstein[2] and Waismann.[3])

---

*[1] I should have consistently used "*Ereignisfolge*" instead of "*Ereignisreihe*" [i.e., "sequence of events" instead of "series of events"; in the present translation both expressions have consistently been rendered as "sequence of events". Tr.]

[2] [Ludwig Wittgenstein, *Tractatus Logico-Philosophicus* (1918/1922), Proposition 5.154. Ed.]

[3] [Friedrich Waismann, *op. cit.*, p. 246. Ed.]

From this point of view, the purpose of these singular probability statements would, therefore, be not a prediction about the next throw with a die, but rather a (somewhat indefinite) prediction about the average result of a sequence of throws. Universal probability statements would, accordingly, be statements about (somewhat imprecise) laws of sequences of events.

This view agrees well with the actual procedure used in assessing probability statements. If in ten throws I obtain "1" six times, then I will conjecture that something is wrong with the probability prediction; if, say, in the very next five throws I get "1" two or three times again, I will be convinced that the prediction (for this case), and with it the specific assumptions, are falsified: I will try to change the assumptions. Initially, I will not change the natural laws but assume that certain other assumptions were false. Above all, I will examine whether the die is not "loaded" (whether the centre of gravity of this die is at its geometric centre, etc.).

I regard as innocuous the difficulties that are supposed to exist in a view of probability such as the one developed here. They usually result from an *excessively narrow view of the concept of law*. We obtain knowledge by searching for laws; and if they cannot be found in the individual events of a particular type, then we just search for them in sequences of events (or deduce them for sequences of events and verify them through such sequences of events).

Among these problems are the *inaccuracies* of probability statements, or their lack of precision. This also seems to me not to be a serious problem. It is simply another prejudice, namely that every law must be a *precise statement* (the prejudice stems from classical physics, but it has even deeper roots; more on this later). Medical predictions, for example, are usually much more imprecise than probability statements. What is crucial is that predictions are *falsifiable at all*; this must suffice. Moreover, the imprecision itself follows deductively from the assumptions (so that, for example, if in every six throws of a die all sides *always* appeared with equal frequency, we would indeed conclude from this that the assumptions are false).

Some supplementary comments on these questions will follow in a later section (15); in addition, I would like to refer the reader to the paper by Waismann cited above, with whose views (excepting certain details) I largely agree.

To sum up the discussion in this section, I suggest that probability statements are (derived) hypotheses about sequences of events; this, at any rate, establishes an objective concept of probability. As far as the validity of such hypotheses is concerned, for the time being only one thing is certain: their validity is not of a different kind from that of other hypotheses, of natural laws or of the other assumptions from which probability statements are deduced. And with this question about the validity of hypotheses, we have returned once more to the problem of induction.

14. *Probability as an objective degree of validity of universal empirical statements.* The *probability of an event* may be defined as follows: a probability statement is a statement about a series of events [or better: a sequence of events*[1]].

But how should we actually conceive of the *probability of a statement*?

The probability of an event is the *content* of a statement. The probability of a statement (especially the probability of a hypothesis) should refer to the *objective validity* of a statement. The degree of validity of a statement and its content (what is stated by it) are, of course, two fundamentally different things.

Is it possible to specify more precisely what is to be understood by the probability of a hypothesis?

Is it perhaps possible to reduce the probability of a hypothesis to the probability of an event?

Whatever form the elucidation of the concept of the objective probability of a statement may take, one thing is certain: that a statement is probably *valid* can only be expressed by a statement about that statement (by a "judgement of a judgement"). For a statement, or a hypothesis, states only that something is the case or that something is not the case. It can, admittedly, also state that something is probably the case (probability of an event). But if we want to express that one of these statements is not straightforwardly valid, but only probably valid, then this can only be done by a statement about a statement. This should be kept in mind.

Beyond this, it is rather difficult to say *more precisely* what is actually meant by this concept of objective probability as a degree of validity of a statement, or by the probability of a hypothesis. I must confess that I am unable to find a tenable analogy between the probability of an event and the objective probability of a statement as it is usually understood.

The probability of an event is a statement about a sequence of events. However, obviously it is impossible in analogous fashion to conceive of

*[1] See Section 13, note *1.

the probability of a hypothesis as a statement about a sequence of hypotheses.

Certainly, the probability of a hypothesis can only be a probability statement about the question whether events (that is, events as yet unknown to us) will or will not correspond to the hypothesis in question.

But here, too, an analogy with the probability of an event cannot be found. The characteristic feature of a probabilistic prediction (Section 13) is that it says nothing at all about the (individual) next throw of a die, for it is consistent with all possible cases.

It is an entirely different matter when one speaks about a probability of the question whether an event will or will not conform to a natural law. For if the event does not conform to the natural law, which is a statement formulated in strictly universal terms, then the natural law is *false*, and its probability suddenly and definitively drops to zero. The fairly high probability, however, of *not* throwing "2" with the next throw [of a die] (it equals 5/6) neither increases nor decreases as a result of the fact that I just threw "2".

In contrast, the proponents of the concept of the probability of hypotheses assume that the probability will increase if the event has been in accordance with the hypothesis, or if it can be regarded as a verification of the hypothesis. But no one*[2] believes that the probability of throwing "1" will increase if I have just thrown "1".

Thus, we can hardly expect to discover a simple analogy, and the concept of the probability of hypotheses appears in general to be somewhat obscure.

It seems to me that the proponents of the probability of hypotheses of statements are completely mistaken if, like Reichenbach,[1] they maintain that this concept is identical with the concept of the probability of events.

Reichenbach[2] writes in support of this view:

"So far we have regarded as a case of a probability of an event the assignment of a probability 1/6 to any one side being thrown; we could also express this by saying that the statement 'the probability of "1" being thrown is 1/6'."

---

*[2] Some probability theoreticians believe precisely that; for example, Rudolf Carnap. See his book *The Continuum of Inductive Methods* (1952).

[1] Hans Reichenbach, "Kausalität und Wahrscheinlichkeit", *Erkenntnis* 1 (1930), pp. 158 ff.

[2] Hans Reichenbach, *op. cit.*, pp. 171 f.

One can immediately see that this position is untenable. The statement "The side '1' of the die will turn up with a probability of 1/6" will be neither confirmed nor refuted if it turns up or fails to turn up; for the statement is a prediction about a sequence of events. But the statement "The side '1' of the die will turn up" will prove to be true or false after the throw. It is a genuine prediction for this individual event and definitively verifiable. Its "probability" cannot remain 1/6, but must become 1 or 0 after verification. The two cases are, therefore, fundamentally different. The distinction is by no means "a mere matter of terminology".[3]

A typical response to such objections is that the theory of probability cannot be explained within the framework of classical logic, but that the situation will be completely altered if one admits the possibility of a special "probability logic".

And indeed, the crucial point of the question is whether a statement can possess a degree of validity between true and false. According to the "old" logic, however, the law of the excluded middle applies: a statement can have no degree of validity other than true or false. The only consistent way in which to expound the objective probability of hypotheses is, therefore, to abandon classical logic or at least to supplement it by a probability logic; and this, surely, is a drastic step to take.

Thus the difficulties (and with them the probability of being on the wrong track) constantly increase, and the question appears ever more obscure and mysterious. In consequence, I will rely exclusively on the following indisputable fact.

If something like the objective probability of hypotheses exists at all, then this can surely be formulated only in a probability statement about the hypothesis, perhaps in a statement such as the following: "This hypothesis has a higher or lower probability of being valid."

15. *One way of more closely defining the concept of the probability of a hypothesis (primary and secondary probability of hypotheses). The concept of simplicity.* The rather negative conclusions we have reached up to this point regarding the probability of hypotheses are not entirely satisfactory. It is indisputable that we *believe* in hypotheses with varying degrees of probability. And, what is almost more important, it is indisputable that we believe some

---

[3] [Hans Reichenbach, *op. cit.*, p. 171. Ed.]

hypotheses to be more probable than others, and this is motivated by reasons that cannot be denied an element of objectivity. Would it not be possible to indicate the objective reasons motivating the subjective probabilities we assign to hypotheses? It would be very conducive to a better understanding of the situation. It would be particularly satisfying if a relationship with the probability of events could be established, if only an indirect one.

I start from the concept of the *range* of a hypothesis. (On this subject see also Waismann's study cited above.[1])

Compare, for example, the following two hypotheses: (1) All trajectories are parabolas. (2) All trajectories are conic sections.

Since all parabolas are conic sections, and there are conic sections other than parabolas, the second hypothesis permits many more possibilities than the first. Its range is wider. In our case, its range fully encompasses that of the first hypothesis.

This relationship is a purely logical one. If the first hypothesis (with the narrower range) is true, then the second hypothesis, whose range encompasses that of the first, must also be true. However, the second hypothesis could be true without the first one being true as well; for example, if there were hyperbolic trajectories. (The first hypothesis [logically] entails the second hypothesis, but not vice versa.)

This relationship makes the hypothesis with the wider range *more probable* than the other *for purely logical reasons* (that is, *a priori*). This, of course, implies no judgement at all with regard to their actual degree of validity. For example, they might (*a posteriori*) both be true or both be false. It implies only this: the first hypothesis cannot be true without the second hypothesis also being true.

If the second hypothesis is called "*more probable*", it should be clear that it is more probable only *in relationship to the first* hypothesis, that is, that this concept of probability is only relative; for it is based on a logical *relationship* between the two hypotheses.

I call this kind of probability "*primary probability of hypotheses*" (in order to avoid the term "*a priori*").

By comparing any two hypotheses in terms of their range, an entire scale of primary probabilities of hypotheses can be constructed ("scaling").

---

[1] [Friedrich Waismann, "Logische Analyse des Wahrscheinlichkeitsbegriffs", *Erkenntnis* 1 (1930), pp. 235 ff. Ed.]

The following would be an example of such a scale with an increasing "primary probability of hypotheses":

(1) All trajectories are parabolas. (2) All trajectories are conic sections. (3) All trajectories are continuous curves. (4) All trajectories are continuous or discontinuous, unbroken or broken lines.

The last hypothesis (4) is in any case true *a priori*. This is why its primary probability equals 1. But this is also why it is *completely empty of meaning*.

The greater the precision of a hypothesis, the lower its primary probability. The emptier of meaning a hypothesis and the lower its precision, the higher will be its primary probability.

This consideration suggests that there is a close relationship between the primary probability of hypotheses and the concept of law (and thus the concept of knowledge in general).

Universal statements of type (4), that is, with primary probability 1, say nothing at all about reality: these "hypotheses" do not formulate any law at all, and impart no empirical knowledge; there would also be no point in deriving predictions from them. They can be called *empirically insignificant*. With decreasing primary probability, the precision of the statement increases: it progressively develops its law-like character and predictions can be derived from it, i.e., it conveys empirical knowledge. The narrower its range, that is, *the lower its primary probability, the more a statement will say*.

One might even say: the narrower the range of a statement, the lower its primary probability (or the higher its primary improbability), and the more precise the statement, the more knowledge we can gain from it. (That is, if it can be aligned with experience.) This suggests the imposition of a kind of relative scale on the concept of knowledge. The *cognitive value of a statement is inversely related to its primary probability*; it increases with its primary improbability.

In the same way, the concept of law can be regarded as quantitatively scaled, so that one can speak of degrees of law-likeness and of higher or lower specificity. A law is more of a law the more precise it is, or the higher its primary improbability. (Clearly, this is again a kind of analysis of the concept of knowledge; cf. Section 10.)

It is now understandable why, in our search for knowledge, we always seek to make our statements more precise. (It constitutes the legitimate core of the prejudice against imprecise laws mentioned earlier.) If we can bring a more precise hypothesis into line with experience, then we regard the less precise one as obsolete (since it is implied by the new one –

cf. Section 31 – it is implicitly asserted by it). If this orientation towards precision statements is satisfactorily carried through, then we speak of "exact" sciences. The importance of a narrow range also sheds light on the role of mathematics in empirical knowledge (e.g. in physics). It is a logical method that permits the derivation of precise statements and precise predictions with arbitrarily narrow range (within the limits of measurement accuracy). (Without mathematics we could talk not, for example, about a "parabola" but at best about a "curved line".)

Moreover, the highly controversial notion of the "simplicity of a law" and its relationship to the concept of knowledge thereby becomes fully transparent – to the extent that this notion, which plays a very considerable role in inductivist arguments, can be rationally comprehended at all.

Inductivism assumes that from individual observations we reach natural laws through generalisation. Now, if we think of the individual observations as points plotted in a coordinate system (the measured results of each observation are its coordinates), the graphic representation of a law would be a curve (a function) passing through these points. However, it is always possible to draw an unlimited number of curves through a finite number of points (the law is not uniquely determined by the observations). Hence, the important question arises: which of these curves should we choose?

The usual answer is: choose the simplest curve, the simplest function. Wittgenstein, for example, says:[2]

"The procedure of induction consist in accepting as true the simplest law that can be reconciled with our experiences."

It is, however, obvious that very little has been achieved in this way. Why do we accept the simplest function? What does this simplicity consist in?

Inductivism has not yet provided any satisfactory answer to these two questions. The concept of simplicity confronts it with considerable problems.

Thus, Schlick[3] establishes a connection between simplicity and law-likeness, yet "without being able to indicate what is actually meant by

[2] Ludwig Wittgenstein, Tractatus Logico-Philosophicus (1918/1922), Proposition 6.363.
[3] Moritz Schlick, "Die Kausalität in der gegenwärtigen Physik", Die Naturwissenschaften 19 (1931), p. 148.

simplicity . . . The concept of simplicity is . . . partly a pragmatic, partly an aesthetic concept." And he continues:[4]

"It is certain that one can define the concept of simplicity only by a convention that must always be arbitrary. While we may tend to regard a function of the first degree as simpler than one of the second degree, the latter will undoubtedly represent a perfect law if it describes the observed data with a high level of accuracy; the Newtonian formula of gravitation that contains the square of the distance, is usually considered a model of a simple natural law. Moreover, one can, for example, agree that of all the continuous curves that are sufficiently close to a given number of points, the one to be regarded as the simplest is that which has on average the largest radius of curvature (see, on this, a still unpublished work by Marcel Natkin[5]); but such devices appear contrived."

Now, I believe that it is very easy to indicate what this "simplicity" actually consists in, and why it is always the *simplest law* that we attempt to establish. (At issue here is only *that* concept of simplicity that is meant [intended] *in this epistemological debate*; the extent to which this concept corresponds to common linguistic usage will not be discussed.[*1]) The following view will be defended here:

"Simplicity" in the sense of "simplicity of a law" is only another term for "primary improbability"; in other words (as we have already seen), it is nothing but the purely logical concept of a (relatively) narrow range.

If this interpretation is correct, then the concept of knowledge implies that we always seek to establish the simplest law: precisely because the simplest law says more and possesses a greater cognitive value.

Of course, no logical proof can be provided to show that the diffuse pragmatic-aesthetic concept of simplicity employed by the inductivists is identical with the precise concept of logical range. But it can be shown that my definition of the concept of simplicity delivers exactly what inductivism demands from this concept.

---

[4] [Moritz Schlick, *op. cit.*, pp. 148 f. Ed.]

[5] [See note 8. Ed.]

[*1] And, *a fortiori*, nothing is asserted here about the "essence" of simplicity. [Cf. Karl Popper, *Logik der Forschung* (3rd ed., 1969, and subsequent editions), Section 46, *Zusatz (1968). Ed. *The Logic of Scientific Discovery* (6th impression, revised, 1972, and subsequent editions), Section 46, *addendum*, 1972. Tr.]

For example, since it is identical with primary improbability, this concept of simplicity is an indicator of the degree of law-likeness of a hypothesis; therefore, it delivers precisely what Feigl[6] emphasises when he speaks of the "idea of defining the degree of law-likeness in terms of simplicity".

It can similarly be shown, with the aid of the definition of simplicity put forward here, why a straight line (a linear function, cf. the quotation from Schlick) is simpler than, for example, a conic section (curves of the second order): it has a narrower range (a higher primary improbability), since it can be understood as a special case of a conic section. (Its range is encompassed by that of conic sections.) For the same reasons, a circle and a parabola are to be considered as simpler than, say, an ellipse and a hyperbola. In general, we can say: curves (functions) of a higher order are less simple than curves of a lower order. The latter can always be understood as limiting cases of curves of a higher order, but not vice versa. (Their range is encompassed by that of curves of a higher order.) Their range is smaller; this, however, means that (according to my terminology) they are more precise, have a higher primary improbability, and are "simpler".

Admittedly, the proposed concept of simplicity is not in all respects identical with that of the authors cited. But this is precisely what demonstrates its superiority.

Schlick[7] mentions Natkin's[8] definition that the curve that on average has the largest radius of curvature (the smallest average curvature) should be considered simpler. Apart from the difficulties posed by the concept of "average", a cubic parabola, for example, would then be simpler than a regular quadratic one. (Not only does its curvature decrease more rapidly with increasing distance from the point of inflection than that of a quadratic parabola; at its point of inflection the curvature is actually zero.) According to this definition, an ellipse could be simpler than a circle[*2] (and yet, attempts were initially made to interpret planetary orbits as circular!), and an (asymptotic) hyperbola would be even simpler. This view does not seem, therefore, to be very auspicious.

[6] Herbert Feigl, *Theorie und Erfahrung in der Physik* (1929), p. 25.

[7] [Moritz Schlick, *op. cit.*, p. 149. Ed.]

[8] [Marcel Natkin, *Einfachheit, Kausalität und Induktion* (Dissertation, Vienna, 1928), pp. 82 f. Ed.]

[*2] And a larger circle would always be simpler than a smaller circle.

Feigl[9] mentions a somewhat different definition: the deviation of a curve from a straight line should be as small as possible. But then, a highly complicated function oscillating only slightly in long waves around a straight line (and perhaps even asymptotically approaching it) would, for example, be far simpler than a regular parabola.

No, we are not dealing with such "devices" (as Schlick[10] calls them), for which our preference must always remain a mystery. We are dealing with a much simpler simplicity: not with a concept whose definition is just as obscure as the reason for its application, but with a purely logical concept whose application analytically follows from the concept of knowledge. The "simplicity" of a law is just another term for its "primary improbability".

(Supplementary comments on this point can be found towards the end of Section 30.)

Our knowledge, therefore, consists in ordering the given material as well as possible; that is, in trying to describe it through hypotheses with as high a primary improbability as possible, through laws that are as simple as possible and through universal statements that are as precise as possible, and to be able to deduce predictions that are as precise as possible and apply them directly to reality. (These are all analytic statements, tautologies.)

Let us now turn to the *"secondary probability of hypotheses"*.

Whereas the primary probability of hypotheses is concerned only with logical, *a priori* relations between statements, the secondary probability of hypotheses refers to the relationship of these hypotheses (whose primary probability may be regarded as more or less high) to experience. (I call them "secondary" in order to avoid the term "*a posteriori*". Here the concept is introduced only in a preliminary fashion, and will be more closely analysed in the next section.)

The result will be this: the lower the primary probability of a hypothesis, the higher its *secondary probability as a result of a verification of its predictions* – and vice versa: the higher its primary probability, the lower its secondary probability even in the case of a large number of confirmations.

This is only apparently paradoxical.

9 [Herbert Feigl, *loc. cit.* Ed.]
10 [Moritz Schlick, *loc. cit.* Ed.]

Let a hypothesis with an exceedingly high primary improbability (a hypothesis with a very narrow range) be formulated. Take, for example, the following hypothesis (derived from the general theory of relativity):

"If one carefully compares the photograph of any constellation taken at night with a photograph of the same constellation taken at the time of day when the sun is at the centre of the constellation (such a photograph may be taken during a total eclipse of the sun), then, provided the measurement is sufficiently accurate, the following result will always obtain: at the closest proximity to the sun, the distance between the stars increases and they move apart by a minute but precise amount (approximately 1.7 seconds of arc)."

Let us now experiment. Suppose that initially we make only *one* attempt at verification – and we succeed *in spite of all the* [primary] *improbability.* Already after the first verification, we conjecture that a coincidence with such a high primary improbability can be *no accident. For an accident would be too improbable.*[3] The high primary improbability of the hypothesis lends it a considerable secondary probability after only *one* attempt at verification. Even if we may not readily believe that this hypothesis expresses a natural law, we shall nevertheless assume (as long as the results of the verification are unequivocal) that here there is an underlying law-like regularity.[4]

Thus, if we succeed in verifying in only a small number of cases a statement with a high primary improbability, then we attach the greatest significance to this verification – for we regard it as highly improbable that several cases would, by mere chance, fall within the very narrow range of the precise statement.

"Not chance-like" is, therefore, synonymous with "law-like" ("some law-like regularity *is at the bottom of it*").[5] "Chance-like" means "not law-like", unpredictable, unknowable. (No one has as yet been able to discover any order in the sequence of numbers in a game of chance. If an order were to be found, then it would no longer be a game of chance.)

Experience, verification, is very significant in the case of (simple,

---

[3] I return to this important argument in my book *Objective Knowledge* (1972), pp. 101 f., and relate it to the concept of *verisimilitude.* Conversely, one might introduce the concept of verisimilitude with the aid of secondary probability.

[4] That is, a law-like regularity to which the conjectured law-like regularity is at least an *approximation.*

[5] See preceding note.

precise) hypotheses and of predictions with primary improbability – for those with primary probability it is correspondingly insignificant.

We will not readily want to accept (after a few observations) the hypothesis (having high primary probability) that every trajectory must be curved. This is not because of any preference for straight lines; but because it was perhaps only chance that curved the investigated trajectories. Perhaps – we may think – it is after all possible, if we throw with great skill, to throw something along a straight line for a certain distance. The more precise hypothesis, with high primary improbability, that the trajectory is a parabola will already be considered well corroborated after only a few careful experiments. And if it were possible to produce experimental evidence even for the hypothesis that the trajectory is a straight line, then a still smaller number of experiments would suffice to convince us (see [the] example of free fall).

Conversely, however, if a statement is *a priori* true and has a primary probability equal to 1, and if it therefore has no significance for empirical knowledge, then experience is equally insignificant for it. Although – or because – the statement is *a priori* true, experience cannot make it credible. It will not be accepted as a hypothesis, no matter how much experience confirms it. We assign it a secondary probability value of zero.

These results also allow us to show the connections between the "probability of hypotheses" and the concept of the probability of events that we have been searching for.

It is with the notions of *law-likeness* and *chance* that we are able to establish these connections.

The analysis of the *primary probability of hypotheses* has shown that the degree of law-likeness is determined by *primary improbability*.

As the analysis of the *probability of events* has shown, if a sequence of events does not yield the expected average value, that is, if it has an *improbable* distribution, we analogously infer the existence of a law-like regularity.

Thus, if sequences of events deviate from the "probable" or "chance-like" (not governed by rules) distribution, we will always infer the existence of laws; and this applies equally to the probability of hypotheses and the probability of events. Either we consider as refuted our assumption that no law-like regularity exists (probability of events), or we consider as confirmed the assumption that a law exists (probability of hypotheses).

16. *The concept of the corroboration of a hypothesis — positivist, pragmatist and probabilistic interpretations of the concept of corroboration.* What point have we reached in the discussion of the question concerning the validity of hypotheses? Is primary or secondary probability, perhaps, the objective degree of validity of universal empirical statements that we are looking for?

The *primary probability of hypotheses* is a purely logical concept. It is (*a priori*) determined by relations between logical ranges. Experience has no bearing on them whatsoever. As a logical concept, it is objective; as a degree of validity of empirical statements, however, it does not come into consideration, since empirical statements can have no *a priori* degree of validity: only experience can decide their validity.

Whether the *secondary probability of hypotheses* is, perhaps, somehow related to objective validity cannot at first glance be determined. For the concept of the secondary probability of hypotheses can be interpreted in various ways. (I have intentionally introduced this concept initially in a somewhat diffuse, indeterminate fashion.)

I shall start by presenting the view advocated here.

I hold two interpretations of the concept of secondary probability of hypotheses to be admissible (that is, simultaneously admissible).

An *objective* interpretation that leads to the adoption of the concept of *corroboration*, to be attributed to a hypothesis according to the given state of our experience; and a *subjective* interpretation that sees in the secondary probability of hypotheses a description of our *subjective degree of belief* and of its motivation through the (objective) corroboration of hypotheses.*[1]

---

*[1] We are, thus, presented with four probabilities: probability of events (objective) or probability of statements, the latter being primary (objective) or secondary, the latter in turn objective or subjective. Schematically:

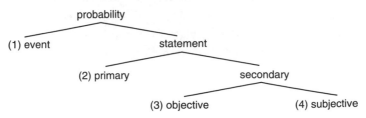

Of these four probabilities, (1) and (2) fulfil the axioms of probability calculus, whereas (3) and (4) do not.

The concept of *corroboration* will be discussed first. It is of the utmost importance.

In order for a hypothesis to be assigned a positive degree of corroboration at all, (1) predictions deduced from it must be *verified*, and (2) all our experiences must be *consistent* with the hypothesis. If one of these conditions is not fulfilled, then the hypothesis cannot be ascribed any positive degree of corroboration.

In addition, the value of a corroboration increases with the primary improbability of the hypothesis and with the number of verifications (as the preceding section has shown with respect to the "secondary probability of hypotheses").

This concept of corroboration certainly is objective. It expresses a particular relationship between a given verification by experience and the primary probability of the hypothesis.

Much could be added with regard to this concept. Only the most important points will be indicated here.

If a hypothesis has any positive degree of corroboration at all, then the effect of its primary improbability on the value of corroboration is to be rated as greater than the effect of the number of verifications: even a very large number of verifications fails to corroborate a hypothesis with high primary probability, while a very small number of verifications corroborates a hypothesis with high primary improbability.

One might say that the magnitude of the primary probability or improbability of hypotheses determines how many verifications will be required for a hypothesis to be assigned a particular degree of corroboration.

This explains why "any scientist who has succeeded in representing a sequence of observations by a very simple formula ... is at once absolutely certain that he has found a *law*" (Schlick).[1] For he can appeal to the relatively high improbability of a *simple* law and the relatively strong corroboration corresponding to it.

The first genuine falsification (observation*[2] of an event which is inconsistent with the hypothesis) destroys the corroboration of the hypothesis.

---

[1] Moritz Schlick, "Die Kausalität in der gegenwärtigen Physik", *Die Naturwissenschaften* 19 (1931), p. 148.

*[2] Better: accepted observation statement, or accepted statement about particular states of affairs (facts).

Further comments on possible ways of measuring the degree of corroboration are beyond the scope of this study. It would be the task of a theory of method.[2]

The (positivist) concept of corroboration thus outlined has nothing to do with the objective probability of hypotheses as a *degree of validity*. It contains nothing to the effect that past corroboration justifies the conclusion that a hypothesis will continue to be corroborated. Corroboration is merely a certain kind of summary report about hitherto observed verifications; admittedly, an evaluative report. By taking into account the primary probability of a hypothesis, it considers whether or not these verifications have any significance at all (and how significant they are).

I now turn to the subjective interpretation.

The subjective belief in probability can be supported by the corroboration of a hypothesis, but this belief goes beyond what corroboration can achieve. It presupposes that a corroborated hypothesis will continue to be further corroborated. It is clear that without this belief we would be unable to act, and therefore unable to live. So there is nothing really puzzling about this belief. Its objective motives are sufficiently illuminated by the concept of corroboration for it not to provoke further epistemological questions.

This analysis of the concept of secondary probability of hypotheses represents a *positivist* standpoint: as does "strict positivism", it conceives objective corroboration as an – always only preliminary – report on experiences, albeit as a special evaluative report on very specific experiences, through which predictions deductively obtained from a hypothesis are verified.

Other views of the concept of corroboration are, however, also conceivable: views intended to make corroboration into an *objective degree of validity* of universal empirical statements.

The first view to be examined is that of *pragmatism*. Pragmatism takes the position that the truth of a statement lies only in its corroboration. It equates truth with corroboration. This is related to an appreciation of the concepts of "prediction" and of "verification", which as such is quite justified. If a prediction (a singular statement) is corroborated by

---

[2] [See Editor's Postscript. Cf. also Karl Popper, *Logik der Forschung* (1934; 2nd ed., 1966; and subsequent editions), Section 82. Ed. *The Logic of Scientific Discovery* (1959; 2nd ed., 1968; and subsequent editions), Section 82. Tr.]

experience, if it has been verified by experience, then it is also definitively verified. It is true.

This truth is timeless. The statement "Napoleon carried a sword" is true not only at the end of the eighteenth century, but is and always will be true (or it has always been false): *validity is timeless*.

With respect to singular statements, the concept of corroboration may [therefore] be equated with that of truth without giving rise to contradictions. It is a different matter, however, when we come to strictly universal empirical statements.

A hypothesis may have been corroborated for a long time, and it may still be corroborated today; but perhaps it will no longer be corroborated tomorrow. This does not, however, allow us to say that it is indeed true today but may be false tomorrow. This would represent a misunderstanding of strict universality and of the concept of validity. Therefore, I entirely agree with Schlick:[3] "'Truth and confirmation are . . . not identical." The pragmatist interpretation seems to me unacceptable.

The position that is really at the centre of this debate is the position of *probability logic*. However, unlike pragmatism it does not simply equate corroboration with truth, but instead assigns to statements a probability value between true and false, corresponding to their degree of corroboration.

The concept of corroboration seems to be extremely well suited to providing a basis for the *objective probability of hypotheses* qua degree of validity. Admittedly, the argument of Section 14 is still correct: it is still impossible to find any genuine analogy to the probability of events; the relations between the two concepts are rather remote.[*3] The concept of corroboration can, nevertheless, be used to describe, in more specific terms, what is actually meant by the objective probability of a hypothesis, by a degree of validity of a hypothesis that is intermediate between true and false.

By introducing the concept of corroboration, I have thus made far-reaching concessions to the position of probability logic. It appears that with the aid of the concept of corroboration, the concept of the objective probability of hypotheses can now be defined in a consistent fashion.

---

[3] [Moritz Schlick, *op. cit.*, p. 155. Ed.]

[*3] The probability of events fulfils the axioms of the calculus of probability, but corroboration does not. See note *1, and *The Logic of Scientific Discovery* (1959; 2nd ed., 1968; and subsequent editions).

But this is only apparently so. The position of probability logic is defeated by the infinite regression of any induction.

17. *The infinite regression of probability statements.* The proponents of the doctrine of the objective probability of hypotheses take the position that universal empirical statements can never be true, but only probable.

This view is logically untenable: not only from the perspective of Aristotelian "two-valued logic", but also from that of any "probability logic".

If one wishes to express the view that a universal empirical statement can be attributed *a posteriori* a certain probability as a degree of validity, then this can be objectively established only by a statement about this statement.

This statement is of a higher type than the hypothesis. But it is, itself, a universal empirical statement that can thus possess only a probability value as a degree of validity; this is demonstrated by the fact that a falsification of the hypothesis will also falsify the statement that assigns it a positive probability value: its validity is dependent on experience, and it cannot be a definitively true statement. If it is, however, only probable, this can in turn only be expressed by a statement of a higher type, etc. *ad infinitum*.

Nothing can break this infinite regression of probability statements.

Views that, for example, state that the probabilities of a higher type will "converge towards 1", or that a probability of the second order will usually be quite close to 1, and other similar arguments, do not help at all in this respect. Even if they were otherwise correct, they could not change anything about the infinite regression. (They would constitute inadequate rationalist attempts to introduce the truth of universal empirical statements into probability logic by the back door.) But they are also untenable in themselves, for the probabilities of higher-order hypotheses simply cannot be more certain than those of a lower order. If the hypothesis is refuted by experience, then the probabilities of all orders will be equal to zero.

This infinite regression of probability statements is possibly even more awkward for inductivism than Hume's argument. This latter still left the dogmatic adoption of a principle of induction as a way out; if one takes the position that empirical statements (and thus any principle of induction) can have *only* a probable degree of validity, then no [apriorist] principle of induction will help.

Probable validity can be expressed only by a universal empirical statement of a higher type, which in turn should, of course, be valid only with a certain probability; therein consists the inescapable infinite regression of the probability position; but all dogmatic-rationalist attempts at making probability logic into metaphysics also break down in this way. Of this kind is, for example, Reichenbach's[1] attempt to declare the principle of induction acceptable because probability logic without a principle of induction would be meaningless (indeed, because even in general "probability statements are not meaningful if we do not already presuppose the principle of induction";[2] yet, natural science cannot do without probability logic as a "conceptual framework for all knowledge of nature in general".[3] This (transcendental) motivation fails its purpose. Probability logic makes no sense even in the presence of a principle of induction.

One might think that the infinite regression of probability statements is, nevertheless, of a somewhat different kind from the infinite regression of induction; that the probability positions may well succeed in avoiding Hume's argument, but that in the process they unexpectedly encounter new difficulties, a new regression. For the regression of induction was a regression of the principles of induction, whereas the regression of probability statements seems to result only from the fact that the probable validity of a statement cannot be expressed by that statement itself.

But this view would be erroneous. This, too, is a case of the regression of induction. The difference in this instance lies only in my somewhat formalistic representation. In order to show this, I will outline another, less formalistic representation of the infinite regression of probability statements.

If we assign to a hypothesis an objective probability value based on observations, then (implicitly or explicitly) we make a presupposition that may be roughly formulated as follows:

"The degree of corroboration of a hypothesis will also give some indication of how well this hypothesis will be corroborated in the future."

---

[1] Hans Reichenbach, "Kausalität und Wahrscheinlichkeit", *Erkenntnis* 1 (1930), pp. 186 ff.
[2] [Hans Reichenbach, *op. cit.*, p. 186. Ed.]
[3] [Hans Reichenbach, *op. cit.*, p. 188. Ed.]

(It should, therefore, not only determine our confidence, but also give us some indication of the objective behaviour of events as yet unknown.)

This statement would be the "principle of probabilistic induction of the first order". Even if it has so far been corroborated, then this can only say something about its objective probability value if we presuppose a corresponding second-order principle, etc.

Hence the infinite regression of probability statements is identical with that of induction. (In the formalistic representation, the regression becomes an infinite one only because none of the statements of a higher order may be regarded as simply true.)

Whether I assume it to be true that a statement is true, or whether I assume it to be (objectively) probable that a statement is probable, has no bearing on the problem of induction.

Thus, once again, this regression demonstrates to us the following obvious result:

If it were possible to know – with a certain probability – whether the natural laws [so far corroborated] will still hold tomorrow, we could indeed know more than we know. We *cannot* know this; of course we must (so far as we have hitherto observed) *believe* it. To objectify this belief is [dogmatic] rationalism.

Chapter VII

THE PSEUDO-STATEMENT POSITIONS

18. *The pseudo-statement positions: new formulation of the problem.* The preceding considerations allow us to make a generalisation that is decisive for the problem situation.

If a statement is not to be regarded as valid, then this must be expressed by a statement about that statement; regardless of whether that statement is to be called "false" or perhaps "probable", or whether we wish to assign to it any other *truth value whatsoever* (except for the value "true").

Only if this second statement, or some other higher-order statement, can be unconditionally true will the regression stop. However, should none of these statements be considered unconditionally true, then the infinite regression will be inevitable. Putting all these statements together, we have in effect said *nothing*.

As a result, we no longer have any reason to add another truth value to "two-valued logic". (In principle, singular empirical statements must always be definitively verifiable or falsifiable; and such a step can be of no benefit to universal empirical statements.)

Universal empirical statements can never be [demonstrably] true (for science) – this was the result of the critique of normal-statement positions.

They cannot have any [demonstrably] (positive) truth value – this is the essential result of the critique of the probability positions.

Now, from this state of affairs the *pseudo-statement positions* draw the conclusion that natural laws, the "universal empirical statements", are not even *genuine statements*.

While admittedly their linguistic guise is that of "statements", often language is imprecise, frequently creating misunderstanding and pseudo-problems. Generally, "we know . . . from modern logic that the external form of a statement gives us precious little from which to infer its actual logical form".[1] The same holds here.

The statement form of natural laws is only their "grammatical veil". They are not finally verifiable in principle, which is a sure sign that, in a logical sense, they are not statements or propositions. They are "pseudo-statements".

This view, therefore, shares with the normal-statement positions the fundamental presupposition (presented above in the words of Schlick[2]) that it "is essential for a genuine statement . . . [to be] in principle definitively verifiable or falsifiable".

Natural laws are pseudo-statements – inductivism is forced into this position. But what are they, if they are not statements?

Merely maintaining that natural laws cannot be statements, or calling them "pseudo-statements", does not in itself say anything. If nothing more could be said about them, then the theory of knowledge might as well be abandoned. In order to speak at all about a "pseudo-statement position" as a solution to the problem of induction, we need a moderately satisfactory answer to the question: "If natural laws are not statements, then what are they?"

This is the problem situation of the pseudo-statement positions.

The only answer so far available, to my knowledge, was provided by Schlick in his paper "Causality in contemporary physics".[3] This paper (as the title suggests) is concerned primarily with problems in the philosophy of nature, and only in this context does it touch on epistemological questions. It was not Schlick's intention to give a final answer to the question of what natural laws really are (and with it, to the problem of induction). While he

---

[1] Moritz Schlick, "Die Kausalität in der gegenwärtigen Physik", Die Naturwissenschaften 19 (1931), p. 154.

[2] [Moritz Schlick, op. cit., p. 156. Cf. Section 7, text to note 1. Ed.]

[3] Moritz Schlick, op. cit., pp. 145 ff.

THE PSEUDO-STATEMENT POSITIONS 173

does provide a short outline of his view, he does so, as he notes explicitly, "without . . . here . . . being able fully to resolve the apparent paradox".[4]

Although I see this attempt at a solution as the last resort of inductivism, at the same time I regard it as one of its strongest positions.

In order to criticise this position as thoroughly as possible, I shall have to try to follow the arguments outlined by Schlick down to their last implications, search for their connections and independently think them through to the end.

It is important to note this, as it explains why parts of my polemic will be directed against imaginary opponents.

19. *Natural laws as "instructions for the formation of statements"*. The answer given by Schlick[1] to the question "If natural laws are not statements, then what are they?", is "that a natural law . . . does not have the logical character of a 'statement', but that it represents an 'instruction for the formation of statements' ". He adds: "I owe this idea and this phrase to Ludwig Wittgenstein." (To my knowledge, Wittgenstein himself has not yet published this idea.)

What does the idea that natural laws are "instructions for the formation of statements" mean?

In order to understand this position, we need only remind ourselves of the *purposes* that natural laws serve in practical life; this will also clarify their role in the process of gaining knowledge about nature.

The purpose of natural laws is certainly not exhausted by their provision of mere descriptions of nature (if that is what they actually do). At any rate, they are not *only* reports about natural events. Their purpose is also to *assist* us in describing nature.

In our lives we never need the natural law itself; we merely use it in order to infer from singular statements (particular events) other singular statements, with whose help we understand other particular events.[2]

---

[4] Moritz Schlick, *op. cit.*, p. 150.

[1] Moritz Schlick, "Die Kausalität in der gegenwärtigen Physik", *Die Naturwissenschaften* 19 (1931), p. 151.

[2] Cf. Ludwig Wittgenstein, *Tractatus Logico-Philosophicus* (1918/1922), Proposition 6.211 and the following comment: "In philosophy the question, 'What do we actually use this word or this proposition for?' repeatedly leads to valuable insights." [This and all other direct quotations from Wittgenstein's *Tractatus* are taken from the second edition of the English translation by D.F. Pears and B.F. McGuinness, London, 1971. Tr.]

No doubt, we always use natural laws ultimately in order to derive *predictions*. As singular statements, these predictions are definitively verifiable, and so they are unquestionably genuine statements.

That natural laws enable us to formulate singular statements, and in particular predictions, is (as I, too, believe) their most important function, not only in practical life but also in science. Wittgenstein's and Schlick's view that natural laws can be characterised as "instructions for the formation of statements" is, therefore, absolutely correct.

But is this enough to give a satisfactory answer to the question, "What are natural laws if they are not statements?"

I believe that it is not enough. Singular propositions, which without a doubt are genuine statements, may be interpreted as "instructions for the formation of propositions" just as much as natural laws may be.

The fact that natural laws can be used for the formation of singular propositions, which this terminology is designed to emphasise, is usually expressed by saying that predictions can be logically derived, or *deduced*, from natural laws. Natural laws, however, share this characteristic with many singular statements from which we can also deduce other singular statements.

The universal law (to return once more to our old example) that all trajectories are approximately parabolic, may (or must, according to Schlick and Wittgenstein) be understood as an instruction for the formation of singular statements. If an artilleryman wants to calculate, that is, predict, the trajectory of a particular projectile, he will proceed according to the "instruction" and formulate the prediction: "The trajectory of this projectile will have approximately the form of a parabola (more precisely, a ballistic curve)."

But even this prediction, this definitively verifiable singular statement, will in turn serve as an "instruction" helping him to derive the further prediction: "The projectile will strike in this place."

Hence, genuine statements may also be viewed as instructions for the formation of statements. And that natural laws can be understood in this way would seem to support rather than contradict the claim that they are genuine [descriptive] statements.

Schlick[3] rightly notes: "We must not forget that observations and experiments are *actions* through which we enter into direct contact with

---

[3] Moritz Schlick, *op. cit.*, p. 156.

nature. The relationship between reality and ourselves sometimes comes to light in statements that have the grammatical form of propositional expressions, whose real meaning however consists in their being instructions for possible actions."

But all this could also be claimed for singular, certainly genuine, empirical statements just as much as for natural laws. If I say to a guest who is in my house for the first time, "The light switch is on the left in the corner", then this undoubtedly is a genuine statement because it is definitively verifiable. And yet one might well say that its "real meaning" consists in being an "instruction for an action", that it contains a rule or an imperative (indeed, a conditional or hypothetical imperative, a rule for a purposive action), and that it should "really" be: "If you want light, turn the switch in the corner on the left!"

(Kant already knew that all these "hypothetical imperatives", all instructions, "rules of common sense", etc., are nothing but concealed empirical statements, that is, either natural laws or singular predictions.)

Another example of this possibility of transforming statements into imperatives, or of translating them into the "pragmatic" mode (and vice versa), seems to me worth mentioning. The statement "Gaining knowledge is the discovery of law-like regularities" is an analytic judgement, a definition. It can easily be transformed into the (hypothetical) imperative: "If you want to gain knowledge, search for laws!" I can, therefore, regard Schlick's view that the "principle of causality" represents "an invitation or a rule to search for regularities, to describe occurrences through laws",[4] only as a veiled definition of knowledge.

Therefore, if quantum physics – apparently for good reasons – claims that we *cannot know* the location *and* the velocity of an electron with arbitrary precision, that our knowledge, that is, our search for laws, faces certain limitations owing to [Heisenberg's] "uncertainty relations" – then of course we can also translate this into the imperative or pragmatic mode. Schlick[5] provides us with just such a translation into a pragmatic form when he states that the "invitation . . . to describe occurrences through laws" is "within those boundaries . . . useless or pointless, unfulfillable". What Heisenberg's "uncertainty relations" establish is that our knowledge, that is, the discovery of laws, is in principle incomplete.

---

[4] Moritz Schlick, *op. cit.*, p. 155.
[5] Moritz Schlick, *loc. cit.*

This itself is knowledge: the range of incompleteness is demarcated by a *law*.

(This law contains the assertion that the principle of causality is false – if, that is, we want to associate with the term "principle of causality" (Sections 3 and 5) the assertion of complete law-like regularity admitting of no exceptions. And to return to the critique of apriorism: Wittgenstein's "proud thesis of the omnipotence of rational science" (the phrase is Carnap's[6]) proves to be fully equivalent to the Kantian principle of causality. Wittgenstein's[7] thesis, "If a question can be framed at all, it is also *possible* to answer it," is *false* from the standpoint of Heisenberg's relations because the question about the precise state of motion of an electron simply *cannot* be answered. And like the principle of causality, Wittgenstein's thesis can be saved if one*[1] views it as untestable, but thus also as *saying nothing*.)

We can now see that not every arbitrary answer to the question "What are natural laws if they are not statements?" suffices as a satisfactory justification of a pseudo-statement position. We must, above all, demand a demonstration that the constructs with which natural laws are to be identified are, indeed, *not genuine statements*; that they are not merely apparent pseudo-statements concealing genuine statements that can be true or false.

This requirement will turn out to be extremely important in what follows. It has, at any rate, become evident here that merely pointing to the undoubtedly practical functions of natural laws, to their pragmatic, imperative or instructional character, does not suffice to establish the pseudo-statement character of natural laws.

I do, nevertheless, consider this indication valuable. It can perhaps direct our attention to where a solution may be sought.

Natural laws and singular empirical statements are – there can be no doubt about this – two different classes of logical constructs (not to say, of statements).

It might well be that what these two classes of constructs have in *common* is precisely that they can be understood as instructions for the formation

---

[6] [Rudolf Carnap, *Der logische Aufbau der Welt* (1928), p. 261. Ed.]

[7] [Ludwig Wittgenstein, *Tractatus Logico-Philosophicus* (1918/1922), Proposition 6.5. Ed.]

*[1] Better: ". . . if one . . . rejects the question about the precise state of motion of an electron as meaningless". (It is "not even possible to pose this question".)

of statements, or as practical rules. This would, then, point the way towards a closer definition of natural laws. Natural laws would be those instructions for the formation of statements, which (in contrast to instructions that are themselves statements) have *specific properties* that still need to be further determined.

What are these properties?

20. *"True – false"* or *"useful – useless"? Consistent pragmatism.* According to the pseudo-statement positions, the specific properties of "genuine" statements consist in their being definitively verifiable or falsifiable. We should, obviously, search for the specific properties of natural laws on this same level.

Thus, Schlick[1] says of a natural law:

"Such an instruction is not true or false, but good or bad, useful or useless."

This, I believe, sums up the basic idea of the pseudo-statement positions. It is in principle impossible to assign to natural laws *any truth value at all* (even a *negative* one in the event of their "falsification"), but purely and simply a *practical value.*

It is the case that there must, at any rate, be particular positive and negative values to be assigned to natural laws. For science *discards* laws while others are maintained (at least for some time). Demonstrating the inadequacy of laws and replacing them with better ones, this is what the progress of science consists in.

But how does science arrive at its decisions, and how does it justify its appraisals?

It is the fate of *predictions* that determines the appraisal of the natural laws from which the predictions were derived. For this reason alone we would be right to regard the formation of predictions as the fundamental function of natural laws.

From natural laws we derive statements concerning events about which we know nothing; that is, prophecies, forecasts, predictions. If the prophecy comes true, if the prediction is verified, then we shall also assign a *positive value* to the natural law. If the prediction is falsified, then we shall consider this a failure of the natural law.

---

[1] Moritz Schlick, "Die Kausalität in der gegenwärtigen Physik", *Die Naturwissenschaften* 19 (1931), p. 155.

The appraisal of a natural law is determined by its *adequacy* with respect to the derivation of true predictions. This is the basis for the view that the appraisal of natural laws is a purely practical, pragmatic affair. A natural law is *useful* for the derivation of predictions if the prediction is *true*; it is *useless* if the prediction turns out to be *false*.

The interpretation of natural laws as "instructions for the formation of statements" does, then, contain an important clue (although on its own it is too indeterminate). Natural laws are defined as a class of "instructions" that do not, as such, have any direct truth value, indeed not even any cognitive value, but that do have a *practical value* for the derivation of predictions. Their role in the cognitive process and their value for knowledge are purely pragmatic.

This view is a consistent synthesis of positivism and pragmatism.

As in the case of strict positivism, it acknowledges only statements about what can be experienced. But it takes account of the fact that science cannot manage with these statements alone. Therefore, it adds to these "genuine" statements the "pseudo-statements" of natural laws, which it regards as purely pragmatic constructs.

However, whereas pragmatism tends to equate usefulness with truth (indeed, it seeks to explain truth in terms of usefulness; cf. Section 16), the "pseudo-statement position" makes everything depend on the existence of an irreconcilable opposition between usefulness and truth, between pragmatic value and truth value.

Validity is timeless (as already emphasised in Section 16). If a statement is true, it is true finally, once and for all. By contrast, *pragmatic value* or usefulness always depends on the specific *purpose* and may change from case to case.

These conclusions seem to apply very well to natural laws, as their appraisal can never be definitive, depending as it does in each case on the verification of the predictions.

While the pseudo-statement position is positivist with respect to "genuine" statements, it represents a particularly radical form of pragmatism with respect to natural laws (which for the problem of induction are, of course, the most relevant). In this analysis (in which only the problem of induction is taken into account) I will call this position, according to which everything depends on the opposition between truth value and pragmatic value, "consistent pragmatism".

Is this position really tenable? Is the opposition really irreconcilable?

21. *Difficulties of consistent pragmatism.* A variety of examples could be given of the conflict between pragmatic value and truth value.

A particularly striking example is that of a lie. If a lie fulfils its purpose, then a *false* statement has proved to be *useful*; for this [its] purpose it is, to say the very least, more useful than the (known) true statement.

The role played by "fiction" (in Vaihinger's[1] sense) in the cognitive process would be analogous, that is, a consciously made false assumption that is valuable for knowledge as a "heuristic principle". In fact, science can be stimulated in a most fruitful way by an error or by a false statement.

A *false* statement may thus be *useful*, even for the purposes of knowledge – certainly a convincing argument for the independence of truth value and pragmatic value, on which consistent pragmatism relies.

Despite these and other examples, there remain problems for the consistent-pragmatist position that need to be discussed. In my view, only if these difficulties are overcome can consistent pragmatism be seriously considered as a solution to the problem of induction.

I agree with Schlick when he writes that "it is truly difficult and requires deep reflection to comprehend the difference between a true statement and a useful rule, and between a false statement and a useless rule".[2]

But (unlike Schlick) I do not see the origin of these problems in the fact that these "instructions . . . [appear] grammatically in the guise of ordinary statements";[3] this (like the so-called "language critique" in general) would not pose a very serious problem.

The real problems are related instead to the observation (cf. Section 19) that genuine statements could always appear in pragmatic translation as "instructions".

In these cases, the pragmatic values "useful" and "useless" (that are to be attributed to these "instructions") usually turn out to be simply translations of the truth values "true" and "false". Therein lies the problem.

Admittedly, such translatability applies not to those "rules" that regulate the interaction between individuals (that is, to laws in the legal sense);

---

[1] [Hans Vaihinger, *Die Philosophie des Als Ob* (3rd ed., 1918). Ed.]

[2] Moritz Schlick, "Die Kausalität in der gegenwärtigen Physik", *Die Naturwissenschaften* 19 (1931), pp. 155 f.

[3] [Moritz Schlick, *op. cit.*, p. 156. Ed.]

but to those (particular) rules concerning "*actions* . . ., through which we engage in direct interaction with nature".[4] Only those rules are of concern here, and they can usually be readily translated.

This may be illustrated by the examples in Section 19. The instruction "If you want light, turn the switch in the corner on the left!" proves to be *useful* if my guest finds the switch and turns on the light. Of course, one could equally well say that through this action my guest has verified the genuine statement, or prediction ("If the switch in the corner on the left is turned, the light will come on"), which in its pragmatic translation would be the "instruction".

To take the other example, suppose the artilleryman who wants to calculate in advance the place where a projectile will strike uses the (particular) instruction that this projectile will follow the trajectory of an exact parabola (instead of a ballistic curve, which, in the case of heavy artillery, deviates considerably from a parabola); if he does so, he will find that this instruction for the prediction of the point of impact is *useless*; once again, this means precisely that the corresponding (genuine) statement "the trajectory of this projectile will have exactly the form of a parabola" has proved to be *false*.

While it is quite correct that pragmatic values and truth values can indeed, under certain conditions, be independent of each other, these examples show that in other cases, pragmatic values and truth values may [be dependent on each other and, indeed,] be virtually *identical*.

Moreover, a true statement is always practically useful for certain purposes; that is, at least for cognitive purposes, namely as an instruction for its own verification. A false statement is likewise always*[1] useless in a practical sense (for the same purposes). (There are, of course, always other purposes for which a particular true statement is totally useless, and so on.) Particularly when testing or verification is required, the pragmatic value always depends on the truth value.

The same applies to the evaluation of natural laws. They will be evaluated positively or as useful if the derived predictions are true; and negatively or as useless if the predictions are false.

---

[4] Moritz Schlick, *loc. cit.*
*[1] "Always" is incorrect: from a false statement both true and false predictions *can* be derived.

Now, we have already established in this analysis that a natural law must never be assigned the truth value "true", since its truth can in principle never be finally decided. It is equally certain that as long as it proves "useful", a positive pragmatic value may well be assigned to it, for pragmatic values can be adopted *tentatively* and can be revised from case to case.

However, what all this really shows is *only* how flexible and imprecise pragmatic values are. It can by no means be considered a sufficient proof of the "pseudo-statement character" of a logical construct that the latter *can* be assigned a pragmatic value. The pragmatic mode of expression must, in general, be treated with great caution. We shall have to examine the pseudo-statement positions very carefully to ascertain whether in fact *only those* pragmatic values that are definitely not truth values in disguise, or mere translations of the values "true" and "false" into [the] pragmatic mode of expression, are assigned to the former's "instructions for the formation of statements" (natural laws as they are used in science).

These problems of "consistent pragmatism" are related to the unreliability of pragmatist terminology, which seems hardly fit for the attainment of "consistency". They compel us to return once more to the question of whether it might not be possible to indicate more clearly what, according to this position, natural laws actually are.

What route should we follow towards a more precise definition?

In the following section I shall suggest a route that initially appears quite feasible. We shall have to examine it, if only because various remarks by logical positivists refer to it. It is the view that natural laws are so-called "propositional functions" (or perhaps also instructions for the use of propositional functions).

This route will, however, turn out to be in the nature of a somewhat protracted detour. It leads to new problems, and (after generating some positive secondary results) will ultimately fail to take us significantly beyond the reservations already expressed. We shall have to return once more to the somewhat vacillating position of pragmatism that we have already reached. Only in Section 36 will we embark again on the straight road of a critical investigation of the problem of induction.

Unfortunately, the unavoidable polemic will force me, in the intervening Sections 23 to 35, to introduce a rather difficult terminology (that of "logistic"*²) and to discuss in detail specific logical questions that might, not unreasonably, be felt to be hair-splitting. It will be an unavoidable critique of certain logistical subtleties, and in order to rebut them I shall sometimes even have to stray away from the topic. However, of these terminological and logical comments only the discussion of "implication"*³ in Section 31 is of any significance for the deductivist-empiricist view of the problem of induction.

22. *Tool and schema as purely pragmatic constructs.* Which route could we follow in order to find a satisfactory answer to the question of what natural laws actually are – in the sense intended by the pseudo-statement position, or by a consistent form of pragmatism?

We should have to look for characteristic and typical constructs that can, in principle, be evaluated only pragmatically, that is, where there can be no question of their practical values being simply truth values in disguise.

If such constructs can be identified, and if they can justifiably be placed alongside natural laws, then perhaps a step has been taken towards a more precise definition of the peculiar character of natural laws, and thus also towards a more precise rendering of the somewhat uncertain position of consistent pragmatism.

I take *tools* to be such purely pragmatic constructs. A tool exists *only* to render purely practical services in specific cases. A hammer or a pair of pliers can never have anything like an absolute truth value. The value of a particular tool always depends on its suitability for a particular purpose to which it happens to be put. Its suitability may, therefore, change from case to case. In addition, there are also tools that serve specifically cognitive purposes, such as apparatus, measuring devices and instruments, which

---

*² The discussion in my *Two Fundamental Problems* is strongly influenced by Rudolf Carnap's *Abriß der Logistik* (1929), a truly excellent textbook of mathematical logic, which, however, became outdated very soon as a result of developments in this field, in particular by the work of Kurt Gödel and Alfred Tarski. Even the terminology of Carnap's *Abriß* is now rarely used, including the term "logistic" (for "mathematical logic").

*³ In *Principia Mathematica* by Alfred North Whitehead and Bertrand Russell, a conditional statement (If . . . then statement) is not clearly distinguished from a logical inference; it is therefore called "implication". Carnap's *Abriß* takes the same position.

are of great practical value for the "formation of genuine empirical statements". Moreover, the value of such instruments, just like that of natural laws, depends on the truth of the statements that are derived with their help; which, however, does not in any sense imply that these instruments themselves should consequently be assigned a truth value.

The analogy, that is, the appeal to the pragmatic character of instruments or tools, seems, in this respect, to be quite suitable for the purposes of consistent pragmatism.

Now, it might still appear questionable whether intellectual [or] logical constructs, such as natural laws, can be compared with tools or with material research instruments. However, I consider these reservations unjustified. There are also intellectual, *logical tools*, namely logical schemata, which may well be compared with material tools.

If, for example, a physicist wants to evaluate a sequence of experimental observations, he usually employs various "schemata". He begins by producing empty tables, empty schemata, that are filled in according to a certain schematically determined procedure. The data that are inserted in the schema are acquired through observations that also follow a certain schematically determined procedure.

Such a schema may be set up in a practical or impractical fashion, it may be useful or useless, but in itself it is never knowledge, never a statement. It is an instrument, a kind of shelf for genuine statements; in itself it is *empty*, it cannot have a truth value.

We use such schemata – intellectual devices, logical tools – in the most diverse fields. Anyone who wants to write a scientific treatise will utilise an outline – a schema that is not true or false like the content of the treatise, but appropriate, clear, applicable and useful.

Such schemata may also play an important part in the formation of scientific concepts, in particular in all *systematic classifications*. Systematic botany and systematic zoology can be regarded as classificatory schemata that cannot be called true or false, but only useful or useless, unified or incoherent (and which, in addition, may or may not fulfil certain purposes, such as that of indicating natural kinship relations).

If it could be shown that natural laws may also be viewed as schemata in this sense, then the problems posed for consistent pragmatism by the mutual translatability of true statements and useful rules would at least be partially solved.

23. *Natural laws as propositional functions.* The possibility of natural laws being logical schemata needs to be more closely examined; all the more so, since there are in fact typical logical schemata that may very well be understood as "schemata for the formation of statements" (though not as "rules" in Schlick's sense). These are the so-called "propositional functions", which play quite an important role in the new logic ("logistic").

What is a propositional function?

A (simple) statement, such as the sentence "Napoleon carried a sword", is true or false only as an *integral whole*. A *fragment* of this statement – whatever it may be – is not itself a statement, it can no longer be called true or false. Now, if we compare this statement with certain other, *similarly constructed* statements (such as "Napoleon wore a hat" or "Mozart carried a sword"), we can see that the statement has various components that can be viewed as relatively independent, namely as independently *exchangeable*.

A *propositional function* can now be more precisely explained as the *fragment* of a statement that remains when one or more independently exchangeable components are deleted from the statement. The "blanks" ("argument spaces"), that is, the places at which a component has been deleted, must somehow be marked (such as by "..." or "x"), for example, "... carried a sword" or "x carried a sword".

In other words, the statement fragments "x carried a sword" or "x carried y" are called *propositional functions*.

It is a fact that such propositional functions *cannot be true or false*. They can only be used as a *schema* for the formation of statements by the insertion of suitable argument values (proper names or universal concepts) into the blanks. In this way, a propositional function is again transformed into a statement that may be true or false.

Thus in the propositional function "x wore y", for example, we could insert the argument "Caesar" for x and "a toga" for y. This creates a statement that is (probably) true. But we may just as easily create a false statement if, for example, we insert "Caesar" for x and "tails" for y.

All (genuine) statements that are created in this fashion, and all the examples presented above, are "similarly constructed". They are constructed according to the same schema, that is, they are based on the same propositional function.

As a "schema for the formation of statements" that cannot itself have any truth value whatever, the propositional function ("statement-function") should never be confused with a statement.

All propositional functions are fragments of statements. They have "blanks" or "argument spaces". The signs marking the blanks are entirely arbitrary. Instead of letters, one could use points or crosses or circles. These signs are often referred to as "variables", in order to indicate that in these spaces different arguments may be inserted. The arguments inserted in the blanks are often referred to as the "values that the variable assumes". But these are only metaphorical forms of expression. One should not forget that "variables", such as "x" or "y", are not signs that refer to any object; they are only "*place-holders*", they mean *nothing* by themselves.

If a propositional function has more than one blank, for instance, "x wore y", then it is of course impossible to say of a single argument (for example, "Caesar") whether it *satisfies* the propositional function (that is, whether its substitution transforms the propositional function into a *true statement*) or does not satisfy it (that is, whether it transforms it into a *false statement*). Only if a *pair of values* is given (for instance, "Caesar" and "toga") can we say whether or not the function is satisfied. The same holds analogously for propositional functions with three or more argument spaces, for example, the propositional function "in temperatures between . . . degrees and . . . degrees, the chemical compound . . . assumes the colour . . .", a propositional function that might serve as a schema for observation. We frequently use similar schemata that through the substitution of several arguments produce true or false statements (for instance, "Mr x lives in the city of y at no. w, z street").

All this is quite simple. But it may not yet be completely clear how these propositional functions are supposed to be related to natural laws.

I shall try to show (with the help of a repeatedly used example) that quite close relationships can be established between natural laws and propositional functions.

Let us carry out an experiment by throwing a number of stones. The individual throws are numbered. (The numbers may be regarded as the proper names of the throws.) The trajectory of each throw will be precisely determined by measurements (for example, with the aid of a film played back in slow motion).

Thus, I throw a stone (throw 1) and find that its trajectory has approximately the shape of a parabola. I can therefore formulate the (singular) statement: "The trajectory that the stone has just traced in throw 1 has approximately the shape of a parabola", or more briefly: "The trajectory of throw 1 is a parabola."

After throws "2" and "3" and the corresponding measurements, I can derive analogous statements concerning these throws. Now I find that these statements are based on the same schema, and that the numbers of the throws (as well as all the information about the stones, the time and the location) are independently exchangeable.

Instead of now making an (impermissible) generalisation, or an induction, I isolate the propositional function on which the statements are based: "The trajectory of throw x is a parabola."

As I already know, this propositional function is *satisfied* by the arguments "1", "2" and "3"; in other words, through the substitution of these arguments it produces *true statements*. I cannot know yet whether other argument values such as "4", "5", etc. will also satisfy my propositional function. I can, however, now use the propositional function as a schema in order to formulate genuine statements by the substitution of these arguments; more specifically – since I do not yet know whether these genuine statements are true or false – I can formulate *predictions*. I can then verify or falsify these predictions.

Should natural laws, perhaps, be identified with propositional functions (say, of the type "The trajectory of throw x is a parabola")?

It is a most attractive solution for the pseudo-statement positions to approach natural laws as propositional functions. There is, in fact, a passage in Carnap[1] in which he seems to be alluding to the position according to which natural laws should be viewed as propositional functions. It reads:

"Is a state of affairs referred to by a propositional function or by a statement? Here a distinction is necessary: *individual* states of affairs are to be expressed by statements, *universal states of affairs* by propositional functions. Linguistic expressions do not distinguish precisely between these two types." Carnap then states that at this point of his study he is dealing with *universal states of affairs*, adding (in parentheses): "The same holds for states of affairs that occur in natural laws."

It is possible[*1] that Carnap is advocating the position according to which natural laws are propositional functions. (I suspect that Schlick

---

[1] Rudolf Carnap, *Der logische Aufbau der Welt* (1928), pp. 65 f.

[*1] "Possible" may have been a little too cautious; I could have written "here evidently". Elsewhere (*Abriß der Logistik*, 1929, 6c, p. 14) Carnap says that laws are represented by "general implications" – hence not by statement functions, but by statements.

and Wittgenstein do not take this position. The view that natural laws are propositional functions is close to an epistemological position that Schlick explicitly – and in my opinion rightly – rejects: so-called *conventionalism*.)

Here we can, in any event, retain, as one possible pseudo-statement position, the view that natural laws can be understood simply as propositional functions. The appraisal of natural laws through the sciences would then be a purely pragmatic matter. The propositional function "The trajectory of throw x is a hyperbola" would, for example, be a *useless schema*, while "The trajectory of throw x is a parabola" would be a *useful schema for the making of predictions*.

This pseudo-statement position, that is, the view that natural laws are propositional functions – it will, in what follows, be briefly referred to as [the] *first pseudo-statement position* – seems to be quite simple and plausible. At first glance, it does not appear that this view could give rise to special epistemological problems.

But those who know the epistemological discussion concerning what is referred to as conventionalism, and have followed the debate between conventionalism and empiricism, will notice that all the objections raised by the empiricist critique of conventionalism can be raised also against the conception of natural laws as propositional functions, [that is] against the first pseudo-statement position.

Conventionalism and most of its empiricist critics (including, for example, Feigl) do not, however, share the basic assumptions of the pseudo-statement positions, but rather see natural laws as *genuine statements*.

In order to put in sharp relief the problems of the pseudo-statement position that regards natural laws as propositional functions, I will now leave the analysis of the pseudo-statement positions. I will move to a presentation of conventionalism and a comparison between conventionalist and empiricist views. Later in my analysis, I will contrast these views with the first pseudo-statement position, which interprets natural laws as propositional functions.

Chapter VIII

CONVENTIONALISM

24. *The pseudo-statement positions will temporarily be put away: conventionalism.* Conventionalism regards natural laws as *genuine statements*. Therefore, it is not *a pseudo-statement position*.

In contrast to all previously discussed views, conventionalism is *deductivist*: this is one reason why it is of interest. Discussing it does not, however, properly belong to a critical analysis of the inductivist positions.

Conventionalism is distinguished from the deductivist and empiricist theory of knowledge (which I advocate) above all by the fact that it must be characterised as *non-empiricist*. According to the conventionalist view, *experience cannot* decide the truth or falsity of natural laws. According to conventionalism, natural laws are *analytic judgements* because they are (hidden) *definitions*, arbitrary stipulations, "conventions".

Although conventionalism is not empiricist, it cannot be characterised as rationalist, either. While according to conventionalism, natural laws are *a priori* valid, they are *not* synthetic *a priori* judgements since they are not *empirical statements* at all. They are analytic judgements (mere conceptual analyses); and the *a priori* validity of analytic judgements is, after all, undisputed.

The presentation of the conventionalist view in the following sections will go only as far as is necessary to facilitate discussion of the pseudo-statement positions; and only for this purpose will conventionalism also be compared with *empiricist* views.

This comparison is designed only to prepare the continuation of the discussion and critique of the pseudo-statement positions, to be resumed in Section 36. The comparison itself is not part of this discussion. This is why those forms of empiricism that regard natural laws as pseudo-statements (Schlick, for example, advocates such an *empiricist* pseudo-statement position) will not appear in it. Rather, conventionalism will here only be compared with those empiricist views that regard natural laws as *genuine statements*.

With the help of these two opposing views – conventionalism and empiricism (in so far as the latter regards natural laws as *genuine statements*) – I intend to narrow down, as it were, the pseudo-statement positions; I want to draw certain boundaries that the pseudo-statement positions cannot transgress without abandoning the thesis of the pseudo-statement character of natural laws (and thus, without undermining themselves).

A fundamental, conclusive critique of conventionalism will not be attempted here. Suggestions for such a critique will, of course, be found in the subsequent sections. However, a fundamental critique of conventionalism will emerge only from the discussion of the demarcation problem.[1]

The point of departure of conventionalist philosophy is its amazement at the apparent *simplicity of the world* that is revealed to us in natural laws.

The simplicity, on the grand scale, of natural laws, says the conventionalist, would be most miraculous if the laws were to be understood in the way that (according to conventionalism) an empiricist must understand them; that is, as revealing to us an internal simplicity of the world which in its external appearance is so diverse and complex.

Whereas theological metaphysics recognises the work of God in this simplicity, and whereas Kant's apriorism explains it by saying that our understanding necessarily prescribes its laws to nature, the conventionalist says:

This simplicity is, indeed, a work of our understanding, but it is a *free creation* that does not imprint itself on nature. For it is not nature that is

---

[1] [Cf. Vol. II (Fragments): [III.] *Transition to the Theory of Method*; [V.] *Outline of a Theory of Empirical-Scientific Methods (Theory of Experience)*. See also Editor's Postscript. Ed.]

simple, only natural *laws* are. We do not, therefore, prescribe the forms of our understanding to nature, but we invent a rational natural *science*.

This science is not a copy of nature, but a purely conceptual construction. Natural laws are not determined by the properties of reality; they determine the properties of an artificial conceptual world that we have created. These concepts do not refer to real events and objects; they are, on the contrary, *defined* by natural laws. From these definitions, all further properties of the world follow – but of course not of the real world, but of the simplified, abstract, conceptual world of which alone theoretical natural science speaks.

Thus, conventionalism regards natural laws not as empirical statements or synthetic judgements, but only as purely conceptual constructs, hidden definitions, *analytic* judgements.

How is this to be understood? Above all: how can a judgement be analytic without being obviously so?

An analytic judgement is one that does not state more about a concept than is already contained in the *definition* of that concept.

At times one still encounters the naive view*[1] according to which a definition can be correct or incorrect in the sense that it more or less adequately reflects the "essence" of a concept. Thus, one might claim that it is part of the concept of "body" that it is extended, but not that it is heavy. According to this view, a "body" should perhaps be defined as "a three-dimensional, completely circumscribed region of space". By contrast, a definition that determines a "body" as a spatial region filled by a ponderable substance, or perhaps even a definition that attributes to a "body" only two dimensions, would be *false*; it would not properly reflect the "essence" of the concept "body".

It must be emphasised with respect to such a view that definitions are *in principle arbitrary*. In science there are *no quarrels about words* [or there should be no such quarrels].

Admittedly, it is true that according to *conventional terminology*, two-dimensional things are referred to as surfaces, "plane figures" or something of this sort, but not as "bodies". But if someone wants to use the term "body" instead of the term "figure", we would not necessarily object

---

*[1] I have later called this view "essentialism", or "essentialist philosophy". [Cf. Section 35, note *1. Ed.]

provided that his terminology is sufficiently clearly established and unambiguously employed.

A terminology can be useful or useless for a given purpose, it can be simple or complicated, and above all it can be unambiguous or contradictory, but it cannot be true or false,*² or correct or incorrect, since from a logical viewpoint it is always arbitrary, always conventional. For a concept is created only by its definition; only through a definition does a symbol receive its particular meaning.

Now, a judgement is called "analytic" if it does not state more about a concept than is already contained in its definition. An analytic judgement as a mere analysis of a definition does not require experience: it is *a priori* valid. If a judgement contains more than is implied by the definitions of its concepts, then it is called "synthetic".² Without having precise definitions we cannot possibly say, in some cases, whether a particular linguistically formulated statement is analytic or synthetic.

For example, the statement "All bodies are heavy" should be called analytic if by definition I understand a "body" ("physical body") to be a region of space filled by ponderable matter. The same sequence of words should be seen as a synthetic judgement if by "body" I want to understand no more than, say, a completely circumscribed three-dimensional region of space.

This does not, however, imply that *the same judgement* can be understood as analytic or as synthetic. From a logical point of view they are two different judgements, since two different concepts occur in them that happen to be referred to by the same word.

Thus, if precise definitions of the concepts used are available, we should be able to specify for each judgement whether it is analytic or synthetic. Conversely, by establishing whether a judgement is analytic or synthetic, we can implicitly indicate how the concepts used should be defined.

When Kant,³ for example, calls the statement "All bodies are extended" analytic, and the statement "All bodies are heavy" synthetic, we can conclude that he does not want the concept of "body" to be defined in such a

---

*² However, a little further below definitions will be subsumed under analytic judgements; and this makes them into analytically true statements.

² Cf. on this and on the following, Moritz Schlick, *Allgemeine Erkenntnislehre* (2nd ed., 1925), § 11.

³ [Immanuel Kant, *Kritik der reinen Vernunft* (2nd ed., 1787), pp. 11 f. Ed.; English translation by N. Kemp Smith (1929), 1965: *Critique of Pure Reason*, pp. 48 f. Tr.]

way that the predicate "filled with ponderable matter" is incorporated in it. Through this remark, Kant implicitly gives a kind of (incomplete) definition of the concept "body".

In this way, *every analytic judgement* can be viewed as a kind of (incomplete, partial) *implicit definition* of the concepts occurring in it. (Here I will not pursue the question of whether definitions are judgements at all, since it is irrelevant to the discussion. I regard definitions, including explicit ones, as a kind of analytic judgement; or, if you prefer, I *define* analytic judgements here in such a way that they include definitions.)

Now, such analytic judgements, or such implicit definitions of the concepts occurring in them, are regarded by conventionalism as *natural laws*.

I shall use, as a simple illustration, the physicist's concept of force. (Although this concept is not indispensable for physics, I use it because it is most suited to an explanation of conventionalism.)

According to conventionalism, the Galilean–Newtonian law of inertia, "A body maintains its state of rest or of uniform rectilinear motion unless the influence of a *force* alters this state", may well be viewed as an implicit definition of the concept of "force". Accordingly, the explicit definition is usually "Force is the cause of a change in the state of motion". Of course, as an implicit definition this statement would in any case be valid, that is, *a priori* valid. Whenever a body changes its state of motion, the cause must by definition be a *force*.

But the other concepts as well, in particular the concept "motion", obtain their precise meaning only through natural laws.

According to the customary view, the concept of motion, in particular that of uniform rectilinear motion, must be defined with the aid of measuring rods and clocks (that is, with the help of a space-time system of measurement).

In contrast, conventionalism views natural laws (thus also the law of inertia) as an implicit definition of the concept of motion (in the case of the law of inertia: as an implicit definition of the concept of uniform rectilinear motion) and thus also as an implicit definition of the space-time system of measurement.

Here the contrast between a "*concrete*" or "*empirical*" *definition* and an *implicit definition by means of natural laws* clearly emerges.

According to the customary view, measuring rods can be "concretely" or "empirically" defined; for example, a "measure of distance" could be defined as "what is determined by two marks fixed on a rigid body".

A measure of time, a "clock", as we know, can only be determined with the help of a periodic motion (with the help of a rhythmic division of time). As a "natural clock", as a concrete definition of a measure of time, it is best*³ to use the motion of the sun (rotation of the earth).

If one were to determine a space-time system of measurement by this kind of definition, the system would *not* be defined by natural laws, it would not be implicitly defined. The concrete concepts denoting real things or objects could then appear in natural laws, they could be *assigned*, through concrete definitions, to the corresponding concepts occurring in natural laws ("assignment definition"). Natural laws in which these externally defined concepts occur would then be synthetic statements (if they state more than is specified by the definitions of these concepts).

But conventionalism (Poincaré) asserts that in defining a space-time system of measurement, we only *apparently* proceed in this fashion. In fact, we set up the *measuring instruments* in such a way that they meet the requirements of natural laws (thus also the law of inertia), and not the other way round. The measuring rod as a concrete instrument is only apparently the "measure of all things"; in fact, we presuppose the natural laws and on their basis determine the properties of the measuring rods.

We know that we have to make certain *adjustments* to measuring rods and clocks (also to the rotation of the earth as a clock); we have, for example, to assume that "rigid bodies" expand when heated. As a result, however, we have abandoned the concrete definition (and are therefore presupposing something else as the ultimate, crucial definition).

What would happen if we did not make those adjustments in our measuring instruments?

We would then define the measuring rods concretely, and our *experience* tells us that if we were to measure the motion of a body with such an unadjusted measuring rod, the laws we would discover in this way would be far more complicated than the natural laws we prefer to have. (For example, they would be dependent on the temperature of this measuring rod.) While those laws would, indeed, be empirical statements

*³ This was written in about 1930. Nowadays better clocks are available. However, three paragraphs below it will be noted that certain adjustments also have to be made to "the rotation of the earth as a clock"; moreover, further below the possibility of "atomic clocks" will be pointed out.

or synthetic judgements, we would be faced with having to make all kinds of adjustments to these *laws* (in a rather opaque fashion) rather than to our measuring instruments.

The following point will be crucial for the whole set of problems raised by conventionalist arguments. We can *either* define concepts explicitly, say, by means of concrete empirical definitions with reference to particular natural events, then coordinate these definitions with the concepts occurring in natural laws. In this case, we shall have to wait and see what experience tells us about the laws that can be formulated with the help of these concepts. Moreover, we simply cannot know whether we shall be able to discover laws at all, and if we do, whether they will be *simple*; that is, we do not know whether we can *gain knowledge*. (As a result, we are confronted with all the difficulties of the problem of induction.)

Or, *alternatively* – and this is the path taken by conventionalism – we establish certain natural laws (which *roughly* correspond to certain empirical statements) by definition or by convention, and we define the concepts occurring in them by demanding that they satisfy these laws; that is, we define them implicitly. We shall then probably find that there exist in nature no objects or events corresponding to the concepts defined in this arbitrary fashion. For example, we can never actualise, in nature, a motion in strict conformity with the law of inertia (a pure force-free motion); similarly, there is no completely accurate clock (conventionalism does not yet take into account the "atomic clock", which, however, in no way provides a decisive argument against it), and there is no measuring rod that would work anywhere without adjustment. But we can artificially produce all this (on the basis of implicit definitions by means of natural laws) by creating "models" that come very close to satisfying the strictly implicitly defined, or ideal, concepts. Any deviation will simply be adjusted with the help of natural laws. (Such a model of an ideal measuring rod would be the Paris "standard metre", or the chronometers that are constantly corrected, etc.) These "models", in effect all scientific measuring instruments, represent attempts to put together constructs that correspond, with a high degree of precision, to the ideal, implicitly defined concepts occurring in natural laws. They are attempts to *realise* ideal concepts. According to this view, natural laws are thus absolute, *a priori* true statements from which there *can* be no deviation, since any deviation would only show that the measuring instrument in question is not a "model" of the corresponding concept in natural laws, that is, it is not even suitable for detecting a deviation. In short, natural laws are analytic judgements.

Therefore, the two possibilities are: either concepts are concretely defined through "coordinative definitions", concepts that subsume real things or objects being assigned to natural laws (empiricism). In this case, natural laws will be synthetic empirical statements and might become very complicated. Or (conventionalism) natural laws are established in a *simple* form. In that case, concepts are implicitly defined, and relating them to reality may become very complicated. (Construction of "models" of concepts.)

Conventionalism appeals to the fact that we actually always take the second route. We always search for *simple* laws.

During the whole process of gaining knowledge about nature, we are guided by considerations of what is useful for our purposes. Such considerations are also decisive for conventions, or definitions. This is, of course, why we search for the kinds of conventions that are not excessively difficult to coordinate with reality ("model construction"). This is essentially what all progress in science consists in (according to the conventionalist view). Other conventions would, in principle, also be feasible; but we select those that prove in practice to be simple, or useful.

This sums up the view of conventionalism. It was originally developed (in a less radical fashion) by Poincaré. In Duhem's work in particular, it becomes evident that conventionalism is actually purely *deductivist*. This is, in fact, quite obvious. If the basic principles of natural science are definitions or arbitrary conventions, then they cannot be "induced"; everything follows deductively from them, and a relationship with reality can be established only by deduction.

Of course, conventionalism does not as such recognise *verification and falsification*, since all statements of the system, like its basic principles, must be *a priori* true.

In this context, I would like to refer especially to Viktor Kraft's book, *Die Grundformen der wissenschaftlichen Methoden*. While Kraft's work is, in some respects, very close to conventionalism, it should nevertheless be viewed as representing an intermediate stage between deductivist conventionalism and deductivist empiricism. It is, at any rate, radically deductivist (the method of science is essentially "hypothetical-deductive") and it also acknowledges the method of verification.[4] As far as I can tell, Kraft directly anticipates the deductivist-empiricist position that I advocate.

(I believe that it is only by explicitly formulating and resolving the two fundamental problems of the theory of knowledge that I move significantly beyond Kraft, who makes rather far-reaching concessions to the "probability positions".[5] For example, in the context of the problem of induction, that is, the question concerning the *validity* of natural laws, I establish the simple fact that natural laws cannot have *any positive truth value*, but *only a negative one*.) Duhem and Kraft are probably the most important defenders of the deductivist modes of thought in the modern theory of knowledge.

In addition to its deductivist aspect, conventionalism is also of interest for its pragmatist aspect. The choice between various possible conventions is made according to the pragmatic standard of usefulness.

25. *The three interpretations of axiomatic systems. (The circle of problems surrounding conventionalism.)* My basic objective in presenting the group of problems surrounding conventionalism is to be able to shed more light on the "first pseudo-statement position", which regards natural laws as propositional functions.

In this and in the following sections, it will not be possible to return to a discussion of this position. But in preparation for this discussion, I will begin here by analysing the connections between *conventionalism*, which regards natural laws as analytic statements, and its counterpart, *empiricism*, which regards them as synthetic statements, with the "first pseudo-statement position", which interprets them as propositional functions.

These three views of natural laws – as analytic judgements (conventionalism), as synthetic judgements (empiricism) or as propositional functions (first pseudo-statement position) – seem to be the three possible interpretations of any axiomatic system, and hence also of any axiomatically constructed theory of natural science.

The aim of constructing theories of natural science is to gain control over, i.e., to predict as precisely as possible, a maximum number of occurrences, or natural events, with a minimum number of basic assumptions,

---

[4] Cf., for example, Viktor Kraft, *Die Grundformen der wissenschaftlichen Methoden* (1925), p. 156.
[5] Cf., for example, Viktor Kraft, *op. cit.*, pp. 184 f.

or universal natural laws. An ideal, theoretically presented natural science (an approximation would be theoretical physics) appears as a closed *deductive system* with a strictly limited number of principles from which all other assertions of this science, i.e., its theorems, are derived in a purely logical fashion.

The development of such deductive systems of natural laws for the purpose of formulating predictions in a most comprehensive fashion is a fact that is, as such, completely independent of the epistemological debate, and also of the debate between the inductivist and deductivist theories of knowledge. For inductivism too, the admissibility of deductive logic and the significance of deductive systems is beyond doubt. (Only with respect to its *value for knowledge* does inductivism rate deduction very low compared with induction.)

At least since Euclid, geometry is rightly considered to be closest to the ideal of a strictly deductive science.

But in other sciences, too, there are attempts to develop systems with a complete deductive structure. In particular, large parts of *theoretical physics* can be developed into a deductive system which in terms of its overall completeness and consistency already closely approaches geometry.

What characterises this scientific form of a theory, i.e., the deductive system?

Every statement of a theoretical, deductive system must be derivable, deducible or "provable" in a purely logical fashion from a particular group of statements (the principles) of the system, or it must itself be one of these principles. For their part, the principles are established without any logical deduction from other statements, that is, without "proof".

A "proof" consists in the logical reduction to *principles*, so that this requirement cannot apply to the principles themselves. To "reduce", "prove" or "deduce" means to transform a theorem in such a way that it becomes evident that *if the principles are true, the theorem to be proved must also be true.*[*1] The logical form of proof suggested here will be discussed in more detail below (in Section 31 on inference and implication). Every

---

[*1] Later I have strictly distinguished between a derivation (deduction) and a proof (derivation from an empty class of premises). A derivation is characterised by the transmission of truth from the premises to the conclusion and by the re-transmission of falsity from the conclusion to the premises (to at least *one* of the premises). [See Karl Popper, "New Foundations for Logic", *Mind*, N.S., 56 (1947), pp. 230 ff. Ed.]

theoretical, deductive system is thus composed of two parts: the system of foundations or basic principles and the system of theorems – that is, the propositions that are deduced or "proved" from the principles.

It is the task of "*axiomatics*" to construct a clear logical order for the statements of a deductive system, one that makes all of its interconnections transparent. It seeks to provide a complete inventory of the basic principles, the "*system of axioms*", in the simplest fashion, and to demarcate it sharply from the *system of theorems*.

These efforts towards axiomatisation originated essentially with Euclid. It was undoubtedly Euclid's programme (even if he did not succeed in carrying it out to the letter) to formulate in his principles (the "definitions", "postulates", "axioms") all those, and only those, assumptions necessary for a purely logical deduction of the theorems.

From this "Euclidean programme", four *fundamental axiomatic conditions* follow that any system of axioms should fulfil:

The basic assumptions made in the system must be:

(a)   *with respect to each other* (irrespective of the system of theorems)

(1) *consistent* and
(2) *independent* (not derivable [from each other]);

(b)   *with respect to the system of theorems*

(3) *complete* (that is, sufficient for a derivation of the theorems*[2]) and
(4) *indispensable* (that is, necessary for a derivation of the theorems).

(In contrast to Carnap,[1] I consider the distinction between the conditions formulated under (2) and (4) essential; for (2) may be fulfilled without (4) being fulfilled.)

"Axiomatics" examines the systems of axioms, particularly whether they satisfy these four fundamental conditions.

Euclid himself set up three groups of principles for geometry. The "definitions" (example: "A point is that which has no parts"), the "postulates" (example: "It is to be required that one and only one straight line

---

*[2] Of course there are other (and more interesting) concepts of completeness.
[1] Rudolf Carnap, *Abriß der Logistik* (1929), pp. 70 f.

can lead from any one point to any other point") and the "axioms" (example: "Two straight lines do not enclose a space"). The distinction between postulates and axioms is not very significant – which is evident from the fact that the famous fifth postulate, the "Euclidean parallel postulate", appears in many manuscripts as the eleventh axiom.

Precisely this parallel postulate or axiom is formulated in Euclid in a rather complicated manner, and – perhaps only for this reason – inspired the first axiomatic analyses. It appeared questionable whether or not it fulfils the axiomatic condition of independence. (As is well known, the failed attempts to deduce it from the other principles through an indirect proof, that is, through the proof that the negation of this axiom *contradicts* the other principles, led to the setting up of non-Euclidean geometries.)

One result of modern axiomatic analyses (especially Hilbert) is particularly significant for the modes of thought of *conventionalism* that are here under discussion. Only this result of axiomatics fully reveals the significance of conventionalism. It demonstrates, surprisingly, that Euclid's definitions (which are explicit definitions), and indeed all explicit definitions (coordinative definitions), are dispensable from the point of view of axiomatics. They do not fulfil the fourth fundamental axiomatic condition (indispensability), and are therefore to be eliminated from the system of axioms. We deduce solely from the axioms (or from the postulates), that is, from statements linking and relating the fundamental concepts to each other, not from any (explicit) definitions.

For example, in deriving some geometric theorem we never refer to statements such as "a point has no parts" or "a line is length without breadth"; we may, however, refer to the statement that two distinct points define one and only one straight line.

Thus from the standpoint of axiomatics, or from the standpoint of a pure, logical-deductive system (without taking into account its potential applications), definitions have no significance whatsoever. They can be seen simply as superfluous phrases. And this is the case not only in geometry: analogous conditions exist in all axiomatically presented deductive systems.

Let us illustrate the dispensability of definitions by a traditional example. The deduction "All men are mortal" – "Socrates is a man" – "Hence Socrates is mortal" is valid regardless of how we might define the concepts "man", "mortal" and "Socrates".

Whether we define these "basic concepts" according to common usage or give them a different meaning does not play any part in the deduction. We do not infer anything from the definition.

An axiomatic deductive system, or a pure "theory" from which everything irrelevant for the deductive relations has been eliminated, thus becomes a combination of basic symbols that are, properly speaking, meaningless, and for which different meanings can be substituted. From the standpoint of pure deductive relations, the deduction above could be represented in the following way: "All x are y" – "a is an x" – hence "a is y". Thus, in a purely axiomatic deductive system, the basic symbols can be viewed as *variables*. The system would then have to be interpreted as one of *propositional functions* rather than as a system of statements.

A second interpretation of deductive systems can appeal to the fact that propositional functions can always be transformed into *propositions* (and that the system is actually meant to be a system of genuine propositions). We only need to assign certain concepts as arguments to the variables, to the place-holders or blanks – in other words, to give certain meanings to the place-holding "basic symbols" through *coordinative definitions* – and we shall obtain genuine statements that may be true or false.

Finally, a third view is possible. We may assume that the basic symbols are to be "implicitly defined" by the propositional functions or by the system of axioms themselves, i.e., that by definition only those arguments are to be substituted for the basic symbols that satisfy the axioms. If we substitute for a deductive system of propositional functions only those arguments that – with the aid of these propositional functions (i.e., of the system of axioms) – are *defined* such that they satisfy the system, we will always obtain *analytic judgements* that are *a priori* true.

Thus three interpretations of any deductive system or theory are possible, corresponding to three epistemological positions.

1. The *first pseudo-statement position*, which regards natural laws as *propositional functions*, corresponds to the view that every theory, or every deductive system, is a system of propositional functions (without coordinative definitions), that is, that the "basic symbols" do not refer to basic concepts, but are only *blanks*: they are *variables*. Depending on the arguments to be substituted for these variables, they may give rise to true or false statements.

2. The *empiricist* view, which regards natural laws as *genuine empirical statements* the validity of which can be decided only by *experience* (that is,

synthetic *a posteriori* judgements), corresponds to the view that the "basic symbols" of (scientific) theories are not *variables* but refer to *certain concepts*; more precisely, that they are defined by coordinative definitions, or that certain concrete meanings are assigned to them. According to this view, a (scientific) theory is a system of *propositional functions in conjunction with coordinative definitions*. However, such propositional functions together with the coordinative definitions are *genuine statements*, since through a coordinative definition certain concepts are substituted, as arguments, into the propositional functions.

3. *Conventionalism*, which regards scientific theories as *analytic* statements implicitly defining the basic concepts, corresponds to the view that for the propositional functions forming the axiomatic system, one may, by convention (or by definition), substitute only those arguments that satisfy the axioms. The variables of these propositional functions are not merely blanks for which any arguments can legitimately be substituted, irrespective of whether or not they satisfy the propositional functions; they are "bound" [in the sense] of being implicitly *defined* as place-holders only for those arguments that *satisfy* the propositional functions (that is, they may only be occupied by such arguments).

These three views of natural laws as propositional functions with or without (concrete) coordinative definitions, with "free" or with "bound" variables, need to be examined more closely. We will proceed in the following fashion:

The conventionalist "implicit definitions" require some further explanation, to be provided in the next two sections (26 and 27).

The view of axiomatic systems as systems of *pure propositional functions*, that is, the interpretation of the first pseudo-statement position, confronts one problem in particular. A propositional function can be neither true nor false; nonetheless, in the context of an axiomatic system we speak about the "proof" of a theorem or [about] its "refutation". Similarly, we say that the solution of a geometric problem, which must of course consist of a proven proposition, is *correct* or that it is *incorrect*. An explanation of this apparent contradiction – propositional functions cannot, of course, be correct or incorrect, just as they cannot be true or false – will be attempted in the following section (28).

Finally, in the subsequent sections (29 and 30) we shall discuss, in greater detail, the relationship between propositional functions and coordinative definitions, that is, the *empiricist interpretation*.

26. *Conventionalist implicit and explicit definitions. Propositional function and propositional equation.* A propositional function, such as "x carried a sword", assumes different truth values or *propositional values* ("function values") when different arguments are substituted for its blank. Depending on the arguments substituted, it can assume the statement value "*true*" or the statement value "*false*".

Thus, there is a formal analogy between propositional and mathematical functions. Depending on the arguments substituted, the function "x + 7" also assumes different values, namely *numerical values*, which may also be called "function values".

This analogy greatly facilitates the understanding of implicit definitions.

In a mathematical as well as in a propositional function, we can arbitrarily fix an argument (by assigning it); but in this way we have, at the same time, determined a certain function value (such as the numerical value "23", or the value "true").

In both types of function, however, we can *fix the function value in an arbitrary fashion,* which will *conversely* establish the argument; and this procedure, that is, this determination of an argument by arbitrarily stipulating a function value, is precisely the procedure used for the *implicit definition of* an argument.

If, for a mathematical function (such as "x + 7"), we arbitrarily fix a function value (such as the numerical value 23), this transforms the function into an *equation:* "x + 7 = 23". The argument of this equation can no longer be established arbitrarily; x is a variable only in appearance. It is [therefore] a "*bound variable*": its value is implicitly determined (implicitly defined) by the equation. For the *equation is not a function.*

Such a bound variable need not always be a constant. True, the function "x + 7" gives one definite argument value for each function value (for the function value 23, for example, the argument value is 16); but even the quadratic function "$x^2 + 7$" produces two argument values, or two "solutions", for each function value (for example, +4 and −4 are the solutions for the function value 23). As we know, the number of solutions, that is, of implicitly defined arguments, increases with the degree of the function *ad infinitum.* There also exist functions that yield equations with an infinite number of solutions, therefore implicitly defining an infinite number of arguments. A simple example is the sine function sin (x). Each of the equations "sin x = 0", "sin x = 0.7" and "sin x = 1" implicitly defines a certain *sequence or class* of solutions. None of the solutions of one equation satisfies any of the other equations, but each of these equations is satisfied by an infinite number of solutions.

Thus an implicit definition, as in the case of the equation of the first degree "x + 7 = 23", *may* establish an argument value *unequivocally*; however, this is by no means *necessarily* the case. It is also possible (and this is the more common case) that *an implicit definition singles out not a certain unequivocal argument but a class of arguments*, which may consist of several or even of an unlimited (infinite) number of arguments.

Thus, the *equation* "sin x = 0" by no means unequivocally picks out one argument. This "x" is, however, no longer a variable such as the variable of the *function* "sin x". The equation simply determines certain arguments (albeit not unequivocally) that satisfy the equation; that is, the "*solutions*" of *the equation*. The "x" in the equation no longer simply refers to a blank: it is a place-holder for specific arguments. It is [therefore] *bound* by the equation or by the implicit definition ("bound variable"*[1]).

The situation is analogous in the case of propositional functions. The propositional function "x carried a sword" assumes the arguments (function values) "true" and "false", depending on whether I substitute the argument value "Mozart" or "Napoleon". I can, however, construct two "equations" out of these propositional functions ("propositional equations"); only *two* because propositional functions can assume only the two values "true" and "false". The one "propositional equation" would be: "x carried a sword" is true (or: "x carried a sword" is a true statement); the other: "x carried a sword" is false. These propositional *equations* are *not propositional functions*. Their "variables" are *bound*. The solutions of the first propositional equation constitute the class of those who carried a sword, while the solutions of the second propositional equation constitute the class of those who did not carry a sword.

Propositional equations may also *unequivocally* single out certain specific solutions (for example: "x is a French emperor who in the nineteenth century was exiled to Elba" is a true statement). But even with respect to propositional equations, the more common case is probably that through these implicit definitions it is not one specific argument value that is

---

*[1] This extension in the usage of "bound variable" [*gebundene Variable*. Tr.] has not become generally established. See Rudolf Carnap, *Abriß der Logistik* (1929), 6e, p. 14.

unequivocally defined but a considerable *number of solutions*, a *class* consisting of many *elements*, more precisely: of these solutions.

Herein lies the major difference between an *ordinary* ("explicit") and an "implicit" *definition*. Usually a definition is understood as an *unequivocal* determination of a concept. When I say "Gold is a metal", this is not yet a definition; the concept "gold" is established only as an element of the class of metals. The concept "gold" is *defined* only if, in addition, I have indicated a *specific difference* that unequivocally distinguishes the concept "gold" from other concepts that are elements of the class of metals. The phrase "Gold is a precious metal" is, therefore, also insufficient; as a specific difference, we will have to indicate its atomic weight, or melting point, or specific gravity.

In general, an implicit definition does *not* unequivocally establish an argument. It provides *only* the class (the *genus proximum*) to which the implicitly defined argument value belongs, the *differentia specifica is missing*. (An argument value can only be unequivocally determined by an implicit definition if this class has only *one* element.) This should not, however, lead us to confuse an implicitly defined (that is, only partially defined) concept with a *variable*. It is in any case *bound*, bound as an element of a class.

(If a propositional function has more than one argument-place, then the corresponding propositional equations do not – according to the terminology of logistic*[2] – establish "classes" but "relations", that is, not individual elements but pairs of elements, triplets of elements, etc. In formal terms, however, relations are exactly analogous to classes; which is why in the present work, for the sake of simplicity, we shall speak only of "classes" and of "elements" even where we should be speaking of "relations" and their "components" – "pairs of elements", etc. This is unlikely to cause confusion, because everything that will be said here about classes can analogously be applied to relations. At this point, it should be emphasised that the theory of relations is the most significant part of logistic.)

If I define "gold" only as "metal" or as "one of the metals", then it is not really defined at all (in the ordinary sense of this word). The same is true of an implicit definition. It does not really create a concept. (Carnap[1]

---

*[2] The term "logistic" has also not become generally accepted. Instead, one speaks of "mathematical logic" or "symbolic logic". See Introduction 1978.

[1] [Rudolf Carnap, "Eigentliche und uneigentliche Begriffe", *Symposion* 1 (1927), pp. 355 ff.; cf. also R. Carnap, *Abriß der Logistik* (1929), p. 71. Ed.]

therefore speaks of "improper concepts".[+1]) But as *bound variables*, these "improper concepts" must be distinguished from *genuine variables*, just as *propositional functions* must be distinguished from *propositional equations*.

A genuine variable is only a symbol for a blank; it says nothing about whether the values to be substituted for the blanks will or will not satisfy the propositional function. And a propositional function can, therefore, never be regarded as true or false (otherwise it would be a genuine statement). If a propositional function is, however, to provide an implicit definition, then the "variables" are to be viewed merely as symbols for those values that *satisfy* the propositional function. But this means that it is not in fact a propositional function, for now it must be *true*. It is a propositional equation, a genuine statement, an analytic judgement, a tautology.

A propositional function that is meant to be "true" or "false" and thus made into a propositional equation is, therefore, no longer a propositional function; just as a propositional function into which argument values have been substituted is no longer a propositional function.[2]

Every propositional equation is, therefore, an *implicit definition* (and vice versa).

But every propositional equation also explicitly defines a concept. This explicitly defined, unequivocally determined concept is the *class of solutions itself*, that is, the class of argument values satisfying a propositional equation.

It is important not to confuse this explicit concept, or the *class itself*, with its *elements*, with the arguments (which the propositional equation defines only implicitly).

For example, in the propositional function "x carried a sword" we can substitute the element "Napoleon" for the x, but not the "class of those who carried a sword". We can say of this class that it probably has more than a thousand elements; what we cannot say, however, is that it carried one (or several) swords. *Not the class but only its elements satisfy a propositional function*. (The class is not even admissible as an argument value.) By the same token, I can say: " 'x is a yellow metal' is satisfied by the argument

---

[+1] ["Ansetzungen über unbestimmte Gegenstände". Tr.]

[2] Contrary to Rudolf Carnap, for example *Abriß der Logistik* (1929), p. 71, View 2. There, Carnap overlooks the difference between an implicit definition or statement-equation and a propositional function, moving from one view to the other without comment.

'gold' "; but I cannot substitute the "class of yellow metals" as an argument value. This class is not a metal, but only a (mental) *collection* of metals.

Every propositional function (and every axiomatic system consisting of propositional functions) may be viewed as a propositional equation, and it will then define an *explicit concept*. But this is *not an argument* of the propositional function. Argument values are only *implicitly defined*, that is, *determined as elements of an explicit concept*.

Thus, there can be several elements of an explicit concept, and thereby several solutions or "models"*[3] (Carnap[3]), which satisfy an axiomatic system (or *systems* of solutions, since axiomatic systems usually have *several* argument-places).

A classic example of the ambiguity of implicit definitions, or of a plurality of models, is the notion of *duality* in projective geometry (of plane and space).

In projective geometry (say, in three dimensions), it is surprisingly the case that *every theorem* remains correct even if we interchange the concepts "plane" and "point". This gives the theorems intuitively a completely different meaning, but they remain, without exception, correct and provable. For example: Three points define three straight lines and a plane – unless they define only *one* straight line (i.e., lie on *one* straight line). The corresponding *dual* statement is: Three planes define three straight lines (the intersecting lines) and one point (spatial corner), unless they define only one straight line (intersect the same line).

The explanation for this peculiar reversibility or duality is that the concepts "point" and "plane" are interconnected and implicitly defined by exactly analogous axioms. Three points define a plane – three planes define a point. Two points define a straight line – two planes define a straight line. Through this *formal* identity they become logically completely equivalent. We obtain a *model* of the axiomatic system if for the *symbols* "point" and "plane" we substitute the *intuitive constructs* "point" and "plane"; but even if we assign to the symbol "point" the intuitive construct "plane", and to the symbol "plane" the intuitive construct "point",

---

*[3] Since 1930, the theory of models has been further developed with great intensity, especially by Alfred Tarski and his school.

[3] [Rudolf Carnap, *op. cit.*, pp. 71 f.; cf. also R. Carnap, "Eigentliche und uneigentliche Begriffe", *Symposion* 1 (1927), pp. 361 ff. Ed.]

we still obtain a *model*: that is, a system of solutions, or a system of arguments that satisfies the axiomatic system. Thus, the "problem of duality" can be resolved by the realisation that, through an implicit as opposed to an explicit definition, certain concepts are not necessarily unequivocally determined, but that several different systems of solutions (models) may be admissible. (Only the internal relationships between the relations are *unequivocally* determined by an axiom system.)

We shall, once again, obtain an entirely different model of geometry (say, of plane geometry) if for every "point" we substitute a pair of numbers, and for every "straight line" a linear function, etc. In this sense, algebraic analysis is only a translation of geometry into numerical language, i.e., it is a specific model of the axiomatic system of geometry. And there are many other such models of the same axiomatic system.

We need only call – *as conventionalism* does – a propositional function (or axiomatic system) an analytic (or tautological) judgement, that is, *a priori* true judgement, in order to transform it into a propositional equation or implicit definition.

However, the analytic judgement determined by the propositional equation can, *as such, be explicitly formulated*. We then have to render it in such a way that the bound character of the "variables" is made explicit. Through this formulation we have to express the requirement that the variables must assume not just *any* value, but exclusively those values that constitute "solutions".

This explicit formulation as an analytic judgement can be achieved with the help of a "general implication"*⁴ (as logistic calls it).

27. *Conventionalist propositional equations as tautological general implications.**¹ What is a *general implication?**² A general implication is always a *genuine statement*. It seems important to me to emphasise, right at the outset, that a general implication is never a propositional function. Since every general implication always contains

---

*⁴ See Section 27, note *2, and *Introduction 1978*.

*¹ The editor and the author have agreed to have Sections 27 to 29 (inclusive) and 31 set in smaller type: by this means the author wants to distance himself clearly from these sections. (See *Introduction 1978*.)

*² The term "general" in the phrase "general implication" was introduced by Rudolf Carnap in 1929 in his *Abriß der Logistik*; see *Abriß*, p. 108, "*Neue Termini*". The term does not seem to have found general acceptance. See *Introduction 1978*. Carnap, *Abriß*, 6c, p. 14, states that general implications express "laws".

propositional functions as components, this could easily give rise to the erroneous view that it is itself a propositional function.

The following formula may serve as an example of a general implication: "Every argument that satisfies*[3] the propositional function 'x is a British officer who lived in the eighteenth century', also satisfies the propositional function 'x carried a sword'."

With the help of this example, I shall discuss in greater detail the peculiar (and in its linguistic guise, rather awkward) form of statement that logistic calls a "general implication".

To begin with, the aforementioned general implication is no doubt a genuine statement. It expresses a proposition that is either true or false. (True if in fact all British officers in the eighteenth century carried swords, and false if this was not the case.) It is, therefore, equivalent to the ordinary statement "Every British officer who lived in the eighteenth century carried a sword".

The example further shows that this general implication consists of two propositional functions. The first ("x is a British officer", etc.) is called the "implying propositional function" or the "*implicans*", and the second ("x carried a sword") is called the "implied propositional function" or the "*implicate*".

A general implication is an assertion that every argument value that satisfies the implicans also satisfies the implicate. More briefly, one might say: the implicans *generally implies* the implicate, and accordingly our example can be rendered (it means exactly the same as) " 'x is a British officer who lived in the eighteenth century' *generally implies* 'x carried a sword' ".

Any genuine statement can be put in the form of a "general implication" (without changing its meaning), and this can be done in several ways. To begin with, a genuine statement, for example, "Napoleon was in Vienna", is transformed into a propositional function, say, "Napoleon was in x". This propositional function is used as the *implicate*. It is premised on a propositional function (the *implicans*) which is satisfied precisely by that argument value or values that were removed from the original statement at the place now occupied by "x". In our case, we might choose*[4] as the implicans "x is the capital of Austria". In this way, we have carried out the transformation of the statement into the "general implication": " 'x is the capital of Austria' generally implies 'Napoleon was in x' ". The "variable" of the implicate is *bound* by the implicans. (In an analogous fashion, the same statement can be formulated in another way as a "general implication", for example: " 'x is a French emperor who was crowned in 1804' generally implies 'x was in Vienna' ".)

---

*[3] Nowadays the term "satisfies" would be regarded as metalogical or metatheoretical.

*[4] A trivial choice is "x is identical with Vienna".

These last examples show also that every *singular statement* can be transformed into a general implication. It is important to emphasise that the adjective "general" here has nothing to do with a universal (a "general") statement.*[5] All genuine statements, whether universal or singular, can be rendered as general implications. The word "general" only serves to characterise a general implication as a statement that asserts that *all* argument values that satisfy the implicans also satisfy the implicate. However, if the implicans is, for example, satisfied by *one* argument only, then the general implication merely asserts that the implicate is also satisfied by this argument.

The arguments that satisfy the *implicans* constitute a *class*. (It is the class that is explicitly defined by the implicans. In the first example, it is the class of British officers who lived in the eighteenth century.) Each element of this class – so the general implication asserts – satisfies the implicate, and transforms it into a true statement.

If the class has only a single element – this is possible, as was discussed in the previous section – then the general implication simply asserts something about *this* argument (as in the second example about Vienna). If a singular statement is to be rendered as a general implication, then (as in this example) we must choose a propositional function as implicans that is satisfied only by those arguments about which something is to be stated (a propositional function that "marks out" those particular arguments).

The claim that every genuine statement, including every singular statement, can in principle be transformed into a "general implication" without altering its meaning will subsequently prove to be significant (cf. Section 32).

If *every* genuine statement can be written in the form of a general implication, then it must be possible to divide general implications (just like ordinary statements) not only into *universal* and *singular general implications*, but also into *analytic* and *synthetic general implications*. And this division is valuable for my present purposes.

An attempt will be made *to formulate the conventionalist implicit definitions*, or propositional equations, *explicitly as analytic judgements*; and [only] for this purpose was the notion of general implication introduced here.

The previous examples of general implications were synthetic, were reworded empirical statements; they will be discussed again in Section 29.

Here we are dealing with analytic, or *tautological, general implications*. With their

---

*[5] This is evidently meant as a correction of the view that general implications correspond to universal statements (laws). (Cf. Rudolf Carnap, *Abriß der Logistik* (1929), 6c, p. 14; see above, Section 23, note *1.)

help it is easy*[6] to formulate implicit definitions, propositional equations, explicitly as analytic judgements.

If, for example, "x carried a sword" is to be understood as a *propositional equation*, this means that "x" is tied exclusively to those arguments that satisfy the propositional function. In other words: for "x" we must substitute only elements of those classes that are defined by the statement-equation "x carried a sword". The aim of the implicit definition might be expressed by the formulation (which clearly reveals its character as an analytic judgement): "Each element of the class of those carrying a sword satisfies the propositional function 'x carried a sword'." Formulated as a general implication in a way that can be more broadly used:

" 'x carried a sword' generally implies 'x carried a sword'." This general implication is evidently analytic, or tautological. However, it says exactly the same as the corresponding propositional equation: the "variable" of the implicate is a bound variable, it is bound by those argument values that satisfy the propositional function.

If we apply these results to *axiomatic systems* and their *conventionalist* interpretation as *implicit definitions*, then we can say:

The "variables" occurring in a particular axiom are implicitly defined by the entire axiomatic system (by the "conjunction" of all axioms). They are *bound* specifically by the solutions of the propositional equation consisting of the conjunction of all the axioms of the system.

According to this (conventionalist) view, it must therefore be possible to write every axiom as that *general implication whose implicans is the conjunction of all the axioms and whose implicate is the individual axiom in question.*

Since the implicate also occurs in the implicans, these general implications can again be readily identified as tautological.

We can, thus, simply equate the conventionalist view, which interprets an axiomatic system as an implicit definition of the concepts occurring in it, with the view that every axiom can be explicitly written as a tautological general implication, with the conjunction of all the axioms as implicans and the axiom in question as implicate. The meanings of "implicit definition" and of "propositional equation" and their rendition as a "general implication" are *completely equivalent.*

Much the same can be said of every *theorem.* The variables that occur in a theorem of a system are bound, or implicitly defined, by the *axiomatic system.* Thus, according to the conventionalist view, it must be possible to render *every theorem as a general implication*, again with the conjunction of axioms as the implicans, but

---

*[6] This was a very uncritical remark; on the contrary, it requires a distinction between object-language and metalanguage.

with the theorem as the implicate. For the conventionalist maintains*[7] that the theorem is valid for those arguments that satisfy the axiomatic system, which are the solutions or "models" of the axiomatic system.

(An individual theorem, just like an individual axiom, cannot be understood as a propositional equation: only the axiomatic system as a whole, the conjunction of the axioms, constitutes an implicit definition, or propositional equation.)

The preceding formulations are significant because with their help it will be shown in the next section how close the "*first pseudo-statement position*", which regards natural laws as *propositional functions*, comes to *conventionalism* as presented here, which interprets natural laws as genuine statements, or as *a priori* true analytic judgements.

28. *Can axiomatic-deductive systems also be understood as consequence classes of pure propositional functions (of pseudo-statements)?* In the previous two sections, the *conventionalist* interpretation of axiomatic systems has been discussed in some detail.

I shall now discuss some of the difficulties that arise from the interpretation of axiomatic-deductive systems as systems of pure *propositional functions*; that is, from the interpretation according to which deductive systems or scientific theories are *pseudo-statements* ("first pseudo-statement position").

It will be shown here that the view of the first pseudo-statement position, which regards deductive systems as systems of propositional functions, leads to certain difficulties, and that these difficulties force it to come very close to the conventionalist view.

Thus, a fundamental *critique* of this pseudo-statement position will not be attempted; but an understanding that the first pseudo-statement position is much closer to conventionalism than to any empiricist view will prepare the ground for such a critique.

The first pseudo-statement position, that is, the conception of axiomatic systems as systems of propositional functions, would seem to deviate quite considerably from the conventionalist view, a view that regards axiomatic systems as analytic judgements. Propositional functions cannot be true or false – whereas conventionalist propositional equations are established as *a priori* true, and can be explicitly formulated as tautological general implications, or as analytic judgements.

The difficulty that the first pseudo-statement position can overcome only at the cost of moving closer to conventionalism consists in the following:

A *theorem* "*statement*" of an axiomatic-deductive system – according to the view of the first pseudo-statement position – is to be regarded not as a proposition, but as a propositional function. Hence it can never be *true*. But what, then,

---

*[7] This assertion, however, belongs to the metalanguage.

distinguishes it from that incalculable number of similar functions that in ordinary language we would call "false theorems"? (In the following, the term "theorem" will be used in a neutral fashion without prejudging whether we are dealing with a proposition or a propositional function.)

For example: take the "theorem" that two straight lines intersect so that any two adjacent angles add up to 180 degrees. This "theorem" can be viewed as a propositional function if we assume that the verbal symbols "straight line", "angle", etc. do not refer to concepts, but are simply place-holders for blanks, that is, variables. Hence, if this "theorem" is a propositional function, then here, like a "theorem" according to which those same adjacent angles add up to 170 degrees, it is neither true nor false. (Only by way of substitution, by assigning certain arguments, can this propositional function become a true or a false statement.)

The conception of axiomatic systems as systems of propositional functions, if it is to be taken seriously, must spell out how to distinguish "theorems" that are usually viewed as true or correct statements from those propositional functions that are usually called "false theorems".

Those who interpret axiomatic systems in the sense of the first pseudo-statement position will answer: "Propositional functions that are usually called 'correct theorems' are distinguished from all other propositional functions (the 'false theorems') only by the fact that they *belong* to a particular *axiomatic-deductive system*, that is, that they are *deducible* from the axioms of that system."

And indeed: whether the "theorems" of a deductive system are viewed as propositional functions or as genuine statements – a "*theorem*" is, in any event, to be *defined* as being logically derivable from the fundamental propositions (or from the fundamental propositional functions).

This answer already implies the manner in which the first pseudo-statement position comes close to the conventionalist view; the following analysis will show this.

What could actually be meant by the claim that a propositional function can be "*deduced*" from other propositional functions?

Let us review the example: "All x are y" – "Socrates is an x" – "Hence Socrates is y." The "inference" or "conclusion" (more accurately: the "concluding propositional function") is obviously *deduced* syllogistically, or "proved"*[1] from the "premises" (more accurately: from the "premise-functions").

But how can a propositional function, which can be neither true nor false, be "proved"? A "proof" was usually understood as a demonstration of the truth of a statement.

---

*[1] Later, I have sharply distinguished between a logical derivation (deduction) and a logical proof. See Section 25, note *1, and Introduction 1978.

Now in the case of a propositional function, the proof or deduction consists in showing that all those arguments that transform the "premise-functions" into true statements must also transform the "conclusion-function" into a true statement (i.e., satisfy the function). For example: the pairs of arguments "human being" and "mortal", or perhaps "Greek" and "southern European", satisfy the "premise-functions", and the "conclusion-function" is indeed also satisfied by them.

But the fact that two propositional functions correlate with each other in such a way that every argument value (or every pair of argument values) satisfying the one will also satisfy the other, means precisely that their relationship with each other is that of a "general implication", for this is how the concept of "general implication" was explained.

To "deduce" or "prove" a propositional function from, or by, other propositional functions ("premise-functions", *axioms*) is the same as showing by means of logical (tautological) transformations that it is "generally implied" by the axioms.

(The demonstration of a *general implication* is for propositional functions what for statements would be the proof of their truth.)

Thus, we see that for a propositional function to belong, as a *theorem*, to an axiomatic system is fully equivalent to this propositional function being generally implied by the axioms of the system (by the "conjunction" of the axioms). From a logical viewpoint it is, thus, itself nothing but a general implication. And the latter is also, like all general implications, a *genuine statement*.

I therefore agree with Carnap when he writes:[1] "Every theorem can be transformed into a genuine statement, namely into a general implication, with the conjunction of axioms as implicans and the theorem as implicate."

But I have to disagree with Carnap[2] when he advances the view that while every "theorem" *can* be understood as a general implication, that is, as a genuine statement, it can also and just as well be understood as a *propositional function*. In my view, a "theorem" of an axiomatic system (in contrast to the "principles", or axioms) can be regarded *only* as a genuine statement.

From the incalculable number of propositional functions all of which have theoretically the same value, that is, are neither true nor false, we mark out individual propositional functions (such as the axioms) only by *arbitrary labelling*.

Labelling a propositional function *as a "theorem"* is, however, *not an arbitrary act*. A propositional function is *defined* as a theorem through being *generally implied* by an axiomatic system (which, from a logical viewpoint, may in turn be arbitrarily

---

[1] Rudolf Carnap, *Abriß der Logistik* (1929), p. 71.

[2] Rudolf Carnap, *loc. cit.*; and R. Carnap, "Bericht über Untersuchungen zur allgemeinen Axiomatik", *Erkenntnis* 1 (1930), pp. 303 f.

chosen). Any symbol by which we set off this particular propositional function from others as a "theorem", and any way or procedure by which we label this propositional function as a "theorem" to distinguish it from others, is, from a logical viewpoint, simply an unstated *assertion* that this propositional function is a "theorem".

By labelling a propositional function a "theorem", we set up a general implication, an assertion or a statement (which may be true or false). And the *propositional function so labelled* is itself a general implication or a genuine statement; for it already contains the assertion that it is generally implied by a particular axiomatic system. This is evident already from the fact that such a label can be rightly or wrongly conferred on a propositional function: rightly, if a general implication actually holds good, that is, if it is a true statement, and wrongly if the general implication asserted is *false*, that is, if it does not hold.

Now one might – from Carnap's standpoint – also attempt to raise the following objection. It may be granted that a *propositional function labelled as a "theorem"* (that is, a propositional function together with its characterisation as a "theorem") must, from a logical viewpoint, be called a general implication, but this by no means proves that the *"theorem" itself* is not identical with the *implicate* of this general implication, and may thus be a propositional function. Even in the case of a genuine statement deduced from genuine premises, the *statement* itself can be clearly distinguished from the assertion that it is derived from those premises, that is, *from characterisation as a theorem* of that system. Why would it not be possible to make a corresponding distinction for propositional functions?

This objection overlooks a fundamental and, in the present context, crucial difference between a theorem or conclusion, which is a genuine *statement*, and the implicate of a general implication, which is a propositional function. (In logistical terminology, genuine *conclusions* would be implicates of "implications",*[2] not of "*general* implications". Concerning the following remarks and, in general, the contrast between "implications" of statements and "general implications" of propositional functions, see Section 31.) By itself a statement may be true or false, it can by itself be asserted irrespective of its deducibility from premises. And according to the rules of logistic – a genuine *conclusion* (the *implicate* of an "implication", but not of a "general implication") can by itself be correspondingly established as an assertion. However, there is no logistical rule according to which the implicate of a general implication can be detached from that general implication and asserted by itself, or distinguished in any other way. There can, moreover, be no such rule, for *a propositional function cannot be asserted*. A propositional function without its label as a theorem is, quite simply, not

---

*[2] More accurately: of tautological (logically true) implications.

labelled, it is not distinguished from the mass of other propositional functions. By distinguishing it from others that are not theorems, we transform it into a general implication.

Thus, I reject as logically (and logistically) impracticable the position of the logistic critique of language according to which the "*theorems*" of an axiomatic system can be interpreted as propositional functions. They are *genuine statements* (and only in appearance "pseudo-statements").

However, the peculiar interpretation of axiomatic systems given by the first pseudo-statement position should *not*, as a result, be regarded *as refuted*. All my objections apply only to *theorems*. *Axioms*, on the other hand, may very well be interpreted as propositional functions; their characterisation is, from a logical viewpoint, completely arbitrary (within certain limits set by the basic axiomatic conditions). As propositional functions, axioms are, as Carnap[3] puts it, free "assumptions about undefined objects"[+1] (about variables).

Viewed as propositional functions, axioms can be neither true nor false. Their choice is determined by extra-logical (for example, pragmatic) considerations.

The first pseudo-statement position will, therefore, continue to be distinguished from the conventionalist interpretation by the fact that it views *axioms* as propositional functions, while conventionalism regards them as genuine analytic statements (implicit definitions).

As far as the conception of the status of the *theorems* is concerned, I cannot acknowledge any difference between the two positions. The pseudo-statement position, too, is forced to admit that the theorems of an axiomatic-deductive system are genuine statements, that is, tautological general implications with the conjunction of axioms as implicans and the "theorem" as implicate. But this is equivalent to the assertion that "theorems" are satisfied by those arguments that satisfy the axiomatic system, that is, by the "solutions" or "models" of the axiomatic system. And this is precisely the view of conventionalism.

Thus, the first pseudo-statement position has to distinguish sharply between axioms and theorems: the former are propositional functions and the latter are statements. According to the conventionalist view, axioms and theorems are general implications constructed in a completely analogous fashion.

The agreement of both interpretations with respect to theorems entails a very considerable proximity between the first pseudo-statement position and conventionalism. The genuine, the epistemologically essential opposition is between these two views on the one hand, and empiricism on the other.

---

[3] [Rudolf Carnap, *Abriß der Logistik* (1929), p. 10. Ed.]
[+1] ["Ansetzungen über unbestimmte Gegenstände". Tr.]

Conventionalism and the first pseudo-statement position regard theorems as *tautological* general implications, or as *analytic judgements* — empiricism regards the axioms and theorems of a scientific theory as *synthetic judgements*.

The essential contrast is not propositional equation (conventionalism) versus propositional function (first pseudo-statement position), but analytic versus synthetic judgements, tautological versus synthetic general implications. Or expressed differently:

Propositional functions with or without coordinative definitions?

29. *The coordinative definitions of empiricism: synthetic general implications.* As was shown in Section 27, every empirical statement can be rendered as a synthetic general implication.

As an example, we used the statement "Every British officer who lived in the eighteenth century carried a sword." When formulated as a general implication, this yields: " 'x is a British officer who lived in the eighteenth century' generally implies 'x carried a sword'."

The two propositional functions that occur in such a general implication, the implicans and the implicate, fulfil rather different functions. We can say that the implicans *assigns* arguments to the implicate, and that a general implication consists in the assertion that a particular propositional function, that is, the implicate, yields *statements* true of the arguments assigned by the implicans. Thus, the implicans may be regarded as a *coordinative definition*, and the entire general implication as a *propositional function (implicate) coupled with a coordinative definition* (implicans).

This coupling of a *propositional function with a coordinative definition* can also be formulated in a manner different from that of a synthetic general implication. A different rendition might be: " 'x carried a sword' is satisfied by assigning any argument denoting an element of the class of eighteenth-century British officers." (Or, more briefly: " 'x carried a sword' is satisfied by any argument referring to a British officer of the eighteenth century", etc.)

Evidently, a rendition as a general implication is not essential for expressing the connection of a propositional function with a coordinative definition. It is only one of the possible ways of rendering this connection. (Specifically, it is a rendition in which the coordinative definition can also be formulated as a propositional function and, as implicans, serve as the premise for the "genuine" propositional function, that is, for the implicate.)

Of course, every *propositional function coupled with a coordinative definition* is a genuine statement, for it asserts that the propositional function is satisfied by certain arguments.

Hence, propositional functions given together with coordinative definitions, which are genuine statements, must under no circumstances be confused with propositional functions.

In terms of their form, tautological general implications may also be regarded as propositional functions coupled with coordinative definitions. Here too, the implicans assigns argument values to the implicate. (For example, " 'x carries a sword' generally implies 'x carries a sword'." This tautological general implication can of course also be expressed in the form: " 'x carries a sword' is satisfied by assigning any element of the class of those who carry a sword.") In earlier sections I have, however, always used the phrase "*coordinative definition*" in the sense of a synthetic, empirical, coordinative definition, and I will continue to follow this usage. When we speak about coordinative definitions in general, this is not meant to refer to *tautological* arguments, that is, the assignment of values *defined* by the condition that they must satisfy a propositional function. (Such a "tautological coordinative definition" does not independently establish any values in order to assign them to a propositional function. It simply asserts that those values that satisfy a propositional function satisfy that same propositional function.)

Provided a "coordinative definition" is understood exclusively as a "genuine", synthetic or empirical definition, excluding all tautological definitions, then we can say:

Every genuine empirical statement can be transformed into a propositional function together with a coordinative definition (such as in the form of a synthetic general implication), and vice versa:

Every propositional function with a coordinative definition (expressed perhaps as a synthetic general implication) is a genuine empirical statement.

Of course, all those forms of *empiricism* that regard natural laws as *genuine statements* view them as synthetic or as *empirical statements*. Or, as we might now also put it: as *propositional functions, coupled with* (empirical) *coordinative definitions* (which can be written in the form of general implications).

To cite examples of such natural laws – formulated as propositional functions with coordinative definitions – it suffices to refer to those empiricist positions that regard natural laws as genuine statements.

For my examples, I will choose two such empiricist positions: the position that regards natural laws as genuine, strictly universal empirical statements (a view that is also in agreement with the deductivist-empiricist view I advocate), and the position of strict positivism that regards natural laws as summary reports (that is, not strictly universal, but genuine singular empirical statements).

A natural law, understood as a strictly universal genuine empirical statement, formulated as a propositional function with a coordinative definition (as a synthetic general implication), would look something like this (I will use our old examples):

" 'x is a stone-throw' generally implies 'the trajectory of x is a parabola' " (the ordinary way of expressing this is: "The trajectories of all stone-throws are parabolas").

In the sense of strict positivism, this statement – as a summary report – might be written as follows:

" 'x is one of those stone-throws whose trajectory has *hitherto* been determined' generally implies 'the trajectory of x is a parabola' " (the ordinary way of expressing this is: "All hitherto observed stone-throws have had trajectories that are parabolas").

In these formulations, empirically defined arguments are assigned to the implicate by the implicans. These are arguments about which there can be no *a priori* answer as to whether they fulfil the conditions of the implicate, that is, whether or not they satisfy the implicate. For the question here is simply whether these empirical statements are true or false.

If we compare these empiricist views with the conventionalist view or with the first pseudo-statement view, we realise that whether propositional functions (or propositional equations) are accompanied by coordinative definitions is a question of crucial importance.

Without a coordinative definition, the concepts or variables of a system are merely connected, via the axioms, *with each other*, i.e., related *to each other*, but not to reality. Only if the concepts of a system have a concrete meaning that is *not* implicitly conferred on them by the axiomatic system can the axioms of a theory be viewed as statements *that speak about reality*. This meaning is conferred on the symbols (the concepts or variables) only by a coordinative definition (which is not necessarily always explicitly formulated; in fact, in most cases it is established only by the *use* of these symbols, by a "working definition"). The concepts – and with them the axioms and theories in which the concepts occur – refer to reality only by way of the coordinative definitions.

A theory conceived in a conventionalist way (or one understood in the sense of the first pseudo-statement position) can also be applied to reality. However, such an application is completely different from one obtained by means of empiricist coordinative definitions. For conventionalism does not provide definite assignments in terms of definite events and objects of reality; it allows us only to consider *those* events and objects that are models of the theory and that satisfy the conditions of the theory. The concepts (or the bound variables) of the theory are defined only within the models, and the theory *speaks only about* these models. But whether a real event will correspond to the theory or not *cannot be predicted* with the help of this (conventionalistically understood) theory, if only because the theory can be applied to the event only if we already know that the event corresponds to it, or models it.

Hence the conventionalist can never make *predictions* about the course of events in reality. He can speak about, and make predictions for, only the models of the theory. Whether or not an event is a model of the theory becomes evident only when this event has or has not been shown to satisfy the conditions of the theory. If it turns out that the event does not satisfy the theory, then the theory simply has not referred to it, and the theory has not made any claims about it. Thus, with respect to a real event we always find out only *post festum* (not "*a posteriori*") whether the theory has referred to it at all, or which concepts of the theory refer to it as their model. Predictions that can be verified or falsified *a posteriori* do not come about in this way; for such predictions can only be empirical statements: propositions that refer to reality in as definite a manner as possible.

Every form of empiricism must demand coordinative definitions or something corresponding to them; the same holds for a pseudo-statement position with an empiricist orientation. For only by means of coordinative definitions do combinations of symbols and conceptual systems become scientific theories. "Only by means of such coordinative definitions does it become possible to speak about reality in the language of a conceptual system."[1]

A propositional function with a coordinative definition can (like any empirical statement) also be understood *pragmatically*.

What a coordinative definition does is to demarcate a particular (empirical) field of arguments, while asserting that these arguments satisfy the given propositional function. This assertion may also be expressed, in pragmatist fashion, as follows: For the field demarcated by the coordinative definition, the propositional function is a *useful schema for the formation of statements*.

It would be possible that every assertion that a propositional function is *useful for a particular empirical domain* is simply a propositional function together with a coordinative definition, that is, a genuine statement; a result that demonstrates how carefully we should examine every "pseudo-statement position" as to whether its "pseudo-statements" are not perhaps genuine statements after all.

Since our analysis has temporarily left the critical discussion of the pseudo-statement positions and addressed the nexus of problems posed by conventionalism, it has made some (preliminary) contributions to its original topic, that is, to the critique of the pseudo-statement positions.

It has shown that conventionalism, which regards natural laws as genuine analytic judgements, and that form of empiricism that regards natural laws as genuine synthetic judgements, are two hazards that must be avoided by any pseudo-statement position that associates natural laws with the concept of propositional function.

---

[1] Herbert Feigl, *Theorie und Erfahrung in der Physik* (1929), p. 108.

Particular difficulties arise, on the one hand, for any theory of knowledge that advocates an empiricist pseudo-statement position and rejects conventionalism, since the question "Empiricism or conventionalism?" is almost equivalent to the question "Coordinative definition or no coordinative definition?" However, every coordinative definition transforms a propositional function into a genuine proposition and every definite indication concerning the empirical domain for which the propositional function is supposed to be useful may turn out to be a hidden coordinative definition.

On the other hand, the derived "propositional functions" ("theorems") of the "first pseudo-statement position" come dangerously close to conventionalism; they are no longer pseudo-statements but tautologies, or analytic judgements.

In the face of all these difficulties it should, however, be recalled that the pseudo-statement positions do not necessarily *have to* associate natural laws with propositional functions. There are still, perhaps, other types of pragmatic constructs that can be taken into consideration as natural laws. The difficulties here presented have, generally speaking, been presented not in order to refute any of the pseudo-statement positions, but only to prepare for their refutation.

30. *Conventionalist and empiricist interpretations, illustrated by the example of applied geometry.*[1] The decisive explanation of the opposition between the conventionalist and the empiricist view will be found only through the analysis of the problem of demarcation (specifically, through the application of the criterion of demarcation). Nevertheless, as a preliminary conclusion of the discussion of the set of problems posed by conventionalism and also as a counterweight to the rather lengthy logical subtleties treated in the previous sections, the opposition between conventionalism and empiricism will, at this point, again be summarised by reference to an example. The problem [of] *geometry and experience* will serve as this example.

In my view, only *applied geometry* as the doctrine of the measurable relationships between physical objects in physical "space" can be regarded as a serious topic of controversy between conventionalism and empiricism. I do not consider *pure geometry*, qua purely mathematical discipline, to be such a topic of controversy. On the whole, even modern empiricism acknowledges the non-empirical character of pure mathematics.

[1] Regarding this section, cf. the more recent formulations in Section 3 of the Appendix: "*Transition to the Theory of Method.*" [This note only in K₂. "*Transition to the Theory of Method*", see Vol. II (Fragments); cf. also Editor's Postscript. Ed.]

Pure geometry, or more accurately, pure geometries, are nothing but arbitrarily chosen axiomatic-deductive systems (that is: chosen within the limits set by the basic axiomatic conditions); they are pure combinations of concepts resting on a freely chosen axiomatic basis. Therefore, depending on the composition of the axiomatic system, very different geometries can exist (topological, projective and metric geometries, and among the latter the Euclidean and non-Euclidean geometries figure prominently).

All these systems – in so far as they are axiomatically fully articulated – are, from a logical viewpoint, completely equivalent in one respect: they are free "postulates about undefined objects"[2] and as such may be interpreted both as implicitly defining postulates (propositional equations) and as propositional functions. They can be postulated without regard to their potential applications, or to conditions obtaining in reality. They are different conceptual games played according to definite rules, that is, according to the rules of logic.

From a historical-genetic viewpoint, naturally even pure geometries originated in field surveying, that is, in a practical or applied discipline. And even today, natural scientists are interested in them primarily on account of their possible applications. They *need* geometry, and accordingly regard pure geometries as tools forged for them by the mathematician – who may not even have had the practical use of these "tools" in mind.

The logical structure and the *validity* of pure geometries are, however, completely independent of their history and of the physicist's pragmatic viewpoint. I consider the debate about whether the theorems of pure geometry are *synthetic judgements* (as Kant believed) – that is, empirical statements – or *purely conceptual constructs* – that is, either analytic judgements (implicit definitions, propositional equations) or propositional functions – to have been finally resolved. The credit for this resolution is due mainly to modern research into the foundations of mathematics and, in addition – from the philosophical side – to conventionalism and to "logical positivism". The result is this: pure geometry belongs to a purely conceptual domain and has, in the first instance, nothing to do with reality.

Only through [their] *application* are geometries related to reality, and this is where we encounter the controversy between conventionalism and empiricism regarding certain still unresolved epistemological questions

---

[2] [Cf. Section 28, note 3 and text to this note. Ed. See also Section 28, note +1. Tr.]

(which, in my view, even the very remarkable analyses by "logical positivists" have not yet fully resolved).

It is these questions that I propose to discuss in this section, in order to illustrate the opposition between conventionalism and empiricism.

A physicist needs a measuring geometry or *metric geometry* in order to make precise, numerical predictions about natural events, more particularly: about motions. (The significance of precise quantitative statements for our knowledge of nature has been mentioned earlier; see Section 15.) But as intimated above, there are among the geometric axiomatic systems *several different metric systems*, in particular the Euclidean and non-Euclidean geometries.

We are immediately confronted by the questions:

Which of these different geometries that are logically on a par should the physicist apply to reality? And what considerations should be borne in mind when deciding between different geometries?

To begin with, I will provide a very brief survey of the best-known views on this question. I shall subsequently discuss in greater detail the conventionalist and the empiricist answers, which in my opinion are the most important ones.

The *rationalist* view, according to which the unconditional (*a priori*) validity of the Euclidean axioms is immediately evident – self-evident also in their application to reality – is still quite widespread. It is plain that the conceptual definition "An axiom is a statement whose truth is immediately self-evident" was still being taught in school geometry lessons long after the acknowledged coexistence of the Euclidean and non-Euclidean axiomatic systems of pure geometry had made it inapplicable. (Two contradictory axioms cannot both be immediately self-evident.*[1])

A *second view* is Kant's doctrine of pure "intuition". Nature appears to us in the spatial and temporal forms of intuition, which "pure intuition" (the intuitive counterpart to discursive "understanding") transcendentally imposes on it. On the basis of pure intuition, we can decide *a priori* that space, as the form of all knowledge about nature, is Euclidean. (I shall not

---

*[1] Or if they are, we cannot infer their truth from the fact that they are immediately self-evident.

examine any further the debate about Kant's philosophy of geometry. On this issue, I largely follow the logical positivists, in particular Schlick's *Erkenntnislehre*.[3])

The main exponent of an *empiricist* philosophy of geometry is probably Helmholtz. According to him, experience decides (*a posteriori*) which of the different metric geometries is to be applied to reality, that is, which geometric axiomatic system has significance for physics, over and above the mathematical-logical significance of any system of pure geometry.

I regard only the arguments of *conventionalism* (Poincaré) as a serious threat to the empiricist view. Poincaré's objection seems to deal a fatal blow even to Helmholtz's empiricism.

Poincaré claims that, in the question of applied geometry, it is impossible "to connect . . . any rational meaning"[4] whatsoever with the empiricist thesis; for *it is, in principle, always possible to bring our experience into line with any metric geometry*, with non-Euclidean geometries just as much as with Euclidean geometry.

But if every experience can be made compatible with any geometry, then an empirical decision about the choice of a geometry is impossible. Conventionalism, accordingly, holds that as far as experience is concerned we have complete freedom of choice, and that only by convention can we single out the geometry in favour of which we want to decide. But which geometry should we choose? In the absence of material empirical grounds for our decision, our conventional decision is guided solely by the greater or lesser *simplicity* of the different systems. We choose Euclidean geometry because its axiomatic system is the *simplest*.

I will now examine in greater detail the conventionalist view, whose basic ideas I consider unassailable (even though I belong to the empiricist opposition).

The different systems of metric geometry are – as pure axiomatic systems, irrespective of their application – distinguished by the fact that a *different metric formula* is valid in each of them. Thus, for example, the quantitative relationship between the diameter and the circumference of a circle is not a constant in the formulae of non-Euclidean geometry, but depends

---

[3] [Moritz Schlick, *Allgemeine Erkenntnislehre* (2nd ed., 1925), pp. 320 ff. Ed.]

[4] [Henri Poincaré, *Wissenschaft und Hypothese* (German translation by Ferdinand and Lisbeth Lindemann, 3rd ed., 1914), p. 81. Ed.; English translation by William John Greenstreet: *Science and Hypothesis* (1905; reprinted 1952), p. 79. Tr.]

on the (absolute) size of the circle. The same thing holds for the sum of the angles in a triangle. In Euclidean geometry it is constant at 180° (irrespective of size). In non-Euclidean geometries the sum of the angles increasingly deviates from its Euclidean value as the triangle grows in size.

That such differences exist between different (pure) geometries is an obvious consequence of the different ways in which the axioms are put together. As we can see (and as was discovered by Kant's friend, J.H. Lambert[5]), the simplicity of Euclidean geometry consists in the fact that its metric formulae for different geometric constructs take no account of the (absolute) size of these constructs. (As formulated by Gerstel,[6] the following axiom applies: "All spatial size is relative."[*2])

The conventionalist position contains, as its most important thesis, the assertion that for a description of nature we can, without any great difficulty, use any of these geometries.

A model of a Euclidean triangle, realised by genuine physical bodies, will, admittedly, look different from the model of a non-Euclidean triangle (with non-Euclidean "straight lines" as its sides) constructed according to the differing conditions specified by a non-Euclidean axiomatic system. But models can be constructed for any of these geometries (and this, to any degree of approximation). This, however, means that (with the help of the coordinate systems accordingly con-structed and realised) each of these geometries is applicable to reality.

Since there are, in these different geometries, different *metric* formulae, their difference is manifested primarily by the fact that the models of the *measuring rods* for these various geometries have *physical properties* that *differ* from each other. A Euclidean model of a measuring rod will have to be physically constructed in a different way from a non-Euclidean model. Thus, if we choose a particular geometric axiomatic system, this choice will simultaneously determine the physical construction of the models of measuring rods for this system (the "*measuring system*").

---

[5] On this subject, cf. Roberto Bonola, *Die nichteuklidische Geometrie* (German translation by Heinrich Liebmann, 1908).

[6] [Adolf Gerstel, "Über die Axiome der Geometrie", *Wissenschaftliche Beilage zum sech-zehnten Jahresbericht* (1903) *der Philosophischen Gesellschaft an der Universität zu Wien* (Vorträge und Besprechungen über das Wesen der Begriffe, . . .), p. 110. Ed.]

[*2] Another formulation is, "there are *similar* triangles, but of different size" (that is, triangles with the same angles but of different size).

The measuring system, or measuring rod, must be constructed in such a way that all measurements agree with the metric formulae of the chosen geometry; for it is these formulae that *implicitly define* the geometry's concept of a measuring rod.

No experience can then come into conflict with the applicability of a freely chosen geometry. If practical measuring results contradict the formulae of a chosen geometry, this does not at all mean that this particular geometry does not agree with the conditions imposed by reality; rather, it is only an indication of the fact that the *measuring instruments* used as measuring rods are inadequate models of this geometry. They must, therefore, be *corrected* according to the formulae, for the deviation shows that, in terms of the implicitly defined ideal model, they have been lengthened or shortened, or at any rate *deformed*.

So much for the conventionalist view. Its fundamental idea – that in principle it must always be possible to describe any physical event, or any natural event, with the help of a freely chosen geometry – seems to me unassailable.

Given this problem situation, how can the empiricist view still appear tenable, that is, the view that experience decides the choice of a geometry?

Now, the empiricist must admit that we *can* adopt a geometry by free choice and, in this way, implicitly fix the concept of a "measuring rod".

We *can*, however, also proceed in the opposite way.

We can – and this is what the empiricist view is based on – concretely define the concept of a "measuring rod" or "measuring instrument" by means of an (explicit) coordinative definition. With this coordinative definition, we transform all the metric statements of the different geometries into empirical statements that can be decided only by experience. Only experience can decide which of the different geometries best represents the empirical measuring relationships; of course, only those measurements can be considered that were taken on the basis of the explicitly defined measuring instrument as a measuring rod.

But which physical body will the empiricist choose as a measuring instrument?

Every definition is conventional, it is freely stipulated. Much like the conventionalist who decides to choose a certain geometry, thus freely establishing a system of implicit definitions, the empiricist is guided by considerations of *simplicity* in the definition of a measuring rod, or in the choice of a measuring instrument. While the conventionalist chooses

Euclidean geometry, the empiricist chooses a "practically rigid" (that is, as solid as possible) physical body as his measuring rod.

Both conventionalism and empiricism thus have to start by giving *definitions*.

The conventionalist chooses a system of implicit definitions, a particular geometrical axiomatic system – such as Euclidean geometry.

The empiricist chooses a particular physical instrument as his measuring rod – such as a practically rigid body.

For conventionalism as well as for empiricism – once these definitions have been established – there can be *no further freedom of choice*.

With the choice of a geometry, the conventionalist has, at the same time, implicitly chosen his measuring rods. He must be satisfied with correcting the models of his system, or measuring rods, according to the conditions of the system. Whether and to what extent a particular (explicitly defined) physical body satisfies the conditions of a model will be shown by the results of measurements carried out with this body.

With the choice of a measuring instrument, the empiricist has, at the same time, implicitly chosen a geometry. He can carry out measurements only by means of this measuring rod and must wait to see which geometry the results of measurement accord with. It will, obviously, be the geometry of the model for which the chosen measuring instrument is appropriate. He too can discover only through measurements made with his measuring instrument whether and to what extent a particular geometry accords with the results of these experiments.

The results of the new physics have given a new impetus to the debate between conventionalism and empiricism.

Poincaré was still able to draw support from the fact that at that time physics gave preference to Euclidean geometry. Since Einstein's general theory of relativity, however, physics favours non-Euclidean (Riemannian) geometries, a fact that without a doubt has significantly strengthened the empiricist position.

But it is also possible – and it *must* be possible in the manner described by conventionalism – to interpret and represent with the help of Euclidean geometry all the facts of the general theory of relativity.

The general theory of relativity gives preference to an empiricist way of representation. It assumes – *on the basis of the results of measurements* – that in a gravitational field a non-Euclidean geometry is valid. (This is usually expressed through the rather daunting formulation – which nevertheless is intended to state exactly the same thing – that in a gravitational field "*space is curved*".)

However, the same empirical facts that lead to the adoption of a non-Euclidean geometry may also be interpreted and expressed in the manner of conventionalism (and, for the layman, in a much more understandable form), namely that all rigid bodies in a gravitational field contract in a certain way. The measuring rods fixed on these rigid bodies are, therefore, shortened when compared with the ideal rods implicitly defined by Euclidean geometry. Rigid bodies are simply not ideal models of Euclidean measuring rods.

We can, thus, interpret the same empirical finding in a *conventionalist* fashion, as the shortening of a measuring rod in the gravitational field (more accurately, as a shortening of a rigid body in relation to the implicitly defined measuring rod), or, in an *empiricist* fashion, as an indication that in a gravitational field non-Euclidean geometries are valid or that space is curved, depending on whether, as a conventionalist, one adopts Euclidean geometry by definition, or, as an empiricist, one adopts a rigid body as a measuring rod.

At this point, one might be tempted to regard this whole opposition between conventionalism and empiricism as a vacuous controversy about words. After all, both positions appear to represent the *same empirical facts*, even if they express them in different ways.

Each of the two positions – or so we could attempt to justify such a view – has to start with definitions. The one chooses an axiomatic system of implicit definitions, while the other chooses coordinative definitions. Once the definitions have been adopted, everything else depends, for both sides, on experience: for conventionalism, how its models are to be physically constructed; for empiricism, which axiomatic system has or has not been corroborated. With respect to both positions, we can thus distinguish between a defining part and an empirical part. Epistemologically, they are essentially *equivalent*, and which position we prefer to follow is merely a question of representation, or a question of style or taste.

I consider the view just presented as unclear, and I regard the attempt to justify it as a misunderstanding of conventionalism. But this view, this misunderstanding, may stimulate us to probe the problem further.

To begin with, it is very obvious that there is no controversy between conventionalism and empiricism about empirical facts. Conventionalism has no reason to enter into a debate about "experience", since in its own view *every* experience can (and must) be interpreted in terms of the theory it has chosen. There is, therefore, no question of a controversy about observed facts; the opposition consists exclusively in the different *interpretations*.

It is, moreover, confusing to construe as necessarily conventionalist all Euclidean interpretations of the results of the theory of relativity. Such interpretations could also be empiricist. And if, within a Euclidean conception of the results of the theory of relativity, it were really possible to distinguish between a defining *and an empirical part* (as is presupposed by the view that denies the opposition between the two positions) – then the term "conventionalism" would indeed be an "ill-fitting name" (Reichenbach[7]) for a view that is thoroughly *empiricist*.

Every empiricist interpretation must arbitrarily stipulate definitions (that is, coordinative definitions) in order to be able to make *empirical statements*, and conversely: every conception that proceeds in this way, that introduces empirically testable statements, is empiricist. It is this "empirical part", that is, these empirical statements, that characterise empiricism: perhaps not the introduction of a non-Euclidean geometry but the decision that this introduction should be judged by experience.

However, it is only if their concepts have acquired a concrete meaning through coordinative definitions that the statements of the different geometries can be related to reality in such a way that experience can decide between them.

The interpretation of the theory of relativity that retains Euclidean geometry and speaks about a shortening of rigid bodies in a gravitational field must, therefore, also provide coordinative definitions if it is to be treated (and perhaps rejected) as being an *empirical theory* at all. It must specify the physical properties of its measuring rod, for example, by precisely indicating the degree of shortening of the rigid body relative to the measuring rod. It must make these specifications explicitly and concretely, and remain *committed* to its explicit definition. There is, in principle, no reason why it should not choose its coordinative definitions in such a way that the results of measurement will agree with the formulae of Euclidean

---

[7] [Hans Reichenbach, *Philosophie der Raum-Zeit-Lehre* (1928), p. 49. Ed.; English translation by Maria Reichenbach and John Freund (1957), *The Philosophy of Space and Time*, p. 36. Tr.]

geometry. These coordinative definitions – and herein lies the opposition to a conventionalist implicit definition – must not, however, be altered as required (*ad hoc*) in order to save the statements of the system from refutation by experience.

Only a connection of the system with sufficiently specified coordinative definitions is empiricist. "Properties of reality are discovered only by a combination of the results of measurement with the underlying coordinative definition", writes Reichenbach[8] concerning the empiricist view.

Conventionalism does not in principle commit itself to any coordinative definition; for it cannot define its concepts twice (once implicitly and once concretely). Its "rigid body" may well be identical with a physically rigid body under certain circumstances; however, under other circumstances – that is, if the results of measurements with the physically rigid body contradict the theory – a conventionalist cannot remain committed to any coordinative definition. The "practically rigid measuring instrument" has then simply been *deformed* in terms of the implicitly defined measuring rod or the "ideal rigid body".

What is asserted about this deformation is of particular interest for the problem.

Either the conventionalist interprets this deformation as *having no real significance*, since it depends on the arbitrary choice of a system: the measuring body instrument in question simply does not conform to the conditions imposed by the implicit definitions of this system, though it might conform to a different system.

Or – and this is the more interesting case by far – he could take the position that the deformation is as "real" as any measurable physical event can be. To be consistent, a radical conventionalist will assume that *every* description of a physical event is carried out in a conventionalist fashion, that is, that it depends on the choice of the system; for this reason, the asserted deformation of a "practically rigid body" is just as "real" as any other event.

Presented in this form, the assertion of a deformation of the measuring instrument takes on the character of a (physical) hypothesis, that is – since it can be introduced *ad hoc* at any time – an *auxiliary hypothesis*.

---

[8] Hans Reichenbach, *op. cit.*, p. 47 [English translation, p. 35. Tr.]; of course I cannot completely concur with the view of conventionalism presented there.

This auxiliary hypothesis permits us to maintain a kind of coordinative relationship between the implicitly defined "measuring rod" and the real measuring instrument in question; but it is a coordinative relationship which – in contrast with an empirical coordinative definition – is never binding but rather, if required, can always be changed through other auxiliary hypotheses. Indeed, it must be changed, should it become necessary to "explain" deviating measurement results.

If a conventionalist wishes to give more detailed indications about applications and so to spell out coordinative relationships, he must necessarily avail himself of such auxiliary hypotheses: not only must he admit them, but he must even declare them to be unavoidable. For he presupposes that science must avail itself of implicit definitions since, with the help only of concretely defined concepts, exact scientific statements are not possible. He is, therefore, forced to fill the gap that he creates between concretely and implicitly defined concepts with auxiliary hypotheses. Hence, to any adjustment of the "model" there corresponds an auxiliary hypothesis about some deviation of the concrete "model" from the ideal [model] that was established by implicit definition.

According to the conventionalist view, there can be no axiomatic system in which such adjustments, such auxiliary hypotheses, are superfluous. If a particular axiomatic system could make the gap between the implicitly defined ideal models and the real objects and events disappear, then we should be in need of no implicit definition. We could formulate concrete definitions, and the whole conventionalist theory of knowledge would be superfluous.

This gap may well be excessively widened by some axiomatic systems and by some implicit definitions, and these will then be eliminated for practical reasons as not useful (but not as false). However, in principle the other axiomatic systems are all on a par. They are all in need of adjustments [and] of auxiliary hypotheses. This is why the decision between them is not made in terms of their more or less difficult practical application; the choice is made exclusively in terms of the *simplicity of the system*.

Once introduced, the chosen system may be fixed and regarded as *unalterable*. Its relations with real events and objects are what become *variable*. The bridge to reality consists of variable adjustments, that is, of auxiliary hypotheses introduced in an *ad hoc* fashion; and to these conventionalism is, in principle, unable to accept any restrictions.

In contrast, empiricism demands the most limited use of hypotheses and adjustments.

Empiricism, too, is forced to make adjustments and to adopt auxiliary hypotheses with respect to its coordinative definitions, and frequently these are not even especially simple. The classic example is that of the temperature adjustment carried out on "practically rigid bodies", which is temperature- and material-dependent.

But here lies a fundamental difference from conventionalism.

An empiricist is unable to adjust his coordinative definitions without thereby altering the axiomatic system. In a certain sense, for the empiricist the axiomatic system and its coordinative definitions form a unit, since changes in the coordinative definitions will also change the meaning of the empirical statements forming the axiomatic system. In addition, he must demand that the adjustment be *founded* on the system itself, that it should be deducible from the latter, and that the system will, if necessary, be altered accordingly.

The following remark illustrates most pointedly the opposition between the conventionalist and the empiricist view concerning adjustments.

For a conventionalist, the system is preserved unaltered regardless of whether many, or only few, auxiliary hypotheses become necessary. The adjustments are the necessary consequences of the absolute, *a priori* validity of the system as a system of implicit definitions.

An empiricist thinks that every adjustment that becomes necessary shakes the foundations of his system; for the fact that an adjustment has become necessary means precisely that his system (in its present form) has been refuted by experience. Admittedly, often he has good reasons why he should not immediately abandon the system as a whole. He knows that even an adjustment, or an auxiliary hypothesis, which was at first introduced merely in an *ad hoc* fashion and with some hesitation, may develop into a brilliantly corroborated component of the theory. But if an auxiliary hypothesis remains a foreign element in the system, if corroborations fail to occur, and above all if *new auxiliary hypotheses should again* become necessary, he will finally stop trying to save the system. He will regard it as refuted and will abandon it. A *new construction* becomes necessary.

An empiricist follows the methodological principle: as few hypotheses as possible! ("Principle of the most parsimonious use of hypotheses.")

If he does not follow this principle, he cannot escape conventionalism.

He could always try, yet again, to prop up the system by adding auxiliary hypotheses; a new construction would then be superfluous, since the system can always be saved through corresponding auxiliary assumptions (and thus by detaching it from binding coordinative definitions). It becomes irrefutable by experience. But then the empiricist position has been ditched and conventionalism has taken its place, for only *analytic* judgements are irrefutable by experience, that is, only they are *a priori* true.

(In order to make a theory unassailable, it is not at all uncommon in various sciences to resort to such a "conventionalist stratagem".)

There is, actually, no necessary opposition between conventionalism and empiricism in the choice of theories. Indeed, it is (as it were) the normal state of affairs that conventionalism and empiricism advocate not different theories but only different *interpretations* of [what at the time are] generally accepted theories. It is always, in principle, possible to view every theoretical system as a system of implicit definitions.

However, a conflict between conventionalism and empiricism must arise when a theory enters a phase of upheaval and crisis, that is, when empiricism regards the dominant theory as *refuted* and begins to undertake a comprehensive new construction.

A conventionalist simply cannot go along with this. He will never understand why precisely these experiences are supposed to refute the theory, since minor adjustments (which are always necessary) could quickly restore order. He sees no reason why the confirmed theory – the confirmed implicit definitions – should be abandoned, and he is *unable* to see one, since implicit definitions are irrefutable.

Of course, I am thinking primarily of the upheaval in physics that took place as a result of the theory of relativity (and of its conventionalist critique by Dingler[9]).

And this brings me back to the problem of geometry.

Conventionalism, too, had to accept the admissibility of the relativist non-Euclidean conception of space. Conventionalism is not wedded to Euclidean geometry; on the contrary, it recognises in principle the objective equivalence of different systems. It is, therefore, quite capable of

---

[9] [Cf. Hugo Dingler, *Physik und Hypothese* (1921), Part IV, pp. 150 ff. Ed.]

adapting itself to any new theory. But there is one thing conventionalism will never admit: that experiences force us to start building anew, and that vis-à-vis the old theory, the new one is a sign that knowledge is advancing.

According to conventionalism, knowledge progresses only when the system is *simplified*. Without a doubt, the theory of relativity represents an increase in complexity when compared with the classical geometrical and physical systems. Its mathematical-geometric apparatus is incomparably more difficult (it operates with four-dimensional non-Euclidean space-time geometries and, what is more, with a different one at every point in space), not to mention the complication arising from the intrusion of physics into geometry.

That a simple system should be superseded by a much less simple one must appear absurd to conventionalism, and even as a backward step in our knowledge. Conventionalism cannot accept the empiricist explanation for this way of proceeding, namely that the new system allows us to represent the new empirical findings much more simply, that is, with fewer auxiliary hypotheses.

An undoubtedly correct basic idea of conventionalism is that – from a logical viewpoint – a theory is never unequivocally determined by experience. This is why a conventionalist chooses a theory for its "simplicity".

A reasonable form of empiricism must also acknowledge the idea that, logically speaking, experience does not unequivocally determine the choice of a theory. An empiricist, too, admits that other empiricist theories, among them some working with Euclidean geometry, would also be capable of representing the empirical findings that led to the formulation of the theory of relativity. And the remarkable thing is that even empiricism appeals to *simplicity* in the choice of these possible empiricist theories. Einstein's general theory of relativity is said to be the *simplest* of these theories, primarily because it has to introduce far fewer auxiliary hypotheses. The simpler system seems to be the one that best satisfies the *principle of the most parsimonious use of hypotheses*; thus, we might also say: the system that proceeds in the least conventionalist fashion.

It is evident that the two views operate with two different concepts of simplicity; for otherwise they could not end up with such different results in the choice of a system. Accordingly, the opposition between conventionalism and empiricism can be represented as the *opposition between the conventionalist and the empiricist concepts of simplicity*.

In Section 15 I examined more closely an epistemological concept of simplicity. There, simplicity (as identical with the degree of law-likeness) was reduced to the concept of *primary improbability* of a law. The greater the primary improbability of a law (or the smaller its primary probability, that is, its range), the greater its degree of simplicity. Is this concept of simplicity related to the conventionalist or to the empiricist concept of simplicity?

It is easy to show that there is no immediate connection between the *conventionalist concept of simplicity* and this concept. If simplicity means no more than primary improbability, then the simplicity of every conventionalist system is equal to zero since the conventionalist system of implicit definitions is true *a priori*, hence has a primary probability equal to 1. According to this concept of simplicity, there can be neither more nor less simple analytic judgements; they are all alike in this respect: none of them is simple. "Simplicity" in the sense of primary improbability can be ascribed *only to synthetic judgements*.

The conventionalist concept must, therefore, refer to a different "simplicity", a simplicity of the internal logical relations within the system. It is a *purely formal concept of simplicity*, and we can perhaps approach it through the following considerations. The (individual) law, that is, the *synthetic judgement* which by virtue of its form, of its logical-mathematical precision, has a higher primary improbability, i.e., is simpler, will also correspond more closely to the conventionalist concept of simplicity if, by a "conventionalist stratagem", it is reinterpreted as an *analytic judgement*. (Such a "conventionalist twist" is always possible. All we need to assume is that the "concepts" occurring in the law are implicitly defined exclusively through their internal relations.)

For example, Euclidean geometry is simpler than non-Euclidean geometry in the sense of primary improbability also. Non-Euclidean geometries contain Euclidean geometry as a limiting case, but not vice versa. (We thus have a relationship fully analogous to that between a straight line and the conic sections; cf. Section 15). The bridge between the two concepts of simplicity is, therefore, constituted by the formal concept of a purely logical "range". But whereas the application of this concept to empirical statements leads to the opposition between *law-likeness and chance* and to the concept of primary improbability, its application to analytic judgements is indeed an "aesthetic", "pragmatic" and "conventional" one (Schlick[10]). Even the "simplest" system of implicit definitions has, in the sense of primary improbability, a zero degree of simplicity. These two concepts of simplicity must, therefore, be clearly distinguished.

(I wish to note that I do not believe that – as held by conventionalism – the reason why Euclidean geometry is so familiar to us is its "simplicity". In my view, the reason is its empirical validity within the limits of terrestrial dimensions; but this, in turn, is related to the fact that it constitutes a limiting case of non-Euclidean geometry and is, therefore, simpler because it lies within the latter's range.)

But what is the relationship between the *empiricist concept of simplicity* – which is discussed in this section – and simplicity in the sense of primary improbability?

It can easily be shown that these two concepts are equivalent. "Simplicity" in the sense of the "principle of the most parsimonious use of hypotheses" is also *identical to primary improbability*.

There is a stark contrast between this view and inductivist probability logic. Kaila,[11] for example, claims the exact opposite. Expressed in my terminology, he holds a view to the effect that the principle of the most parsimonious use of hypotheses can be reduced to *primary probability* in such a way that the simpler system (in the sense of a system with *fewer* hypotheses) has a greater primary probability. He maintains that this system has (*a priori*) fewer opportunities for conflicting with reality. Our own arguments lead to the opposite result. The *more* presuppositions (auxiliary hypotheses) a theory introduces, the greater are its prospects for adapting itself to any experience whatsoever, or for evading any conflict with experience. In the absence of any restrictions on the introduction of auxiliary hypotheses, a theory can be brought into line with any possible experience. Its "empiricist simplicity" disappears, and with it any cognitive value (as well as any predictive value) in the sense of empirical knowledge.

Here it becomes clear why the empiricist concept of simplicity can be formulated also as the (methodological) demand: As far as possible, avoid

---

[10] [Moritz Schlick, "Die Kausalität in der gegenwärtigen Physik", *Die Naturwissenschaften* 19 (1931), pp. 148 f.; see Section 15, text to notes 3 and 4. Ed.]

[11] Eino Kaila, *Die Prinzipien der Wahrscheinlichkeitslogik* (1926), p. 140.

proceeding in accordance with the spirit of conventionalism! Each step taken in the spirit of conventionalism, each adjustment and each auxiliary hypothesis gives a theory a much higher primary probability, and moves it closer to conventionalist analytic propositional equations, which are true *a priori*.

The opposition between conventionalism and empiricism may be summed up as follows:

Either one opts for the unbridled use of hypotheses, for no commitment to coordinative definitions but also for an unbridled application of the formal (that is, of the conventionalist) concept of simplicity in the choice of an *a priori* valid system of implicit definitions; or else one opts for the most parsimonious use of hypotheses, for a firm commitment to coordinative definitions and for an application of the empiricist (and not only formal) concept of simplicity which, in the choice of a system of empirical statements, is kept within bounds by experience.

I have made no secret of my partisanship for empiricism. My description of the conventionalist-empiricist opposition might, therefore, be perceived almost as a critique of conventionalism. Nevertheless, I regard conventionalism as by no means refuted by the considerations and comparisons presented here. Indeed, I consider it essentially irrefutable.

I cannot justify my rejection of conventionalism by arguing that it is *false*, but only by arguing that it does not succeed in solving epistemological problems, more particularly: the problem of demarcation and the methodological questions related to it. However, the conventionalist view is always practicable, and the *problem of applied geometry* can always be interpreted in a conventionalist sense.

Therefore, I come to the conclusion that it is not sufficient to distinguish between pure and applied geometries. Within applied geometries, two possible kinds of application must be distinguished: applications in the sense of conventionalism and applications in the sense of empiricism.

An applied geometry in the *conventionalist* sense is irrefutable; *it is protected against every falsification.*

Experiences and observations cannot decide against it, and thus not in favour of it either. Such a geometry does not, however, say anything about experience. Its application is based on adjustments of the measuring instruments so that the resulting observations will agree with the definitions adopted in the system.

Admittedly, an applied geometry in the *empiricist* sense also starts from arbitrary basic assumptions, but it does not keep to them under all circumstances. Rather, it adopts methodological rules about how geometry is to be applied (for example, rules about the admissibility of adjusting measuring instruments) that make it possible for this geometry to *come into conflict with experience*. It is, therefore, not protected against falsification; it is falsifiable and *experience can cause it to fail*.

The results of observation can confirm or refute it. Observation says something about the usefulness of the theory, and the theory says something about experience. It is a part of empirical science and of physics. (It is the physics of space.)

And *only to empirical science* does Einstein's[12] famous dictum apply:

"In so far as the statements of mathematics speak about reality, they are not certain, and in so far as they are certain, they do not speak about reality."

---

[12] Albert Einstein, *Geometrie und Erfahrung* (1921), pp. 3 f.

Chapter IX

STRICTLY UNIVERSAL STATEMENTS AND SINGULAR STATEMENTS

31. *Implication and general implication.* Our critical discussion of the pseudo-statement positions was interrupted in order to enable us to analyse (in sections 24–30) the set of problems posed by conventionalism, above all in order to allow a closer characterisation of the first pseudo-statement position.

On that occasion, logical (logistical) questions were discussed in perhaps greater detail than was absolutely necessary. This was done in part because a polemical treatment was desirable, but also because the terminological machinery acquired in that process will be needed in a further discussion, which is also polemical. Only after concluding this discussion can we return to the critique of the pseudo-statement positions.

This second polemic concerns the relationship between *general implications* on the one hand and *universal and singular statements* on the other.

The problem at the centre of this debate will be examined in the next section; the present section has the task of providing a recapitulation of the concept of general implication.

For this purpose, we discuss first the logistical concept of "implication" and then the concept of "general implication". For a more detailed discussion of the latter, the concept of "*implication*" is almost indispensable.

The concept of "implication" is, however, important for other reasons too. Its examination will shed considerable light on certain aspects of the *problem of induction* itself. This important additional result will be used in the subsequent analysis – though it should be clearly understood that the analysis has, at the present stage, different objectives.

While a *"general implication"* asserts that a particular relationship holds between *propositional functions*, an *"implication"* asserts that a similar relationship holds between genuine *statements*. (The "implicans" and the "implicate" of an "implication" are thus statements and not statement functions.) Both "general implications" and "implications" are assertions; they are themselves genuine statements. An "implication" might, therefore, also be called a "statement about statements", and a "general implication" a "statement about propositional functions".*[1]

An "implication" connects statements (its implicans and its implicate), thus forming a *conditional proposition* ("hypothetical judgement"). The latter is usually expressed linguistically by means of the connective "if . . . then . . ." ("If" introduces the implicans, "then" the implicate.) For example, "If Napoleon carries a sword, then he also wears a hat."

This example was intentionally chosen so that no *"internal" dependence whatever* exists between the two interconnected statements involved ("Napoleon carries a sword", "Napoleon wears a hat"). An "implication" should not be regarded as an assertion about the internal relations, or about the *content* of the two statements; it asserts only a relationship between their *truth values*.

What it asserts is only that if the implicans is *true*, then the implicate is also *true*.

Therefore, it asserts nothing about the content of the statements, nor does it say that "something is the case", that an event will or will not occur (it asserts neither that Napoleon carries a sword, nor that he wears a hat). Only if the one event occurs (that is, if the implicans is true) will the implication also assert something about the other event (about the implicate).

The truth or falsity of such a conditional statement, or implication, depends exclusively on what *truth values* are assumed by its implicans and its implicate.

With reference to our example, let us look at the following cases (in the sense of "Wittgensteinian schemata"[1]):

---

*[1] These formulations (in particular the word "about") again demonstrate the absence of a distinction between object language and metalanguage. What is meant is that an implication is a statement containing (two) statements, while a general implication is a statement containing statement functions.

[1] [Ludwig Wittgenstein, *Tractatus Logico-Philosophicus* (1918/1922), Propositions 4.441, 4.442, 5.101. Ed.]

a)   implicans and implicate are *both true*;
b)   implicans and implicate are *both false*;
c)   the implicans is *false*, the implicate is *true*.

In these three cases, the "implication" itself is *true* and it is correct to say that the relationship between the two statements is that of an implication.

d)   the implicans is *true*, the implicate is *false*.

In this case, and *only* in this case, is the implication also *false*, and no implication holds between the two statements.

In accordance with this schema, an implication can be *defined* as a statement about the truth values of two statements – implicans and implicate – that is false only if the implicans is true *and* the implicate false.

It is important to note that (according to b and c) an implication will be true in all circumstances where the implicans is false (i.e., if Napoleon does not carry a sword), regardless of whether the implicate is or is not true. A *false statement* implies *any statement whatever*.

An implication is proved whenever it has been demonstrated that either the implicans is *false* or the implicate is *true*.

Depending on whether its proof is of an empirical or of a logical nature, an implication can be classified as *synthetic* or *analytic*.

Synthetic implications can be confirmed or refuted only by experience. The example "If Napoleon carries a sword, then he also wears a hat" is, of course, a synthetic implication. It only becomes false when there is empirical evidence to show that Napoleon carries a sword but does not wear a hat.

Analytic implications are identical with what is usually called *inference*, drawing a conclusion or *deduction*.

An inference or logical derivation asserts only that if the basis of the deduction (the premise) is true, then the same will hold also for the propositions that are deduced (conclusions). This assertion evidently constitutes an implication. However, we speak of an inference only if the asserted relationship does not need to be confirmed by experience but can be proved *a priori* by means of a logical transformation. The concept of inference (more precisely, that of an inferential or of a deductive relationship) is, therefore, identical *not* with the concept of "implication" in general, but only with that of analytic (tautological) implication.

The purpose of an inference, or deduction, is to derive conclusions or *implicates* – for example, predictions – from the theory, and then to assert them separately from the theory; perhaps in order to compare them with experience, to verify or to falsify them. It must, therefore, be possible to *separate* an implicate from an implication and to assert it by itself, for this is why we carry out deductions (in order to obtain conclusions from premises).

Logistic expresses the admissibility of this procedure through the locution "*inference rule of implication*":[2] "If we have two assertions, one of which is an implication and the other its implicans, then we are permitted to infer its implicate."

This rule simply expresses the logical purpose of an implication. It applies to all implications, whether synthetic or analytic.

Two problems that we have touched on earlier in this work will give us the opportunity of applying the concept of implication.

Its applicability to the *problem of induction* seems to me to be of special importance.

The infinite regression of induction demonstrates that universal empirical statements are not verifiable or falsifiable, *at least not directly*. The *predictions deduced* from them are, however, directly verifiable or falsifiable.

If a prediction is deduced from a theory, then the former relates to the latter as implicate to implicans: they stand in a *relationship of implication* to each other. The following remarks, directly derivable from the definition of implication, therefore hold for theories and their predictions:

1. The empirical verification of a prediction never allows us to infer the truth of a theory or natural law. (Even if the implicate is true, the implicans may be false: "A true statement is implied by every statement"[3] and therefore the implicans is left completely undetermined.) This, however, means that it is impossible empirically to verify natural laws by way of their predictions, either directly or indirectly.

2. From the empirical falsification of a prediction, on the other hand, it necessarily follows that the theory or natural law must also be false. (If the implicate is false, then – provided the implication holds – the implicans must also be false; this is the rule of "*modus tollens*" of traditional logic.) Therefore, it is *perfectly possible empirically to falsify* natural laws (admittedly not directly, but) *indirectly*.

These quite trite propositions (which, of course, are valid only provided natural laws are genuine statements) already contain the deductivist-empiricist solution to the problem of induction. This solution states that while there is no bridge linking the empirical verification of singular empirical statements to that of universal statements, there is a bridge linking the empirical falsification of predictions to the empirical falsification of the universal statements from which they were deduced. According to this thesis, *universal empirical statements can never be proved to be true, but may well be proved false.*

---

[2] Quoted from Rudolf Carnap, *Abriß der Logistik* (1929), p. 11.
[3] [Cf. Rudolf Carnap, *op. cit.*, p. 7. Ed.]

Apart from this application of the concept of implication, which for my purposes is the most important, there is a second application that seems to me noteworthy. With the help of this concept, it is possible to highlight the crucial importance of the "first fundamental condition of axiomatics", namely the *standard of consistency, or freedom from contradiction.*

While the other fundamental conditions of axiomatics, such as that of logical independence (cf. Section 25), can easily be derived from the notion of an axiomatic system – from the contrast between fundamental principles and theorems – it is not at first glance as easy to provide a justification for the standard of consistency. Consistency is, nonetheless, more fundamental than all the other conditions; there is no doubt that it rightly takes first place.

We could try to justify this condition by saying that a logically inconsistent statement, or a "contradiction", indeed any logically inconsistent system of propositions, is in any case *a priori false*. (The deduction of a logical inconsistency is the only purely logical, analytic method of proving statements to be false. The negation of a contradiction is tautological.) Correct as this remark may be, it does not quite suffice to explain the fundamental character of the standard of consistency. For if we compare a *false but logically consistent axiomatic system* (one that has been empirically refuted by the falsification of some of its predictions) with a *logically inconsistent one*, there remains one fundamental difference between the two. This difference is that there follow, even from a false theory (for example, from a geocentric system of astronomy), fairly precise predictions for certain domains (e.g. for eclipses), while a logically inconsistent theory will always be useless for such purposes.

But, then, wherein lies the importance of the standard of consistency?

The purpose of an axiomatic system is to stipulate a very limited number of assumptions, from which we can obtain in a purely logical fashion all the propositions (thus also all the predictions) belonging to a scientific domain.

This may also be expressed as follows:

By means of an axiomatic system, out of the infinite class of all possible statements a determinate subclass – consisting of the theorems of the system – is implicitly (but in a purely logical fashion) *marked out as true;*[*2] and thus another subclass, that of the statements that contradict the system, is *marked out as false.*[*3]

A *logically inconsistent* axiomatic system cannot carry out this fundamental task.

[*2] Provided that the axioms are true.
[*3] Under the same proviso.

For it is possible to *deduce any statement whatever* (and thus always its negation, too) from a logically inconsistent axiomatic system. Hence, by means of such an axiomatic system it is impossible *to single out any statement at all*, for all statements are characterised as both true and false.

This assertion may be considered established if it can be demonstrated *purely logically* that an arbitrary proposition is implied by every logically inconsistent system, deduction being the method by which the validity of an implication may be demonstrated purely logically.

This demonstration can easily be provided. A logically inconsistent axiomatic system is *false* for *purely logical* reasons; but a false proposition – a false "conjunction" of a system of propositions – implies *any arbitrary proposition.* (Cf. above.)

It may be admitted that an *empirically false* axiomatic system that is not logically inconsistent also implies any statement whatsoever. Nevertheless, such an axiomatic system performs the task of marking out only a very restricted class of statements as theorems. Only the statements belonging to this restricted class can be *logically deduced*, since only they bear the *analytic* relationship of implication to the system. Since the system is false, all other statements are admittedly implied, but the implication is *synthetic*. They *cannot be deduced*, since the implication relationship (the *synthetic* implication) cannot be purely logically demonstrated.

Thus, the consistency standard can be justified by the fact that a logically inconsistent (contradictory) axiomatic system does not single out any theorems at all – since it is compatible with any conclusion and allows the deduction of any arbitrary statement; it is completely empty.

(Thus, in direct opposition to Wittgenstein's[4] view, not [only] a tautology but [also] a *contradiction* allows "*all* possible situations" in the "whole – in the infinite whole – of logical space".)

It should be pointed out that the "first fundamental condition of axiomatics", as presented here, is particularly significant for the analysis of the demarcation problem. It enables us to establish an exact formal analogy between the "*criterion of demarcation*"[5] and that of "logical consistency".

The applications presented here are intended to draw attention to the significance of the concept of implication, and in particular to that of analytic

---

[4] Ludwig Wittgenstein, *Tractatus Logico-Philosophicus* (1918/1922), Propositions 4.462 and 4.463. Cf. also Proposition 5.14.

[5] [Cf. Appendix: Section V; Karl Popper, *Logik der Forschung* (1934; 2nd ed., 1966; and subsequent editions), Section 24. See also Editor's Postscript. Ed.; English translation, *The Logic of Scientific Discovery* (1959; 2nd ed., 1968; and subsequent editions), Section 24. Tr.]

implication. Since natural laws, according to the deductivist-empiricist theory of knowledge, are to be regarded solely as premises of *deductions*, it is not surprising that for this theory of knowledge the concept of *analytic implication* is of great importance: for this is nothing other than the *concept of deduction*.

The concept of "*general implication*", which has – for polemical purposes – been used rather frequently in the present work, is not comparable in epistemological significance with the concept of implication.

A "general implication" asserts the existence of a certain relationship between *propositional functions*. This relationship cannot, of course, be identical with an implication. For an "implication" is a relationship between *truth values* (the truth values of the implicans and the implicate); whereas propositional functions can have no truth values.

Yet there is a far-reaching analogy between the two concepts.

If two propositional functions stand in a relationship of "*general implication*", then all pairs of statements formed from them will stand in a relationship of "*implication*", provided that these propositions are obtained from the two propositional functions by substitution of the *same* argument, which can otherwise be freely chosen.

A "general implication", therefore, asserts the existence of a relationship of implication between *all* pairs of statements formed in this way: hence its name.

It can easily be shown that this explanation of the notion of "general implication" is strictly identical with the definition given earlier (a "general implication" is the assertion that all the arguments that satisfy the implicans also satisfy the implicate). Both formulations state precisely that *if* an argument turns the implicans into a true proposition, *then* the same holds for the implicate.

This connection with the concept of implication enables us to conceive of general implications in a different way from that adopted in earlier sections, namely, as a *schema for the formation of "implications"*.

This view can be applied to both synthetic and analytic general implications; it is on a par with, and is indeed logically equivalent to, the views presented earlier.

A *synthetic general implication* (we may recall the example of Section 29: " 'x is a stone-throw' generally implies 'the trajectory of x is a parabola' ") has previously been interpreted as an ordinary empirical statement about all the elements of a class ("The trajectories of all stone-throws are parabolas") or, equivalently, as a propositional function coupled with a coordinative definition. Equally valid is the interpretation according to which a "general implication" is a schema for the formation of a very large number of synthetic "implications". Asserting a "general implication" accordingly amounts to asserting that *each* of the statements formed from the statement function that constitutes the implicans implies the corresponding statement formed (by substitution of the same argument) from the statement function that constitutes the implicate. (If this argument is not a throw of a stone, but perhaps that of a boomerang, then the implicans becomes false and, for this reason alone, the whole implication will be true.)

An *analytic* or *tautological general implication*, in which the implicate occurs also in some form in the implicans, was earlier understood in two different ways: as an *analytic judgement* about the elements of a class (propositional functions together with a tautological, pseudo-coordinative definition) and as an *inference* between propositional functions. Now a third conception is added, namely, that of a propositional function as a schema for the formation of analytic implications. All three views may be applied to the following example: " 'All x are y and Socrates is x' generally implies 'Socrates is y'." Viewed as an analytic judgement, this general implication signifies: We can say about Socrates whatever can be said about every element of every class to which Socrates belongs. Viewed as an inference, it signifies: Through logical transformation, we can derive the implicate from the implicans, regardless of which arguments are substituted for the variables. Viewed as a schema for the formation of "implications", it signifies: Every substitution transforms a general implication into a true analytic implication; and this includes the substitution of arguments not satisfying the implicans.

Whichever way we conceive of a general implication, it must in any case be viewed as a genuine statement. Even as a "schema for the formation of implications", it asserts something (and it will be false if this assertion does not hold); that is, that no (correct) substitution can yield a false implicate unless the corresponding implicans is also false.

(Being a genuine statement, every "general implication" – as well as every "implication" – can itself be the implicans or the implicate of an "implication", but never the implicans or the implicate of a "general implication".)

"The inference rule of implication" may, of course, be applied to any "implication" that is formed from a "general implication"; that is, the implicate of an "implication", which is now a genuine statement, may be detached from this "implication" (if we assume the implication itself, as well as the implicans, to be true). Can there be an analogous "inference rule" for a "general implication"?

I have already answered this question in the negative in Section 28. I advanced the argument (against Carnap) that there is not, and cannot be, a rule that permits us to detach in any way the *implicate* of a general implication.

It is a fact that there exists no such rule, that is, that logistic has so far not formulated such a rule. But is there, perhaps, a gap in the system here? Perhaps such a rule can still be incorporated?

I believe that this summary survey of the notion of "general implication" can establish full clarity on this point. The different views concerning this concept are strictly logically equivalent. But only one of them, the one that regards it as an "inference", allows us even to think of anything similar to an "inference rule of general implication". With respect to the other two views – namely, that a general implication is an ordinary analytic or synthetic judgement or that it is a schema for the formation of implications – it is immediately obvious that any analogy with an "inference rule" is out of the question.

The "ordinary method" simply consists in detaching the implicate – in accordance with the "inference rule of implication" – in the case of those values (of the elements of the class) for which the implicans can be asserted. We cannot, of course, apply another analogous "inference rule" to this detached implicate.

The impossibility of such an "inference rule" becomes even clearer if we consider the conception of a general implication as a "schema for the formation of implications". Here, implications must first be formed in order to apply the "inference rule of implication" to those among them whose implicans is "asserted". This "inference rule" does not apply to all implications, however, but only to those whose implicans is asserted. The application of an analogous inference rule to the general implication, or schema, would be equivalent to an extension of this "inference rule" to all implications, including any whose implicans is assumed to be false – which of course contradicts the definition of an implication.

In summary, we can say that the fundamental difference between "implication" and "general implication" finds its precise expression in the existence of the "inference rule of implication", but not of an [analogous] "inference rule of general implication".*[4] As propositional functions, the implicans and the implicate of a "general implication" simply cannot have any truth value, and therefore they can be neither asserted nor denied.*[5]

32. *General implication and the distinction between strictly universal and singular statements.* The contrast between "strictly universal" and "singular" statements is fundamental for the *problem of induction.* The latter cannot even be formulated without this distinction. From the start of our analysis, it has therefore been necessary repeatedly to contrast universal with singular

---

*[4] This is not quite correct. For from the general implication

$$(x)\ (Fx \supset Gx)$$

one can deduce the implication

$$(x)\ (Fx \supset Gx)$$

to which *modus ponens* is then applicable.

*[5] This is correct; but if a *generalised* implicans is asserted (or a *generalised* implicate is denied), then this yields a generalisation of the implicate (or the negation of the generalised implicans).

statements; for example: in the "Formulation of the Problem" and in the presentation of Hume's argument. Almost everything that was said there and subsequently would collapse if this contrast proved untenable.

Up to this point, however, there has been little reason to regard as problematic the distinction between universal and singular statements. Anyone dealing with the problem of induction almost always presupposes this distinction more or less consciously. If, however, doubts emerge about its admissibility or if it is in any way unclear, the fundamental importance of the distinction makes further discussion unavoidable.

This, now, is indeed the case. In Schlick's presentation of the *pseudo-statement position*, we find a remark that upon further reflection forces us to examine in detail the distinction between universal and singular propositions.

Schlick's remark concerns the logistical concept of *"general implication"*; it was impossible to discuss his remark earlier, since any discussion would have required that this term was already understood.

In Sections 27 and 29, it was maintained that strictly universal as well as singular statements can be rendered as general implications. The examples I used were, among others, the strictly universal statement "The trajectories of all stone-throws are parabolas" and the singular statement, or summary report, "The trajectories of all *previously* recorded stone-throws are parabolas."

Rendered as general implications, these two propositions read as follows:

" 'x is a stone-throw' generally implies 'the trajectory of throw x is a parabola' " (strictly universal general implication), and " 'x is a stone-throw whose trajectory has been recorded' generally implies 'the trajectory of throw x is a parabola' " (singular general implication).

"Strict *positivism*" objects to the view that natural laws are strictly universal propositions. Its argument (the "strict positivist argument") is that such laws cannot be verified for *all* cases.

This position (and this argument) is, of course, directed only against "strictly universal" general implications, and is quite compatible with the existence of "singular" general implications.

It is a different matter with the *pseudo-statement positions*. They must oppose *every* view that purports to regard natural laws as general implications; they must indeed be opposed to *every* form of general implication, for every general implication is a *genuine proposition*.

Thus, Schlick too rejects general implications. But one remark in his justification is striking:[1]

"Natural laws are not (in the logician's language) 'general implications', because they cannot be verified for *all* cases . . ."

As we can see, Schlick bases his rejection on the "strict positivist" argument. The latter can be directed only against "strictly universal" propositions, and never against general implications as such. Admittedly, a general implication is always a statement about "*all* cases" (all elements) belonging to some class, but this class (as the example of "singular" general implications shows) can sometimes also be so defined that the statement *can be verified for all cases.*

Schlick undoubtedly identifies "strictly universal propositions" with "general implications" (which is also evident from the global structure of his argument). This may well be just a minor slip that we need hardly mention. But further reflection shows that there are deeper reasons for this confusion.

In the language of logistic, Schlick was unable even to express the concept of "strictly universal proposition", since logistic does not have any means for conceptually grasping the contrast between "strictly universal" and "singular" propositions.

If this is true, then it is certain that we can no longer regard the distinction between universal and singular statements as unproblematic. This distinction is the problem to be examined in the following sections (33–35); then (in Section 36) we shall finally resume the long-interrupted discussion of the pseudo-statement positions.

We begin the analysis with a brief terminological survey.

The opposition of "strictly universal" and "singular" propositions (which resembles a distinction made by Kant; cf. Section 7) takes as its point of departure the terminological needs of the *problem of induction.*

The division into *universal and particular* judgements arises from the entirely different needs of the old logical *theory of inference* (syllogistic): "universal judgements" are judgements about *all* elements of a class, while "particular judgements" are exclusively about *some* elements of a class.

---

[1] Moritz Schlick, "Die Kausalität in der gegenwärtigen Physik", *Die Naturwissenschaften* 19 (1931), p. 156.

(But particular judgements – for example, "Some humans are fair haired" – can always be transformed into "universal judgements" such as "All fair-haired humans constitute a [non-empty] subset of the class of humans"; which means that this distinction was in fact significant only for syllogistic rules.) What this means is that the "universal judgement" of the *syllogistic* has a completely different meaning from that of a "strictly universal" proposition in my terminology: for it means exactly the same as the "general implication" of *logistic*.

As has been shown earlier, all kinds of singular propositions, including "*particular judgements*", can be written as general implications. In other words, the syllogistic counts "particular judgements" among "universal judgements" (as Kant[2] also emphasises): they, too, are statements about all – and not only some – elements of a class (namely, a class with only *one* element).

Both traditional syllogistic logic and logistic, that is, use terminology that fails to meet the needs of the problem of induction. In order to work on this problem, we must divide the "universal judgements" of traditional logic and the "general implications" of logistic into "strictly universal" (or "universal", if there is no risk of confusion) and "singular" propositions.

Traditional logic, which employs the language of words, has no problems with such a distinction. But logistic, which employs a precise symbolic language, is (in its present form) incapable of grasping the distinction. (I believe that what prevents it from grasping the distinction is an inductivist prejudice that already plays a part in its fundamental presuppositions.)

Since "universal" as well as "singular" propositions can be formulated as general implications, so that both are statements about *all* the cases belonging to some class, the distinction between them – should it be sustainable – must obviously correspond to a difference between the classes in question.

In the next section, the two groups of "classes" underlying this distinction will be presented: universal concepts and individual concepts.

---

[2] [Cf. Immanuel Kant, *Kritik der reinen Vernunft* (2nd ed., 1787), pp. 96 f. Ed.; English translation by N. Kemp Smith (1929), 1965: *Critique of Pure Reason*, p. 107. Tr.]

33. *Universal concept and individual concept – class and element.*[1] The distinction between strictly universal statements and singular statements can be reduced to the classical distinction between universal concepts (universals) and individual concepts. But this reduction only shifts the problem, it does not constitute a solution; for, conversely, we might just as well reduce the distinction between universal and individual concepts to the distinction between universal and singular statements. We may, therefore, say only that the two traditional distinctions are interdependent; that neither can be given up without simultaneously giving up the other.

The analogy between the two distinctions is far-reaching. The opposition of universal and singular statements gives rise to the *problem of induction*, and a similar opposition of universal and individual concepts gives rise to the classical *debate about universals*. The connection between these two problems will be further discussed below.

In its present form, logistic cannot even formulate the opposition of universal and individual concepts. It tends to regard this distinction of traditional logic as inadmissible, and the problem of universals as a *"pseudo-problem"*. It attempts to replace the traditional distinction between *universal and individual concepts* by the (logistical) distinction between *class and element.*

---

[1] [In this section, a page was enclosed with the following note:]

33. Universal concept and individual concept; – class and element.

This (and the two following sections 34 and 35) are presently [1932] being reformulated. In Section 36, the most important results of the analysis up to that point will be recapitulated so that the reader can continue from there without any difficulty.

Brief summary of contents of [the newly planned] Section 33:

In Section 33 it will be shown that logistic and "logical positivism", for example, Carnap, recognise only *classes* and *elements*, but not the distinction between universal concepts and individual concepts. Every universal concept and every individual concept, however, can always be understood as a *class* of elements as well as an *element* of a class. Since logical positivism recognises only classes and elements, it identifies "universal concepts" with classes and "individual concepts" with elements; consequently it can easily assert the *relativity* of the distinction between universal and individual concepts.

[The first sentences of this note refer to earlier – and now lost – versions of sections 33, 34 and 35. The summary of contents for the newly planned Section 33 corresponds quite closely to the version of Section 33 reproduced here and with Section 14 of *Logik der Forschung* (1934; 2nd ed., 1966; and subsequent editions). Ed. *The Logic of Scientific Discovery* (1959; 2nd ed., 1968), Section 14. Tr.] *See also Vol. II (Fragments): [III.] *Transition to the Theory of Method*, Section 7.

(On an equal footing with "classes and their elements", logistic deals with "relations and their components"; cf. Section 26. As was pointed out there, relations need not be discussed separately; everything to be said here about "classes" can be applied *mutatis mutandis* to "relations".)

Notwithstanding the efforts made by logistic, the two distinctions – universal and individual concepts on the one hand, class and element on the other – will, from the start, be portrayed here as *fundamentally different*. Even though only the distinction between universal and individual concepts is of interest for the present analysis, its presentation will be based directly on the opposition between this conceptual pair and that of class and element.

According to the view advocated here, the distinction between universal and individual concepts is *unambiguous* – a universal concept can never be also an individual one – whereas the distinction between class and element is *not an absolute one*.

Every class can always occur also as an element, that is, as an element of a class of a higher type.

To begin with, this claim about the distinction between class and element will be clarified by means of examples. Next, a similar relationship will be pointed out between superordinate and subordinate concepts (in the sense of traditional logic). The only purpose of all this is to arrive finally at a position from which the *unambiguous* character of the distinction between universal and individual concepts can also be defended against the objections of logistic.

I shall begin by giving examples that illustrate the distinction between class and element.

The chemical concept "iron" can be understood as a class whose elements are "things" ("physical bodies") that have certain chemical properties. (In the logistical representation, this class is defined by the propositional function "x has the chemical properties of iron". The arguments that satisfy this propositional function are the elements of the class "iron".) This class, however, not only *has* elements; it can *itself* be regarded *as an element*, such as an element of the class of "metals" (defined by the propositional function "x is a metal"). This class, in turn, can also occur as an element of a class, and so on. In their turn, individual "iron things" (the "physical bodies"), that is, the *elements* of the class "iron", can be understood as *classes*. Every physical body can, perhaps, be understood as a class of its "states". A physical body occupies a particular region of space for a particular time, that is, a space-time region. If we think of this region as divided into instantaneous slices of space, we can call such an instantaneous cross-section a "*state*" of a physical body. The "body itself" is, accordingly, a class whose elements are "states".

Each (individual) "state" of a physical body could, in the same way, be understood as a class, for example, as a class whose elements are the "states" of molecules lying in a certain region of space, and so on.

This example would yield something like the following hierarchy of types (type hierarchy of classes):

The "state" of a molecule; the "state" of a class of molecules (= "state" of a physical body); the physical body itself as a class of its states; "the element iron" as a class of physical bodies; "the metals" as a class of classes of bodies (of iron, copper, aluminium, etc.). This hierarchy could be extended further.

The example should serve to illustrate what I wish to refer to by the expression "*relativity* of the distinction between class and element": namely, that *every* concept that can be understood as a *class* can also always be interpreted, under a different aspect, as an *element* of a class (of a "higher type"). The distinction between class and element is, therefore, *not unambiguous*.

The idea of a *type hierarchy* has become known especially through Russell's "theory of types" (a critique of which is beyond the scope of this investigation). In a type hierarchy, the concepts are ordered in such a way that a particular concept appears, on the one hand, as a class whose elements are concepts of a lower type and, on the other, as an element of classes that are concepts of a higher type. But within each type, classes can be ordered according to their *extension*, that is, according to whether they possess more or fewer elements (of a lower type). This ordering by extension creates, within each type, *superordinate concepts* and *subordinate concepts* subsumed by the superordinate ones. Traditional logic, which did not take into account a hierarchy of types, called this ordering by extension a "hierarchy of concepts".

Within the type of physical bodies, the following "hierarchy of concepts" could thus be set up as an example of a hierarchy ordered by extension:

"Cast-iron rod", "cast-iron body", "iron body", "heavy-metal body", "metal body", "solid body", "physical body", and so on.

Each of these "bodies" is a superordinate concept in relation to the preceding subordinate one. That is to say, this distinction too is *relative*. The *relativity* of the distinction between superordinate and subordinate concepts (between "genus" and "species") is *all that we need to say here about this distinction* (in order to contrast it with the "absolute" distinction between universal and individual concepts, which is a distinction of a completely different kind).

A type hierarchy has, incidentally, more dimensions than a hierarchy of concepts ordered by extension, which is always confined to one type.

The hierarchy of concepts and the hierarchy of types will now be compared by means of an example.

Hierarchy of concepts:

"German shepherd dogs living in Vienna"; "German shepherd dogs living in Austria", etc. . . . "dogs living in Austria"; "dogs" . . . "mammals" . . . "animals". All these classes are of the same type. This is evident from the fact that, for example, my dog Lux is an element of each of them; or from the fact that we can formulate the general implication: " 'x is a Viennese dog' generally implies 'x is an animal' ", in which a single argument can be substituted for "x" at each occurrence.

Hierarchy of types (this example follows Carnap,[2] though it has been slightly modified):

"My dog Lux" is an element of the class "dogs living in Vienna", which in turn is an element of the class "animal classes of Vienna"; but "my dog Lux" itself constitutes a class, that is, the class whose elements are the "states of the dog Lux"; an individual "state of Lux" is (according to Carnap[3]) "a class whose elements are points of the perceptual world", and so on.

While the contrast between class and element (or between superordinate and subordinate concepts) is a *relative* one, that between universal and individual concepts is absolute; on this point I fully endorse the position of traditional logic.

---

[2] [Cf. Rudolf Carnap, *Der logische Aufbau der Welt* (1928), p. 213. Ed.; English translation by Rolf A. George (1967): *The Logical Structure of the World and Pseudoproblems of Philosophy* (1967), (London), p. 247 (§158). Tr.]

[3] [Rudolf Carnap, *loc. cit.* Ed.; English translation, *loc. cit.* Tr.]

A single dividing line runs through the hierarchies of types and of extensions and through *each individual type*. This line divides the whole system of concepts into two fields – the realm of *universals* (example: "dog breed"; "a large brown dog") and that of *individual concepts* (example: "the dog breeds of Vienna"; "my dog Lux").

Each of the two realms has hierarchies of types, and also classes and elements; and each has hierarchies of concepts, that is, concepts of greater or lesser extension.

According to the view advocated here, this line between universal and individual concepts is *unambiguous*. Whereas one and the same concept can, depending on our viewpoint, be interpreted both as a class and as an element and both as a superordinate and as a subordinate concept, we must always be able to answer unequivocally the question whether it is a universal concept or an individual concept.

What is this line? In what does this absolute distinction consist?

I should emphasise that I consider the notions "universal" and "individual" to be basic undefinable logical concepts. (They could presumably be defined, but only if the distinction between universal and singular statements were presupposed.)

Although they are undefinable, a very simple and unequivocal *criterion* can, nonetheless, be suggested for determining whether a concept is universal or individual.

It is an old logical rule that a particular individual can never be uniquely characterised through a universal concept alone. For a unique characterisation of an individual, we always need to draw upon *proper names* in some form or another. This means that

universal concepts have to be so determined that *no proper name* could be used in their definition; whereas for

individual concepts at least one proper name (in some form) is used in their definition.

I hold the concept of a proper name also to be undefinable: I believe that paraphrasing it is sufficient. A proper name is a symbol (like a dog tag) that can, if necessary, be directly attached to the object in question, and if it needs to be used at all, will be used only *one time*, only for this object. (If the object is of a kind where attaching such a name is not possible – names of countries and the like – then a proper name might be posted on the country's borders; or the object could be defined with the *help* of actual proper names – [example:] "The meeting of 8 February

1893." Concerning exact dates, cf. further below.) Direct (demonstrative) *references* such as "This dog here" or "Today" and so on can be treated as proper names.

In order to show that the suggested criterion captures what we understand by universal and individual concepts, I shall here propose two guidelines that will be discussed by means of examples. I expect a discussion of Carnap's view in particular, which is diametrically opposed to mine, to contribute to the clarification of this question.

The two guidelines to be discussed are:

1. A particular *individual* can never be unequivocally characterised by universal concepts alone, without the use of proper names.

2. A *universal concept* can never be defined by means of proper names or by means of a class of particular individuals.

Comments on guideline 1.

No matter how precisely I describe my dog Lux by means of universal concepts, perhaps as a one-year-old, brown German shepherd dog with bright green eyes, etc., I shall never be able, in this way, to characterise it uniquely as an individual. However far I push this "specification", I shall always be able to speak about *all* one-year-old, brown German shepherd dogs and so on. Even if the description were so precise that there could in *practice* be no second dog to which it applied, I would not have achieved anything. From a *logical* viewpoint, it is always an entire class that is circumscribed by the description, even if I so narrowed the description that perhaps it ceased to fit any individual dog.

It would be a completely different matter if I made use of proper names: "my dog"; "the beautiful German shepherd dog of N-street in Vienna"; "the dog that in the year 1930 in Vienna wore tag no. 17,948" and so on. Such characterisations can be unambiguous.

Exact places and times in particular make an unambiguous characterisation possible. This point is important. We should not overlook the fact that times and places must be *exact*; for these, in turn, *always originate in proper names*. The origin of a temporal and spatial coordinate system can be fixed only through the use of proper names (for example, Greenwich or Christ's birth) or by direct ostensive reference, which amounts to the same thing. (Only one specific point fixed in this way within an "individual" coordinate system can be considered as a potential *principium individuationis*.) A person, such as Napoleon, can thus be unambiguous characterised by specifying the place and date of his birth. For we should thereby have used individual concepts or proper names.

A particular individual object – such as the soap bubble that in an experiment carried out one week ago I filled with a mixture of oxygen and hydrogen – occupies a determinate connected space-time region, but only if we are dealing with a physical body. That soap bubble came into being at a determinate instant in the year 1931, in a determinate place in Vienna, grew to a diameter of 6 cm and burst after three minutes.

It would, however, be erroneous to believe that occupying a connected space-time region is what characterises individual concepts. What matters is the characterisation of the region by *proper names*, which are provided by a specified spatio-temporal coordinate system. "A soap bubble having a diameter of 6 cm that was filled with a mixture of oxygen and hydrogen and burst three minutes after it came into being" would be a *universal concept*, since a spatio-temporal specification by ostension or by proper names is missing.

There are, moreover, individuals such as the battle of Waterloo that are not physical bodies. It is hardly possible, and it would hardly accord with this kind of concept, if we were to specify for it a *precisely circumscribed* interval of time (or even region of space). It is, nonetheless, possible to characterise this battle unambiguously by specifying exact individual places and times or by another use of proper names. This is so, of course, only if the meaning of the universal concept "battle" is known.

And this leads us to an important point.

It is always possible for an individual concept to be an element of a class of a higher type, regardless of whether the latter is itself an individual concept or a universal concept.

The battle of Waterloo is, in this way, an element of the class of "Napoleon's battles" (individual concept), but it is also an element of the class of "battles between armies equipped with firearms" (universal concept), and an element of the class of "battles" in general (universal concept). And my dog Lux is both an element of the class of "dogs living in Vienna today" (individual concept) and an element of the class of "dogs" in general.

The *elements of a universal concept* ("dogs") can, therefore, be *individual concepts* ("Lux"), and universal concepts ("dogs") can be *superordinate concepts* of individual concepts ("Viennese dogs"). This is as elementary as it is important. The *applicability* of universal concepts rests on the fact that individual concepts can be subsumed under, or they can be elements of, universal concepts. Simply expressed, the only purpose of universals is to be applied to individuals (or individual concepts).

It is clear that the elements (or the subordinate concepts) of a universal concept can be, but need not *necessarily* be, individual concepts. "An element of the class dog" is a universal concept (under which "my dog Lux" can be subsumed, so that this individual concept becomes a subordinate concept on the one hand, and an element on the other).

That universal concepts can stand to individual concepts in the relation of "class to element" or "superordinate to subordinate" is, therefore, a trite point. But this does not support the view that the distinction between universal and individual concepts is *ambiguous*, i.e., that it is *relative* – in the way that the distinction between class and element is.

Everything that has been said in this discussion of guideline 1 is best confirmed by noting how the sciences actually proceed.

Where it is concerned with propounding universal laws (from which individual predictions can be unrestrictedly deduced), science, that is, "theoretical science", employs only universal concepts (in order to apply them to individual cases, or to subsume individual cases under them). But where it is concerned with describing individual conditions, such as in geography (or in history), science always employs *proper names* in addition to universal concepts. No science that seeks to characterise individual objects achieves this characterisation without the use of proper names. When Carnap[4] advances the thesis "that each object which appears in a scientific statement can in principle . . . be replaced by a structural definite description" (by which is meant a purely formal characterisation without the use of proper names), then we can only reply that no science dealing with *individual* objects proceeds in this way, least of all geography (from which his examples[5] are drawn). Geography uses exclusively proper names for "characterisation", and like all "individualising" sciences is not in the least interested in "structural characterisation".

Comments on guideline 2.

Although *universal concepts* can stand to individual concepts in the relation of "class to element", they can never be defined or

---

[4] Rudolf Carnap, *Der logische Aufbau der Welt* (1928), p. 20. [English translation by Rolf A. George (1967), *The Logical Structure of the World*, pp. 28 f., §16. Tr.]

[5] Rudolf Carnap, *op. cit.*, pp. 16 ff. [English translation, *op. cit.*, pp. 27 f., §15. Tr.]

"constituted"*[1] as classes of particular individuals or of individual concepts. All concepts that can be defined only with the help of proper names are themselves individual concepts, even if they are classes of arbitrarily high type.

The three persons who are presently in my room thus form a class, the "class of persons who are presently in this room". This class is, of course, an individual concept. The "class of classes of three persons who were together in some room in Vienna yesterday at 12 noon" is also an individual concept (for it is simply a collection of individual classes).

That an individual concept can subsume not only elements but also individual classes is never an argument against the unambiguous character of the distinction between universal and individual concepts, but only a result of the relativity of the distinction between class and element. Only those who confuse these two distinctions can infer the "relativity of the distinction between universal and individual concepts" from this state of affairs. (This confusion plainly arises from a failure to distinguish between what is true of "the majority of individuals" and what is true "universally".)

From the relativity of the distinction between class and element, it follows that an individual (such as my dog Lux) can also be understood as a class, for example, the class of its "states". "State of my dog Lux" is, of course, an *individual concept*, in contrast (say) to the universal concept "state of a dog". The concept "state of the dog Lux" by no means refers to a particular or "individual" state; but the states to which it does refer are characterised by *elements of an individual class*. "State of my dog Lux" is, therefore, a very indefinite concept. According to Carnap[6] (cf. Section 26 above) it is an "improper" but nonetheless individual concept, in contrast to the improper universal concept "state of a dog".

In the same way, I can, for example, view a sphere (in geometry) as a class of points. "Point of a sphere" is, accordingly, an (improper) universal concept. But "this sphere here", or "this globe", can also be understood as the class of its points. And of course, "a point of this globe" is an individual concept.

---

*[1] "Constituted" is a fundamental concept in Rudolf Carnap's *Der logische Aufbau der Welt* (1928). ["Constructed" in the English translation by R.A. George, *The Logical Structure of the World*. Tr.]

[6] [Rudolf Carnap, "Eigentliche und uneigentliche Begriffe", *Symposion* 1 (1927), pp. 355 ff.; cf. also R. Carnap, *Abriß der Logistik* (1929), p. 71. Ed.]

In this connection, many criticisms could be raised against logistic. We should especially have to examine more closely Carnap's attempt[7] to constitute the most important universal scientific concepts from a limited number of particular, that is, of individual experiences. For example, when Carnap[8] tries to "constitute" a certain colour, e.g. the universal concept "brown", as a class of experiences that evoke one another because of the brown colour common to all of them, we should have to raise the objection *inter alia* that experiences that (temporally) occur after the constitution of such a universal concept can no longer belong to this class; a class that is defined by particular individuals is unsuitable for subsumption. If the classes are reconstituted after each new experience, this yields "universal concepts" the extension and content of which are constantly changing.

The situation is such that, while a class of particular individuals represents what is common to them (or, as Carnap[9] puts it, the "generality" of these objects), these common or "*general*" characteristics are not universal enough to constitute a universal concept. By listing all persons who in all countries on earth are now looking out of a window and by putting them together in one class, we can never constitute the universal concept "The persons who are looking out of a window", but only the individual concept of persons who are looking out of a window *now* and *in any country on earth* – a class whose size (a certain finite number) can, in principle, be precisely determined. The individual class displays more common characteristics than the universal one. The property of looking out of a window now is not the only property the persons in question possess: they have, in addition, innumerable properties and relationships in common that ought not to be included in the universal concept.

A further discussion of Carnap's undertaking is beyond the scope of our investigation. One more passage should, however, be discussed because in it Carnap directly concerns himself with the question of the difference between universal and individual concepts.

I am quoting from that part of his *Der logische Aufbau der Welt* that deals with the "clarification of some philosophical problems on the basis of

---

[7] Rudolf Carnap, *Der logische Aufbau der Welt* (1928) [pp. 213 ff. Ed.; English translation by Rolf A. George (1967), *The Logical Structure of the World*, pp. 247 ff. Tr.].

[8] [Rudolf Carnap, *op. cit.*, pp. 213 f. Ed.; English translation, *op. cit.*, pp. 248 f. Tr.]

[9] [Cf. Rudolf Carnap, *op. cit.*, p. 213. Ed.; English translation, *op. cit.*, p. 248. Tr.]

construction theory". Carnap[10] stresses that "the virtue of the construction system" lies "only in achieving a uniform *ordering of concepts which allows a clearer formulation of the question for each problem and thus brings us closer to a solution*". The first "clarification" already impinges on our problem. Carnap writes:[11]

> *About the difference between individual and general concepts*
>
> Concepts are usually divided into individual concepts and general concepts; the concept Napoleon is an individual concept; the concept mammal, a general concept. From the standpoint of construction theory, this division is not justified, or, rather, it is ambiguous, since every concept, depending upon one's point of view, can be considered either an individual concept or a general concept. . . . Now that we know the constructional forms . . . we realise that, just as the general concepts, (almost) *all of the so-called individual concepts are classes or relation extensions.*
>
> > EXAMPLE. Let us use for clarification the following descending sequence of objects (or concepts). The dog (species) is a class to which my dog Luchs belongs. Luchs is a class whose elements are the "states" of Luchs. An individual state of Luchs (as a perceptual thing) is a class whose elements are points of the perceptual world. One such point is a many-place relation extension whose terms are four numerical terms (namely, the space-time coordinates) and one or more sense qualities; a sense quality is a class "of my experiences". The latter are here envisaged as basic elements.
>
> In the ordinary view, some of the concepts in this example would have to be called individual and others general. But each of them (except for the last one) is constructed as a class or relation extension, and each of them is an element of the preceding class or a term of the preceding relation extension; thus, each of them is a generality of other objects.
>
> What is the reason that, in the ordinary view, e.g., the species dog and the sense quality brown are considered something general while the dog Luchs, and a given world point, and a given experience are con-

---

[10] Rudolf Carnap, *op. cit.*, p. 211.
[11] Rudolf Carnap, *op. cit.*, p. 213. [English translation, *op. cit.*, pp. 247 f.]

sidered something individual, and that frequently only the latter are called "objects", while the former are called "mere concepts"?

After what has already been said, the criticism of this quotation should be obvious.

The first sentences are, in my view, particularly important because Carnap's examples ("mammal", "Napoleon"), as well as his subsequent examples, show that the terms "general (universal) concept" and "individual concept" are used in the same sense as usual (and as they are used here). We are not therefore at cross-purposes, but speaking about the *same* distinction.

Because he immediately conflates this distinction – which makes no sense in logistic – with the logistical distinction between class and element, Carnap considers it not to be an absolute one. This is shown especially by his examples. He moves from a *universal* class (dog) to its individual elements ("my dog Luchs"), which is not a problem. All further concepts, such as "states" of this particular dog, or experiences, or classes (and relations) of experiences, that "constitute" a specific state, are *individual concepts* in so far as these classes and relations are comprised of particular individual experiences.

Carnap's subsequent arguments too are untenable. He believes he can reduce the usual distinction between universal and individual concepts, which, however, according to him, is not univocal, to the significance that the special spatio-temporal order has for us. "Individuals" are character-ised by the fact that we assign to each a particular, *connected* spatio-temporal region, whereas for universal concepts "the sense quality brown . . . has many unconnected space-time areas assigned to it".[12]

But *disconnected* spatio-temporal regions also correspond to individual concepts, such as the class of native Austrians who have lived abroad for five years, and who drank a glass of milk yesterday and one month ago. Adoption of the spatio-temporal order as a *"principium individuationis"* is based solely*[2] on the fact that by means of a particular space-time coordinate system, it is very simple to assign proper names to individual concepts.

---

[12] [Rudolf Carnap, *op. cit.*, p. 214. Ed.; English translation, *op. cit.*, p. 248. Tr.]
*[2] It is also based on the fact that individuals are primarily physical things.

34. *Strictly universal statements – the problem of induction and the problem of universals.*[1] If the distinction between universal and individual concepts is given, then strictly universal statements and singular statements can be defined. The former are propositions about *all the elements of a class* defined only by *universal concepts*, while the latter are propositions about single individuals, or [about] classes defined by means of individual concepts (proper names). I am not of the opinion that much has been gained by this definition; the difference between universal and singular statements, and its importance for the problem of induction, probably were never unclear. It has already been clearly established that universal statements can never be verified. But now it has become evident that not even *all* singular statements can be verified, even though for many of them there is the possibility of verification. (An example of a singular statement that is in principle unverifiable: "The trajectories of all – or even only some – stones that were thrown today but *not measured*, are parabolas.")

That *natural laws* must be strictly universal statements is implied by the use of the term "natural law".

[1] Previously Section 35. This rearrangement still has to be taken fully into account in the text.

[In this section, a page was enclosed with the following note:]

34. Strictly universal statement.

This section is at present [1932] being reformulated.

Brief summary of contents of [the newly planned] Section 34:

A strictly universal proposition can (in the case of empirical statements) be viewed as a (non-tautological) statement about a *universal concept* (or about all elements of a class that is referred to by a *universal concept*).

A universal concept and a universal statement are *correlatives*.

Since it is never finally verifiable, yet allows the deduction of definitively verifiable predictions, a strictly universal statement may be called a *heuristic fiction* (in Vaihinger's sense). But contrary to Vaihinger, it must be maintained that *this* notion of fiction is *logical* and has nothing to do with the psychological concept of fiction.

It is, of course, because he considers them to be definitively verifiable, or rather, because they are formulated in the hope that they correctly represent a general state of affairs, that Vaihinger himself stresses that *hypotheses* are not fictions.

[The first sentences of this note refer to an earlier (now lost) version of Section 34. Cf. Section 33, note 1. The summary of contents for the newly planned Section 34 corresponds quite closely to the version of Section 34 reproduced here. Ed.]

We acknowledge a rule to be a genuine natural law only if it is always, and in all circumstances, confirmed. Should deviations from a natural law be discovered one day, then a new law must be formulated that subsumes these deviations (and, if possible, entails the old law as a special case, or as an approximation*[1]).

This accords with the fact that the "nomological" or "theoretical sciences" (such as physics, geomorphology or macroeconomics) have no interest in proper names, except in so far as the verification of predictions, which are singular statements, is concerned; for these sciences propose natural laws. In contrast, as we mentioned earlier, the "individualising sciences" work with proper names and with singular statements.

(From an epistemological viewpoint, the theoretical sciences are far more interesting. The problem of induction relates only to these sciences.)

The arguments here put forward have all been external to our debate, so to speak. They apply only under the proviso that the pseudo-statement positions are mistaken, [and hence] that natural laws are genuine statements.

From the position of the deductivist-empiricist theory of knowledge (and given the above proviso), how are the problem of induction and the problem of universals related?

Science is concerned with knowledge. Knowledge can be represented only by statements and not by concepts. Epistemologists and logicians can be divided into two groups: those primarily interested in propositions, and those more interested in *concepts*.*[2]

For example, Russell,[+1] with his "no-class theory", belongs to the first group, but Carnap, with his conceptual system, does not. Logistic views a "concept" as a class of argument values that transform a propositional function into a proposition that is true. (It makes no fundamental

---

*[1] The remark in parentheses is exceedingly important: it refers to what I have later called "the rationality of scientific resolutions". [See Karl Popper, "The Rationality of Scientific Revolutions", in *Problems of Scientific Revolution: Progress and Obstacles to Progress in the Sciences* (The Herbert Spencer Lectures 1973, ed. Rom Harré, 1975), pp. 72 ff. Ed.]

*[2] On this important distinction, see *Logik der Forschung* (2nd ed., 1966) [English translation, *The Logic of Scientific Discovery* (1959; 2nd ed., 1968). Tr.], Section 4, note *1, and *Conjectures and Refutations* (1963), p. 19.

[+1] [See Bertrand Russell, "On Some Difficulties in the Theory of Transfinite Numbers and Order Types", *Proceedings of the London Mathematical Society*, series 2, 4 (March 1906), pp. 29–53, § IIc. Reprinted in *Essays in Analysis* (1973). Tr.]

distinction between strictly universal and singular statements, and with this view of concepts it is incapable of making a distinction between universal and individual concepts.)

The deductivist-empiricist position must also be counted among those interested primarily in propositions, Therefore as far as this position is concerned, the problem of universals can be satisfactorily solved only together with the problem of induction.

In Section 31 it was explained that from the deductivist-empiricist standpoint, genuine empirical statements fall into two classes: singular propositions, which, generally speaking (cf. above), can in principle be definitively verified or falsified as relevant, and universal propositions, which can be falsified but in principle cannot be definitively verified.

According to this view, the purpose of a universal proposition is solely to provide a starting point for the deduction of singular statements and, especially, of predictions. But for a conclusion (implicate) to be deducible from a premise (implicans), not only must that conclusion be entailed by the premise (analytic implication), but the premise must also be *assumed to be true*.

In order, therefore, to be able to perform a deduction, we must *assume* the truth of universal statements. But we know that they *can never be verified* and so, in keeping with the fundamental empiricist principle "The truth or falsity of an empirical statement can be decided solely by experience," they must *never* simply be regarded *as true*.*[3]

The apparent difficulty is very easily resolved. Example: I come home, assuming that no one is in. I find my flat locked from the inside with a security chain. Since it can be deduced from my assumption, *provided it is true*, that the chain must be off, I conclude that my assumption is false. In this way it is perfectly admissible, for the purposes of deduction, (tentatively) to assume a false statement to be true.

It might be objected that this assumption is a singular statement that *might* have been true, though it happens to be empirically false. But a universal empirical statement can, for logical reasons, never be *accepted* as true. Given this fact, is it admissible to adopt, for the purposes of deduction, a universal empirical statement as true, albeit provisionally?

---

*[3] It would have been more accurate to say: "they must not be regarded as having been decided to be true". (But this is very ugly.)

Such reservations, however, are unjustified. What do we do when we set out to demonstrate the falsity of a mathematical proposition? We show that its consequences (deduced either with the help of the rest of the system, or from the proposition on its own) lead to *logical inconsistencies*. The statement is proved to be contradictory, so it *cannot*, for *logical reasons*, be true. In order to be able to deduce the contradictory consequence, we must nonetheless provisionally assume it to be true. There is, therefore, no reason to object to the (provisional) assumption, for the purposes of deduction, of the truth of a statement that for logical reasons cannot be true.

This is, consequently, the reason [or at least one of the reasons] why we usually regard a universal statement, or a natural law, as *true* as long as it has been confirmed.

For it is nothing but the starting point of a deduction, and it can perform this function properly only if we (provisionally) assume it to be true.

Thus, natural laws, being universal propositions, are assumptions − *assumptions that are in principle provisional*, and regarded as true as long as they have not been falsified.

In Vaihinger's[2] terminology (which does full justice to this concept), such assumptions are, however, "fictions".

Vaihinger[3] calls fictions "intentionally" false assumptions. Since the word "intentionally" can also be psychologistically interpreted, I prefer to say: assumptions that *cannot, in principle, be true*.*[4]

If we assume a false or contradictory mathematical proposition to be true, in order to be able to draw conclusions from it, this assumption of the truth of the proposition is undoubtedly a *genuine fiction*.

But then, all universal propositions, natural laws and hypotheses would, for the same reason, be *genuine fictions*.*[5]

Vaihinger[4] himself rejects the view that hypotheses are fictions, arguing that they are, after all, proposed in order to be proved true (wherever

---

[2] [Hans Vaihinger, *Die Philosophie des Als Ob* (3rd ed., 1918). Ed.; English translation by C. K. Ogden, *The Philosophy of "As If"* (1924; 2nd ed., 1935), based on the 6th German ed. Tr.]

[3] [Vaihinger, *op. cit.*, p. 130. Ed. English translation, *op. cit.*, p. 109. Tr.]

*[4] This is a poor formulation: instead of "be true", it should read "demonstrated to be true". See *Introduction* 1978. I have, by now, completely abandoned Vaihinger's terminology. It is utterly inappropriate.

*[5] No: since they *can* in fact be true without ever being *demonstrably* true.

[4] [Cf. Vaihinger, *op. cit.*, pp. 143 ff. Ed.; English translation, *op. cit.*, p. 125. Tr.]

266 STRICTLY UNIVERSAL STATEMENTS AND SINGULAR STATEMENTS

possible). As a Kantian, he believes in the possibility that *natural laws* are true. But nothing fits his concept of fiction as closely as do natural laws*⁶ (which – according to the view advocated here – cannot be distinguished from hypotheses, except perhaps through their degree of corroboration).

But if universal empirical statements are in principle fictional assumptions because they are always provisional, the *fictionalist view of universals* takes on a new significance.

Universals, after all, are precisely those concepts (Vaihinger:⁵ "artifices") that we have to introduce in order to formulate fictional, strictly universal propositions that can in principle serve – always and everywhere – as premises for the uniform deduction of predictions.

Just as universals can be explained in terms of universal statements (as "the concepts that can occur in strictly universal statements"; which again⁶ agrees with Ockham's view), so can their fictional character be reduced to that of universal statements, that is, to the fact *that an empirical statement about universals can never be demonstrated to be true.*

35. *Comments on the problem of universals.*¹ The problem of universals is usually understood to be the question "of the validity of universal

---

*⁶ This is completely false; for a natural law can in fact be true.
⁵ [Cf. Hans Vaihinger, *op. cit.*, pp. 15 ff., 28 ff. Ed.; English translation, *op. cit.*, pp. 10 f., 17 f. Tr.]
⁶ [See note 1 and Section 35, note 5 and the text to this note. Ed.]
¹ [In this section, a page was enclosed with the following note:]

35. Problem of induction and problem of universals.

This section is presently [1932] being reformulated.

Brief summary of contents of [the newly planned] Section 35:
The "problem of universals" is, in its ordinary formulation, a pseudo-problem.
This statement is, however, rather unsatisfactory; the "*pseudo-problem method*", that is, the method of declaring problems to be pseudo-problems and to "dispose" of them in this way is rejected. We should attempt to find and formulate in an unobjectionable way the *genuine* problem that, in almost all cases, underlies an inadequately formulated "pseudo-problem".
In the case of the problem of universals, we then arrive at a fictionalist solution (analogous to the solution for universal *statements*).

[The first sentences of this note refer to an earlier (now lost) version of Section 35. Cf. Section 33, note 1. The summary of contents intended for the newly planned Section 35 corresponds quite closely to the version of Section 35 reproduced here. Ed.]

concepts", or of their "essence", or even the question "What are universal concepts?"

Such formulations of the problem are inadequate. The question "What are universal concepts?" cannot be answered if "universal concept" is an indefinable notion. (In most cases, incidentally, this question has a *psychological* rather than an epistemological meaning.) The question about essence is too unspecific, for we should first have to ask about the meaning of "essence". And finally, the question about validity makes good sense when taken to refer to *propositions*: the validity of a proposition lies in its truth value. A *concept*, however, can never be true or false (at most it can be consistently or inconsistently defined). The question of validity, when applied to concepts, is therefore most unclear.

Were we to content ourselves with dismissing the problem of universals, along with these inadequate formulations, as a *pseudo-problem*, then I should regard our procedure as equally inadequate. Even if we were to supplement this *pseudo-problem method* (which we owe to Wittgenstein[2]) with psychologistic considerations about the motives, about the psychological causes that led to the posing of the traditional pseudo-problems, I believe that nothing would have been gained thereby. If it is to be satisfactory, the assertion that a problem is a pseudo-problem must be supplemented by a search for the *genuine problem* (not the problem of psychology but the genuine problem of *epistemology*) that underlies the inadequately formulated problem.

For example: underlying the question about the validity of universal concepts is the question of the validity of universal propositions, that is, the problem of induction; and underlying the question of the essence of universal concepts is the problem of the *relationship between universal and individual concepts*. It is this question that I should like to examine under the heading of "the problem of universals".

Is the strict distinction between universal and individual concepts sustainable or not?

In the light of this question, the possible positions regarding the problem of universals fall into two groups.

First group: The strict distinction between universal and individual concepts is not acceptable. They are *reducible* to each other.

---

[2] Ludwig Wittgenstein, *Tractatus Logico-Philosophicus* (1918/1922), Proposition 6.53.

Second group: The thesis that universal and individual concepts are *not* *reducible* to each other is acceptable.

In the *first group*, two views are possible. One of them seeks to reduce (so-called) individual concepts to *universal* ones (universalist view); the other tries, conversely, to reduce (so-called) universal concepts to *individual* ones (individualist view).

The *universalist view* is deductivist. It corresponds to deductivist rationalism as regards the validity of universal statements (problem of induction).

Our reason, or understanding, has knowledge only of the universal. The individual is, admittedly, "known" through the senses, but this is not genuine knowledge, for knowing always consists of recognising, or of discovering, the universal (in the singular), of subsuming. Hence, even so-called proper names are universal concepts. By means of the name "Socrates", I denote a number of different sense perceptions in which I always recognise the same universal, "Socratesness" (Champeaux[3]). Only the universal is *essential*, the individual is *accidental*; the facet of Socrates that I happen to look at is accidental; what is *recognised* is only what is universal in him. The more universal, the more essential. (The "Socratesness" of Socrates is accidental in comparison with his "humanity".)

The *individualist view* is inductivist. It corresponds to inductivist empiricism (and was, in fact, elaborated by British empiricists, especially by Berkeley). According to this view, even so-called universal concepts are reducible to individuals, that is, to proper names; they are abbreviations of proper names. In order to be consistent about the validity of universal statements, this view has to assume that there are no genuinely universal propositions. Natural laws must, therefore, be either singular propositions ("strict positivism") or not statements at all ("pseudo-statement position").

Both views, universalism and individualism, must of course attempt to *explain* the apparently irreducible difference between [(so-called) universal and] (so-called) individual concepts; for according to both views, this difference cannot be something final or indefinable; it must be explicable.

The explanations offered by these two positions are very similar. Both acknowledge that we can associate so-called individuals or individual

---

[3] [William of Champeaux; cf. Carl Prantl, *Geschichte der Logik im Abendlande* II. (1861), pp. 128 ff. Ed.]

concepts with certain spatio-temporal, or at the very least with temporal, specifications: the temporal character of the individual is thus the *principium individuationis*. So-called universal concepts, on the other hand, are regarded either as *timeless* (like the truth or falsity of a statement, which is timeless; cf. Section 16), or at least as not sharply localisable in time, or as in principle assignable to different time spans (perhaps even different space-time regions).

But *the interpretations* of these results diverge as follows.

Rationalism maintains (according to the doctrine of manifest truth) that reason obtains knowledge of the universal by intuitively grasping or intuiting it. The universal is [a] recognisable object, it is at least as much an object as is the individual or accidental. Universals exist in intuition. The timelessness of universals is interpreted as *eternity*, the temporality of individuals as *transience*. In this way, universal concepts are invested with a *higher reality* (Plato); they are the "truly" real, the essence; knowledge of them is obtained through the *intuition of essences* (*universalia sunt realia*, realism*[1]).

Apriorism is more inclined to view universal concepts as forms that cognitive understanding imposes on sense perceptions. Universals are thus produced, but not intuited, by the understanding (according to Kant, there is no knowledge intuited by reason); they are not "real". The temporality of everything real is acknowledged, whereas timelessness turns all universals into unreal fictions (fictionalism).

The same applies to deductivist conventionalism. Universal concepts are logical constructions. (*Rationalism*, which, like individualism, regards universals not as timeless but merely as not sharply localisable in time – for they exist at many different points of time – corresponds to the position: *universalia in rebus*.)

Inductivist individualism regards universal concepts as mere abbreviated labels for collections of proper names or for particular constructions of proper names, in which individual objects are ordered according to psychological aspects (memory associations) or formal aspects (similarity). They possess no independent meaning. Their "time-

---

*[1] I referred later to this "realism" as "essentialism" or as "essentialist philosophy". [See Karl Popper, "The Poverty of Historicism I.", *Economica*, N.S., 11 (1944), p. 94 (*The Poverty of Historicism*, 1st ed., 1957, and subsequent editions, p. 27, cf. also Karl Popper, "Intellectual Autobiography", *The Philosophy of Karl Popper* I. (ed. Paul Arthur Schilpp, 1974), p. 13 (= Karl Popper, *Unended Quest: An Intellectual Autobiography*, 1976, p. 20). Ed.]

lessness" consists in the fact that they pertain to many disparate periods. Everything that can be said about these universal concepts is, in principle, fully translatable into statements about proper names, individual objects or particular experiences (*universalia sunt nomina*, extreme nominalism).

There is no question that among the views of the *first group*, nominalism is the most self-contained. It is far more satisfactory to reduce universal concepts to proper names than the other way round. But the strict positivist position too is distinguished by its simplicity and consistency. The question is whether extreme nominalism is not just as much of a philosophism as is strict positivism.

The *second group* of views recognises that universal and individual concepts are *not reducible* to each other.

Like the views of the first group, they recognise the timelessness of universal concepts and the temporality of individual concepts; but this temporality appears to be reducible to the fact that particular periods of time can be fixed only by means of proper names. The special status of the individual is also acknowledged in that proper names and demonstrative references are equated.

This apart, realist, fictionalist and nominalist interpretations are all possible. But it is clear that the controversy between competing views has become far less acute:

Realist and *fictionalist* interpretations are no longer opposed on matters of any real substance. The special status of the individual is acknowledged, and it is no longer necessary to play down its importance or to portray it as accidental. It no longer makes sense to attribute a *higher* reality to universal concepts or to make similar appraisals. The value and importance of universal concepts for knowledge can, of course, still be emphasised. Should any kind of reality be attributed to universal concepts, this position will acknowledge, too, that it is a *different kind of reality* from that of individual objects. The "ordinary" reality, as attributed to particular persons or to particular experiences, that is, the reality of the individual objects to which we can point, is subject to the condition of temporality ("the temporality of the "real"[4]). The "reality" of timeless universals is of a different kind; it no longer makes sense to call it a "higher reality" (Plato), since the individual is no longer viewed as an instance or as a special case

---

[4] Moritz Schlick [*Allgemeine Erkenntnislehre* (2nd ed., 1925), pp. 172 ff. Ed.; English translation by Albert E. Blumberg (1974), *General Theory of Knowledge*, p. 188 ff. Tr.].

of the universal. But then it becomes no more than a semantic dispute whether this special kind of reality ought still to be called "reality" or whether perhaps it should be called "irreality". The recognition that universals are different in kind from the individual objects that are usually called real is the only point of *substantive importance*; and here, this form of realism agrees with fictionalism. As a result, however, it is necessary to abandon the doctrine of intellectual intuition (which is the doctrine of manifest truth adapted to concepts). In view of the common linguistic usage that describes individual objects and experiences as "real", it is no doubt preferable to stress the different character of universals by terminological means and to speak about "irrealism" or "fictionalism".

But the opposition to nominalism disappears, too, as soon as we recognise that universals cannot serve as *proper names*.

There is no question that universal concepts are verbal symbols or *names*; yet they are not *proper names* (but perhaps terms or generic names, as long as this word is not understood to mean anything like a class of proper names). There is, thus, no objection to a nominalism (or terminism) if the expression "nominalism" is used in this sense, and if its use succeeds in highlighting the opposition to rationalist-metaphysical realism. (Ockham's nominalism was of this kind.[5])

It is important to emphasise that the "timelessness" of universal concepts (more accurately, the temporal unrestrictedness of their application) implies that these concepts pick out classes of individuals whose *extensions cannot be restricted*.

In my opinion, the discussion up to this point of the problem of universals has not been entirely satisfactory. This is because the views just discussed can appear satisfactory only in the context of the *problem of induction*. The problem of universals has to do with concepts; *but concepts exist only to enable knowledge to be formulated in propositions*.[*2]

The view referred to as "fictionalism" will, more particularly, gain greater significance as a result of the analysis of the problem of induction.

As far as the problem of universals goes, I do not believe that we can say much more about the relation between universal and individual concepts than that it is of such a kind that neither can be reduced to the other.

---

[5] [William of Ockham; cf. Carl Prantl, *Geschichte der Logik im Abendlande* III. (1867), pp. 343 ff. See also Section 34, text to note 6. Ed.]

[*2] See also text to note *2 in Section 34.

Chapter X

BACK TO THE PSEUDO-STATEMENT POSITIONS

36. *Return to the discussion of the pseudo-statement positions.* A brief recapitulation, from the start of our discussion of the pseudo-statement positions, should serve to recall the course of our analysis so far.

The pseudo-statement positions deny natural laws the character of genuine propositions to which truth values can be assigned. If this position were accepted, the problem of induction, or the question of the validity of natural laws, would disappear. It would be not a genuine problem, but only a pseudo-problem caused by the misunderstanding by which natural laws are regarded as genuine statements.

This idea – which we owe to Wittgenstein and Schlick – leads to the question being posed in a new form: What are natural laws if they are not genuine propositions?

The answer[1] that natural laws are "rules for the transformation of statements" was accepted here tentatively, but it was not considered

---

[1] [Moritz Schlick, "Die Kausalität in der gegenwärtigen Physik", *Die Naturwissenschaften* 19 (1931), p. 151. Cf. Section 19, text to note 1. Ed. There exists an English translation, "Causality in Contemporary Physics", by David Rynin, *The British Journal for the Philosophy of Science* 12 (1961), pp. 177–193, 281–298. The page reference in the English version is

satisfactory. For such rules might also be *genuine propositions*. To the new formulation of the question had to be added the demand that natural laws be so defined that their character as pseudo-statements is put beyond doubt.

The analysis thus arrived at was the formulation of a consistent pragmatism: in that it can, in principle, only be a provisional evaluation, an evaluation of natural laws cannot be an assignment of (absolute) *truth values*, which can be ascribed only to *genuine propositions*.

In the search for a more specific characterisation of a still highly uncertain and shifting problem situation, the analysis reached the concepts of "purely pragmatic constructs" and of "tool and schema", and subsequently of the logical schemata for the formation of statements, that is, of the *class of statement functions*.

Are natural laws propositional functions? (First pseudo-statement position, Section 23.) In order to gain an overview of the implications of the question thus formulated, the discussion of the pseudo-statement positions was temporarily abandoned. The extended digression that was then undertaken consisted of two fairly lengthy parts. The first part (Sections 24–30) started from the question whether natural laws are propositional functions, and dealt with the *problems posed by conventionalism*. The second part (Sections 31–35) started from the logistic concepts of implication and of general implication, discussed in the first part, in order to secure the *distinction between strictly universal and singular propositions*, a distinction that is fundamental for the problem of induction.

For the analysis to resume the critical discussion of the pseudo-statement positions, it must return to the point where we left off, that is, to the first pseudo-statement position and to the question:

Are natural laws propositional functions?

p. 190, where the translation is "a natural law . . . represents 'a direction for the formulation of propositions' ". On p. 312 of *The Logic of Scientific Discovery*, Popper translates his own transcription of Schlick in *Erkenntnis* 11 as "rules for the transformation of statements", and adds a footnote: "In order to get Schlick's intended meaning, it might be better to say 'rules for the formation or transformation of statements' . . . [since] 'Bildung' had, at that time, hardly any of the technical connotations which have since led to the clear differentiation between the 'formation' and the 'transformation' of statements." Tr.]

It may be admitted that the discussion of conventionalism has yielded no unambiguous resolution of this question; it nevertheless produced some rather remarkable results.

It showed that the conception of natural laws as *propositional functions* is close to the *conventionalist theory of knowledge*, and accordingly *unacceptable* to an *empiricist*. Yet even this pseudo-statement position, for all its apparent logical precision, does *not* establish the pseudo-statement character of natural laws. On the one hand, those natural laws that are not axioms of a theory but theorems derived from the axioms are not pseudo-statements (but analytic judgements, like any conventionalistic natural laws; cf. Section 28). On the other, propositional functions taken in conjunction with coordinative definitions have to be regarded as *genuine* empirical statements, and it seems relevant to ask whether establishing the utility of a propositional function does not, in fact, assign to it a certain domain of arguments. This would imply, however, that it is a propositional function only in appearance; in reality it is a genuine statement (cf. Section 29).

In sum, we have to say that the analysis of the problems of conventionalism only reinforced our scepticism concerning the pseudo-statement character of natural laws. Even such precise logical (logistic) constructs as propositional functions are unable to strengthen the shaky foundations of the pseudo-statement positions.

None of this should, however, be seen as a criticism. These reservations are almost as vague and unspecific as the positions against which they are directed. They should, therefore, be excluded from any fundamental critique of the pseudo-statement positions. Such a fundamental critique has to start from a completely different place.

The point on which the attacks of a fundamental critique have to focus will be reached only in the next section. It suffices to say here that the critique will ultimately be directed against any form of the *pseudo-statement positions*.

In order to make the critique as general as possible, the pseudo-statement positions that our considerations have so far called into question will be *explicitly acknowledged as admissible positions* (only temporarily, of course: only until they are refuted by the fundamental critique).

I have in mind particularly the following pseudo-statement positions, which (I believe) have in fact been advocated.

1. Natural laws are *propositional functions* (a view that is *perhaps* advocated by Carnap; cf. Section 23). This position is to be regarded as unobjectionable. It presupposes only *one* thing (and it must presuppose it): that an *evaluation* of these propositional functions by natural science cannot assign them any definitive truth values.

2. Natural laws are *propositional functions, taken in conjunction with pragmatic rules* for their application. This view would be closer to *empiricism*; for these pragmatic *rules* would exclude a conventionalist interpretation. The obvious objection that such rules would probably be identical with co-ordinative definitions (and propositional functions would, thus, be identical with genuine statements) will not be considered. It will provisionally be assumed that this view leads to an unobjectionable pseudo-statement position. Just as propositional functions (as schemata) correspond to tools, so these pragmatic rules for their application correspond to the practical *instructions* we get with tools. Such instructions may well be called practically useful or practically useless, but not definitively true or false. (With this position I am attempting to render what Wittgenstein and Schlick might have meant by "rules for the transformation of statements".[2])

3. But have natural laws perhaps nothing whatever to do with propositional functions? In order that the critique be as general as possible, it will be directed against a pseudo-statement position that, while admittedly rather vague, *encompasses all the others*. This is a standpoint according to which natural laws are "constructs" that might not even be susceptible of any more precise definition but are not, in any event, genuine statements because they can *in principle* be *evaluated only in a tentative fashion*.

If the critique refutes this most general form of the pseudo-statement positions, it will refute all the others too. It will, therefore, be sufficient for the critique to concentrate solely on this most general formulation.

Our reservations about the pseudo-statement character of the constructs to be examined will, therefore, be put aside for the time being. Only after the fundamental critique is concluded will it become evident whether these reservations were justified or not.

---

[2] [See note 1. Ed.]

37. *Symmetry or asymmetry in the evaluation of natural laws?* The critique of the pseudo-statement positions will be an immanent critique. The purpose of drawing on the deductivist-empiricist position in this section is not to demonstrate its advantages vis-à-vis the pseudo-statement positions; the intention here is only to find the point from which a fundamental critique of the pseudo-statement positions has to start. For if the deductivist-empiricist view is correct, then it must also be possible to use it as a key to the critique of all other views. The point at which the incorrect views deviate from the correct one in a substantive and unambiguous fashion is the best starting point for a critique that seeks to demonstrate their immanent contradictions (cf. also Section 9).

Such a key, or such a guideline, is almost indispensable in the case of a critique of the pseudo-statement positions. Since we moved on from the normal-statement positions, the difficulties have constantly grown. The probability positions, and even more so the pseudo-statement positions, have proved to be such incomplete, unspecific and, I am tempted to say, amorphous constructs that a critique must begin by trying to give them somewhat sharper contours. It would, otherwise, be almost impossible to present the often quite intricate problems to which a consistent pursuit of the arguments leads. The analysis of the pseudo-statement positions up to this point has certainly shown one thing, if nothing else: the real need for a key, or a heuristic principle, to enable us to discover the points at which the opponent can be attacked; where he stands firm instead of vanishing – like "The Lean One" in Peer Gynt[1] – just when we think we have cornered him.

At this point, I shall make my presentation somewhat more subjective and report the considerations that have led me to my critique of the pseudo-statement positions.

When I heard for the first time about Schlick's *pseudo-statements* – his "rules for the transformation of statements"[2] – it was immediately clear to me that this could only be a dispute about semantics; whether we call

---

[1] [Henrik Ibsen, *Peer Gynt* (1867), pp. 80 ff.; German translation by Georg Brandes, Julius Elias and Paul Schlenther (1901), pp. 260 ff. Ed.; English translation by Rolf Fjelde (revised ed., 1980), Act II, Scene VII, pp. 64 ff. Tr.]

[2] [Moritz Schlick, "Die Kausalität in der gegenwärtigen Physik", *Die Naturwissenschaften* 19 (1931), p. 151. Ed.; English translation by David Rynin, "Causality in Contemporary Physics", *The British Journal for the Philosophy of Science* 12 (1961), p. 190. Tr.]

natural laws "statements" or "pseudo-statements" cannot make much difference to the real problems.

What I found far more important about Schlick's approach was that he made rather significant concessions to *deductivism*. As the phrase "rules for the transformation of statements" suggests, the purpose and the importance of natural laws are seen primarily in the formulation of predictions, that is, in the possibility of deducing singular empirical statements. However, I took the emphasis on the pseudo-statement character of natural laws to be an indication that the inductivist prejudice had not yet been abandoned. The term "pseudo-statement" could mean only that Schlick still agreed with strict positivism that there are no strictly universal statements, but *only singular empirical statements*. Since he himself acknowledged that the strict positivist position does not accord with the actual procedures of science and with the actual role of natural laws, he had to come up with his "rules for the transformation of statements".

The semantic dispute over calling natural laws "statements" seemed to me rather unappealing. If it is true that the pseudo-statement position is still fundamentally inductivist despite its partly deductivist approach, then it must be possible to find in it a *substantive* conflict with the deductivist view; and the pseudo-statement position must then founder on the fundamental contradiction besetting inductivism, that is, *infinite regression*.

At first glance, there seemed to be no hope of demonstrating any such conflict. The pseudo-statement positions give the impression of having been created for the purpose of evading infinite regression.

How does the infinite regression arise? It always arises whenever an attempt is made to use experience as a foundation for more than it can actually support. The pseudo-statement positions certainly make no such attempt. They always assert only a *provisional* utility of natural laws, and they are in full agreement with the deductivist position in considering a final justification of strictly universal statements impossible.

Indeed, Schlick also believes that he has in this way overcome all the difficulties:[3]

"For the problem of induction consists in the question of the logical justification of general propositions regarding reality, which are always extrapolations from individual observations. We recognise, as Hume does,

---

[3] Moritz Schlick, *op. cit.*, p.156 [English translation, *op. cit.*, p. 286. Tr.]

that there is no logical justification for them; there cannot be one because they are not real propositions."

Could it be that Schlick's position is, after all, simply the deductivist one, translated into a pragmatic mode of expression?

I decided to examine the two positions *without regard to their terminology*, but only with regard to their substantive differences. When I did this, I noticed the following:

The deductivist-empiricist view is distinguished by a pronounced *asymmetry* in the evaluation of universal propositions.

For while singular empirical statements can, in principle, be definitively *verified or falsified*, this is not so for universal empirical statements. True, the latter (as premises for deduction; cf. Section 31) can be definitively *falsified* or assigned a final *negative truth value*, but [we must] never [attribute to them] a positive truth value: the positive value is, in principle, of a *different kind* from the negative one; it is, if you will, a pragmatic value that might be called a "corroboration value" (words should not matter here); in any event, such a value can, *in principle, be only* provisionally attributed to a natural law.

In contrast to this *asymmetry between positive and negative evaluation*, all inductivist views exhibit a *symmetry*. *Normal-statement positions* hold that natural laws can be true or false,*[1] while *probability positions* hold that natural laws can be *probable* or *improbable*. Both are defeated by infinite regression (or by apriorism).

"*Pseudo-statement positions*" exhibit this *symmetry*, too. This, evidently, is the substantive deviation from the deductivist-empiricist position that we have been looking for. If this is right, then the symmetry must lead to an internal *contradiction* also in the case of the pseudo-statement positions.

Identifying this contradiction thus becomes a *crucial test* of the *pseudo-statement positions*.

But can we, perhaps, specify more precisely the critical point of the pseudo-statement positions? For this purpose, we need only look more closely at the difference implied by this symmetry.

The *normal-statement positions* (and the probability positions) agree with the deductivist-empiricist view that natural laws can be assigned definitive *negative values*. But they also seek to attribute to them definitive *positive values*.

---

*[1] Instead of "can be true or false", I should have written: "can be demonstrably true or demonstrably false".

At this point they depart from the deductivist-empiricist view, and at this point they immediately become subject to the contradictions produced by the infinite regression.

The *pseudo-statement positions* are in agreement with deductivism with respect to *positive evaluation*. For both, a positive evaluation is, as a matter of principle, a tentative one. As far as the positive side of the evaluation is concerned, we can in fact find no evidence of any infinite regression or other internal contradiction in the pseudo-statement positions; but there is *a departure* from the deductivist-empiricist view *with respect to negative evaluation*: the pseudo-statement positions do not admit *any definitive negative values* for natural laws – in contrast to the deductivist-empiricist view which asserts the possibility of *definitive empirical falsifiability* *² for universal empirical statements.

If the deductivist-empiricist view is right, then it is at this point, that is, the question of the *negative evaluation* of natural laws, that all those internal contradictions that are characteristic of the problem of induction should appear also in the case of the pseudo-statement positions. And it must be possible to express these difficulties *formally*. The term "truth value" or "practical value" should not matter; what should matter is only the question whether a negative evaluation carries the *same* weight as a positive one, which is always only provisional ("symmetry of evaluation"), or whether a negative evaluation can carry *more* weight than a positive evaluation, whether it may be specially privileged vis-à-vis the positive evaluation ("asymmetry of evaluation").

Formulating the question in this way – symmetry or asymmetry of evaluations? – makes the critique, for the present, independent of the dispute over whether natural laws should be interpreted as "statements" or as "pseudo-statements". Therefore, it makes possible an immanent critique of the pseudo-statement positions.

38. *The negative evaluation of universal statements. Critique of the strictly symmetrical interpretation of pseudo-statements.* The pseudo-statement position advocated by Schlick unambiguously adopts a symmetrical standpoint with regard to the positive and the negative evaluation of natural laws. Positive and negative evaluations are, without exception, made *only provisionally*.

---

*² In the sense that if particular singular facts are recognised, certain universal statements must be false. See also Introduction 1978.

At first glance, this most simple interpretation of pseudo-statements – I shall call it the "*strictly symmetrical*" *interpretation* – ought to appear as the only one possible. For if an *asymmetry* is admitted, if it is recognised that a negative evaluation of natural laws can, in principle, be different in kind from a positive one, that it does not have to be provisional but can be *final* – then presumably it must be acknowledged also that laws can have a truth value, that is, that they are *genuine statements*.

This impression may, however, be *too restrictive*. It will, therefore, be assumed that a refutation of the strictly symmetrical interpretation of pseudo-statements cannot completely defeat the pseudo-statement positions. They are flexible (or vague) enough to be, if necessary, compatible with an asymmetrical interpretation. Indeed, even in Schlick's presentation we find suggestions that *may* point in this direction: that with the help of rules that should, in principle, be evaluated *only* provisionally (that is, with the help of "strictly symmetrical rules", or rules interpreted in the sense of a "consistent pragmatism"), a certain asymmetry can also be expressed. (This may be achieved by demanding that greater weight, or a special "*privileged status*", be assigned to some negative evaluations.)

These "asymmetrical" interpretations of pseudo-statements will be examined in the following sections. Their critique will make it clear that the pseudo-statement positions can, in fact, no longer evade the typical contradictions of *induction*, once the question about the "symmetry or asymmetry of evaluation" has been resolved. It will also be shown (in Section 41) – something that, in this section, is still difficult to see – that the strictly symmetrical pseudo-statement position is *identical* with that of strict positivism; identical, of course, only *formally*, because the terminology and the interpretation are very different.

To begin with, the critique – in this section and in the two that follow – will be a *purely formal* one. It is immanent (and it takes place independently of all terminological questions). Whenever it speaks of "truth values", one could always use the expression "definitve or specially privileged utility values", if preferred; and one could use the expression "pseudo-statements" instead of "universal propositions". This would not affect the argument. And it is for the sake only of simplicity and clarity that this substitution will not, for the most part, be made in the presentation.

In this section, only the strictly symmetrical interpretation of pseudo-statements will be criticised.

The *positive evaluation* of natural laws does not give rise to any substantive opposition of the deductivist-empiricist view and the pseudo-statement positions. Natural laws and, in general, strictly universal empirical statements – whether regarded as genuine propositions or as pseudo-statements – can, in principle, never be positively evaluated. "Subsequent observations can, after all, always belie the presumed law . . ." (Schlick[1]).

But what about *negative evaluation?*

On calm reflection, one might think that the asymmetry (the special privilege accorded to a negative evaluation) cannot be seriously disputed. The argument by which a definitive positive evaluation is disputed, itself supports this. If "subsequent observations" *can* "belie the presumed law", that is, if *experience* is at all *able* to refute the law, then it can also *definitively* refute it; for natural science will never adopt a natural law that is *unequivocally inconsistent* with some experience.

This is, in fact, also the view of deductivism.

The discussion of the concept of implication (Section 31) has shown that, while the premises of a deduction can never be retrospectively verified *by the verification* of the consequences (predictions) deduced from them, they can be retroactively falsified *by the falsification* of the conclusions. (In the logistic mode of expression: If an implication is given, and if the implicate is false, then the falsity of the implicans follows.)

Natural science makes extensive use of this procedure (*modus tollens*). For it takes for granted that deductive logic is justified and may be applied to natural laws as (genuine) universal propositions. But natural science thereby already embraces the *asymmetry* thesis. It introduces a form of negative evaluation that is privileged in a completely different way from that of a positive evaluation. A negative evaluation is entailed by a strict logical deduction from an empirical statement; it is distinguished from a positive evaluation in the same way that *deductive inferences* are distinguished from so-called "*inductive inferences*". (And though the justification of the deduction is not called into question, the inadmissibility of "inductive inferences" constitutes the foundation of the pseudo-statement positions in the same way as it constitutes the foundation of the deductivist view.)

The objection that experiences can never unequivocally contradict natural laws cannot (in this form) be discussed here. It leads directly to

---

[1] Moritz Schlick, "Die Kausalität in der gegenwärtigen Physik", *Die Naturwissenschaften* 19 (1931), p. 150.

conventionalism, that is, to the view that natural laws are *a priori* true (precisely because experiences cannot contradict them); from the empiricist standpoint, it leads to *completely contentless* natural laws, which one might as well call pseudo-statements.

A similar objection that might be raised should, however, be discussed in more detail.

We must consider the fact that *a whole range* of premises is usually involved in the deduction of predictions: these are in general deduced not from an *individual* "natural law" but from a system of statements, or "theory". The retrospective falsification of the predictions affects the premises of the deduction taken as a whole; it affects the *"conjunction" of the assumptions*. But this does not mean that each individual assumption has been falsified, but only that among the assumptions there is *at least one* false statement.

Thus, from a logical viewpoint, the falsification of the deduced predictions leaves us uncertain which of the assumptions contained in the premises of the deduction are false.

From considerations of this sort, it has been concluded (for example, by Duhem[2]) that there exists no actual falsification of natural laws. Only a *theory taken as a whole* can be rejected, which by no means implies that *all* the contentions of the theory have been rejected. On the contrary, we should always be prepared for individual propositions or parts of a falsified theory to re-emerge later (or in a different context). They cannot, that is to say, be regarded as *definitively* falsified.

The results of our analysis (that is, the demonstration that natural laws cannot be verified) seem to make the force of Duhem's argument even more compelling. If there were a *verification* of natural laws, then we could in principle know of any assumption of a theory whether it is true. If a theory is falsified as a whole by the falsification of its predictions, then there might be a case where we know that all assumptions but *one* are true; this assumption would then be falsified. But we know that none of the

---

[2] [Pierre Duhem, *Ziel und Struktur der physikalischen Theorien* (German translation by Friedrich Adler, 1908), pp. 243 ff., 266 f. See also Volume II (Fragments): [VII.] The *Problem of Methodology*, Section 1, note *1. Ed. *La Théorie Physique, son objet, sa structure.* (1906; 2nd ed., 1914. English translation of the 2nd ed. by Philip P. Wiener (1954), *The Aim and Structure of Physical Theory*, pp. 183 ff., 199 f. See also note 9 to §4. Tr.]

assumptions can be finally verified, and this knowledge seems to confirm the view that no assumption is definitively falsifiable.

If the situation were like this, then the symmetrical view would be superior to the asymmetrical one, and the pseudo-statement position would thus be superior to the deductivist-empiricist view. But the situation is different.

For the moment, let us take no account of the form of any actual theory in natural science. If we generalise the question and inquire into the falsifiability of universal empirical statements in general, then there can be no doubt that, on the basis of experience, we are justified in making a definitive negative evaluation of at least some simple universal empirical statements.

The statement "All books are bound in red leather" is indubitably a universal empirical statement, and it is without a doubt *false*. How does the falsification proceed? It is very simple. This statement, in conjunction with the further assumption "This is a book," provides premises for the deduction of the prediction "This book is bound in red leather." This prediction is one that I can falsify. One of the assumptions must therefore be false. The second assumption was a *singular empirical statement* that can be definitively verified. Hence the other assumption is *definitively falsified*.

Can objections be raised against these trivial considerations? I do not think so. Any objection would have to be directed against the *final verifiability of singular empirical statements*. (Such reservations are, however, beyond the scope of the problem of induction and, as already explained in Section 9, are not to be taken seriously.*[1]) What then does this example tell us? It tells us, first, that it is in principle possible to falsify universal empirical statements. Statements such as "All human beings have black hair", "All electrons are visible with the naked eye", "Whoever holds an office has the intelligence for it" are undoubtedly refuted by experience. The example tells us, *secondly*, that a universal empirical statement is falsifiable if, in order to deduce predictions, we have to introduce as additional assumptions singular empirical statements that are definitively verifiable. We can generalise this result in this way: a single universal empirical statement can be retrospectively falsified by predictions deduced from it, provided that the truth of the other assumptions can in some way be

---

*[1] This passage sounds almost as if it was written before the analysis of the last part of Section 11 (Fries' trilemma).

secured. (This will also be the case, however, if these assumptions, while not being singular empirical statements, are *analytic judgements*; for example, definitions.)

Many examples could be cited to show that there are also *scientific* statements of this kind, and that individual *"natural laws"* can be definitively falsified. One of the best-known examples is Galvani's theory (refuted by Volta). If we disregard its vitalistic-metaphysical elements, we have a natural law with the following content: the (electrical) processes in question originate in substances derived from *living animals* (or plants). Volta falsified this law by replacing the experimental substances in question by inorganic fluids (with which he recreated those characteristic processes).

The objection that natural laws can never be finally refuted because we can never know to which premises of the theory the falsification refers, cannot be accepted. It is not of general and major importance.

This (Duhemian) objection is, nevertheless, not unimportant. It encourages the formulation, in a particular direction, of more precise concepts of "natural law" and of the "premises of a (scientific) deduction".

It must be admitted that there are many theories to which the objection would apply. (A classic example is Newton's emission theory of light. Despite its falsification by Foucault, despite the victory of Huygens' theory, a number of Newtonian views reappeared in some modern quantum-mechanical theories of light.) What is the status of these "natural laws", which can occur only in the context of such a theory?

Taken individually, these assumptions certainly are not definitively falsifiable (unless we are able to separate from the theory at least some of its more doubtful premises [and test them in isolation]). But the *whole theory*, the "conjunction" of all assumptions, is in any event definitively falsifiable. And this is all that matters.

The discussion of this objection thus yields the following result. Under certain conditions, complicated theoretical systems can be definitively falsified only as wholes (or as large, coherent parts); that is, falsification can mean only that this theory in this form must be definitively and finally rejected. Some components may, of course, reappear (in a different context).

From a deductivist standpoint, this result is self-evident. It regards natural laws as premises for deduction, as strictly universal propositions from which *predictions* can be *deduced*, which in turn are testable by experience. A (dependent) assumption from which no predictions whatever can be deduced without the use of other assumptions (because it is by itself too vague) is to be treated as a premise (or as a natural law) only in the presence of these other assumptions. The universal proposition is, then, the conjunction of these assumptions. It can undoubtedly be evaluated asymmetrically; that is, it is definitively falsifiable.

The development of modern physical theories shows that the falsification of definite predictions can bring about the collapse of entire theoretical systems. And it shows also by what *purely logical* considerations a physicist can try to separate the falsified premises from the theoretical system (take Einstein's *special* theory of relativity). All these considerations proceed in the direction of *modus tollens*, that is, asymmetrically.

The distinctive quality of scientific development, the character of natural laws as *progressive approximations*, would be inconceivable without this asymmetry in evaluation. That positive evaluations are intrinsically provisional is the precondition for science not to be stagnant. But only the supplementary principle of privileged negative evaluation can introduce an *element of order* into this process. Without it, there would be as much quarrelling among the systems of natural science, and as much chaos as there is in philosophy. For order is not produced by unanimity in the positive construction of hypotheses. Here controversy reigns, and there is outright chaos. But the whole of science ultimately bows to a *refuting* experience. A privileged negative evaluation makes possible uniformity in the rejection and *elimination* of useless theories. It makes *selection* possible, and increasingly better adaptation, that is, *progressive approximation*.

("And even if one is not in possession of the truth, it is at least something to have discovered those places where it is not to be found," says Martin du Gard's[3] Jean Barois.)

---

[3] [Roger Martin du Gard, *Jean Barois* (1913), p. 441; 64th ed. (1930), pp. 443 f.; German translation by Eva Mertens (1930), p. 440; in the German edition of *The Two Fundamental Problems* (*Die beiden Grundprobleme der Erkenntnistheorie*, 1979), this translation is reproduced with the changes that Popper inserted in K_1, K_2, K_3 and K_4. Ed. ["Et c'est déjà quelque chose, à defaut de posséder la vérité, que d'avoir bien repéré les endroits où elle n'est pas!" There is an English translation by Stuart Gilbert (1950): "There was, anyhow, some merit, even though the truth itself was not attained, in charting out the places where it was not to be found." Tr.]

Natural science never regards a natural law as finally verified; but only *because* it never ignores a new experience that *defeats* the natural law.

These arguments in no way aim to refute, in a purely logical fashion, the strictly symmetrical pseudo-statement position. I consider a *purely logical refutation* of this position to be as impossible as a logical refutation of *strict positivism*. In neither case do I attempt to demonstrate an *internal contradiction*; what I wish to show is only that this position fails to account for the *actual procedures of science*. (This is why the critique is a "transcendental" one.) And, as in the case of strict positivism, the strictly symmetrical pseudo-statement position, though admittedly not inconsistent, looks like an *empty philosophical ideology*. Anyone who refuses to acknowledge the special privileged status of negative evaluation over positive evaluation has a conception of natural law different from that of natural science.

We have, therefore, to try to construct an *asymmetrical* pseudo-statement position; that is, a position that adequately deals with the privileged negative evaluations of natural laws, and thus with the actual procedures of natural science.

39. *An infinite regression of pseudo-statements.* That the internal contradictions of the pseudo-statement positions are, in fact, those of the *problem of induction* can be most clearly seen if we try to interpret the pseudo-statement positions in terms of an *asymmetry* between positive and negative evaluations. And as was shown in the preceding section, such an interpretation must be attempted if the pseudo-statement positions are to deal adequately with the actual methods of natural science.

It was, therefore, the central task of the preceding section to show that such an attempt is necessary, and in so doing to clear the way to a demonstration that the pseudo-statement positions face exactly the same formal difficulties as the normal-statement positions.

While the strictly symmetrical interpretation is, in certain respects, analogous to the normal-statement position of strict positivism, the two asymmetrical interpretations exhibit far more explicit analogies with the two other normal-statement positions. The interpretation attempted in the present section (the *"naive" interpretation of pseudo-statements*) corresponds to naive inductivism (Bacon): this attempt is also defeated by an infinite regression. And the attempt to avoid this regression leads (in the next section) to an *apriorist* solution.

The value of this discussion lies in this analogy between the pseudo-statement and the normal-statement positions: the discussion leads to a critique of all pseudo-statement positions, and at the same time provides clues for their *interpretation*.

The "naive" interpretation of pseudo-statements will be discussed first. The critique, which consists in the demonstration of an *infinite regression*, can again be described as immanent. The ("naive") position is constructed without going beyond the pseudo-statement position as such. It is the result of trying to create, with the means available to the pseudo-statement positions, an asymmetry between the positive and the negative evaluations of natural laws; that is, from an attempt to single out the negative evaluations as being, in some form or other, especially privileged.

I shall consistently adopt the terminology used by Schlick in describing the pseudo-statement positions,[1] but only in order to emphasise that my criticism proceeds immanently. The use of quotations should, therefore, not give the impression that Schlick himself has advanced such an asymmetrical interpretation. It is merely designed to show that the position to be presented can be developed from Schlick's approach — if, that is, the (transcendental) demand for asymmetry is added.

According to Schlick,[2] natural laws, "as a strict analysis shows, do not even have the character of statements", but "rather represent 'rules' for the transformation [of] statements".[3]

The positive evaluation of natural laws, which is always only tentative, is expressed by the fact that "the usefulness of a rule can never be demonstrated in a purely and simply absolute way, since subsequent observations may always prove it to be inappropriate".[4]

[1] Moritz Schlick, "Die Kausalität in der gegenwärtigen Physik", *Die Naturwissenschaften* 19 (1931), p. 145 ff. [English translation by David Rynin, "Causality in Contemporary Physics", *The British Journal for the Philosophy of Science* 12 (1961), pp. 177–193, 281–298. Tr.]

[2] Moritz Schlick, *op. cit.*; all other quotations in this section come from this source.

[3] Moritz Schlick, *op. cit.*, p. 155. [English translation, *op. cit.*, p. 285: "natural laws, strictly analysed, are not propositions that are true or false, but are, rather, 'directions' for the construction of . . . propositions". Tr.]

[4] Moritz Schlick, *op. cit.*, p. 156. [English translation, *op. cit.*, p. 286: "the usefulness of a direction can never be absolutely proven because later observations may still prove it to be inappropriate". Tr.]

In terms of this pseudo-statement position, natural laws can be interpreted as practical rules or, if preferred, as *imperatives* or *postulates*. We should not, of course, use these expressions as they are used in a rationalist system of philosophy. A *postulate*, in the sense in which this concept occurs in earlier philosophies . . . means a rule that should be adhered to *under all circumstances* (Schlick[5]). Natural laws cannot, of course, be such postulates, since their evaluation is a conditional, *tentative*, one.

Within this pseudo-statement position, an attempt will now be made, using the means available to the position itself, to create the asymmetry or to confer privilege on negative evaluations. For this purpose, we have to pay particular attention to the procedure this position follows in making a negative pragmatic evaluation. How is a decision reached about the *non-utility* of a rule or postulate?

". . . natural laws themselves decide the limits of utiliy: this constitutes the new element of the situation. Postulates, in the sense of classical philosophy, do not even exist. Rather, every postulate can be limited by a counter-rule gained from experience; that is, it can be recognised as inappropriate and can in this way be eliminated" (Schlick[6]).

If a natural law is to be regarded as falsified, in the sense intended by one of the normal-statement positions, then, within the framework of the pseudo-statement position, evidently this can be interpreted as meaning that the natural law has been "limited by a counter-rule gained from experience; that is, it can be recognised as inappropriate and can in this way be eliminated".

This would be the negative evaluation – but it would typically be provisional (that is, also typically symmetrical). Evidently, *asymmetry* can be achieved only by a *specially privileged form of "elimination"*.

How could such a thing be accommodated within the "pseudo-statement position"? Obviously only by means of a *rule*, that is, by means

---

[5] Moritz Schlick, *op. cit.*, p. 155. [English translation, *op. cit.*, p. 285: "*postulate*, in the sense in which this concept occurs in earlier philosophers . . . means a rule to which we must adhere *under all circumstances*" Tr.]

[6] Moritz Schlick, *loc. cit.* [English translation, *loc. cit.*: "natural laws themselves decide the limits of utility. In this lies the novelty of the situation. There are no postulates in the sense of the older philosophy. Each postulate may be limited by an opposing rule taken from experience, that is, may be recognised as inappropriate and thus nullified." Tr.]

of a "guideline for that kind of activity that is called natural science" (Schlick[7]).

This rule or "guideline" would have to prescribe that in certain cases (namely, those in which the normal-statement position would speak of a definitive falsification) the counter-rules gained from experience are given a *special weight*, or a *special privilege*, vis-à-vis natural laws; that is, the guideline would have to demand that such counter-rules could not themselves simply be restricted or nullified.

Such a guideline would, of course, itself have only a pragmatic and tentative character. It would be obtained from experience, but not quite in the sense in which natural laws are obtained from experience. It would be obtained from experiences with natural laws. It would not be, like a natural law, a "behavioural rule for the scientist to find his way in the real world, to discover true statements and to expect particular events" (Schlick[8]). Instead, it would be a behavioural rule with which the scientist could find his way in the world of natural laws (that is, in a world of behavioural rules), and could anticipate the non-utility of a natural law. In short, this guideline would be of a *higher type* than natural laws.

The question "symmetry or asymmetry?" is here no longer a matter for discussion; only the asymmetrical interpretation is being discussed. Nevertheless, I wish to illustrate by means of an example how necessary such a guideline is; and that where it is absent, we regard it as a matter of course that we can discard the counter-rule and return to the previous rule.

A man has adopted the practical rule, the imperative, not to jump out of the first-floor window but to walk down the stairs. During a fire, which has also engulfed the staircase, he considers this rule superseded or nullified by a counter-rule, and acts accordingly. He jumps out of the window. The counter-rule proves of great utility (for he survives). The man is unlikely to think of maintaining this very useful counter-rule from now on as a privileged one, but (until the next fire) will revert to his old rule and use the stairs.

---

[7] Moritz Schlick, *loc. cit.* [English translation, *loc. cit.* "guiding thread to the activity that is called investigation of nature". Tr.]

[8] Moritz Schlick, *op. cit.*, p. 156. [English translation, *op. cit.*, p. 286: "rules, instructions, aiding the investigator to find his way about in reality, to discover true propositions, to expect certain events". Tr.]

The example shows that it is by no means self-evident that a counter-rule is entitled to a privileged status, and that we are much in need of a guideline telling us in which cases an empirically won counter-rule against a natural law should be regarded as having special privilege.

We may express this point in the language of the normal-statement positions, as follows: In cases where a definitively falsified natural law nevertheless proves to be empirically *applicable* – and such cases occur time and again – the falsifying evidence would, without such a guideline, be regarded as superseded by the new experience; for the latter demonstrates the utility of the law.

If the necessity of such a guideline is recognised (as already mentioned, we in no way question this *here*), then we find ourselves already in the midst of an infinite regression. The "guideline" in question is of a higher type than natural laws. Only if it cannot itself be "restricted" or eliminated at any time, that is, if it is itself treated as privileged, can it ensure that the "counter-rules" (the falsifications) are treated as privileged in the way that it requires. But "postulates" [that are privileged *a priori*] "in the sense of classical philosophy simply do not exist". The "guideline" that is so crucial for "that kind of activity that is called natural science" must, therefore, be protected by a practical rule of a higher type that ensures its privileged status, and so on – *ad infinitum*.

40. *An apriorist pseudo-statement position.* Where the preceding section – the presentation of the "naive" asymmetrical interpretation of pseudo-statements – had the primary purpose of indicating the analogies between pseudo-statement and normal-statement positions, the same applies *a forti-ori* to the present section, the presentation of the "apriorist" interpretation. For I do not think for a moment that any proponent of the pseudo-statement positions would actually choose this way out. But of course, we have seen that probability theoreticians end up on the path leading to the much-maligned apriorist version. It is, therefore, safer briefly to discuss this apriorism, which in any event appears to be a possible escape from the infinite regression of pseudo-statement positions.

The situation is simple enough:

To satisfy the transcendental demand that the actual methods of science are adequately described, one of guidelines of higher type – or simply the first of them (that is, the one that is at the level immediately above that of natural laws) – is decreed *a priori* to be privileged. In this way, of course, this rule, this postulate, this imperative becomes a binding rule, or a "postulate in the sense of classical philosophy"[1] (a kind of categorical imperative).

No one can be expected to adopt such a position. Someone who is already an apriorist will, of course, choose a postulate in line with the normal-statement position: a guarantee that we can have knowledge of the world, a guarantee of the possibility of true natural laws; but one would not choose an imperative demanding that useless rules should no longer be used, an imperative that – as it were – guarantees the possibility of false pseudo-statements.

41. *Interpretation of the critique up to this point; comments on the unity of theory and practice.* The critical arguments of the past three sections have shown that the pseudo-statement positions are just as exposed to the dangers besetting induction as are the normal-statement positions. Like strict positivism, only the strictly symmetrical pseudo-statement position avoids being drawn into the infinite regression and the *a priori* situation. But like strict positivism, the strictly symmetrical interpretation of pseudo-statements cannot adequately deal with the (transcendental) requirements that natural science must impose on any theory of knowledge.

How is this result to be interpreted?

After everything that has been said, it should come as no surprise. Reservations emerged already in Section 19 about the pseudo-statement character of Schlick's "rules", and despite all efforts to dispel them, we never succeeded completely. Even propositional functions, which apparently are constructs of pure logic, did not escape from the suspicion that they can be evaluated *as useful* only if they are genuine propositions.

In spite of these reservations, however, we could not quite pin down the pseudo-statements, and clear proof of their identity with genuine propositions was difficult to establish. We could never be sure that the critical onslaught might not be evaded. The positions were too vague even to allow us to mount a decisive attack on them. Only a comparison with the deductivist-empiricist solution (Section 37) supplied the resources with which to banish all the temptations of the verbal dispute about "pseudo-statement" or "proposition", about "useful" or "true", and to

---

[1] [Cf. Section 39, note 6 and text to this note. Ed.]

track down the *formal* differences between these positions, differences that could be guaranteed to be not merely linguistic, but of a substantive nature.

The analysis of these differences in the preceding sections has produced a result that can, without doubt, be interpreted as a confirmation of all our reservations. As Kant knew well, every genuine scientific statement, more particularly every natural law, can be formulated as a rule, or as an imperative, and (more importantly for our present purposes) vice versa:

It is not that natural laws are, as Schlick believes, rules that appear "grammatically in the guise of ordinary statements",[1] but on the contrary, Schlick's rules are *genuine statements appearing in the pragmatic guise of rules*.

Let us, for the time being, leave the "linguistic critique" whose results are not very encouraging. Let us rather discuss the substantive issues.

Schlick's natural laws can never be evaluated other than *provisionally*. At this point, the interpretation of pseudo-statements as genuine propositions (in a pragmatic guise) encounters a formal, substantive problem: if pseudo-statements are to be formally identified with genuine propositions, then it must be possible to assign them absolute, definitive *truth values!*

The contradiction disappears once we realise that pseudo-statements must be interpreted as pragmatic translations of *singular* propositions – or at most of summary reports. Every summary report can, indeed, be assigned a definitive truth value, but the report itself is only a tentative one and may become superseded as a result of new evidence. And precisely the same applies to pseudo-statements and to their pragmatic evaluation. If a pseudo-statement has been corroborated up to now, then this fact can never be changed; but new evidence can, of course, (provisionally) show the pseudo-statement to be out of date.

In the light of this interpretation of pseudo-statements as singular empirical statements, the pseudo-statement position appears to be formally identical with that of strict positivism.

If this interpretation is correct, then it must also be possible to apply it to the *positive* evaluation of natural laws, which (according to the *deductivist*

---

[1] [Moritz Schlick, "Die Kausalität in der gegenwärtigen Physik", *Die Naturwissenschaften* 19 (1931), p. 156. Ed.; English translation by David Rynin, "Causality in Contemporary Physics", *The British Journal for the Philosophy of Science* 12 (1961), p. 286: "grammatically in the form of ordinary propositions". Tr.]

view) is, in principle, provisional. And such an application is, in fact, possible (indeed, virtually necessary). The pragmatic, provisional degree of *corroboration* of a natural law can be interpreted, in an unobjectionable way, as a *provisional report*, as a report on previous verifications of deduced predictions. That is to say (as already explained in Section 16), it can be interpreted as an evaluative report that takes into account the primary improbability of the natural law (as well as other related factors).

Schlick's "pseudo-statements" (in their "symmetrical" interpretation) admit *only* provisional values, and so they are *only* summary reports. For this reason, this symmetrical view may be described not only as analogous to that of strict positivism, but virtually as *formally identical* with it. For it departs from the deductivist view at precisely the same point as does strict positivism.

But Schlick himself opposes strict positivism (cf. Section 8) with the argument that no *predictions* can be deduced from mere summary reports. Does this not amount to an important substantive difference between strict positivism and Schlick's pseudo-statement view? Schlick's "rules for the transformation of statements" were, after all, conceived of as rules for the formulation of predictions (cf. Section 19).

We can answer only: Everybody knows how to deduce propositions from propositions, and knows that the premises have to be assumed to be *true*. The deductivist position takes this into account. Nowhere, however, has Schlick shown how to deduce predictions from his *pseudo-statements*, which in principle can *only be useful*. What is more, the phrase "rules for the transformation of statements" does not allow us to work out how such a transformation is to be carried out. Despite the terminology, we are confronted with the same substantive difficulty as in the case of strict positivism. We do not know how predictions are to be deduced from natural laws.

In this light, how are we to interpret the infinite regression and the apriorist position? In such a way, evidently, that internal contradictions must arise from any attempt to construe as summary reports the negative evaluations of universal propositions.

I should like to discuss this point further, since it is not completely straightforward, and since it casts a somewhat different light on the problem of induction.

The (usual) regression of induction (which occurs in the case of a positive evaluation) arises from calling on experience to justify more than it can properly justify. The new regression that occurs in the case of a negative evaluation cannot arise in the same way. If I have seen one book that is not bound in red leather, then I know from experience that the statement "All books are bound in red leather" is false. How does an internal contradiction arise here?

The contradiction arises from the assumption of the pseudo-statement position that every evaluation of a natural law or of a rule for scientific research must in principle be provisional. In other words: this view does not recognise the existence of any universal statements whatever. Note, however, that the experience that one book is not bound in red leather falsifies only that one universal statement. Related singular statements such as "All books that my friend N has ever observed are bound in red leather" are not falsified by my observation. If I conclude, relying exclusively on this experience of my own, that perhaps my friend too has seen books that are not bound in red leather, then this is a typical (inadmissible) inductive inference, which therefore promptly succumbs to infinite regression. It is, therefore, inevitable that any attempt to make a privileged negative evaluation of singular statements – that is, to invest the falsification with a more general significance – will lead to the difficulties encountered by any inductive inference.

(One might try to object to this argument by claiming that the special nature, the greater weight and the definitive character of falsification should somehow manifest themselves also in summary reports. And indeed, one falsifying observation is sufficient to falsify any summary report that makes a corresponding assertion about all books that have been hitherto observed. Yet this very objection can be expressed only through a universal statement; for it refers to every summary report. Since it asserts something about the content of all possible summary reports that include all books observed theretofore, it is a universal empirical statement. It only paraphrases the assertion that it will be for ever false that all books are bound in red leather. Hence a theory of knowledge that does not recognise universal empirical statements cannot even express this idea; that is, it cannot assert that all summary reports of this kind have been falsified. According to such a theory of knowledge, there might thus still be reports that have not been falsified; the "medium of the universal"[2] is unavailable for drawing a logical conclusion.)

---

[2] [Cf. Section 8, text to note 8. Ed.]

The problem of induction arises not only if one tries to infer universal from singular propositions, but also if one tries to infer singular propositions from other singular propositions; this is also why singular propositions are not suitable for the deduction of predictions. And the same applies to Schlick's pseudo-statements.

Natural laws are, however, above all *premises for deductions*. They possess those and only those properties that they must possess in order to function as premises for deductions, premises that can be empirically tested, not in any direct way, but only by way of their consequences. The asymmetry of truth values counts among these properties. *Any* deviation from this asymmetrical pattern leads straight into all the difficulties raised by the problem of induction. Our identification of the critical point of the pseudo-statement positions should, therefore, be considered as a confirmation of the deductivist-empiricist view.

It may be that the intertranslatability of the theoretical and pragmatic modes of expression requires a few further comments.

We might say:

If a tool is useful, then there is always a statement that is true, namely the statement that asserts the utility of the tool. If it is useful for a particular case, then the statement is a singular one. Should we *conjecture* its general utility for "typical" cases, i.e., for a universal class of cases, then the conjecture can be expressed in a universal statement. Because we do not know whether the tool will, indeed, prove its utility in all cases, this statement is, in principle, never [demonstrably] true; it may, moreover, be replaced by a much better tool. But if it has proved only once not to work, then its general utility can no longer be asserted.

This example shows that it is completely misguided to set up an irreconcilable opposition of pragmatic and theoretical constructs.

It may be admitted that Schlick himself, in many passages, indicates clearly the pragmatic aspect of everything theoretical when, for example, he writes:[3] "We must not forget that observations and experiments are *actions*." But should he believe that the problem of induction can be solved by maintaining that natural laws are *not genuine propositions but pragmatic constructs* (rules, etc.), then he must hold the view that there is, after all, an opposition of genuine statements and rules, or between theoretical and

---

[3] [Moritz Schlick, *loc. cit.* See Section 19, text to note 3. Ed.]

pragmatic constructs. In this vein, he emphasises the "difference between a true proposition and a useful rule", and so on.[4]

One of the most serious misgivings one can have about Schlick's pseudo-statement position is, in my view, that it opens a rift between "theory" and "practice" that does not, in fact, exist. From a biological-pragmatist viewpoint, empirical science or *theory* is nothing but a route, that is, *an indirect route to practice*; it is a "method" (which is what is meant by "indirect route"), but it is an economical method, "*roundabout production*"[+1] (a term of Böhm-Bawerk's,[5] which in this application appears to be well suited for reconciling Schlick's logical principle of the economy of thought with the biological principle of Mach, Spencer et al.[6]). This view should prove itself valuable not only epistemologically, but in other fields too (psychology of knowledge, biology, sociology).

It is a fact that the pseudo-statement positions – the strictly symmetrical interpretation, the infinite regression and the apriorist standpoint – can be interpreted in the sense suggested here. Yet this is only one *interpretation* of the critique – though, I believe, a rather convincing one.

A rigorous *proof* that the pseudo-statements *must* be interpreted in this sense cannot be furnished and cannot even be demanded. In a dispute over the application of *terminology* (either pragmatist or everyday terminology), only the consistency of the *application* can be proved, never the *necessity* of using this particular terminology. In this battle of words, the only thing one could still show would be the appropriateness of the one terminology, and the inappropriateness of the other.

And this raises the question: What *purposes* does the terminology of the pseudo-statement positions serve? Is its purpose only to solve the problem of induction? Or are there, perhaps, other important problems behind this point of view, which is so firmly opposed to acknowledging natural laws

---

[4] [Cf. Section 21, note 2 (p. 179) and text to this note. Ed.]

[+1] [The German term is *Produktionsumweg*. In the 2nd ed. of 1909–1914 (and also the 4th) what had been Bd 2 was split into two volumes, Abt. 2, Bd 1 (which is what is referred to here) and Abt. 2, Bd 2. Cf. *The Positive Theory of Capital*, translated by William Smart (1891; reprinted 1971), pp. 18–20 (Book I) and 81–89 (Book II). Tr.]

[5] [Eugen Böhm-Bawerk, *Kapital und Kapitalzins* II.: *Positive Theorie des Kapitales* (1889), pp. 15 ff., 81 ff.; *Positive Theorie des Kapitales* I. (4th ed., 1921), pp. 11 ff., 107 ff. Ed.]

[6] Cf. Moritz Schlick, *Allgemeine Erkenntnislehre* (2nd ed., 1925), p. 91. [English translation by Albert E. Blumberg (1974), *General Theory of Knowledge*, pp. 98 f. Tr.]

as genuine propositions? To the extent that it was immanent, the critique could so far deal only with the formal side of the question. There has, therefore, been no opportunity to clarify sufficiently the reasons for which the pseudo-statement *terminology* was created. But even the terminological question cannot be satisfactorily answered without some knowledge of the objective reasons for its introduction.

In order to examine in isolation from other questions this question of the ultimate reasons for the pragmatist terminology, we can take the following route.

The intertranslatability of the pragmatist and theoretical modes of expression has so far been used as a heuristic principle in the *critique* of the pseudo-statement positions. But it can be employed in the other direction too:

It must also be possible to translate the deductivist-empiricist position into the pragmatist mode of expression. This would lead us to a pseudo-statement position that is in no way affected by the immanent-formal critique. Only one objection would remain: that evidently we are dealing with a translation into the pragmatist language. But this objection (which is not immanent and is on the same level as the *interpretations* presented in this section) may be excluded.

It is evident that the discussion of such a pseudo-statement position would have to take place in the realm of terminology, since the formal differences have been reduced to a minimum. The discussion should bring out clearly the advantages and disadvantages of the two terminologies and, if followed through consistently, should reveal the ultimate reasons behind the terminology of pseudo-statements.

In the next section, we shall try to construct this "ultimate pseudo-statement position".

42. *A last chance for the pseudo-statement positions.* Should the deductivist-empiricist position be translatable into the pragmatic language, then the proponents of the pseudo-statement positions can yet stave off defeat.

A critique of this "ultimate pseudo-statement position" that is directed exclusively against its formal side must inevitably fail. The only line remaining is to ask what reasons there are in favour of calling natural laws "pseudo-statements" at any cost. But even this formulation of the question, that is, the question of the justification of the terminology, will prove to be fruitful.

The ultimate pseudo-statement position, which construes natural laws in exact formal analogy to the deductivist-empiricist view, albeit as pseudo-statements, has nevertheless to contend with a number of problems. It has to create an *asymmetry* in evaluations; but how is it to do that?

The infinite regression has shown that such an asymmetry can never be achieved if one *starts from symmetrical values of utility*. This is why the new position must, from the start, assume asymmetrical values of utility; it must *a priori* make negative evaluations *privileged over* (essentially tentative) positive evaluations.

In order to avoid slipping thereby into apriorism, however, it must not assert the privileged status of negative evaluations in the form of a (methodological) rule – a guideline, or anything like it; for this would be tantamount to a synthetic *a priori* rule. Rather, it must *by definition* introduce "inutility" as a *privileged* form of evaluation. This would correspond (as far as possible) to the deductivist procedure that *defines* natural laws as premises of deductions and derives everything else from this definition. But whereas the deductivist approach is simple and transparent, the same cannot be said for the corresponding definition of the pseudo-statement positions. The definition that opposes "inutility" as a privileged evaluation to (the essentially tentative) "utility" not only is *arbitrarily adopted*, but threatens and obscures the essential *character of the pragmatic evaluation* as something that is in principle provisional. In this way, consistent pragmatism is abandoned. A substantive and not merely terminological difference between "utility", as thus defined, and "falsity" as a genuine *truth value*, which may be assigned only to genuine propositions, can no longer be maintained.

From a formal viewpoint, the disadvantages of this ultimate pseudo-statement position vis-à-vis the deductivist view arise in the following way.

In the deductivist view, the asymmetry of truth values results from an analysis of the (logical) concept of a deductive premise that is not directly verifiable. Unlike the logical concept of a deductive premise (implicans), the concept of a "rule for the transformation of statements" does not have any specific content but is an arbitrarily introduced term. Its special properties can, therefore, be stipulated only by arbitrary definition; that is, by the definition that confers on negative evaluations a privileged status.

We have in this way, however, finally discovered a substantively unobjectionable pseudo-statement position – at least one that, from the deductivist-empiricist standpoint, is no longer open to formal but only to *terminological* objections. It is now possible to focus the analysis on the terminological domain and to ask what reasons there might be for favouring the pseudo-statement terminology.

What advantages might the choice of a pseudo-statement terminology offer that would compensate for the considerable disadvantages of this ultimate pseudo-statement position when compared with the deductivist standpoint?

In my view, this terminological question is in fact at the root of the *problem of the concept of meaning*, with which the following sections will deal. But I am aware that a committed supporter of the pseudo-statement positions is hardly likely to admit the question in this form.

He would adopt a position according to which the terminological advantages and disadvantages do not even enter the discussion: the decision between the two modes of expression would in his view be completely clear. Treating natural laws as genuine statements (in the sense of deductivism) would be completely out of the question, since this view is demonstrably *false*. With the help of the *concept of meaning*, the terminological conflict may definitively and unambiguously be decided in favour of the pseudo-statement terminology.

Every genuine statement must have a *meaning*. But "the meaning of a statement" (Waismann[1] writes) "is the method of its verification. Indeed, whoever utters a statement must know under what conditions he will call the statement true or false; if he is not able to specify this, then he does not even know what he is saying. A statement that cannot be definitively verified is not verifiable at all; for it lacks any meaning . . ."

---

[1] Friedrich Waismann, "Logische Analyse des Wahrscheinlichkeitsbegriffs", *Erkenntnis* 1 (1930), p. 229. ["A Logical Analysis of the Concept of Probability". In Friedrich Waismann, *Philosophical Papers* (ed. Brian McGuinness, 1977), pp. 4–21. The passage, which is on p. 5, reads: "The sense of a proposition is the method of its verification. In fact, whoever utters a proposition must know under what conditions he will call the proposition true or false; if he cannot tell this, then he does not know what he has said. A statement which cannot be conclusively verified is not verifiable at all; it just lacks all sense . . ." Tr.]

This would amount to a substantive (rather than a merely terminological) decision, and a final judgement on natural laws would have been passed. They would have to be declared pseudo-statements, for there is of course no longer any doubt that they are in principle not [definitively] verifiable.

The pseudo-statement view is thus ultimately based on the *concept of meaning*. Does the concept of meaning conceal more than a merely terminological problem?

Does the introduction of the concept of meaning really transform the terminological conflict into a substantive one, or does it only shift the terminological problem elsewhere?

Chapter XI

PSEUDO-STATEMENT POSITIONS AND THE CONCEPT OF MEANING

43. *The concept of meaning in logical positivism.* In the writings of logical positivists, the concept of meaning is of paramount significance. There can be no doubt that Wittgenstein's and Schlick's pseudo-statement positions can be understood only in connection with the *concept of meaning*, which is why this concept will be presented here in detail. (To the extent that the structure of my presentation permits it, I shall use quotations.)

Before one can even ask about a proposition being true or false, one must know whether it has a *meaning* or whether it is *nonsensical*. The (putative) proposition "Socrates is identical" is *nonsensical*; and it would also be nonsensical to ask whether it is true or false.

It is one of Wittgenstein's fundamental ideas that the grammatically correct form of a proposition offers no guarantee that it is *meaningful*.

As a result, there is the danger that on account of their grammatically correct form, meaningless combinations of symbols – *pseudo-statements* – might be regarded as genuine, that is, as meaningful propositions.

According to Wittgenstein, misunderstandings of this kind play a considerable role in philosophy:

"Most of the propositions and questions to be found in philosophical works are not false but nonsensical. Consequently we cannot give any answer to questions of this kind, but can only point out that they are nonsensical . . .

(They belong to the same class as the question whether the good is more or less identical than the beautiful.)"[1]

It is clear that pseudo-statements, pseudo-arguments, pseudo-problems, in short, that *nonsense* must be recognised as such and be excluded from scientific debate. That is the task of philosophy:

"All philosophy is a 'critique of language' . . ."[2]

It is its meaning that turns a proposition into a genuine proposition, not its grammatical form. For a proposition, only its meaning is essential:

"A proposition possesses essential and accidental features.

"Accidental features are those that result from the particular way in which the propositional sign is produced. Essential features are those without which the proposition could not express its sense."

"So what is essential in a proposition is what all propositions that can express the same sense have in common."[3]

This something that constitutes the character of a genuine proposition and that alone is essential for the proposition, that is, its meaning, is not something ultimate that cannot be further reduced. The concept of meaning can be logically analysed.

A meaningful proposition (and *only a meaningful* proposition) represents a *state of affairs*, one that may really exist or may only be imagined. And only by virtue of the fact that it represents an (existent or non-existent) state of affairs does a proposition have *meaning*.

"In a proposition a situation is, as it were, constructed by way of experiment.

---

[1] Ludwig Wittgenstein, *Tractatus Logico-Philosophicus* (1918/1922), Proposition 4.003. [This and all other direct quotations from Wittgenstein's *Tractatus* are taken from the 2nd ed. of the English translation by D.F. Pears and B.F. McGuinness, 1971. Tr.]

[2] Wittgenstein, *op. cit.*, Proposition 4.0031. *"Though not in Mauthner's sense," Wittgenstein adds. [The reference is to Fritz Mauthner, *Beiträge zu einer Kritik der Sprache* I./III. (1901/1902; 2nd ed., 1906/1913); F. Mauthner, *Wörterbuch der Philosophie: Neue Beiträge zu einer Kritik der Sprache* I./II. (1910/1911). Ed.]

[3] Wittgenstein, *op. cit.*, Propositions 3.34 and 3.341.

"Instead of, 'This proposition has such and such a sense,' we can simply say, 'This proposition represents such and such a situation.' "[4]

The sense of a proposition is that which it represents:

"A proposition is a picture of reality."

"A proposition states something only in so far as it is a picture."

"What a picture represents is its sense."[5]

A statement is true if the state of affairs that it represents exists; it is false if this state of affairs does not exist.

"Reality is compared with propositions."

"A proposition can be true or false only in virtue of being a picture of reality."[6]

We have understood the meaning of a proposition if we can indicate the state of affairs it represents, in other words, if we know what state of affairs must exist if the proposition is to be true.

"To understand a proposition means to know what is the case if it is true.

"(One can understand it, therefore, without knowing whether it is true.)"[7]

Only if we can indicate (or if we have determined) what state of affairs a proposition represents, that is, under what conditions it is to be called "true", do we know and understand its meaning:

". . . in order to be able to say:" [about a proposition (let us designate it "p")] "p is true (or false), I must have determined in what circumstances I call 'p' true, and in so doing determine the sense of the proposition."[8]

Waismann's remark (cf. the quotation at the end of the preceding section) is in complete accord with Wittgenstein's analysis of the concept of meaning:

"A statement describes a state of affairs. A state of affairs exists or it does not exist . . . If there is no way of indicating under what conditions a statement is true, then the statement has no meaning at all; for the meaning of a statement is the method of its verification."[9]

[4] Wittgenstein, op. cit., Proposition 4.031.

[5] Wittgenstein, op. cit., Propositions 4.01, 4.03 and 2.221.

[6] Wittgenstein, op. cit., Propositions 4.05 and 4.06.

[7] Wittgenstein, op. cit., Proposition 4.024.

[8] Wittgenstein, op. cit., Proposition 4.063.

[9] Friedrich Waismann, "Logische Analyse des Wahrscheinlichkeitsbegriffs", Erkenntnis 1 (1930), p. 229.

One question in particular is important from the standpoint of the *problem of induction*: What is the relationship between the logical-positivist concept of meaning, and the distinction between strictly universal and singular statements?

The preceding quotations do not bode well for universal statements: they cannot, in principle, be verified; no one can state under what conditions they are to be called true, since there can be no such (experiential) conditions: *they do not represent empirical states of affairs.*

One might attempt to speak about universal and singular *states of affairs* (so that universal propositions would represent universal states of affairs, and singular propositions would represent singular states of affairs). But although in the case of singular states of affairs we can decide, on the basis of experience, whether they do or do not exist, we can never, in principle, know whether there is such a thing as a universal state of affairs. The question whether universal states of affairs exist, the question of whether law-like regularities exist in nature, and the question whether there is a *principle of induction* (cf. Section 5) — all these questions are equivalent to the question of whether a natural law can be empirically true:*[1] it can, in fact, be true only if the universal state of affairs (the law-like regularity) that it represents really *exists*.

According to deductivist empiricism too, the thesis that natural laws can never be [demonstrably] *true* is equivalent to the thesis that we have no possible empirical (and certainly no *a priori*) justification for asserting the existence of *universal states of affairs*.

(We can, therefore, only assert the existence of those states of affairs that can be represented by singular statements; that is, only the existence of singular states of affairs.)

On the question whether or not *experiential*, empirical universal states of affairs exist, deductivism is in agreement with logical positivism: both answer this question in the negative.*[2] (This is, according to deductivism, why natural laws are *fictions*, since they do not represent any real state of affairs. The assertion that universal states of affairs exist is rationalist. In the problem of universals, it leads to realism. But oddly enough, the

---

*[1] Or better: "can be empirically demonstrated to be true".

*[2] As long as the emphasis is on the words "experiential" and "empirical", this statement is correct. It follows that the proposition "universal states of affairs exist" is metaphysical; but it does not follow that natural laws are fictions.

logical-positivist Carnap has no difficulty in speaking about universal states of affairs as opposed to individual ones; cf. the quotation in Section 23.)

Logical positivism establishes the concept of meaning through the concept of a state of affairs: every meaningful statement represents a state of affairs.

If there are no universal states of affairs, then there are no universal statements. The putative universal statements are meaningless, they are pseudo-statements.

That logical positivism advocates this view is illustrated most clearly by the fact that it declares natural laws to be pseudo-statements, that is, by its pseudo-statement position. Schlick [writes]:[10]

"As has frequently been remarked, we can never actually speak about an absolute verification of a natural law since we tacitly always reserve the right, as it were, to be allowed to modify it on the basis of subsequent experiences. If I may be allowed to make an incidental comment on the logical situation, then what has just been said also means that a natural law fundamentally lacks the logical character of a 'statement', but rather represents a 'rule for the transformation of statements'. (I owe this idea and this phrase to Ludwig Wittgenstein.)"

The view that the putative "universal statements" are pseudo-statements is a necessary consequence of Wittgenstein's concept of meaning. This will be illustrated further by means of several quotations.

The following passage shows that Wittgenstein does not use the concept of state of affairs in the sense of a universal state of affairs:

"A proposition must restrict reality to two alternatives: yes or no.

"In order to do that it must describe reality completely."[11]

Only a singular statement (in the terminology I use) can restrict a singular state of affairs to either yes or no (of course, not every singular statement); for with respect to a universal statement we can never say [with certainty] that things are, in fact, the way that it asserts they are.

The problem of universal statements is illuminated especially by those passages in which Wittgenstein speaks about the possibility of answering questions.

---

[10] Moritz Schlick, "Die Kausalität in der gegenwärtigen Physik", Die Naturwissenschaften 19 (1931), p. 151; cf. also the quotation in Section 19.

[11] Wittgenstein, op. cit., Proposition 4.023.

With regard to *questions*, Carnap writes:[12] "In a strictly logical sense, a question consists in being presented with a statement and with the task of establishing as true either this statement or its negation."

If every genuine statement *restricts* reality to yes or no, then every genuine question must, in principle, be decidable by yes or no (otherwise it would constitute a *pseudo-problem*). According to Wittgenstein also:

"*The riddle* does not exist.

"If a question can be framed at all, then it is also *possible* to answer it."

"And it is not surprising that the deepest problems are in fact *not* problems at all."[13]

If one attempts to understand natural laws, in the deductivist sense, as genuine statements, and the question whether they are true or false as a genuine problem, then Wittgenstein's views would have the most peculiar implications. Any question would be answered only after all (conceivable) natural laws had been falsified; for since a natural law is not verifiable, the question about its truth value will remain unanswered as long as it has not been falsified: the solution of all riddles would be the end of theoretical natural science.

But it is clear that Wittgenstein's view (Carnap[14] calls it the "proud thesis of the omnipotence of rational science"), that is, the view that it is, in principle, possible to answer all questions, is based on the assumption that natural laws are pseudo-statements, and that the question about their truth or falsity [is] a pseudo-problem.

It should be noted that not all proponents of logical positivism have fully embraced Wittgenstein's concept of meaning. Carnap, who in his *Der logische Aufbau der Welt* endorses Wittgenstein's thesis, adopts a completely different concept of meaning (in *Scheinprobleme in der Philosophie*,[15] published at the same time). Even if one uses his narrowest formulation (in terms of the concept of "grounding"[+1]), "natural laws" would still have to be acknowledged as meaningful statements. Deductivism cannot, of course,

---

[12] Rudolf Carnap, *Der logische Aufbau der Welt* (1928), p. 254.

[13] Wittgenstein, *op. cit.*, Propositions 6.5 and 4.003.

[14] Carnap, *op. cit.*, p. 261. [See also R. Carnap, *op. cit.*, p. 255. Ed.]

[15] Rudolf Carnap, *Scheinprobleme in der Philosophie: Das Fremdpsychische und der Realismusstreit* (1928), pp. 28 f.

[+1] ["Fundierung" in the German. Tr.]

appeal to this concept of meaning; for Carnap defines the concept of "grounding" by employing that of "inductive inference" without indicating what is meant by inductive inferences. This concept, therefore, is not available for an analysis of the problem of induction.

In sum, the logical-positivist concept of meaning could be characterised as follows:

Every genuine statement describes a state of affairs: therein lies its meaning. If a putative statement does not represent a state of affairs, then it is a *pseudo-statement*, it is *meaningless*. There are no universal states of affairs and hence no universal statements. All meaningful statements can be definitively decided – by yes or no.

(Whereas in Section 32 it was found that logistic, and with it logical positivism, cannot formulate the distinction between strictly universal and singular statements, we see here that logical positivism does not fail to make such a distinction. Logical positivism knows that demarcation; not, admittedly, as a demarcation between universal and singular statements, but as a demarcation between pseudo- and genuine statements, between nonsense and meaning.)

If natural laws are pseudo-statements, then the problem of induction must be a pseudo-problem. It is the question about the truth of natural laws; but we cannot ask about the truth of pseudo-statements.

44. *The concept of meaning and the demarcation problem – the fundamental thesis of inductivism.* At this point, we could proceed by way of a critique of the concept of meaning; then the next section (following a well-established heuristic principle) would, once again, raise the question of what serious reasons and substantive problems underlie this concept of meaning. But the answer to this question shows that the concept of meaning takes us to the very limits of the problem of induction (and, indeed, beyond it). The critique of the concept of meaning, therefore, will be the *final* critique not only of the pseudo-statement positions, but, more generally, of *the problem of induction*.

The sequence will be reversed accordingly. A critique of the concept of meaning will be dealt with only in the later sections, for if this critique is to *conclude* our discussion, it has to assume a full understanding of the ultimate substantive reasons behind this problem.

We will, therefore, inquire into these reasons in the present section.

It is the *"demarcation problem"* (according to my terminology) that lies behind Wittgenstein's concept of meaning: the concept of meaning in Wittgenstein's philosophy plays the role of a *demarcation criterion*.

The solution of the demarcation problem, that is, the establishment of a criterion that allows us to draw a sharp boundary between natural science and metaphysics, is (as we shall see) precisely the *task* that was set in the *Tractatus Logico-Philosophicus*.

Much like Kant, who sets a limit to our *knowledge* (to the use of our understanding and reason), Wittgenstein wants to "set a limit to thought".

Kant sees a certain difficulty in our having to possess *knowledge* of the very limits of knowledge; but he does not consider this a serious difficulty. By means of an apt analogy, he attempts to show that nothing fundamental stands in the way of establishing such limits through an investigation of *internal* conditions.

"Our reason is not like a plane . . . the limits of which we know in a general way only; but must rather be compared to a sphere, the radius of which can be determined from the curvature of the arc of its surface – that is to say, from the nature of synthetic *a priori* propositions . . . Outside this sphere (the field of experience) there is nothing that can be an object for reason."[1]

Wittgenstein considers the same question; but it is evident that he does not regard such an "internal survey", such a demarcation from within, as possible.

"Thus the aim of the book is to draw a limit to thought, or rather – not to thought, but to the expression of thoughts: for in order to be able to draw a limit to thought, we should have to find both sides of the limit thinkable (i.e., we should have to be able to think what cannot be thought)."[2]

What is the more encompassing domain within which the limit is to be determined? We already know that Wittgenstein's criterion of demarcation, the *concept of meaning*, sets the limit within the domain of *grammatically*

---

[1] Immanuel Kant, *Kritik der reinen Vernunft* (2nd ed., 1787), p. 790. [English translation by N. Kemp Smith (1929), 1965: *Critique of Pure Reason*, pp. 607 f. Tr.]

[2] Ludwig Wittgenstein, *Tractatus Logico-Philosophicus* (1918/1922), Preface; see also Proposition 5.61.

correct statements, that is, in the domain of language (even if not in the domain of *meaningful* speech).

"It will therefore only be in language that the limit can be drawn, and what lies on the other side of the limit will simply be nonsense."[3]

The problem of demarcation appears as a major task in Wittgenstein's philosophy:

"Philosophy sets limits to the much disputed sphere of natural science."

"It must set limits to what can be thought; and, in so doing, to what cannot be thought.

"It must set limits to what cannot be thought by working outwards through what can be thought."[4]

The domain of the thinkable, of the meaningful, is that of the statements that represent "the existence and non-existence of states of affairs"[5] (that is, the domain of the definitively verifiable "*singular empirical statements*"); it is the *domain of natural science*:

"The totality of true propositions is the whole of natural science (or the whole corpus of the natural sciences)."[6]

On the other side of the limit, beyond the concept of meaning, lies the unthinkable, nonsense, the playground of philosophical pseudo-problems; here be *metaphysics*. The following quotation appeared in the previous section:

"Most of the propositions and questions to be found in philosophical works are not false but nonsensical. Consequently we cannot give any answer to questions of this kind, but can only point out that they are nonsensical."[7]

This pointing out, this activity of demarcating, cleansing, clarifying, is the real task of philosophy. For philosophy itself cannot teach true statements: only natural science can do this.

"Philosophy is not one of the natural sciences . . ."

"Philosophy aims at the logical clarification of thoughts.

"Philosophy is not a body of doctrine but an activity.

"A philosophical work consists essentially of elucidations.

---

[3] Wittgenstein, *op. cit.*, Preface.
[4] Wittgenstein, *op. cit.*, Propositions 4.113 and 4.114.
[5] [Wittgenstein, *op. cit.*, Proposition 4.1. Ed.]
[6] Wittgenstein, *op. cit.*, Proposition 4.11.
[7] Wittgenstein, *op. cit.*, Proposition 4.003.

"Philosophy does not result in 'philosophical propositions', but rather in the clarification of propositions.

"Without philosophy thoughts are, as it were, cloudy and indistinct: its task is to make them clear and to give them sharp boundaries."[8]

Philosophy cannot teach any propositions. (If, nevertheless, it tries to do so, these will be metaphysical pseudo-statements.) Meaningful propositions exist only in natural science.

The correct method of philosophising, the activity of elucidating and demarcating, consists in recognising metaphysical pseudo-statements and pseudo-problems for what they are ("pseudo-problem method"). This activity is negative, "sterile" (this is how it is characterised by H. Gomperz[9]), unsatisfying – but it alone meets the requirements of the task of philosophy. If one intends to speak *meaningfully*, then one might just as well utter only the propositions of the natural sciences.

Pseudo-statements and pseudo-problems arise from the use of *empty words* that usually have an emotional meaning for us but that are logically meaningless.

If a proposition "has no sense, that can only be because we have failed to give a *meaning* to some of its constituents.

"(Even if we think that we have done so.)

"Thus the reason why 'Socrates is identical' says nothing is that we have not given *any adjectival* meaning to the word 'identical'."[10]

From this follows the programme of philosophical demarcation, the *programme of applying the "pseudo-problem method"*:

"The correct method in philosophy would really be the following: to say nothing except what can be said, i.e. propositions of natural science – i.e. something that has nothing to do with philosophy – and then, whenever someone else wanted to say something metaphysical, to demonstrate to him that he had failed to give a meaning to certain signs in his propositions. Although it would not be satisfying to the other person – he would not have the feeling that we were teaching him philosophy – this method would be the only strictly correct one."[11]

At this point, it becomes especially clear that Wittgenstein does, in fact,

---

[8] Wittgenstein, *op. cit.*, Propositions 4.111 and 4.112.
[9] [Cf. Heinrich Gomperz, *Weltanschauungslehre* I. (1905), pp. 14 f. Ed.]
[10] Wittgenstein, *op. cit.*, Proposition 5.4733.
[11] Wittgenstein, *op. cit.*, Proposition 6.53.

intend to set a limit that is designed to achieve precisely the purpose that I have set for a demarcation criterion. His meaning criterion divides the field of language into two large domains, it separates sense from nonsense, statements from pseudo-statements; and, as a demarcation criterion, *natural science from metaphysics*.

True philosophy, which does not attempt to teach us anything, belongs [according to Wittgenstein] to neither of the two domains. It is the *activity* of demarcating. It has to defend the domain of meaning, of natural science, against the claims of metaphysics (and, very likely, vice versa); it has to separate the domains clearly and cleanly.

On the *boundary* between sense and nonsense (on the nonsense side) lies *logic*.

"The correct explanation of the propositions of logic must assign to them a unique status among all propositions."

"The propositions of logic arc tautologies."

"Therefore the propositions of logic say nothing. (They are analytic propositions.)"

"Tautologies and contradictions are not pictures of reality. They do not represent any possible situations . . ."

"Tautologies and contradictions lack sense . . .

"(For example, I know nothing about the weather when I know that it is either raining or not raining.)"[12]

But even though they lie beyond the boundary, they are not yet inside the domain of metaphysics (of actual "nonsense") but simply at the *boundary*:

"Tautology and contradiction are the limiting cases – indeed the dissolution – of the combination of symbols."

"Tautologies and contradictions are not, however, nonsensical . . ."[13]

There are, therefore, two forms of meaninglessness: (metaphysical) nonsense and the meaninglessness of silent logical (and mathematical) tautologies. If we include logic, we must, therefore, distinguish between three domains in the field of language:

The meaningful statements of natural science, the meaningless tautologies of logic (and mathematics) and the nonsensical pseudo-statements of metaphysics.

---

[12] Wittgenstein, *op. cit.*, Propositions 6.112, 6.1, 6.11, 4.462 and 4.461.

[13] Wittgenstein, *op. cit.*, Propositions 4.466 and 4.4611.

The demarcating *activity* of philosophy is, however, engaged in all domains: it is the "critique of language", by means of which Wittgenstein determines these boundaries.

But where is there room for natural laws? Are they meaningful? Are they meaningless or nonsensical? Or do they, perhaps, belong to the domain of philosophical activity?

As we have already seen, it is a necessary consequence of the concept of meaning that natural laws be regarded as *pseudo-statements*. They *cannot* belong to the domain of meaningful propositions.

Schlick's emphasis on their pragmatic character might suggest that they are in the domain of *activity*, of philosophy. But this is impossible; for philosophy itself is negative, it is "sterile". It cannot produce anything. This solution must be rejected.

Do natural laws belong to the border region of meaningless tautologies? There is considerable evidence that supports this view, at least according to *conventionalism*. But this view is incompatible with that of Schlick: time and again, he emphasises the *empirical* aspect of natural laws when contrasted with conventionalism.

Are natural laws metaphysical, then?

If we do not want to assume a third form of meaninglessness alongside meaningless tautologies and nonsensical metaphysics, the only apparent course of action open to us is to declare natural laws to be metaphysical.

It may, however, be possible to regard them as a special type of pseudo-statements (that is, unlike the pseudo-statements of nonsensical metaphysics).

I cannot state with certainty whether natural laws are metaphysical (in other words, nonsensical) or whether they form a discrete group of pseudo-statements. Only *one* thing is clear: they cannot be meaningful, they lie beyond the limits that the demarcation criterion of meaning has drawn for the natural sciences. Perhaps they belong somehow to "scientific activity", but certainly not to scientific *theory*; for we know already (see above):

"The totality of true propositions is the whole of natural science (or the totality of the natural sciences)."[14]

---

[14] [Wittgenstein, *op. cit.*, Proposition 4.11. Ed. The English text is by the present translators and revisers. Tr.]

Natural laws cannot, therefore, belong to natural science, for they can never be (demonstrably) *true*. (What is more, they cannot even belong to the "totality of propositions", but are pseudo-statements.)

Whereas natural laws do not belong to natural science, *all* true statements are to be regarded as part of natural science; for example: "The 'Tractatus' is lying open on my desk," or "Like Klopstock, Kant is more admired than read," or "One of my friends has not kept his promise to visit me today."

In the present section, I shall not in any way embark on a critique of the *concept of meaning* itself. The view that natural laws are meaningless pseudo-statements will not, therefore, be disputed here.

But the *one* question that I do wish to pose here is whether Wittgenstein has accomplished the task he himself had chosen for his philosophical activity: has his *demarcation* been successful or not?

From this perspective, that is, from the position of the demarcation problem, Wittgenstein's solution *cannot* be accepted, for the following reason: Wittgenstein's *concept of "natural science"* has nothing whatever to do with the natural sciences as they exist in fact. His demarcation criterion excludes natural laws from his "natural science"; but thereby he also excludes natural science as it actually exists from his "natural science".

Natural laws belong, without a doubt, to what the natural sciences themselves regard as "scientific". But are natural laws, perhaps, not of *central* importance in the domain of the natural sciences? Is it perhaps the case that only [demonstrably] *true* statements (singular empirical statements) should primarily be called "scientific", whereas natural laws should be described as "scientific" only in so far as they can help in the formulation of such *true* statements (in the formulation of singular predictions)?

If this were the case, Wittgenstein's concept of meaning would still not be an entirely satisfactory *demarcation criterion* (it would be much too vague and indeterminate for a *result* of philosophical activity, for it does not distinguish sharply between natural laws and metaphysical pseudo-statements); but at least some part of existing natural science would lie within the demarcated domain of his "natural science".

The situation, however, is completely different. The more highly developed natural sciences, in particular, consist almost entirely of natural laws (universal statements):

"We ought not to forget that any description of the world by means of mechanics will always be of the completely general kind. For example, it will never mention *particular* point masses: it will only talk about *any point masses whatsoever.*"[15]

Mechanics, as correctly characterised here by Wittgenstein, is a natural science according to the viewpoint of natural science. It can, however, never be included in Wittgenstein's concept of a natural science. The philosophical critique of language maintains that the putative strictly universal empirical statements of mechanics are actually *pseudo-statements*, and it excludes them from the domain of scientific *statements*, that is, it sharply demarcates "natural science" so as to keep them out.

Wittgenstein's "natural science" contains, instead, an incalculable number of true statements that, while representing some states of affairs, have never been of interest to the natural sciences and probably never will be.

By saying that, I do not wish to restrict Wittgenstein's right to determine philosophically what is "genuine" natural science by means of his conceptual constructions. Nor do I wish to dispute the thesis that natural laws are nonsensical, that they belong to the domain of the unthinkable and unspeakable and therefore not to that of natural science. I am leaving all these questions aside.

I pose only *one* question here (quite unphilosophically and soberly): Has Wittgenstein succeeded, given the natural sciences that actually exist, in demarcating science? For the problem of demarcation is unambiguous. Its task is the clean separation of the domains, that is, the clear and sharp demarcation of this natural science from (as understood by this science) unscientific speculation, or from "metaphysics".

It seems to me that this task has not been accomplished.

The analysis of the pseudo-statement positions leads our discussion of the problem of induction to the problem of demarcation. This problem does not merely constitute the background of the logical-positivist concept of meaning: on closer examination it becomes evident that it is in fact the *problem of demarcation that underlies the problem of induction.*

The fundamental problem of *empiricism*, that is to say, of that epistemology that attaches a special value to the empirical sciences, consists in the

---

[15] Wittgenstein, *op. cit.*, Proposition 6.3432.

task of determining more closely the peculiar "*empirical*" character of natural science (in contrast to "speculative" metaphysics).

For empiricism, this value consists in the fact that the empirical sciences alone are capable of conveying well-founded *knowledge* of reality. The empiricist theory of knowledge (empiricism) seeks to account for this capacity in terms of the special character of the *empirical method* used by the natural sciences (as opposed to the metaphysical method).

But for this purpose it must, above all, *determine* the special character of the empirical method as against that of the metaphysical method. The fundamental problem of empiricism, therefore, is the *demarcation problem*, that is, the question:

What method distinguishes natural science from metaphysics?

The most obvious and apparently self-evident answer is: natural science refrains from speculation and *proceeds only from experience*.

This answer, however, is that of *inductivism*.

Inductivism is nothing but a (primitive) solution of the demarcation problem: fear of metaphysics (a fear that is only too justified as long as no useful demarcation criterion is available) leads the (inductively oriented empiricist) to cling as tightly as possible to the immediate data of experience.

The inductivist demarcation criterion is the inductive method. We can obtain legitimate scientific concepts and statements (that is, non-metaphysical concepts and statements) only *from experience*.

(From its very inception, inductivism has always led to false demarcations. Bacon confused theory formation with metaphysics: by appealing to the evidence of the senses, he refused to give up his geocentric convictions; compare also Mach's attacks on atomism.)

This is not the place to discuss in further detail inductivist efforts to resolve the problem of demarcation. There is only *one* point I wish to make here: namely, that the *inductivist prejudice* also underlies the logical-positivist criterion of demarcation (for only in this way will it be demonstrated that the pseudo-statement positions are, in fact, "inductivist"; cf. Section 37).

The inductivist solutions, as we know, related primarily not to *statements* (that are asserted) and to their (objective) *validity*, but to concepts (that we should "possess") and to their (subjective-psychological) "origin" (cf. also Sections 11 and 33–35). The following demarcation criterion would correspond approximately to this formulation of the problem:

All legitimate concepts of science must be reducible to elementary experiences (perceptions, impressions).

If we ask about the analogous demarcation criterion for *statements* – this is of much greater interest to us here – and avoid the *subjectivist-psychologistic mode of expression*, then inductivism must arrive at the following criterion, which I call the *fundamental thesis of inductivism*.

All legitimate statements of science must be reducible to elementary empirical statements. In other words: the truth of all legitimate statements must depend on the truth values of some elementary empirical statements.

("Elementary empirical statements" are to be understood as (objective) descriptions of the simplest states of affairs, which can be tested directly (in principle, by any subject) through "perceptions"; cf. Section 11.)

As long as *induction*, or the inference of universal statements from singular experiences, is accepted as justified, the "fundamental thesis of inductivism" proves to be an exceedingly useful *demarcation criterion* with the help of which natural laws can also be demonstrated to be "legitimate". But should genuine inductive inference be regarded as impermissible and self-contradictory (Hume), then natural laws can no longer be reduced to elementary empirical statements. Put another way:

Legitimate statements can no longer be elevated to the rank of generalisation, that is, to the level of natural laws. They are cut off from natural laws by the demarcation criterion (by this very "fundamental thesis"); the boundary runs below the level of natural laws. Legitimate statements remain confined to experience, that is, to the singular.

And from here we can go back to the logical-positivist criterion of demarcation:

Wittgenstein introduces the *concept of the (meaningful) proposition* twice (the two definitions are completely identical): the first time with the help of the concept of states of affairs and the concept of meaning; the second time, he *formally* defines the general concept of proposition, namely as a "truth function" of "elementary propositions".

Wittgenstein's concept of elementary propositions corresponds to what I have called here "elementary empirical statements":

"The simplest kind of proposition, an elementary proposition, asserts the existence of a state of affairs."[16]

---

[16] Wittgenstein, *op. cit.*, Proposition 4.21.

If the truth value of a statement depends on that of other statements (to which it is thus reducible), then it is a "truth function". The statements to which it can be reduced are its "truth arguments".

(Here I can refer only briefly to Wittgenstein's interesting *formal theory of "truth functions"*, the *"Wittgensteinian schemata"* already mentioned in Section 31.)

If we express the *"fundamental inductivist thesis"* using this terminology, we arrive at the following formulation:

All legitimate statements of science are truth functions of elementary statements.

Wittgenstein defines the (formal) concept of *"proposition"* in exactly the same way:

"A proposition is a truth-function of elementary propositions.

"(An elementary proposition is a truth-function of itself.)"

"Elementary propositions are the truth-arguments of propositions."[17]

Used as a demarcation criterion, this formulation draws the boundary between the (legitimate) statements of natural science and metaphysical pseudo-statements along the same lines as does the *concept of meaning* when used as a demarcation criterion. (That is, according to my terminology, between singular and strictly universal statements.) Consequently, we always have to do with the *inductivist criterion of demarcation*, regardless of whether it occurs in the form of the concept of meaning or in the form of the "fundamental inductivist thesis".

We see that the pseudo-statement positions are, indeed, inductivist; and we are justified in calling the concept of meaning on which they are founded the *"inductivist concept of meaning"*.

The *concept of meaning itself* has not, so far, been affected by these considerations, but only by its use as a demarcation criterion.

It is quite possible that there is another, more suitable (and also sharper) demarcation criterion that does full justice to the existing natural sciences (that is, it does not exclude natural laws), while also accepting the inductivist concept of meaning as such. Although *"meaning"* would not, in that case, constitute the boundary between natural science and metaphysics, natural laws would nevertheless be *"meaningless pseudo-statements"*.

---

[17] Wittgenstein, *op. cit.*, Propositions 5 and 5.01.

We have to admit that according to this view, the concept of meaning would not solve the problem of demarcation, but it would still have an epistemological function. It would get rid of the problem of induction, for one cannot ask about the validity of pseudo-statements.

Within the context of these investigations into the *problem of induction*, a critical discussion of the pseudo-statement positions compels us to embark on a *critique of the inductivist concept of meaning itself*.

45. *Critique of the inductivist dogma of meaning.* The logical-positivist, or inductivist, concept of meaning is *dogmatic*.

In justifying this assertion and the rejection it implies, it will hardly be necessary to provide an explicit definition of [the concept of] "dogma" (or of "dogmatism"). The investigation will demonstrate sufficiently how these words are used here and that this use is justified.

In order to analyse the inductivist concept of meaning, I shall distinguish between two possible interpretations of this concept.

1. The concept of meaning is *reducible* to other concepts (it is definable).

2. The concept of meaning is *indefinable* (it is an indefinable basic concept).

On the first interpretation:

If Wittgenstein's concept of meaning is regarded as reducible, then the only possibility is to reduce it to *that of a state of affairs* (the concept of situation):

"Instead of, 'This proposition has such and such a sense,' we can simply say, 'This proposition represents such and such a situation.' "[1] (This passage has been quoted earlier.)

It should here be assumed – and we need to remember this – that the concept of meaning is reducible. On this assumption, Wittgenstein's formulation can be used as a "practical definition", as a translation rule. His formulation allows us to transform every statement in which the word "meaning" occurs[*1] into one from which this term is eliminated and replaced by the term *state of affairs* (of course, a singular state of affairs).

---

[1] [Ludwig Wittgenstein, *Tractatus Logico-Philosophicus* (1918/1922), Proposition 4.031. Cf. Section 43, text to note 4. Ed.]

[*1] In the sense of "the meaning of a statement".

The translation rule would go as follows: "To have meaning" is to be understood as "to represent a (singular) state of affairs".

For example, the assertion "All (grammatically correct) statements that can be definitively verified, in particular all true statements, *are meaningful*", can be reformulated with the help of this translation rule as follows: "All . . . statements that can be definitively verified . . . *represent a* (singular) *state of affairs*".

If the position is adopted that the concept of meaning can *by definition* be reduced, in the way indicated here, to the concept of (singular) state of affairs, then the following translation must also be allowed:

The assertion "this natural law *has no meaning*", or "this natural law is *meaningless*", states nothing other than "this natural law does not represent a (singular) *state of affairs*".

We are already aware that a natural law does not represent a (singular) state of affairs. By *referring* to this fact through expressions such as "meaningless", "nonsensical", "unthinkable", "unsayable", "unspeakable", etc. (all of them expressions that can be reduced to the concept of meaning), we can neither pose nor solve a problem: replacing one name by another is merely a matter of *terminology*.

The choice of a suitable or unsuitable terminology may, admittedly, contribute to the clarification of a problem or to its obfuscation, but such renaming alone cannot, of course, alter anything about the problem itself.

A natural law does not represent a (singular) state of affairs. So much is fact. It *cannot* possibly represent a (singular) state of affairs, if it is to act as a *universally applicable deductive premise*. For this very reason it is also *unverifiable*. If *for these reasons* we wish to call it a "pseudo-statement", or "meaningless", or "unspeakable", etc., there can be no objections in principle to this terminology. But practice shows that it is *very* unsuitable, because it is *very* misleading.

It should be remembered that I am discussing only the interpretation that regards the concept of meaning as *definable*. If this interpretation is accepted, then no locution that belongs to the pseudo-statement terminology will enable us to say more than that natural laws do not represent (singular) states of affairs.

But, as we know, laws may still be *false*, and the terminology cannot, of course, change this fact.

It now becomes evident that this terminology is *highly unsuitable*: it suggests the impermissible construal that natural laws cannot have any truth value whatever (not even a negative one). But such construal has nothing to justify it (in the context of this interpretation). If "having meaning" means nothing but "representing a (singular) state of affairs", this certainly does not justify the conclusion that only those statements that represent a (singular) state of affairs (that is to say, have meaning) can be false.

If, however, we do not allow ourselves to be misled by the term "meaningless", and if we admit that the statement "All apples are dark green" is false, this terminology may appear even more unsuitable: one would then call false statements (that is, statements that have a truth value) "meaningless".

One obvious reason why this terminology, more particularly the expressions "nonsense", "the unthinkable", etc., is completely unsuitable, is that ordinary language burdens it with (to some extent derogatory) valuations. Certainly, though, these valuations cannot be derived from the sober definition "To have meaning" is to be understood as "to represent a (singular) state of affairs".

Wittgenstein too emphasises this valuation. Consider his examples of meaningless statements, for example, the "question whether the good is more or less identical than the beautiful".[2]

This valuation can, evidently, lead us to draw hasty conclusions that in no way may be justified by the terminology or the definition alone; that is, the conclusions that "meaningless" natural laws cannot have any truth value and that they are, moreover, unfalsifiable.

(A method that reads into a definable concept more than was, by definition, put into it – and especially one that reads into it unjustifiable valuations – may well be called "dogmatic".)

In the present case, we seem to be dealing with the view that it is of the "essence" of the concept of meaning that only a meaningful statement can have a truth value. Be that as it may; if we wish to define the concept of meaning through the concept of (singular) state of affairs, then by way of this definition we have already decided the fate of this term: we have made use of it in a different way. We cannot subsequently ask about its "essence" [again].

But this renders untenable the interpretation that regards the concept of meaning as definable, or reducible.

---

[2] [Wittgenstein, op. cit., Proposition 4.003. Cf. Section 43, text to note 1. Ed.]

The same argument could be used against any other definition of the concept of meaning. If, for example, we define the "meaning of a statement" as the "method of its verification" (cf. Waismann[3]), then once again we are not permitted to read into the assertion "Natural laws are meaningless" anything but "There is no method of verifying natural laws". No progress can be made this way. Introducing a terminology cannot change anything in the logical situation. It follows that it must be possible to describe it *without* using the terminology in question.

This result, namely the rejection of the first (purely terminological) interpretation, is therefore not accidental; it does not depend on the particular definition of the concept of meaning in terms of a state of affairs.

On the second interpretation:

Here I shall discuss only the view that the concept of *meaning* is an *indefinable basic concept*. (Every theory of knowledge must, of course, admit such indefinable basic concepts in order to define other concepts.)

The attempt (conversely) to define the concept of a state of affairs through the concept of meaning can change nothing in the situation we have reached so far, and also is certainly not in line with Wittgenstein's thinking. (If, for example, we propose the definition "A state of affairs is that which is represented by a meaningful statement", once again we shall only have a symbol rule, or a translation rule, and shall reach the same results as in the purely terminological interpretation.)

We have no other choice, therefore, but to assume that we cannot define either the concept of meaning by that of the state of affairs (as was attempted by way of the first interpretation) or the concept of state of affairs by that of meaning. The two concepts cannot be reduced to each other by *definition*.

The inductivist concept of meaning is, therefore, to be regarded as *indefinable*, for it must contain far more than is expressed in an assertion such as "To have meaning means to represent a (singular) state of affairs". It must also contain all those *valuations* – even if they are not stipulated by definition – with which we usually invest expressions such as meaningful – meaningless; conceivable – inconceivable; expressible – inexpressible, etc.

---

[3] [Friedrich Waismann, "Logische Analyse des Wahrscheinlichkeitsbegriffs", *Erkenntnis* 1 (1930), p. 229. Cf. Section 42, text to note 1; Section 43, text to note 9. Ed.]

But if a corresponding definition of the concept of meaning cannot be given, how is it possible to *justify* Wittgenstein's assertion "To have meaning means to represent a (singular) state of affairs" (and many similar assertions)? This question is important, since this assertion is fundamental for the *pseudo-statement positions*.

In any event, such an assertion *cannot* be *tautological*, it cannot be the result of a *purely logical analysis* of the concepts in question; the statement would not, therefore, represent the result of a conceptual analysis or an analytic judgement, it would have to be regarded as a *synthetic judgement*; that is, as a (formal) *synthetic judgement a priori*, since it says nothing about the experiential states of affairs themselves (instead, much like Kant's synthetic *a priori* judgements, it would be of a type higher than that of "empirical statements" in that it says something about the concept of states of affairs and empirical statements in general).

The pseudo-statement positions (the view that natural laws are pseudo-statements) could, therefore, be secured through one (or several) synthetic *a priori* judgements, for example through the following (and already familiar) judgements in which the concept of meaning must be understood as implying a *valuation*, as opposed, say, to "utter nonsense": "The *meaning* of a statement consists in the method of its verification", or: "The meaning of a statement consists in that it restricts a state of affairs to yes or no".

No experience can teach us anything about the "essence" of the concept of meaning; these synthetic judgements would, without a doubt, be *a priori*, and any attempt to justify them could only lead to the *doctrine of self-evidence* (for example, in the form of the phenomenological method of intuiting essences).

Furthermore, this apriorism, as opposed to the Kantian one, could not be justified by any "transcendental method". No analysis of the assumptions of the existing sciences could ever yield the view that natural laws are meaningless.

But a philosophy that introduces synthetic *a priori* judgements without being constrained by transcendental considerations should undoubtedly be characterised as rationalist and – in Kant's sense – as *dogmatic*.

It appears to me that the investigation of these two possible interpretations has demonstrated the impermissible (because it is dogmatic) use of the logical-positivist concept of meaning.

But one *objection* remains possible, one that shatters this whole line of reasoning and allows the inductivist concept of meaning to rise unscathed from its ruins.

The main thrust of this objection is that the argument presented in this section cannot be held to be *an immanent critique*: from the position of the inductivist concept of meaning, *only* an argument that relies on a *scientific* (singular) *state of affairs* can be accepted as valid (or legitimate). Any other line of reasoning works with pseudo-arguments; and this applies also to the one presented here.

But this objection can be put in even stronger terms. Not only does my critique fail to be immanent, not only does it fail to be founded on the inductivist concept of meaning: by assuming without proof (even if not explicitly) that its argument signifies anything at all, that it is more than shadow-boxing, it tacitly introduces a *completely different concept of meaning* as an (unproven) assumption. It is only too evident that on the basis of this assumption, the inductivist concept of meaning becomes entangled in contradictions. The result of the critique, in so far as it is not a pseudo-result and therefore meaningless, cannot possibly be any different; for the inductivist concept of meaning contradicts the assumptions of the critique and, for this reason, must appear contradictory from the viewpoint of these assumptions.

The objection outlined here should not be regarded as simply a *possible* one. From Wittgenstein's standpoint, it *must* be raised if logical positivism is not to be accused of gross inconsistency. (This will become clear below.)

The fact that Wittgenstein's standpoint *must* ultimately lead to this objection is the reason why I call the inductivist concept of meaning a specially privileged dogma, or a "*protected dogma*".

The dogmatism of a doctrine may consist in propositions being set up without sufficient justification and asserted as *true* ("*unprotected dogma*"). Spinoza's ethics, for example, would be "dogmatic" in this sense: its axioms and so on are meant to be accepted and adopted as immediately evident, or as internally justified (or something of that nature). In this form of dogmatism, nonetheless, it would still be conceivable that such a proposition could be (logically or empirically) *refuted* by demonstrating an inconsistency, whether it be an internal one or an incompatibility with experience.

But there is also a form of dogmatism ("*protected dogma*") whose "dogmatic character" is much more pronounced: dogmas can be secured by other dogmas in such a way that they must remain *untouchable* in all circumstances.

Hegel's dialectic, for example, offers such privileged protection.

Although Kant believed himself able to make all speculative metaphysics and all dogmatic rationalism impossible by demonstrating that pure speculative reason will necessarily lose itself in *contradictions* (and in pseudo-problems), there is *one* possibility he had not anticipated: dogmatic metaphysics can protect itself against his objection simply by *appraising contradictions* in a different way, namely positively.

Hegel does not even attempt to refute Kant's demonstration. Rather, he constructs his dialectic directly on the concept of *contradiction* as a necessary and eminently productive factor in all thinking. This move undermines not only Kant's attack, but also all conceivable objections: any such attack is not even defended against, for it cannot confront the system (it always confronts only its own antithesis). Any conceivable objection to the system could consist only in a demonstration of its internal contradictions. But such demonstration does not shake the dialectical system; instead, it reinforces and confirms it.

Under the special protection of the dialectic, the system is outside and above any discussion. It rests in a "higher sphere of reason", it has burned all bridges (or perhaps better: all ladders) that lead up to it from the plain of the discussable.

An analogous form of dogmatism is Tertullian's*[2] "*credo quia absurdum*": if absurdity, or internal contradiction, is elevated into a motive of one's faith, then faith is on a level that cannot be reached by argument. (And this is, presumably, also the innermost "essence" of faith.)

Precisely the same privileged protection is also achieved by introducing the *inductivist concept of meaning*. Once introduced, the struggle against it becomes futile; any objection is condemned to meaninglessness, for no objection directed against the concept of meaning can be "scientific" [and therefore meaningful], since the concept of meaning itself is not a scientific one. It is on a higher level; it will always remain inaccessible to those arguments it admits as valid.

---

*[2] Troels Eggers Hansen has informed me that the attribution of this quotation to Tertullian is no longer accepted; see *Historisches Wörterbuch der Philosophie* I. (ed. Joachim Ritter, 1971), pp. 66 f.

It is also, of course, not possible to provide a *meaningful justification* of the concept of meaning: "the true philosophical method" does not consist in justifying the concept of meaning by way of argument, but only in rejecting any *objection as meaningless*, as a pseudo-objection. (It is, therefore, an *apologetic pseudo-problem method*.) Enthroning the concept of meaning is, therefore, meaningless if undertaken by means of argument. At least, it must be recognised in retrospect as a meaningless venture, that is, as soon as it has been carried out.

This realisation, therefore, that any discussion of the concept of meaning, even its enthroning by way of argument, is *meaningless*, is the *final word* of philosophical argumentation; and then it falls silent. The boats have been burnt, the bridges torn down, the ladders thrown away.

Wittgenstein, too, has this to say in conclusion:[4]

"My propositions serve as elucidations in the following way: anyone who understands me eventually recognizes them as nonsensical, when he has used them – as steps – to climb up beyond them. (He must, so to speak, throw away the ladder after he has climbed up it.)

"He must transcend these propositions, and then he will see the world aright."

"What we cannot speak about we must pass over in silence."

Once the logical-positivist has thrown away the ladder, having climbed it, he is safe from any attack. No argument can reach or pursue him now to his own sphere from the plain of the discussable. The concept of meaning is *absolutely unassailable*, an immanent *critique* (even an immanent *justification*) *impossible*.

Whereas the nonsensical character of the (enthroning) *argument* is one necessary consequence of the concept of meaning, the unassailability of the *result* is another; and it is this consequence that is most crucial for dogmatism.

Wittgenstein judges his enterprise quite correctly when he says:[5]

"On the other hand the truth of the thoughts that are here communicated seems to me unassailable and definitive. I therefore believe myself to have found, on all essential points, the final solution of the problems . . ."

---

[4] Wittgenstein, *op. cit.*, Propositions 6.54 and 7.
[5] Wittgenstein, *op. cit.*, Preface.

It would, therefore, be a mistake to see a contradiction between this remark and the final propositions (in the immediately preceding quotation) of the *Tractatus* (since nonsensical propositions cannot be definitively true). Both remarks are, in the same way, consequences of the dogma of meaning: it is precisely *because* any discussion of the concept of meaning is nonsensical that the impregnable and definitive truth of all the results that follow from it can be asserted: they are "*protected*".

Like any dogma, Wittgenstein's doctrine too has found its adherents; and so has his certainty in providing final solutions to problems.

In order to show that the *severity of my polemic* is justified; indeed, that it is made necessary by the determined self-assurance of the position (of the school of logical positivism) against which it is directed (but perhaps also by its close relationship with certain transcendental final judgements); I am quoting here at length from a programmatic paper by Schlick.[6] This passage refers to Wittgenstein's philosophy, that is, to the "pseudo-problem method". Schlick writes:[7]

"I permit myself this reference to the frequently described anarchy of philosophical views, so as not to leave in any doubt that I am fully aware of the import and weight of the conviction that I now wish to express. For I am convinced that we are in the very midst of an ultimate turning point in philosophy, and that we are objectively justified in regarding the fruitless quarrel of systems as finished. I am saying that we already have the means at our disposal to render any such quarrel unnecessary in principle; all that matters is to apply them resolutely.

"These means have been created quietly, unnoticed by the majority of philosophy teachers and writers, and thus a situation has emerged that cannot be compared with anything in the past. It is only by familiarising oneself with the new routes, and by looking back from the position to which they lead at all the endeavours that have ever been considered 'philosophical', that one can realise that the situation is genuinely unique and that the change really is final."

Schlick concludes this paper with the following remarks:[8]

---

[6] Moritz Schlick, "Die Wende der Philosophie", *Erkenntnis* 1 (1930), pp. 4 ff.

[7] Schlick, *op. cit.*, pp. 5 f.

[8] Schlick, *op. cit.*, pp. 10 f.

"Thus after the great turning point, philosophy reveals its character of finality more than ever before.

"For only by virtue of this character can the quarrel of the systems be ended. I repeat that as a consequence of the insights discussed above, we may already regard this quarrel as ended in principle . . .

"There will, no doubt, be rearguard action, and certainly there will be many who continue to tread the beaten paths for centuries to come. Authors will go on discussing old philosophical pseudo-questions. But in the end no one will listen to them any more, and they will resemble actors who continue declaiming for a while before noticing that the audience has gradually stolen away. Then it will no longer be necessary to speak about 'philosophical questions', because one will speak about *all* questions philosophically, that is, meaningfully and clearly."

If the author of *Erkenntnislehre*[9] (an opus, I am convinced, that will always retain its eminent place in philosophical literature) advocates a view with such conviction, only one thing remains for anyone unable to follow him in this: he will attempt to "discuss" those "old pseudo-questions" — such as the *problem of induction* — using the kind of arguments to which one cannot turn a deaf ear, which one *must* "listen to". He will attempt to mount such an intense "rearguard action" that his opponent will be unable to "steal away" in boredom (as he had planned to do); forced to change fronts, he must turn and fight.

From the work cited above it emerges clearly that Schlick counts the problem of induction among those "old pseudo-questions": for according to this work (just as in Wittgenstein) there are no genuine "philosophical" or "epistemological" *questions*; to designate [or to expose] such apparent questions as "pseudo-questions" is simply its *only* legitimate "answer".

It is only now, therefore, that we comprehend the astonishing certainty also manifested in Schlick's presentation of the *pseudo-statement positions*; that is, in his application of the pseudo-problem method to the problem of induction, which promptly reveals itself as "*devoid of content*" (the passage has been quoted earlier *in part*):[10]

---

[9] [Moritz Schlick, *Allgemeine Erkenntnislehre* (1918; 2nd ed., 1925). Ed.]

[10] Moritz Schlick, "Die Kausalität in der gegenwärtigen Physik", *Die Naturwissenschaften* 19 (1931), p. 156. [Cf. Section 37, text to note 3. Ed.]

"The informed reader will note that considerations such as the preceding ones render the so-called problem of 'induction' devoid of content . . . For the problem of induction consists in the question about the . . . justification of universal statements . . . We recognise . . . that there cannot exist for them . . . any justification; it cannot exist, because they are not even genuine statements."

We now know that this certainty is all too well founded. Its foundation is unshakeable. My attempt at an immanent critique was also bound to fail.

We recognise that no immanent critique of the pseudo-statement positions exists; it cannot exist, because they are as irrefutable as they are unjustifiable:

Under the special protection of the inductivist concept of meaning, they are outside or above any discussion, beyond the reach of any admissible argument.

After its hazardous voyage between the Scylla of infinite regression and the Charybdis of the *a priori*, the ship of inductivism limps home to the safe harbour of dogma.

46. *Fully decidable and partially decidable empirical statements – the antinomy of the knowability of the world. (Conclusion of the critique of the pseudo-statement positions.)* Does the introduction of the concept of meaning substantiate the terminological opposition between the deductivist-empiricist view and the "final" pseudo-statement position? Or does it merely move the terminological problem elsewhere?

This question suggested itself at the end of section 42, when we introduced the concept of meaning – the final and undoubtedly the strongest argument of the pseudo-statement positions. Even then, it did not seem quite plausible that a conflict which, after the victory of all the objective arguments of one party ("asymmetry"), had degenerated into a mere dispute about words, should once again become a substantive issue through the introduction of a new concept.

It is now possible to answer this question more precisely.

If one tries to discover behind the (inductivist) concept of meaning more than a mere term, a mere name for the class of singular empirical statements, then dogmatism becomes inescapable.

What is open for discussion is only the purely terminological ("first") interpretation of the concept of meaning. Viewed in this way, the introduction of the expression "meaningful" as a label for singular empirical statements alone proves to be a highly inappropriate convention; as inappropriate as the pseudo-statement terminology in general, once it has been deprived of its substantive or, if you will, its formal basis ("symmetry"). This "concept of meaning" is loaded with unjustified valuations, and therefore is misleading.

I propose, therefore, to eliminate this concept from the epistemological debate. One should seek to express in a different way what is actually intended by the concept of "meaning". And once it has been differently and unobjectionably expressed, it does not matter a great deal whether or not the concept of meaning is reintroduced. For my part, I hold that it flies in the face of linguistic usage to call universal statements such as "All ravens are black" or "All humans are mortal" (whether or not they may be *demonstrably true*) "*meaningless*". Similarly, I would prefer not to call evidently metaphysical statements (such as Schopenhauer's metaphysics) "meaningless". I should be content to call them "metaphysical", "*unscientific*" (in the sense of the empirical sciences and of the demarcation problem) or perhaps "*empirically empty*" [with emphasis on "empirically"]. I do not believe, furthermore, that someone who has read Schopenhauer will easily accept that everything he has read is pure nonsense. But I do not want to enter into a debate about the "correct" use of the term "meaning": what it may contribute to philosophy should be achievable by other means.

In this connection, only an investigation of the *demarcation problem* [1] can be fully satisfactory. It will show that any desired demarcation (of empirical statements, of metaphysics and of logic) is possible without using the concept of meaning or any similarly loaded concept. But once this has been achieved, there is no longer any reason to object to further use of the concept of meaning. It will become merely a question of *convention*.

However, Wittgenstein's concept of meaning determines a boundary that is of interest not only in terms of the demarcation problem: the boundary between "singular" and "strictly universal" empirical statements, drawn with the help of the inductivist concept of meaning, is of particular interest from the perspective of the *problem of induction* and of the discussion of the *pseudo-statement positions*.

The remaining demarcating functions that have to be fulfilled by the inductivist concept of meaning will be discussed as part of the

---

[1] [See Editor's Postscript. Ed.]

demarcation problem.[2] At this point (in order to clarify what aspects of these functions lie within the domain of the problem of induction) I shall have to discuss once more, in summary fashion, the distinction between singular and strictly universal empirical statements.

We already know that only singular empirical statements can, in principle, be verified and falsified, whereas strictly universal empirical statements are, in principle, only falsifiable.

These properties can be used in order to distinguish, with sufficient precision, between singular and strictly universal empirical statements. To this end, however, it is above all necessary to define more precisely the expressions "in principle verifiable" and "in principle falsifiable". For without such a definition, the statement "Singular empirical statements are, in principle, verifiable and falsifiable" would be ambiguous. Its wording could be so understood as to make it permissible for one and the same statement to be both true and false. Similarly, the statement "Universal empirical statements are in principle only falsifiable" could be misinterpreted as stating that universal empirical statements can, in principle, only be false.

I propose, therefore, the following more precise definition: the phrase "in principle verifiable" is to be understood as saying that no logical reasons stand in the way of empirical verification.

The statement "Singular empirical statements are, in principle, verifiable and falsifiable" is to be understood as saying that no logical reasons stand in the way of empirical verification or falsification of singular empirical statements. Similarly, "Universal empirical statements are, in principle, only falsifiable" is to say that experience can, for logical reasons, decide only their falsity but never their truth.

No logical statement justifies our saying a priori that universal empirical statements are false (otherwise they themselves would be logical contradictions, and experience could in no way decide them); we can, however, say a priori that their truth cannot be demonstrated by experience.

(It would be quite erroneous to think that this view is incompatible with the "law of the excluded middle"; on the contrary, it assumes this law, for this view is based on the following analytic-hypothetical

---

[2] [See Editor's Postscript. Ed.]

statement, or tautological implication: even if a universal empirical statement is true, its truth can never be demonstrated empirically. Incidentally, the so-called "crisis of the law of the excluded middle" rests completely, in my opinion, on misunderstandings, on confusing logical with psychological and empirical relationships.)

On the one hand, therefore, "strictly universal" empirical statements can (for *logical reasons*) never be confirmed by experience; that is, they can never be verified. On the other, it is again for *logical reasons* that they can be falsified by experience. The form of this refutation (*modus tollens*) is a form of *logical deduction*: it is the retrospective falsification of the *implicans* by the falsified *implicate*.

The more precise definition of the expression "in principle verifiable" and the like is important, since lack of clarity on this point can lead to serious misunderstandings.

When, for example, Schlick[3] says (in the passage already quoted) that "it is essential for a genuine statement that it be, in principle, definitively verifiable or falsifiable", the literal wording of this formulation fits also *universal* empirical statements, or natural laws, for these are "in principle falsifiable". In this wording, Schlick's "statement" would be identical with what I call "empirical statement", and it would include singular *and* universal empirical statements. But this agreement is only one of wording, for as Schlick's *pseudo-statement position* proves, this passage is intended to have a different meaning: he wants to subsume *only* the singular empirical statements under "statements".

(Similarly, the corresponding passages in Carnap[4] are not entirely free from ambiguity. Carnap, too, provides a more precise definition of the phrase "in principle", but I am not entirely sure whether or not his comments should be interpreted in accordance with the pseudo-statement position.)

I believe that my aforementioned definitions have established with sufficient precision the distinction between singular and universal empirical statements. "Singular" empirical statements are, in principle, verifiable *and* falsifiable, universal empirical statements are *only* falsifiable.

---

[3] Moritz Schlick, "Die Kausalität in der gegenwärtigen Physik", *Die Naturwissenschaften* 19 (1931), p. 156. [Cf. Section 7, text to note 1; Section 18, text to note 2. Ed.]

[4] Rudolf Carnap, *Der logische Aufbau der Welt* (1928), p. 254.

And by clarifying this distinction we have drawn that boundary which the inductivist concept of meaning had to draw (to the extent that this must be done within the domain of the problem of induction).

Yet the inductivist concept of meaning contains a *valuation*. Is this valuation manifested in the deductivist distinction presented above, or is it perhaps completely inappropriate there?

This question also will be discussed here only in so far as it falls within the domain of the problem of induction.

It should be noted, above all, that the deductivist distinction also contains a valuation; indeed, on closer inspection it contains two valuations (they are at different levels, as it were). And *these* valuations can be precisely specified and justified.

First, the deductivist distinction establishes that the truth of universal empirical statements can never be demonstrated. They cannot have a positive truth value, they *cannot be "valid"* [more accurately, their validity can never be demonstrated]. Now this is, undoubtedly, a precise and also a radical restriction of the "value" of such universal empirical statements. Whereas they may well be positively appraised, their positive value, or their corroboration value, is never final. As we know already, this value is nothing but a general account of previous attempts at verification; or, as I prefer to put it, of previous (unsuccessful) *attempts at falsification*.

This *first valuation*, contained in the deductivist distinction between singular and universal empirical statements, undoubtedly restricts and significantly reduces the value of universal empirical statements.

But does this not fully accord with what the *pseudo-statement position* asserts? Is this downgrading evaluation not the same appraisal (the one I have called "derogatory") that the inductivist concept of meaning is designed to express? Are we not fully justified in *not* calling such ("inferior") logical constructs "empirical statements", since in any case they belong to a class of logical constructs completely different from that of singular empirical statements?

We are confronted here, for the last time, with the terminological question: Is it useful to call natural laws "empirical statements" even though they can never be empirically verified?

(The answer to this question will lead also to a discussion of the *second valuation* contained in the deductivist view of natural laws.)

My position on the terminological question is this: in so far as we can even speak about "justification" with regard to such questions, it is not only useful but even *justified* to call natural laws "empirical statements".

To begin with, it is imperative to recognise natural laws as "propositions", or "statements" (if we want to avoid terminological confusion). First, because they can have an empirical truth value (that is, a *negative* one). Second, because they enable us to deduce genuine consequences, that is, they imply genuine statements. Third, because for the purpose of deduction they must, provisionally, be assumed to be true (cf. Sections 31 and 34). Fourth, because their negation is implied by falsified consequences. In short, since the logical theory of deduction is applicable to natural laws, they must be regarded as propositions or as statements in the logical sense.

But are they, perhaps, not statements in the empirical sense, that is, "empirical statements"? Perhaps they are only "free posits" or "arbitrary suppositions"?

Certainly we may describe natural laws as "free posits" or "arbitrary suppositions", for they are formulated tentatively and they are not, from a logical viewpoint, dependent on experience. We should, however, not overlook the fact that they must not be regarded as "free posits" in the sense of definitions or conventions. As "posits", they are not *a priori* true (nor are they *a priori* false), but they can be *defeated by experience; experience* can *refute* them. The only truth value that can be assigned to them definitively is one that is *based on experience*. And it seems to me quite useful to call an empirically false universal statement, such as "All humans have fair hair," an "empirical statement". And if we call universal statements that have already been falsified "empirical statements", we shall have to use the same name for those that have not been falsified yet. (Incidentally: if among the so-called "natural laws" there are, perhaps, some that are genuine conventions, this would be only a reason for not calling those particular ones "natural laws".)

With regard to this terminological question, the following considerations seem to me even more important than the eternal falsifiability argument:

Why are natural laws not verifiable? Is it, perhaps, because they are "empirically empty"? Or is it because of their "fictitious character"?

The appeal to this "fictitious character" cannot resolve these questions, for I have (by definition) called natural laws "fictitious" only because it is impossible, in principle, to demonstrate their truth.*[1]

What, then, are the logical reasons that stand in the way of an empirical verification of natural laws?

If we compare the distinction between singular and universal empirical statements made in this section, with the distinction (Sections 32–35) that goes back to the opposition between individual and universal concepts, we note that the two distinctions are strictly identical.

The reason why universal empirical statements are not definitively verifiable is that they are statements about all cases that belong to a *universal* class (universal concept). Every universal class, however, has in principle an unlimited number of elements (cases). The scope of a universal concept, compared with that of another universal concept, may be greater or smaller (superordinate concept and subordinate concept). But it is, in any case, fundamentally *unlimited*; and in particular, it is not restricted to specific spatial and temporal regions.

Regardless of the number of observed cases included under a universal concept, there will always be cases that have not been observed.

This is the logical reason, then, that stands in the way of empirical verification: universal empirical statements do claim something about observable cases, they are not empirically empty and they make assertions about empirical reality, but they state *more* than can be empirically tested.

This becomes especially clear if we compare them with empirically empty statements. In Section 15, the statements that are *a priori* true and, as hypotheses, have primary probability 1, were called "empirically empty". These (analytic) judgements state nothing about reality; experience cannot decide them. This also is why they should not be called "empirical statements" (but perhaps "conceptual analyses").

But universal empirical statements are, so to speak, the opposite of these empirically empty statements: they assert so much about reality that their primary improbability is very high. They have *unlimited* opportunities to be false, and also unlimited is the number of empirical cases about which they assert something.

---

*[1] The phrase "only because" seems to me incorrect, and the label "fictions" for natural laws should be abandoned. See *Introduction 1978*.

In Section 15 I discussed only the probability of hypotheses, and refrained from comparing the ranges of *universal* statements with those of *singular* statements. But it is evident that among singular empirical statements also, there must be relationships between ranges and, therefore, between probabilities that are analogous to the relationships between those of universal empirical statements. (Waismann,[5] to whom I referred in that section, speaks only of the latter.) A singular consequence deduced from a precise law (that is, from a simpler law, one with a higher primary improbability), will [can] itself be more precise (be simpler, have a higher primary improbability), have a smaller range, than a singular consequence deduced from a less precise law (one with a higher primary probability, less simple). The relationships between the ranges of singular empirical statements, therefore, correspond exactly to those that obtain between the corresponding hypotheses.

But if we try to compare the range of a universal empirical statement with that of a singular empirical statement (that is, if we compare the primary probability of a hypothesis with that of a singular consequence), we note that a universal empirical statement is always infinitely more improbable than any singular empirical statement, and its range infinitely smaller. More accurately, their probabilities are of entirely different orders of magnitude. (On account of its smaller range, a universal statement [taken in conjunction with singular statements] can imply an unlimited number of singular statements; it can be their premise.)

The fact that universal empirical statements are not verifiable is, therefore, associated with their high primary improbability. Put another way: they are far from being empirically empty.

Consequently, the *cognitive value* of universal statements is of an entirely different order of magnitude from that of singular statements, for the cognitive value of a statement increases with its primary improbability.

This is why we rate the theoretical (or "nomothetic" [or "nomological"]) natural sciences, that is, the ones that formulate *laws*, so much higher than the individualising (or "idiographic") sciences, and why we attribute to them the character of a science to a much higher degree: they are "scientific" to an entirely different order of magnitude from the individualising sciences.

---

[5] [See Section 15, note 1. Ed.]

This *second valuation*, therefore, based on the distinction between singular and universal empirical statements, accords an incomparably *higher* status to universal than to singular empirical statements. And that derogatory first *valuation* must be revised also at this point. It cannot detract from this higher status in any way; for although universal empirical statements can never be empirically verified, because they state too much about reality, their positive value, or their corroborative value, is never lower than the truth value of a singular empirical statement; for the corroborative value of a universal empirical statement has always, at the same time, the truth value of a summary report.

The *incomparably* (in the precise sense of this word) higher value of universal statements for empirical knowledge undoubtedly justifies the rejection of the pseudo-statement terminology and a recognition of the empirical sciences' ordinary view of natural laws: it sees in them especially valuable *empirical statements*.

If the justification of the deductivist terminology is recognised, or at least its consistency and usefulness, then all the considerations of Section 41 will become applicable once again. The controversy about the pseudo-statement positions and about the concept of meaning will necessarily lead us to a critique of the normal-statement positions, undoubtedly made more difficult by an original but unsuitable terminology.

In order to emphasise the empirical character and the special properties of singular and of universal empirical statements, I shall call singular empirical statements (empirically) "*fully decidable*", and universal statements (empirically) "*partially decidable*".

These expressions correspond to the symmetry and the asymmetry of truth values.

A statement will be called *fully decidable*, therefore, if an empirical decision can, in principle, be made about its truth *and* falsity (cf. Section 11); it will be called *partially decidable* if experience can, in principle, decide only *one* of the two, its truth or its falsity.

(As previously, "in principle" here means "for logical reasons".)

If a statement is fully decidable or partially decidable, it can be called "decidable", or "empirical", or an "empirical statement".

Every *empirical statement* is *decidable*; *singular* empirical statements are *fully decidable*, *universal* empirical statements are *partially decidable*.

In addition to *only falsifiable* natural laws, there are other *partially decidable* statements, that is, those that are, in principle, *only verifiable*, hence not falsifiable. Such statements are *negations* of strictly universal empirical statements. The statement "It is not true that all ravens are black" can, in principle, *only* be verified, but it can never be definitively falsified.

These statements can be formulated positively also, in the form of "there-is statements". For example, the statement "It is not true that all ravens are black" (or "Not all ravens are black") is strictly equivalent to the formulation "*There is* a raven whose colour is not black". Any such universal "there-is" statement, that is, any statement that asserts that something exists without restricting the scope of its assertion to a particular region, is equivalent to the negation of a universal statement. (I call these "there-is" statements "*universal [there-is statements]*", in contrast to such statements as "There are – at present – white ravens in *Vienna*"; such statements can be falsified also, and therefore are fully decidable.)

Whereas experience can only *defeat* natural laws, it can *only confirm* their negations, the universal "there-is" statements. (A falsification would be equivalent to a verification of a natural law.) Their primary improbability is, therefore, very low, and so is their cognitive value: it is even lower than the cognitive value of a *singular* empirical statement, since a *singular* empirical statement that refutes a natural law confirms its negation, the "there-is" statement; the former implies the latter [but not vice versa]. The singular empirical statement, therefore, has a smaller range and a greater cognitive value.

These partially decidable universal "there-is" statements are, nonetheless, often of great scientific interest; more precisely, the experience that confirms them, the singular empirical statement, is especially interesting since it falsifies a natural law.*[2]

Such "there-is" statements and their confirmation can play a considerable role in science generally, if only because they can be deduced from natural laws, and their confirmation, therefore, is capable of corroborating a natural law. Take, for example, the discovery of new elements (according

---

*[2] At that time I was, apparently, still inclined to regard partially decidable universal there-is statements as scientific, whereas later (see Volume II (Fragments): [III.] *Transition to the Theory of Method*, Section 4, note 1 and *Logik der Forschung*, 1934) I have regarded these statements as metaphysical (except when they are part of a falsifiable theory), since their empirical content is too small (that is, nil). [Cf. Karl Popper, *Logik der Forschung* (1934; 2nd ed., 1966), Section 15 and Section 23, text to note *1. Ed.; English translation, *The Logic of Scientific Discovery* (1959; 2nd ed., 1968). Tr.]

to the periodic table), which appears in the form of a verification of such "there-is" statements.

Universal "there-is" statements are of some interest also for the critique of Wittgenstein's concept of meaning. For one might think that since they are verifiable, they can represent a (singular) state of affairs; that is (according to the *Tractatus*), that they have meaning. Their meaning would be "the method of their verification". But then it would be far from obvious why the meaning of a natural law should not lie in the *method of its verification*;*[3] the more so since all experimental and other investigations of a natural law may well be regarded as attempts to falsify the law. But Wittgenstein would, no doubt, refuse also to recognise partially decidable "there-is" statements as meaningful. They do, admittedly, restrict reality "to yes or no" (that is, to "yes"), but not to yes *and* no; as a result, the conclusions about the "meaning" of natural laws become inapplicable.

(The concept of partial decidability, and more particularly those statements that are only verifiable, may remind some readers of Brouwer's[6] mathematical "intuitionism". In my view, the considerations that lead to the concept of partial decidability are, in principle, applicable to empirical statements *only*, as a result of which Brouwer's sceptical and mystical implications become irrelevant. It seems curious, therefore, that partial decidability was first recognised in the case of *non-empirical* statements (to which it is inapplicable), and furthermore in the less important case of "there-is" statements. My own investigations, and the concept of partial decidability, assume the applicability of Aristotelian logic, including *tertium non datur*. My "deductivist" position (as far as I can judge) corresponds to

---

*[3] I suspect that what was intended here was "*falsification*" rather than "*verification*". But (in respect of my earlier strong rejection of the concept of meaning) this remark must not be regarded as proposing to replace verifiability with falsifiability as a concept of meaning.

[6] [Luitzen Egbertus Jan Brouwer, *Intuitionisme en Formalisme* (1912; *Intuitionism and Formalism*, English translation by Arnold Dresden, *Bulletin of the American Mathematical Society* 20 (1913), pp. 81 ff.); "Über die Bedeutung des Satzes vom ausgeschlossenen Dritten in der Mathematik, insbesondere in der Funktionentheorie", *Journal für die reine und angewandte Mathematik* 154 (1924), pp. 1 ff.; "Zur Begründung der intuitionistischen Mathematik", *Mathematische Annalen* 93 (1925), pp. 244 ff.; 95 (1926), pp. 453 ff.; and 96 (1927), pp. 451 ff.; "Mathematik, Wissenschaft und Sprache", *Monatshefte für Mathematik und Physik* 36 (1929), pp. 154 ff. See also L.E.J. Brouwer, *Collected Works* I.: *Philosophy and Foundations of Mathematics* (ed. Arend Heyting, 1975). Ed.]

[Karl] Menger's[7] "implicationist" approach, translated of course into the empirical. And does not the role of the concept of meaning in Wittgenstein correspond to that of Brouwer's intuitionist concept of meaning? It is, after all, only one step from dogma to scepticism and mysticism.)

The discussion so far seems to have covered the entire range of functions governed by the inductivist concept of meaning within the domain of the problem of induction. One question only remains to be considered: the *existence or non-existence of "universal states of affairs"*.

Natural laws are decidable (that is, partially decidable); they are empirical statements; they state something (in fact, very much) about what can be experienced; they can conflict with experience. And *they also, undoubtedly, represent something:* a (strictly) *universal state of affairs* whose existence can, of course, never be asserted.

The existence of universal states of affairs, therefore, remains a "fiction".*[4] But at least it remains as fiction (in the sense specified in Section 34): it is *conceivable* that universal states of affairs exist. Wittgenstein, it is true, asserts that everything "meaningless" is unthinkable, unspeakable and so on. According to his concept of meaning, therefore, a universal state of affairs is altogether *inconceivable*. But with the rejection of the concept of meaning, these arguments melt away also.

Let us, nonetheless, briefly look at the implications of the doctrine that universal states of affairs are inconceivable. The universal state of affairs represented by the statement "All humans have fair hair" can be called "inconceivable" only if the concept of an unlimited, infinite class is declared "unrealisable", "unthinkable", "nonsensical" and so on. But then, the concept of the transfinite would collapse, and with it the transfinite numbers and a very large and valuable part of mathematics. (And consistent with this, Wittgenstein's concept of number permits *only finite numbers*.)

If we do not regard the concept of an infinite class as unthinkable, an understanding of universal states of affairs is *conceivable* also. (We should

---

[7] [Karl Menger, "Der Intuitionismus", *Blätter für Deutsche Philosophie* 4 (1930), p. 325. Ed. Karl Menger, "On Intuitionism", English translation by Robert Kowalski, in: Karl Menger, *Selected Papers in Logic and Foundations, Didactics, Economics*, Vienna Circle Collection 10 (ed. Henk L. Mulder, 1979), p. 57. Tr.]

*[4] I consider this to be false, or at least terminologically misguided. Since universal states of affairs can exist (even if we *cannot know with certainty* whether they do exist), we should not call them fictitious.

then simply think "that things will always go on as they have done before", that, for example, "all other humans" have fair hair also. Such ideas are, indeed, very popular: "It was ever thus and it will always be thus.")

Natural laws, therefore, represent universal states of affairs. However, their "fictitious character" does not consist in that such universal states of affairs cannot (for logical or other a priori reasons) exist, or that we know that they do not, in fact, exist; rather, what we know, and know for logical reasons, is only that we can never achieve empirical certainty about their existence or non-existence, and this is the only kind at issue here.

Here we encounter, for the second time in this investigation, the antinomy of the knowability of the world (cf. Section 10).

The thesis of this antinomy (in the formulation underpinned by the "state of affairs" concept) is this: there are universal states of affairs; universal states of affairs exist. (This thesis is identical with the "first" principle of induction formulated in Section 5.) It is relatively unimportant how this thesis is justified, whether in an overtly rationalist fashion or in a Kantian apriorist way, according to which the understanding prescribes its own laws to nature; for the thesis is rationalist:*[5] it asserts something about reality that experience cannot decide (it can do so neither in a positive nor in a negative sense). It asserts that there are law-like regularities in nature; that it must, therefore, be possible (in principle) to gain knowledge of the world (since gaining knowledge, in the sense of the theoretical natural sciences, consists in discovering law-like regularities).

The antithesis of the antinomy is: there are no universal states of affairs, only singular states of affairs exist. This antithesis is advocated by Wittgenstein. This has been made clear earlier in the discussion, but will be shown here in greater detail.

According to Wittgenstein, there are no law-like regularities; or (which amounts to the same thing) they exist only in logic:[8]

"The exploration of logic means the exploration of everything that is subject to law. And outside logic everything is accidental."

It is of some interest that this antithesis is already prejudged in the assumptions of the Tractatus, in the first propositions. In order to show this,

---

*[5] Today I would say not "rationalist" but "metaphysical". I myself advocated this realistic metaphysics in Logik der Forschung (1934).

[8] Ludwig Wittgenstein, Tractatus Logico-Philosophicus (1918/1922), Proposition 6.3.

we shall briefly interrupt our discussion of the antinomy of the know-ability of the world.

What I want to show here is that even Wittgenstein's fundamental assumptions exclude the possibility that something like universal states of affairs or law-like regularities can exist.

Wittgenstein distinguishes between "states of affairs" ["situations"*6] and "facts". A "state of affairs" can "exist" or "not exist", it can "be the case" or "not be the case". If a "state of affairs" factually exists, then it is a "fact":[9]

"We also call the existence of states of affairs a positive fact, and their non-existence a negative fact."

Wittgenstein introduces the concept of a state of affairs with the help of this concept of a fact and that of its *fundamental concept*: "being the case":[10]

"What is the case – a fact – is the existence of states of affairs."

Wittgenstein not only introduces the concept of "being the case" as the first of these concepts, he also formulates it in such general terms that it includes everything fact-like, everything that can exist.

But even this concept in Wittgenstein is insufficiently general, insufficiently indefinite to allow the possible existence of universal states of affairs, or of law-like regularities. Wittgenstein narrows down, from the outset, his definition of the concept of "being the case" by way of the proposition:[11]

"Each item can be the case or not the case while everything else remains the same."

This statement cannot be reconciled with the assumption that law-like regularities also can "be the case". According to Wittgenstein, facts (that which "is the case") stand unconnected side by side:[12]

"The world divides into facts."

---

*6 I do not think that *originally* Wittgenstein intended a distinction between "*Sachverhalt*" and "*Sachlage*" as rendered in the translation approved by him ("atomic facts" and "state of affairs"). [In line with the new translation of Wittgenstein's *Tractatus*, "*Sachverhalt*" is here always translated as "state of affairs" and "*Sachlage*" always as "situation"; cf. Section 43, note 1. Tr.]

[9] Wittgenstein, *op. cit.*, Proposition 2.06.
[10] Wittgenstein, *op. cit.*, Proposition 2.
[11] Wittgenstein, *op. cit.*, Proposition 1.21.
[12] Wittgenstein, *op. cit.*, Proposition 1.2.

Wittgenstein introduces his basic concept of "being the case" in a way that leaves no room for universal states of affairs. (This agrees with what we noted earlier: Wittgenstein recognises *singular* states of affairs only. Translated into our terminology, his phrase "state of affairs" always means "singular state of affairs".)

But *in addition to this* "being the case" in Wittgenstein's world, could there be a different kind of existence, or of "so being", that leaves room for something such as law-like regularities? Even this last possibility is excluded by the wording Wittgenstein uses to introduce his phrase "being the case", for the *Tractatus* begins with the words:

"The world is all that is the case."

The world view of the "antithesis", that of "logical positivism", splits into a kind of mosaic; although this world is not composed of things, it consists, mosaic-like, of unconnected "facts" that lie next to each other by happenstance.

So as not to fragment this picture even further, I will quote the crucial propositions from the beginning of the *Tractatus* in their proper order:[13]

"The world is all that is the case."

"The world is the totality of facts, not of things." . . .

"The world divides into facts."

"Each item can be the case or not the case while everything else remains the same."

From these follows the necessary result:[14]

"And outside logic everything is accidental."

Wittgenstein advocates here, even if not explicitly, the *antithesis* of the antinomy of the knowability of the world. *The antithesis is rationalist* [or better: *metaphysical*] *also*, for all the things that it tells us about the world are *synthetic a priori judgements*. At any rate, our empirical sciences do not tell us anything about it. (It is an "attempt to make metaphysics out of logic", as Kant would have said.) We cannot know anything about any of this, just as we cannot know whether natural laws are true, or whether universal states of affairs exist.

It is, therefore, relatively unimportant how this antithesis is justified: whether by overtly rationalist means, through an appeal to a doctrine of

---

[13] Wittgenstein, *op. cit.*, Propositions 1, 1.1, 1.2 and 1.21.

[14] Wittgenstein, *op. cit.*, Proposition 6.3.

self-evidence (for example, to the argument that universal states of affairs are inconceivable or ineffable), or along aprioristic lines through an analysis of our cognition or representation, perhaps by way of a "reflection on the essence of expression, of representation, that is, of every possible 'language' in the most general sense of the word".[15] Such reflection may yield the result that every representation, being an "image", can represent only something with which this image can be compared or with which it can stand in a "mapping relationship". However this justification is attempted (Wittgenstein adopts both methods), it cannot alter the rationalist [or metaphysical] character of the antithesis.

This is, perhaps, best illustrated by considering the surprising *consequences* of this antithesis (to do this one needs, of course, to *leave* the domain of an *immanent* critique of Wittgenstein).

For if the antithesis is true — it can have *a priori* validity only — then all universal empirical statements must be *a priori false*; since if it is known *a priori* that there are no universal states of affairs, this can only mean that *all* statements representing such states of affairs are false. But this would also mean that the *negations* of all conceivable natural laws, that is, any imaginable universal "there-is" statement, must be *a priori true*. One would be allowed to assert *a priori* not only that every conceivable event can really occur, but also that every conceivable event and every conceivable sequence of events *must* occur (at some time or another) by *a priori* necessity. Everything that is *conceivable* (all singular states of affairs) would *a priori* be *real* also.

Indeed, *experience* could never decide that no universal states of affairs exist, that there are no law-like regularities of any kind (neither of a statistical nor of any other conceivable class); *we could not have* such an "experience"; the empirical falsification of the very last natural law that is even conceivable (the verification of the very last conceivable "there-is" statement) would be something that we are unable to "experience". (Chaos would, so to speak, long since have swallowed us up before our cosmos dissolved.)

The antithesis, the statement that there are no law-like regularities, would therefore be the only natural law, the only *universal* empirical statement; it would be a *synthetic a priori judgement*.

---

[15] Moritz Schlick, "Die Wende der Philosophie", Erkenntnis 1 (1930), p. 7.

Wittgenstein escapes the consequences of the antithesis, but only with the help of his dogma of meaning. This dogma simply forbids us to speak about universal states of affairs and the like. (Therefore, to the extent that the critique disregards this rule it is *not an immanent one*.) But prohibiting speech cannot eliminate these consequences; and it does not stimulate philosophical discussion.

How can the antinomy of the knowability of the world be resolved?

By asserting the logical, the *a priori* true analytic statement:

Empirically and logically, we can know nothing about the existence of universal states of affairs; not even that they do not exist.

We can, therefore, frame natural laws *as if* universal states of affairs exist. We can frame them in this way *only*, that is, as provisional assumptions: this is the reason they are "fictions", and they are fictions in this sense only. And formulate them we *must*, if (in the sense of the theoretical sciences) we want to *gain knowledge*, to devise predictions and to test them.

The formulation that I have used several times, namely, that natural laws "*cannot be true*", should not, therefore, be understood as declaring the *impossibility* of a natural law being true. Its sole purpose is to express the logical impossibility of ever *deciding* the truth of natural laws; for "only experience can decide the truth or falsity of an empirical statement" ("fundamental thesis of empiricism").

It seems important to me that acknowledging the empirical inability to decide this question is not a metaphysical or rationalist assertion. It is, admittedly, *not empirical* (but rather, logical), but certainly it is *empiricist*: it fully agrees with the "fundamental thesis of empiricism". Only a positive or a negative answer to this question is rationalist (metaphysical).

In the deductivist-empiricist theory of knowledge, this concept of the empirical undecidability of the question about the existence of law-like regularities, the *unknowability of the existence of universal states of affairs*, corresponds precisely to Kant's *unknowability of the "thing-in-itself"*.

(In the same way that I ask, above all, about the validity of *statements* and not about the genesis of *concepts*, one should ask about *states of affairs* and whether they exist, instead of asking about *things* and how they are.)

The analogy between the unknowability of the "thing-in-itself" and the unknowability of universal states of affairs is almost perfect.

The only difference is that in Kant's "thing-in-itself", the distinction between the universal and the singular does not seem to have the same significance. (In Schopenhauer's interpretation, however, even this imperfection in the analogy would disappear.)

The analogy is perfect in all other respects. And not only that: the typical problems created by the Kantian concept are, I believe, illuminated only by the concept of the unknowability of universal states of affairs.

The argument that a "thing-in-itself" is conceivable (asserted by Kant, but well known as one of the most controversial features of his doctrine) must be asserted also for universal states of affairs. *Experience* can decide nothing about a thing-in-itself, nor anything about the existence of universal states of affairs. And both concepts play the part of indispensable *limiting concepts*.

Kant shows that *rationalism* (dogmatism) holds a thing-in-itself to be knowable. This is what gives rise to the *antinomies* of pure reason. Asserting something about the existence or non-existence of universal states of affairs is, undoubtedly, dogmatic; it is *rationalism*. This rationalism leads to *antinomies* also. The "antinomy of the knowability of the world" is resolved by acknowledging the limiting character of unknowable universal states of affairs, just as Kant's antinomies are resolved by acknowledging the limiting character of the unknowable thing-in-itself (through transcendent idealism).

And does not "material idealism" (as Kant puts it) or, what amounts to the same thing, the *positivist denial of the thing-in-itself* in Wittgenstein's erudite doctrine, correspond to logical positivism, which presumes to know that universal states of affairs do not exist?

The underlying tendency of positivism is, therefore, always the same. Not only does "logical" positivism attribute to logic our inability to know ("what we cannot know with certainty is inconceivable"); its "thesis of the omnipotence of science"[16] is nothing but the general positivist dogma: "What we cannot know with certainty *does not exist*."

In this way, positivism *objectifies our inability to know for certain*, it attributes it to the objective "world" (which logical positivism, very much in contrast to natural science, regards as a mosaic of unconnected "facts"). One might say: it attributes our ignorance to Creation.

Once again, this reveals its rationalism.

---

[16] [Cf. Rudolf Carnap, *Der logische Aufbau der Welt* (1928), p. 261. Ed.]

In all its variants (depending on the emphasis attaching to the concepts of "perceiving", "recognising", "thinking", "knowing", "speaking" and so on), positivism teaches the same thing always, that is: the *identity* (which in Schlick's *Erkenntnislehre* [17] is still described as "adventurous") of *thinking* (more recently: of speaking) *and being*.

---

[17] [Cf. Moritz Schlick, *Allgemeine Erkenntnislehre* (2nd ed., 1925), pp. 307 ff. Ed.]

Chapter XII

CONCLUSION

47. *The dialectical and the transcendental corroboration of the solution.* The critique of inductivist attempts to solve the problem of induction has been concluded. What has it achieved?

Even the sharpest polemic in this investigation was designed, first and foremost, to serve a positive purpose. But what is this purpose, and how should it be assessed?

I see the primary value of the critical-polemical form in being an *acid test* of the positive solution. We should not, of course, overrate this form of testing. Its sole value consists, essentially, in making the proposed solution fit for discussion.

One might also call this critical-polemical test a *dialectical corroboration* of the solution, because (to characterise this method in the words of H. Gomperz[1]) it "lets every attempted solution ... emerge from the *contradictions* that another attempt has encountered, either with its own assumptions or with concepts of the individual sciences or of scientific practice", and because it seeks to show that the proposed solution "contains within itself, in 'preserved' form, the justified elements of earlier attempted resolutions".

---

[1] Heinrich Gomperz, *Weltanschauungslehre* I. (1905), pp. 296 f.

I do not, however, regard this method of dialectical corroboration (in contrast to that of Gomperz, whose procedure I have, to a certain extent, used as a model) as a kind of "*verification*" of the proposed solution, but rather, as I have suggested already, merely as a demonstration of its *fitness for discussion*.

For there is another form of corroboration that, even though I should not wish to call it "verification", might be more deserving of this name; a form of corroboration that is, to a large extent, analogous to the corroboration of natural laws by verification of the consequences derived from them. I call this second and more important form "*transcendental corroboration*".

The concept and the method of a "transcendental corroboration" can be outlined here in brief only; the "dialectical corroboration" of the deductivist-empiricist solution will be discussed later in somewhat greater detail as a (tentative) final summary of the investigations into the problem of induction.

We need to clarify, above all, to what extent we can speak about "verification" or "corroboration" within the bounds of the theory of knowledge advocated here.

The resolution I am proposing for the problem of induction consists entirely of a few definitions and a few statements derived from them; that is, entirely of analytic judgements. This already means that we cannot talk about verification, since analytic judgements are *a priori* true.

What can justifiably be asked, however, is whether those definitions are consistent and useful.

Whether or not they avoid contradictions can, in part, be established by dialectical corroboration, namely, for those contradictions that have defeated older systems.

The question of usefulness can, however, be put more precisely by asking whether the definitions (and the basic concepts) of the system do justice to the actual method of science.

Does the definition of natural laws as "partially decidable premises for the deduction of fully decidable consequences", in particular, accord with the method of the individual sciences? Is the analysis of the concept of knowledge, is equating cognitive value with primary improbability, justified by the method of the individual sciences?

Only questions such as these can ultimately decide the appropriateness and usefulness of the solution; compared with this form of corroborative testing, which can justifiably be called "transcendental" (cf. Section 9), the "dialectical" test is of secondary, merely stage-setting significance.

As shown in Sections 25 ff. already, the question about the corroboration or applicability of a *scientific* theory can be viewed as follows also: can particular real concepts be assigned consistently to a theory established on an axiomatic system? One might also regard the theory as a system of implicit definitions, that is, of analytic judgements, and ask whether the assignment of real concepts by way of coordinative definitions leads to contradictions. Or one may ask whether the theory is applicable in the way required by the coordinative definitions.

The question about the corroboration of a theory of knowledge is completely analogous. Is it possible, without contradictions, to make the system (and especially the concept of "natural law") correspond to the natural sciences and to their method? This is, as it were, the question about a higher "type" of a corroborative or a falsifying method, that is, one step higher than the corroborative methods used for natural laws.

But how should we *decide*? An inductivist epistemologist will probably say that the inductive method of science (for example, as described by Ernst Mach in *Die Mechanik in ihrer Entwicklung* [1]) demonstrates the inadequacy of the deductivist theory of knowledge. The deductivist, in reply, can invoke Duhem's views and Viktor Kraft's *Die Grundformen der wissenschaftlichen Methoden* [2] (cf. the reference at the end of Section 24). There appears to be little prospect, therefore, of reaching an objective decision by means of "transcendental corroboration".

I believe, however, that on this point I have already taken a significant step forward. The deductivist-empiricist theory of knowledge permits us to take considerably further the analogy between transcendental corroboration and the corroboration of a natural law through the verification of its consequences.

One could almost speak of an *epistemological formulation and verification of consequences*.

As I have mentioned more than once, from the deductivist-empiricist theory of knowledge it is possible to deduce a *general theory of method*.

---

[1] [1883; 8th ed., 1921; English translation by T.J. McCormack (1919), *The Science of Mechanics: A Critical and Historical Account of its Development.* Tr.]

[2] [1925: *The Fundamental Forms of Scientific Methods.* Tr.]

(Because of its deductive, *theoretical* form, I use this term in preference to "methodology".) The assertions made by such a theory about the methods of the empirical sciences can, at least in part, be *decided* (verified or falsified) by the methods actually followed by them.

The *critical* conclusions reached by the theory of method, the *critique of method*, seem to me even more promising for a "transcendental corroboration"; for the implications of the theory of method lead to a criticism of the method followed by some "empirical" sciences: it is characterised partly as metaphysical, partly as unproductive (because it is governed by the inductivist prejudice). At the same time, the critique of method offers suggestions for reforming the methods in question.

In this way, deductivist epistemology could prove its *productivity*; and even the bare *possibility* of being able to develop productive implications for scientific methods is something that otherwise cannot easily be claimed by a theory of knowledge. (From the position of deductivist epistemology, only such a procedure could be called a transcendental *method*.)

If this productivity can be demonstrated, if the reform of the method succeeds and leads to useful results for particular sciences, only then can the transcendental corroboration be regarded as successful and satisfactory.

Within the bounds of this book, therefore, it is quite impossible to carry out this transcendental corroboration itself; this task must be left to individual sciences. Only the *basic outline* of the general theory of method can be provided, *after* presenting the analysis of the *demarcation problem*.[2] But it seems to me that even an indication of the possibility of such a productive test offers new prospects for the theory of knowledge.

We are left, therefore, with the merely preparatory *dialectical corroboration* as the only test that can be performed within the domain of this book.

But the dialectical corroboration is also necessary; for only such corroboration can justify any claim by a new attempted solution that it be taken seriously. Without closer investigation, it is not always immediately evident whether a "solution", if it is not altogether too primitive, avoids at least those difficulties already overcome by older positions (let alone whether it avoids all the difficulties).

---

[2] [See Editor's Postscript. Ed.]

The dialectical form is, without a doubt, the most productive in which to carry out such an investigation. Not only does it allow us to illuminate questions that we should hardly have encountered in a merely descriptive, positive presentation of the solution; it also keeps raising the question whether those points that could rightfully (that is, without internal or external contradictions) support the arguments of earlier attempted solutions have found their place in the new one. It forces us, therefore, to treat the old attempted solutions fairly, not to ignore their positive contributions but rather to let them "all [be] affirmatively contained as elements in a whole" (Hegel[3]).

It is precisely the critique of logical-positivism as presented in this book that illustrates the importance of the dialectical procedure; for neither in the form of probability positions nor in that of pseudo-statement positions has positivism moved, on any essential points, beyond the problem situation created by Hume and Kant. As valuable as its opposition to Kant's *open* (but critical) apriorism may be, its unduly summary rejection of Kant has only led to a *hidden* (and uncritical) apriorism and rationalism, and this has hopelessly confused the problem situation.

Positivism fails to examine (dialectically) the problem situation that leads to apriorism. Since it does not recognise the situation, it fails to escape apriorism.

With his transcendental programme, Kant showed the way for a theory of knowledge, for a theory of science and for a critique of method. From a historical perspective, the systematic attempt by positivism to discredit Kant's project has, undoubtedly, seriously harmed the development of epistemology (and of the "scientific world view").

(See, for example, the historical address[4] to the Prague Congress [1929] on the "epistemology of the exact sciences". One searches in vain for Kant's name among those of the very many philosophers of all periods. Finally we find it, when Franz Brentano is boldly praised[5] for having "*spared himself the Kantian interlude*". We can only wonder: Why Brentano in

---

[3] [Georg Wilhelm Friedrich Hegel, *Vorlesungen über die Geschichte der Philosophie* I. (ed. Karl Ludwig Michelet, *Werke: Vollständige Ausgabe durch einen Verein von Freunden des Verewigten* XIII., 1833), p. 50. Ed. English translation by E.S. Haldane (1892/1955): *Hegel's Lectures on the History of Philosophy* I., p. 37. Tr.]

[4] Otto Neurath, "Wege der wissenschaftlichen Weltauffassung" ["Ways of the Scientific World View". Tr.], *Erkenntnis* 1 (1930), pp. 106 ff.

[5] Neurath, *op. cit.*, p. 120.

particular? Does such an evaluation of Kant not suggest that it should, instead, have been this or that positivist boasting of this?)

In order to emphasise my commitment to Kant, if not to Kant's apriorism, I should like to quote in full several paragraphs from the *Critique of Pure Reason* ("The Regulative Employment of the Ideas of Pure Reason").[6] This passage might well serve as a motto for my work. In any event, it is appropriate to quote it at this point in the argument, which deals with dialectical corroboration and therefore with historical justification, for it sheds light on one of Kant's ideas:

"If, however, the universal is admitted as *problematic* only . . . the particular is certain but the universality of the rule of which it is a consequence is still a problem. Several particular instances, which are one and all certain, are scrutinised in view of the rule, to see whether they follow from it. If it then appears that all particular instances that can be cited follow from the rule, we argue to its universality, and from this again to all particular instances, even to those which are not themselves given. This I shall entitle the hypothetical employment of reason.

"The hypothetical employment of reason . . . is not, properly speaking, *constitutive*, that is, it is not of such a character that, judging in all strictness, we can regard it as proving the truth of the universal rule that we have adopted as hypothesis. For how are we to know all the possible consequences which, as actually following from the adopted principle, *prove* its universality? The hypothetical employment of reason is regulative only; its sole aim is, so far as may be possible, to bring unity into the body of our detailed knowledge, and thereby to *approximate* the rule to universality.

"The hypothetical employment of reason has, therefore, as its aim the systematic unity of the knowledge of understanding, and this unity is the *criterion of truth* of its rules. The systematic unity (as a mere idea) is, however, only a *projected* unity, to be regarded not as given in itself, but as a problem only. This unity aids us in discovering a principle for the understanding in its manifold and special modes of employment, directing its attention to cases which are not given, and thus rendering it more coherent."

I have not quoted this passage until now because it is, perhaps, only at this point that it can be fully appreciated. It supports my view that the

---

[6] Immanuel Kant, *Kritik der reinen Vernunft* (2nd ed., 1787), pp. 674 f. [English translation by N. Kemp Smith (1929), 1965, *Critique of Pure Reason*, pp. 534 f. Tr.]

thread of the epistemological debate has to be rejoined at the point where post-Kantian metaphysics had torn it: with Kant.

(On the subject of the dialectical method that originates with Hegel – although it is used and viewed here in a way different from that of Hegel – I should clearly state my conviction that post-Kantian metaphysicians, and especially Hegel, have had a very negative influence on the development of the theory of knowledge. Without a doubt, they are to blame for the fact that after such a promising start, the *epistemological* debate about Kant's work fizzled out so quickly – except under Fries.)

Returning to the dialectical consideration of modern positivism, we must acknowledge also the latter's great achievements. It has sought to re-establish a close connection between epistemology and natural philosophy on the one hand, and *natural science* on the other. (In this way it has resumed Kant's transcendental programme, a programme to which only positivism and conventionalism attempt to do justice.) Even if positivism has failed to avoid the pitfalls of the problem of induction, has failed to solve it (and especially, failed to escape apriorism), it has – and this is its major achievement – vigorously opposed apriorism (and in particular, the rationalist concept of causality). It has, in this way, succeeded in bringing Kant back into the epistemological debate. And it has, without a doubt, attacked Kant at the right point: it is the merit of positivism (and to some extent, of pragmatism) that it is the only modern theory of knowledge that has fought for strict *empiricism*.

The merits of positivism, therefore, need to be fully acknowledged here, especially its often exemplary efforts to use a simple, comprehensible and yet precise mode of expression. This is not the least among the conditions on which a productive epistemological debate depends.

What positivism should be criticised for is only that by being unfaithful to its own true nature, it has succumbed to all those tendencies it is opposing, even to the attempt to solve problems merely by inventing new words. Positivism, therefore, illustrates the fact (to quote a remark used by Gomperz to indicate the significance of the *dialectical method*) "that concealed behind that seeming radicalism which purports to break with tradition and to return directly to the facts of experience, in truth, there always lies an *uncritical acceptance* of traditional conceptions".[7]

---

[7] Heinrich Gomperz, *Weltanschauungslehre* I. (1905), p. 35. [Emphasis not in the original. Ed.]

To conclude the critique of inductivism, and at the same time to supplement and summarise the dialectical corroboration, I shall now provide a brief survey of the positions that have been discussed (and to some extent, of those only mentioned in passing).

This survey will not recapitulate the entire dialectical development; it will simply let the *solution* emerge from the internal contradictions of the other positions. It will briefly emphasise those points that (for logical or transcendental reasons) should be rejected, and those that will be accepted; this will prepare the ground for the subsequent *presentation of the solution*. It will become evident that the solution avoids those elements that are to be "rejected", but encompasses the other elements.

In keeping with the sequence so far (starting from Section 3), I will begin with a discussion of:

Rationalism (cf. Sections 3, 9): The dogmatic assertion of "evident" principles is rejected (indeed, over and above this I deny the admissibility of any answer – whether apodictic or assertoric – to the question whether there are [*demonstrably*] true universal empirical statements). The purely deductive procedure, the logical theory of deduction, is accepted.

Empiricism: The inductive method is rejected. The idea that "experience" alone can decide the truth value of an empirical statement (cf. Sections 3, 31, 46) is elevated into a fundamental principle (that is, into the definition of the concept "empirical statement").

Intuitionism: It is likely that the truth of a *singular* empirical statement (in physics, particularly the coincidence of points) can be decided only "intuitively" (through intuition, perception). But this aspect of intuitionism is not problematic. (Like Kant's or Brouwer's *mathematical* intuitionism, it is not in the domain of the problem of induction.)

Only the form of "intuitionism" that allows the possibility of "intuitively grasping" *universal* empirical statements, or natural laws, is of interest here.

The sharp separation between the theory of knowledge and the psychology of knowledge permits us to do justice to this view; it should be rejected, however, if it makes epistemological claims: there is no intuition (or evidence) that guarantees the truth of a natural law.

But intuitionism may well be right in terms of historical genesis or the psychology of knowledge. In any event, the deductivist theory of knowledge is closer to an intuitionist psychology of knowledge than to an inductivist (say, sensualist) one. For according to the deductivist view, there is no rational path, no scientific method leading from experience to natural laws; only the path from natural laws to experience is rational.

The formulation (or discovery) of a natural law, therefore, contains in any event an *irrational element* (an element of *intuitive, creative adaptation* in Bergson's sense). Or as Einstein[8] puts it, "there is no logical bridge between the phenomena and their theoretical principles . . .; only intuition, resting on sympathetic understanding of experience, can reach them".

The theory of induction of Bacon (and Mill): Induction in an epistemological sense is rejected: there is no inductive rational method. It is accepted that in a historical genesis sense, the empirical sciences evolve towards ever increasing universality. The fact of this "ascending" or, if you will, "inductive" direction of scientific evolution (I call it "*quasi-induction*") needs to be not only recognised, but also explained by a theory of method (cf. Section 48).

Hume's theory of habituation belongs to the domain of the inductivist psychology of knowledge, not to that of epistemology. (I consider it psychologically mistaken also — but this question is not relevant here.[9]) *Hume's argument* against the epistemological admissibility of any induction is accepted in full: *there is no induction.*

Strict positivism is rejected, in so far as it regards natural laws as singular empirical statements, or as summary reports (cf. Section 8). It is accepted that only singular empirical statements can have a [demonstrated] positive truth value, and that a positive appraisal of a natural law — its corroboration value — should be interpreted as the truth value of a summary report (a report on unsuccessful falsification attempts; cf. Sections 41 and 46).

Apriorism is rejected in so far as it asserts (epistemologically) the truth of universal empirical statements (synthetic *a priori* judgements). The view of natural laws as strictly universal empirical statements (cf. Sections 7 and

---

[8] Albert Einstein, "Motive des Forschens", *Zu Max Plancks sechzigstem Geburtstag: Ansprachen, gehalten am 26. April 1918 in der Deutschen Physikalischen Gesellschaft* (1918), p. 31 [= A. Einstein, "Prinzipien der Forschung", *Mein Weltbild* (1934), pp. 168 f. Ed.; English translation by Alan Harris (1934), revised by Sonja Bargmann, 1954: "Principles of Research", in *Ideas and Opinions* by Albert Einstein, p. 226. Tr.]

[9] [See Section 4, note 1 (p. 31), and text to this note. Cf. also Karl Popper, *Conjectures and Refutations* (1963), pp. 42 ff.; Karl Popper, *Logik der Forschung* (1934; 2nd ed., 1966) [*The Logic of Scientific Discovery* (1959; 2nd ed., 1968). Tr.], New Appendix *X, (1); Karl Popper, "Replies to my Critics", *The Philosophy of Karl Popper* II. (ed. Paul Arthur Schilpp, 1974), pp. 1023 ff. Ed.]

32) that have no inductive truth is accepted. In particular, the transcendental formulation of the question that regards the truth of natural laws (their "possibility") as a fundamental epistemological problem (since knowledge is possible through laws only; cf. Sections 10 and 11) is accepted. Psychological apriorism (cf. Section 4, conclusion), that is, the position that universal empirical statements have no *a posteriori* truth but instead are preformed, they *occur* in *a priori* anticipatory fashion (even though they are not *a priori* true), is accepted also.

The probability positions are rejected in so far as they claim that by introducing the concept of probability they contribute anything of value to the (epistemological) problem of induction. In particular, the view that between true and false there is an (objective) truth value such as a "probability" or the like is rejected. The subjective belief in probability (secondary probability of hypotheses), based on objective corroboration values (cf. Sections 12–16), is accepted. Moreover, the position that natural laws are empirical statements and are not definitively verifiable (they are not "normal statements", that is, they are not "fully decidable") is accepted.

The pseudo-statement positions are rejected as vague and dogmatic at the same time. It is accepted that they state – along with Hume – that natural laws cannot have a [definitive] positive truth value, that their *empirical* justification is logically impossible and that their positive appraisal is, in principle, provisional, or pragmatic. (Also accepted is Wittgenstein's assessment of the *demarcation problem* as a fundamental problem in the theory of knowledge.)

Pragmatism is rejected (a position reached by Schlick also; cf. Section 16) where it *equates* truth with corroboration. But the assertion that a positive appraisal of natural laws consists in their *corroboration through the verification of derived consequences* only, and that a non-corroboration should be equated with a *falsification*, is accepted. More generally, it should be pointed out that there is considerable agreement between my position and those of the pragmatic approaches (cf. Section 41).

Conventionalism is rejected where it regards the [theoretical] premises of deduction exclusively as those "free suppositions" that experience cannot decide (more on this in the discussion of the demarcation problem below[10]). It is accepted where it regards them as "free posits" the purpose

[10] [See Editor's Postscript. Ed.]

of which is to underpin a theoretical system (deductivism). It is accepted also that not every "axiom" of a scientific theory is decidable. Here I must draw attention again to Kraft's position (cf. Section 24, conclusion).

Finally, Vaihinger's *fictionalism* is rejected in so far as he refuses to grant to natural laws the character of fictions (a position he evidently reaches also by way of a somewhat psychologistic formulation of the concept of fiction; cf. Section 34). It is accepted where it emphasises the fundamental importance of heuristic fictions. Natural laws are *heuristic fictions*, they are regulative ideas (principles); see the quotation from Kant in this section.

This summary renders a detailed presentation of the solution superfluous. More accurately: the positive solution is of a kind that would make a detailed presentation pointless.

The discussion up to this point has, perhaps, eliminated the most important prejudices that stand in the way of an understanding of the solution.

In any case, once the conditions for the proposed solution exist, the solution itself can be presented without much effort, even with some marginal comments, within the smallest space (on Kirchhoff's quarto-size sheet of paper[11]).

The problem of induction, the question of the truth of universal empirical statements, is answered as follows: universal empirical statements can never have a [definitive] positive truth value, but only a [definitive] negative truth value.[*1]

This solution will be explained further, as follows:

The problem of induction arises from an apparent *contradiction between the basic empiricist requirement* (only experience can decide the truth or falsity of a scientific statement) and Hume's insight into the logical *impermissibility of inductive decisions* (there is no empirical justification of universal statements).

---

[11] [It appears that Gustav Robert Kirchhoff wrote somewhere that every scientific discovery can be communicated "on one quarto-size sheet of paper". The editor has been unable to find the source of this passage. Ed.]

[*1] Here we have, once again, one of those questionable formulations, even though correct formulations were given a little earlier. (See Section 46, text between notes 7 and *5; and the resolution of the antinomy associated with our ability to gain knowledge about reality, near the end of Section 46.) I ought to have written something like "we cannot attribute to universal empirical statements . . ." (The text in the following paragraphs is free of these erroneous formulations.)

This contradiction exists only if we assume that empirical statements must be *empirically "fully decidable"*, that is, that experience must be able to decide not only their falsity, but also their truth.

The contradiction is resolved once "partially decidable" empirical statements are admitted:

Universal empirical statements are empirically *falsifiable*, they can be *defeated by experience.*

But as a result, the inductive method (already shown to be inadmissible) becomes *superfluous*: the method of empirical testing (partial decision) by experience is that of *deriving fully decidable consequences* (elementary empirical statements, "empirical basic statements").

Induction in the logical or epistemological sense does not exist.

The theoretical natural sciences are "hypothetico-deductive systems" (Kraft). Natural laws are statements (fundamental propositions) in these systems, or conjunctions of these propositions: they have the logical properties of *deductive premises* that can be tested, not directly but *only* through their consequences.

They can, therefore, never be *demonstrably true.* They always remain "problematic regulative ideas" (Kant) only, "heuristic fictions" (Vaihinger). But as deductive premises, they can be *corroborated*; if they are not corroborated, they are *falsified.* Their cognitive value (and their corroboration value) increases with the primary probability of their falsification, that is, with their *primary improbability.*

48. *Is the problem of induction solved?* [1] I shall not discuss here whether my proposed solution of the problem of induction is correct; for it is the

---

[1] [In this section, a page was enclosed with the following note:]

48. Is the problem of induction solved?

This section is at present [1932] being reformulated.

Summary of contents of [the planned new] Section 48:
Comments on quasi-induction.
Preview of the problem of demarcation.
The criterion of demarcation is formulated:
A statement makes an *empirical statement about reality*, only if it is *empirically falsifiable*, that is: if it can conflict with experience.

[It is not possible to determine whether the first sentences in this note refer to the version of Section 48 presented here or to an earlier version, now lost. Ed.]

task of this entire book to justify my conviction that this is the case. As explained in the previous section, only a critical discussion can decide this question – and indeed, not so much a "dialectical" as a "transcendental" discussion.

What will be discussed here, however, is to what extent the proposed solution is satisfactory.

Has the problem been completely resolved? Or is it still intractable?

I see two questions, above all else, that the problem of induction still leaves unresolved if the proposed solution is accepted: the *problem of demarcation* and the question of *quasi-induction*.

These two questions should not be correlated in any way. They differ entirely in importance, and they are on quite different levels.

From an epistemological viewpoint, the *problem of demarcation* is, in fact, the only *fundamental* one. The problem of induction arises as a result of the problem of demarcation only. The "inductive method" plays the part of a criterion of demarcation (cf. Section 44): it is meant to be the central characteristic of empirical science.

The problem of demarcation, therefore, is not merely the only important problem, the *only fundamental problem*, behind the problem of induction; it is the only fundamental problem in the theory of knowledge as a whole. This was probably recognised most clearly by Wittgenstein. Put another way: in a "correct" theory of knowledge that can avoid all polemical digressions, one that does not need to deal with the historical-dialectical problem situation, admittedly one would have to speak about the problem of demarcation (as in Wittgenstein's profound book); but the problem of induction and the concept of induction need not be mentioned at all.

For there is no induction in the epistemological sense.

This fundamental thesis of deductivism says two things:

First, that there is no inductive logic, that genuine inductive inferences cannot be justified logically; that induction, therefore, is not a scientific method, that is to say, it cannot be a scientific procedure for justification.

Secondly, however, it says (for otherwise this claim would be trans-cendentally meaningless) that empirical science *does not, in fact, make use of any such inductive method*, but instead proceeds deductively.

This second assertion does seem to be rather audacious.

Is it conceivable that the inductive method of the empirical sciences is merely a hallucination of inductivist epistemologists, one that does not correspond to anything in the actual method employed by the empirical sciences?

Here we encounter the question that can only be answered satisfactorily by an *investigation of quasi-induction*[2] (as part of the general theory of method).

It would seem, at any rate, desirable to discuss the concept of quasi-induction, if only to show that this concept does not serve to disguise a covert return to inductivism.

Let us, then, introduce a terminological definition:

The statements, [or] the field of a science, can be traversed in various directions. The one that leads from the most general principles to individual singular statements (that is, the deductive direction) will be called, without implying a value judgement, the *downward* direction, the direction from top to bottom; the reverse (inductive) direction will be called the *upward* direction.

In general, of course, the *direction of deductive inference*, or the direction of deduction, is *downward*. But we should not forget that *pure deduction can lead in the upward direction also* (that is, in the inductive direction). We are familiar already with an example of such deduction moving in the upward direction, in the very important retrospective falsification of the *implicans* by the *implicate* in *modus tollens* (cf., for example, Sections 31 and 38).

This "retrospective falsification" is, without a doubt, genuine deduction. (This is most evident in the fact that, according to the rules of deductive logic, the negated *implicate* can be written as the *implicans* and the negated *implicans* as the *implicate*.*[1]) It is just as certain that this pure deductive inference moves in the upward ("inductive") direction: it is an inference from a singular empirical statement to a natural law (namely, to its falsity).

---

[2] [Cf. Karl Popper, *Logik der Forschung* (1934; 2nd ed., 1966) [*The Logic of Scientific Discovery* (1959; 2nd ed., 1968). Tr.], Section 85; Karl Popper, *op. cit.* (2nd ed., 1966), *Sachregister*: Quasiinduktion, deduktive Schlüsse in induktiver Richtung [2nd ed., 1968, *Index of Subjects*: Inductive direction, deductive movement in, quasi-induction. Tr.]. See also Editor's Postscript. Ed.]

*[1] That is, if "$p \supset q$" is analytic, then "$\sim q \supset \sim p$" is analytic also.

Such strictly deductive (deductivist) methods that move, nonetheless, in an upward, "inductive" direction, I call "quasi-inductive".

Quasi-induction is, accordingly, any systematic procedure which, based on purely deductivist methods, advances in an upward direction. (The possibilities of quasi-induction are by no means exhausted by *modus tollens*.)

Quasi-induction will be treated in the general theory of method: as the *modus tollens* example shows, quasi-inductive methods are an important part of deductivist-empiricist methods. They can be derived deductively from the principles of the general theory of method.

An investigation of these principles will show that it was, indeed, the *quasi-inductive* method that led the inductivist theory of knowledge to the theory of *induction*. It becomes clear also why the "inductive method" was regarded as a *criterion of demarcation*: the opposition to deductively proceeding, rationalist metaphysics can manifest itself most visibly in the quasi-inductive method of empirical science; rationalist metaphysics does not, for example, recognise retrospective falsification. It would be quite incorrect, nevertheless, to regard the quasi-inductive method as the criterion of demarcation.

It is not possible here to discuss quasi-induction in more detail. The general theory of method can be outlined only after investigating the *problem of demarcation*.[3] The reason is not only that the *demarcation criterion* is the most important principle of the general theory of method, but also that the rest of its assumptions arise directly from the investigation of the problem of demarcation.

Returning now to this problem, only its investigation can provide satisfactory answers to a whole range of questions thrown up by the problem of induction. I have pointed this out on a number of occasions. The reader may recall the discussion of the inductivist concept of meaning (Section 44) and of conventionalism (Sections 24 and 30). But the critique of strict positivism also will gain in clarity by an investigation of the demarcation problem, and the same is true for the critique of apriorism and the "antinomy of the knowability of the world".[4]

---

[3] [See Editor's Postscript. Ed.]

[4] [Cf. Volume II (Fragments): [V.] *Outline of a Theory of Empirical-Scientific Methods* (*Theory of Experience*), Section 2; Karl Popper, *Logik der Forschung* (1934; 2nd ed., 1966) [*The Logic of Scientific Discovery* (1959; 2nd ed., 1968). Tr.], Section 78. See also Editor's Postscript. Ed.]

The demarcation problem's main task is to bound empirical science against all rationalist speculation based on pure reason. Not only is this the task, or problem, that Kant identified in the very title of his major work as the most important undertaking of the theory of knowledge; it will be shown also that Kant's solution to the problem of demarcation indicated the right way to follow.

Appendix

THE CRITIQUE OF THE PROBLEM OF INDUCTION IN SCHEMATIC REPRESENTATIONS

The purpose of the following schematic representations is to indicate clearly, for each position, what assumptions it makes and by which assumptions it differs from other positions. (This method of schematic representation was first developed by Leonard Nelson.[1]) The tables provide a fairly *comprehensive summary of the critique of the problem of induction.*

In order to show how such representation should be read, the first table ("The three inductivist groups of positions") is accompanied by an *analysis.* The other tables should be analysed similarly.

[1] [Cf. Leonard Nelson, "Die kritische Methode und das Verhältnis der Psychologie zur Philosophie: Ein Kapitel aus der Methodenlehre" ["The Critical Method and the Relationship of Psychology to Philosophy: A Chapter from the Theory of Method". Tr.], *Abhandlungen der Friesschen Schule neue Folge* 1 (1904), pp. 56 f. Ed.]

Analysis for Table I

(a), (b), (c) are three assumptions that are incompatible when taken together, but any two of them are compatible.

If we assume (a) and (b), we must abandon (c). We then arrive at Position (1). If we assume (a) and (c), we must abandon (b). We arrive at Position (2). In the same way, abandoning (a) leads to Position (3).

The table can be read in two directions:

A) Starting from the *inferences* (*positions*), we check which two *assumptions* each of the positions is based on, or which of the assumptions this position had to reject.

B) Starting from the *assumptions*, we check which two *inferences* (*positions*) each assumption can lead to, and how the choice of one of these two inferences leads to the acceptance or rejection of one of the two other assumptions.

Table I The three inductivist groups of positions (see Section 6)

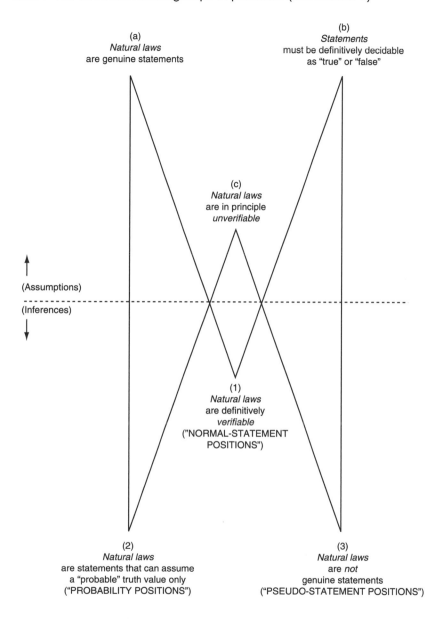

Table II The "normal-statement positions" (see Section 7 and especially Section 8)

Common assumption: Natural laws are verifiable (fully decidable) empirical statements (synthetic judgements)

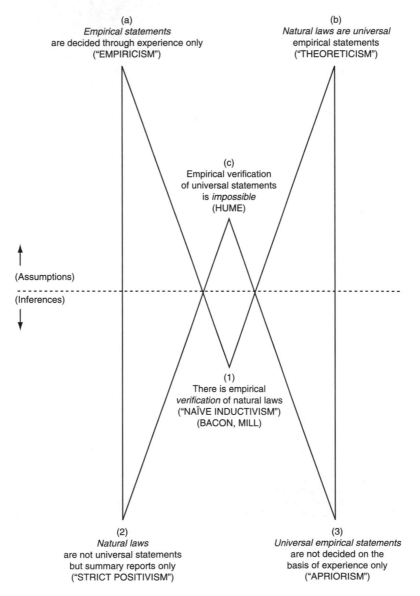

(a)
Empirical statements
are decided through experience only
("EMPIRICISM")

(b)
Natural laws are universal
empirical statements
("THEORETICISM")

(c)
Empirical verification
of universal statements
is *impossible*
(HUME)

(Assumptions)

(Inferences)

(1)
There is empirical
verification of natural laws
("NAÏVE INDUCTIVISM")
(BACON, MILL)

(2)
Natural laws
are not universal statements
but summary reports only
("STRICT POSITIVISM")

(3)
Universal empirical statements
are not decided on the
basis of experience only
("APRIORISM")

Note: Table VI has somewhat different concepts of "empiricism" and "theoreticism".

Table III The *probability positions* resolve the conflict of the normal-statement positions "dialectically" (see Section 12)

(Hume's argument — Table II(c) – is assumed)

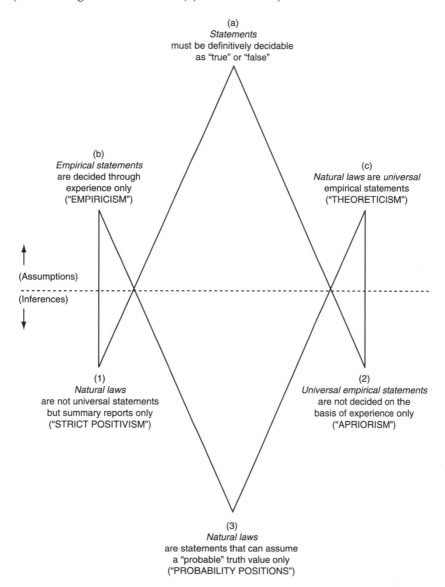

Note: See the note to Table II.

Table IV The "pseudo-statement positions" (see Section 18)

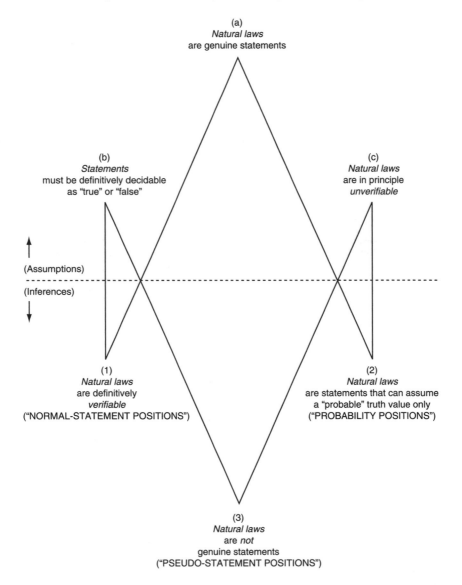

Note: This is the same as Table I, but arranged differently. Here, the pseudo-statement positions play the part of a "dialectical resolution" of the conflict between the normal-statement and the probability positions.

Table V Pseudo-statement positions and conventionalism (see Section 24)

("Theoreticism" is assumed)

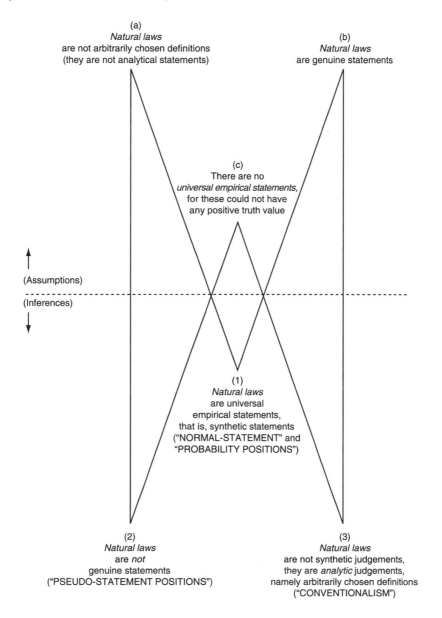

(a)
Natural laws
are not arbitrarily chosen definitions
(they are not analytical statements)

(b)
Natural laws
are genuine statements

(c)
There are no
universal empirical statements,
for these could not have
any positive truth value

(Assumptions)

(Inferences)

(1)
Natural laws
are universal
empirical statements,
that is, synthetic statements
("NORMAL-STATEMENT" and
"PROBABILITY POSITIONS")

(2)
Natural laws
are *not*
genuine statements
("PSEUDO-STATEMENT POSITIONS")

(3)
Natural laws
are not synthetic judgements,
they are *analytic* judgements,
namely arbitrarily chosen definitions
("CONVENTIONALISM")

Table VI Conventionalism, derived from the normal-statement positions (Table II)

(Hume's argument – Table II(c) – is assumed)

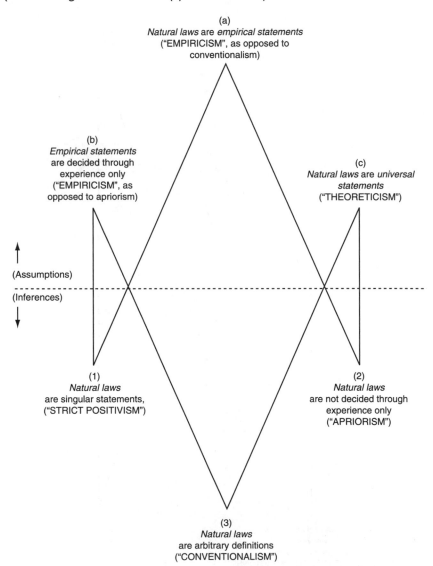

(a)
Natural laws are *empirical statements*
("EMPIRICISM", as opposed to
conventionalism)

(b)
Empirical statements
are decided through
experience only
("EMPIRICISM", as
opposed to apriorism)

(c)
Natural laws are *universal
statements*
("THEORETICISM")

(Assumptions)
- -
(Inferences)

(1)
Natural laws
are singular statements,
("STRICT POSITIVISM")

(2)
Natural laws
are not decided through
experience only
("APRIORISM")

(3)
Natural laws
are arbitrary definitions
("CONVENTIONALISM")

Note: Compare with the concepts of "empiricism" and "theoreticism" in Table II.

Table VII Resolution

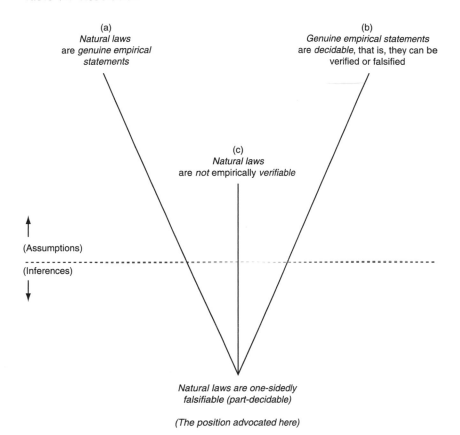

(a)
Natural laws
are *genuine empirical*
statements

(b)
Genuine empirical statements
are *decidable*, that is, they can be
verified or falsified

(c)
Natural laws
are *not* empirically *verifiable*

(Assumptions)

(Inferences)

Natural laws are one-sidedly
falsifiable (part-decidable)

(The position advocated here)

Book II

The Problem of Demarcation

Experience and Metaphysics

The Two Fundamental Problems
of the Theory of Knowledge
Volume II (Fragments)

PART ONE

FRAGMENTS 1932

DRAFT OF AN INTRODUCTION

Is there a philosophical science? (Introductory considerations on the problem of demarcation.)

1. An investigation in an *individual science*, say in physics, can begin straight away with the formulation of the problem. It is possible "to enter the house through open doors", as it were; for a "house" exists: a structure of scientific theory, a generally recognised problem situation. The researcher can count on the reader (who can be expected to be familiar with the discipline's prerequisites) to fit the new work into the overall context of scientific knowledge.

A philosopher finds himself in an entirely different situation. He faces not a theoretical edifice but a heap of ruins. He cannot take as his starting point a *generally recognised* problem situation; for the only thing that is generally recognised is, most often, that there is none. Indeed, it is even fashionable in philosophical circles to assert that nothing like a genuine philosophical problem can exist at all.

A philosopher who does not wish to commit himself to any of the quarrelling schools, or to resign himself to accepting the sad state of philosophical debate, will be forced to begin from the beginning.[1]

---

[1] [The first section of this *Draft of an Introduction* is an earlier version of the *Preface* (Vienna, Autumn 1934) to Karl Popper, *Logik der Forschung* (1934; 2nd ed., 1966). Ed. *The Logic of Scientific Discovery* (1959; 2nd ed., 1968). Tr.]

2. This, however, will be no easy task. Before we have even taken the first step, or at least, while believing that we have not taken it yet, it appears that we have already gone too far; on all sides we hear a resounding "Stop!"

It is modern ("logical" or "logistical") *positivism* on the one hand, and modern *Weltanschauung philosophy* on the other (regardless of the immense differences separating them otherwise), that equally oppose certain assumptions that we have tacitly introduced into our first statements.

For these statements evidently contain an implicit message, namely that the state of philosophy described above is an *unhealthy* one and that healing, or reform, or a *scientific reconstruction of philosophy, is possible and necessary*.

But this is precisely what is denied by modern "positivism" and by modern *Weltanschauung philosophy*; both hold the view that a *philosophical science does not and cannot exist* – that is, if we take *"science"* (in the sense of the various individual sciences) to mean an *objectively justifiable* theoretical structure. According to either position, there is no *science* outside (or above) the individual sciences (among which, of course, one would then have to include *logic*, usually considered a part of philosophy).

3. Modern *positivism* (we are thinking, more particularly, of Wittgenstein) regards the traditional *problems of philosophy* in part as genuine *problems that do not belong to philosophy at all* (they should be dealt with, for example, by logic or by mathematics, by physics or by empirical psychology); and in part – that is, in so far as *typical philosophical* problems are concerned, such as the problem of reality, the problem of causality and the problem of free will – not as genuine problems but as *pseudo-problems*. They cannot even be precisely formulated, and only linguistic lack of clarity and misunderstanding give rise to the false impression that these "problems" are genuine questions. This view implies that there can be no philosophical *doctrine* or philosophical *science*: where there is no question, there can be no answers. "Philosophy is not a body of doctrine but an activity," says Wittgenstein.[2] This *"activity"* of philosophising, in dispensing with all philosophical *assertions*, restricts itself to clearing up the linguistic misunderstanding and misuse that have brought about the philosophical pseudo-problem whose elimination is being pursued.

---

[2] [Ludwig Wittgenstein, *Tractatus Logico-Philosophicus* (1918/1922), Proposition 4.112. Ed.]

According to this view, there can be no philosophical *system*, not even a system of philosophical errors and pseudo-problems (although there are *typical* and also *traditional* linguistic misuses); for we can never know which new linguistic misuses may appear one day. In contrast, there is a kind of *method* of philosophising, a method of philosophical activity. It consists in *reflecting on the rules of linguistic usage* (of grammar in the widest sense), for these rules alone determine the "sense" and "meaning" of our statements and words.

The view of modern positivism outlined here will necessarily regard the inclination to undertake a *scientific reconstruction of philosophy*, to which we have alluded at the beginning, as the cardinal error of all previous philosophising. This view explains also why such attempts have always failed. With its doctrine that there is no system of philosophical "problems", that is, the doctrine of grammatical misuse, it also explains the existing anarchy of philosophical systems.

4. Similar outcomes, albeit from a completely different direction, are reached by modern *Weltanschauung philosophy* (we are thinking particularly of Scheler, Heidegger and Jaspers). Admittedly, it acknowledges the legitimacy of philosophical problems, it makes philosophical assertions and it regards philosophy as a *doctrine* – but a doctrine of *a different kind* from that of the objectively justifiable sciences. Deliberately, and sometimes explicitly, denying the scientific nature of philosophy, it regards the work of philosophers as confessions of *individual and subjective Weltanschauungen*, that is, *world views*. Idiosyncrasy, depth and original intuition, rather than scientific objectivity or rational-critical testability, are the elements that make philosophical projects significant and valuable. A philosopher can, indeed must, desist from any attempt to justify a proposed doctrine against objections. Unlike a scientist, he should be persuasive not through reasoning but by expressing what profoundly moves him (and those "travelling along the same road", as Jaspers[3] says).

Much like modern positivism, *Weltanschauung philosophy* too can explain the existing anarchy of philosophical systems; for it too, there can be no conclusive philosophical system, or even a conclusive or final system of

---

[3] [Cf. Karl Jaspers, *Philosophie I.: Philosophische Weltorientierung* (1932), p. VII. Ed. English translation by E.B. Ashton (1969), *Philosophy I.: Philosophical World Orientation*, p. 1. Tr.]

philosophical problems, for we can never know what new philosophical problems may be revealed one day.

Similarly, modern *Weltanschauung philosophy* must regard the inclination to undertake a scientific reconstruction of philosophy, to which I have alluded at the beginning, as the cardinal error of previous philosophising. It is the orientation towards (individual) *science*,*[1] the striving towards objective justification, towards an exclusively valid and dominant system, that generates these unhealthy phenomena: the mutual lack of understanding and intolerance of philosophical schools seldom giving a fair hearing to the world views of other systems and constantly criticising their (necessarily) inadequate rational "*justifications*".

5. If we want to pursue our intention of starting at the beginning, we must not ignore the objections raised by positivism and by *Weltanschauung philosophy*. We must not, simply and uncritically, assume the possibility of a scientific reform of philosophy, or even the possibility of a philosophical-scientific debate.

What needs to be critically discussed, first, is the *problem: Is there a philosophical science?*

But does this formulation of the problem offer an escape from the objections discussed above? Evidently not: the question about the scientific nature of philosophy is not a problem of an individual science, but a philosophical problem; the possibility of critically analysing it, therefore, is disputed.

6. At this point, however, we need not fear such objections. On the contrary: if positivism or *Weltanschauung philosophy* dispute our problem and the possibility of discussing it scientifically, this gives us (in turn) an opportunity of proceeding critically against both views.

These two views, whether implicitly or explicitly, take a position on the scientific nature of philosophy. They answer this problem, and this answer is negative. (If they do not recognise it explicitly and discuss it as a problem, this can mean one thing only: that their response is uncritical and that they have simply become resigned to the anarchic state of philosophy.)

---

*[1] Many years later, this scientific orientation was referred to and opposed as "scientism". See also my book *Das Elend des Historizismus* (1944/1945; German translation by Leonard Walentik, 1965), pp. 48, 53. ["The Poverty of Historicism II.", *Economica*, N.S., 11 (1944), pp. 120 f., 123 (*The Poverty of Historicism*, 1st ed., 1957, and subsequent editions, pp. 60, 66). Ed.]

But if the two views were to apply their negative response to the problem itself, they would necessarily become entangled in inconsistencies and paradoxes (of the Liar's Paradox kind).

For if positivism applies its thesis that "There is no philosophical problem and hence no philosophical assertion" to our problem, this thesis will become contradictory since the thesis itself is a philosophical assertion, therefore it also acknowledges the existence of a philosophical problem (our problem). Positivism must, therefore, proceed more cautiously (in such a way as not to assail our formulation of the problem).

Similarly, *Weltanschauung philosophy* would become entangled in contradictions if it were to take a stand against our formulation of the problem. For it can only do so if it regards its own thesis, namely that philosophy does not establish any scientific (justifiable) statements, as a scientific (justifiable) statement, and employs it against us. In that case, however, this statement will be contradictory (since it is itself a "philosophical" statement). But if it regards it not as a scientific statement but as a commitment to a world view, it cannot object to our formulation of the problem; for then we could also assert the opposite (non-contradictory) statement that there can be scientific-philosophical statements (and discussions).

(Here, evidently, we are dealing with one of those classic contradictions that reveal the close logical relationship between *scepticism* and *mysticism*; in our case, between positivism and *Weltanschauung philosophy*. It is the contradiction that Socrates must have sensed when, so it is said, he followed his statement "I know that I know nothing" with the comment "and I barely know that.")

These remarks should not be regarded as particularly polemical in character. They are intended to show merely that no serious objections can be raised against the *formulation of the problem: Is there a philosophical science?*

But does this problem even merit serious interest?

7. We would not have drawn out these introductory remarks to such an extent were we not convinced that this problem merits our deepest interest. It can be seen as the very key to the fundamental problems of philosophy.

Even formulating this problem yields the following (provisional, not entirely accurate, but illustrative) conception:

We have before us a domain ([that] of the individual sciences), the scientific nature of which is to be regarded as undisputed. There is a second domain (philosophy), the scientific nature of which is to be regarded as problematic.

We can formulate this problem as follows: where in this second, philosophical domain should we draw the boundary between science and *Weltanschauung* (or between science and linguistic misuse)? Should we draw it in such a way that the entire second domain lies outside this boundary, or should it be drawn inside the philosophical domain, or should the latter as a whole lie within science?

If we want to investigate this problem scientifically, this conception will have to be slightly modified: we shall have to introduce a third domain (above or between these other two, so to speak), namely the domain within which this investigation will be conducted. It will have to be assumed (provisionally, at least, once we have formulated the problem) that this domain is (on the one hand) scientific and (on the other) philosophical. It is situated, as it were, on the boundary of the domain assumed to be scientific, and also on that of the philosophical domain of which the scientific nature is in doubt.

More precisely: the task of this third domain is to examine the boundaries between the first and the second domains, to determine where the boundaries of science are drawn.

We shall call this domain of the philosophical investigation assumed to be scientific, the domain of the *theory of knowledge*. Should it, furthermore, transpire that there is a philosophical domain outside science, we shall call it "metaphysics" – regardless of whether we want to appraise it negatively (as positivism does) or positively (as *Weltanschauung philosophy* does).

On the basis of this conception, we can now formulate our problem "Is there a philosophical science?" as follows: where is the boundary between science and metaphysics? Alternatively, in a formulation that does not appeal quite so strongly to our intuitive conception, we can ask:

Is there a criterion that allows us to distinguish between scientific and metaphysical assertions?

If we call such a criterion the "*demarcation criterion*", and if we call the question about the demarcation criterion the "*demarcation problem*", we can say:

The question "Is there a philosophical science?" leads to the formulation of the "demarcation problem" as the most general philosophical problem.

I.

FORMULATION OF
THE PROBLEM

1. *The problem of demarcation.* What distinguishes the *empirical sciences* from the *non-empirical sciences* and from *extra-scientific* domains?

Is there a criterion that demarcates the empirical sciences from non-empirical domains? A criterion that marks out some statements or systems of statements as empirical, and others as non-empirical?

I call the question about such a *demarcation criterion* the "*demarcation problem*".

The demarcation problem is the fundamental problem of the theory of knowledge: all epistemological questions can be reduced to it.

2. *Scope of the problem of demarcation.* Instead of the question:
What is knowledge?
(which, in this form, can surely lead to little but a fruitless quarrel about nominal definitions, for definitions are always arbitrary), we could start by asking the narrower question:
What is *scientific* knowledge?
Since scientific *knowledge* can always be represented in the form of *statements* or of *systems of statements* (so that we can say very briefly: scientific *knowledge* consists of *statements* or *systems of statements*), we can transform the

question "What is *scientific* knowledge?" into the following ones (which are equivalent to it):

"What statements constitute scientific knowledge?" or "What is it that characterises particular statements as 'scientific'?" or "What criterion makes it possible to demarcate science from extra-scientific domains?"

It is evident that the various formulations are generalisations of the demarcation problem articulated above.

Much like the question "What is knowledge?", this demarcation problem (in its shortest formulation: What is science?) is too vague and too general, in this form, to serve as a fundamental question for investigation. The immediate question is one of *terminology*, that is, of establishing by definition what we wish to *call* "scientific" and "extra-scientific". Whether or not we wish to regard, say, a *metaphysical system* as science is, to begin with, only a matter of convention, at least as long as we cannot put forward substantive arguments in support of introducing particular investigations or particular demarcations. (Naming will, of course, be of secondary importance even then; what is important is only where the boundary is drawn and the arguments in support of it.)

If we restrict the question further, however, and if we do not ask (bearing the generalised demarcation problem in mind) for a criterion of science in general, but ask instead – using the *demarcation problem* itself – for a criterion of *empirical* science, this will reduce the risk of losing our way in terminological arguments. For there is, by and large, agreement about which sciences should be called "empirical" and which should not. (To the extent that linguistic usage moves away from ambiguity, the question loses its arbitrary terminological nature.)

The *generalised demarcation problem*, the question about a criterion of the nature of science (*What is science?*), was introduced here as a restriction on the question *What is knowledge?*, up to a point even as a substitute for it. Analogously, the *demarcation problem* itself, that is, the question about a criterion of being empirical-scientific (*What is empirical science?*), corresponds to the question "What is empirical knowledge?" or "What is experience?"

The *demarcation problem* can, therefore, also be seen as a form of the *problem of experience* (in some respects, a more specific form).

The most important boundary that the demarcation criterion has to draw is the one between empirical science and metaphysics.

(The term "metaphysics" is controversial also. *Provisional definition*: we call non-empirical statements about reality "metaphysical". According to this definition, all non-empirical assertions that state something about existing, real objects are metaphysical; so too are all non-empirical assertions that lay claim to being empirical, thus *violating the boundary* drawn by the criterion of demarcation.)

Historically, all the empirical sciences arose from non-empirical, speculative-philosophical "metaphysics", and the traces of their metaphysical past still cling visibly to the less highly developed among them. For those, a *demarcation from metaphysics* is of great importance.

Should we want to circumscribe the narrower sphere of the demarcation problem, this might best be achieved by means of the keywords *"experience"* and *"metaphysics"*.

3. *The problem of induction.* We can *observe* particular *individual events* only, and just a *limited number* of these. That is why we can directly test, by observation, *particular (singular) statements* only, that is, statements about individual events or about a limited number of such individual events. In the empirical sciences, nonetheless, *universal (general) statements* do occur, statements that say something about an *unlimited number* of events. Foremost among such statements are what we call *"natural laws"*.

The *problem of induction* is the question about the truth (or about the *justification*) of universal statements in the empirical sciences. Put differently: can *empirical statements* (statements about reality that are based on experience) have *universal truth*?

4. *Scope of the problem of induction.* The problem of induction, the problem of (the truth of) *universal empirical statements*, is a particular form of the *problem of law-like regularity in nature* (and of the *problem of causality*).

To "explain" ("causally explain") some occurrences, means to *derive* from universal statements (from natural laws, theories) statements that describe these occurrences, and to do so in a purely *logical-deductive* fashion.

(If a particular *individual occurrence* is to be explained, the derived statements must be *singular*. In addition to the theoretical system, that is, to the universal statements (major premises), their derivation requires that we assume singular minor premises, since without the substitution of singular conditions we cannot infer singular statements from universal statements.)

For any given statement (unless it is contradictory), it is possible to construct a variety of universal statements from which the given statement can be deduced. It is trivial, therefore, to say that in principle, any occurrence whatever can be (causally) explained in a variety of ways.

(A more difficult task, albeit one that can, in principle, always be performed in several ways, is to construct an explanatory theory, that is, major premises for deduction, for an entire (consistent) *system* of given statements.)[1]

---

[1] [The conclusion of this section cannot be found and must be presumed lost. Ed.]

[II.]

ON THE QUESTION OF ELIMINATING SUBJECTIVIST PSYCHOLOGISM

The deductivist, transcendentalist and objectivist view of science advocated here, differs in a truly fundamental way from any inductivist, psychologistic and subjectivist view of science such as the one advocated by (for example) modern positivism. Inductivism (positivism) regards our perceptions (and perhaps other experiences also) as the foundation of all knowledge, of all science. This basic theme is common to all positivist approaches, although they interpret it in a variety of different ways. Some go so far as to regard scientific *statements* as being "only" logical constructions of experiences; others regard the *concepts* of empirical science as "only" logical constructions (classes of classes, classes of relations) of elementary experiences. The transcendental untenability of this view, and the logical difficulty of treating irrational elements (which is what our experiences are) logically and rationally, lead positivism ultimately (while not abandoning its basic position) to replace irrational experiences with rational constructs, namely with perceptual *statements* ("protocol *sentences*"). The foundations of science are to be constituted no longer by our irrational perceptions, but by the rationalised linguistic expression of these perceptions.

In this way, positivism believes it has overcome the psychologism [and the] subjectivism inherent in the irrational original material. Comparison with the deductivist view reveals how unsuccessful this undertaking has been. According to the deductivist view, objective *science* must not be confused with our experiences (hypothetically posited by psychology), those we call "*knowing*".

The study of our subjective knowledge, our subjective convictional experiences, is a matter for the *psychology* of knowledge; it is not relevant to the *theory* of knowledge. The psychology of knowledge will, presumably, offer the trivial proposition that our experiences of knowing or of believing – to the extent that they can be explained at all – should be seen as caused by other experiences; in particular, by what are called "perceptual experiences", be they the perception of an event or of written symbols, of language sounds or the like.

From a subjective, psychological viewpoint, therefore, science is a system of visible or audible statements, the perception (and mental processing) of which aids us in the formation of our subjective convictions.

The objective, epistemological viewpoint is entirely different.

The deductivist theory of knowledge regards science not as a system of convictions, but only as a hypothetico-deductive system of statements formulated according to certain methods.

This system has the nature of objectivity or [of] intersubjective testability; that is, anyone willing (and able) to make the effort can, in principle, test it. Both the system's deductive derivations and the final derived singular basic statements (the singular predictions derived by hic-et-nunc substitutions) have this nature of objectivity, of intersubjective testability. The tests can be performed by the various subjects in entirely different ways. This is a matter for each individual subject who wishes to form an opinion, and it is the case both for the derivations and for the final derived basic statements. The only task of science is to provide its derivations with a "clear" form (which means only: an intersubjectively testable form) and to take the derivations to the point where statements (instructions for observation) are reached that can be tested easily by anyone ("non-problematic basic statements"). Ascertaining how the subjective tests are performed in each case is a matter for the psychology of knowledge; and its statements are subject to the same methodological rules that apply to any other empirical, hypothetico-deductive science.

This position is generally accepted with regard to the logical deductions of science. Nobody would maintain, for example, that the sciences explicitly take into account the psychological convictional experiences that may accompany the testing of deductions, and adduce these experiences as a basis for logical deduction. (Only explicit inductivist approaches attempt sometimes to support a deduction by presenting mental convictional experiences.)

What is, however, not accepted at all is the deductivist position that science should stop at non-problematic (that is, easily testable by anyone) basic statements, and that further testing is no longer a matter for science unless special difficulties are encountered (in which case, the scientific derivation should be carried on until non-problematic statements are reached).

The dominant (inductivist-positivist) view regards science not as an aid for individuals to form their own convictions, but as a system of convictions; not as a system of statements that satisfies particular formal conditions and must, in particular cases, be modified according to particular formal rules, but as a system of "true" or at least "probable" statements, these terms being understood in the sense of our [subjective] convictional experiences.

This view is shared also by that variant of positivism that replaces perceptual and convictional experiences with protocol statements. This becomes evident in that perceptual or protocol statements are simply statements made by individual subjects about particular experiences. Science [so it is assumed] builds on these experiences, whether in inductive form, or by deriving consequences from hypotheses in combination with protocol statements, these consequences in turn being compared with protocol statements. In any event, protocol statements, that is to say, reports about subjective perceptions, constitute the foundation of science itself: they are integral components of the scientific system, one that is presented to a certain extent as a system of logical constructions erected upon protocol statements.

A deductivist epistemologist is not *as such* *[1] interested in the question whether there are subjective perceptual experiences or "only" protocol statements. He can, therefore, accept (at least provisionally) that whenever

---

*[1] What is meant is this: unless he happens to be interested in the *psychology* of knowledge also (as in the second part of this paragraph).

we wish to discuss subjective observations, we need to speak about protocol statements instead. Using this terminology, he would say: every subject tests science with the help of his own protocol statements. On the one hand, he tests a deduction and records that it appears to him to be "conclusive" or "non-conclusive". On the other, he tests the last derived non-problematic basic statements *about* easily observable events, and records whether they appear to him to agree with his observations and therefore "true", or not to agree and therefore "false". But all these tests by way of all these protocol statements no longer belong to the science being tested; they belong to what we have called the "formation of subjective conviction". They belong, therefore, to the hypothetico-deductive psychology of knowledge, a science of facts that must ascertain whether the procedure being described corresponds to the facts, one to [which] the same methodological rules apply as to any other empirical science.

[III.]

TRANSITION TO THE THEORY OF METHOD[1]

1. *An objection to the criterion of falsifiability.* The following objection can be raised, and quite rightly so, to the proposed solutions to the demarcation problem[2] and to the problem of induction:

Admittedly, so this objection may be formulated, scientific theories represent non-verifiable systems; they are not, however, *unverifiable* only, but *unfalsifiable* also. Every theoretical system can be protected against empirical falsification, and in a variety of ways. One can introduce auxiliary hypotheses to "explain" the observations that threaten the theoretical system, that is, to bring them into agreement with the system; or one can amend the "*coordinative definitions*" (or whatever takes their place if not working with "coordinative definitions", as in the view advocated here). In other words, one can alter the empirical meaning assigned to the concepts ([or] the terms) that occur in the theory. Finally, one can simply exclude the unfavourable observations by declaring them to be "fabricated",

---

[1] [As stated in Volume I: Section 30, note 1, it had been considered to add *Transition to the Theory of Method* as an appendix to Volume I; this was not, however, the original plan; see Editor's Postscript. Ed.]

[2] [See Editor's Postscript. Ed.]

"unscientific", "non-objective" or something of this sort. Any one of these procedures, and even more so in combination, makes it possible to protect a theory against falsification. The reference to the one-sided falsifiability of theories, therefore, is not a sound argument and is incapable of paving the way for a solution of the epistemological problems. There is, moreover, no asymmetry between positive and negative truth values, between verification and falsification. The proposed solution to the problem of induction should be rejected, because natural laws are not "partially decidable" but not decidable at all. The proposed solution to the demarcation problem should be rejected because scientific theories are not falsifiable, which entails that falsifiability as the criterion of demarcation would exclude them from science (as a result of which, the arguments raised against Wittgenstein's criterion of meaning[3] would now be turned against the position advocated here).

The objection just described (in what follows it will be called the "*conventionalist objection to falsifiability*") is of *fundamental importance* for all further discussion.

This objection *is justified, but it does not affect the epistemological view advocated here*. It is true that a particular theoretical system should never be described as absolutely "*falsifiable*"; there always exist procedures that can make falsification impossible. But *there also exist procedures* that achieve the opposite, *that render the theoretical system "falsifiable".*

This point reveals very clearly the opposition between viewing the theory of knowledge as a theory of method and every other epistemological view; in particular, any view that aims to examine the theory of knowledge not as a methodology but only as logical analysis of knowledge.

Where it is not only the logical properties of a theory that make it falsifiable but also certain procedures, that is, certain *methodological decisions*, this means that demarcation is not a logical matter only but a methodological one also, and that the demarcation problem is not just a logical but a methodological problem. Similarly, the demarcation criterion cannot be a logical criterion only: it must be a methodological one also, one that relates not to a given theory and to its logical structure only, but

---

[3] [Cf. Volume I: Section 44; Appendix: Section V; Karl Popper, *Logik der Forschung* (1934; 2nd ed., 1966) [*The Logic of Scientific Discovery* (1959; 2nd ed., 1968). Tr.], Section 4. See also Editor's Postscript. Ed.]

to its treatment in science also. The "conventionalist objection to falsifiability" [as I have called it], therefore, has threefold significance for the present investigation:

a) In so far as this objection is justified, it can be levelled *against any* non-methodological demarcation attempt; and it is used in this sense here.

b) It allows us to pursue the thesis of the methodological character of the theory of knowledge, and to formulate and to treat the demarcation problem as a concrete methodological one.

This point is important because it permits us to apply the transcendental method, turning the demarcation problem into a *decidable (that is, partially decidable)* question whose solution rests not on purely arbitrary definitions of the concepts of "metaphysics" and "empirical science", but on definitions whose usefulness and productiveness can be decided by the success of the scientific method.

c) The objection suggests that the deductivist theory of scientific method should be based on the question: *What methodological definitions would render a [scientific] theory falsifiable?* The answers to this question, answers that can be obtained by way of logical analysis and deduction, constitute the theorems of the theory of method.

These three points will be discussed in turn in greater detail; points (a) and (b) in the following sections, and point (c) in the chapter "Outline of a deductivist theory of empirical-scientific methods".[4]

2. *Critique of non-methodological theories of knowledge.* For the purpose of this section, it shall be assumed that the falsifiability criterion performs the demarcation in a substantively correct way, that is, [such] that the methodological results derivable by assuming this criterion are transcendentally corroborated.

What is to be shown here is that given this assumption, any non-methodological demarcation attempt must prove inadequate; in other words, that the empirical criterion of falsifiability cannot be replaced by any non-methodological criterion and especially not by a logical one. The argument used to demonstrate this contention will be, essentially, the "conventionalist objection to falsifiability". In order to carry out this

---

[4] [A reference to Volume II (Fragments): [V.] *Outline of a theory of empirical-scientific methods (theory of experience).* Ed.]

demonstration, a theory of knowledge will be assumed that agrees with the one advocated here excepting on one point only, namely in its methodological considerations. Such a theory of knowledge would be deductivist, first and foremost: it would regard natural laws, or theoretical systems, as premises for the derivation of singular empirical statements, that is, of fully decidable predictions.

This view seems to lead to a demarcation criterion that is, in a certain sense, more convenient than the one advocated in the present work; for it suggests that *those, and only those, statements should be called empirical and scientific that either are fully decidable or imply fully decidable statements*; put another way: the observation statements, and those statements from which observation statements can be derived strictly deductively, are empirical and scientific.

At first glance, such a demarcation criterion appears to be equivalent to the criterion of falsifiability. For if we can derive from a theory fully decidable consequences, then by virtue of *modus tollens* the theory is evidently falsifiable (as has been explained above[1]). Falsification of consequences derived from a theory in purely logical fashion invalidates its major premises, thus falsifying the theory.

A theory of knowledge that sets up such a demarcation criterion, that is, the criterion "Statements that imply observation statements are called empirical" (since every statement implies itself, this formulation*[1] includes observation statements also), would come as close to the view advocated here as is logically (that is, non-methodologically) possible. To date, no theory of knowledge has come to my attention that would advocate such a criterion of demarcation, explicitly or even implicitly. Hahn's formulations, communicated to me privately, would seem to come closest to this demarcation criterion; some of Carnap's formulations appear less close. (Discussions of both positions will follow further below.[2]). But even if the demarcation criterion formulated above were to be explicitly promoted by some theory of knowledge, it would *not* be *equivalent* to the one advocated here.

This demarcation would differ from the one advocated in the present

---

[1] [Cf. Volume I: Section 31. Ed.]

*[1] As does the criterion of falsifiability.

[2] [These "discussions" cannot be found and must be presumed lost; see Editor's Postscript. Cf. also Hans Hahn, "Logik, Mathematik und Naturerkennen", *Einheitswissenschaft* 2 (1933), pp. 22 f. Ed.]

study primarily by failing to distinguish between conventionalist-tautological and empirical systems; that is to say, it fails to characterise the *empirical method* (which can be comprehended by a methodological formulation of the problem only). As a result, it cannot but fail to illuminate the concept of *experience* (of which H. Gomperz rightly says that "almost all controversial philosophical questions can be expressed also as questions about the scope of the concept of experience"[3]); the concept of experience that, in this study, is illuminated through being replaced by a methodological concept: *that of the empirical-scientific method*.

In order to justify these objections to an exclusively logical criterion of demarcation, we shall start (in the next section) by examining a comparison, albeit a provisional one, between *conventionalist* and *empiricist* ideas.

3. *Comments on the question: conventionalism or empiricism?* Naive inductivist empiricism holds, usually, the untenable view that it is possible to speak of "correct" and "incorrect", "true" and "false" theoretical systems (systems of *universal* empirical statements) in exactly the same sense in which we speak of "correct" and "incorrect", "true" and "false" observation statements (*singular* empirical statements). It regards universal empirical statements, then, as fully *decidable*, not as falsifiable only but as verifiable (inducible) also.

Conventionalism is fully justified in opposing this naive view. It emphasises that an unambiguous decision about theoretical principles cannot be attained through observation statements. It should always be possible, therefore, to have *several* theoretical systems that permit [us] to explain a given system of observation statements (to link them deductively).

This is why, so conventionalism further concludes, a certain freedom of choice exists with regard to the fundamental principles of a theoretical system: these principles are freely introduced conventions, and it is not "experience" that decides between them but aesthetic and practical considerations. All theoretical systems that allow us to explain a given system of observation statements (to connect them deductively) are, so it would seem, fully equivalent empirically. The choice between them can only be made according to a viewpoint that takes into account, for

---

[3] Cf. Heinrich Gomperz, *Weltanschauungslehre* I. (1905), p. 35.

example, which system is more practical in its application, [or] is more symmetrical, elegant and so on in its logical structure. This viewpoint goes by the name "principle of economy" or "principle of greatest simplicity".

In so far as conventionalism opposes the naive-inductivist view that theories are empirically verifiable, that they can be decided unambiguously by observations, its position is justified, as noted already: there exists, no doubt, some freedom of choice between theoretical systems, and the only choice between two such systems whose consequences are *completely equivalent* would be according to aesthetic-pragmatic aspects. (According to the view advocated here, incidentally, this decision is not especially important. Theories that are equivalent in all their consequences can themselves be called equivalent, that is, they differ from each other terminologically only.)

But the conventionalist view goes much further: it opposes, too, the view that theories are empirically *falsifiable*, thereby implicitly opposing the *deductivist* empiricism advocated here. The arguments that conventionalism can offer on this question were mentioned above ("conventionalist objection to falsifiability").

Conventionalism *must* arrive at this rejection of falsifiability. For conventionalism, the principles, or "axioms", of a theory represent "free stipulations", that is, implicit definitions of the basic concepts. Definitions, however, are *irrefutable*; they cannot be [judged as] "true" or "false", but only "practical" or "impractical" (or "simple" and "complicated", or the like).

The best-known example is as follows: if we decide to adopt a particular metric geometry (say, Euclidean geometry), this decision can never conflict with observation because it defines what a "measuring rod" (or a "rigid body") is. The measuring instruments must always be corrected in such a way that the measurements correspond to the metric forms of the chosen geometry. But this makes falsification impossible: a measurement inconsistent with the metric formulae of the chosen geometry will force us to correct the measuring instruments, but never to modify the chosen axioms. As shown by Dingler especially, this idea (which goes back to Poincaré) can be generalised; as noted by Carnap, three different kinds of stipulations must be made: a "spatial law" (geometrical metric), a "temporal law" (a standard for time measurements) and a "causal law" (a metric for some basic intensities, for example "mass" or "charge").

These stipulations, representing irrefutable definitions, determine the system of theoretical physics in its basic outlines.[1]

The conventionalist view might be characterised by the statement that a scientific *theorist can never be put right by "experience"*; only an experimenter can be put right by experience – even he, however, not about the truth of scientific statements but only about the practical-experimental success of theories.

In opposition to this view, "empiricism" (including the variant advocated here) can be characterised, quite generally, by saying that it regards the natural sciences (including the theoretical ones) as *capable of learning from "experience" (observations)*.

The conventionalist view can, in principle, *always be applied*. As Carnap notes, "for any arbitrary axiomatic system we can achieve what is called 'agreement with reality' ".[2]

Logical analysis, therefore, can never decide whether a given scientific system is "conventionalist" or "empiricist". Such a question cannot even be posed about the logical properties of a system since every system can, in any case, be consistently construed in a conventionalist way. If any systems exist to which an empiricist view can be applied also (besides the conventionalist one, which is always possible), evidently this empiricist "view" can only consist in *deciding not to aim*, at all costs, "at what is called 'agreement with reality' ". Put another way: it consists of introducing *methodological decisions* that *exclude particular procedures* by which a theory is made consistent with reality. (For example: if the results of measurements conflict with the chosen geometry, we need not necessarily correct the measuring instruments; we could, for example, do so only if an error in the measuring instruments [or in the results of measurements] can be detected by some other methods also.)

Scientific systems "as such" cannot, therefore, be divided into conventionalist or empiricist; such a distinction is, moreover, irrelevant as long as "everything is going well" in science, that is, as long as all measurements lead only to the anticipated, or *predicted*, results. Only if *unanticipated results* occur will the distinction become important. In that event, the

---

[1] [Cf. Rudolf Carnap, "Über die Aufgabe der Physik und die Anwendung des Grundsatzes der Einfachstheit" ["On the Task of Physics and the Application of the Principle of Greatest Simplicity". Tr.], *Kant-Studien* 28 (1923), pp. 90 ff. Ed.]

[2] Rudolf Carnap, *op. cit.*, p. 106.

empiricist will demand a revision of the system, perhaps even its complete *reconstruction*. The conventionalist, however, will not see any reason to deviate from his stipulations; for him, "unanticipated" results are not unexpected at all. To some extent they are even a matter of course, for only such circumstances can bring about corrections to his measuring instruments, but on the other hand the measuring instruments are defined as the "results of corrections".

The opposition between conventionalism and empiricism becomes relevant, therefore, only in the event of a scientific "crisis", when its existence is denied by conventionalists and asserted by empiricists. *The methodological decisions according to which science proceeds in the event of a "crisis" – that is what characterises the "empirical method",* that is what characterises the view that science can learn from experience.

Empirical science, therefore, is not determined by its results; it is not its statements as such that have a scientific nature: only its *method* does.

4. *The empiricist character of colloquial language – the logical view as a prerequisite for the methodological view.* If we assume – as we did in Section 2 – the utility of falsifiability as a methodological criterion of demarcation, then any exclusively logical demarcation attempt should be regarded as a failure, since it can never be equivalent to a methodological demarcation. It fails to draw the boundary between empirical and conventionalist-tautological systems.

The conventionalist objection to falsifiability, therefore, has the merit of drawing attention to the non-equivalence of the logical and the methodological methods of the theory of knowledge.

But drawing the boundary logically, that is, logically separating statements into singular and universal empirical statements, into metaphysical and logical ones (as shown above . . . in the Table of Statements[1]), does constitute, in a sense, the foundation for the methodological demarcation. This table summarises the true picture, except that we have to understand "*empirical falsification*" (or "*verification*") as that which the empiricist methodology, the theory of "experience", has yet to define more precisely.

---

[1] [Only the following draft of this Table of Statements (opposite) has been preserved (see Editor's Postscript)]

This should be taken into consideration, more particularly, if we apply the table to such complicated constructs as scientific theories. A scientific theory can, in most cases, be falsified as a whole only. The theory *as a whole*, therefore, has the nature of a universal empirical statement. If, for example, statements happen to occur in a theory that look like "there-is" statements, these statements will not necessarily represent metaphysical elements of the empirical theory, for they constitute one component of the theory, that is, of the universal empirical statement.

If we apply the Table of Statements to simpler fields, however, more particularly to the statements of our colloquial language, then (oddly enough) no special precautions need be taken. The statement "All humans have (by nature) hair that ranges between very fair (white), red and dark brown (black)" is easily recognised as falsifiable, that is, as a genuine empirical statement. A *"conventionalist stratagem"* – perhaps consisting in failing to regard the observation of humans with blue or green hair as falsification, but instead not recognising such people as "humans", or their hair as "hair", or its green colour as "green" – should not, in general, be feared where such statements of colloquial language are concerned. It is just as easy to recognise that the statement "This stone is sad" (or "All rock crystals are sad") is metaphysical, since obviously no falsifying observations exist.

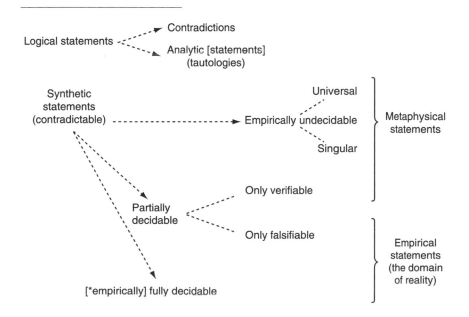

It is the case that "conventionalist stratagems" are always logically possible, even for the statements of colloquial language. But the fact that *colloquial language usage* is, in general, sufficiently clear so as to exclude conventionalist stratagems, demonstrates that such linguistic usage is *empiricist*. The methods we usually apply when testing the statements of our colloquial language are, therefore, *empiricist methods* (without being inductivist methods as a result, as often assumed). The practical usefulness of language in everyday life depends, after all, on allowing ourselves to be taught by "experience".

Although the utility of the Table of Statements rests, *in any event*, on methodological conventions – whether explicitly formulated in a theory of method or, as in the case of colloquial language, implicitly established by practice – the logical considerations leading to the formulation of the table constitute, in a sense, the *prerequisite* for drawing the boundary methodologically. For even though it is impossible, without taking certain methodological decisions, to demonstrate that empirical statements are falsifiable, we can (near enough) identify all statements that do *not* imply observation statements, and all contradictions, as non-empirical.

The relationship between the merely logical demarcation and the methodological one can, therefore, be characterised in the following way: whereas logical analysis suffices for characterising particular statements as non-empirical, it is never sufficient for characterising other statements as empirical. That a statement cannot be identified as non-empirical by logical analysis is a necessary condition but not a sufficient one for characterising it as "empirical".

5. *Concerning the critique of non-deductive and non-transcendental theories of knowledge.* We can put forward, in support of the deductive-transcendental method of the theory of knowledge advocated here, some further important arguments, related also to the "conventionalist objection to falsifiability" (cf. point b) in Section 1). These arguments, too, are directed against the logical method of demarcation, that is, they emphasise the advantages of the methodological, or transcendental, method.

But they do so in a different way: what is to be stressed here is the significance of the *deductive* nature of the theory of method, making this theory a *decidable* (that is, partially decidable, falsifiable) system of statements.

The problem of demarcation is, to begin with, purely one of *definition*.

Only the demarcation criterion provides a sharp definition of what should and what should not be called "empirical science".

Most theories of knowledge are, therefore, at risk of "solving" the problem of demarcation through sterile nominal definitions.

Of course, every theory of knowledge that seeks, somehow, to take account of existing science will attempt to formulate its definitions in such a way that what everyone calls "science", and what everyone calls "metaphysics", are demarcated accordingly. (Wittgenstein was unsuccessful in this respect, too.)

Some fields are controversial, however, and opinions differ as to whether they should be counted as science or as metaphysics. It is here that demarcation becomes interesting and important; but it is precisely here that the theory of knowledge seems unable to proceed except in a completely *arbitrary* fashion. For it is its task to pin down what we understand, or what we mean, when we speak about "empirical science" or about "metaphysics". But as soon as we set foot in a controversial border-line area, this task is not unambiguously formulated and cannot, in principle, be unambiguously accomplished: the various demarcation criteria represent diverging opinions, but are unable to resolve the controversy.

These comments concerning the problem of demarcation apply, in principle, to any scientific definition. In some sciences, nevertheless, we prefer one definition over another, and not only because it agrees more closely with our subjective inclinations but for objective reasons also: we favour one definition on account of its (theoretical) *productiveness*.

For example, Karl Menger writes:[1] "Any particular definition, therefore, contains a certain degree of *arbitrariness*, whose justification can be furnished only by the *productiveness* of the definition."

But what does the productiveness of a definition consist in? If one does not regard the theory of knowledge as a deductive science, or a deductive theory of method, it is difficult to see to what extent one arbitrary definition might be distinguished from another in terms of its special productiveness. Logical positivism, for example, finds itself in this situation, regardless of whether it views the theory of knowledge not as a *doctrine* but as an activity of clarifying and imparting meaning (as do

---

[1] Karl Menger, Dimensionstheorie (1928), p. 76.

Wittgenstein and Schlick), or whether (as does Carnap) it calls epistemological statements "metalogical" or "semantic" and advocates the "metalogical thesis" "that meaningful philosophical statements are metalogical, that is to say, they speak about the forms of language".[2]

If one views the theories of knowledge in this or in a similar way, tendentious arbitrariness becomes unavoidable; for whatever "imparting of meaning" or "language-critical conventions" may be established in the matter of the demarcation problem, one would always have to presuppose what one actually means by the words "empirical science", "metaphysics" and so on.

The situation is entirely different if we take our arbitrary definitions as the basis of a *deductive theory*.

"It is the purpose of a strict definition," writes Menger,[3] "to be the starting point of a deductive system. Definitions are dogmas, only the deductions derived from them are knowledge. It is a *requirement*, therefore, *that the content of any definition prove to be a source of knowledge by being the starting point of a comprehensive, aesthetically perfect theory*."

(The requirement of aesthetic perfection is unlikely to be met by the theory of method developed here, of course.)

Menger continues: "Fulfilling this *content-related* requirement is the only possible *justification of any definition*. If we are dealing specifically with the definition of a concept that is called by a name taken directly from everyday life, the fulfilment of the *formal* requirement (which in itself is secondary for the concept) provides a *justification for the naming of the concept*."[4]

If a definition can be justified by its productiveness, therefore, that is to say, by leading to interesting theoretical consequences, this means, in the special case of an *empirically applicable* theory, that the theory – together with its underlying definitions – leads to empirically decidable consequences. But this means that the theory is decidable (one-sidedly falsifiable), and in the analogous case of a transcendental theory for the definition in its consequences [leads] to decidable methodological assertions, so that the *scientific success* of the derived methodological consequences either justifies the definition or demonstrates its inadequacy.

---

[2] Rudolf Carnap, "Die physikalische Sprache als Universalsprache der Wissenschaft" ["Physical Language as a Universal Language of Science". Tr.], *Erkenntnis* 2 (1932), p. 435.

[3] Menger, *loc. cit.*

[4] [Menger, *loc. cit.* Ed.]

The fate of epistemological assertions and definitions is decided, therefore, by the *success* of the derived "empirical method".

6. *Is there a methodology?* The view advocated here about the significance of methodology is unlikely to remain undisputed. It can safely be assumed that not only the *significance* of methodology, but the justification of its very existence will be disputed also; since according to some epistemologists, there can be no science beyond the individual empirical sciences, and in particular there can be no "philosophical" discipline to which the individual sciences are subordinated.*[1]

First, concerning the question of the *significance* of methodology, it may well be impossible to discuss this question objectively and seriously. Other disciplines, especially those of a higher degree of abstraction, are accused often enough of being meaningless also; for example, n-dimensional geometry. The way in which one judges the significance of a science is, no doubt, a matter of taste to a certain degree. And yet, at least two (*ad hominem*) arguments can be offered in support of the "significance" of methodology. First, that it is precisely the old philosophical controversies, so often held to be unsolvable, that are transformed by methodology into a new and decidable form. Second, that methodology is far from being devoid of practical utility. It is, admittedly, not very likely to succeed in influencing a highly developed science such as modern physics; on the contrary, it can probably only learn from physics.*[2] But it might well have an influence on the less highly developed sciences (biology, psychology, sociology). These sciences, which have often rightly attempted to take the method of physics as their model, undoubtedly suffer from a faulty methodological analysis of physics, in particular from a superficial analysis of the relationship between theory and experiment, what has been called the "experimental method". Not only is it the most important *practical* task of methodology to offer assistance: this may be its most important opportunity to prove itself theoretically also.

*[1] This was, in fact, the position of the Vienna Circle: mathematics and logic consist of analytic statements, whereas natural science consists of synthetic verifiable statements; everything else is meaningless. This was the main objection to my theory of knowledge, also. See especially Moritz Schlick, "Die Wende der Philosophie", Erkenntnis 1 (1930), pp. 4 ff., quoted above in Volume I, Section 45, text to note 6.

*[2] This was certainly meant seriously, but has turned out to be somewhat pessimistic.

More important than the charge of meaninglessness is the objection that calls into question the possibility of a methodology at all.

This objection, too, can be linked to the "conventionalist objection to falsifiability"; for if it is shown that the conventionalist objection is invalid, that is to say, that there are systems of statements that are *empirically falsifiable by virtue of their logical form alone*, without any further methodological decisions, all the arguments presented in the preceding sections to demonstrate the necessity of methodological decisions will become irrelevant. Logical analysis will then suffice for proving the empirical nature of a statement.

We could base this line of argument on the example given above ("All humans have fair, reddish or dark brown hair"). Whether or not such a statement is falsifiable, one might argue, depends not on methodological decisions but quite simply on the meanings we associate with the different words mentioned in it; that is, on the *definitions* of the *concepts* that occur in it. If we use the statement in an empiricist fashion in one instance and in a conventionalist fashion in another, we will not be using the same statement at all but only the same sequence of words. Logical analysis shows that a conventionalist who declares, when encountering a green-haired person, "This is not even a human" (and so on), simply *defines* the concept "human" in a different way from the empiricist. It must always be possible, therefore, through logical analysis of the concepts used or through appropriately strict definitions of these concepts, to establish the empirical or non-empirical nature of a system of statements. No methodology is necessary, for the "methodological decisions" would at best be equivalent to logical definitions.

Methodology will be defended against this argument by three counter-arguments. Each of these, taken by itself, seems to me sufficient to safeguard the methodological position against the objection described above.

1. Even if those substantive reasons were valid, they would not be sufficient to support the anti-methodological conclusions. For even if the methodological decisions could be replaced by definitions, there might well exist a science that is completely equivalent to what is here called "methodology". The definitions used to ensure the *empirical nature* of the concepts and of the corresponding statements would, evidently, have something in common: namely, the very trait that characterises them as "empirical". The definitions would, therefore, exhibit regularities that could and should be formulated as definitional rules. The theory of

definitional rules would, however, be analogous to logic (the theory of inferential rules) and *equivalent* to "methodology" (the theory of statement usage); but equivalent at best, and that only if it really manages to accomplish what methodology accomplishes.

2. As the following considerations show, however, such equivalence – replacing methodological decisions with rules of definition – cannot be attained. Definitions cannot prevent science from simply ignoring observations that do not agree with it. Only methodological decisions can do this. Empirical science is, evidently, characterised by the fact that in the event of contradiction between theory and observation, it never resorts to the ultimate device of saying, "so much the worse for the facts" – even though, often enough, it happens that individual scientists refuse to acknowledge facts that are inconsistent with their theories. Now, it is quite *conceivable* for such devices, the ones used by some individual scientists, to evolve into a method, that is, a "science" might emerge that recognises only facts that fit its theories, simply excluding conflicting observations as "unscientific", "inconsistent" or "unreal". Clearly, we would not call such a procedure "empirical-scientific". Empirical science is, evidently, characterised by proceeding differently. But it is rather difficult to see how this difference in procedure might be expressed in the definitions of the concepts used. (Going back to our example: the conventionalist response "But this is not even a human" may modify the definition of the concept [human] – but the response "If you believe this is a human with green hair, you suffer from pathological hallucinations" does not.)

3. The most important counter-argument can be outlined only at this point, and cannot be sufficiently justified. It can be formulated through the thesis that it is impossible to define concepts completely; that is, to define them in such a way that their empirical application is determined unambiguously.

The situation, according to this view, is the reverse of the one assumed by the proponents of definitions: instead of the application of a concept being determined by its definition, it is the application that establishes what we call its "definition" or its "meaning". In other words, there exist only *working definitions*.

This view will be explained by way of some additional comments.

a) The existence of what we call "explicit definitions" is, of course, not being denied. But it is well known that these are only rules through which terms can be translated among themselves, that is, they are abbreviation rules for linguistic usage only; they are, in principle, dispensable (for, by definition, the *definiendum* may always be replaced by the *definiens*).

b) Putting aside these dispensable explicit definitions, therefore, we can advance the thesis that *all concepts are defined implicitly only*, whether they occur in the most fundamental principles, in the axioms of a theory or in the final derived consequences. They are determined, always, by being used within statements in particular ways.

c) Concepts become "empirical" through the empirical use of the system of statements in which they occur. We may call concepts "empirical basic concepts" if they occur in the "empirical basic statements", that is, in the lowest singular consequences of the relevant deductive system (the observation or elementary empirical statements). As a result of the empirical use of these statements, the concepts that occur in them are used empirically also. The empirical basic statements (and their empirical application) are, therefore, the implicit (working) definitions of the empirical basic concepts.

d) According to the deductivist-empiricist view, a system is to be called empirical if it is falsifiable through the empirical falsification of the derived consequences. These consequences – the singular empirical statements – are the empirical basic statements (if they can be tested directly and empirically). It follows that it must be possible to eliminate deductively (by substitution) the fundamental concepts that occur in the axioms of an empirical theory, since only empirical basic concepts occur in the final consequences.

e) Coordinative definitions in the old sense, that is, definitions through which something real is assigned to a concept (not a proper name, but a universal), do not exist. What were taken to be*[3] coordinative definitions are, for the most part, explicit definitions in which primitive empirical basic concepts, that is, concepts of (empirical) colloquial language usually, occur as *definiens*.

f) Similarly, there are no concepts that can be constituted*[4] or defined empirically.

If the view just outlined is correct, it is impossible to establish, through the definition of concepts, how statements are to be used. The reverse is

---

*[3] Including by me, in Volume I.

*[4] "To constitute", "constitutable" and "constitution" are concepts that play a central role in Rudolf Carnap's *Der logische Aufbau der Welt* (1928). See Volume I, Section 33.

the case: what usually we call the meaning of a concept is established by the way in which the statements containing the concept are used.

Investigating how statements are used is, however, the task of methodology.

7. *Universal concept and individual concept – class and element.* According to the view advocated here, it is impossible, for logical reasons, to "constitute" or to define scientific concepts empirically. The concepts of empirical science are always defined implicitly only, by the statements in which they occur. This implicit definition is, as such, only logical-formal; it does not confer on the implicitly defined terms any specific meanings (implicitly defined terms are variables). The implicitly defined terms acquire a "specific meaning" (that is, an empirical "meaning") through the *empirical use* of the statements in which they occur, and through them only.

The mistaken view that it is possible to define concepts empirically, either explicitly (by constitution) or by denotation (using what is known as a coordinative definition), can be refuted by pointing to the unbridgeable gap between universals (universal concepts) and individuals (proper names).

The distinction between "universals" and "individuals" is fundamental. For example, "mammal" and "typewriter" are universals, "Napoleon" and "a painting by Holbein" are individuals.

Universals are distinguished by the fact that proper names do not enter into their definitions; individuals by the fact that they are defined with the help of proper names.

We should regard as "proper names" not only proper names in the colloquial sense, but any specific concrete reference also (such as a *gesture* or a *demonstrative pronoun*, for example, "this painting here" or "that person there"). The most common method for replacing proper names with other proper names is that of *specifying particular space-time coordinates*. In this way, we can dispense with the introduction of new proper names, reducing all proper names to the proper names "Christ's birth" and "Greenwich".

It is a trivial fact that we cannot define a universal concept by a class of proper names, and similarly we cannot define a proper name through the specification of universal concepts.

It is, for example, a futile attempt to define the universal concept "dog" by listing any number of proper names of dogs (or by pointing to "this animal here", "that other animal there" and so on). The universal concept "dog" encompasses not all living dogs only, not even all the dogs that have ever lived only: it is a characteristic of this universal concept that it encompasses those dogs also that were not referred to when it was established. A universal concept, then, is a symbol for a class of elements that is, *in principle, unlimited in number.*

It would be equally futile [conversely] to define, by specifying the universal concept "dog" *without introducing proper names*, a concept with the same scope as the proper name "my dog Rustan". By progressive specification I can, it is true, arrive at the concepts "a Newfoundland dog", "a slim Newfoundland dog", "a slim, large Newfoundland dog with black, silky fur", "a slim, large Newfoundland dog with black, silky fur and white paws" and so on. But however far I may take the specifying description, as long as I do not introduce any proper names I will always be describing a *class with an unlimited number of elements.*

There is no continuity between individual and universal concepts, therefore, in the sense of individuals being definable through universals or vice versa. There exists between them a relationship of substitution only: every individual concept may occur as an element not only of an individual class but also of a universal one (but not vice versa). For example, the individual concept "my dog Rustan" is an element not of the class "the dogs of Vienna" only (individual concept), but of the class of all dogs also (universal concept); and the individual concept "the dogs of Vienna", in turn, is an element of the universal concept "the class of classes of dogs" also (or "the class of classes of dogs living in cities"), and not an element of the individual concept "the class of classes of dogs living in European cities" only. It is, therefore, possible to set up a class hierarchy of universals and a separate class hierarchy of individuals. The class-type of a universal concept is comparable with the class-type of an individual concept, since every individual concept can occur as an element of a universal concept of a higher type, and as an element of an individual concept of a higher type also.

Since all our concrete experiences are of an individual nature, any attempt to construct universals from experiences (to "constitute" universals as classes or as a relationship of classes of experience) is as futile as the attempt to make universal concepts correspond to reality (or to objects of reality) by assignment, [through] coordinative definitions or the like.

In order to be consistent, the proponents of a "theory of constitution" and of "coordinative definitions" should, therefore, ignore the difference between individual and universal concepts, or reject this distinction as ambiguous or the like. Carnap, for example, does this in his *Der logische Aufbau der Welt*.[1]

8. *Concerning the language-critical objection to the possibility of a methodology.* According to Wittgenstein's view, a view adopted by Schlick in particular, it is singular empirical statements *only* (that is, those statements that represent a singular "state of affairs", a particular "slice of reality") that are "meaningful statements".

Other than these statements [including their truth functions], there exist logical tautologies and contradictions that are empty of meaning (even if not nonsensical). All other statements are "*meaningless*".

It has been mentioned already that in this way, natural laws and with them almost the whole of natural science are implicitly declared to be meaningless. Here we shall only discuss the consequence of Wittgenstein's concept of meaning, namely that philosophy and methodology seem to be regarded as meaningless also.

For Wittgenstein, therefore, philosophy is not a body of doctrine or a system of statements but an *activity* (of demarcation, of clarifying). It consists, according to Schlick, of the acts of clarifying and of giving meaning. Wittgenstein's school expresses this*[1] in the concise and memorable words: "It is impossible to speak about language."

Much as this position seems to be entailed by the concept of meaning, it appears inconsistent when we look at Wittgenstein's own view of language, for according to him, statements are states of affairs also; that is, states of affairs that have a projective relationship with those of reality. One should, therefore, assume that those states of affairs of reality that are called "linguistically formulated statements" can themselves be represented. This would be similar to the following situation: for any structure that has a projective relationship with a second structure, we can form a third whose relationship with the first structure is projective and analogous to that of the first with the second.

---

[1] [Cf. Rudolf Carnap, *Der logische Aufbau der Welt* (1928), p. 213. The end of this section can no longer be found and must be presumed lost. Ed.]

*[1] Roughly in the years 1931–1933.

(It should be emphasised that these remarks are not meant to be an acceptance of Wittgenstein's linguistic theory of the projective relationship between a statement and a state of affairs.)

Carnap, in his "*semantics*",[1] developed a position that permits us "to speak about language". Among others, he formulated the "*thesis of semanticism*", holding that every meaningful philosophical statement is a "semantic" one, that is, a statement that speaks about the forms of language.

But Carnap's semantic statements are not *statements of philosophy only*: he shows that the overwhelming majority of all treatises in the individual sciences are of a semantic nature. For example, he analyses one specific paper in physics (the beginning of Einstein's "On the Electrodynamics of Moving Bodies", 1905): the statements he analyses prove, without exception, to be semantic ones. (The only apparent exception is a passage in which physical laws are presented; and even this passage is not an exception, as these laws are presented solely in order to justify and explain a semantic thesis that had just been advanced.) Carnap's analysis is very valuable, describing in brilliant and striking fashion the dogmatic character of Wittgenstein's positivism and its destructive impact on natural science, from which it is alienated. The analysis shows that even scientific papers do not consist entirely of "meaningful" (singular) empirical statements and of natural laws that are of a higher type than the

---

[1] [I suspect that this description of Popper's alludes to an earlier version (1932) of Rudolf Carnap's *Logische Syntax der Sprache* (1934) [English translation by Amethe Smeaton (1937), *The Logical Syntax of Language*, p. xvi. Tr.], mentioned by Carnap at the end of his preface of May 1934, since the description accords closely with § 85 of the published *Syntax*, but not in its terminology. I suspect (see R. Carnap, *Erkenntnis* 3 (1932/1933), pp. 177 ff.; *Logische Syntax der Sprache* (1934), pp. 1 f.) that in the earlier version Carnap used the term "*semantic*" wherever in the subsequent published version he speaks about "*syntax*". Popper remembers that Carnap, in 1932, brought along an early manuscript of the later *Syntax* to Tyrol, but cannot recall any details. Popper's manuscript, which Carnap read at that time (see Karl Popper, *Conjectures and Refutations* (1963), pp. 253 f.; "Intellectual Autobiography", *The Philosophy of Karl Popper* I., ed. Paul Arthur Schilpp (1974), p. 71 = Karl Popper, *Unended Quest: An Intellectual Autobiography* (1976), pp. 89 f.; also "Replies to My Critics", *The Philosophy of Karl Popper* II., ed. P.A. Schilpp (1974), pp. 968 f.), ends with the Appendix of Tables. This would explain his allusion to Carnap's earlier version. Later, Carnap distinguished sharply between *syntax* and *semantics*, and it is important that Popper's references in the present book to Carnap's "semantics" should always be interpreted as references to Carnap's *Syntax*. See Editor's Postscript, Section 2, note 14. Ed.]

singular statements, but also consist of statements of an even higher type also, that is, statements that speak about natural laws, for example, about the relationships between laws. It is quite trivial that "philosophical" statements – such as the statements (decisions) of the general method-ology of the natural sciences – are not, for the most part, of a lower type than those that occur in the scientific papers themselves; and since, according to Carnap, all statements of a higher type than natural laws are called "semantic", there can be no objection to his "thesis of semanticism".

Indeed, all statements that are here called methodological (much like the statements that express Carnap's thinking *about* semantics) should be characterised as statements *about* formal relationships between scientific theoretical systems (or between scientific theories and the singular empirical statements through which the theories are tested). They are, therefore, purely semantic statements in Carnap's sense. (This is not to say that I agree with Carnap's position.) Some general remarks about the language-critical method of Wittgenstein's school seem appropriate here.

Wittgenstein's language-critical method is opposed to the psycho-logical method of the earlier philosophy of knowledge. He rightly notes[2] that his method entails risks similar to those of the earlier method: here too, there is a danger of being diverted from the main path and losing sight of the end in pursuit of the means.

But this end, as demonstrated especially by the preface and conclusion of Wittgenstein's book, is primarily the epistemological end, or the epistemological problem that is here called the demarcation problem. And had Wittgenstein himself, through his thesis that there are no philosophical problems but only scientific ones, not taken a position against this view, one might well have called him the philosopher who – since Kant – has most decisively put the demarcation problem (in the form of the "problem of meaning") at the centre of his philosophical investigations.

In my view, however, he and his school have strayed from this main path. The language-critical method has led logical positivism astray, just as earlier philosophy was led astray by the psychological method. The linguistic critics constantly end up in conflict with positive science, and it

---

[2] [Ludwig Wittgenstein, *Tractatus Logico-Philosophicus* (1918/1922), Proposition 4.1121. Ed.]

is this conflict that forces them to abandon one position after another. The transcendental method is forced on them as a result: instead of using it consciously, they use the language-critical method, of which the transcendental failures are so evident and so constant that this philosophy is finally forced to develop in a direction that more closely agrees with the methodological situation. This development seems obvious to anyone who is aware that all language-critical considerations are disguised conventions. Which linguistic formulations are meaningful and which are meaningless, what is legitimate and what is illegitimate, what is permitted and what is prohibited, cannot be regarded as a property of linguistic constructs in the same way that green is a property of a leaf, or usefulness (or uselessness) is a property of a tool (with regard to a particular purpose). All such labels rest on arbitrary ("grammatical" or "logical" or "semantic") conventions. Only two possible restrictions apply to this arbitrariness: first, an orientation towards colloquial language. This orientation fails at the crucial points, since language critique is, after all, a critique of colloquial language, and it seeks to create more definite, more determinate linguistic usage than the colloquial one. Second, there is an orientation towards the needs and procedures of science. This *transcendental method* is the only one possible for placing restrictions on naive arbitrariness, prejudice and bias when it comes to creating sharper demarcations, conventions and definitions than exist in colloquial language.

Even what the Wittgenstein School calls the language-critical method, therefore, can prove ultimately to consist of no more than transcendental conventions, once it has overcome the naive-naturalist position that some combinations of words are meaningful (legitimate, permitted) by their nature, whereas others are meaningless (illegitimate, not permitted), once again by their nature.

It should not go unmentioned that Wittgenstein's and Schlick's view, namely that philosophy consists of acts of clarification, of imparting meaning and so on, does in a certain sense find its justification in the methodological methods of epistemology also. For it has been shown that only through their application, one that is regulated by methodological decisions, do the terms of natural science acquire a particular "meaning" (and statements acquire thereby, if you will, a particular "sense"). And methodological statements, in so far as they are free decisions, are acts or actions; such decisions, of course, having to be justified in a deductive-transcendental fashion.

(It seems to me that the naturalist view has not been completely over-come in Carnap's "*semantics*".[3] For example, in the most interesting passage as far as the present investigation is concerned, the passage where Carnap deals with the question of falsification, he writes: "Should two mutually contradictory formulae be derivable, then the system must be changed. But there are then no strict rules that would determine, in every instance of inconsistency, which concrete and general formulae should be struck out or changed; for this purpose there are only loose method-ological suggestions." From this approach, Carnap correctly concludes: "There is evidently *no refutation* (falsification) of a law in the strict sense, but only what one might call a practically sufficient refutation." If, in these passages, we replace the naturalist view by the one advocated here, namely that all these relationships can be regulated or altered by methodological decision, instead of "there are then no strict rules" Carnap should obviously have written either "in this situation, for logical reasons, it is not possible to devise strict rules", or "we have, so far, not succeeded in devising strict rules". Similarly, the later passage should have read: "due to the absence of appropriate definitions, there is evidently no refutation . . . in the strict sense". But such a non-naturalist formulation would, at the same time, imply a call for the introduction of appropriate definitions that would secure a refutation; a call that Carnap cannot make, on account of his naturalist approach.)

The critique of the linguistic critique too, therefore, results in a justifi-cation of the call for a deductive-transcendental theory of method.

[3] [See note 1 and Rudolf Carnap, *Logische Syntax der Sprache* (1934) [English translation by Amethe Smeaton (1937), *The Logical Syntax of Language*. Tr.], § 82; cf. also Karl Popper, *Logik der Forschung* (1934; 2nd ed., 1966) [*The Logic of Scientific Discovery* (1959; 2nd ed., 1968). Tr.], Section 10, note 6. Ed.]

[IV.]

THE METHOD OF EXHAUSTION. – "STATE OF AFFAIRS" AND "FACT". – UNIVERSAL DIVERSITY

Eddington[1] says, the mind exhausts;
we can say, theories exhaust.

The term "method of exhaustion" was coined by Dingler.[2] He is probably unique among modern methodologists in forcefully emphasising that we address reality with our theoretical questions, and "exhaust" it with the help of our theories. We capture only those things that find space in our receptacle (the theory).

Conventionalism was able to arrive at this insight because it has,

---

[1] [Cf. Arthur Stanley Eddington, *Das Weltbild der Physik und ein Versuch seiner philosophischen Deutung* (German translation by M. Fr. Rausch v. Traubenberg und H. Diesselhorst, 1931), pp. 237 ff. Ed. [*The Nature of the Physical World* (1928), pp. 239 ff. Tr.]]

[2] [Hugo Dingler, *Grundlinien einer Kritik und exakten Theorie der Wissenschaften insbesondere der Mathematischen* [Outline of a Critique and Exact Theory of the Sciences, the Mathematical Sciences in Particular. Tr.] (1907), pp. 29 f. Ed.]

in principle, nothing to do with inductivism. Within a deliberately deductivist view, this idea can give rise to further consequences.

It was noted above[3] that an individual concept can never be defined by the specification of universal concepts. Contained in this logical fact lies what one might call the irrationality of reality, or the universal diversity of reality.

The impossibility of defining individual concepts by universals alone entails that not even the most precise description of an object, or of an event, allows us to assume that it has determined the object unambiguously. On the contrary: we must assume that even the most precise description we are capable of at a particular time will, in principle, capture an unlimited number of objects or events, for the scope of the class defined by that description will remain fundamentally unrestricted.

This situation can be expressed as follows also: any real-life descriptions we provide will contain a finite number of specifications. Since the class of all objects described by a finite number of specifications is transfinite, a transfinite number of specifications would be necessary to specify an individual concept, or an individual. This fact can be expressed realistically also, by saying that any individual object can be "completely described" by a transfinite number of characteristics only, so that any "actual description" arbitrarily selects from [the] transfinite number of characteristics a finite (and compared with the non-described remainder, a vanishingly small) set of characteristics. Continuing in the realist mode, this situation may be called "universal diversity". Notice, however, that we are dealing with a logical fact; we are merely expressing it in realist form. However uniform our world might be, this "universal diversity" would still exist. It relates to our way of labelling the world only, to the distinction between universal and individual concepts, not to the empirical diversity of real objects.

The relationship that exists between statement and fact is analogous to that between concept and object.

A statement represents a state of affairs. This state of affairs, that which the statement represents, can (according to H. Gomperz[4]) be distinguished from the fact, from the irrational slice of reality to which the

---

[3] [See *Transition to the Theory of Method*, Section 7; cf. also Volume I: Section 33. Ed.]

[4] Heinrich Gomperz, *Weltanschauungslehre* II. (1908), pp. 76 f.

statement refers and of which the state of affairs constitutes a "rational partial moment". (Examples according to Gomperz.[5]) The characteristics of every object can be expressed. Every statement that expresses a characteristic represents a state of affairs.

Just as an object has a transfinite number of characteristics, a fact has a transfinite number of states of affairs as rational partial moments.

This second mode of expression that relates to facts, states of affairs and statements, is without a doubt more important than the first, the one that speaks about objects, characteristics and concepts. But just as an object does not consist of characteristics, and just as the characteristics prove to be applied by us to the object by the fact that (seen logically) they always prove to be selected arbitrarily (from a transfinite set of possible characteristics); states of affairs prove to be rational coordinates that we import into a non-rationalised reality.

Naive inductivist empiricism regards statements as images of reality. It holds that statements represent what is here called "facts"; and [it] ignores the difference between "state of affairs" and "fact".

It regards not facts but states of affairs as – in some sense – "given" or "observable".

A less naive position, one that distinguishes between states of affairs and facts, and if proceeding in inductivist fashion, has to deal with the puzzle of how rational states of affairs emerge from irrational facts.

This is not a fundamental difficulty for deductivism. Its theoretical statements (and so on) are all rational constructions.

For deductivism, a state of affairs proving to be a rational partial moment of a fact means simply that it is possible for facts to be inconsistent with rational states of affairs. Expressed in biological-pragmatist terms: reactions can turn out to be expedient or inexpedient.

---

[5] [Cf. Gomperz, op. cit., pp. 74 ff. Ed.]

[V.]

OUTLINE OF A THEORY OF EMPIRICAL-SCIENTIFIC METHODS (THEORY OF EXPERIENCE)[1]

Principle of falsifiability. Empirical scientific statements or systems of statements are distinguished by being empirically falsifiable.

Singular empirical statements can be empirically verifiable also; theoretical systems, natural laws and universal empirical statements are, in principle, one-sidedly falsifiable only.

The theory of method explains in further detail what is to be understood by "empirical falsification" and "empirical verification". It explains also the conditions (the "methodological decisions") designed to ensure the empirical falsifiability of empirical statements and systems of statements.

1. *Principle of continuity.* So long as any system of hypotheses is to be regarded as not falsified, the application of the following rules

---

[1] [In K_2, written in pencil above this heading:] Freedom from contradiction.

notwithstanding, it is regarded as corroborated. The rule is: all *admissible means* of escaping falsification should be used.

2. *Thesis against strict positivism.* Strict positivism, as we use this term, is the view that natural laws are not universal empirical statements but summary reports only; that is, summaries of singular empirical statements. More precisely, they are truth functions of a finite set of "elementary experiential statements". A methodological decision to restrict the number of attempted tests ([or] falsifications) of a theory, that is, to restrict these attempts numerically, spatially or temporally and to dispense with further falsification attempts, would be equivalent to this view to quite a large degree (but it would take deductivism into consideration). Such a decision could bring about a symmetry of truth values: the theory would not be falsifiable only, but definitively verifiable also. This "strictly positivist turn" of deductivism is eliminated by the following methodological decision:

The series of falsification attempts is, in principle, unlimited. (No attempted falsification is designated the last one.)

This principle should secure the (*one-sided*) *non-verifiability* (the *asymmetry* of truth values) for theoretical systems.

It is only through this principle that the "strict universality" of "universal empirical statements" (theoretical systems) is secured (these two versions being equivalent). Put another way, this principle is an instruction for the use of "all" statements (it regulates the use of those statements through which the word "all" is implicitly defined).

3. *First thesis against conventionalism: principle of system closure.* Falsification of a theoretical system can always be avoided by introducing an auxiliary hypothesis. If we want to ensure falsifiability through methodological decisions, these decisions must restrict the introduction of auxiliary hypotheses. The first of these restrictions can be expressed as the "principle of system closure":

The axiomatic system of an "empirical theory" is closed, that is, the introduction of a [new] theoretical axiom (not deducible from the system) is equivalent to *falsification* of the theoretical system.

The introduction of a new axiom may only, therefore, be carried out in accordance with the rules (to be stated later) for the reconstruction of a falsified theory.

Whereas the thesis against "strict positivism" (as a user instruction for "all" statements) ensures the asymmetry or non-verifiability of theories, the "principle of system closure" provides, as it were, the first half of a working definition for the concept of the "*falsification*" of a theoretical system.

4. *Second thesis against conventionalism: principle of restricting singular auxiliary assumptions (ad hoc hypotheses)*. Even a closed system of theoretical axioms can always escape falsification, for falsification occurs when derived (*singular*) *consequences* fail to take place. But their derivation always requires the introduction (in addition to the universal theoretical major premises) of a *singular minor premise*. Now, without using a singular minor premise, the derivation can always be taken to the point where this singular minor premise need only take the form: *hic et nunc* there is a case that belongs to the class of cases legitimately substitutable in the derived rule.[1] The assertion of the *hic et nunc* statement that this substitution is admissible can always be disputed; in this way, however, one disputes the admissibility of the derivation of the consequence, whose falsification, therefore, can no longer falsify the theoretical system.

The statements used to deny the admissibility of the substitution can be universal or singular statements. Examples: (universal statement) All measuring rods contract in a gravitational field; (singular statement) This measuring rod is incorrect.

Universal statements of this kind must either be derivable from the axioms of the system or constitute a new, non-derivable axiom, that is, they must be treated in accordance with the "principle of system closure". Singular statements of this kind, pertaining to the singular minor premises only, may be called "ad hoc hypotheses".

Ad hoc hypotheses are mostly assertions of the kind that the measuring instruments are faulty, that the observer is suffering from hallucinations or simply that an error has occurred.

Ad hoc hypotheses are admissible under some conditions; their use is not prohibited but only restricted in particular ways by methodological decisions. This restriction follows already from the "principle of system

---

[1] Cf. "Excerpt", p. 20 [= Appendix: Section VIII, A. First approximation of the method].

closure", which would be inapplicable in the absence of such a restriction, or from the distinction between singular ad hoc hypotheses and universal auxiliary assumptions, the latter being subject to the principle of system closure. If the use of ad hoc hypotheses were to be unrestricted, such use would be equivalent to using a universal auxiliary assumption, that is, it would serve as a means of circumventing the principle of system closure. (One might, for example, in any given case, replace the universal auxiliary assumption "All measuring instruments show false results under such and such conditions" with the ad hoc hypothesis "This particular measuring instrument shows false results in this particular case.") The following methodological decision must be introduced in order to eliminate this circumvention:

Ad hoc hypotheses are admissible if and only if their non-universal, singular character is demonstrable; more precisely: if their possible direct generalisations are falsified.

Example: the ad hoc hypothesis "This (otherwise accurate) clock showed the wrong time under such and such conditions", or "This (otherwise accurately observing) individual hallucinated (or lied) under such and such conditions", can only be recognised as admissible ad hoc hypotheses if the universal statement "All (otherwise accurate) clocks show the wrong time under such and such conditions", or "All (otherwise accurately observing) individuals hallucinate (or lie) under such and such conditions", can be taken to be falsified, that is, refuted by counter-examples.

If an ad hoc hypothesis was shown to be admissible (non-universal), the derivation of the singular consequence in question may be considered invalid; the particular case in question, therefore, loses its scientific meaning. Such a procedure seems all the more justified as the working rule for the admissibility of ad hoc hypotheses, as quoted above, implicitly contains the condition that repeat tests must be performed.

It is an important point that every time the introduction of an ad hoc hypothesis becomes necessary, the whole system appears to be in doubt; namely, until the admissibility of the ad hoc hypothesis seems secured by the appropriate falsification attempts.

The principle of the restriction of ad hoc hypotheses, together with the principle of continuity, seems to ensure the *objectivity* of falsification; in other words, the theory should only be considered falsified if its falsification is, in principle, testable.

At the same time, this principle of restriction provides, so to speak, the second half of the working definition for the concept of a theoretical system's falsification; for it assigns a privileged status to a negative appraisal, or falsification. If, based on the principle of continuity and with the help of ad hoc hypotheses, one attempts to avoid falsification, this will only be successful if another hypothesis, the *generalised* ad hoc hypothesis (which is subject to the continuity principle also), can in turn be falsified. The avoidance of falsification, in turn, rests therefore on (another) falsification. If this second falsification fails, the first will come into effect. As a result of this methodological stipulation, that is, of the principle of the restriction of ad hoc hypotheses, the "conventionalist objection to falsifiability" has been defeated completely. Provided that a system permits the derivation of empirically testable consequences in the first place, the objection that this system is, in principle, not falsifiable has been shown (through the principle of the restriction of ad hoc hypotheses) to be inconsistent. This principle provides a working definition of the concept of "falsification", such that the non-falsifiability of any hypothesis (including of a generalised ad hoc hypothesis) would entail the falsifiability of other hypotheses (that is, the falsification of the original axiomatic system). Clearly, this is contradictory.[2]

---

[2] [Here follow, in K_1, these three handwritten notes:]

[A] We can, therefore, say: a theory is falsifiable if, for at least one of its derived statements of a lower degree of universality, there is a) a statement that contradicts it, and b) a procedure that allows crucial experiments to be performed.

[B] A theory can only be refuted by a *singular* statement if this singular statement is intersubjectively testable at any time, for example, by examining a museum piece (including the certificates associated with it, and suchlike).

[C] If a (corroborated) *universal* statement a that has refuted a theory T is refuted in turn, this does not imply the rehabilitation of the original theory T; statement a must, in turn, be incorporated into the reconstruction, just like the statements that corroborate T.

PART TWO

FRAGMENTS 1933

ORIENTATION

The situation in contemporary philosophy is characterised by the opposition between the proponents of "*metaphysics*" and those of "*anti-metaphysics*".

The question at the centre of this controversy is the one about the relationship between philosophy and the empirical sciences.

The metaphysician is quite wary of empirical science. Recent upheavals in the natural sciences in particular, having rocked the very foundations of their systems, strike him as an alarming symptom of an internal crisis, as a consequence of the alienation of empirical research from its philosophical basis; for only philosophy can provide the ultimate justification of empirical science.

The anti-metaphysician admires the rapid developments in modern natural science. It appears to him that the more profoundly these developments rock its foundations, the more powerful its empirical, non-philosophical character will become. Empirical science seems to be freeing itself from the inhibiting prejudices of its metaphysical past. In the attitude of metaphysics towards modern natural science, the anti-metaphysician can see only uncomprehending presumptuousness. Empirical science is autonomous. It needs no philosophy to provide it with any "foundations". There is no longer any need for a philosophical science superordinate to the individual sciences. The supposed problems of philosophy prove to be meaningless or even nonsensical pseudo-problems. Much like Kant[1] ("philosophy can never be learned . . . we can at most learn to *philosophise*"), although more radically, the anti-metaphysician declares that philosophy is not a body of doctrine but an activity.[2]

The task of this philosophical activity is the struggle against metaphysics, against philosophy as a body of doctrine. Its intended result is not the construction of a new philosophy: the goal of this struggle is to leave the construction of theories to natural science alone. Even though this kind of philosophising does not seek to construct a theory, indeed it strongly opposes the construction of any philosophical theory, it would be quite superficial to characterise it as destructive or as anything of that sort: rather than combating any position, it shows that such a position never even existed. And this is why it fights not for the recognition of a new position, but for the promotion of a new mental attitude: the attitude of saying what can be said; of saying what is and what is not; and of remaining silent about the inexpressible.

[1] [Cf. Immanuel Kant, *Kritik der reinen Vernunft* (2nd ed., 1787), pp. 865 f. Ed.; English translation by N. Kemp Smith (1929), 1965. *Critique of Pure Reason*, p. 657. Tr.]

[2] [Cf. Ludwig Wittgenstein, *Tractatus Logico-Philosophicus* (1918/1922), Proposition 4.112. Ed.]

[VI.]

PHILOSOPHY

[Introduction.] Is there a philosophical science? Are there, beside the empirical sciences, beside logic and mathematics, other sciences that have a specific, a "philosophical" character?

I believe that to pose the question is to answer it. By speaking *about* empirical science, *about* logic and mathematics, about the relationships between these sciences, by asking whether there is a "science", we have already constituted a system of concepts that belong to a domain we should probably have to identify as "philosophy". The concept "empirical science" is not a concept of empirical science. The concept "logic" is not a concept of logic. The concept "mathematics" is not a concept of mathematics. All these concepts belong to a theory of science.

It would seem obvious, furthermore, that the concept of a "theory of science" cannot be a concept of the theory of science. And this is quite true. We arrive at a kind of hierarchy of analytical types, each one investigating the nature of the type subordinate to it.[*1] But this does not create a problem: we are not facing an infinite regression, for the truth of the statements that belong to the subordinate science is not deduced from

---

[*1] Evidently, what I had in mind was a hierarchy of metatheories. I wrote this passage, apparently, before I became acquainted with the expressions "metalanguage" and "metascience".

that of the superordinate one. Each of these sciences has to fend for itself. (Compare Nelson's critique.[1])

We can take the name "philosophy" to mean a whole variety of things; and these surely include metaphysical speculation. Our thesis is the following. We assert that something like a philosophical science exists also, that it is a theory of science, and that its main task is to investigate what science is ("science" here in the sense of the sciences subordinate to it). In summary, "scientific philosophy" is a science of demarcation.[2]

It follows from this idea that scientific philosophy is *methodology*, as we believe our investigation has demonstrated already.

I wish to go further even: I assert that almost all those endeavours that have ever been deemed philosophical, that is to say, scientific-philosophical, were either methodological endeavours or metaphysical hypostatisations of methodological arguments.[3] Indeed, this idea proves to be a most productive heuristic principle for the discovery of method-ological arguments and for the illumination of supposed philosophical problems.

In speaking here about philosophy, namely about philosophy as methodology, as the science of demarcation, we find ourselves already, so to speak, standing on a higher level (and by stating this fact, we move up one level again), and so on *ad infinitum*. We reached this level earlier, in our investigation into the nature of methodology.[4] In so far as we never need to come to an agreement about methodological issues, philosophy as methodology is not an empirical science, for it is practical behaviour, practical evaluation, that motivates philosophy, or methodology. It is, therefore, neither an empirical science nor pure logic; one might call it metaphysics (on account of its objective non-decidability), but it would be better to reserve this expression for those undecidable assertions that have a theoretical character, that is to say, those that claim to represent facts, but without the clear insight of drawing the boundaries convention-ally and arbitrarily, guided by value judgements only. (Even transcen-dental corroboration starts off from value judgements about the sciences;

[1] [See Volume I: Section 11, text to notes 42 and 43. Ed.]

[2] [Cf. Volume II (Fragments): Draft of an Introduction, Section 7. Ed.]

[3] [CF. Karl Popper, *Logik der Forschung* (1934; 2nd ed., 1966) [*The Logic of Scientific Discovery* (1959; 2nd ed., 1968). Tr.], Section 11, note 3; see also Editor's Postscript. Ed.]

[4] [See Volume II (Fragments: [III.] Transition to the Theory of Method. Ed.]

they are acknowledged to be sciences and successful ones. Things are somewhat different with regard to what we call "dialectical corroboration" only: it causes open problems to vanish, which shows that these problems have arisen on the assumption of equal valuation. For even a shared valuation basis can give rise to problems, but such questions only that are solvable in this case on the basis of shared valuation.)

1. *The problem of induction and the problem of demarcation.* Kant was probably the first philosopher who placed the demarcation between empirical science and metaphysics at the centre of his philosophical considerations, albeit without precise formulation or clear awareness. We shall not discuss his attempted solution in further detail, but instead emphasise one idea only: that of the doctrine of the antinomies. Its underlying idea, if we get rid of some formalistic and other restrictions, is that one can debate metaphysical assertions *ad infinitum* without reaching any conclusion. Kant does not go so far as to declare that for *any given* metaphysics, it is always possible to construct a counter-metaphysics and to show that no decision can be reached between these two mutually contradictory entities; but elaborating his ideas would lead to this outcome.

We can regard this endless debate between metaphysical opponents, this possibility of constructing an antithesis to any thesis and a rebuttal to this antithesis, as the hallmark of the metaphysical nature of an assertion. The occurrence of such antinomy motivates us not to resolve it (as Kant still attempted to do), but to reject the whole question as metaphysical: anyone is welcome to try his hand, and perhaps will manage to recast the question in non-metaphysical terms that render this new, modified question decidable.

The antinomous nature of metaphysics is not used here directly for definitional purposes; it follows from our demarcation criterion of falsifiability. If a theoretical, that is, non-verifiable statement is unfalsifiable also, it must be possible always to adduce a statement that contradicts it and is unfalsifiable also. For if that contradicting statement were falsified, the statement it contradicts would be verified thereby. Here lies the root of the antinomous nature of metaphysics.[1]

The view that philosophy is a science of demarcation and that the demarcation problem is its main problem is supported decisively by our

---

[1] [Cf. Volume I: Section 10, text to note 6; see also Editor's Postscript. Ed.]

ability to show that the problem of induction can be reduced to that of demarcation: for the inductivist prejudice arises as a result only of demanding, or hoping, that theories be verified; and the hope of verification is born of the belief that it is the only way of escaping endless metaphysical argument. Inductivism has always been motivated by the idea of clinging to direct experience in order to avoid slipping into metaphysics. But this endeavour is what inevitably has plunged it into the wildest metaphysical adventures: induction without synthetic *a priori* judgements is unthinkable.

In its efforts to hold fast to certainty, to start from subjective convictions, inductivism was thrust into another adventure, that of subjectivism, and finally even into solipsism, albeit one moderated by the adjective "methodical".[2] Science, however, requires not certainty but only successful predictions; not convictions but objective testability. We can show, therefore, that the two main problems of the *Critique of Pure Reason*, that is to say, Hume's problem of induction and Kant's problem of demarcation from metaphysics, are *one and the same*: the problem of demarcation. That is how Hume would have seen the problem of induction also; at least, he sees demarcation as the task of philosophy.[3]

[2] [See Hans Driesch, *Ordnungslehre: Ein System des nichtmetaphysischen Teiles der Philosophie* [*Theory of Order: a System of the Non-Metaphysical Part of Philosophy*. Tr.] (2nd ed., 1923), p. 23; Rudolf Carnap, *Der logische Aufbau der Welt* (1928) [*The Logical Structure of the World*. Tr.], pp. 86 f. Cf. also Karl Popper, *Conjectures and Refutations* (1963), pp. 265 ff. Ed.]

[3] [See Karl Popper, *Logik der Forschung* (1934; 2nd ed., 1966) [*The Logic of Scientific Discovery* (1959; 2nd ed., 1968). Tr.], Section 4, note 2, and text to this note, also the new note *3 and text, in which the last page of David Hume's *Enquiry concerning Human Understanding* (1748) is quoted. Ed.]

[VII.]

THE PROBLEM OF
METHODOLOGY

1. *Methodology and the possibility of falsification.* We began by examining
theoretical statements, in order to see whether by virtue of their logical
form they permit strict verification through singular statements. This has
proved not to be the case. Instead of trying, as it were, to circumvent this
negative result and replace a strict form of verification with a more relaxed
form, which would have entangled us in the difficulties of the problem of
induction, we abandoned the idea of verification in any form and turned
to falsification. It seems to us that falsification attempts offer the only
possibility of testing a theory empirically.

We had to turn to a logical investigation of the falsifiability of a theory.
We were able to develop falsifiability as a relationship between a theory
and its possible empirical basic statements. This shifted the question
logically to the problem of basic statements.

By introducing the concept of a "falsifying hypothesis",[1] we were able
to make falsification, to some extent, independent of the basic statements.

---

[1] [Cf. Karl Popper, *Logik der Forschung* (1934; 2nd ed. 1966) [*The Logic of Scientific
Discovery* (1959; 2nd ed., 1968). Tr.], Section 22; see also Editor's Postscript. Ed.]

But always, of course, the basic statements and the problems associated with them remained in the background.

In order to resolve these problems, we had to introduce methodological rules the task of which was to limit the arbitrariness that is, in a sense, unavoidable in decisions that deal with basic statements.[2]

It seems that in the end, the whole problem has shifted to the question of these methodological rules. How would it be possible to justify these rules?

We can arrive at the same question in a slightly different way.

We started, in the immediately preceding paragraphs, from the logical prerequisites of falsifiability, and have seen that in pursuing them we were forced into the domain of methodology. Even though we consider this to be at the core of the whole issue, there is no doubt that in addition to a logical aspect, the question has its practical aspect also. It has been emphasised many times, probably by Duhem[3] first, that the difficulties associated with the empirical testing of theories involve not the positive aspect of the question only, namely verification, but falsification also. The main reason is that the retrospective falsification of theoretical assumptions through the falsification of derived consequences, that is to say, *modus tollens*, affects all the deductive assumptions equally. As a result, the decision as to which of these assumptions to regard as falsified and which as upheld*[1] is always a largely arbitrary one.

Whether or not this view is justified, it should be stressed, at any rate, that the asserted asymmetry between verification and falsification cannot be affected by such arguments, be the difficulties encountered by the idea

---

[2] [Cf. Volume I: Section 11 towards the end; see also note 6 and Editor's Postscript. Ed.]

[3] [Pierre Duhem, *Ziel und Struktur der physikalischen Theorien* (German translation by Friedrich Adler, 1908), pp. 243 ff., 266 f. Ed.; English translation by Philip P. Wiener (1954), *The Aim and Structure of Physical Theory*, pp. 183 ff., 199 f. Tr.]

*[1] In the British and North American literature of the philosophy of science, the logical problems discussed in this and in the following two sections are known as the "Duhem–Quine thesis". Quine and myself discovered these problems independently of each other and of Duhem, and we both established Duhem's priority independently of each other. Later (in *Logik der Forschung* (1934)) I forgot some of the things I had discovered about Duhem; or perhaps they fell victim to the radical cuts, and this was what made me forget about them. [Cf. Volume I: Section 38, text to note 2. See also Willard Van Orman Quine, "Two Dogmas of Empiricism", *The Philosophical Review* 60 (1951), pp. 38 ff.; Quine, *From a Logical Point of View* (1953; 2nd ed., 1961), pp. 41 ff. Ed.]

of falsification for the reasons stated above insurmountable or not. They are, in any event, of an entirely different kind from those that arise for verification. Verification is logically impossible, whereas falsification will, at worst, face practical impossibilities. This is evident from the fact that in the inductivist direction (that is, from singular statements to universal statements), *modus tollens* functions as a strictly logical inference, but there is no *modus ponens* proceeding in this direction.

But even if the logical asymmetry asserted by us were to be conceded, one might still argue [against us] that this asymmetry does not hold in practice, that the practical constraints compensate for the logical ones. In any experiment that we conduct in order to test a theory, so many theoretical assumptions come into play that it is almost impossible to analyse them all. Whenever we read a dial, we rely on the hypotheses of geometrical optics: the hypothesis of rigid bodies, the hypothesis that Euclidean theory is valid in small regions, the "thing hypothesis" and a large number of others. From a logical viewpoint, falsification prejudices all these assumptions in the same way: not that each individual assumption is falsified by the falsification of a derived consequence, but their simultaneous assertion – their conjunction – is falsified. The trouble is that on account of the fundamental impossibility of verification, we can never know which of these assumptions it is; *any* of them may be the one that is falsified.

The situation is alleviated, admittedly, by "quasi-induction";[4] or more generally, by the possibility of showing that falsification affects only certain assumptions that are additional to a basic set. When those supplementary assumptions are left out, no falsification takes place. This circumstance is certainly not unimportant, but it cannot greatly alter the fundamental indeterminacy; for we cannot doubt that sometimes it is possible to save the supplementary assumption by modifying the basic set. This situation explains why, according to some, the possibility of falsification is sufficiently remote for unambiguous, strict falsification of a theory to be ruled out.

This is the point of departure for our methodological considerations.

To contrast the approach discussed above with ours: we consider it entirely misguided to view the conditions under which theories are tested, and similar situations encountered in science, practically from such

---

[4] [Cf. Volume I: Section 48, note 2 and text to this note; see also Editor's Postscript. Ed.]

a natural-scientific [naturalistic[5]] position, as we prefer to call it, and to take cognisance of particular difficulties or problems in the *same* way that one would take cognisance of natural laws, for example. It is, we admit, quite possible to take such a position vis-à-vis the methods of natural science, to define our task as examining the situation purely descriptively and acknowledging the facts. This would not, however, be an investigation conducted within the theory of science. (It should, instead, be called an investigation within the sociology of science.)

The task of the theory of science, or of methodology, as understood here, is completely different. We proceed along an analytic-descriptive path as long as we are investigating logical circumstances. Elsewhere, we assume that it is largely in our power to influence the circumstances and to conduct science according to a method we consider useful.

Applied to our problem: the logical asymmetry between verification and falsification is fundamental for us. It exists for universal statements only, but not fully for basic statements. In fact, where basic statements are concerned, we can only speak about such asymmetry at all if the basic statements are assumed to make empirical decisions possible. With basic statements, it is within our power to proceed in such a way, that is, to establish methodological rules by arbitrary decision, that the statements, even if not verifiable, at least become one-sidedly decidable, namely falsifiable.

And in a way similar to the one with which we solve the basic statement problems, by cutting through the Gordian knot, as it were, with the help of our methodological decisions, so we have to defend falsifiability by means of our methodological decisions against the objections of Duhem and of other conventionalist thinkers.

In our investigation of the basic statement problems, we justified the effect of particular methodological decisions by showing that the introduction of some decisions is necessary, indeed unavoidable: since the derivation [of further basic statements] would never bring the infinite "regression" to a *natural* conclusion, we must impose an arbitrary conclusion if only because, in science, we have other things to do besides continuously investigating questions that have been answered with

---

[5] [Cf. Karl Popper, *Logik der Forschung* (1934; 2nd ed., 1966) [*The Logic of Scientific Discovery* (1959; 2nd ed., 1968). Tr.], Section 10; see also Volume II (Fragments): [III.] *Transition to the Theory of Method*, Section 8, note 1 (p. 413), and text to this note. Ed.]

sufficient precision already, at least for practical purposes.[6] Similarly, we can defend ourselves adequately against Duhem's conventionalist objection, as outlined above, with the realisation that we can make no progress at all without general methodological guidelines to regulate our procedures and our treatment of natural laws.

The following is an especially trivial example of the necessity of such methodological guidelines:

We tend to take it for granted that once a theory has been introduced and as long as it has not been rejected, we test it over and over again, especially if improved measurement accuracy or extension of the theory's range of applications create new testing opportunities. This scientific tradition, which a naturalistically inclined methodologist is likely to over-look or at best note in passing, conceals a practical methodological rule; as does any practical attitude towards science. This can be seen most easily in the fact that we might have adopted the procedure of testing a theory just *once* (or not at all), and decided to be content with that. Such a procedure would be, of course, "not in the spirit of science", it would be "unscientific". But these are words only. What we want to show here is that when examined logically, this "spirit of science" can be captured by practical methodological rules for a practical attitude towards science.

Methodological rules, therefore, can be regarded as defining what is meant by scientific conduct. But are we not, once again, adopting a naturalistic perspective? Are we not forced to construe the methodological rules from the actual, observable behaviour of scientists?

2. *The demarcation criterion and the theory of method.* We believe that we can, in fact, avoid a naturalistic conception of scientific methods. We want to attempt a deductive derivation of the scientific methods from the assumption that our theory is correct, that is, essentially [from the assumption] of the demarcation criterion.

The criterion of demarcation is, in essence, nothing but a definition of what we want to call "science" and of what we want to call "meta-physics". If the methodology is meant to describe the scientific spirit naturalistically, as it were, it could proceed deductively also; that is, attempt to derive that description systematically from some hypothesis. To

---

[6] [Cf. Volume I: Section 11 towards the end; Appendix: Section IX; Karl Popper, *op. cit.*, Sections 29 and 30. See also Editor's Postscript. Ed.]

this end, a useful hypothesis might be that the task of science is to erect a theoretical edifice as far removed from metaphysics as possible. This naturalistic, deductive theory of method would have to derive the greatest possible abundance of implications from its hypothesis, and could test these implications against the actual methodological conduct of scientists; against methodological experience, so to speak.

But we reject such a scientific [or naturalistic] method for the methodology. Put briefly, we do not want to accept an empirical decision based on the scientist's actual behaviour. We do not want to derive everything that a scientist does in practice, but those methods only that lead him *to success.*

Even though we do link a deductive theory of method to the demarcation criterion in the way indicated above, we view this theory not in an empiricist or naturalistic fashion but as a fairly practical doctrine, one that is corroborated if it is successful in practice.

What is the nature of scientific success? We decline to believe that such a question can be answered theoretically. We assert that the answer will depend on what we regard as scientifically valuable. The theory of method, therefore, is a discipline based on particular scientific values, or to put it more plainly, on particular scientific goals or objectives. There can be very different scientific goals or objectives. I regard a rational decision between them as impossible. One might regard the goal of science, for example, as consisting in the production of a theory that is as certain as possible, perhaps even one that is absolutely certain. To those who pursue such goals, developments in physics since the early twentieth century must appear as the collapse of science. It is not difficult to fend off such a collapse by means of methodological decisions; one decides to hold on, under all circumstances, to a particular system that has been singled out as useful and simple, and to supplement it, but where necessary only, with auxiliary hypotheses. This, near enough, is Dingler's conventionalism.[1] We do not wish to oppose such an appraisal through a naturalistic appeal to the evident fact that today's science is not conducted like that. When confronted by such a naturalistic objection we would, on

[1] [Cf. Hugo Dingler, *Die Grundlagen der Physik: Synthetische Prinzipien der mathematischen Naturphilosophie* [*The Foundations of Physics: Synthetic Principles of Mathematical Natural Philosophy*. Tr.] (2nd ed., 1923); Dingler, *Der Zusammenbruch der Wissenschaft und der Primat der Philosophie* [*The Collapse of Science and the Primacy of Philosophy*. Tr.] (1926). Ed.]

the contrary, side with Dingler and agree with his view that it is always in our power to determine what the ultimate foundation should be; this choice can never be imposed on us, in primitive fashion, by the facts. If, nonetheless, we are on the side of modern natural science, this is not because science is, in fact, the way it is, but (in rough and ready terms) because we like it the way it is. Our *valuation* differs from that of Dingler. Our goal is not a system of securely founded knowledge; what we seek to do is to penetrate ever more deeply into the undreamt-of connections within nature. We are never more certain of having taken a step towards this goal than when we succeed in refuting, in a surprising way, a statement that hitherto had been considered certain.

We approve of the methods of modern science not because they are modern but because, with their bold theories, they lead us to new empirical insights, to unexpected basic statements that may even have been seen as inconceivable, insights we would never have gained without these grandiose, simple theories that border on the paradoxical and on the contradictory.

Nothing can support our valuation other than the fact that it accords with our overall world view, with the biological role that science plays in this view. Science is our farthest outpost, it is the pioneer of adaptation; therefore it has to be exposed to the process of selection. And if modern science corresponds, to a substantial degree, to our methodological ideal of a science (it is far from identical with it, as is clear from our non-naturalistic fundamental position), this is easily explained, in our world view, as an effect of natural selection.

We share with conventionalism, therefore, the position that the ultimate foundations of all knowledge should be sought in an act of free determination, that is, in pursuing a goal that is, in itself, no longer rationally justifiable. This, in a different form, is Kant's idea of the primacy of practical reason.

[VIII.]

COMMENTS ON THE SO-CALLED PROBLEM OF FREE WILL

[1. *Introduction.*] The supposed problem of free will emerges with full force within a "deterministic" world view only, that is, where physics (to put it a little simplistically) draws a picture of the world that resembles the movement of a clock. Modern quantum physics, with its "non-deterministic" probability statements, seems more likely to blur the problem of free will than to solve it. More precisely, this blurring of the problem is caused not by physics itself, of course, but by impermissible interpretations.

I believe that we shall gain a much clearer understanding of the question of free will, if we stand back completely from contemporary physics and ask ourselves how the problem would appear if we imagined a completely deterministic physics.

Let us pose the problem as specifically as possible, if only in an "*ad hominem*" fashion. If, as a consequence of a deterministic world view, we regarded the creations of Bach or of Michelangelo, for example, as nothing but the outcomes of necessary physical processes, the products of an automatic physical apparatus, something in us would rebel against accepting such a consequence. If we imagined all the physical processes in the world as determined by the constellation of initial conditions and natural laws, then whether we liked it or not we would have to assume that the works of Bach and of Michelangelo were contained in them already in *nuce*, that is, we would find ourselves almost irretrievably within a metaphysics of pre-established harmony.

This, however, is merely one aspect of the problem. Sometimes we experience immediate situations when we feel that something depends on our decision, whereas at other times we feel clearly that our decisions and actions are conditioned by a variety of external circumstances. The feeling that our decisions are important tends to occur in those cases when, as one usually says, we become conscious of having a clear "responsibility". Although, on sober reflection, this subjective feeling does not seem to me to play as large a part in the problem of free will as the considerations suggested earlier, we would have to require from a satisfactory formulation that it adequately take account of the problem of "responsibility".

It appears to us possible, without assuming a non-deterministic physics, to offer a satisfactory solution to the problems outlined above. Indeed, if we assumed a non-deterministic physics, we should find ourselves in the alarming situation of easily "solving" more than we intended to solve. If we were to eliminate the "causal connection" between our experiences, decisions and so on, we should obtain a theory of "free will" but never one of responsibility, for responsibility assumes the existence of *accountability*, and breaking the causal experiential chain would, in general, imply non-accountability only.

It seems to me that the way to treat this problem is foreshadowed by the positivist critique of the concept of causality.[1]

The historical, metaphysical concept of causality is closely associated, when regarded historically, with that of *genesis*, of generation, of calling into being, of creation by *someone out of something*. The German word Ur-sache,[+1] the Ionian speculation about a primordial substance, these and similar ideas point clearly to this method of "explanation". Our instinctive attitude also towards natural events contains still a distinct animistic element. This causal instinct, as we might call it, implies a kind of empathy

---

[1] [In the manuscript, this paragraph begins "P. 18 ..."; the editor was unable to interpret this reference. Ed.]

[+1] [See Volume I, Section 11, note [+2], and text to this note. Tr.]

with causes: the cause is regarded as active, as a human agent, it "brings forth the effect".

The critique of this animistic conception of causality, one that continues to play a part in modern philosophy, is very old. Beginning with the sceptical physician Sextus Empiricus around 200 CE, albeit building on some preparatory work by his predecessors, and continuing with the Arab Al-Gazzâlî in the eleventh century CE, Nicolaus of Autrecourt in the fourteenth, Malebranche and Joseph Glanvill in the seventeenth and so on down to Hume, the critics of the concept of causality emphasise that claiming a causal necessity in the sequence of events cannot be justified either logically or empirically: we can never observe that one event causes another, only that *one event of this type tends to follow regularly after an event of that other type.*

Following on from this concept of causality as reformed by positivist concepts, in this book we have adopted the position also that we shall speak about "causality" and so on in the sense of being able to predict an event from natural laws and from initial conditions, and in this sense only. If, according to this view, we want to speak about two events being in a "causal relationship", this can mean only that by relying on a law together with the first event, we can infer the second.*1

It seems to me that the implications of this view of causality solve, almost by themselves, the supposed problem of free will; we need only be resolute in drawing all the implications.

In the view just described, the deterministic hypothesis can be characterised as follows: we assume that every event can be predicted to an arbitrary degree of accuracy, even though we might not yet know all the natural laws necessary for doing so; provided, of course, that the statements about the "causing event", about the initial conditions to be substituted, are sufficiently precise.

2. *The "event" and the "slice of reality".* The view described above makes it clear that we can infer from statements (natural laws, statements about events) to statements (predictions about events) only.

---

*1 This is a formulation of what nowadays is called the "deductive model" of causal explanation. See also *Logik der Forschung* (1934; 2nd ed., 1966) [*The Logic of Scientific Discovery* (1959; 2nd ed., 1968). Tr.], Section 12. What is there called "boundary condition" ("initial conditions" would have been better), here seems to be called "first event".

Every statement leaves some latitude for "reality". If we want to avoid a metaphysical-realist mode of expression, this can be worded formally also in the following way: every existential statement, however detailed, is logically compatible with an arbitrarily large number of possible existential statements; and among these, in turn, there is an arbitrary [arbitrarily large] number of existential statements that are spatially-temporally adjacent to the first existential statement, this adjacency being of arbitrarily close proximity.

There exists, therefore, neither an existential statement nor any conjunction of such statements that would unambiguously describe to us even the smallest "slice of reality" (that is, a spatial-temporal region). Instead, every such statement only provides, as it were, answers to questions that happen to interest us at the time. And whereas we can, in principle, [answer a finite number of questions only, we can always] "conceive" of an infinite number of questions, or state rules and schemata according to which an unlimited number of questions about some spatial-temporal region can be constructed. We can, consequently, say also that only a vanishingly small part of all possible questions can be posed and answered.

This is what we describe intuitively when we say that even the most precise description leaves some latitude for reality. We might add that even the most precise description can never reduce this latitude noticeably: speaking metaphorically, this could be achieved by an infinite number of statements only.

[IX.]

THE PROBLEM OF FREE WILL[1]

5. *Individuals and universals*. Even though we can never provide anything approaching a complete description of a "slice of reality", we can always give it a name; we can characterise it in individual terms. Here, once again, we encounter the problem of universals. We have established already[2] that it is impossible to replace an individual concept, or to identify an individual unambiguously, by any number of universals. We encounter the same opposition in the relationship between "event" and "slice of reality"; for if we could describe a "slice of reality" unambiguously, we could replace its name by a description.

Every scientifically predictable event must, in principle, be repeatable, or reproducible: this is a fundamental requirement that follows from the principle of scientific objectivity. An event, viewed as "a slice of reality", is fundamentally individual, can be named only, and is, therefore,

---

[1] [Sections 1–4 can no longer be found and must be presumed lost; see Editor's Postscript. Ed.]
[2] [See Volume I: Section 33; Volume II (Fragments): [III.] *Transition to the Theory of Method*, Section 7. Ed.]

unrepeatable in principle. Compared with concrete individuals, our scientific descriptions are nothing more than abstract extracts.

The image of a net of theories by means of which we seek to capture reality[3] confronts us here for the last time, and in an entirely different form: the net has holes, and they are so large that any amount of reality can escape. However fine the mesh, reality is finer still. Only the coarsest pieces are caught in the net.

We wish to show that in all those moments when the problem of free will seems to us relevant, we always are dealing with individual events in all their uniqueness.

First, the Bach example. We readily concede that every *describable partial event* during the conception and the writing [of the composition] is, in principle, repeatable. But nobody assumes that there will be two identical Bachs or two identical compositions. The assertion, which alone could be considered deterministic, that an identical individual placed in the same situation would react in the same way, is fundamentally untestable, therefore, at the very points we are concerned with; it is causal metaphysics. Two events at different times cannot be completely identical (at least, according to the deterministic view), if only because the second is influenced by the first. And if we assume that each lies outside the other's sphere of influence, identity in the deterministic sense would be conceivable but there would remain the objection that this identity can extend only as far as does our description. The deterministic approach leads to the necessary assumption that there exist several spheres of influence, completely separated from each other but otherwise absolutely identical; an assumption that betrays its metaphysical character clearly enough. If the spheres of influence are not completely separated, determinism can never establish an identity even as a hypothesis, not even where the description fails to identify a difference.

---

[3] [Cf. Novalis: "Hypotheses are nets, only he who casts will catch . . .", *Novalis Schriften* II. (ed. Friedrich Schlegel and Ludwig Tieck, 1802), Dialogue 5, p. 429; Karl Popper, *Logik der Forschung* (1934; 2nd ed., 1966) [*The Logic of Scientific Discovery* (1959; 2nd ed., 1968), Tr.], p. 11. See also Editor's Postscript. Ed.] *I had this image of a net of theories long before I discovered it – to my happy surprise – in Novalis. But it seems that this passage does allude to Novalis.

All that is individual, therefore, in so far as it is individual, appears as scientifically non-describable.*[1]

This leads to the conclusion that there is no conflict between the view that everything describable is predictable, and the view that everything individual is non-predictable.

6. *The doctrine of the two worlds.* Kant's solution to the problem of free will, which tries also to reconcile a determinism of natural events with an indeterminism that allows room for responsibility and creative action, rests on his doctrine of the two worlds. He distinguishes between the world of "nature" and that of the "thing-in-itself". Nature is organised by the activity of a knowing consciousness; by science, as we would say today. The world of the things-in-themselves is unknowable; it is not as a citizen of this world of things-in-themselves, however, that the individual is subject to the laws recognised by science, but as an object of nature only. Wherever we engage in scientific examination, therefore, there prevails law-like regularity that we do not know from the world of the things-in-themselves, and that (for this reason) we cannot assert.

This view, often criticised and surely contradictory, appears nevertheless to have a core of truth. In so far as we are dealing with our present question, we need only substitute, for Kantian "nature", the extract rationally captured by the net of theories. And for the world of the "thing-in-itself" we substitute not a world inaccessible to our consciousness, one that not only can we never know but can never even experience; on the contrary, what we substitute is the concrete world that we experience through unrepeatable individual occurrences.

If we approach the problem of free will from this position, it takes the following form: in as much as we can repeat events (repeat them, in principle, any number of times, by creating the same initial conditions), we can formulate theories and test them. We can move, in principle, towards ever increasing precision, we can pose ever more specific questions and undertake more and more detailed analysis, without this process ever coming to an end. Science does not have a border area (Kant's

*[1] These ideas go back to my first publication in 1925. [Cf. Karl Popper, "Über die Stellung des Lehrers zu Schule und Schüler: Gesellschaftliche oder individualistische Erziehung?" ["On the Attitude of the Teacher to School and to Pupils: Social or Individualistic Education?" Tr.], Schulreform 4 (1925), pp. 204 ff.; see also Section 6, note *2 (p. 445) and text to this note. Ed.]

example of a curved, sphere-like scientific domain[1]). Science can, in principle, provide answers to any theoretical questions that can be posed about the world; for every question can be posed in such a way that it need be answered with a "yes" or a "no" only. By formulating a theoretical question, however, we construct (by means of universals) a conceivable and repeatable "event", and every repeatable event can, in principle, be researched. (This is where we should take modern quantum physics into consideration. It has created fundamentally different conditions, but for the present investigation we imagine a deterministic [classical*[1]] world view.)

No theoretical questions, however, will ever allow us to get to the individual, not even to an individual stone. We may be able to describe the stone, perhaps predict its trajectory to an arbitrary degree of precision. But no stone will ever have been thrown in exactly the same way as this one, and whatever is unrepeatable will remain non-predictable and cannot even be asked.

That we tend to view stones in terms of natural science and humans more as individuals is due simply to the fact that we are interested in stones as means but in individuals as ends. All our actions have goals, or ultimate ends; science deals with the means only, those we can apply systematically and rationally in order to achieve certain ends.

Humans can, of course, become an object of scientific analysis just as stones can. But it is significant that unlike stones, only types*[2] and typical, repeatable phenomena describable by universals can be comprehended scientifically; never individuals, or that which is simply individual.

This is where the question of unique works of art is solved, and what we mean by artistic originality becomes clear. This is where the problem of responsibility is elucidated also.

Whenever we speak about responsibility, we think of that aspect of an event that is not scientific and is not repeatable. Every individual event is, in principle, unrepeatable, but its typical features can be repeated. If we are

---

[1] [Cf. Immanuel Kant, *Kritik der reinen Vernunft* (2nd ed., 1787), p. 790 [English translation by N. Kemp Smith (1929), 1965, *Critique of Pure Reason*, p. 607. Tr.]; see also Volume I: Section 44, text to note 1. Ed.]

*[1] Cf. my paper "Indeterminism in Quantum Physics and in Classical Physics", *The British Journal for the Philosophy of Science* 1 (1950), pp. 117 ff., 173 ff.

*[2] Again, the position I took in my first publication. Cf. Section 5, note *1.

interested in what is typical only, and do not regard the individual event as unique, what we call responsibility never occurs.*³

Physicists feel responsible for their scientific assertions. But they feel no responsibility for any easily repeatable experiment. If we entrust them with expensive apparatus, they feel some responsibility: they know that the apparatus is not easily replaced or repaired. The responsibility is even greater where we deal with an irreplaceable, unique work of art, and it is greatest where human individuals are concerned. One might say that the degree of responsibility is, to a first approximation, a measure of the non-repeatability of the event in question; non-repeatability in the sense that it is a measure of what interests us about this event: the aspect that can, or cannot, be repeated.

In sum, we can say: if by causality we mean law-like regularity, pre-dictability, we can speak about the causal determination of repeatable typical events only. We must never use the idea of law-like regularity, in the scientific sense, where we are interested in the individual. Applying this idea to individuals goes far beyond what science justifies us in doing: this is an application of the old animistic genetic concept of causality, which would involve us in causal metaphysics.

The non-metaphysical*⁴ view of the concept of causality necessarily implies that the idea of law-like regularity should not be applied where we are interested in the individual, but only where we are interested in the typical. It becomes evident that this false application, this causal meta-physics, is precisely what we rebel against instinctively when we sense

---

*³ This assertion, that "responsibility" is *always* associated with individuality, does not strike me as correct. I may have had my reasons, but I cannot recollect them.

*⁴ These remarks were written in a somewhat anti-metaphysical frame of mind, one that does not completely accord with the much less anti-metaphysical attitude of my published work, "Ein Kriterium des empirischen Charakters theoretischer Systeme" ["A Criterion of the Empirical Character of Theoretical Systems". Tr.], *Erkenntnis* 3 (1933), pp. 426 f., and the first German edition (1934) of *The Logic of Scientific Discovery* (1959; 2nd ed., 1968) of about the same time. Even later, however, and even today, I take the view that we will have made significant progress if we could make a meta-physical theory falsifiable and therefore scientific. [For an earlier version of "A Criterion of the Empirical Character of Theoretical Systems (Preliminary communication)", see Appendix: Section V. This "Preliminary communication" was republished in *The Logic of Scientific Discovery* (1959; 2nd ed., 1968), New Appendix *I as well as in *Logik der Forschung* (2nd ed., 1966), Neuer Auhang *I. Ed.]

that the application of deterministic ideas to unique acts of creation is untenable.

Musicians often come from musical families. If we consider the case of Bach in this way, we look at it with a scientific interest. The events that take place during musical composition can, without a doubt, be analysed psychologically, as can the occurrence of scientific intuition. But the event "the composition of the St Matthew Passion" cannot be investigated scientifically, because it can never be reproduced. We cannot describe it; all we can do is name it. We can only describe it to the extent that it is typical and repeatable. If we say of this event that it is causally determined, we may believe (correctly) that everything about this event that we can describe could, presumably, be investigated psychologically. If, however, we went further and asserted, for example, that an individual exactly like Bach would, in exactly the same situation, have also written the St Matthew Passion, we would be making unfalsifiable and therefore metaphysical assertions. We will never find another individual exactly like Bach, and we will never find another situation exactly like the one in which Bach wrote his St Matthew Passion.

It is not asserted here that this analysis captures precisely what is meant by the problem of free will. The situation here is the same as for the problem of simplicity;[2] it can always be asserted, after the event, that the problem being solved is quite a different one.[3] But here too, as we did there, we can show that our formulation of the question, at least, coincides in part with the ill-defined one underlying the discussion: its application to the problem of responsibility has always been one of the fundamental questions, and equally so the question of unique creative acts. The analogy between our solution and the Kantian one shows, without implying that we adopt Kant's metaphysics, that we are dealing with a closely related problem.

This question too, therefore, can be resolved by way of demarcation between science and metaphysics.

7. Has quantum physics changed the situation? So far we have assumed a deterministic physics. It seems to us that even modern quantum physics

---

[2] [See Volume I: Section 15; Karl Popper, *Logik der Forschung* (1934; 2nd ed., 1966), Chapter V. Ed. *The Logic of Scientific Discovery* (1959; 2nd ed., 1968), Chapter VII. Tr.]

[3] [Cf. Volume I: Section 15, note *1, and text to this note. Ed.]

cannot change the fundamental ideas underpinning our view. The idea, probably advanced first by Medicus[1] and later suggested by Niels Bohr[2] also, that the solution of the free will problem is heralded by the loosening of physical causality, seems to me (as indicated already[3]) to miss the core question.

The only consideration worth discussing, so it would appear to me, is an opposite one: not physical insights contributing to the solution of the evidently*[1] logico-epistemological problem of free will, but the reverse: epistemological considerations (these, as we have seen, are applicable not to free will only but to any arbitrary event) contributing to the solution of those physical questions that are concerned not so much with direct problems of physics (derivation of consequences) but with [their] interpretation.

Even if science, as we have imagined up to now, were capable in principle of answering any theoretical question, that is, any question relating to law-like regularities and to the prediction of events, even then it could not give us answers to non-theoretical questions that are motivated by an interest in individuals.

Now, because of quantum physics, it looks as though physics may be fundamentally unable to answer some theoretical questions, too [or could offer a probabilistic answer only, such as "the probability is one-half"]. We might ask how this limit on physical knowledge is related to the occurrence of individual, non-repeatable events. We might be tempted to argue as follows: physics has reached a limit in posing theoretical problems, and this limit is set by the individual who cannot be analysed physically any further, by the individual aspect that underlies all physical events.

We might say this: when we make a statement about the behaviour of particular personality types in particular situations, we are making it not about single individuals but about average values that occur in all of them.

---

[1] Fritz Medicus, *Die Freiheit des Willens und ihre Grenzen* [*Freedom of Will and its Limits.* Tr.] (1926).

[2] Niels Bohr, "Light and Life", [IIe Congrès international de la lumière (1932), p. XLV]; German translation by Hertha Kopfermann, "Licht und Leben", *Die Naturwissenschaften* 21 (1933), pp. 249 f.

[3] [See Volume II (Fragments): [VIII.] *Comments on the So-called Problem of Free Will*, Section [1]. Ed.]

*[1] Today this does not seem to me evident.

Similarly, physics can make statements not about individual particles, but about classes of particles and their average values only.

This view could be expressed as follows: the difference between individuals and universals is more pronounced than we assumed to begin with.

It is true, admittedly, that in principle we can always ask questions that are answerable by science, that the number of these questions is unlimited and that in this way, nonetheless, we shall never come close to the individual. But the other idea, that if, for example, we observe two events or two bodies of the same kind, we shall keep encountering differences by subdividing them further and further, this idea was erroneous in two ways: first, it operated on the false assumption that we can, in principle, refine our observations ever further. Since this assumption is false, there being absolute limits on the degree to which we can refine our observations, it might have been possible to say of two events or two bodies that they are identical within the achievable limits of observation. We have shown, however, that such a statement would not take account of the fundamental distinction between individuals and universals: while we may be able to reach the limits of precision in our observations, we shall never find there things of the same kind but individually different things only. The result is that the limits of observation become, at the same time, the limits of scientific prediction.

I regard such a view as metaphysical also, for the reasons indicated earlier (section . . .[4]): it draws excessively far-reaching conclusions from the present situation, in evident unawareness of the logical status of probability statements. I should like to remark, nevertheless, that such a view appeals to me far more than its reverse, that is, the application of the results of quantum physics to the problem of free will. And if we are looking for an "explanation" of the (perhaps) permanently non-deterministic nature of quantum physics, it appeals to me far more also than the form of indeterminism advocated by quantum physicists who resort to a causal-metaphysical explanation, with the idea of the observing subject interfering unpredictably with the observed object. It is able, instead, to "explain" this "explanation": the unpredictability of the interference appears as a consequence of the uniqueness of the situation.

---

[4] [This section can no longer be found and must be presumed lost; see Editor's Postscript. Cf. Karl Popper, Logik der Forschung (1934; 2nd ed., 1966) [The Logic of Scientific Discovery (1959; 2nd ed., 1968). Tr.], Sections 76 and 78. Ed.]

[X.]

THE PROBLEM OF
THE RANDOMNESS OF
PROBABILITY STATEMENTS

[Introduction.] Only from the vantage point of the frequency inter-pretation[1] of probability statements is it possible to formulate precisely the distinctive paradox inherent in all probability arguments, a paradox that constitutes the one aspect of probability that is most in need of an epistemological clarification.

This paradox consists in the following: there are particular classes of events to which we tend to apply a very characteristic and perplexing form of expression. When it becomes apparent, for particular series of events*[1] that belong to such a class, that we are unable to come up with predictions for the individual events in these series, from this impossi-bility of predicting an individual event we infer the possibility of making a prediction for the whole series; that is, a frequency prediction.

---

[1] [See Karl Popper, *Logik der Forschung* (1934), Chapter VI (2nd ed., 1966, Chapter VIII) [*The Logic of Scientific Discover* (1959; 2nd ed., 1968), Chapter VIII. Tr.]. Ed.]

*[1] Here and in the next three sections, I should have changed "series of events" to "sequences of events".

In a game of dice, for example, we infer from the fact that we can offer no rational method of making a prediction for a particular throw (only a clairvoyant could predict the next throw of the die, and we are not aware of a rational theoretical method of making such a prediction) that it is possible to make a prediction about a whole series of throws, that is, a frequency prediction. Quite generally, for some events (whether in atomic theory or in the statistics of mortality) where individual predictions fail, we think that we can assume, precisely for this reason, that statistics or the application of probability calculus will not fail.

This distinctive paradox, one that consists in deriving predictions from the impossibility of some other prediction, has always been recognised. Lacking clear understanding of the frequency interpretation, subjective probability theory[2] was unable to articulate this paradox precisely. It was clear to its proponents, nevertheless, that the peculiarity of probability statements consists in somehow inferring information from lack of information (problem of indifference[3]). [R. von] Mises' frequency theory[4] sees, with great clarity, the relationship between the randomness of individual events and the applicability of probability calculus to series of events. This theory elucidates how particular probability calculus statements (the special multiplication theorem and the propositions dependent on it) rely on this randomness of individual events, such that some justification does reside in this paradoxical inference. But it does not

[2] [See Popper, op. cit., Section 48. Ed.]

[3] [Cf. John Maynard Keynes, A Treatise on Probability (1921), Chapter IV; see also Popper, op. cit., Section 57, note 2 and text to this note. Ed.]

[4] [Richard von Mises, "[Karl] Marbes 'Gleichförmigkeit in der Welt' und die Wahrscheinlichkeitsrechnung" ["Karl Marbe's 'Uniformity in the World' and Probability Calculus". Tr.], Die Naturwissenschaften 7 (1919), pp. 168 ff., 186 ff., 205 ff.; "Fundamentalsätze der Wahrscheinlichkeitsrechnung" ["Fundamental Statements of Probability Calculus". Tr.], Mathematische Zeitschrift 4 (1919), pp. 1 ff.; "Grundlagen der Wahrscheinlichkeitsrechnung" ["Foundations of Probability Calculus". Tr.], Mathematische Zeitschrift 5 (1919), pp. 52 ff. and 7 (1920), p. 323; Wahrscheinlichkeit, Statistik und Wahrheit (1928; 4th ed., edited by Hilda Geiringer, Library of Exact Philosophy 7, 1972) [2nd revised English ed. prepared by Hilda Geiringer: Probability, Statistics, and Truth (1957). Tr.]; "Über kausale und statistische Gesetzmäßigkeit in der Physik" ["On Causal and Statistical Regularities in Physics". Tr.], Die Naturwissenschaften 18 (1930), pp. 145 ff. (Erkenntnis 1, 1930, pp. 189 ff.); Vorlesungen aus dem Gebiete der angewandten Mathematik I.: Wahrscheinlichkeitsrechnung und ihre Anwendung in der Statistik und theoretischen Physik [Lectures in Applied Mathematics I: Probability Calculus and its Application in Statistics and Theoretical Physics. Tr.] (1931). See also Karl Popper, op. cit., Section 50. Ed.]

resolve the paradox; indeed, it cannot even grasp its full import because it speaks, from the start, about those series of events only to which, by definition, probability calculus should be applicable: about those series for which frequency predictions can, by definition, be devised.

If we were to express this in the terminology of Mises' theory, our paradox would consist in this: under some conditions, conditions that are not identical with Mises' requirement of a limiting value of relative frequency, we can infer such a limiting value from the existence of randomness. Still using Mises' terminology, a resolution of the paradox would only be possible if it could be demonstrated that probability calculus can be constructed on the axiom of randomness alone, without one that requires a limiting value for relative frequency; or with the help of some other, weaker axioms that would replace the limiting value axiom.

We can frame this task in the following way also: it needs to be shown when, and under what conditions, we are justified in a tautological inference of the possibility of frequency prediction from the existence of randomness, that is, from the impossibility of an individual prediction.

6. *Sets of the first kind for infinitely extendable series.*[1] We want to examine how far we can free ourselves from explicit restriction to finite classes,[2] without having to include the concept of a limit in the definition of probability statements.

In order to avoid the concept of a limit, let us start by reviewing the objectives achieved by introducing this concept.

We would be justified in saying that *one* of the most important objectives is to replace the empirical, relative frequencies that vary in each series of experiments with a definite, fixed value that makes it possible to perform calculations. It seems to us that this objective can be achieved in another way also, without introducing the concept of a limit. We need to bear in mind that the limit of probability sequences can never be reached; it is introduced hypothetically [only]. Its introduction is motivated, in general, by the discovery of empirical frequencies that appear to be converging towards some limit, but this motivation does not interest us here;

---

[1] [Sections 1–5 can no longer be found and must be presumed lost; see Editor's Postscript. Ed.]

[2] [Cf. Karl Popper, Logik der Forschung (1934; 2nd ed., 1966) [*The Logic of Scientific Discovery* (1959; 2nd ed., 1968). Tr.], Sections 52 ff.; see note 1. Ed.]

its discussion belongs among the epistemological set of problems.[3] The important point is this: the introduction of the limit is hypothetical.

We should remember that relative frequencies can be associated hypothetically with finite classes also (based on some assumptions about this finite class). By counting the class we can determine whether our hypothesis and its assumptions were correct; and if we were wrong, the magnitude of the error. The assumptions on which such a hypothesis is based can include, for example, a partial or even a full empirical count of the relevant class; or particular assumptions about its composition, of which we may have some theoretical or empirical knowledge. A hypothetical relative frequency is present also where the frequency is estimated on empirical grounds, as soon as we make such an estimate and use it in our calculations; for the calculations are valid under the assumption of that estimate only, and it is irrelevant to them where the estimate came from. Instead of the hypothetical limit, therefore, we shall simply speak about the hypothetical relative frequency.

The *second* function of the concept of a limit is, obviously, to allow the application of the frequency concept to infinite series. But we should be clear that although under some conditions we can use probability calculus with infinite series also, that is, wherever we can apply the (epsilon) test to the computation of an exact limit; in general, probability calculus involves not infinite sequences but finite segments of sequences that are, of course, infinitely extendable, and in a sense that makes them similar to exponentiations. Should we be forced to define our concept of probability at once for infinite sequences, [then] we would be quite unable to get around the problem of the limit, for the relative frequency of an infinite sequence will, in general, have the value of a fraction, infinity divided by infinity, that is, be indefinite; it will only have a definite value if approached through the computation of a limit. But since, in general, we always deal with finite segments, as already mentioned, we can manage with our concept of hypothetical relative frequency. Where we encounter infinitely extendable series, we might say: we have reasons (what they are remains unsaid, for now) to assume that in each finite segment of this infinitely extendable series, there will [approximately] occur some hypothetical relative frequency.

The *third* reason for introducing the concept of a limit becomes clear in this last formulation. It is a peculiar characteristic of probability calculus

---

[3] [Cf. Popper, *op. cit.*, Section 51, text to note 2, and Section 66. Ed.]

that we expect the relative frequency corresponding to the hypothetical relative frequency to occur not in *every* finite segment, but only in *large* finite segments. We should, therefore, modify our concept of hypothetical relative frequency and say that we do not expect the same hypothetical relative frequency to occur every time; instead, we expect deviations that decrease with increasing series size. Alternatively, we should provide our own additional rules for handling this concept of hypothetical relative frequency. We shall embark on this latter route: the issue, evidently, is merely to specify when we can expect less precise or more precise values when we perform empirical testing of hypothetical relative frequencies.

Finally, in Mises' work, the concept of the space of relative frequencies still has a clearly defined formal meaning: his theory is so constructed that from the existence of the limit of the relative frequency and of the randomness principle, one can infer the existence of such a limit and the applicability of the randomness principle in the *derived sets*; that is, the limit of the relative frequency has the formal function of being transmitted to derivations (to use a legal phrase, [the existence of] a limit of relative frequency is "hereditary"). It can be shown that the concept of a limit is irrelevant to this function. Our hypothetical relative frequency (especially in conjunction with some particular randomness requirements) can perform the same formal function also.

We should note that our concept of hypothetical relative frequency achieves the following: we have seen that Mises' theory excludes the problems of the *estimation* of probability from probability calculus: from particular assumed probabilities, probability calculus infers others. We can accept this view without developing dogmatic-empiricist theses about the way to arrive at the probability estimate; in our opinion, this is something that Mises' theory does, at least *implicitly*. For in terms of its genesis, Mises' theory is distinctly inductivist-empiricist,[4] and still today there exist signs that indicate these origins. Even though the estimation problems are excluded from probability calculus, Mises suggests more than once that it

[4] [Cf. Richard von Mises, "[Karl] Marbes 'Gleichförmigkeit in der Welt' und die Wahrscheinlichkeitsrechnung" ["Karl Marbe's 'Uniformity in the World' and Probability Calculus". Tr.], *Die Naturwissenschaften* 7 (1919), pp. 172 ff.; "Fundamentalsätze der Wahrscheinlichkeitsrechnung" ["Fundamental Statements of Probability Calculus". Tr.], *Mathematische Zeitschrift* 4 (1919), p. 76; "Grundlagen der Wahrscheinlichkeitsrechnung" ["Foundations of Probability Calculus". Tr.], *Mathematische Zeitschrift* 5 (1919), pp. 60 ff. Ed.]

is experimental series that do and must give us the probability estimate.[5] Even if these suggestions are downplayed in his later writings and the hypothetical nature of the estimate more strongly emphasised, it is just this inductivist-empiricist aspect of Mises' approach that has found strong adherents (Reichenbach,[6] among some others).

Let us consider Mises' separation of the probability estimation problems from probability calculus. For us [as for Mises], probability *calculus* consists in the calculation of new probabilities from particular initial distributions, but we do not exclude the estimation problems from probability *theory*. It is our very recognition that probability estimates come into probability calculus as hypotheses that makes possible a clear formulation of the question about which assumptions must be made when framing these hypotheses. This commits us neither to an empiricist nor to an "apriorist" theory; as far as the "*a posteriori*" probabilities[7] are concerned, it leaves the way open to accepting statistically determined frequencies as the main foundation of our estimate. We are clearly aware, of course, that some constancy hypothesis should accompany these empirical data. (This hypothesis might take the form of the assumption that the frequencies remain approximately constant, as long as some empirically controllable "boundary conditions" do not change.) We retain the option of utilising the so-called "*a priori*" probability also, that is, of estimating hypothetically some relative frequencies not on the empirical basis of experimental series but on that of natural laws and of a reformed indifference principle.[8] This removes, as regards our position, the objection that makes Mises' theory unacceptable to Waismann, as already mentioned:[9] Waismann objects to Mises' theory for being unable to explain why, without conducting any experiments, we assume that in a die whose

---

[5] [Cf. Mises, *Wahrscheinlichkeit, Statistik und Wahrheit* (1928; 4th ed., edited by Hilda Geiringer, Library of Exact Philosophy 7, 1972). Ed. [2nd revised English ed. prepared by Hilda Geiringer: *Probability, Statistics, and Truth* (1957). Tr.].

[6] [Cf. Hans Reichenbach, "Kausalität und Wahrscheinlichkeit" ["Causality and Probability". Tr.], *Erkenntnis* 1 (1930), pp. 167 ff., "Axiomatik der Wahrscheinlichkeitsrechnung" ["Axiomatics of Probability Calculus". Tr.], *Mathematische Zeitschrift* 34 (1932), pp. 613 ff. Ed.]

[7] [See Karl Popper, *op. cit.*, Section 57, note 3 and text to this note. Ed.]

[8] [See [Introduction], note 3. Ed.]

[9] [See note 1 and Editor's Postscript. Ed.]

centre of gravity differs from its geometric centre, the frequencies of landing on its different sides will depart from those of a true die.[10]

We note that the classic concept of probability, too, agrees with Mises' concept of limit in that the probability 1 is a fixed value (in contrast to empirical frequencies under constant conditions) and has the property of being "hereditary".

The estimation problems discussed above are not, admittedly, tasks for probability calculus, which for us consists also in the derivation of one hypothetical relative frequency from another; they belong, nonetheless, to the group of mathematical logic problems that investigate the assumptions underlying estimation. We shall discuss this estimation problem in greater detail, and begin by asking: "For what kinds of 'infinitely extendable series of events' or 'event classes' are we able to make such an estimate or introduce a hypothetical relative frequency?"

Supplement. A constant hypothetical relative frequency permits a strict limiting process; the latter, in turn, results in another hypothetical relative frequency only, but this time for infinite classes. This is trivial. If the hypothetical relative frequency is constant for all finite partial classes of an infinite class, it is merely another way of expressing this assumption if we perform the limiting process and say that the hypothetical relative frequency has the same value for the infinite class also.

7. Conditions for infinitely extendable sets of the first kind. The first condition we must require from a class of "events" if we want probability calculus to be applicable to it, is for it to be countably infinite. This is related directly to the concept of relative frequency: we must be able to count the events, that is, they must be discrete. The characteristics may be discrete or continuous. In the first case we speak of an "arithmetic" set, in the second of a "geometric" set[1] (the theory of arithmetic-geometric sets will be

[10] [Friedrich Waismann, "Logische Analyse des Wahrscheinlichkeitsbegriffs" ["Logical Analysis of the Concept of Probability". Tr.], Erkenntnis 1 (1930), pp. 230 f. Ed.]

[1] [Cf. Richard von Mises, "Fundamentalsätze der Wahrscheinlichkeitsrechnung" ["Fundamental Statements of Probability Calculus". Tr.], Mathematische Zeitschrift 4 (1919), p. 72; "Grundlagen der Wahrscheinlichkeitsrechnung" ["Foundations of Probability Calculus". Tr.], Mathematische Zeitschrift 5 (1919), pp. 70 ff.; Vorlesungen aus dem Gebiete der angewandten Mathematik I.: Wahrscheinlichkeitsrechnung und ihre Anwendung in der Statistik und theoretischen Physik [Lectures in Applied Mathematics I: Probability Calculus and its Application in Statistics and Theoretical Physics. Tr.] (1931), pp. 28 f. Ed.]

discussed later[2]). This requirement ensures that we can "number" the different events of any subclass.

The *second* condition is associated with the problem of the *constancy* of relative frequencies. Without having any detailed information about the distribution of the relative frequencies, often we can know something about their constancy or about their variation, or we can make a hypothetical estimate of their constancy or variability. An example will illustrate this point: imagine a jet of water directed horizontally against a wall, and consider the frequency with which drops of water hit a particular section of the wall per minute. Without knowing anything about this frequency, obviously we shall assume that the frequency increases with increasing water pressure (or with an increasing quantity of water drops per minute) and decreases with decreasing pressure. We can further assume that given constant pressure, the frequency for a particular section of wall will decrease when the distance of the hosepipe from the wall increases. Such considerations show that we can know whether, and in which direction, particular conditions affect the frequency, without necessarily knowing the actual values of the frequency under these conditions. Our example shows, too, that we need not assume constant conditions. It is not too difficult a task for probability theory, given certain assumptions, to compute probability functions, say under continuously changing conditions. What we assume in this case also, however, is that holding the conditions constant will cause the frequency to be constant too, at some phase during its changing. A constant frequency should not be understood as absolutely fixed. What is meant is the following: we assume a relationship between the frequency and the conditions such that changing the conditions affects the frequency perpetually in a very specific sense, that is, in such a way that the latitude of the fluctuations that occur under constant conditions is exceeded definitely in one particular direction. Conditions of this kind will be called boundary conditions. What we need to assume about a set is this: either, its boundary conditions must not change uncontrollably, that is, we need to know whether they are constant or changing and how they change; or, if they do change uncontrollably or are unknown to us, we need to know that their change is not law-like but "random". In other words, the changes in the uncontrolled boundary conditions must not exhibit a perpetual trend in

---

[2] [See Editor's Postscript. Ed.]

one particular direction; they should be *able* to assume all possible values in the course of the experimental series. The experimental conditions must not privilege a particular value or trend, but should be so arranged as to prevent any one value being singled out.

Comment. The terminology needs to be modified slightly. Instead of boundary conditions we should say relevant conditions. Non-compensating relevant conditions will be called boundary conditions, and the others will be called "compensating conditions".

It is important to be aware that we cannot examine all the relevant conditions, and that we assume hypothetically that all those conditions not included in our calculations compensate for each other. The *hypothetical nature* of the whole procedure is crucial. If the hypothetical assumptions were unjustified, this would show itself in disagreement between the calculated and the observed results.

If we make these two assumptions about a series of events, we already assume the applicability of probability calculus as developed above[3] to this series of events.[4]

8. *The problem of random sequences.* The two assumptions in the previous section are not equivalent. The [first] assumption of a countable class is necessary so we can devise any evidently hypothetical relative frequencies at all. The second assumption refers already, as it were, to the success of this test. We can only expect a successful probability prediction, that is, a prediction about the relative frequency of a series of events, if we have reason to assume that we know the boundary conditions or that they are constant or that they vary in a particular law-like manner known to us. If probability calculus proves to be incapable of successful application in

---

[3] [See Editor's Postscript; cf. also Section 6, note 1. Ed.]

[4] [Here the manuscript continues:]

Comments on Section 5. Discussion of the "non-empty" assumptions.

[In view of Karl Popper, *Logik der Forschung* (1934; 2nd ed., 1966) [*The Logic of Scientific Discovery* (1959; 2nd ed., 1968). Tr.]: Section 58, note 4 and text to notes 4 and *3, it seems clear that the expression "non-empty" refers to the question whether the concept of set is "empty" (contradictory) or "non-empty" (non-contradictory). The "comments" and the "discussion" announced here can no longer be found and must be presumed lost. See also Section 6, note 1, and Editor's Postscript. Ed.]

an area that satisfies the first condition, our assumptions concerning the second condition must have been false, that is, the boundary conditions varied in a law-like manner that we failed to take into account.

For the purpose of our two arguments, we can ignore the case of law-like variation in the boundary conditions and confine ourselves to constant probabilities, that is, to constant boundary conditions. The concept of boundary conditions, however, implies this only: that if these conditions are constant, the relative frequency will remain confined within particular limits. The assumption of constant boundary conditions is so general that it covers sequences of events of the most diverse types. It does not restrict the application of probability calculus to sequences that exhibit the distinctive and intuitive character of randomness discussed above. Sequences that change with law-like regularity – for example, 0, 1, 0, 1, 0, 1 or 0, 0, 1, 1, 0, 0, 1, 1, 0, 0, 1, 1 or even sequences consisting only of ones – in brief, the most diverse sequences that display law-like regularity, are as amenable to calculation as the random sequences of games of chance. This has to do with the fact that up to now, all we have done was apply the concept of relative frequency to infinitely extendable sequences. To do this, we used the concept of hypothetical relative frequency and, as a basis for application to infinitely extendable sequences, the concept of constant boundary conditions. This concept is applicable without any difficulty to sequences the law-like nature of which is known to us. The problem we turn to next is the following:

Distinctively *random* sequences, such as the ones that occur in games of chance, permit extensive application of the special multiplication theorem, as follows: if, instead of considering all the elements of a sequence, we consider every second or every third element (in the terminology of [R. von] Mises,[1] this is the selection operation), this will

---

[1] [Richard von Mises, "[Karl] Marbes 'Gleichförmigkeit in der Welt' und die Wahrscheinlichkeitsrechnung" ["Karl Marbe's 'Uniformity in the World' and Probability Calculus". Tr.], *Die Naturwissenschaften* 7 (1919), pp. 171 f.; "Grundlagen der Wahrscheinlichkeitsrechnung" ["Foundations of Probability Calculus". Tr.], *Mathematische Zeitschrift* 5 (1919), pp. 57 ff.; *Wahrscheinlichkeit, Statistik und Wahrheit* (1st ed., 1928), pp. 38 f. (4th ed., edited by Hilda Geiringer, Library of Exact Philosophy 7, 1972, pp. 45 f.) [2nd revised English ed. prepared by Hilda Geiringer: *Probability, Statistics, and Truth* (1957). Tr.]; *Vorlesungen aus dem Gebiete der angewandten Mathematik I.: Wahrscheinlichkeitsrechnung und ihre Anwendung in der Statistik und theoretischen Physik* [*Lectures in Applied Mathematics I: Probability Calculus and its Application in Statistics and Theoretical Physics*. Tr.] (1931), pp. 74 f. Ed.]

not alter the distribution of relative frequencies by reference to this selection as a reference class. The set is said to be insensitive to ordinal selection. There is another type of ordinal selection to which empirically given sets of games of chance are known from experience to be insensitive: it is the selection obtained by making the position to be selected dependent, in a law-like manner, on some property of the rest of the series (in particular, [on a property] of its neighbourhood). If, for example, we select the positions followed by a zero, or [those] preceded by two zeros and followed by two ones, the set proves to be insensitive to the reference class generated by such ordinal selection; that is, the new reference class exhibits the same relative frequencies (approximately only, of course) as in the original set.

Supplement. The more accurate our knowledge of the relevant conditions, and the greater the number and importance of the relevant boundary conditions, the smaller will be the fluctuations of the relative frequencies and the smaller their dispersion. Problem: are we observing a transition to strict law-like regularity?

Compensating conditions play no part at all in the first probability estimate. Dispersion analysis relates to higher-order probability. The first probability estimate relies on the boundary conditions only. The discussion thus far suffices for *a posteriori* probabilities.

(Mises has been taken to task on the grounds that his concept of ordinal selection cannot be pinned down with sufficient precision.[2] I consider this objection inappropriate.[3])

How does the distinctively intuitive nature of the randomness of chance-like sequences (or the applicability of the special multiplication theorem) relate to the applicability of the selection operation?

This question takes us back to the one that we have described as the fundamental paradox of probability calculus. How can we infer the applicability of probability calculus (in our case, the applicability of the

---

[2] [Cf. Herbert Feigl, "Wahrscheinlichkeit und Erfahrung" ["Probability and Experience". Tr.], *Erkenntnis* 1 (1930), p. 256. Ed.]

[3] [cf. Karl Popper, *Logik der Forschung* (1934; 2nd ed., 1966) [*The Logic of Scientific Discovery* (1959; 2nd ed., 1968). Tr.], Section 58, notes 2 and *1, and text to these notes. Ed.]

special multiplication theorem) from our inability to provide a rational prediction for any element of a sequence?

The following answer might seem plausible: if, based on the outcomes so far of an experimental series, we can frame a prediction, evidently the result (according to our hypothesis, at least) depends on these outcomes; a selection that takes this dependence into account must (according to the hypothesis, once again) produce a sequence that *no longer* has the random nature of the original sequence. For example, it may consist of *ones* and nothing else. But this answer is unsatisfactory, for two reasons:

First, because it offers no answer about the robust nature of the new relative frequency. It does explain why, if we cannot make predictions, we do not obtain a strictly law-like sequence by ordinal selection; but it fails to explain why the relative frequencies are the same as before.

Second, this answer takes account of the structure of the series only, of the order of its elements. The answer would, therefore, apply also to a series whose elements follow each other in a chance-like sequence but that consists of event-elements that were all predictable and of nothing else.

(Here we encounter an important point, for probabilistic considerations apply not only to chance-like series of events, that is, to series whose elements are all unpredictable, but to those series of events also that contain individually predictable elements and nothing else, and yet there is no association between the elements that regulates their sequence. It is important to note that this is the more general case. Chance-like sequences are an important special case only. Probability calculus, as a theory of sequences with a chance-like structure, is much more general than probability theory as a theory of games of chance.)

APPENDIX

SUMMARY EXCERPT (1932)

from

The Two Fundamental Problems
of the Theory of Knowledge

PRELIMINARY NOTE

The following brief item is a summarising excerpt from the manuscript of my book (planned to consist of two volumes) *The Two Fundamental Problems of the Theory of Knowledge*, Volume I: The Problem of Induction (Experience and Hypothesis), Volume II: The Problem of Demarcation (Experience and Metaphysics).

In this note, Sections I to V, VII, IX and X are taken from Volume I, which is in publishable form. Some of these are verbatim excerpts (for example, Section I), sometimes with additions. Section V will appear under the title "A Criterion for the Empirical Character of Theoretical Systems" as a "Preliminary Communication" in the next issue of *Erkenntnis*.[1] It can be regarded as the shortest *summary* of the basic ideas.

The Appendix of Tables[2] is meant to serve as a substitute for the detailed critical investigations that define the spirit of the book but that could not be included in this excerpt.

---

[1] [*Erkenntnis* 3 (1933), pp. 426 f.; Karl Popper, *Logik der Forschung* (1934; 2nd ed., 1966) [*The Logic of Scientific Discovery* (1959; 2nd ed., 1968). Tr.], New Appendix *I. Section V is an *earlier* version of this "Preliminary Communication". Ed.]

[2] [This "Appendix of Tables" is omitted here because it is reproduced in Volume I: *Appendix: The Critique of the Problem of Induction in Schematic Representations.* Ed.]

I. FORMULATION OF THE PROBLEM

The problem of induction and the problem of demarcation. This investigation focuses on two questions: the problem of induction and the problem of demarcation.

The problem of induction:

We are able to observe particular events only, and always a limited number of them. The empirical sciences, nonetheless, propose *universal statements*, for example, natural laws; that is, statements that are meant to apply to an unlimited number of events. What is the justification for proposing such statements? What does one mean by such statements? These questions suggest an outline of the problem of induction, a problem that I pose as a question about the truth of the universal statements of the empirical sciences. Put another way: can empirical statements based on experience be universally true? Or more casually: can we know more than we know?

The problem of demarcation:

Most empirical sciences, as their history shows, were born out of metaphysics: their last pre-scientific form was speculative-philosophical. Even physics, the most highly developed among them, may not have rid itself completely of the last traces of its metaphysical past. In recent times it has been subjected to a violent cleansing process: metaphysical ideas (Newton's absolute space and absolute time, Lorentz's ether at rest) have been ruthlessly eliminated. The less highly developed sciences (for example, biology, psychology, sociology) have always been more strongly pervaded with metaphysical elements than has been (and still is today) the case for physics. Even the view that metaphysics must be eliminated as "unscientific" is strongly contested by some proponents of these sciences.

Is metaphysics justifiably rejected or not? What do we mean by the terms "metaphysics" and "empirical science"? Is it even possible to establish strict distinctions and definite limits? These questions (they outline the scope of the demarcation problem) are of general and decisive importance. Any form of empiricism must, above all, demand from the theory of knowledge that it should secure empirical science against the claims of metaphysics.

The theory of knowledge must establish a strict and universally applicable criterion that allows us to distinguish between the statements of empirical science and the assertions of metaphysics ("criterion of demarcation"). I call the question about the criterion of demarcation the "demarcation problem". Put another way: when in doubt, how can we decide whether we are dealing with a scientific statement or "merely" with a metaphysical assertion? Or more casually: when is a science not science?

I regard these two questions, the problem of induction and the problem of demarcation, as the fundamental problems of the theory of knowledge. It seems to me that the problem of demarcation is of greater interest. Far from being of theoretical-philosophical significance only, it has the deepest relevance for the individual sciences, more particularly for research practices in the less highly developed sciences. From a philosophical perspective, it proves to be the fundamental problem to which *all other epistemological questions*, including the problem of induction, can be reduced.

These *epistemological* questions are of a quite different nature from the *psychological* question about how our knowledge, in actual fact, comes into existence. We are asking not about the way that scientific statements are discovered, how they arise, but about their *justification*, about their *truth*: the *epistemological* questions, as questions of justification or of truth (Kant: "*quid juris?*"), must be distinguished strictly from *psychological* (and historical-genetic) *questions of fact* ("*quid facti?*"), that is, from questions about the *discovery* of knowledge.

The view that the theory of knowledge should deal with questions of truth only, not with those of fact, makes it, in a sense, into a general methodology for empirical science. For method in science is not the way that something is *discovered*,[1] but a procedure through which something is *justified*.

II. THE TRANScENDENTAL METHOD OF THE THEORY OF KNOWLEDGE

The theory of knowledge is a general *methodology for empirical science*. It does not determine the methods of empirical science descriptively only but attempts to *explain* them, that is, to *derive* them *deductively* from a small number of principles or definitions. It is a *theory of method*.

---

[1] [See Volume I: Section 1, note *1. Ed.]

The most important of these definitions is that of the concept of "*empirical science*", a concept that originates in the "demarcation criterion"; that is, in a criterion for distinguishing between empirical-scientific and metaphysical systems.

Other important concepts in the theory of method (some of which can be introduced as fundamental, whereas others can be defined) include those of "theory", "prediction", "deduction" and "empirical falsification".

The fundamental statements of the theory of method are controversial. How can this controversy be resolved? There are two ways:

1. Inconsistent solutions can be eliminated *logically*.

2. By way of the *transcendental method*: the results of the theory of method are compared with those that are used successfully in practice by the empirical sciences. Theories of knowledge that do not successfully describe the actual methodological procedures (herein consists the transcendental method) should be regarded as having failed.

The conflicting theories of knowledge must enter into a transcendental competition with each other. Some of them appear to be internally consistent and satisfactory, but fail when faced with the methodological problems revealed by *other* theories of knowledge. It should be noted, however, that only *transcendental failure* can decide this question, that is, inconsistency with an actual scientific justification method.

(Such transcendental critique can be viewed as an *immanent critique* of a particular theory of knowledge, for the theory's task is defined as describing the methods of science. This procedure should be distinguished from *transcendental critique*, commonly used in the theory of knowledge but unjustified[1] nonetheless: it consists in rejecting a theory of knowledge for being inconsistent when viewed from the vantage-point of another, in the sense of conflicting with the theoretical assumptions of an alien approach.)

The competition leads to the uncovering of *contradictions* between the theories, and sometimes transcendental decision between them is possible. (This method of competition can be called the "dialectical method".)

According to the view presented here, the theory of knowledge is a theoretical science. It does contain freely adopted rules (for example, definitions), but it consists *not of arbitrary conventions* only but of refutable

---

[1] [Cf. Volume I: Section 9, note *1 and text to this note. Ed.]

statements also: they are refutable through comparison with the method of justification used in scientific practice.

Its relationship to science is the same as that of science to empirical reality; the transcendental method is analogous to the empirical method.

The theory of knowledge is a science of science, a second-order science, a science of a higher type.

So as to leave no doubt about the view advocated here concerning the concept of "transcendental", let us express the fundamental trans-cendentalist thesis as follows:

Epistemological assertions and conceptualisations must be tested critically against the justification method used in empirical scientific practice; and this (transcendental) test is the only one that can decide the fate of such assertions.

III. DEDUCTIVISM AND INDUCTIVISM

Theories of knowledge may have a *deductivist* or an *inductivist* orientation, depending on how they assess the significance of deduction (logical deri-vation) and of induction (generalisation). *Classical rationalism* (Descartes, Spinoza), for example, has a strictly *deductivist* orientation (its model is geometrical deduction), whereas classical empiricism is *inductivist*. Radical inductivist positions (such as that of Mill) deny deduction any significance at all; an analogous *deductivist* position, one that denies induction any si-gnificance, is the fundamental idea of the view advocated here.

The thesis of this *consistent deductivism* may be presented as follows: there is no induction of any kind; the widespread view that generalisation is a scientific method rests on an *error*. The only admissible inferences that proceed in the inductive direction are the deductive inferences of *modus tollens*. (Deductions of any kind are admissible, but their premises are always hypothetical.)

This idea of a strictly "deductivist" theory of knowledge can be carried through consistently; if applied systematically, it leads to simple solutions of all the epistemological problems we have encountered so far.

The view advocated here links *deductivism* with *empiricism*; that is, it adopts the position of the *fundamental empiricist thesis* that experience, and experience only, can decide the truth or falsity of any empirical statement.

("Experience", accordingly, is a particular *method* of deciding on state-ments, or systems of statements.)

IV. THEORETISM. SCIENTIFIC OBJECTIVITY

"Theoretism" is the term by which I refer to the position (one that follows from deductivism) that the task of natural science (and of empirical science in general) is not the description of individual facts but the formulation and testing of theories. (It is substantively identical with those positions that, in an older form of words, saw the task of science in the *systematic explanation* of facts.) Theoretism, according to Kant, can be supported by the concept of scientific objectivity.

Scientific objectivity consists in the fact that anyone (with sufficient *critical training*) is capable, in principle, of testing scientific results (*intersubjective testability*). (Any attempt to *explain* the existence of such intersubjectively testable knowledge leads to the unsolvable "antinomy of the knowability of the world", that is, to metaphysics.)

Testing, and especially intersubjective testing, assumes the formulation of theories (hypotheses). Only what is (in some sense) repeatable can be testable; that is, only a conjectured law-like regularity is testable.

Scientific objectivity assumes, therefore, the construction and testing of theories ("*theoretism*"). Scientific knowledge (as Kant already knew) is only possible if we succeed in discovering laws that are corroborated.

The *empiricist theoretism* that is advocated here is the position that states: empirical-scientific theories must have the character of hypotheses, or of provisional assumptions.

V. OUTLINE OF THE SOLUTIONS TO THE TWO FUNDAMENTAL PROBLEMS OF THE THEORY OF KNOWLEDGE[1]

1. (Preliminary question.) The "problem of induction" (Hume's problem), the question about the truth of natural laws, arises from the (apparent) contradiction between the "*fundamental thesis of empiricism*" (only "experience" can decide the truth or falsity of empirical statements) and Hume's realisation of the *inadmissibility of inductive (generalising) proofs*. Inspired

---

[1] This section (with the exception of the last sentence) is identical with the communication "A Criterion for the Empirical Character of Theoretical Systems" (see Preliminary Note). [Section V is an *earlier* version of this "Communication"; see Preliminary Note, note 1 (p. 465). Ed.]

by Wittgenstein, Schlick[2] believes it is possible to resolve this contradiction by assuming that natural laws "are not genuine statements at all" but "rules for the construction of statements", that is to say, a particular kind of "pseudo-statements". This attempted solution (it seems to me purely terminological), in common with all earlier attempts (for example, "apriorism", "conventionalism" and so on), relies on an unjustified assumption: that all *genuine statements* must be "*fully decidable*" (verifiable *and* falsifiable), that is, (definitive) empirical verification and empirical falsification must be *logically possible* for all genuine statements. If we abandon this assumption, the contradiction created by the "problem of induction" can be resolved in a simple way: natural laws ("theories") can be regarded without inconsistency as "*partially decidable*" (unverifiable, for logical reasons, but *one-sidedly falsifiable*) genuine empirical statements, systematically tested through attempts to falsify them.

This attempted solution has the advantage of paving the way also for a solution of the second (and truly fundamental) problem of the "theory of knowledge":

2. (Main question.) This, the "demarcation problem" (Kant's question about the limits of scientific knowledge), can be defined as the question about a criterion for *distinguishing between "empirical-scientific" and "metaphysical" assertions* (statements, systems of statements). Wittgenstein's attempted solution[3] is that the "concept of meaning" provides this demarcation: every "meaningful statement" (as a "truth-function of elementary statements") must be fully reducible, logically, to (singular) observation statements (it must be derivable from them). If a supposed statement cannot be so derived, it is "meaningless", "metaphysical", it is a "pseudo-statement": *metaphysics is meaningless*. With this criterion of demarcation, positivism seemed to have achieved a more radical overthrow of metaphysics than had earlier anti-metaphysical positions. But along with metaphysics, this radicalism destroys natural science also: natural laws, too, are not logically derivable from observation statements (the induction problem!); under consistent application of Wittgenstein's criterion of meaning, they would become nothing but "meaningless pseudo-statements" or "metaphysics" also. This puts paid to the attempted

---

[2] Moritz Schlick, "Die Kausalität in der gegenwärtigen Physik" ["Causality in Contemporary Physics". Tr.], *Die Naturwissenschaften* 19 (1931), p. 156.

[3] Ludwig Wittgenstein, *Tractatus Logico-Philosophicus* (1918/1922).

demarcation. The dogma of meaning with its pseudo-problems can be replaced, as a demarcation criterion, by the "*falsifiability criterion*" (the criterion of at least *one-sided* decidability): statements that can be defeated by "empirical reality", those for which we can specify the conditions under which they should be regarded as empirically refuted, are the only ones that assert something about it.

The acceptance of *partially decidable* statements, therefore, solves not just the "problem of induction" (there is *one* type only of inference that proceeds in an inductive direction: the deductive *modus tollens*), but the "demarcation problem" also (which underlies virtually all "epistemological" questions). The "falsifiability criterion" allows us to demarcate, with sufficient precision, the empirical sciences from the metaphysical (and from the conventionalist-tautological) systems, without requiring us to declare that metaphysics, the historical source from which empirical science arose, is "meaningless". By using a generalised variant of Einstein's well-known phrase,[4] therefore, we could define the empirical sciences as follows: *in so far as scientific statements speak about reality, they must be falsifiable, and in so far as they are not falsifiable, they do not speak about reality*.

Logical analysis shows that for empirical-scientific systems, the criterion of (*one-sided*) "*falsifiability*" plays formally an exactly analogous role to the one played by "*consistency*" for scientific systems in general: an *inconsistent* system of principles is compatible with any statement whatever (and, therefore, with any conjunction of statements also),[5] and does not single out any statements from the set of all possible statements. Similarly, a *non-falsifiable* system is compatible with any conceivable "empirical statement", and does not single out any statements from the set of all possible "empirical" statements.

VI. PREREQUISITES OF FALSIFIABILITY, CONSTRUCTION OF THEORIES

Individual statements are not falsifiable: in the strict sense, whole theoretical systems only are falsifiable. In some circumstances and under particular conditions, however, it is possible to test part-systems of

---

[4] Albert Einstein, *Geometrie und Erfahrung* [*Geometry and Experience*. Tr.] (1921), pp. 3 f.
[5] [Parentheses inserted in K_1, July 1933. Ed.]

theories in relative isolation. This case is of great methodological importance ("quasi-induction", "levels of support").

Only a *closed* system, furthermore, is falsifiable. If one permits the *ad hoc* introduction of auxiliary hypotheses, the theory can always be protected against any falsification and becomes empirically empty, conventionalist-tautological or metaphysical.

If the falsifiability requirement is tightened, the requirement for the system to be closed takes on a stricter form also: it is replaced by the principle of the most parsimonious use of hypotheses.

The axioms of a theory, non-empirical and empirical, can be regarded as implicit definitions of its basic concepts. This is conventional in non-empirical theories. In the case of empirical theories, however, one tends to suppose that the basic concepts should be thought of as non-logical constants or the like, and that there is something in reality that corresponds to them. This view is untenable in this form (especially the stated view of coordinative definitions); for if a basic concept could be assigned to its object in reality, this would imply that universal concepts refer to demonstrable objects (that is, the thesis "*universalia sunt realia*" in its most primitive form).

The situation is such that even the basic concepts of the *empirical* sciences are defined implicitly. What corresponds to reality are not the basic concepts but the *theory as a whole, with all its concepts* (through the specification of the conditions under which it should be regarded as refuted). In other words, the correspondence takes place through the method of deciding about the singular *consequences* of the theory, through decisions about the derived predictions *in which the basic concepts no longer occur*. (The assignment is the *application* of the theory, it is scientific *practice*, it rests on practical decisions; a remark that makes a discussion of the difference between the transcendental viewpoint and that of the psychology of knowledge a pressing matter.)

VII. TRANScENDENTAL AND PSYCHOLOGICAL METHOD. ELIMINATION OF THE SUBJECTIVE-PSYCHOLOGICAL BASIS

Almost all theories of knowledge up to now (conventionalism might be mentioned as the sole exception, and even then with serious reservations), when asking about the basis of our empirical knowledge, confuse transcendental and psychological elements. The reason for this is simple enough (and probably was most strongly emphasised by Fries): if statements are not to be introduced *dogmatically*, they should be justified. The question about the justification of statements leads nowhere if one avoids psychologistic (that is, subjective) answers. For if one does not wish to rely on one's conviction, perception, evidence, immediate knowledge and the like (all of these are subjective, psychologistic), one can *justify statements by other statements only*; and if these are not to be introduced dogmatically, they in turn require justification. (Fries constructs his doctrine of "immediate knowledge" on this argument; perception and intuition are, for him, immediate knowledge that needs no further justification and from which empirical statements originate.) All positivist theories proceed in similar psychologistic fashion, even in their most modern forms (Wittgenstein's elementary propositions, Carnap's protocol sentences – whether assumed "inside" or "outside" the language of the system; the same is true of Neurath's protocol sentences).

None of these views stands up to a transcendental critique, for such critique shows that perceptions and observations (more accurately: perception and observation statements), if not intersubjectively testable, will never be recognised or taken seriously by science; not even if backed subjectively by the strongest force of conviction (one may call to mind the reports of sea-serpents!). They enter science not so much in the form of preliminary material, but *at best* as suggestions or as problems to be solved.

In science, therefore, no subjective convictions of any kind can ever be of methodological significance, but they can be of historical-genetic significance only; that much is demanded by the concept of scientific objectivity (see IV): statements are scientific if they are "objective", that is, intersubjectively testable. (The attempts involving elementary propositions and protocol sentences are, obviously, intended also to eradicate from science any subjective psychological basis, albeit not so much for transcendental, objectivist reasons but because of physicalist tendencies. But this attempted eradication is unsuccessful. All it does is translate psychological perceptual statements into physiological reports about the perceptual statements made by physiological persons; it is nothing but a physicalist reconstruction of the psychologistic doctrine about the perceptual basis of the empirical sciences.)

The only possible eradication of the subjective psychologistic basis from science is by accepting particular statements as true, and doing this *arbitrarily, by convention*; that is, without any further scientific justification. Science invokes these statements when it declares other statements (theoretical systems) to be corroborated or falsified. They constitute the foundation, they are the (arbitrary) endpoints of deductive derivation; they are the statements at which deduction from theories stops, they are the major premises for *modus tollens*. (They do not have to be *explicitly* instituted as true or as false; this happens usually as a result of applying to them logical inference rules, first and foremost *modus tollens*.)

A view such as the one just put forward is bound to rouse fierce objections. It appears, at first glance, to open the floodgates to dogmatic adoption of basic statements, or (and this would be no better) to transform empirical science into a system of conventions, blurring the differences between empirical and non-empirical theoretical systems, that is, between conventionalist-tautological systems (such as mathematics and pure geometry) and empirical science (mathematical physics, physical geometry).

These objections call for clarification (and for a problem formulation). The conventional adoption of basic statements is not arbitrary in the sense that any statement at all can serve as a basic statement; it is arbitrary in the same sense only in which conventions are called arbitrary because they are statements stipulated as true by *decision* and not by virtue of *justification*. The decisions by which the basic statements of *empirical* science are established are not "arbitrary"; they are regulated, in a very particular way, by methodological principles. What is crucial is this only: we are dealing not with *justified* statements but with *stipulated* statements, and the *methodological regulation of decision-making* is something entirely different from *the justification of a statement*.

The essential question is this: by what methodological regulation or stipulation of its basic statements is empirical science distinguished?

How, travelling between conventionalism and positivism, does one establish an accurate view of empirical science? From a positivist perspective, the position developed here is a significant concession to conventionalism. And because, on the other hand, empiricism is to be retained, there must be (as seen from the conventionalist viewpoint) some move towards positivism: not towards its theories, of course, but towards some of its tendencies; the empiricist ones.

Historical note. (The view advocated here remains much closer to that of Kant and Fries than to positivism, for the former has the merit of acknowledging that there must exist some final, *objective* statements in science (namely, the perceptual statements that are central to the present discussion of the basis, but others also) that cannot be derived objectively from any others. The Kant–Fries method recognises the fundamental opposition between the final basic statements, still a constituent of objective scientific investigation, and that psychological something – the "immediate knowledge" – by which these basic statements are supported. This view recognises also the discontinuity in the method that consists, until we reach these statements, of a process of logical derivation, whereas the basic statements themselves rest on irrational intuition or on something like it. This is analogous to the position advocated here, that the logically derived justification of a statement is something different from the methodological regulation of a decision. In contrast, positivism always subjectifies science, for its approach is to introduce that psychological something on which the perceptual statements and so on are supposed to rest, into the very *contexts of justification*. Earlier positivism recognised still, at least, the opposition between the "given", which is irrational-subjective, and the statements that express this given directly and are, therefore, rational even if *subjective* still. But modern positivism tends to abolish even these oppositions. It replaces the given with elementary statements or with protocol sentences, or simply leaves out the "given" and tries instead to secure for its protocol sentences and so on the greatest possible immediacy; that is to say, it introduces into science, to serve as its foundation, sentences that are completely impossible to test objectively and the subjective character of which, furthermore, is emphasised and elaborated to the greatest possible degree. In short, it attempts to build science on a subjective basis that is either solipsistic – "first-person psychological basis" – or constructed from the subjective statements of several subjects. This betrays clearly its original *inductivist* reasoning process. The Kant–Fries method shares with ours the view that one comes to an end with the scientific-objective method, and then starts something else – even though it fails to distinguish this something else sufficiently sharply from the scientifically-objectively justified method. Positivism, however, incorporates the subjective elements into science, which loses its objective nature as a result. It should be noted also that it strives to avoid subjectivism, by virtue of providing a behaviourist translation of everything psychological into "physicalist language". But because this translation is underpinned still by the old conception of the psychological foundation, little is gained by such rephrasing.)

VIII. THE METHOD OF EMPIRICAL FALSIFICATION

The question about the "empirical nature" of science was answered (in Section V) by way of the falsifiability criterion. The question about the *empirical basis* of knowledge can be replaced, therefore, by the question about the *method of empirical falsification*.

A. First approximation of the method. Theories permit deductive derivations even without the substitution of singular conditions (that is, conditions that hold in a particular individual case); in other words, derivations of natural laws of a *lower level of universality* from those of a *higher level*. For example, the principles of mechanics permit the derivation of the natural law that says: In an empty homogeneous gravitational field, all projectile trajectories are parabolas. By adding assumptions, we can derive a natural law of lower universality: Shots fired in the atmosphere at such and such velocity describe ballistic curves of this and that type. Natural laws of a sufficiently low level of universality (for example, all shots fired from a cannon of such and such construction, at this particular angle and with this particular charge and so on, and in the absence of wind and on level terrain, land at this particular distance, say 2,456 metres, within such and such a margin of error, say ± 15 metres) can be called "directly testable universal statements". They are *not verifiable* (this is self-evident from Section V), but *falsifiable only* (and capable of provisional corroboration). The universal statements referred to here as "directly testable" are natural laws, but of such a low level of universality that for the purpose of stating a *singular prediction*, a *particular individual case* is determined with sufficient precision by saying: *hic et nunc* is a case that belongs to the class of cases described by the natural law. No further special conditions, other than the spatial-temporal individualisation of the case, need to be substituted: all the other conditions could have been substituted earlier without destroying the character of the *universal* statement (of the natural law). Empirical falsification of such a directly testable universal statement falsifies the whole system retrospectively, by *modus tollens*. Falsification of *one* directly testable universal statement falsifies the *whole* system, even though an *unlimited number* of directly testable universal statements can follow from it.

B. *Second approximation of the method.* How does the testing (provisional corroboration or falsification) of such directly testable universal statements take place?

A singular statement, that is, a *prediction*, can be derived by substituting the *hic et nunc* (a shot as described was actually fired here ten minutes ago). In our example: "The distance between cannon and impact will be at least 2,441 metres and at most 2,471 metres."

If the prediction comes true, the theory is corroborated provisionally. If the prediction does not come true, if a singular, *correctly derived* statement is false, the "directly testable universal statement" is falsified and with it the whole theoretical system.

It should be noted that correct derivation of a prediction consists not just of a logically, formally correct deduction, but of justification of the last substitution also, that is, the truth of the singular statement "a shot as described was actually fired here ten minutes ago". Whereas, so far, we have had to do with *universal* statements that are, in principle, *non-verifiable* (or at best one-sidedly falsifiable), evidently there must exist fully decidable *singular* statements if there is to be any retrospective falsification of theories at all.

C. *Third approximation of the method.* What is the situation with regard to such "fully decidable" singular statements? (Singular statements are statements about a *particular* spatial-temporal region.)

It is clear that if there exist falsifiable *singular* statements, there must exist verifiable *singular* statements also (in contrast with the universal statements). Example: falsification of the statement "My watch is correct" verifies the statement "My watch is wrong". (But falsification of the statement "All watches are correct" verifies *not* the universal statement "All watches are wrong" but merely the *non-universal* statement "Not all watches are correct", or "There exist watches that are wrong" and so on.)

If singular statements are decidable *at all*, therefore, there must exist both false and true singular statements; but then, nothing prevents the retrospective falsification of theories (as described in B).

(In our gunnery example, it should be possible to ascertain the truth of the statement that the cannon is pointing, within a given margin of error, at a particular angle to the horizon, that the terrain is (approximately) level and so on, and the *falsity* of the statement that the projectile landed within the range of 2,456 ± 15 metres.)

There is little doubt that the verification and falsification of *such* singular statements pose no *methodological difficulty* in scientific practice.

We could let matters rest at that, but this is where epistemological misinterpretations tend to occur. Psychologism in particular, in all its varieties, intervenes at this very point and asserts that the truth or falsity of such singular statements rests on "perceptions" or on "protocol sentences". (Whatever the truth of this assertion, this has to do with the *psychology* of knowledge and not with the *theory* of knowledge; cf. also Section X.)

D. *Fourth approximation of the method.* The singular statements that enter science as true or false (thereby rendering theories falsifiable) can themselves, in principle, be justified by scientific (that is, objective) singular statements only. It follows that those statements (cf. Section VII) that must be stipulated by convention, or by decision, as "true" or "false" will be found among the singular statements.

But which singular statements? And how are the decisions regulated?

The best way of answering these questions is by examining how science actually proceeds.

What we find is, first, that singular statements act in the role of transit stations only, of short stopping points during the testing of *universal* statements. Second, that these stations (as mentioned already) do not, for the most part, pose any further practical-methodological difficulties.

If we want to carry the epistemological analysis further, we shall have to focus on those (relatively rare) cases where practical-methodological questions do surface at this point in scientific practice. These are, obviously, cases where one DOUBTS whether a singular statement should be stipulated as true (or false); in other words, whether a fact does or does not exist.

What do non-scientists do if they doubt a fact? What can I do if I doubt whether or not the inkstand here is "really" in front of me? I can (a) look at it from all sides, (b) touch it, (c) ask other people, and so on. If we consider all this not *psychologically* but *methodologically* (cf. Section X on the psychological aspect) we note that here, too, the *hypothetico-deductive method* of testing is applied. If the inkstand is really here – so I conclude – then it should be possible to look at it from other sides also, to touch it, for other people to see it and so on. Such considerations emphasise *seeing, touching* and so on; this is not an epistemological process but a psychological one. Here, emphasis will be placed instead on the words "If-then": *the method of testing a singular statement* (where further corroboration is needed) *consists in deriving from the statement* (and from the theoretical system) *further singular statements (predictions) and testing them.*

In scientific practice, this method is applied also wherever doubts arise. If, for example, we doubt whether a particular object placed before us is (say) made of gold (a singular statement is being tested), we derive from this assumption and from chemical laws (of a fairly low level of universality) particular "directly testable universal statements", perform the experiment (that is, create the conditions described in these universal statements) and test the predictions.

The action of (*objective*) singular statements towards some other singular statements is similar, therefore, to that of hypotheses. Every *objective* (that is, intersubjectively testable) singular statement contains theoretical, hypothetical, law-like elements. It asserts a particular law-like relationship between other singular statements[1] (otherwise it would not be *testable*). For this reason, singular statements that are *scientific*, that is, *objective*, that is, intersubjectively *testable*, can be called *natural laws of the lowest level of universality*.

Because the objective-methodical testing of such objective singular statements can, in principle, lead to other such statements only, the *endpoints* of the deduction, the statements at which finally we let matters rest, *are arbitrary and, in principle, not supported further.*

(This still holds if we use observation statements, "protocols" or the like in the hypothetico-deductive process of testing; for the statement that I see this inkstand, for example, is merely of hypothetical value for science: from a scientific viewpoint, it is a psychological hypothesis, a natural law of the lowest level, one that can be tested through further psychological experiments (through questions and further statements, say) but never proved objectively; cf. also Section X. The objective scientific process of deduction stops mostly (almost always?), in practice, at physical hypotheses of the lowest degree of universality, seldom at psychological ones; for we choose statements that are *most easily amenable to intersubjective*

---

[1] An infinite number of them, in principle, such that even objective singular statements will never be fully testable. I have made detailed reference to this situation in my "Critique of strict positivism" (Section 8) and in my "Presentation of apriorism" (Section 9) in my book [Volume I] ("Transcendence of Representation in General").

testing, that is, about which anyone can easily acquire individual subjective conviction. Even though objective science is not built on these convictions, it does take them into account in the *arbitrary establishment of the endpoints*. Not as a *substantive-logical foundation*, then, but for *methodological regulation of decision-making only*.)[2]

A theory retains its *empiricist* nature, therefore, through a particular methodological regulation of its stipulations. The most important of these regulations is that *singular* statements only may be stipulated as true, and in case of doubt it is never the superordinate, the more universal, the theoretical statement that decides*[1] the issue: further deductive testing continues until it is judged that sufficient reliability has been achieved.

The empirical basis of objective science, therefore, has *nothing absolute* (or given) about it; science is not constructed on solid bedrock. Its building site is more like a swamp, its foundations are pillars driven into the swamp *from above*, not down to any naturally "given" ground but just as deeply as is required; down to the point where we *decide* that we have reached sufficient depth, because (according to our calculations) the pillars will support the building. If the building becomes too heavy nonetheless, the pillars sometimes need to be replaced or driven deeper still.

The objectivity of science must be bought at a price, and this price is relativity (those desiring the absolute must remain with the subjective).[3]

IX. METHODOLOGICAL PRINCIPLES OF THE CONVENTIONAL STIPULATION OF SOME BASIC STATEMENTS AS "TRUE" OR "FALSE"

1. (Fundamental statement.) "Singular" statements only, and intersubjectively testable statements only, may be stipulated as true or false. (Empiricism = singularist basis.)

---

[2] K_3 in the margin: personal equation!

*[1] That a universal statement "never decides" does not mean that we never take into account a well-corroborated universal statement.

[3] Cf. Max Born [Die Relativitätstheorie Einsteins und ihre physikalischen Grundlagen [Einstein's Theory of Relativity and its Physical Foundations. Tr.] (1920), Introduction], Hermann Weyl [Philosophie der Mathematik und Naturwissenschaft [Philosophy of Mathematics and Natural Science. Tr.] (1927), p. 83], Robert Reininger, Das Psycho-Physische Problem [The Psycho-Physical Problem. Tr.] (1916), pp. 290 f. [See Volume I: Section 11, text to notes 15, 16 and 58. Ed.]

2. The stipulation may be made in those cases only where no methodologically admissible doubts exist.

3. Such doubts exist whenever:

a) The singular statement falsifies a well-corroborated "directly testable universal statement".

b) The calculated margins of error are unfavourable.

c) The conditions for intersubjective testing are objectively unfavourable, that is, observational difficulties are encountered.

d) An intersubjectively well-testable statement (of the "sociology of science") asserts that intersubjective testing has resulted in (subjective) confirmation and in (subjective) refutation also, or in (subjective) doubt also; that is, no intersubjective accord can be reached.

Note to a): Conflict between an objective, *otherwise well-tested* singular statement and the universal statements of a theory should not constitute an absolute obstacle to its stipulation (it was merely the motive for testing it), otherwise there would be no falsification at all.

4. If methodologically admissible doubts exist, the singular statement must not be stipulated as "true" or "false"; it should continue to be tested, as would a hypothesis, or a natural law (of the lowest level of universality).

5. Particular attention should be focused on testing the last substitutions that lead from the directly testable *universal* statement to the prediction.

6. All these tests take place by deriving further intersubjectively testable singular statements, that is, further singular predictions, always in accordance with the same principles; but point 3a) is eliminated as grounds for methodologically admissible doubt as soon as the other grounds (b to d) no longer exist *and* an "always testable statement" can be specified as a falsifying statement. Such statements are: (a) a testable theory that conflicts with the first (so that at least *one* easily testable crucial experiment to decide between them is possible); (b) a natural law of a low level of universality (a directly testable universal statement); (c) a singular statement in which the *hic et nunc* is specified but which is permanently testable with the help of "*corpora delicti*" (described also by singular statements about spatial-temporal regions) such as archival documents, museum pieces and the like (and with the assistance of well-corroborated theories). For example, conservation of energy could be refuted by a *perpetuum mobile* exhibited in a museum even if we failed in duplicating this apparatus, that is, in specifying an experiment that is directly testable at all times.

These methodological principles can be more uniformly summarised as METHODOLOGICAL REALISM. Even though a "realist" thesis cannot be *explicitly formulated* within science (realism is defeated by "antinomy of the knowability of the world"), science proceeds methodologically *as though universally true laws* (law-like regularities, universal states of affairs) existed and it were the task of science to describe them.[1] The thesis that *there exist natural laws* is, however, *epistemologically equivalent to realism.*[2]

X. JUSTIFICATION OF PSYCHOLOGISM

The psychological conception of knowledge is not unjustified *as such*; it is unjustified within the *theory of knowledge* only. It is very much in its rightful place within the psychology of knowledge. (This question is completely independent of psychological method, "*behaviourism* = physicalism" or "introspection" and so on.) The psychology of knowledge investigates, *inter alia*, how and when subjective convictional experiences come into being, whether and how they depend on "perceptions" and so on.

The results of these investigations, the assertions of the psychology of knowledge (especially its universal assertions and theories) *are tested in accordance with exactly the same methods* as all other scientific assertions, being scientific (that is, intersubjectively testable) assertions.

The *scientific nature* of the assertions of the psychology of knowledge, that is to say, the requirement that they be *methodically tested*, is sufficient for showing that methodological considerations can never rely on the psychology of knowledge as the final justification.

We might mention, among the results of the psychology of knowledge, its description of "intersubjectivity": to become convinced, subjects conduct their own tests (that is, make measurements and so on), but these tests mostly do not possess absolute convictional power unless they can be repeated or compared with external results. That such comparison, once again, is performed through the subject's "perceptions" (of linguistic signs and other responses) and so on, that is to say, that for *each subject* the convictional experience results from other experiences of his *own* and not from the experiences of others, this circumstance in the psychology of

---

[1] [See Volume I: Sections 10 and 46. Ed.]
[2] K_3 in margin: Com[ment]: intersensual test[ing] and "method[ological] realism".

knowledge should be regarded as *too trivial*[1] to be called "*methodological solipsism*"[2] or the like. This name is misleading also, or false, since it cannot help but betray the *epistemological* subjective-psychological position.

CONCLUDING NOTE

Some of the questions discussed in my book, mentioned in the Preliminary Note, were left out of this summary for lack of space. Of those, let me mention *the deductive theory of method;*[1] it deals *inter alia* with:

1. Levels of reliability and "quasi-induction".

2. The corroboration concept and the simplicity concept; the "principle of the most parsimonious use of hypotheses", derived from the concept of higher and lower degrees of falsifiability (or precision, or statement content).

---

[1] I have emphasised this often against Carnap.
[2] [See Volume II (Fragments): [VI.] *Philosophy*, Section 1, note 2. Ed.]
[1] [See Editor's Postscript. Ed.]

EDITOR'S POSTSCRIPT[1]

1. Introduction. This edition of *The Two Fundamental Problems of the Theory of Knowledge* contains everything that could be found[2] of the original copies of the manuscript. Despite tireless efforts[3] to track down the missing parts, it has proved impossible to publish a complete edition of this two-volume work, written in the years 1930–1933. Volume I: *The Problem of Induction* appears to have been preserved in its entirety,[4] whereas almost the whole manuscript of Volume II: *The Problem of Demarcation* must be presumed lost. Of this volume, there exist a few fragments only and the drastically abridged version published in 1934 under the title *Logik der Forschung*.[5] This book and two short papers (1933–1935) on induction and demarcation in the

---

[1] In the notes to *The Two Fundamental Problems*, many references appear to the Editor's Postscript. Volume II (Fragments): [III.] *Transition to the Theory of Method*, Section 8, note 1 (p. 409) refers to the Postscript, Section 2, note 1 (p. 490); [IX. *The Problem of Free Will*], Section 5, note 1 (p. 443) refers to the Postscript, Section 5 and Section 6, note 30 (p. 496) and to the text of this note. All other references to the Editor's Postscript refer to Section 6 of this Postscript.

[2] See Section 2, notes 1, 4 and 6 (p. 488), and Section 5.

[3] See Section 6.

[4] See Section 6, note 1 (p. 497) and text to this note.

[5] Karl Popper, *Logik der Forschung: Zur Erkenntnistheorie der modernen Naturwissenschaft, Schriften zur wissenschaftlichen Weltauffassung* [*The Logic of Research: on the Epistemology of Modern Natural Science, Writings on the Scientific Worldview.* Tr.] (eds. Philipp Frank and Moritz Schlick), Volume 9, Vienna: Julius Springer, published in December 1934 (dated 1935). The text is included in *Logik der Forschung* (2nd ed., 1966) [*The Logic of Scientific Discovery* (1959; 2nd ed., 1968). Tr.], *Die Einheit der Gesellschaftswissenschaften* [*The Unity of the Social Sciences.* Tr.] (ed. Erik Boettcher), Volume 4, Tübingen: J.C.B. Mohr (Paul Siebeck).

journal Erkenntnis[6] are all that has been published to date (January 1979) of *The Two Fundamental Problems of the Theory of Knowledge*.[7]

My intention, naturally, was to be as faithful as possible to the original text of the preserved copies of the manuscript. But in order to obtain a publishable text from the many manuscripts, none fully edited and many incomplete, it was necessary to make some changes. The next four sections of this postscript describe these changes in some detail, and offer an overview of the copies available to the editor. As a supplement to Book II (Volume II, Fragments), the sixth and final section contains an overview of the many references to the lost volume that are found in the preserved copies of the manuscript and in a note in *The Logic of Scientific Discovery*.

Work on this edition of *The Two Fundamental Problems* began in 1972, and was greatly facilitated by the assistance I have received from many sides. Margit Hurup Nielsen, Jeremy Shearmur and Martin N. Hansen helped me in resolving a variety of problems. Robert Lammer, Paul K. Feyerabend and Arne Friemuth Petersen helped me to track down copies of the manuscript. Gunnar Andersen and Ernst A. Nielsen assisted me in translating my own contributions. I am very grateful to them all. First and foremost,

---

[6] Karl Popper, "Ein Kriterium des empirischen Charakters theoretischer Systeme (Vorläufige Mitteilung)" ["A Criterion for the Empirical Character of Theoretical Systems (Preliminary Communication)". Tr.], Erkenntnis 3 (1933), pp. 426 f.; " 'Induktionslogik' und 'Hypothesenwahrscheinlichkeit' " " 'Inductive Logic' and Probability of Hypotheses' ". Tr.], Erkenntnis 5 (1935), pp. 170 ff. These two papers were republished in Karl Popper, Logik der Forschung (2nd ed., 1966) [The Logic of Scientific Discovery (1959; 2nd ed., 1968). Tr.], New Appendix *I. For an earlier version of the "Preliminary Communication" (1933), see above, Appendix: Section V.

(Karl Popper, "Zur Kritik der Ungenauigkeitsrelationen" ["On the Critique of Uncertainty Relations". Tr.], Die Naturwissenschaften 22 (1934), pp. 807 f. is a summary of The Logic of Scientific Discovery, Section 77.)

[7] Some of Popper's results were reported in late 1932 by Rudolf Carnap; see R. Carnap, "Über Protokollsätze" ["On Protocol Sentences". Tr.], Erkenntnis 3 (1932), pp. 223 ff. Cf. also Karl Popper, Conjectures and Refutations (1963), p. 254; Karl Popper, "Intellectual Autobiography", The Philosophy of Karl Popper I (ed. Paul Arthur Schilpp, 1974), p. 71 (= Karl Popper, Unended Quest: An Intellectual Autobiography (1976), pp. 89 f.); Karl Popper, "Replies to my Critics", The Philosophy of Karl Popper II (ed. Schilpp, 1974), pp. 969 f.; Karl Popper, Logik der Forschung (1934; 2nd ed., 1966) [The Logic of Scientific Discovery (1959; 2nd ed., 1968). Tr.], Section 29, note 1 and New Appendix *I: 1, note 3 (*addition 1957).

however, I am greatly indebted to Karl Popper for entrusting me with this important task and for checking, and here and there amending, the edited manuscript. (All these changes are indicated.)

2. *The original copies and editing of the manuscript.* As the manuscript existed in early 1934,[1] it consisted of two parts of approximately equal lengths: Volume I (*The Problem of Induction*) and an almost completed Volume II (*The Problem of Demarcation*), and probably ran to more than 1,200 typed pages. There existed also several earlier versions of parts of Volume II and a *Summary Excerpt* (1932). Old letters indicate that four copies of Volume I were produced (K_1 and three carbon copies: K_2, K_3 and K_4[2]). It is unknown whether four copies of Volume II and of the *Summary Excerpt* were produced also, but it must be regarded as highly probable. Of this very extensive manuscript material, it has been possible to find the following copies only, all of which[3] were used in preparing this edition:

Title page: K_1.
The mottos:[4]
    Novalis: K_1; Schlick (1930) and Kant (1786): K_2 and K_3; Kant (1781): K_3.
    Exposition [1932]:[5] K_2; Exposition [1933]:[6] K_2.

---

[1] This follows from a letter of the author of 3 February 1934.

[2] K_2, K_3 and K_4 indicate carbon copies; the numbering, however, does not indicate their order.

[3] See notes 7, 10 and 12, and Section 5.

[4] See Section 5.

[5] This version of the Exposition, enclosed with Volume I (K_4), can be reconstructed from the Exposition [1933] with the help of the critical textual notes [these are in the German edition (1979) of *The Two Fundamental Problems*. Tr.].

An earlier version of the second paragraph of the Exposition [1932]: Section [1] is included in a letter to Egon Friedell dated 30.6.1932. This letter includes also the following interesting paragraph:

> "My book is a theory of knowledge, or more accurately: a theory of method. It is a child of its time, a child of the crisis – albeit first and foremost the crisis of *physics*. It asserts the *permanence of crisis*; if it is right, then crisis is the normal state of a highly developed rational science."

[6] Exposition [1933] was one of three enclosures in a letter to Julius Kraft dated 11.7.1933. Cf. Section 6: D).

Volume I: *The Problem of Induction:*[7]
    Contents: K_1, K_2, K_3 and K_4; Sections 1–33 and 36–47: K_1, K_2, K_3 and K_4; Sections 34, 35 and 48: K_1, K_2 and K_3; Sections 33–35 and 48: "Summary of Contents":[8] K_1, K_2, K_3 and K_4; Appendix: The Critique of the Problem of Induction in Schematic Representations ["Appendix of Tables"]: K_1, K_2, K_3 and K_4.[9]

Volume II (Fragments): *The Problem of Demarcation:*[10]
    Draft of an Introduction: K_2; I.: K_2; [II.]–[V.]: K_1 and K_2; [III.], Section 4, note 1 ("Table of Statements"): handwritten draft; Orientation: K_2; [VI.]: K_1 and K_2;[11] [VII.]: K_2; [VIII.]: K_1, K_2 and K_3; [IX.]: K_1 and K_2; [X.]: K_1.

Summary Excerpt (1932): K_1, K_2 (with "Appendix of Tables") and K_3.[12]

It seems that Popper's custom, while working on the manuscripts of *The Two Fundamental Problems* in the years 1930–1933, was to insert his numerous handwritten amendments and additions in one of the carbon copies (here referred to always as K_2), after which they were transcribed to the two other carbon copies (K_3 and K_4) and to K_1. The texts of the four copies are not, however, quite identical: amendments and additions in K_2 were, occasionally, not transferred to the three other copies, or were transferred to one or two of them only. In each of the copies K_1, K_3 and K_4, moreover, there are amendments and additions that were not transferred to the three other copies at all, or were transferred to just one or two.

---

[7] Besides the manuscript copies mentioned here, a copy of an earlier version of Sections 1 and 2 has been preserved also, together with individual pages of earlier versions of the other sections.

[8] See Volume I: Section 33, note 1; Section 34, note 1; Section 35, note 1; Section 48, note 1.

[9] Table VII: K_1, K_2 and K_3.

[10] Almost all the fragments of Volume II were found in a folder labelled "Logik der Forschung: Ur-Version" [*Logic of Research: original version.* Tr.]. Besides these fragments, the folder contained a large number of sections, for the most part incomplete, of earlier versions of *Logik der Forschung*. Since these deviate only slightly from the version published in 1934, however, they were not incorporated into this edition.

[11] The first four paragraphs are not in K_2.

[12] In K_1 and K_3 there is an earlier version of the Preliminary Note.

The editor's manuscript (MS) is based on careful comparison between the copies, and contains all the amendments and additions. In the relatively few cases (I found twenty-eight) where it is not entirely clear which of two possible versions should be regarded as the final text, the version not used is indicated in the critical textual notes included in the German edition of *The Two Fundamental Problems* (1979). All quotations and all references to the literature and to other sections in the book were checked in the course of compiling this manuscript, and errors were corrected without special indication. Spelling mistakes were corrected also, and the format of references was standardised.

There were no footnotes in the original copies, and all references to other sections and to the literature were enclosed in parentheses within the main text. In line with the system followed in *The Logic of Scientific Discovery*, references to other sections in the book were left in the text, but references to the literature are given in footnotes. The editor's additions to these footnotes are enclosed in square brackets, and normally identified by "Ed." also. While editing the manuscripts, I discovered many quotations with no references given at all or with the author's name given only. The missing references were established and added in footnotes in virtually all such cases. These notes, like the other editor's notes, are enclosed in square brackets and normally identified by "Ed." also.

Unlike Volume I and the Summary Excerpt (1932), where the order of sections is shown clearly in the original manuscripts, there is no unambiguous indication in the preserved fragments of Volume II of where individual sections belong, except for I. *Formulation of the Problem*. The order of the fragments in this edition was, therefore, chosen by the editor in reliance on the information about Volume II contained in Volume I, in the preserved fragments of Volume II and in the Summary Excerpt (1932).[13]

The division of Volume II (Fragments) into *Part One: Fragments 1932* and *Part Two: Fragments 1933* is somewhat uncertain also. It does seem, of course, from the way the manuscripts were typed and from their content, that the two parts belong to different phases in the writing of Volume II. We cannot exclude the possibility, however, that some sections of *Part One* were written in 1933 and conversely for *Part Two*. It is highly probable,

---

[13] See Section 6.

nonetheless, that some sections at least of *Part One* were written in 1932,[14] and it is quite certain that some sections of *Part Two* were written in 1933.[15] For the sake of clarity, therefore, I decided to ignore the uncertainty surrounding the dates and used the headings shown in this edition.

3. *Popper's revision of the MS in 1975.* The manuscript prepared by the editor (MS) was reviewed by the author in 1975,[1] resulting in many new notes and additions. In line with the system followed in *The Logic of Scientific Discovery*, Popper's new notes are numbered separately and identified by an asterisk (*), and his additions to other notes are introduced with an asterisk. His additions to the text (these are stylistic improvements and additions that help to clarify and to improve the argument[2]) are enclosed in square brackets. Many of the author's new notes and additions are supplemented by the editor's bibliographical annotations and by references to other sections and notes; *these* additions are enclosed in square brackets and identified by "Ed.".

The author deleted the occasional word in the original text in order to improve the style, replaced one word with another or rearranged the word order. In the German edition of *The Two Fundamental Problems* (1979), these changes are identified in the critical textual notes.

The stylistic amendments include many changes in punctuation, and the deletion of a great many quotation marks unnecessary for an

[14] Cf. Karl Popper, "Intellectual Autobiography", *The Philosophy of Karl Popper* I (ed. Paul Arthur Schilpp, 1974), p. 67 (= Karl Popper, *Unended Quest: An Intellectual Autobiography* (1976), p. 85), which indicates that Popper must have begun work on Volume II in 1932. See also Volume II (Fragments): [III.] *Transition to the Theory of Method*, Section 8, note 1 (after the typesetting of this note I found a copy of a letter from Popper to Carnap dated 16.1.1933, which indicates that Popper had borrowed from Carnap a manuscript headed "Semantik"; this must have been the earlier version of Carnap's *Logische Syntax der Sprache* (1934) [English translation by Amethe Smeaton (1937): [*The Logical Syntax of Language*, p. xvi. Tr.] that Carnap mentions at the end of his Preface of May 1934).

[15] Cf. Volume II (Fragments): [IX. *The Problem of Free Will*], Section 7, note 2.

[1] Volume II (Fragments): Part Two: *Fragments 1933* was added only in 1976/1977, but the editing of these fragments proceeded in the same way exactly as that of the other manuscripts.

Some of these fragments were written at a time when Popper used a shorthand typist. What is preserved is the typist's uncorrected clean copy only, and it contains many peculiar mistakes ("concept of heaven" for "concept of limit", for example). These mistakes were corrected without special indication.

[2] See Introduction 1978, Section 2.

understanding of the text and distracting to the reader. In several places, the use of italics and the division into paragraphs were changed also. These amendments to the editor's manuscript (MS) are not indicated in the German edition's critical textual notes: this would have been quite awkward and would have required an inordinate number of rather uninteresting notes.

4. *Title and table of contents.* According to the original plan, *The Two Fundamental Problems* was to appear in two volumes of roughly equal size. The overall title chosen by the editor for the two volumes is the one that appears on the title page of Volume I (K_1), and the titles chosen for the two volumes are those that appear in Summary Excerpt (1932) (K_2).[1] It is unfortunate that we have been unsuccessful in locating more than a few fragments of Volume II and that it has been impossible to adhere to the original plan. The book now appears in one volume, and the editor and the author decided that it is more appropriate to refer to Volume I as Book I and to Volume II (Fragments) as Book II in the table of contents and on the opening pages. In line with the original plan, however, the notes refer to Volume I and Volume II (Fragments), and that is why these titles appear also in the table of contents and on the opening pages.

The original table of contents in Volume I (K_1, K_2, K_3 and K_4) was arranged in the following way:

I. FORMULATION OF THE PROBLEM. Section 1. II. DEDUCTIVISM AND INDUCTIVISM. Sections 2–4. III. THE PROBLEM OF INDUCTION. Sections 5–6; *The Normal-Statement Positions:* Sections 7–11; *The Probability Positions:* Sections 12–17; *The Pseudo-Statement Positions:* Sections 18–48; *Appendix:* The Critique of the Problem of Induction in Schematic Representations.[2]

For the sake of clarity and in order to give the book a form that resembles that of *The Logic of Scientific Discovery* as closely as possible, the 1975 revision of the manuscript (MS) by the author and the editor introduced

[1] See Appendix: Preliminary Note. In the earlier version of the Preliminary Note in the Summary Excerpt (1932) (K_1 and K_3), the corresponding titles are: *The Two Fundamental Problems of the Theory of Knowledge (The Philosophical Assumptions of Natural Science);* Volume I: *The Problem of Induction (The Problem of Law-like Regularities in Nature);* Volume II: *The Problem of Demarcation (Experience and Metaphysics).*

[2] Unlike this edition, Analysis of Table I follows Table I in the original manuscripts.

a division of Volume I (Book I) into chapters.³ It would have been more consistent to enclose the numbering and most of the titles of these chapters in square brackets, to make it clear that they do not exist in the original manuscripts; but this would have been most unattractive and was not implemented.⁴

5. *The mottos.* In the editor's manuscript (MS), the book is introduced through four mottos. The first three are:

Hypotheses are nets, only he who casts will catch . . .

Novalis¹

The suggestion . . . that man has finally solved his most stubborn problems . . . is small solace to the thinker, for what he fears is that philosophy will never go so far as to pose a genuine "problem".

Schlick (1930)²

I for my part hold the very opposite opinion, and I assert that whenever a dispute has raged for any length of time, especially in philosophy, there was, at the bottom of it, never a problem about mere words, but always a genuine problem about things.

Kant (1786)³

These mottos were used in *The Logic of Scientific Discovery*,⁴ which is why the author and the editor decided to include the fourth motto only in this

---

³ Chapter VIII and Chapter IX: see Volume I, Section 36, seventh paragraph.

⁴ Where the fragment numbers in Volume II are enclosed in square brackets, this is to emphasise that their order is uncertain. As mentioned already, this order was chosen by the editor; the same applies to the title of [IX.].

¹ Novalis (Friedrich von Hardenberg), *Novalis Schriften II.* [*Writings II* Tr.] (eds. Friedrich Schlegel and Ludwig Tieck, 1802), Dialogue 5, p. 429. Cf. Volume II (Fragments): [IX. The Problem of Free Will], Section 5, note 3 and text to this note.

² Moritz Schlick, "Die Wende der Philosophie", *Erkenntnis* 1 (1930), p. 5.

³ Immanuel Kant, "Einige Bemerkungen von Herrn Professor Kant" ["Some Comments by Professor Kant". Tr.], *Prüfung der Mendelssohnschen Morgenstunden oder aller spekulativen Beweise für das Daseyn Gottes in Vorlesungen von Ludwig Heinrich Jakob* [*Examination of the Mendelssohn Morning Hours or of all Speculative Proofs of the Existence of God in Lectures by Ludwig Heinrich Jakob.* Tr.] (1786), p. LIII.

⁴ Novalis: Karl Popper, *The Logic of Scientific Discovery* (1959; 2nd ed., 1968), p. [11] ; Popper, *Logik der Forschung* (1934; 2nd ed., 1966), Section [XI].

Schlick (1930) and Kant (1786): Popper, *op. cit.*, Section [III.] *The Logic of Scientific Discovery*, p. 13.

book: Kant (1781),[5] and this, moreover, in a somewhat shorter version than the one found in K_3.

6. *Volume II: The Problem of Demarcation.* A few sections only could be found of the drafts for Volume II that Popper wrote in the years 1932–1933. All these fragments are included in this edition. It has proved impossible, however, to locate the final version, known to be nearly completed in early 1934[1] and approximately of the same length as Volume I. The only thing that could be discovered for certain about the fate of this volume is that it was preserved completely intact for more than ten years after World War Two, together with several other Popper manuscripts. It must be regarded as likely that Volume II is lost, as a result of several unfortunate misunderstandings.

Even though the search for Volume II failed, the attempts to track down this manuscript have been very useful for the publication of this book. Two copies of Volume I (K_3 and K_4), Exposition [1932], Exposition [1933] and several old letters and smaller manuscripts were obtained thanks to the great help I received from Robert Lammer of Vienna. I am greatly indebted also to Paul K. Feyerabend, Berkeley, California for similar assistance.

The much abridged version of Volume II published in autumn 1934 as *Logik der Forschung*[2] does, of course, convey a fairly accurate picture of large parts of the lost manuscript. The drastic abridgement has resulted, however, in the omission of many sections, and *Logik der Forschung* has little or nothing to say about their content.[3] As a supplement to Book II (Volume II, Fragments), therefore, we provide below an overview of the numerous (but unfortunately, far from exhaustive) indications about the content and structure of the lost Volume II that can be found scattered in the form of references in the preserved manuscript copies, and to which a single note in *Logik der Forschung* and one remark in an appendix to Exposition [1933] refer.

---

[5] Immanuel Kant, *Kritik der reinen Vernunft* (1st ed., 1781), p. XIII. [English translation by N. Kemp Smith (1929), *Critique of Pure Reason*, p. 10. Tr.]

[1] See Section 2, note 1.

[2] See Section 1, note 5.

[3] See note 7.

From references in Volume I[4] and in the preserved drafts of Volume II[5] it appears that after the Introduction and I. Formulation of the Problem, Volume II contained, or was meant to contain, the following three parts in this order:

Investigations of the Problem of Demarcation

Transition to the Theory of Method[6]

Outline of the General Theory of Method.

Investigations of the Problem of Demarcation contained, or was meant to contain, inter alia:

(1) an attempt "to show that the problems of the classical and modern theory of knowledge (from Hume via Kant to Russell and Wittgenstein) can be traced back to the 'problem of demarcation', to the problem of finding the criterion of the empirical character of science";[7]

(2) a discussion of "the demarcating functions that the inductivist concept of meaning has to satisfy"[8] – it is shown "that any desired demarcation (of empirical statements, of metaphysics and of logic) is possible without using the concept of meaning or a similarly loaded concept";[9]

(3) investigation of the "question whether . . . all synthetic judgements are empirical statements, and . . . a closer analysis of the concept of empirical statements, experiential reality and so on";[10]

(4) a "Table of Statements";[11]

---

[4] See Volume I: Section 47, text to note 2; Section 48, text to note 3.

[5] See Volume II (Fragments): [III.] Transition to the Theory of Method, Section 1, text to notes 2, 3 and 4; Section 4, text to note 1.

[6] As it appears from Volume I: Section 30, note 1, Popper considered adding Transition to the Theory of Method as an appendix to Volume I; but that was not the original intention (cf. note 5).

[7] See Karl Popper, Logik der Forschung (1934; 2nd ed., 1966) [The Logic of Scientific Discovery (1959; 2nd ed., 1968). Tr.], Section 11, note 3. Cf. also Volume II (Fragments): I. Formulation of the Problem, Section 1; [VI.] Philosophy, [Introduction], text to note 3.

[8] See Volume I: Section 46, text to note 2; Section 48, text to note 4.

[9] See Volume I: Section 46, text to note 1; cf. also Volume II (Fragments): [III.] Transition to the Theory of Method, Section 1, note 3 and text to this note.

[10] See Volume I: Section 3, text to note 3; Section 10, text to note 12; Section 11, text to note 55.

[11] See Volume II (Fragments): [III.] Transition to the Theory of Method, Section 4, note 1 and text to this note.

(5) a demonstration that Kant[12] is right when his *theory of antinomies* reaches the conclusion "that in those cases where there is an undecidable antinomy, both assertions are to be rejected as unjustifiable and therefore as *unscientific* (dogmatic-metaphysical)";[13]

(6) a discussion of the "antinomy between realism and idealism";[14]

(7) justification of the view that "both thesis and antithesis of the antinomy of the knowability of the world should be eliminated from the theory of knowledge as unscientific, as *metaphysical*";[15]

(8) a demonstration of "the existence of an exact formal analogy between the *criterion of logical consistency* and the 'criterion of demarcation' ";[16]

(9) a critique of strict positivism and of apriorism;[17]

(10) "a fundamental, conclusive critique of conventionalism".[18]

Transition to the Theory of Method appears to have been preserved almost entirely.[19]

Outline of the General Theory of Method contained, or was meant to contain, *inter alia*:

(1) the methodological regulation of the stipulation of basic statements (derived "from the principle of *methodological realism*");[20]

---

[12] Cf. Immanuel Kant, *Kritik der reinen Vernunft* (2nd ed., 1787), pp. 448 ff. [English translation by N. Kemp Smith (1929), 1965: *Critique of Pure Reason*, pp. 393 ff. Tr.]; see also Kant, *Prolegomena* (1783) [English translation by Paul Carus, extensively revised by James W. Ellington (1977), Tr.], § 51 f.

[13] See Volume I: Section 10, text to note 6; cf. also Volume II (Fragments): [VI.] *Philosophy*, Section 1, text to note 1.

[14] See Volume I: Section 10, text to note 7.

[15] See Volume I: Section 10, text to note 13; Section 48, text to note 4.

[16] See Volume I: Section 31, text to note 5; cf. also Appendix: Section V, text to note 5.

[17] See Volume I: Section 48, text to note 4. Cf. also Volume II (Fragments): [V.] *Outline of a Theory of Empirical-Scientific Methods (Theory of Experience)*, Section 2.

[18] See Volume I: Section 24, text to note 1; Section 47, text to note 10. Cf. also Volume II (Fragments): [III.] *Transition to the Theory of Method*; [V.] *Outline of a Theory of Empirical-Scientific Methods (Theory of Experience)*, Sections 3 and 4.

[19] See Volume II (Fragments): [III.] *Transition to the Theory of Method*, Section 2, note 2 and text to this note; Section 7, note 1; cf. also the German edition of *The Two Fundamental Problems* (1979), Volume II (Fragments): [III.] *Transition to the Theory of Method*, Section 8, critical textual notes a and b.

[20] See Volume I: Section 11, text to note 56; Appendix: Section IX. Cf. also Volume II (Fragments): [VII.] *The Problem of Methodology*, Section 1, text to notes 2 and 6.

(2) "*the deductive theory of method,*[21] dealing *inter alia* with the following: 1. levels of reliability and 'quasi-induction';[22] 2. the concept of corroboration[23] and the concept of simplicity; the 'principle of the most parsimonious use of hypotheses', derived from the concept of higher or lower falsifiability (or precision, or statement content)".

The remaining information about the lost Volume II relies on references that do not indicate explicitly how they should be incorporated into the three aforementioned parts. In what follows, this information is ordered by its location.

A) From *Volume I* it appears that Volume II contained, or was meant to contain, a demonstration that the *transcendental definition of knowledge* leads in its "ultimate implications directly to *deductivism*".[24]

B) From *Volume II (Fragments)* it appears that Volume II contained also, or was meant to contain,
(1) an "introduction of the concept of the 'falsifying hypothesis' ";[25]
(2) a frequency theory for finite classes;[26]
(3) a "theory of arithmetic-geometric sets";[27]
(4) a "probability calculus";[28]
(5) a "discussion of 'non-empty' assumptions".[29,30]

---

[21] See Appendix: *Concluding note*, text to note 1.

[22] Cf. also Volume I: Section 48, text to note 2; Volume II (Fragments): [VII.] *The Problem of Methodology*, Section 1, text to note 4.

[23] Cf. also Volume I: Section 16, text to note 2.

[24] See Volume I: Section 10, text to note 15.

[25] See Volume II (Fragments): [VII.] *The Problem of Methodology*, Section 1, text to note 1.

[26] See Volume II (Fragments): [X.] *The Problem of the Randomness of Probability Statements*, Section 6, text to notes 1 and 2.

[27] Ibid., Section 7, text to note 2.

[28] Ibid., Section 7, text to note 3.

[29] Ibid., Section 7, text to note 4.

[30] Volume II (Fragments) contains five further references that should be interpreted as referring to lost sections of Volume II; see [IX. *The Problem of Free Will*], Section 5, note 1 and text to note 2 and 3; Section 7, text to note 4; [X.] *The Problem of the Randomness of Probability Statements*, Section 6, text to note 9.

C) *Appendix: Summary Excerpt* (1932): The Preliminary Note seems to suggest that the content of Sections VI and VIII was derived from the lost drafts of Volume II.

D) *Exposition* [1933] was one of three enclosures in a letter to Julius Kraft dated 11 July 1933. The two other enclosures, now missing, are described in the following appendix to the *Exposition*, at the end of which some information is provided also about the lost Volume II:

"*Comments on the enclosures.* Two small booklets are enclosed with this exposition, one headed 'Drafts of a *preface* and an *introduction*[31] – *Table of Contents* of the book' (etc.), the other headed 'Excerpt' (etc).[32]

"The booklet 'Excerpt' contains a preliminary orientation note.

"It should be noted that these enclosures offer a very incomplete picture of the book.

"In particular, the detailed critical investigations in the book, those intended to demonstrate that the problems regarded by the author as 'the fundamental problems of the theory of knowledge' do lie at the root of the most important questions and debates in epistemology, are reproduced in the form of an appendix of tables only.[33] Of these critical investigations, special mention should be made of the discussions about Hume, Kant, Fries and the 'probability philosophers' (Reichenbach, Kaila and others). The positive results, too, could be included in the 'Excerpt' to a limited extent only. Not included were, above all, the theory of the law-likeness degree of a hypothesis*[4] and that of the relationship between law and randomness, and the investigation into *laws of 'causal form'* and the form of '*possibility statements*', into the 'problem of simplicity' and into the 'principle of economy'."

Troels Eggers Hansen
Roskilde, Denmark, January 1979

---

[31] These drafts may be identical with Volume II (Fragments): Draft of an Introduction and Orientation. It is possible also, however, that they refer to lost sections of Volume I.

[32] This "excerpt" must be identical with Appendix: Summary Excerpt (1932).

[33] See Appendix: Preliminary Note, note 2 and text to this note.

*[4] *Addition* (1983). The phrase "law-likeness degree of a hypothesis" denotes (as pp. 157 ff. show) what later I called the "*content*" of a hypothesis or theory – a central idea in my theory of knowledge. K.R.P.

INDEX OF NAMES

n. indicates that the entry is to be found in a note
Page references to tables are in **bold** print

INDEX OF SUBJECTS